T0355154

Of Age

Of Age

Boy Soldiers and Military Power in the Civil War Era

FRANCES M. CLARKE AND REBECCA JO PLANT

OXFORD
UNIVERSITY PRESS

OXFORD
UNIVERSITY PRESS

Oxford University Press is a department of the University of Oxford. It furthers
the University's objective of excellence in research, scholarship, and education
by publishing worldwide. Oxford is a registered trade mark of Oxford University
Press in the UK and certain other countries.

Published in the United States of America by Oxford University Press
198 Madison Avenue, New York, NY 10016, United States of America.

Library of Congress Cataloging-in-Publication Data
Names: Clarke, Frances M., author. | Plant, Rebecca Jo, 1968- author.
Title: Of age : boy soldiers and military power in the Civil War era /
Frances M. Clarke, and Rebecca Jo Plant.
Identifiers: LCCN 2022053524 (print) | LCCN 2022053525 (ebook) |
ISBN 9780197601044 (hardback) | ISBN 9780197601068 (epub) | ISBN 9780197601075
Subjects: LCSH: United States—History—Civil War, 861–1865—Participation, Juvenile. |
United States—History—Civil War, 861–1865—Children. |
Children and war—United States—History—19th century. |
Children and war—Confederate States of America. |
Child soldiers—United States—History—19th century. |
Child soldiers—Confederate States of America.
Classification: LCC E540 .C47 C53 2023 (print) | LCC E540 .C47 (ebook) |
DDC 973.7083—dc23/eng/20221108
LC record available at https://lccn.loc.gov/2022053524
LC ebook record available at https://lccn.loc.gov/2022053525

DOI: 10.1093/oso/9780197601044.001.0001

1 3 5 7 9 8 6 4 2

Printed by Sheridan Books, Inc., United States of America

To the young people in our lives:
Frances Clarke, Kathleen Clarke, and Samuel Philip Steiger

Contents

Acknowledgments   ix
Note on Terminology   xiii

Introduction   1

I: PARENTAL RIGHTS AND THE DUTY
TO BEAR ARMS: CONGRESS, COURTS,
AND THE MILITARY

1. Competing Obligations: Debating Underage Enlistment
   in the War of 1812   27

2. A Great Inconvenience: Prewar Legal Disputes over Underage
   Enlistees   49

3. Underdeveloped Bodies: Calculating the Ideal Enlistment Age   68

II: THE SOCIAL AND CULTURAL ORIGINS
OF UNDERAGE ENLISTMENT

4. Instructive Violence: Impressionable Minds and the
   Cultivation of Courage in Boys   91

5. Pride of the Nation: The Iconography of Child Soldiers and
   Drummer Boys   111

6. Paths to Enlistment: Work, Politics, and School   142

III: MALE YOUTH AND MILITARY SERVICE
DURING THE CIVIL WAR

7. Contrary to All Law: Debating Underage Service in the
   United States   167

8. Preserving the Seed Corn: Youth Enlistment and Demographic
   Anxiety in the Confederacy   197

9. Forced into Service: Enslaved and Unfree Youth in the Union
   and Confederate Armies   227

Epilogue: A War Fought by Boys: Reimagining Boyhood and
   Underage Soldiers after the Civil War   262

Appendix A: Counting Underage Soldiers   289
Appendix B: Using the Early Indicators of Later Work Levels, Disease,
   and Death *Database to Determine Age of Enlistment in
   the Union Army, by Christopher Roudiez*   295
Notes   301
Bibliography   385
Index   425

Acknowledgments

The ten years or so that it has taken us to write this book have been absorbing, joyful, and challenging. Along the way, we've relished archival discoveries, learned how to write together, and squabbled about whether this or that footnote or sentence should be cut. Our first thanks go to each other, for maintaining a friendship that has enabled us to create work that combines the best of us both.

Many other people have contributed to this project over these years. To start at the beginning, back in 2009 an archivist at the National Archives in Washington, DC, took Frances on a behind-the-scenes tour of the stacks. That tour revealed one of the main sets of records that we eventually used to write this book—a collection containing letters from parents trying to get their underage sons discharged from service. We'll be forever grateful to Mike Musick for bending the rules and introducing us to this untapped treasure trove. He had retired by the time we returned to NARA to start our research, so we relied on Trevor Plante and DeAnn Blanton thereafter to figure out the intricacies of military history records. On multiple trips to NARA over the years, their expertise was invaluable.

Early on, we had help of various other kinds. Geoffrey West, Hilary Coulson, and Danielle Thyer provided research assistance. Hilary also worked on our behalf at the National Archives, as did Michael Henderson. Kate Flach and Jordan Mylet helped us with the laborious process of transcribing documents. Bill Plant, Rebecca's father, pitched in to assist with the equally time-consuming process of searching Ancestry.com for birthdates and other available information for soldiers enlisted in the 64th New York Infantry Regiment.

In addition, archivists at various institutions directed us to invaluable sources or facilitated archival trips. Among those who went above and beyond are Ashley Cataldo, Paul Erickson, Lauren Hewes, and Laura Wasowicz at the American Antiquarian Society; Jim Green at the Library Company of Philadelphia; Peter Drummey, Elaine Grublin, Conrad Wright, and Kate Viens at the Massachusetts Historical Society; and Kevin Shupe at the Library of Virginia. For help identifying court martial records of underage soldiers who served in the Union army, we extend our appreciation to Tom Lowry. Thanks also to Richard Dobbins for responding to our queries about the American Civil War Database.

Researching and writing this book has been a labor-intensive process, complicated by the fact that one of us lives in Sydney, Australia, and the other in San Diego, California, while most of the archives we needed were in eastern, midwestern, and southern cities in the United States. We are very much indebted to the American College of Learned Societies and the Australian Research Council (DP140100983), which generously funded our project. Without their support, which gave us the great gift of time to work together, this book would not exist. In addition, we want to thank the American Antiquarian Society, the Library Company of Philadelphia, the Massachusetts Historical Society, the Newberry Library, the Virginia Historical Society, and the US Army Military History Institute for grants that allowed us to conduct research in their collections. The University of Sydney provided additional support through a Thompson Fellowship, while the University of California, San Diego, supported our work with Academic Senate research grants and a Manuscript Forum Fellowship from the Institute of Arts and Humanities.

The Manuscript Forum Fellowship proved to be especially fortuitous, because it allowed us the opportunity to have Laura Edwards comment on our work at a critical stage in the process. She read our bulky draft with extraordinary care. She posed questions and shared insights, based on her vast knowledge of nineteenth-century legal history, that helped us to clarify and sharpen our central arguments, while offering editorial suggestions that refined our prose. We cannot thank her enough for her generosity.

Our writing has also been informed by dozens of other interlocutors. Susan Ferber, our editor at Oxford University Press, has been wonderful, counselling us without ever being prescriptive, and going over every sentence with an eagle eye. She also found excellent readers for the press who have helped to improve this work substantially. One of these readers was Jim Marten, whose own work on the history of childhood and youth in the Civil War era has been foundational in the field. To Jim and the anonymous reader who offered astute comments on our manuscript, we are immensely appreciative for the time you expended on our behalf. Jim has assisted our work in other ways, including by extending an invitation to contribute to a forum on age and the law in his role as editor for the *Journal of the History of Childhood and Youth*. We are also grateful to Corinne Field, Nicholas Syrett, and the

American Historical Association for organizing a series of seminars on the significance of chronological age that allowed us to present a portion of chapter 3 to a lively group of experts. Thanks especially to Holly N. S. White, who commented on our paper, sharing insights from her own work on the social and legal significance of age in early America.

No thanks could be sufficient for Catherine Jones, who has read multiple drafts of each chapter and provided countless hours of expertise. Few scholars are better able than Kate to help sharpen an argument, interpret sources, or parse an academic debate. Not only has she generously answered questions and commented on successive drafts, but she also organized a special forum on our book for the 2021 Biennial Conference of the Society for the History of Childhood and Youth. We very much look forward to returning the favor.

Among others who have extended their support and expertise is our incomparable friend Carolyn Eastman—sounding board, editor, supplier of inspiration and distraction, and creator extraordinaire. Our lives are infinitely better with you in them. In the United States, Rebecca's colleagues in the History Department at the University of California, San Diego, have provided a warm and supportive intellectual home. Thanks especially to Rachel Klein, a wonderfully generous mentor and insightful reader, and to Pamela Radcliff, Frank Biess, Ulrike Strasser, and Deborah Hertz for helping to keep a semblance of community alive during the pandemic. Kate Flach, Mary Klann, and Samantha de Vera provided helpful feedback on drafts of the introduction and chapter 9, along with the great pleasure of experiencing former PhD students as present-day colleagues. Michelle Hovet read chapter 6 and provided constant encouragement. For final proofreading, Michael Henderson stepped in again and helped eliminate errors.

In Australia, Andy Kaladelfos provided advice on legal sources and read early versions of chapter seven. Michael McDonnell offered helpful comments on chapters one and two, while members of reading groups at the University of Sydney (which included Thomas Adams, David Brophy, Ann Curthoys, John Gagné, Miranda Johnson, Chin Jou, Judith Keene, Cindy McCreery, Kirsten McKenzie, Andres Rodriguez, Penny Russell, Rebecca Sheehan, and Sophie Loy Wilson) workshopped multiple chapters at different stages.

Parts of chapter seven appeared in our article *Law and History Review*, "No Minor Matter: Underage Soldiers, Parents, and the Nationalization of Habeas Corpus in Civil War America." We are grateful to the anonymous readers whose responses continued to inform our thinking, even after we had published the piece.

Finally, we thank our relatives. For Frances, this includes the extended Clarke family, who provided respite during writing breaks and celebrated some of the milestones along the way. When they were small, my nieces, Frances and Kathleen, asked if I could dedicate my next book to them. You had to wait a while, but I kept my promise. It's my greatest wish that neither of you ever know what war is like.

For Rebecca, thanks go first to Bill and Allene Plant. My parents have long supported my aspirations and valiantly tried, with moderate success, to suppress questions concerning this book's publication date. I am fortunate to be able to turn to my sister, Alisa Plant, and my brother-in-law, James Boyden, for practical as well as emotional support. Alisa helped us craft a book proposal, edited our introduction, and offered sage advice on publishing. Jim also weighed in on our introduction when there was little time to spare.

Finally, my greatest debts are to my husband, Rand Steiger, whose buoyancy keeps us all afloat. Expressions of gratitude seem paltry in the face of your unwavering love and support. And to my son, Samuel Steiger, who grew from a boy to a man during the writing of this book, watching you come of age has been my greatest joy and privilege. This book is for you.

Note on Terminology

Some of the terms used in this book reflect an ongoing reassessment of language that has long been employed when discussing slavery and the US Civil War. To underscore the fact that slavery was a labor system in which some people continually exerted power over others, not a set of fixed and uncontested identities, we generally use the adjective "enslaved" rather than the noun "slaves," and the label "enslaver" rather than "slaveowner." We also avoid the sweeping and politically neutral terms "North" and "South" to refer to the two sides in the conflict, since these geographical references evoke too tidy a picture when it comes to mapping people's social and political affiliations. Such framing also implies that western states and territories were entirely removed from the war, while cordoning off conflicts between the United States and Native Americans as unrelated to the effort to sustain the Union. Instead of North and South, we usually refer to the United States and the Confederacy.

We have not, however, followed the decision of the Army University Press to substitute "US Army," "Federals," or "Federal Army" for "Union army." "Union," they argue, refers to the nation undivided; to accept the term "Union army" as a descriptor for forces that hailed overwhelmingly from the northern half of the country is thus to accept the truncated definition of "Union" that Confederates hoped to realize. Others argue that the term "Union army" tends to obscure the reality that US military forces during this period were not only fighting to restore the nation, but also engaged in conflicts with Native Americans over land dispossession. The fact that some Civil War era Americans used the terms "Union army" and "US army" interchangeably, especially during the latter years of the war, would seem to support the case for dropping the former in favor of the latter. After all, "US army" best underscores the historical connection between the force that defeated the Confederacy and the present-day army, puncturing any attempt to portray both sides as somehow equally "American."

These are worthy points. The problem is that "US army" tends to suggest a singular and unified force, whereas the army at the war's outset was in fact much like the nation itself—highly decentralized, with power divided between the states and the US government. To many, "US army" connoted the US government's professional army—a small but permanent standing force. Often referred to as "the regulars," these forces were thought of very differently from the mass of volunteers who mobilized to defeat the Confederacy. Though volunteer units ultimately served under federal control, to conflate the two forms of service is to confuse categories that mattered greatly at the time. Indeed, a major goal of this book is to show how the war tended to erode the dual military system—a shift that is illuminated by the controversies surrounding underage soldiers. To best tell this story, we have retained language that reflects the distinction that Americans continued to draw between volunteer forces and the professional federal army, even as differences between the two became increasingly blurred.

Introduction

Monroe Township, Missouri, was a hotbed of secessionism, but Union sentiment ran strong in the household of John Gudgell.[1] Just four days after federal troops arrived in the area in mid-June 1861, the family's youngest child enlisted in a home guard unit.[2] By fall, fourteen-year-old Julian M. Gudgell was determined to join a proper regiment. Although his father foiled his first attempt, he ran away again a few weeks later and managed to enlist in the 18th Missouri Infantry. He claimed to be seventeen years old.[3]

Julian was just one of more than two hundred thousand youths below the age of eighteen who served in the Union army during the Civil War. Constituting roughly 10 percent of Union troops and most likely a similar proportion of Confederate forces—though surviving records allow for less certainty—these young enlistees significantly enhanced the size and capabilities of the armies on both sides. They also created a great deal of drama and chaos. They upended household economies by absconding with their vital labor power. They caused loved ones to suffer untold anxiety for their welfare. And they generated myriad encounters between ordinary people and the institutions of government, at times resulting in dramatic showdowns between military and civilian authorities. Family members desperate for their sons' release showed up at military camps to confront officers, appealed to judges for writs of habeas corpus, and petitioned elected representatives and government officials. When such efforts failed, many embarked on costly and often futile quests, chasing after regiments on the move, combing city streets near enlistment offices, or traveling to Washington to plead their case in person. These conflicts would ultimately have far-reaching consequences, not only for the individuals and families involved, but also for the battered nation that emerged from the war. Yet for all that has been written about the Civil War, we know little about its youngest soldiers and even less about the parents who so doggedly pursued their release from service.

Consider John Gudgell's attempts to recover his son. He first sought the help of a general stationed in the area, who assured him that Julian would soon be sent home. But six months later, Julian had not been released. In a letter to US Representative Francis P. Blair, Jr., Gudgell explained that he was a stalwart "union man" and would not have intervened had his son been "older & more experienced." But given Julian's youth, he begged Blair to consider "a fathers feelings." He described his special bond with his youngest child, whose mother had died soon after his birth. He explained that his son suffered an infirmity that would be aggravated by the southern climate. And he pointed to the hard times afflicting farmers in his region, where a terrible drought had parched the fields and baked the earth "so we can't plow old Ground attall."[4] Yet no matter what Gudgell emphasized—his social standing and loyalty to the Union, his emotional distress and economic woes, Julian's age and delicate health—he could not get his boy discharged.

It should not have been so hard. After all, the law was on his side: when Julian enlisted, minors below age twenty-one legally needed the consent of a parent or guardian to enlist in the Union army. Even after February 1862, when Congress lowered the bar to eighteen, Julian at fourteen still fell well below the age threshold. What is more, John Gudgell enjoyed political connections that would soon win him a seat in the Missouri House of Representatives and might have been expected to work in his favor.[5] He had even managed the rare feat of obtaining the support of Julian's captain, who wrote to the US Adjutant General's Office that a discharge would be in keeping with army regulations. Besides, the captain added, "such boys are of little or no use to the army in the field."[6]

Julian's service history, however, tells a different story. He fought in the Battle of Shiloh in April 1862 and earned a promotion to corporal in early 1863, just a few months after his sixteenth birthday. No disciplinary infractions, no charges for lost or damaged equipment, not so much as an absence due to illness marred his record. By dismissing the value of young soldiers in general terms, rather than addressing the specific case at hand, Julian's captain managed to skirt the truth: this particular boy was rendering meaningful service, and his discharge would be a loss to the Union army.

While Julian may have been unusually capable for one so young, an enormous number of youths like him helped to sustain the war effort. A large majority of them served as regular soldiers, and around 80 percent were sixteen or seventeen years old. Spindly teens on the cusp of manhood, most did not immediately attract attention. If one searches for them in photographs taken in army camps, their still-smooth faces are not hard to detect, but otherwise they blend in with the men, as they did in real life. It is the youngest and smallest boys who draw the eye and seize the imagination. Some of these pint-sized soldiers were celebrated for heroic feats during the war, the most famous being Johnny Clem, who unofficially joined a Michigan regiment at age nine and was finally mustered into service three years later. But even boys who were merely the pets of their regiments—allowed to ride while others marched, kept behind the lines while others fought—performed important roles. They helped carry the wounded from the field, ran messages, filled canteens, tended to the horses, built campfires, cooked, mended clothes, and lifted men's spirits with their buoyancy and childish antics. They may not have been of age, but they were definitely of use, which is precisely why the military was loath to release them.

This was especially true of the Union forces—a finding that at first seems counter-intuitive, even confounding. After all, the United States boasted roughly 3.5 times as many white men of military age as the Confederacy.[7] To address its population disadvantage, the Confederate Congress resorted to far-reaching measures, achieving a substantially higher rate of service among eligible men than the United States could ever claim. It adopted a policy of universal conscription in April 1862; in February 1864 it lowered the age of conscription from eighteen to seventeen (while also raising the upper limit from forty-five to fifty). At the same time, some Confederate states enrolled boys as young as sixteen for service in state-controlled units.[8] Meanwhile, the United States retained a minimum age of eighteen for voluntary enlistment and drafted only those age twenty or above. Given all this, it seems logical to conclude that the Confederacy mobilized its youth far more willingly and completely than the United States. Many Unionists at the time believed as much, accusing Confederates of "robbing both cradle and grave" to fill the ranks.

But closer scrutiny reveals a more complex reality. Most political leaders balked at the idea of conscripting youths below eighteen directly into the Confederate army, insisting that such a measure would amount to "grinding the seed corn." They instead enrolled seventeen-year-olds and older men in state reserve units, which generally entailed less dangerous service that could be performed without leaving home for extended periods of time. Even near the war's bitter end, when the Confederacy enacted legislation allowing for the enlistment of slaves, it declined to conscript anyone below the age of eighteen into the regular army. Of course, many tens of thousands of underage youths—possibly over a hundred thousand—nonetheless served in the Confederate army. But all things considered, it is the Confederacy's

Sgt Johny Clem

Figure I.1 One of the most photographed subjects of the war, Johnny Clem (originally Klem) was born in 1851, ran away at age nine, and ended up tagging along with 22nd Michigan Regiment before officers relented and mustered him into service. The most commonly known "facts" about Clem are also those most subject to doubt—that he shot a Confederate colonel, and that he was the real-life "Drummer Boy of Shiloh." More verifiable aspects of his life cast a shadow on the celebratory narrative surrounding him. His mother died in a gruesome train accident less than a year before he left home; his family searched desperately for him and mourned him as dead; and General Ulysses S. Grant arranged for him to attend West Point, but Clem could not pass the entrance exam, having spent so little time in school. Grant nonetheless commissioned him as an officer after he graduated from high school in 1871, and Clem remained in service for the rest of his career. Library of Congress Prints and Photographs Division, LC-DIG-ppmsca-34511.

efforts to shield the young from hard service, more than the attempts to mobilize them, that calls out for explanation.

If notions of the Confederate army dragooning boys into service are misleading, so too is the belief that underage enlistment in the United States was mainly limited to drummer boys and other musicians.[9] Leading historians of the Civil War have long held that youths below age eighteen made up a minuscule portion of all Union enlistees. In support of this claim, they point most often to the first modern history of Union soldiers, Bell Irvin Wiley's *The Life of Billy Yank*, published in 1952. Drawing on a large sample of muster rolls, Wiley concluded that only around 1.6 percent of Union soldiers were below the age of enlistment when they joined the army. Although he recognized that an unknown number of youths lied about their ages, he did not think such subterfuge pervasive enough to call into question the basic veracity of the Union army's military records.[10] Since then, a number of historians and diligent amateur researchers have demonstrated that specific regiments included a much higher percentage of underage enlistees.[11] But because scholars have not attempted to discredit the 1.6 percent figure for the army as whole, it continues to be widely cited, not just in scholarship, but also on popular Civil War websites.[12]

The most basic argument of this book is that underage youths constituted at least 10 percent of Union army enlistees.[13] When soldiers' reported ages can be checked against census records and other sources, it becomes clear that military records mask an epidemic of lying. As detailed in the appendices, around half of those who claimed to be eighteen at the time of their enlistment, and some who claimed to be even older were actually underage. While most shaved somewhere between a few months to a few years off their actual ages, the more extreme cases—like that of eleven-year-old George S. Howard, who enlisted in the 36th Massachusetts Infantry as a nineteen-year-old—are positively jaw-dropping.[14] Codified as facts by enlisting officers who often knew better, the lies told by underage boys were subsequently incorporated into historical accounts, skewing our view of the Union army up to the present day.[15]

Calling attention to the vast number of underage soldiers, however, is the beginning rather than the end of our inquiry. Not only did boys and youths enlist in greater numbers than generally thought, they also preoccupied contemporaries to a greater extent than previously recognized. Again, this was especially true in the United States. Early in the war, parents and guardians had two main avenues of redress. They could follow policies that predated the conflict and submit affidavits to the War Department. If they could show that a youth was underage and had enlisted without consent, the army was legally obliged to release him. The other option was to seek a writ of habeas corpus. If granted, an officer had to bring the youth to court, where the judge would rule on the validity of his enlistment contract, either discharging him on the spot or remanding him to service. As soon as the fighting began, petitions and affidavits started pouring into Washington— so many that in September 1861 the War Department simply decreed that it would no longer discharge soldiers on the grounds of minority. But until late 1863, judges in state and local courts continued to hear habeas cases involving minor enlistees, releasing them from service more often than not. Endlessly litigated in courts, debates over underage soldiers also played out in the press, the halls of Congress, government offices, and military and medical circles. All the while, writers, artists, and musicians blanketed the nation with idealized depictions of heroic drummer boys and young soldiers, which appeared in every imaginable genre—from paintings and lithographs to sentimental poems, songs, and plays.

To account for why underage soldiers took on outsized significance in the United States but not the Confederacy is to begin to understand the larger issues at stake. As a political and cultural symbol, the boy soldier or drummer boy resonated in the United States in ways it simply could not in the Confederacy. Rooted in an artistic tradition that dated back to the French Revolution, the figure embodied the democratic republic that the nation imagined itself to be—youthful, incorruptible, and forward looking. These were not the values most prized by the Confederate States of America, a nation founded by self-styled patriarchs seeking to uphold a hierarchical social order based on slavery. When they inaugurated Jefferson Davis on George Washington's birthday, and later when they selected an image of the first US president for the Confederacy's official seal, the rebellion's leaders telegraphed their social and political vision; they pronounced themselves the true heirs of the American Revolution, but they clearly identified more with the revered father of the nation than the revolutionary sons of liberty.[16] Like Unionists, Confederates celebrated particularly heroic youths as evidence of their people's unconquerable spirit, but only in the United States did the generic boy soldier or drummer boy become a symbol that personified the nation.

Likewise, only in the loyal states did youth enlistment become an important political issue, a pressing legal question, and a bureaucratic nightmare.

This is because the debate over underage enlistees in the United States was simultaneously a debate over the limits of military power. It all boiled down to whether the government could legally breach the relationship between a father and a minor son, holding an underage enlistee to service regardless of parental wishes.[17] Contests over the status of enlisted boys and youth thus raised fundamental questions over how much authority household heads, communities, and states could expect to retain while fighting a prolonged and bloody war. Could officers ignore writs of habeas corpus, disregarding what they saw as meddlesome interference by courts and civilians? Or would local communities and courts retain the ability to check enlistment abuses by military officers?

Underage soldiers stood in the middle of this tug-of-war. On one side were parents and guardians, often supported by neighbors, political representatives, and state or local judges who defended parental rights and state and local oversight of military forces. On the other side were federal officials and army officers, who argued that victory required a strong central government and a military unfettered by constant pleading for the release of this or that individual soldier. All parties involved placed a high value on the service of underage enlistees, and all expressed a sense of righteous entitlement to youths' labor and loyalty. Because so much was at stake, these conflicts could quickly escalate. What hung in the balance was not only control over the vital manpower of male youths, but also cherished emotional attachments and deeply felt beliefs concerning the preservation of a Union dedicated to liberty and the dangers of concentrated power. In the eyes of many aggrieved parents, the government's refusal to release their sons represented an unlawful exercise of authority of the very worst kind, for it allowed the military to violate the sanctity of the home.

The Confederacy was also wracked by disputes over how much authority should be ceded to the central government and the military. If anything, such debates were even more heated than in the United States, as one might expect in a nation whose leaders found it necessary to impose heavy-handed policies after having loudly championed states' rights. Within the Confederacy, however, legal conflicts over the concentration of power rarely centered on underage enlistees.[18] Due to the comprehensive nature of Confederate conscription, aggrieved civilians had even bigger concerns: their appeals to authorities typically focused on absent husbands and fathers—adult male providers—rather than underage sons.[19] In any event, Confederate families overall had an easier time recovering youths who enlisted without consent.

The suspension of habeas corpus was more episodic and less effective at putting a stop to such cases than in the United States, and the Confederate government neither enacted laws nor issued general military orders designed to prevent minors' release.

In other words, what happened to John and Julian Gudgell is very much a Union story: the father of a fourteen-year-old who had never consented to his son's enlistment would almost certainly have been able to get him discharged from the Confederate army. But Julian was still on the rolls as of late 1863, when he reenlisted as a veteran volunteer and was rewarded with a thirty-day furlough. That was when his problems began, for once he returned home, his father decided to claim and hold what he saw as rightfully his. John Gudgell went to St. Louis to seek his son's discharge, directing Julian to remain at home and assuring him that the attempt would likely succeed. It did not. Maybe Gudgell told Julian upon his return that he was now a free man. Maybe Julian knew the effort had failed but stayed home anyway, possibly to care for his father—a reasonable supposition, given that Gudgell died soon thereafter. All we know for certain is that an anxious father had been trying for well over two years to reclaim his son through legitimate channels, and a young soldier with a previously unblemished service record failed to return to his unit.[20]

Julian found himself caught between two masters, both relentless in their demands for his presence and service: his father and the US federal government. His decision to privilege filial obedience over his obligations as a soldier would cost him dearly. Deemed a deserter in April 1864, he was arrested in December, just a week after his father died and less than a month after he turned eighteen. A court martial panel heard his case in March 1865 and sentenced him to a dishonorable discharge and a year in prison. Two months later, some leading citizens from Julian's hometown succeeded in having the sentence commuted, assisted by a brigadier general who attested that Julian had been a good soldier and "would not have stayed at home but at the insistence of his father." Yet while he regained his freedom, Julian would never reap the financial rewards and public accolades that accrued to other veterans. His dishonorable discharge barred him from receiving a military pension, and a regimental history published in 1891 fails to list him as a surviving member, even though he was still living at the time.[21] The takeaway seems clear: no matter a soldier's underage status, no matter his parents' desire, he would be held to account if he violated his military contract. Over the course of the war, thousands of Union soldiers and their families would learn this same hard lesson about the growing primacy of federal and military power.

* * *

The boy soldiers of the Civil War era are not the child soldiers of today. Since the 1970s, humanitarians have defined the use of children in war as a breach of international law and a violation of human and children's rights. Dystopian images of young boys draped with ammo belts have proven highly effective at mobilizing moral outrage in wealthy nations: because children are understood to be uniquely vulnerable and especially worthy of care and protection, their use in adults' political and military disputes strikes observers as particularly abhorrent. But the contemporary discourse surrounding child soldiers has proven unhelpful when it comes to promoting a cleareyed understanding of the causes and contours of the problem.[22] It is even less useful as a framework for illuminating the plight of young combatants in the American Civil War, an era that predates contemporary understandings of trauma, childhood, and human rights.[23] Still, it is instructive to consider the present-day construction of the "child soldier" alongside Civil War–era representations of boy soldiers, if only to drive home the stark contrast: whereas today's child soldiers are viewed as the ultimate victims, entirely devoid of agency, the boy soldiers of the Civil War were—and are still— portrayed as heroic authors of their own destiny, even when their military service ended in death.[24]

A desire to tell and hear inspirational stories of boy soldiers was evident from the very beginning of the Civil War. The first Union soldiers killed were four Massachusetts militiamen, en route to Washington with their regiments, who were attacked in Baltimore by an anti-Republican mob. Seventeen-year-old Luther C. Ladd, the youngest of the four, was by far the most widely celebrated, his image appearing in national publications and reprinted on patriotic stationery. Though Ladd never set foot on a battlefield, the press quickly sanctified him as the "Union's first martyr."[25] Stories of other boy soldiers highlighted their quick thinking and heroic actions. In the thick of the fighting at Vicksburg, a wounded twelve-year-old named Orion Howe managed to track down General William Sherman to convey a critical message: the 55th Illinois had run out of cartridges. Sherman's account of the incident, related to the secretary of war, appeared in newspapers throughout the country: "What arrested my attention then was . . . that one so young, carrying a musket-ball wound through his leg, should have found his way to me on that fatal spot, and delivered his message, not forgetting the very important part even of the calibre of his musket."[26] Whether underage soldiers featured as sacrificial young martyrs or precociously brave-hearted boys, the public found their stories irresistible.

This remains true to the present day. With few exceptions, a biographical and anecdotal approach has dominated writing about the war's youngest enlistees.[27] Several authors have published compilations of biographical sketches, and numerous books aimed at juvenile readers center on the story of a particular drummer or boy soldier.[28] These narratives tell of boys coming of age in confronting camp life and combat, of youths performing heroic deeds, and of young lives cut tragically short. Their celebratory tenor may explain why few trained historians have concerned themselves with the subject.[29] Inescapably mired in sentiment, boy soldiers seem to lack academic gravitas. They are just too, well, *popular.*

Of Age offers a different take on this subject. Although underage youths appear throughout these pages, this book is not primarily a history of their wartime experiences. We focus instead on the social context that made those

Figure I.2 Luther C. Ladd was among the first soldiers killed in the war. When his body and that of his comrade and fellow mill worker, twenty-one-year-old Addison Whitney, were returned Lowell, Massachusetts, the town shut down the mills and staged a massive joint funeral. In 1865 the community erected a monument in honor of the two youths, but national attention singled out only Ladd, suggesting the appeal and propaganda value of boy soldiers. "Luther C. Ladd" (1861). *Lincoln Envelopes.* Brown Digital Repository. Brown University Library. https://repository.library.brown.edu/studio/item/bdr:575834/

experiences possible and the significance of the debates they provoked. Examining everything from the labor boys performed to the books they read, we uncover the factors that propelled so many of them into military service. We then trace how underage enlistment rippled outward, affecting households and institutions much farther afield. By signing up for war, boys and youths acted independently, but with ramification that extended well beyond their own lives. Collectively, their acts constituted a family dilemma, a social and cultural phenomenon, a legal conundrum, and a military and governmental problem. Looking beyond young enlistees' experiences to these broader issues reveals a previously untold story about the Civil War's impact on childhood and youth, households, American legal culture, and military and federal power.[30]

Understanding the significance of Civil War–era controversies over underage enlistment necessitates a broad timespan. Our book therefore opens with the War of 1812, when the enlistment of minors first emerged as a major issue. In that conflict, anger focused on proposals legalizing the unauthorized enlistment of youths aged eighteen to twenty-one. Critics argued that the claims of parents, masters, and guardians to minor sons, apprentices, and wards ought to be as secure as enslavers' hold on their "property." By the end of the nineteenth century, far fewer parents depended on children economically, and analogies between children and slaves had become outdated and offensive. Influenced by new conceptions of child and adolescent psychology, Americans now regarded military service as inappropriate for boys and youths in their mid-teens and younger. Yet even as American society redefined one group of underage youths as strictly off-limits to the military, the federal government retained the expanded authority it had acquired over older minors during the Civil War. Only a timeframe encompassing the whole of the nineteenth century can reveal such trends.

Since not all boys or youths who went to war were formally enlisted, *Of Age* also takes an expansive view of its topic. Young males ended up in army camps for a host of reasons. They appeared not just as soldiers but as military laborers, camp followers, refugees, and onlookers. In the Confederacy, officers forced enslaved youths to accompany them to war to serve as cooks and body "servants." Confederate officials impressed other young African Americans, both enslaved and free, to work on fortifications and perform other grueling and often hazardous labor. As the war progressed, increasing numbers of children fleeing from slavery sought refuge with the Union army.

Many of these boys and youths eventually made it onto muster rolls, but others, especially the very young, worked in return for whatever soldiers provided in the way of food, shelter, clothing, and wages. White children also attached themselves to particular companies or individual soldiers, driven from home by poverty, loss of parents, difficult family situations, or a desire for adventure.

To grasp why so many male children and youths were present in and around Civil War armies requires an appreciation of certain fundamental aspects of nineteenth-century American culture. First is the sheer prevalence of the young. Since the nation's founding, Americans liked to describe themselves as a young people, contrasting the vigor and vibrancy of the New World to the stagnation and corruption of the Old. Behind such jingoism lay a potent demographic truth: the American population was, in fact, remarkably youthful. On the eve of the Civil War, the median age was just 19.4 years.[31] This fact is all the more striking when one considers that puberty arrived later than today, on average around age sixteen for boys.[32] Visitors from abroad viewed the population's tilt toward youth as both obvious and consequential. To their minds, the brashness and energy of America—its boisterous character and outlandish ambitions—sprang from the country's distinctive demographics as well as its novel form of government. Influencing everything from the tenor of the political culture to the percentage of white males available for military service, the simple fact that children and youth predominated in the population set the stage for all that followed.[33]

How people thought about and experienced age also differed markedly from the present day. Antebellum Americans lacked a high degree of "age consciousness," meaning that numeric age played comparatively little role in shaping personal identity or structuring social life.[34] The major exception to this rule was when white males turned twenty-one; at this point they shed their minority status and acquired the right to vote.[35] But in an era when birthday celebrations remained novel, inattention to precise age gradations was the norm. This is reflected in the nebulous language that people used to situate individuals on the spectrum of the human lifespan. A "youth" usually meant someone who was no longer a child but not yet a fully independent adult. A "boy" could refer to either a prepubescent child, a young white man in his twenties, or a Black man of any age—a verbal power play meant to reduce African American men to the status of children. The variations "large boy" and "small boy" further underscore the fact that people in this period focused more on size, strength, and ability than on age when appraising young males and their capacities.[36]

It was not just a comparative lack of age consciousness, however, but a specific understanding of youth that both facilitated underage enlistment and informed parents' strong objections to it. When Civil War-era Americans used "youth" to refer to a life stage, they meant something quite different from our modern concept of adolescence. A time of physiological transformation and emotional upheaval, adolescence is now generally seen as a period that demands parental sympathy and forbearance. In the mid-nineteenth century, "youth" carried far more positive connotations. It referred less to changes occurring in young people's bodies and minds and more to their evolving status, as they grew from beloved but burdensome dependents into household assets on whom their parents could rely. It also lasted longer, especially for sons (who tended to leave home later than daughters), often stretching from their early or mid-teens well into their twenties.[37] Male youths generally pulled their own weight by the age of sixteen—an assumption reflected in the US Census, which in 1850 and 1860 required enumerators to record a "profession, occupation, or trade" for "each person over 15 years of age."[38] But many boys went to work at much earlier ages. Compared to the present day, antebellum Americans expected more from young males in terms of labor productivity, assistance to families and communities, and military service, even as they withheld legal and political rights for longer.

This protracted period of dependence existed alongside an expansive notion of parental authority. Anglo-American common law held that a boy was an "infant" until he turned twenty-one.[39] He remained in the legal custody of his father or guardian, and any contract he signed was considered voidable. Because married women had almost no legal authority over their minor children (and even a widow could be deprived of decision-making powers if her husband named a guardian in his will), parental rights in this period typically meant paternal rights. Few fathers exercised their power to its full extent, although some did—including Thomas Lincoln, who rented out his son between the ages of fourteen and twenty-one and retained his wages, instilling in young Abraham the fervent belief that every man should have "the right to eat the bread . . . that his own hand earns."[40] Over the course of the nineteenth century, legal developments softened but did not fundamentally challenge the patriarchal order. Judges began to award custody to mothers in cases involving children of "tender years," for instance.[41] They also used the common law concept of *parens patriae* to extend the state's reach into the private home, asserting custodial power over dependents in the absence of proper paternal rule.[42] Still, at the outset of the Civil War, the vast majority of white fathers could rest secure in their legal right to control their minor children.

Minor sons' legal subordination and extensive duties to households meshed well with militia duty, as popularly conceived, but not at all well with enlistment in the regular US army. The sharp distinctions that nineteenth-century Americans drew between these two forms of military service were at the heart of the debates over underage enlistees. Following the Revolution, Americans' deep suspicion of standing or professional armies led to the establishment of a dual military system, based on the belief that the nation should rely primarily on state militias for protection. Although the Constitution allowed for the establishment of a federal army and navy, these forces remained small throughout the pre–Civil War period, and regular soldiers were frequently disparaged as desperate men, willing to sign away their liberty for sustenance. When Americans envisioned youths in the US military, they often conjured up images of moral corruption and coercion or even impressment; when they imagined youths serving in the militia or voluntary forces, they pictured the embodiment of the nation itself.

Parents therefore accepted that minors above age eighteen (or even younger) should participate in locally raised militias and voluntary companies, while angrily protesting policies that allowed anyone below age twenty-one to enlist in the regulars without their consent. This was not because they believed children should entirely be barred from the US army or navy. The army accepted musicians from the age of twelve, while the navy relied heavily on boys as young as thirteen to serve in such roles as powder monkey, cabin boy, and midshipman. In these cases, however, the father or guardian signed a military contract, similar to an apprenticeship contract but wholly binding. Such an arrangement may have been the best available option for poor families, but it required parents to relinquish all rights to the child for a term of five years, including any say over where he might be sent. In contrast, militia service was short term and geographically bounded—usually restricted to within the state—and typically performed under the watchful eyes of male relatives and neighbors. Even as the militia system deteriorated in the decades preceding the Civil War, these longstanding practical and conceptual distinctions between different types of military service significantly influenced Americans' attitudes toward underage enlistment.

Yet another critical context for making sense of Civil War–era disputes over underage enlistees is the decentralized legal system that existed in antebellum America. Because a large majority of Americans in this period resided in rural areas and small towns, court days often meant face-to-face interactions among people who knew one another quite well. In contrast, the federal judiciary was seen as a wholly separate and remote system that dealt with matters of concern only to the central government. When federal authorities usurped the power of state and local courts, as in the much-publicized fugitive slave cases of the 1850s, Americans often responded with outrage.[43] People looked to local and state courts for day-to-day justice, to such an extent that lower-level courts functioned almost as governing bodies.[44] The decentralized nature of the antebellum legal system is also evident in state laws that protected access to the writ of habeas corpus, allowing individuals to file for relief at the local and state as well as federal level, ensuring that people did not have to travel far to reach a judge. When Americans spoke of the "Great Writ" in this period, they were not referring to an abstruse legal concept, but rather to a practical tool to guard against unwarranted detainment or imprisonment—including by military officers.

In sum, to comprehend the nineteenth-century preoccupation with youth enlistment requires an imaginative leap into a very different world—one in which numeric age had little bearing on daily life, households relied heavily on the labor or wages of minor children, and both military power and legal authority were to a large extent locally rooted. During the Civil War, people viewed the volunteer companies that formed in their local areas more as extensions of the community than as components of an institution that stood apart from it. Populated by their own relatives and neighbors, the army camps that sprang up nearby were not sealed-off citadels, despite officers' efforts to curtail civilian access. They were spaces where young boys might sneak in to watch troops drilling and fathers could show up to retrieve underage sons, expecting no resistance to their claims. When decrees from Washington disrupted this face-to-face world, closing off familiar ways of seeking redress, the war's transformative effects hit home.

* * *

Looking at the history of the Civil War through the lens of underage enlistment provides an original perspective on this much-studied conflict. In the chapters that follow, we show how the war accelerated the growing emphasis on chronological age. We unravel the seeming paradox of mass

youth enlistment in an era renowned for its celebration of childhood innocence. We offer a fresh account of the importance of household economies,
showing how expectations of young males shaped responses to underage enlistment, and how young enlistees' removal from the home affected parents
and families. We uncover what amounted to a traffic in boys and youths that
emerged in the United States near the war's end, and we show how the ideal-
ization of the Confederate boy soldier in the postwar era contributed to the
rise of the Lost Cause mythology. Finally, we provide a groundbreaking interpretation of the causes and consequences of Lincoln's wartime suspensions
of habeas corpus and reassess the war's lasting effects on the nation's dual
military system. By looking at memoirs and other sources with an eye to age,
and by scrutinizing suspect military records, the war we thought we knew
begins to look less familiar.

The large-scale military mobilization on both sides transformed the
Civil War into a great age-consciousness-raising event. Historians who
have tracked the growing importance of chronological age have primarily focused on late nineteenth-century developments in the realms of
education and medicine, such as the rise of age-graded schools and the
emergence of pediatrics. But, as we show, the military played a pioneering
role in promoting age consciousness at a much earlier date. In the mid-
nineteenth century, it was among the few institutions that imposed strict
age limits, at least in theory, and the only one preoccupied with understanding the process of physiological development in relation to precise
age gradations. By 1860, US and European army physicians without exception argued that males in their teens or younger had no business in
uniform. Although calls to raise the age of enlistment during the Civil
War lost out to the relentless demands for more men, warnings about age-
related debility convinced US legislators to set the minimum age for conscription at twenty instead of eighteen—a discrepancy that historians have
not previously explained. More broadly, army physicians shaped public
consciousness by creating what became a widely told cautionary tale of
seemingly healthy young soldiers who broke down on long marches, filling
hospital and draining military resources. The result was a curious situation: although the Civil War included a higher proportion of underage
enlistees than any other conflict in US history, it was fought at a time when
concerns about the hidden physical frailties of youth—including lanky
young men in their upper teens or even early twenties—were more widespread than either before or since.

The war also propelled the slow-moving trend toward age documentation and a preference for written records rather than oral testimony as a means of verifying age.[45] With the Confederate army enlisting almost all white males of military age, and Union enrollment officers going door to door inquiring about people's birthdates, the conflict helped to normalize on a mass scale what would become a mundane and unavoidable part of life in the twentieth century: stating one's age or birthdate and recording it on a government form.[46] It also drove home how much fine gradations in age could matter. "I was only 16 years 8 months old when I joined the company, and am now 17 years 2 months and 9 days old," wrote one unhappy Union soldier in November 1861. "I wish to leave the Army and return to my home."[47] Such pleas were often rejected, but when successful, the consequences for the petitioner could be huge. He might gain release rather than enduring a full enlistment term, or he might be sentenced "on account of extreme youth" to a month's confinement on bread and water, versus a year's hard labor with a ball and chain. With so much at stake, petitioners quickly learned to be precise when referring to age.[48]

While Civil War Americans regularly sounded the alarm about the susceptibility of young bodies to breakdown or disease, they showed little concern about the effects of war on childish minds. Highlighting the vast numbers of boys and youths who experienced this conflict, we question one of the main pillars of scholarship on the history of childhood: the notion that middle-class parents, wedded to an ideal of childhood innocence, sheltered the young from adult interests and concerns. To the contrary, we show how parents of all classes allowed boys and youths to participate in war, either directly or vicariously. They took young boys off to watch battles, allowed them to follow the armies, or purchased books steeped in bloodshed. A burgeoning celebration of childhood innocence instead coexisted with—and perhaps contributed to—a sense that the young required early knowledge of a perilous world, better to equip them to confront its dangers. At a time when the young made such significant contributions to family economies, most parents necessarily thought about their sons in both sentimental and material terms; the two were not antithetical but thoroughly intertwined, and even mutually reinforcing.

Indeed, parental expectations regarding minor youths' economic contributions lay at the heart of their resistance to underage enlistment, even as the very same expectations drove many poor youths to enlist. Negotiations between parents and older sons were supposed to work something like

this: when seventeen-year-old Leander Stillwell expressed his desire to enlist in the summer of 1861, his father mulled things over for a moment and
replied, "Well, Leander, if you think it's your duty to go, I shall make no objection. But you're the only boy I now have at home big enough to work, so
I wish you'd put it off until we get the wheat sowed, and the corn gathered."
Leander quickly assented to these terms.[49] When boys enlisted without consent, they refused to engage in such negotiations, usurping authority not yet
theirs to claim and spurning obligations still owed to parents. As a mother
from Illinois explained in a letter to Lincoln, military pay was no compensation for the loss of an older youth's labor on a family farm: "My son leaving
us we had to hire help and pay 16 dollars a month, and my boy only gets
13."[50] Poor widows and disabled fathers suffered most from the enlistment
of minor sons, resorting to such expressions as "my only dependence" or "all
my dependance" to convey the magnitude of their losses.

By exposing parents' economic reliance on minor children, cases of underage enlistment reveal the endurance of a communal vision of the household during this vaunted age of individualism. Both Confederates and
Unionists who petitioned government offices tended to view wartime sacrifice as something demanded of households rather than individuals.[51] Even
as the US and Confederate governments established universal parameters
for service that applied to individual men, civilians tended to assess what
each family owed on a case-by-case basis, looking at the overall household
situation. The economic status and health of the parents, the number of dependent siblings who remained at home, whether other family members
were currently serving or had already become casualties—these were among
the key factors that people weighed when judging the government's claim to
any given man. The US draft policy acknowledged public sensibilities in this
regard by exempting the only sons of dependent widows or infirm parents,
but this provision was of no help to parents of sons who ran off to volunteer.[52]
And in an era with essentially no social safety net, many parents in less dire
circumstances felt an equal claim to hold back their sons.

Along with a focus on the war's effects on households, this book illuminates
one of the uglier sides of conflict: the widespread exploitation of youth. The
Civil War initially looked like a bonanza for young males, opening a range of
military-related jobs that paid substantially more than they could earn from
civilian employers. For every young enlistee who secured a decent bounty
and an adult wage, however, there was another who found himself trapped
in an exploitative situation. Viewing soldiering as work and concentrating on

the changing nature of the wartime labor market, we show that the coerced labor of the young, especially in the United States, increased significantly over time as the draft raised the value of young recruits. Boys of all kinds ended up performing military work against their will—from indentured free Black boys and enslaved youths to white boys living in rural areas and large cities—confounding traditional stereotypes of boy soldiers as plucky heroes authoring their own fate. Presenting both unprecedented opportunities for the young and unprecedented risks, the Civil War simultaneously expanded the extent of unfreedom in some ways and narrowed it in others, as the federal government emancipated masses of enslaved youths while holding others to service.

By moving underage enlistees to the heart of the story, *Of Age* also offers a new perspective on Lincoln's wartime suspensions of habeas corpus. Scholars in recent years have debated not only whether Lincoln's actions were constitutional, but the extent to which they paved the way for the extraordinary expansion of executive privilege during George W. Bush's presidency.[53] While clearly an important question, the all-but-singular focus on political prisoners has obscured the broader significance of the writ during the Civil War. It was parents' frequent recourse to the writ that helped to convince Lincoln and other federal officials of the need for a blanket suspension to stanch the loss of military manpower. And for many ordinary Americans, it was the inability to recover minor enlistees, more than the suppression of political dissent, that drove home how this suspension threatened individual freedom.

The central role that parents and families played in Civil War–era habeas jurisprudence has been obscured by the fact that cases involving minor enlistees turned on the issue of jurisdiction: the central legal question being debated was not whether federal and military needs superseded parental rights, but whether state and local courts had the authority to hear such cases at all. Today, federal jurisdiction over the US military seems like the natural order of things; the idea of state or local courts discharging men from the US army is all but unthinkable. But at the time, the Lincoln Administration's claim to exclusive federal jurisdiction over habeas cases, including those involving minor enlistees, struck many American as an outrageous, even shocking attempt to usurp the power of states and local communities. Only by grasping that the issue of parental rights was implied in these jurisdictional struggles—that Civil War Americans tended to view the defense of state and local judges' authority *as* a defense of parental rights—can we fully appreciate the stakes involved as people at the time perceived them.

By setting the age of enlistment without consent at eighteen, both the United States and the Confederacy established what in many ways amounted to a new age of majority for male youths. They empowered or, in the case of the Confederacy, required minors eighteen and older to leave their homes, without compensating parents or ensuring that they would receive any portion of their children's bounty or pay. Beyond this, the US federal government insisted on holding even younger soldiers who had fraudulently enlisted, which meant asserting that boys of fourteen years—and in rare cases, even younger—could sign binding contracts. Never before had the United States claimed the right to hold minor soldiers en masse during wartime, regardless of parental consent. Given how radically this departed from past practices, it is no wonder that parents responded with anger and bewilderment when told they had no means of legal redress.

If looking at underage enlistment casts a very different light on wartime debates over habeas corpus, it also leads us to think differently about the mobilization of military force and its transformation over the course of the war.[54] The standard narrative begins with men rising up alongside members of their neighborhoods and communities. In this telling, wartime volunteerism and the state-based organization of the Union army exemplify America's citizen-soldier tradition. But debates over underage enlistment spotlight the fact that the Civil War led to an overhaul of the old dual military system and the establishment of an entirely new military order. By changing militia laws and enrolling volunteers in a federally controlled force—one in which men served for extended periods in the cause of national defense—the Civil War altered the legal and conceptual basis of the distinction between militia service and service in the regulars, ultimately paving the way for Americans' embrace of a national military.

This new order essentially took ideas about the appropriate age for militia service and applied them to a situation that in many respects more closely resembled service in the regulars—one in which enlistees signed up for long periods of time, travelled vast distances from their homes, and served in a large, centralized force. Civil War volunteers—centrally controlled and bound to protect their respective nations—took on duties that were quite foreign, even anathema, to militia service as traditionally defined. It is therefore not surprising that resistance to the growing centralization of military authority and the expansion of federal power should take the form of disputes over young soldiers. For it was in these disputes that the federal government most forcefully asserted the new authority that it would eventually claim over its citizens, as parents found themselves powerless to retrieve their offspring from the military, and state judges lost the right to inquire into underage enlistment. And it was therefore in these disputes that ordinary people most loudly said no to centralized military authority.

The fact that so many boys and youths served in the military during the Civil War does not mean that people took children's military service for granted. They grappled with this issue, but for very different reasons than we do today. They cared little about war's potentially traumatic effects on young minds, but they worried a great deal about the ability of young bodies to withstand the hardships of service. They did not blanch at the notion of young males bearing arms, but they had strong opinions regarding the forms of military service appropriate for youths to perform. They would not have understood the tendency to associate armed youths with failed states, for their own fears concerning underage enlistment went hand-in-hand with anxiety over the consolidation of government power. Finally, they did not see young casualties of war as victims of adults' moral and political failures, but rather as heroic martyrs, whose very youth made them all the more inspirational. To the extent that Civil War Americans perceived youth enlistment as a humanitarian crisis at all, its victims were not the boy soldiers themselves, but their abandoned parents, unjustly deprived of the economic and emotional support to which they were entitled.

* * *

Americans now widely accept eighteen as the minimum age of enlistment and look back with a mixture of awe and horror at the children who served in Civil War armies. But the focus on the conflict's youngest soldiers, who in truth created a sensation even at the time, has distorted the larger story of youth enlistment during the Civil War. Early in the nineteenth century, Americans typically viewed service in the US regulars as a man's job—a harsh, subordinate position that those below age twenty-one should enter into only with parental consent. A feckless minor who signed a fraudulent contract could usually escape its terms if a parent protested, and sometimes even if he himself had a change of heart.

The Civil War fundamentally altered this reality by blurring the distinction between volunteer and regular service and normalizing the idea of youths enlisting in a national military while still in their teens. The story told here, then, is not one of an ever-rising minimum military age, as Americans gradually came to view childhood and youth as a special stage of development requiring protection from the rigors of service and the horrors of war. Instead, by allowing youths of eighteen to enlist without parental consent, and by refusing to release even younger enlistees more often than not, the Lincoln Administration strengthened the federal government's sense of a rightful claim to boys below the age of majority. In 1868, when Congress published *Statutes Relating to the Army of the United States*, it set the standard minimum age for privates at sixteen, lower than ever before.[55] In a broad sense, the Civil War helped to pave the way for the military policies of World Wars I and II, which subjected males as young as eighteen to a national draft—a proposition that the US Congress had rejected in 1863, when it set the minimum draft age at twenty. During the Vietnam War, outrage over the fact that youths could be drafted before they could vote finally led to a nationwide movement to close the three-year gap. But the solution (lowering the voting age to eighteen) appeared so obvious, and manpower needs so pressing, that the other alternative (raising the draft age to twenty-one) was never seriously contemplated.[56]

Contemporary culture has extended adolescence, and neuroscientists today argue that young people's brains predispose them to greater impulsivity well into their twenties, yet relatively few Americans question whether an eighteen-year-old should be able to enter into a binding military contract.[57] The law is now definitive: the federal government has a right to hold such youths, regardless of what their parents think, and whether or not young enlistees themselves get cold feet. That reality is not the natural order of things, but rather an unrecognized legacy of the Civil War: the outcome of the heated battles over federal power and parental authority waged during the nineteenth century. It was a shift that went together with the breakdown of the dual military system and a new willingness to embrace a national military. So complete was this transformation that it eventually became difficult to find traces in mainstream American politics and culture of what was once a powerful and widespread sentiment—a deep hostility to the very notion of a standing army.

The Americans who entered into the Civil War held far more apprehensive views of what a fully nationalized military might mean for individual freedom. That is why some outraged parents referred to the army in ways that strike us as odd and inappropriate. They complained that their children had been "kidnapped," for example, or called for their release from "service imprisonment." Such was the view of C. S. Barton, a "loyal sitizen of the State of Iowa" who wrote to the Secretary of War in December 1862 to "demand" the discharge of his nineteen-year-old son, Joseph. According to Barton, he had forbidden officers from mustering Joseph into service after the youth had enlisted without his consent. His son was still a minor, he had argued, and physically unfit for army life. But another officer subsequently came to their house and "took the boy from a sick bed to iowa city," where he was sworn into service. "[I]t is a hard thing for parents to submit to have their children kidnaped and draged from them in this free country," Barton bitterly complained, "especially those that have had father and grandfather that fought in the revelution and in 1812 for their own rights and their childrens."[58]

Legally, Barton's claim had no merit. By that point in the war, the army could enlist minors above age eighteen without parental consent, and Joseph probably wanted to join the fight. But Barton did not register or accept this new reality. Because Joseph had "never been from under my control," he felt that his authority could not be legitimately breached: his minor son was *his*. That rogue officers could come to his home, roust his son, and carry him off to be mustered into the army could mean only one thing—that the liberties his ancestors had sacrificed to secure were in abeyance. For this was precisely the kind of scenario that the nation's republican system of government had been founded to guard against.

Barton no doubt opposed Joseph's enlistment for self-interested reasons, but he did so by drawing on principles that were deeply embedded in prewar American political culture. His understanding of centralized military power as something inherently dangerous to the republic, his sense that his rights as a citizen derived from his membership in a particular state rather than the nation, and his conviction that one of those rights was the authority to control his minor son—these beliefs were central to the social and political world bequeathed by the American Revolution. What must have been hard for parents like Barton to fathom was how quickly that world was receding, as the immense effort to defeat the Confederacy called forth new convictions about federal power, military service, and national belonging.

Barton's petition went unheeded, and Joseph remained in the army until January 1865, when he was discharged for wounds sustained earlier at the Battle of Cedar Creek. After the war, he married and raised a family, claimed 160 acres of land under the Homestead Act, and joined his local chapter of the Grand Army of the Republic.[59] Due to his injuries, he received a veteran's pension, and he could rest secure knowing that his wife would continue to receive assistance if she outlived him.[60] Unlike his father, Joseph surely did not view the nation's military as a force that ran roughshod over civilians' rights. Nor would he have located his citizenship in any given state, for his sacrifices had been on behalf of the Union, and the rewards he reaped flowed from the federal government. In this sense, his story embodies the United States' transformation from a plural entity into a singular one.

Historians have paid far less attention to the stories of people like Joseph's father—loyal Americans who nonetheless resisted changes that proved necessary to keep the nation whole. In the end, the US government took many unprecedented steps to defeat the Confederacy, from establishing a system of internal taxation to enacting a federal draft to abolishing slavery. It also had to squelch beliefs about the sanctity of parental rights and the dangers of military and federal overreach that threatened to imperil the war effort. When considered in isolation, the conflicts over minor enlistees look like mere family dramas. Yet they added up to something much more significant—a struggle over the extent to which power should be centralized and how it ought to be checked to prevent it from becoming tyrannical. For better and for worse, the war would lead many Americans to shed their ancestors' wariness and embrace a more benign view of centralized political and military power.[61]

PART I
PARENTAL RIGHTS AND THE DUTY TO BEAR ARMS

Congress, Courts, and the Military

1

Competing Obligations

Debating Underage Enlistment in the War of 1812

Nineteen-year-old Nicholas Flynt got himself into trouble in the fall of 1813, when war made its presence felt in his small town in eastern Georgia. Reports from the Mississippi Territory told of a horrifying attack on Fort Sims by a faction of Creek Indians allied with the British.[1] The federal government called up the militia, and "in a moment of hilarity" Nicholas volunteered. When he then failed to show up at the appointed time and place, a junior officer tracked him down and brought him to the camp. Nicholas's father, however, contested the militia's right to hold his son. Pursuing the matter in court, he hired lawyers who argued that he had "not only a legal but a moral right" to his son's "services and labor." "[T]o one who has protected and supported us in the tender period of infancy, we owe allegiance till the age of 21," they argued, "respect and attention ever after."[2] The judges had to agree, despite their support for the war effort: in the absence of legislation that explicitly expanded the military's reach, a father could not legally be deprived of the "person & labor" of his minor son. "The public mind," however, apparently saw the case as less clear-cut. According to the local paper, the decision to discharge Nicholas left the community "considerably agitated."[3]

The enlistment of minors emerged as a major point of controversy during the highly divisive War of 1812. Five months into the conflict, the Democratic Republican majority sought to address the shortage of troops by lowering the age at which a youth could enlist without parental consent to eighteen. The Federalists, who had unanimously voted against President James Madison's request for a declaration of war, were equally united in their opposition to the legalization of minority enlistment. Anger was especially intense in New England, where it eventually helped to fuel a virtual rebellion against federal authority. But such opposition was by no means limited to a single region or political party. Siding with the Federalists, a number of prominent Democratic Republicans in the House, and all but four in the Senate, rejected the proposals to jettison parental consent that were floated in

1812. One Pennsylvania newspaper went so far as to decry the four senators who supported "this *kidnapping* section of the bill" as unworthy of public respect.[4] In short, the battle over minor enlistees reflected the era's sharp partisan divide and regional tensions, but it cannot be reduced to a proxy conflict over broader issues.[5]

Instead, by calling attention to the liminal status of a subset of free, white male youth, the controversy raised questions of both practical importance and profound theoretical significance. Free, white men assumed their legal majority at the age of twenty-one, but their military responsibilities to their home states began three years earlier. That discrepancy created ambiguity about the status of those between the ages of eighteen and twenty-one. Were they fundamentally domestic dependents, lacking political rights and subject to the authority of household heads? Or were they citizens with duties and obligations that lay beyond their family?[6] In regions where labor was in chronically short supply, the answer to this question had immediate, real-world effects. Yet the struggles over minority enlistment also raised thorny theoretical issues that mattered greatly to Americans anxious to protect their fledgling nation—issues that concerned the appropriate balance between state and federal power, the form of military organization best suited to a republic, and the proper scope of parental authority.

Both sides in the debate attempted to legitimize their arguments by appealing to precedent, even though the controversy over minority enlistment was essentially new, a product of the American Revolution. When Democratic Republicans declared that eighteen-year-olds should be allowed to enlist without leave from parents, guardians, or masters, they presented the idea not as a novelty but as part of a long tradition. In a way, they were right: it was unexceptional for boys in colonial America to shoulder arms in their early to mid-teens. Many of the country's most celebrated heroes had begun military careers at a young age—from George Washington, who served in the militia at the age of fifteen during the Seven Years' War, to Andrew Jackson, who fought in the Revolution as a fourteen-year-old.[7] But as opponents were quick to counter, the proposed legislation would enable minors to enroll not in a temporary militia, but rather in the regular US army. Allowing a boy to join relatives and neighbors in defending his home community was one thing. Putting him in a federally controlled, professional army was another matter entirely. Not only did such service remove the youth from community oversight, potentially plunging him into a world of professional soldiers and harsh military discipline, it also altered his legal status by releasing him from parental control. Military service as a regular soldier emancipated minors; service in the militia did not.[8]

For their part, Federalists and the Democratic Republicans who opposed minority enlistment also clad fundamentally novel arguments in the trappings of tradition. They condemned the proposed legislation as an assault on age-old parental rights that were, in fact, of recent date. Legal scholars once traced the "empire of the father" to ancient precedents, but historian Holly Brewer has convincingly shown that it arose in the seventeenth- and eighteenth-centuries, when the notion of consent, based on experience and reason, began to challenge blind obedience to hierarchies.[9] Before this time, children as young as seven or eight could enter into apprenticeships or bind themselves in marriage; the young could be hanged for law breaking, vote if they met the property requirements, or be elected to high office. But as contractual relations were figured as the basis for legal relations and political authority, all those under twenty-one—regardless of class or social status—became minors in the eyes of the law, incapable of signing legally binding contracts, serving on juries, voting, or exercising any of the other prerogatives now understood as properly belonging to adults. As Brewer puts it, the American Revolution reduced children and youth to "a more complete kind of dependence."[10] Meanwhile, writers and social commentators in the new republic further accentuated parental influence by depicting domestic life as the seedbed of public virtue.[11] The notion of parental rights as sacrosanct, in other words, was modern rather than longstanding, and those who opposed minority enlistment were as selective in their use of the past as their opponents.

Despite their enhanced legal authority over children, free white parents in the new republic often struggled to hold on to restive sons. In fact, many parents felt that recent developments had undermined rather than strengthened their authority. With its celebration of liberty over constraint and tradition, the Revolution had emboldened sons and apprentices to shrug off their obligations and strike out on their own. Longer-term trends, including the rise of out-of-wedlock pregnancies and a lessening of parental control over children's marriage choices, also raised alarm.[12] These developments were particularly concerning to New England farmers, who historically had depended on their minor children's labor, exploiting "with doubled intensity the only labor resource available to them—their sons."[13]

As the subdivision of land reached its limits and rural youth began to be drawn into an emerging wage labor market, this tight intergenerational dependence began to fray.[14] By the War of 1812, many New Englanders feared the tenuousness of their control over sons, even as they adamantly defended parental claims to minor children's labor as a form of household property.

Regional differences and competing labor systems thus loomed large in the debate over minority enlistment. Opponents contrasted the plight of hardworking New England farmers and honorable mechanics in cities like Philadelphia and New York to the situation of wealthy southern planters. The former, they argued, would suffer the loss of their most valuable asset—their property in children's and apprentices' labor—while the latter remained untouched by the legislation. This depiction of a stark regional contrast did not accurately reflect how things looked on the ground. Non-elite households in the southern states, including those headed by small-scale enslavers like Mr. Flynt, also leaned heavily on their older children to get by.[15] Likewise, many northern states still had enslaved populations that numbered in the thousands or tens of thousands.[16] By obscuring these realities, Federalist legislators constructed a misleading but politically potent dichotomy, positing a north that relied on sons and apprentices, and a south that relied on enslaved labor. In the process, they helped to lay the intellectual foundation for the free labor ideology that would loom so large in sectional politics.[17]

Notably absent in the debates over minority enlistment was any concern with children's safety or wellbeing. These were first and foremost property disputes, focused on the question of whether parents' claims to children's labor would prevail over the demands of the federal government. But they were also arguments that extended beyond the interests of parents and children, encompassing America's dual military tradition as well as the balance of power among its new governing institutions. The War of 1812 did not resolve the question of who could ultimately lay claim to enlisted minors; controversy simmered throughout the antebellum era, returning to a full boil during the Civil War. In the end, the federal government would succeed in wresting control from parents and local communities, decisively settling the debate in favor of centralizing military power. Only by going back to the early republic is it possible to grasp the extent and significance of this shift.

The Creation of a Dual Military Order in Post-Revolutionary America

The question of who should control the labor of the young—parents or federal officials—was a peculiarly American one. In Britain, the Crown lent the military such vast powers as to all but abrogate parental rights. Not only could minors be enlisted in the Royal Navy without parental consent, they could also be "forcibly impressed into it, against the joint consent of their parents and themselves," as US Supreme Court Justice Joseph Story observed in 1816.[18] British officers who enlisted minors faced no legal penalties, and British parents had little recourse if minor children ran off to join the military. By contrast, politicians and judges in post-Revolutionary America typically rejected the military's right to enlist and hold minors absent specific wartime legislation. Several characteristics of the early republic enhanced the parental rights of free, white fathers, including an emphasis on the family as the basis of social order, and a tendency to augment the powers of the household head by reifying the subordinate status of his dependents. From the outset, courts and legislators interpreted property in children as inviolable and a fundamental aspect of household governance.

Americans' wariness of centralized military power lay at the heart of disputes over how to weigh the relative importance of parents' property in their children against the federal government's right to the service of its citizens. Many who emigrated to America arrived with a fierce hatred of the regular armies that had once oppressed them, feelings that were further amplified by the colonists' experience at the hands of British soldiers during the Revolution. Throughout the first half of the nineteenth century, professional forces were commonly seen as "undemocratic, un-American, and almost unnecessary: caste-ridden, cliquish, hidebound," as historian Marcus Cunliffe puts it.[19] These attitudes explain the passionate support for the dual military system created in the aftermath of the Revolution, which retained the old colonial-era militia system alongside the new US army and navy.

English colonists brought the militia system to America. Each colony had its own militia system, based on slightly different rules, but all were composed of local men, with boys joining their kinfolk and neighbors at some point between the age of sixteen and eighteen. In times of peace, service was obligatory but not especially arduous. Militiamen simply showed up on muster days with a weapon in hand to drill, after which they drank and socialized. Typically confined to propertied males of a particular age, militia membership was understood both as a duty and as a privilege, symbolizing full citizenship and a commitment to the public good.[20]

The situation was quite different in wartime. Although all eligible males had to enroll in their local militia, only a select portion were ever mobilized to fight. Colonies relied on a variety of systems to determine which militiamen would serve, but a general pattern existed: most of those sent to war were poor, unmarried, or socially marginal. Some received bounties or other inducements to volunteer, while others were pressed into service against their will.[21] In the post-Revolutionary era, a powerful but mythical narrative arose that held that independence had been won when a unified mass of citizen soldiers voluntarily rose up to defeat the British. In reality, the question of which militiamen should be called up and under what conditions had provoked fierce class conflict in some colonies, leading to calls to centralize or dramatically reform the militia system.[22]

Few had stronger opinions on this topic than George Washington. He had helped to establish the Continental Army in 1775, in which enlistees signed up for multi-year terms to serve under officers appointed by the Continental Congress. As the commander-in-chief of this force, Washington viewed militia units—which followed their own command structures and often refused to venture beyond their local areas—as disorderly, militarily feeble, and impossible to manage. In debating the shape of the new nation, nationalists like Alexander Hamilton and James Madison joined Washington in pushing for the creation of a permanent US military force. To make their case, they pointed to the incontestable fact that Continental Army soldiers and professional French forces—not militiamen—were primarily responsible for securing the patriots' victory.[23]

Support for the creation of a federally managed force found broad acceptance given the obvious need for troops to guard the new nation's southern and western frontiers and to provide for coastal defense. But the establishment of a professional army and navy was also famously contentious, with some of the most vigorous debates over the Constitution focusing on the composition and nature of the regulars and the status of the militia. While Washington and his supporters favored centralizing power, opponents led by Thomas Jefferson feared and distrusted standing armies. This concern had been a staple of Revolutionary politics, as when Samuel Adams penned a letter denouncing such forces as "always dangerous to the Liberties of the People." Prone to developing their own rules and forms of discipline, they soon came to consider themselves "a Body distinct from the rest of the Citizens," he warned, and thus needed to be "watched with a jealous eye."[24] Looking back to ancient precedent, delegates to the Constitutional Convention agreed that a professional military could easily become a tool to subvert republicanism and insisted that any such force should be placed firmly under civilian control. These beliefs lay behind the constitutional provisions that made the president commander-in-chief yet granted only Congress the power to declare war and mandated the reauthorization of military funding at least every two years.[25]

Profound distrust of standing armies also ensured that delegates refused to yield full control over state militias to the federal government. Virtually all saw a state-based militia system as an essential bulwark of the new republic, even as they conceded that the recent experience of relying on haphazardly trained and often unreliable militiamen had shown that some federal oversight of the militia system was necessary. In the compromises hammered out over the Constitution, delegates agreed that Congress would have the authority to "provide for organizing, arming, and disciplining, the Militia, and for governing such Part of them as may be employed in the Service of the United States." Another centralizing measure gave Congress the right to call forth the militia to "execute the Laws of the Union, suppress Insurrections and repel Invasions." But the states still retained significant autonomy, including the prerogative of appointing officers and training the militia, as well as responsibility for mobilizing militiamen in response to federal calls.[26] To further guard against the consolidation of military force, the second amendment fatefully proclaimed the militia system so vital for guaranteeing "a free State" that "the right of the people to keep and bear arms shall not be infringed."[27]

A series of domestic uprisings among farmers, debtors, and other ordinary Americans in the 1780s and 1790s prompted additional reorganization of the militia system. In Shays' Rebellion (1786–1787), the Whiskey Rebellion (1794), and other internal uprisings, local militia units either actively supported insurgents or refused to turn out to enforce laws or policies that benefited the elite.[28] In response, Congress passed a number of laws to federalize the militia system and to clarify when and how the president could call militia units into service. Sweeping away the varying age restrictions of the past, the Militia Act of 1792 made service obligatory for every "free ablebodied white male citizen" between the ages of eighteen and forty-five. It laid out a militiaman's duty to equip himself and to muster at designated times and provided a broad organizational structure for state militias.[29] In addition, the act mandated that the president could call up a state's militia units whenever he deemed necessary. Further buttressing executive authority at both the federal and state level, another militia law passed in 1795 specified that in cases of internal insurrections, a state's legislature or governor could empower the president to call forth any number of militia units from that or any other state to "suppress such insurrection."[30]

Political leaders may have regarded the militia as a useful way to protect existing power structures—a "statutory instrument of the state"—but militiamen tended to see their own service quite differently. Viewing their companies and regiments as "associational and community-centered," they resisted "even the relatively limited claims of authority that they faced under a weak system of federal and state militia organizations."[31] They routinely refused to fall into line if required to serve in ways they felt were unreasonable or outside the proper scope of their duties. Popularly understood as service geared toward the defense of one's local area, a militia commitment was expected to be short-term, relatively decentralized, and performed among one's peers.[32] Militia laws registered this general understanding. Congress may have enhanced the president's authority to use state militias, but he could do so only after making a request of a state legislature or governor. Even then, militia units remained under their own command structures and disciplinary regimes, and they could be called into federal service for no more than three months in a single year.

Americans in the first half of the nineteenth century tended to view the regular army as the antithesis of the militia. Rather than serving a brief stint, army recruits signed up for five-year terms. On entering the federal military, enlistees lost many of the rights guaranteed to them under the Constitution, such as the right of free speech and assembly, and found themselves subject to rules, procedures, and legal codes that applied to no other aspect of American life. Anyone charged with violating these policies faced a separate court system—the court martial panel—that handed down decisions entirely free from judicial oversight. While the nation's civilian legal system initially borrowed heavily from British precedents and then became increasingly Americanized over time, military justice remained inflexible, hierarchical, and undemocratic.

Just as conditions in the regulars set them apart from independent militiamen, the professionalization of the military widened the gulf between army officers and militia leaders. In contrast to the militia system, which remained largely rooted in community values, with officers drawn from local communities and popularly elected by their men, US officers developed a sense of exclusivity based on specialized knowledge, distinctive education, and disciplinary codes derived from European practice. In 1802, the federal government established the United States Military Academy in West Point, New York, to produce an officer corps equipped with technical knowledge in fields like engineering and mathematics. Modelled after similar institutions founded in Europe in the previous century, West Point closely followed their example. Cadets learned military drill using French manuals and studied the latest developments in tactics and strategies by reading the works of Carl von Clausewitz and analyzing the actions of famed generals like Napoleon Bonaparte and the Duke of Wellington.[33] Based on foreign customs and procedures, the US military appeared to embody its aristocratic origins.[34]

The increasing distinction between locally raised militia units and regular US forces led by a professional officer corps set the stage for the debates over underage enlistment in the War of 1812. Those who prioritized filling the ranks would argue that boys had long served alongside older men; it was irrelevant whether they did so as militiamen or US soldiers. But for parents like Mr. Flynt, the distinction was critical. Flynt did not question that his son, having reached the age of eighteen, was liable for militia service. In fact, prior to Nicholas's aborted enlistment, he had already "stood a draft," meaning that he had presented himself to be selected for militia duty. But the circumstances that led Flynt to seek Nicholas's discharge were different: the call had come from the federal government, the militiamen would be crossing the state line into the Mississippi Territory, and the unit might be commanded by regular army officers. Such service—performed far from home and under the auspices of distant authorities—is where many parents drew the line.[35]

1812: The Debate over Minority Enlistment

The War of 1812 proved so controversial that it threatened to tear the new republic apart. The conflict stemmed from long-brewing maritime disputes that arose during the Napoleonic Wars, when Britain brushed aside the United States' claims to neutrality and denied it the right to trade freely with Europe. The Royal Navy compounded matters by impressing American merchant sailors, causing outrage and reviving the anti-British and anti-monarchical sentiments that had fueled the Revolution.[36] A group of Democratic Republicans clamored for the invasion and annexation of British

North America, insisting that Canadians would welcome Americans as liberators. New England Federalists, fearing that war with Britain would lead to a coastal invasion and disrupt maritime commerce, vehemently disagreed. Resentful of the three-fifths compromise and Virginia's seeming lock on the presidency, they also jealously guarded their region's political influence, eschewing the acquisition of Canada and western territories that would further dilute their power.[37]

Rancor between parties and regions only grew once the United States entered the war in June 1812 and Congress began to debate how to raise troops. In November 1812, Representative David R. Williams of South Carolina, chair of the Committee on Military Affairs, introduced a bill to bolster lagging enlistments. It proposed to increase army pay, forgive recruits' debts, offer land bounties for service, and—most controversially—allow those between eighteen and twenty-one to enlist without the consent of parents, masters, or guardians.[38] Williams anticipated no trouble with the first three measures, but he allowed that the fourth might generate "some objection." To preempt such opposition, he pointed out that enlisting eighteen-year-olds without parental consent was consistent with the long tradition of requiring all males above that age to serve in the militia.

Democratic Republican Silas Stow of New York, among the first legislators to speak out against the proposal, put forward a four-fold critique. First, he countered that empowering the US military to usurp parental prerogatives was a far cry from militia service, which kept a minor under "the wholesome and wise control" of masters and father. Second, he argued that it would break up newly established factories and undermine the moral order if the military were authorized to "go into the private family, the workshops, and the manufactory, regardless of the opinion of the father and superintendent, and seduce the young man from learning some useful and honorable employment."[39] Third, Stow opposed minority enlistment on constitutional grounds, denouncing it as a "dangerous innovation" that violated the sanctity of contracts.[40] Here, he referred to parents' property in the labor of their minor children and to apprenticeship contracts that parents and guardians signed with masters. Finally, Stow condemned youth enlistment on the grounds that it disproportionately affected the northeast, a region of small farms and nascent industries. "The property which a parent has in the services of his son. . . is as real and oftentimes more important than the farmer has in his personal estates, or the planter in his slave," he argued. In sum, Stow charged that the unauthorized enlistment of minors threatened social and economic stability, flouted elemental constitutional rights, and unfairly disadvantaged one section of the country.

All of these arguments would be repeated and elaborated by Federalist legislators in the debates that unfolded over the next few days. In a blistering speech reprinted in dozens of newspapers across the northeast, Josiah Quincy of Massachusetts asserted that the youth who turned eighteen "has hardly paid to the parent or master the cost of his clothing and education." Yet it was at precisely this moment that he began to find his subordination hard to bear, making him an easy target for unscrupulous recruiters who offered "wages and bounty for disobedience." Legalizing minority enlistment would thus deprive parents and masters of their charges just as they were starting to receive recompense for all their trouble and expense. Federalists similarly echoed Stow in declaring parents' investment in their offspring every bit as important as slaveholders' property rights in human chattel. Although some voiced distaste for the slave system, the point of drawing this analogy was not to critique slavery; quite the contrary, it was to legitimize parental control by suggesting that property rights in minor children's labor should be just as secure as the property rights of enslavers.[41] Quincy, for instance, held that "the only real property in the labor of others which exists in the Northern States is that which is possessed in ... minors."[42] The proposed bill would allow the military to seize "the most valued and most precious" assets of citizens in one section of the country, while leaving the property of those in another section intact.[43]

A tendency to portray property rights in the young as the bedrock of social order constituted another key element of the case against minority enlistment. To critics, enlisting youths without parental consent taught defiance against authority in general, rendering young men ungovernable and thus useless to both parents and society at large. These concerns would not have seemed farfetched to some northeasterners, who had begun to witness the gradual transfer of families off the land and into new forms of employment opened up by the expanding commercial economy. Parents may have retained legal control over minors, but their ability to exercise that control was hampered if fathers had little or no land to bequeath, as was often the case when New England farms had been subdivided generation after generation. The resulting downward mobility undercut the power of churches and communities to discipline wayward youths; the law could do little when sons simply abandoned their families and sought anonymity in burgeoning cities. Stow's New York had felt these trends most keenly due to early urbanization.[44] Many of his constituents no doubt nodded in agreement as they read his speech, having seen or heard about the large number of young, footloose men roaming urban neighborhoods. Congress would only compound this problem by condoning or even encouraging youths to run off and join the army.

Underlying all the arguments against minority enlistment was the vital importance of children's contributions to household economies. During this period, all family members generally worked as soon as they were able. White children either labored alongside parents on farms or small shops, or they were apprenticed to masters who provided education and training in exchange for faithful service. The rise of industry and wage work gradually shifted the locus of labor, leading many parents to send children and youths outside the home to supplement the family's earnings. According to one study, the entire northeastern manufacturing sector witnessed a "disproportionate demand for women and children as workers" that accompanied the surge in manufacturing that began with the embargo of 1807 and continued during the War of 1812. By 1832, the percentage of wage-earning women and children in the northeast who labored outside the home had risen dramatically, from about 10 percent early in the century to around 40 percent.[45] These developments created new options for young people and new challenges for parents, who struggled to retain control over children's labor power.

These same economic changes heightened apprehensions about wayward apprentices. Courts continued to protect masters' and parents' authority over minors, and municipalities did their best to rein in "saucy apprentices" and youthful "rowdies" with laws against gaming, noise making, or swearing.[46] Yet this did not stop youth from chafing against their subordination. A spate of state laws enacted in the first quarter of the nineteenth century, many of which concentrated on the problem of runaways, indicate that even before the war, masters struggled to keep apprentices in check. Federalists from urban areas expressed concern over the bill's potential to further erode their authority. Philadelphia's once-thriving maritime trade had been devastated by the nation's self-imposed embargo, but the decline in foreign imports had bolstered local industries.[47] Championing the cause of urban manufacturers, James Milnor of Pennsylvania warned of workshops of "industrious mechanics" and "artisans" coming to a standstill as apprentices were enticed into military service. As he and other Federalist commentators pointed out, the proposal to enlist minors without consent also departed from traditions established during the Revolution, while significantly enhancing the federal government's power at the expense of parents' and masters' rights.[48]

The forceful assertions of property in children evident in these debates contrast with scholarship that charts a growing tendency to see childhood as a special phase worthy of protection, embodied in developments like the decline in corporal punishment or proliferating images of angelic youngsters. Scholars have acknowledged that many children's lives failed to fit the ideal, but they tend to depict understandings of childhood as bifurcated, with middling parents adopting sentimental attitudes in contrast to the pragmatic and proprietary attitudes of those who relied on children's wages.[49] The debates around youth enlistment suggest that there was no inherent conflict between proprietary claims to children and emotional characterizations of parent-child relationships. Stow, for instance, spoke in one breath in economic terms—decrying the plan to "defraud" parents and masters of their property—while in the next warning his fellow legislators not to imperil the "strongest ties of affection and gratitude." Quincy likewise merged the concerns of the pocketbook with those of the heart when he implored, "Touch not private right,—regard the sacred ties of guardian and master,—corrupt not our youth,—listen to the necessities of our mechanics and manufacturers—have compassion for the tears of parents."[50] Conflating minors' economic and emotional value, both speakers acknowledged the productive value of children and apprentices in ways that diverge from the typical portrait of Victorian childhood.[51]

Contrasting conceptions of youth are also apparent in the discussions concerning minority enlistment. Federalists tended to imagine the years between eighteen and twenty-one as a time of great peril, when those on the cusp of manhood were buffeted by a riot of confused emotions: the desire for glory, the anticipation of independence, and the need to make a name for themselves beyond their family circle. One misstep during this hazardous time and all could be lost, as young men who strayed from the path of duty and morality found themselves hopelessly mired in dissipation. Quincy identified the age of eighteen as the time when youthful "passions" were "in their most ungoverned sway," when judgment was "not yet ripe," and youths easily grew "infatuated and corrupted by the vain dreams of military glory."[52] Such depictions of the young being "enticed" or "lured" from the path of virtuousness strongly echoed the era's wildly popular seduction novels, which featured young women who fell prey to rakes and suffered the consequences of lost virtue and early death.[53] These works imagined adolescence in terms of emotional vulnerability, reflecting the belief that self-control was essential for navigating the modern world. In the interim, parents needed to maintain a watchful eye over children's development.

This anxiety-ridden view of the nation's male youth thoroughly exasperated Democratic Republicans. To their minds, youths between the ages of eighteen and twenty-one were fully capable of free thought and competent to navigate their own lives. Young men whose patriotic sentiments drove them to enlist should be commended rather than denounced as disobedient ingrates or unwitting dupes, they argued, even if obligations to parents or employers went unfulfilled as a result. Representative George Troup of Georgia, for one, portrayed Quincy's speech against minority enlistment as ridiculously overwrought. "If a stranger in the gallery had listened to the member from Massachusetts, he would have supposed that the provision of the bill . . . authorized the recruiting sergeant to enter the house of the citizen, drag from it the young man, and transport him, loaded with chains . . . to the armies," he declared. "Who would have supposed that the provisions merely authorize the recruiting sergeant to accept the voluntary service of the young man between eighteen and twenty-one?" Though Troup and his fellow partisans shared Federalists' understanding of youth as a time of heightened emotions, they celebrated rather than feared the "impetuosity" and "ardor" that fueled young men's patriotism and desire for glory.

Most fundamentally, Democratic Republicans who supported minority enlistment differed from Federalists in their understanding of young men's competing obligations. They believed that white male youths had certain responsibilities to the government once they reached eighteen, even though they did not yet enjoy the prerogatives of full citizens. Thus, while parents could typically claim the labor of their minor children, their rights over those of military age were not unqualified. An unsigned letter from "a citizen of Massachusetts," first sent to a congressman and subsequently published in the press, expressed this point clearly: such youths were "members of society, and . . . under equal obligations, moral and political, to contribute in their various capacities, to the defence and support of the government." As able-bodied members of the community and citizens-in-the-making, they had a "paramount obligation" to their country that, in unusual circumstances, took precedence over "service to master, parent or guardian."[54]

To critics' charge that the proposed law unfairly disadvantaged independent farmers vis-à-vis enslavers, Democratic Republican congressmen had very little to say, no doubt because it was impossible to refute. But a "citizen of Massachusetts" took up the issue from a different angle, denouncing the analogy between white minor children and the enslaved as "a radical and gross error." The notion that parents, guardians, and masters enjoyed an "exclusive and absolute right to the services of their wards, apprentices, and sons" akin to the planter's right to his slave, he argued, degraded the nation's youth. The real threat to "the *morals*, the *dignity*, and the *usefulness* of our young men" lay not in their exposure to the dissipations of army life, but rather in the demoralization that came from being reduced to "mere pecuniary personal property."[55]

Despite such pushback, Federalists' outcry did not fall on entirely deaf ears. Along with Stow, several other Democratic Republicans echoed their concerns. Most notably, Representative John Randolph of Virginia reminded his Democratic Republican colleagues of their party's conviction that the military "of all classes in society" needed to be closely watched and limited in its powers. By elevating military rule, their bill would impair "the obligation of contract" and undermine civilian laws.[56] Along with eight other members of his party, most from northeastern states, Randolph refused to support the proposed legislation, as did every Federalist in the House. Their combined efforts helped ensure that the provision to enlist minors without consent was struck down when it came before the Senate.[57]

The Federalists' arguments about parental rights outlived the party itself. In subsequent decades, as anger grew over the disproportionate influence that enslavers wielded at the federal level, it evolved into a full-throated defense of free labor that ultimately provoked the southern states to secede. But in the early nineteenth century, it was New Englanders who threatened violent opposition to federal policies. Addressing legislators who jealously guarded their enslaved "property," while deeming it a "common affair" to "seduce a son worth all the slaves Africa ever produced," Quincy promised a rude awakening should their measure pass: the French government had similarly underestimated the power of ordinary people denied justice.[58] Even as the controversy over minority enlistment that unfolded in 1812 inflamed partisan hostilities, it also exposed the beginnings of an ominous regional divide that would eventually widen into a breach.

1814: The Legalization of Minority Enlistment and the Hartford Convention

Although opponents managed to stave off the legalization of minority enlistment in 1812, the federal government's failure to raise sufficient troops put the issue back on the table in 1814. In late August of that year, British troops sacked and burned much of Washington, leaving the nation humiliated and on the brink of disaster. The president's house was destroyed and the Capitol building reduced to "a most magnificent ruin," in the words of architect Benjamin Henry Latrobe.[59] When Congress convened for a special emergency session a few weeks later, members squeezed into the stifling rooms of the Patent Office, located in the only intact building in the capital that could accommodate them.[60]

It was there that Congress considered two new bills to fill out the ranks. The first proposed to legalize the enlistment of all white males aged eighteen and above, regardless of parental consent. It also doubled the land bounty given to regular army enlistees upon completion of service—a move decried by critics as rewarding youths for filial disobedience. The second bill aimed to bypass the existing militia structure to raise some additional 80,000 troops. Fed up with poorly trained and often unreliable militiamen, Secretary of War James Monroe wanted to prosecute the war with regular troops and volunteers who would serve directly under federal command. Designed to satisfy his request, the bill proposed to classify all eligible men aged eighteen to twenty-five into groups of one hundred, with each group responsible for producing four men for service. To their critics, both measures entailed an expansion of federal authority that imperiled parents' rightful control over minor sons.[61]

Responding to the bill to legalize minority enlistment, Federalist lawmakers argued that the army was already ignoring restrictions on the enlistment of minors. They painted a picture of armed men trampling on civil law, violating parental rights, and robbing youths of their personal liberty. Speaking to his colleagues in the House of Representatives, Cyrus King alleged that "Minors have been often enlisted without the consent of their parents; and when these parents have demanded them of your officers, they have laughed them to scorn; and when they have called in the civil authority to enforce their demands, it has been resisted by force of arms; and the unhappy youth marched off, in the dead of night, and concealed from his parent."[62] It is hard to know the extent to which such overwrought rhetoric captured events on the ground, but newspaper notices concerning runaway sons and apprentices, which appeared interspersed among the far more numerous advertisements seeking to recover those who fled slavery, reveal frustration with the military. In 1813, a Virginia paper carried an ad regarding a sixteen-year whose father had twice retrieved him from the army, only to see him take off again. Should recruiting officers enlist the boy, the advertisement warned, "they may expect to be dealt with as the law will direct."[63] Other notices adopted a similarly suspicious and adversarial tone vis-à-vis the military in threatening to prosecute recruiters who enlisted runaway minors and apprentices.[64]

Reiterating arguments they had advanced in 1812, Federalist critics portrayed the parent-child bond as the very foundation of civil society. "No one rule of the common law" was "more universally known" than that pertaining to the disability of minority, argued Representative Jeremiah Mason of New Hampshire. "It is one of the first a child learns. Till the age of twenty-one the parent has a power over the child, for government and education, and has a right to his services." To question the father's right to his child was to question everything—if a minor child or apprentice could sign an enlistment contract on his own accord, then why not a wife or, more realistically, a slave? Thomas P. Grosvenor of New York made the same point when declaring himself in agreement with Daniel Webster, the leading Federalist in the House: if the army was prepared to enlist minor sons or apprentices in defiance of their contractual obligations, then why not also accept enslaved men who preferred military service to perpetual bondage?[65] To undermine a father's claim to his son's labor and personhood, according to this line of reasoning, was to destabilize the other hierarchical relationships that constituted a well-ordered household and society.

With the nation's very survival at stake, however, such arguments proved hard to defend. Should parents and masters really be able to prevent the enlistment of healthy young patriots eager to defend their country from an enemy who had destroyed the seat of government? Concluding that, in this instance, the nation's needs trumped parental rights, Congress passed the bill legalizing the unauthorized enlistment of minors above age eighteen in early December of 1814. The final legislation included one small but telling concession to its critics. It granted enlistees below age twenty-one a four-day grace period during which they could back out of their commitment, a nod to the fact that minors were typically judged incompetent to sign binding contracts. This provision, however, did nothing to ameliorate the loss of parental rights; a minor could escape his enlistment if he himself changed his mind, but his parents could only plead their case, not exert their will. Unappeased by this provision, the editor of Boston's *Weekly Messenger* posed a rhetorical question: what would happen if the military violated enslavers' property rights in a like manner, accepting male slaves who desired to escape their present circumstances? Every planter would resist the measure "to the last extremity," he answered, no matter how great the public need. Yet why should his "title to the slave, whom, like his cattle, he has reared or bought," hold more sway than the father's claim to a son "who is attached to him by love and the nearest tie of relationship"? The law was so manifestly unjust, the editor implied, that fathers would be well within their rights to resist it with force.[66]

If anything, the measure to reorganize the militia generated even more heat. Calls to classify the militia were not new, but they had always met with resistance, especially outside of the southern states.[67] In 1790 and 1791, Secretary of War Henry Knox had promoted a classification scheme to divide the militia into three age-based classes, with the greatest responsibility falling on an "advanced corps" of youths aged eighteen to twenty-one years who would train for thirty days annually at federal expense.[68] The 1792 Militia Act, however, did not separate minors from the main body of militiamen or burden them with special responsibilities. Nor did subsequent proposals place the onus of service so squarely or exclusively on the shoulders of minor youths—a shift that reflected the growing deference accorded to parental claims in the post-Revolutionary era. In fact, a scheme proposed in 1812 by South Carolinian David Williams, the Democratic Republican who chaired the House Committee on the Militia, shielded the "minor class" from arduous service. It would have required youths eighteen to twenty-one to serve for no more than three months and only within state lines, leaving those aged twenty-one to thirty-one to bear the brunt of service. The 1814 version, drafted when the situation on the ground had become far more dire, returned minor youths to the first class of service but also extended the upper age limit to twenty-five, making it somewhat harder for critics to discredit it as a "minor conscription" bill.

Still, fierce resistance ultimately defeated the legislation. From a contemporary perspective, the debates over classification seem rather abstruse, but congressmen's frequent references to the French and Prussian armies point to their underlying concerns. They feared the measure was "calculated to destroy the militia system, and . . . the sovereignty of the states" by subjecting the militia to centralized control. Daniel Webster claimed that the plan "foully libelled" the Constitution, because it attempted to "raise a standing army out of the militia by draft." To his mind, states could require men to perform militia service, but the federal government had no authority to force men into regular service. "Where is it written in the Constitution," he queried, "that you may take children from their parents, and parents from their children, and compel them to fight the battles of any war in which the folly or the wickedness of government may engage it?"[69] Representative Morris Miller of New York similarly stressed the many differences between service in the regular army and the militia. Begging his colleagues and fellow parents to reject a system that deprived them of their children, he melodramatically proclaimed that he would rather see his sons dead and follow them to the grave than have them compelled to serve in the regular army.[70]

Opposition to the national government's wartime measures reached its apex at the Hartford Convention, a series of secret meetings held between December 15, 1814, and January 5, 1815. During these three weeks, leading Federalists aired their grievances, debated secession, and cobbled together a list of proposed constitutional amendments. Among the delegates' chief concerns was the law, signed just five days before they convened, that legalized minority enlistment. Asserting that, with this action, "the power of the Executive over all the effective male population of the United States is made complete," they implied that the legislation had transformed the republic into a military dictatorship, since the president as commander-in-chief could now violate the rights of every American father, guardian, or master. According to some Federalists, this situation was so corrosive to liberty that, when considered in tandem with other government outrages, it justified secession. Most, however, stopped short of promoting this radical step.[71] The convention was ultimately rendered moot by the Treaty of Ghent, signed on December 24, 1814. But until word of the treaty reached American shores in mid-February, intense battles continued to rage in both the field of war and the political arena.[72]

Meanwhile, military officers and their political allies argued that it was resistance to minority enlistment (and the war effort more broadly) that threatened the republic by undermining the legitimacy of the central government. In January 1815, the Madison Administration sent Colonel Thomas Sidney Jesup to Hartford, allegedly on a recruiting mission, but really to keep an eye on the proceedings in Hartford in case the threat of secession materialized.[73] Seeking to win over the community with appeals to martial valor and patriotism, Jesup staged boisterous military parades and arranged for local Democratic Republican elites to host balls that showcased his handsome officers.[74] State and local authorities, however, remained cold to the colonel's charm offensive and tried to obstruct his activities. On January 7, Jesup requested instructions from the War Department "in the event of the state authorities interfering" with his recruitment efforts. By January 20, he had grown considerably more exercised about the situation. Local officials were seizing soldiers who owed debts and throwing them in jail to prevent their service, Jesup reported to Secretary Monroe, while his regiment was "threatened daily with prosecutions in consequence of the enlistment of minors." Most concerning, the Connecticut legislature had convened for a special session, which he suspected would promote "resistance to the laws of the union."[75]

Jesup was correct in his prediction. In attempt to nullify federal legislation, both the Connecticut and Massachusetts legislatures passed laws that prohibited the enlistment of youths under age twenty-one without the consent of parents, guardians, or masters. Recruiters who ran afoul of these measures faced hefty fines and prison sentences of up to three years.[76] "If this act of unparalleled usurpation be submitted to," Jesup fumed, "it will but embolden the unprincipled faction who rule this country to commit greater outrages and to make further encroachments upon the rights and authority of the United States." Several years later, an anti-Federalist newspaper reflecting on these developments characterized Connecticut's law as the "first act of a legislature that *declares* a law of the Union, which by the constitution is a supreme of the land, unconstitutional, and that provides for the punishment of those who obey it," adding, "In ordinary times this would look somewhat like a declaration of war."[77] It was indeed a remarkable display of defiance. When it came retaining control over minor children, New England Federalists were willing to go to the mat, even if that meant rejecting the legitimacy of the federal government.

As things turned out, however, the Federalist Party overplayed its hand. Amid the surge of patriotic sentiment that followed Andrew Jackson's improbable triumph in New Orleans on January 8, 1815, the Hartford Convention drew widespread scorn. Democratic Republicans had little trouble painting their opponents as unpatriotic obstructionists at best, traitors at worst. This turn of fate, which allowed the Madison Administration to emerge from the war claiming victory, despite having virtually nothing to show for it, delivered a blow from which the party never recovered. The beliefs that critics of minority enlistment voiced regarding the danger of military power and the sanctity of parental rights, however, would persist for decades to come.

* * *

During the War of 1812, critics of youth enlistment confronted a set of economic and legal realities that pulled in opposing directions. On the one hand, parents had gained new rights under common law to control minor children and to profit from their labor. But on the other, their ability to exert those rights frayed as youths increasingly asserted their independence by seizing new opportunities for wage work and embracing the many pleasures and freedoms to be found beyond parental oversight. Calls for troops and promises of glory inevitably clashed with parents' competing needs and rights. The emotive power of these cases—involving, as they did, people's most intimate relationships and sacrosanct rights—stemmed from the problem of cross-cutting allegiances: familial love pitted against patriotism, the needs of the country against those of the family, and the rights of states and localities against those of the federal government.

The war's end defused but did not resolve the conflict over minority enlistment. Less than six months later, the US army ordered released, upon the request of a parent or guardian, all soldiers below age twenty-one who had enlisted without consent.[78] Then, in February 1816, Congress allowed the law authorizing the enlistment of minors to lapse, restoring the situation to the prewar status quo. In the legal realm, however, judges continued to grapple with fundamental disagreements over the relative importance of parental rights versus state interests, the proper form of the military, and the relationship between military and civilian law. To what degree, and under what conditions, should military needs be allowed to override the common law right of parents, guardians, or masters to control minor children and profit from their labor? And in cases of conflict between military and common law—two areas with radically divergent precedents and procedures—which should have primacy?

The disagreements ignited by these questions informed some of the most explosive political problems in the first half of the nineteenth century, including debates over free labor, family governance, legal consent, and the expansion of the US military. Central to these questions lay an issue that was anything but arcane for Americans at this time: to what extent would service in the militia resemble service in the regulars? The Civil War would ultimately render the distinctions drawn between these two forms of service all but meaningless, as the rules, regulations, and procedures governing regular service were extended to cover combatants in general. But that process was neither smooth nor automatic. It required those in favor of treating all forms of military service alike—a group that included regular army officers and their supporters in Congress and the judiciary—to advance arguments that were bitterly contested.

2

A Great Inconvenience

Prewar Legal Disputes over Underage Enlistees

In 1812, eighteen-year-old William Bull left his job and enlisted in an infantry regiment. Since he was an orphan, he signed up on his own, later explaining that he was "induced into the service by reason of his poverty." Military service apparently proved worse than he expected, for he absconded while his regiment was stationed in Vermont and returned to his home in Massachusetts. After his arrest for desertion, Bull's attorney filed a writ of habeas corpus on his behalf with the Massachusetts State Supreme Judicial Court. Portraying a rash youth who had entered the service "unadvisedly," influenced by "undue solicitations," his attorney appealed to legal understandings of minority that had solidified in the post-Revolutionary era, when minors had come to be seen as incapable of understanding the implications of their decision-making and thus incompetent to sign binding contracts. Why should a young man's decision to enlist in the military be treated differently from any other contractual obligation, he asked. In response, the opposing counsel put forward three counterarguments that in the long run proved critical in shifting power from the states to the federal government and foreclosing the ability of state courts to intervene in the US military. They claimed that the militia enlisted eighteen-year-olds and that service in the regulars was not essentially different; that the federal government had a constitutional right to raise an army; and, finally, that in exceptional instances contracts signed by minors could be held binding, provided they were deemed to be in the individual's interests.

Like most legal authorities at the time, the justices found these claims unpersuasive. They dismissed attempts to conflate the militia and the US army, pointing out that militia duty was performed "at home, under officers generally deriving their commission from popular elections." In contrast, army enlistment was "a very distinct thing . . . subject to a very different discipline, and to hardships and dangers unknown to militia service." The justices saved their strongest argument for last: refusing to allow a minor to escape an unwise enlistment contract would be "unduly harsh," they argued, violating "a fundamental principle of the common law"—namely, that "infants . . . were incapable of making any contract binding on themselves except in a very few instances." If the government wanted to hold minors in service, in other words, Congress had to enact legislation to that effect. In the absence of such laws, the court implicitly agreed that enlistment contracts were neither uniquely binding nor in minors' interests.[1]

This case highlighted several legal conflicts underlying the enlistment of minors in the first half of the nineteenth century. One concerned the nature of an enlistment contract. Given the common law precept that contracts signed by minors were generally voidable, could a minor invalidate his enlistment at will, or did entry into the military, like marriage, alter his status, transforming him into a fictive adult? That question led to another: Were enlistment contracts governed by contract law, or by the constitutional provision allowing the government to raise and administer a military force? A third, related question concerned the conflict between parents' (or masters' or guardians') right to control minor children and profit from their labor, versus the states' right to enlist citizens regardless of age. Whereas judges accepted that the federal government had a constitutional right to enlist any male citizen in wartime by passing laws to this effect, did this same right exist absent explicit legislative sanction? Finally, when parents, guardians, or masters of young enlistees applied to the court system for relief, who determined the limits of civil and military authority? Minors who signed enlistment contracts placed themselves under federal control. Did state courts have the right to inquire into the legitimacy of this authority and to release individuals from the military, or did only federal judges hold this power?

Although numerous state courts and even the US Supreme Court weighed in with decisions relating to minor enlistees, the result was a mass of conflicting rulings rather than a clear line of precedent-setting decisions. This confusion stemmed from the fact that the relatively clear hierarchy that characterizes the modern American legal order—wherein state courts operate in a separate domain, yielding when necessary to the greater authority of the federal judiciary—did not yet exist. The power of state courts was particularly evident when it came to habeas corpus—the legal procedure that many people used in enlistment cases. Rooted in common law and enshrined in the US Constitution as well as state constitutions, habeas corpus protects citizens from arbitrary detention by allowing them to appeal to a judge for a writ. These writs require that the detaining authority "produce the body" of the detainee in court so that a judge can determine whether a detention is legal. If the judge deems the detention unlawful, the detainee is immediately set free. Prior to the Civil War, habeas corpus could be claimed everywhere throughout the nation's legal system—at the local, state, and federal levels. Judges at this time generally accepted the principle of concurrent jurisdiction, meaning that state as well as federal courts had a right to adjudicate cases involving federal detentions, including those relating to military enlistments. Indeed, that principle was so well established that the two most authoritative legal treatises on this topic confidently deemed the matter "settled."[2]

It might seem odd that a military enlistment could once have been considered as a potentially illegal form of imprisonment. After all, in the modern era habeas corpus is mostly used as a legal remedy for prisoners, and few would draw parallels between service in the armed forces and prison confinement, precisely because enlistment contracts are presumed to be freely chosen, while prison sentences are not. The fact that Americans once thought of officers as would-be kidnappers speaks to how differently many viewed the US military in the past. Their wariness of centralized power and familiarity with the long history of men being coerced or decoyed into service, coupled with scandals involving the British Royal Navy's impressment of merchant seamen during the War of 1812, made Americans particularly keen to retain local and state courts as checks on military overreach. As the author of a legal treatise pointed out in 1832, recruiting officers' extraordinary clout meant that they were apt to commit "oppressive acts" of various kinds. The ability of ordinary people to go before a local judge and swear out a writ to thwart any "abuse of an authority given by the United States" was thus one of the essential protections of American citizenship.[3]

Naturally, military officers did not see themselves as potential oppressors. In fact, by the antebellum decades, many viewed their profession as beleaguered and unfairly targeted by newspaper editors, state court judges, and other nosy outsiders who thought they should have a say in enlistment decisions. Their biggest bone of contention was the massive number of recruits who signed up before reaching the age of majority, only to secure discharges when parents or guardians sought their release. Military officials continually fought such cases in court, arguing that only federal judges should be allowed to oversee federal detentions. When that failed, they tried to hold youngsters to account by charging them with perjury for lying about their age. They also repeatedly objected to the trouble and expense incurred when officers were forced to appear in court and to release men who had already been outfitted and sometimes partially trained.

In the long run, a series of legal rulings relating to minor enlistees would vindicate those who advocated federal power and a centralized military. Interpreting the nature of enlistment contracts, parents' rights vis-à-vis the military, and the question of state courts' jurisdiction over federal detentions, these cases had far-reaching implications. They helped to reshape state and federal relations, transformed the citizen-soldier tradition, and dramatically expanded military power and autonomy. But no one could have predicted this outcome given the nature of legal decision-making in the years leading up to the Civil War. Rather than a foregone conclusion, these transformations resulted from struggles played out over many decades as officers fought with parents and their judicial allies over the fate of boys and young men.

The Transformation of the Dual Military System

The dual military system that the founders imagined fell apart in the second quarter of the nineteenth century, as growing numbers of people began opposing the principle of compulsory militia service. The Militia Acts passed after the Revolution had established an organizational structure for state militias and prescribed militiamen's duties, setting up the so-called uniform militia system. All free white males between eighteen and forty-five years of age were obliged to appear for training on specified muster days, armed with weapons and ammunition. Since the federal government provided no means to supervise or fund this uniform system, however, it existed solely on paper. Successful implementation would have required tremendous effort at every level. Officers of militia companies, for instance, were supposed to maintain detailed rolls of their members—a task that involved keeping track of who had aged in or out of service, and who had arrived or departed from a locality that might cover many miles and encompass a sizeable population. It was also their duty to report any absentees or missing equipment on muster days to the state's adjutant general. He, in turn, was required to forward this information to the War Department so that government officials could ascertain the strength and readiness of militia units. Given the tremendous mobility of Americans in the first half of the century, this was virtually an impossible job, especially since it was part-time, poorly compensated work performed without administrative support.

If the burden on militia officers was great, the financial onus placed on militiamen was even greater. In most states prior to the 1840s, eligible men had to equip themselves with a long list of items detailed in militia statutes. Failure to appear for practice, or appearing without any requisite item, was punishable by fine. Add to this the lost income or time off work and the expense of travel—which might stretch over multiple days for those in rural areas—and the outlay could be considerable, especially for fathers who had to bear their own costs and those of sons between ages eighteen and twenty-one. Over time, the uniform militia system generated increasing levels of class conflict.[4] Some complained that it was unfair to expect poorer men to equip themselves to protect the property of the rich. Spreading the burden equitably, they argued, would require those in greater need of protection to pay more for the privilege. Others raged against the exemptions for militia service, which disproportionately allowed social elites to evade militia duty.[5]

As states began to abandon property and residency requirements for voting and the franchise came to be linked to age, the practice of requiring eighteen-year-olds to sign up for militia service also came under fire. "The right of calling into service our children before they have any voice in the affairs of government, appears to be so manifestly wrong, that I have been astonished that our Legislators . . . should thus long have submitted to a law so unjust," editorialized the *Citizen Soldier* in 1840. "Is not a father the natural guardian of his sons till they arrive at the age of 21 years?" Echoing arguments advanced by Federalists during the War of 1812, he pictured militia service corrupting impressionable youths, undermining laws that gave "mechanics and manufacturers" control over their apprentices, and annulling parental rights.[6] Such arguments carried no weight with judges who, in line with congressional mandates, continued enforcing militia duty for white males above eighteen.[7] Elected officials proved more amendable to demands to end compulsory militia training, however, and by the 1840s the uniform militia system had become moribund across much of the United States.[8]

The erosion of this system cannot be attributed to the rise of anti-war sentiment, nor to growing respect for the US military. The few peace societies established after the War of 1812 remained small-scale and mostly confined to the northeast, while commentators continued to depict large professional military forces as fundamentally un-American.[9] In fact, if anything, the distinctions drawn between militiamen and regular enlistees grew stronger in the post-Revolutionary decades, even as states allowed the principle of compulsory militia training to lapse. In the 1830s and 1840s, the dream of a uniform state militia system gave way not to pacifism or military profession-alism, but to the growth of volunteer militia companies that were privately organized and financed. These companies stood apart from, yet were linked to, the state-based militia system. Chartered by state governments, they could be called into service under existing militia laws. They were also obliged to accept the chain of command established under the old uniform system, even though they largely determined their own membership, training, and dress. As masses of new immigrants began arriving in northeastern cities in the 1830s and 1840s, volunteer militia companies were increasingly organ-ized along ethnic lines, providing a vehicle for native-born citizens to flex their muscle in public or for new arrivals to protect neighborhoods and dis-play pride in their heritage. In slaveholding states, elites might organize a militia company to demonstrate their capacity for leadership, while men of middling wealth might agree to serve under them to establish their "standing in gentry society."[10]

By mid-century, volunteer militias served multiple roles. They carried out the many civic functions that militia companies had long performed, including putting down threats to the status quo, protecting prisoners from lynching, assisting volunteer fire companies, and participating in public events and celebrations.[11] They also constituted the main social clubs of their day in an era before the rise of organized athletics and college life, offering their mostly young members a venue for camaraderie and manly preening.[12] Distinguished from the compulsory militia by their splendid uniforms, fancy clubrooms, and elaborate bands, they held welcome dinners for fellow companies and sham battles and military balls for the public, as well as taking center stage in parades, celebrations, and public dedications in town squares and neighborhoods across the country. Establishing their own rules when it came to membership, volunteer companies did not typically follow rigid age restrictions, and some had junior wings that allowed boys and youths to join in exhibitions of martial skill and display.[13] In the decades leading up to the Civil War, these volunteer companies proliferated alongside the remnants of the old uniform militia system, with many dozens from across the country offering to serve when the United States went to war with Mexico in 1846.

Comparing the conditions faced by US enlistees to those who joined mi-litia or volunteer companies, it is little wonder that Americans continued to draw a sharp distinction between these different kinds of armed service. The enlistment contracts they signed were much stricter than the more fa-miliar labor arrangements that increasingly governed nineteenth-century workplaces. Labor contracts in this period strongly favored employers, allowing them to fire workers at will, dictate employment terms, and even withhold pay if a worker quit before the end of the period for which he contracted.[14] But these unfair and even coercive contractual provisions pale in comparison to the disadvantages faced by recruits who tried to evade their enlistment oaths. Desertion carried punishments ranging from hard labor in prison to death by firing squad. Similarly, the sort of physical correction that had become increasingly unacceptable outside of chattel slavery persisted unchecked in the military.[15] Enlistees who ran afoul of regulations might find themselves clapped in leg irons or stocks, confined in a guardhouse without food or water, or subject to humiliating and painful punishments—from hanging by the thumbs to bucking and gagging—that defined military justice up through the Civil War. Governed by the logic that public shaming and physical violence were essential to order and obedience, the coercive practices of military life diverged sharply from the experiences of free Americans, at times resembling treatment of the enslaved.

Enlistees' low monthly pay rates helped to bolster the sense that independent-minded American men were above service in the regulars. Privates received barely enough to cover subsistence, paid five dollars a month until 1833, with a brief pay rise during the War of 1812, then six dollars from that point until 1854, when their pay increased to ten dollars. Added to the measly incentives and brutal discipline, many recruits were sent to live in sparsely populated frontier regions where hazards were many and enjoyments few. Unsurprisingly, the US military therefore mostly attracted men too poor or desperate to find work elsewhere. By the early 1850s, this largely meant new immigrants, who comprised over 70 percent of all US enlistees.[16] Widely viewed as incapable of achieving success in a competitive economy and willing to surrender their freedoms to enter an autocratic system, enlistees continued to arouse significant contempt and fear.[17]

Likewise, the sense of exclusivity cultivated by regular officers only grew stronger as the nineteenth century progressed. Distinguishing their professionalism from what they increasingly perceived as the rank amateurism of militia units, they created their own publications, traditions, and esprit de corps. The fact that US officers faced repeated challenges to their authority during this period undoubtedly cemented this growing sense of fellowship. Continued denunciations of standing armies as un-American and a threat to the republic saw critics repeatedly assail the nation's military budget and call for West Point to be shuttered. These criticisms ensured that the US military saw no significant expansion in numbers or funding prior to the 1850s.[18] Judging by the contents of military publications like the *Military and Naval Magazine* (1833–1842) and the *Army and Navy Chronicle* (1833–1841), this public censure generated widespread defensiveness in military circles, with regular hand-wringing over the lack of public support for US forces and insistent declarations on the need for an organized and well-trained federal military.

If this weight of public criticism was not sufficient to anger US officers, they also faced a flood of minors who signed enlistment contracts only to be released after parents or guardians filed writs of habeas corpus. Between the War of 1812 and the outbreak of the Civil War, this issue enraged military spokesman like few others. Hard as it was to attract recruits in the first place, they were forced to operate in a legal system where jurisdictional lines were indistinct. Local and state judges regularly invalidated enlistments, ignoring or defying federal court decisions that required enlisted minors to remain in service. As state-level courts took it upon themselves to shield parents and guardians from military officials, US officers seized every opportunity to protect their own authority by promoting a more robust federalism.

Clashes between US Officers and Parents in Local and State Courts

The resentment within the US military caused by the issue of minority enlistment can be glimpsed in the writing of Major William Birkhimer, one of the nation's foremost experts in military law at the turn of the century. Looking back to a time before he was born, Birkhimer could still muster palpable outrage in thinking about how state judges had once seemed determined to undermine military authority. He charged that state courts "well nigh disbanded the army" during the War of 1812 by releasing large numbers of minors. Meanwhile, the "hopeless" federal government, unable to respond effectively to judicial challenges by the states, had left its "faithful" officers hanging out to dry.[19] Even if this characterization was exaggerated, Birkhimer's enduring indignation speaks to the depths of anger that some officers felt over what they viewed as egregious civilian meddling in the military sphere, and to the institutional memory that kept these decades-old slights alive.

The anger is understandable given the procedures governing habeas corpus, which held officers personally responsible for any enlistments deemed fraudulent. When judges issued writs at the request of parents seeking to recover underage recruits, they directed them to individual officers, who had to stop whatever they were doing and accompany enlistees to court. If they refused, state-level habeas corpus statutes allowed courts to form *posse comitatus* to enforce their rulings. In instances when the court ruled in favor of petitioners, those swearing out petitions could also personally sue the officer for damages. It is impossible to calculate the number of citizens who filed these suits, since they were heard in local courts where recordkeeping was minimal. But it is clear that some officers were left to foot the bill.

One such instance occurred at the very end of the War of 1812, just after the law reverted back to requiring parental consent for all minors under twenty-one. In this case, a US army captain enlisted a nineteen-year-old named Noah Hasty, who had claimed to be of age. After a local court discharged Hasty, his father filed suit against the officer and was awarded $60 in damages and $55.27 in costs by the Supreme Judicial Court for the County of York in Massachusetts. This particular case is preserved in the historical record because the officer unsuccessfully petitioned Congress for indemnification in an attempt to avoid paying out of pocket himself. Congress denied his request, citing a law that compelled officers found guilty of enlisting minors without consent to reimburse the cost of any bounty or clothing the minor had received. Whether the government docked his pay to compensate for Hasty's enlistment is unclear, but the fact that he remained responsible for paying all of the legal costs resulting from this action must have been galling.[20] Little wonder that military men remained bitter about these cases decades later.

That some federal and even state court decisions affirmed the military's right to hold minors to service must only have added to officers' frustration. Early in the nineteenth century, several rulings explicitly rejected the principle of determining cases relating to minor enlistees by reference to the common law principles governing contractual relations or parental rights. In 1809, Chief Judge Hooper Nicholson of the Maryland Court of Appeals, Sixth District, denied a petition for the release of Emanuel Roberts, a sixteen-year-old who was allegedly drunk at the time of his enlistment. Taking aim at the notion that anyone below the age of majority was unfit to sign a valid contract, Roberts refused to release the youth, stating that the only legitimate grounds for invalidating the contract would be "an actual imbecility of mind owing to his tender years." Had Roberts been a "child of eight or ten,"

Nicholson conceded, he would have ruled differently, but he did not define more precisely when "imbecility" ended and the capacity to reason began. He simply noted that sixteen-year-old Roberts was "remarkably well grown," implying that judges would know the line when they saw it. On the question of jurisdiction, he argued that state courts should not "be inquiring into the abuse of the exercise of the authority of the general government."[21] For this judge, youths sufficiently "grown" could be held to service, and no state court should be allowed to release them once they were under federal control.

A few years later, Supreme Court Justice Joseph Story issued an even more emphatic defense of federal power in the 1816 case *United States v. Bainbridge*. The case revolved around a nineteen-year-old who had enlisted in the navy without consent and then immediately deserted. After a court martial sentenced Bainbridge to fulfill his enlistment contract, his father filed a writ seeking his discharge. Acknowledging that parents held rights over their children under common law, Story nonetheless argued that those rights could be "enlarged, restrained and limited as the wisdom or policy of the times may dictate." He scoffed at the notion that the founders had intended for youths under age twenty-one to remain off limits to military recruiters even in moments of national peril, should they lack parental consent. The notion struck him as especially preposterous when it came to the navy, which relied so heavily on boys and youth. "How many of our own brilliant victories have been won by persons on land and at sea, who had scarcely passed the age of manhood?" he asked. Naval skills took years to acquire and could only be "attained in the ardour and flexibility at youth," rendering "the employment of minors . . . almost indispensable." Story's ruling thus plainly endorsed the authority of the federal government, affirming its power to "authorize the enlistment" of minors, "independent of the consent of their parents," flowed directly from Congress's constitutionally mandated authority to "provide and maintain a navy." Yet even as he confidently sustained congressional authority to override parents' common law rights, Story took pains to emphasize that he was not addressing the question of whether state courts could release individuals from national service through the habeas process. Intuiting battles on the horizon, he predicted, "Whenever that question shall arise, it will deserve very grave consideration."[22]

Although the US Supreme Court early on sided with the military over parents in a case of minority enlistment, concurrent jurisdiction empowered state and local courts to ignore or dismiss the relevance of Story's emphatic decision. Over the next few decades, a few state supreme courts followed his lead in rejecting petitions for the release of underage enlistees, but most state judges apparently took the opposite tack. It is difficult to be definitive on this point, because the vast bulk of habeas petitions were heard by local and state judges and went unrecorded. Only a few dozen cases relating to enlisted minors that reached appellate courts found their way into law reports, and these tend to be brief and focus on legal precedent.[23] But newspaper coverage of local court rulings, War Department policies in relation to enlistment practices, and precedent-setting cases all strongly suggest that judges generally ruled in favor of petitioners.

In fact, supreme courts in multiple states in the 1830s and 1840s unequivocally endorsed parents' right to the labor and earnings of minors in the absence of legislation authorizing minority enlistment. In 1836, for instance, the Massachusetts Supreme Judicial Court heard the case of *Commonwealth v. Downes*, which involved a twenty-year-old orphan, John H. Lord, who had been apprenticed to a shoemaker around the age of sixteen. After an exchange of harsh words, Lord ran off to join the navy, and his master filed for a writ seeking his return. In this case, the court confirmed that the Constitution theoretically granted Congress the power to enlist minors without consent, but it held that existing laws did not currently authorize such enlistments. Presenting the court's unanimous opinion, Chief Justice Lemuel Shaw went even further, suggesting that laws allowing minors to enlist should never be allowed in peacetime. "It is well settled that by the law of this Commonwealth, and probably by that of most of the States [that] a father has a legal right to the custody of the person of his minor son," Shaw maintained. Defending the critical importance of parental rights, Shaw concluded: "If, at the sound of the drum and fife . . . all the boys of a city or village, of whatever age, could quit the parental roof, and, without consent . . . enlist for the navy and march off. . . it would lead to a state of society very much like anarchy."[24] In other words, only a wartime emergency could justify the temporary legalization of minority enlistment.

The Supreme Court of Pennsylvania echoed this rousing defense of parental rights when it discharged underage enlistee Thomas Webster in December 1847, even though the boy had deserted. Chastising the military officer who had enlisted Webster for failing to query relatives about his age, the justices declared that they would "take the law as we find it, and regard the claim which the law of God, of nature, of the state and of the United States, gives the father to the services of his child, until he arrives at the age of majority, and which renders the minor unable to make a valid contract."

They conceded that their ruling conflicted with the US Supreme Court's *Bainbridge* decision but brushed aside the inconsistency, declaring that only the navy had a unique need for the services of boys and young men. Congress had acknowledged this reality by passing laws that permitted a certain number of youths below military age to enlist in the navy with parental consent, they pointed out, but similar laws were not in place for the army.[25]

State legislators occasionally weighed in as well, adding to the jurisdictional fog surrounding the issue. Legislatures levied substantial fines against recruiters who enlisted underage youths without parental permission or took minors or apprentices outside the state, thereby placing them beyond the reach of state courts. From 1821 onward, recruiters in Maine hazarded a whopping $500 penalty or six months' imprisonment for knowingly enlisting anyone under twenty-one without a parent's or master's sanction.[26] Lawmakers in Massachusetts and Connecticut had imposed even longer prison sentences for the same acts a few years earlier. Similarly, Indiana passed legislation in 1843 nullifying the enlistment of apprentices and imposing $100 fines on anyone who sought to entice them into breaking their contracts.[27] In the two decades preceding the Civil War, efforts to protect citizens from threats to their liberty would increasingly come to focus on fugitives from slavery, with numerous northern states enacting laws that banned state authorities from cooperating in the capture and return of escaped slaves, or that declared free any enslaved person brought within their borders.[28] But from the War of 1812 through the 1840s, both judges and legislators were also preoccupied with the illegal seizure and transport of minors for service in the military.

Newspaper reports and army circulars suggest that a growing number of young men flocked to enlist in the antebellum decades, which helps to account for lawmakers' concerns. Throughout the 1840s, the secretary of war issued one circular after another telling recruiting officers to be vigilant in rejecting anyone who looked underage and warning that they would be held responsible for unauthorized enlistments. The secretary of navy also complained that the illegal enlistment of minors was "an abuse of great importance" in his annual report to Congress of 1839. Dismissing the notion that parents and minors were the aggrieved parties in these cases, he argued that the real victims were military officers imposed on by fraudsters trying to take advantage of government largesse. He described young men appearing at recruiting stations with someone claiming to be a parent or guardian, enlisting, and then remaining in service "until they were sufficiently educated, and capable of being useful." Only after they had been "maintained . . . at the public expense" would their real parents come forward to reclaim them. This depiction of parents plotting with children to secure a free education strains credulity, given that parents generally pursued habeas petitions as soon as they learned of an enlistment. Nonetheless, the secretary of the navy argued that legislators should enact laws allowing recruiters to charge minors for lying about their age if they hoped to prevent widespread abuses.[29]

The bellicose nationalism of the 1840s may have contributed to this wave of underage enlistments, but growing immigration probably played a larger role. New arrivals, mainly fleeing poverty in Ireland and Germany, were lured to America by the promise of political freedom and steady employment. Most instead found irregular work that paid wages insufficient to meet even their most basic needs. Crowded into northeastern cities, desperate newcomers frequently turned to military employment as a stop-gap solution that would at least provide basic subsistence. Much to the annoyance of military officials, a sizeable percentage later sought to evade their enlistment contracts by filing suits claiming status as either an alien or a minor. In 1843, one unnamed officer sent the press copies of a decision by Virginia's High Court of Appeals that invalidated habeas petitions filed on the basis that the enlistees were not US citizens. Hundreds of enlistees had been discharged by this means over the past two years, he griped, causing "great inconvenience" and breeding discontent and insubordination in the ranks as men watched others gain release.[30]

Similar cases heard in lower courts involving minor enlistees generally did not make their way into the press. But in the last months of 1846, the *New York Tribune* suddenly became interested in habeas corpus petitions for the discharge of minors, likely because the stream of cases had suddenly become a flood as regiments were raised for active service in the war with Mexico. On August 24, the paper reported that Judge Aaron Vanderpoel of the Superior Court of New York had just released a youth at the request of his father. The same day Judge Michael Ulshoeffer of New York City's Court of Common Pleas discharged another minor in response to a petition filed by his brother, while the day before a father had secured his son's discharge before an unnamed court.[31] All of these young men served in Colonel John D. Stevenson's California Regiment, then stationed at the recruiting depot on Governor's Island in New York Harbor. The writs would therefore have been directed at the men commanding this particular regiment. A few days later, on August 27, those officers were back before Judge Vanderpoel on the charge of holding a minor named McAdam and a "young colored man named Charles Miller." That same day, they were called yet again, this time to appear before Judge Ulshoeffer to answer petitions from a "widow lady" for the release of her young son and from a wife whose husband had allegedly enlisted in a state of intoxication. All of these enlistees were discharged.[32]

The records do not usually provide direct evidence of officers' exasperation with such decisions by local judges. But in the case of George Buckingham, whose widowed mother had petitioned for his discharge, the press gave an unusually detailed account that highlighted officers' anger as well as their attempts to circumvent the law. One of Colonel Stevenson's officers brought the young recruit before Judge Ulshoeffer and "closely cross-questioned the lad" about whether he had lied about his age on enlistment. When the judge released Buckingham, the officer immediately had him arrested for "false pretensions and for perjury in swearing that he was twenty one" and ordered him marched back into service. The youth's distraught mother and uncle then returned to the judge to recount these events. Incensed at such blatant disregard for his ruling, Ulshoeffer accompanied the pair to Colonel Stevenson's camp and demanded Buckingham's immediate release, threatening to bring suit for false imprisonment if they failed to comply.[33] Foiled in their attempt to assert the primacy of military authority, the officers had no choice but to turn Buckingham back over to the judge.

The following week, Judge John Worth Edmonds in the Circuit Court of New York heard six additional habeas corpus petitions demanding the release of still more recruits in Colonel Stevenson's regiment on the grounds of minority. Each of these cases resulted in a discharge. All told, Colonel Stevenson lost at least a dozen recruits to petitioners in the space of just over a fortnight, while officers' attempts to evade judicial rulings came to naught. This was almost certainly an exceptional moment, given that the New York Tribune suddenly reported on a series of individual cases. But the paper's more typical silence concerning habeas petitions cannot be taken to mean that none were being filed; far more likely, such proceedings were standard occurrences that only became newsworthy when the volume of petitions grew to the point that simmering animosity between civil and military authorities threatened to boil over.

Frustrated over judicial support for parental rights, the federal government appealed several habeas cases while the Mexican American War was ongoing, one of which was heard by the Supreme Court of Appeals in Virginia in 1847. Having answered the call for 50,000 volunteers to fight in this conflict, George W. Blakeney had abandoned his apprenticeship and enlisted, claiming to be twenty-one. His father, Edward, along with his master, denied this claim, filing a writ testifying that George was in fact nineteen years old. The judge who heard the case followed the path laid down by most of his predecessors and released George from military service. According to newspaper coverage of the case, Judge John Clopton based his decision on the common law principle that contracts entered into by minors were not binding and dismissed the idea that the state's militia laws should be used as a guide for the minimum age for military service more broadly.[34]

The federal government decided to challenge this particular ruling, no doubt worried about attracting sufficient recruits in a time of war. In arguing *United States v. Blakeney*, federal officials conflated militia service and enlistment in the regulars, which allowed them to claim that all males aged between eighteen and forty-five should be subject to military duty. Opposing counsel rejected this claim, pointing out that these modes of service were substantially different and that no law currently authorized the enlistment of minors. Nonetheless, the court found against the petitioners. Presenting the majority's opinion, Judge Briscoe G. Baldwin held that American common law should be subordinate to international and British law. In the former, he argued, a citizen's duty to serve the nation was understood to take precedence over any "municipal or domestic law." And in Britain, no law had ever "defined for kings which subjects were fit to enlist in the military." Despite centuries of lawmaking, he went on, "not a single effort had been made" in Britain "to rescue [a minor] from service on the ground of infancy," nor had any judge "supposed that parents or guardians have the right to reclaim them from military service." In short, Baldwin explicitly rejected any distinction between state laws governing the militia and federal laws governing the regulars, arguing that the military age should simply be set by common sense. "A man of eighteen is old enough to die for his country," he concluded, "and not too young to render her effectual service."

Whereas the majority sided with Baldwin in this case, the court's president, Judge John J. Allen, put forward a dissenting opinion. Acknowledging that the government had the power to override parental rights, he argued that this could only be done through legislation lowering the enlistment age. The "whole superstructure of civil society" in America hinged on parents' control over their children until they reached the age of majority, Allen stressed. "Under our law, there can be no interference with [this right], except in cases of gross neglect." Taking a swipe at Baldwin's Anglophilia, he urged judges to "look to the common law as existing amongst ourselves, modified and adapted to our peculiar institutions, to ascertain whether the party entering into a contract of this kind, possesses the legal capacity to bind himself by such an engagement." As for citing British sources, he sniffed, "I should not consider them as entitled to much consideration."[35]

Neither did the Circuit Court of Petersburg, Virginia, which similarly challenged Baldwin's interpretation of the law that same year. In a case relating to a habeas corpus petition for the release of George Lipscomb, who had enlisted at the age of twenty, the court ruled that common law principles in relation to minors should take precedence unless Congress ruled otherwise. "The common law is the general law of the land, recognized alike by the general and state governments; and the common law rights of the citizen remain unimpaired, except so far as altered or abridged by some constitutional provision or statute," argued Judge Thomas Gholson. Under the nation's current laws, contracts made by minors were voidable. If the military was allowed to "change or impair private rights under the common law" in the absence of an explicit statutory declaration, Gholson declared, then there would be nothing to stop the government from impressing or conscripting citizens to fill the ranks.[36] Concerned with preventing untrammelled military power, even in wartime, he sided with those in lower courts who continued upholding parents' claims.

An end to active campaigning in Mexico did not resolve the issue for the military. The adjutant general reported that less than 15 percent of the nearly twenty thousand individuals who sought to enlist in 1850 were accepted as fit for service. While most of those rejected were non-citizens, a sizeable portion (more than 13 percent) were excluded on the grounds of minority. These high figures suggest that at least some military recruiters attempted to stem the tide of underage enlistments. Nonetheless, given how hard it was to verify a potential enlistee's exact age, some minors inevitably managed to sneak through. To mitigate the problem, the adjutant general followed other military officials in strenuously urging a policy that would not simply discharge those who lied about their ages but would "prescribe some adequate penalty or punishment." In the absence of such penalties, he warned, the military would continue to enlist young men, parents would continue to demand their return, and judges would continue to release them, leaving recruiters and officers to face the constant hassle of court appearances.[37]

Military officials had been railing against this situation for decades, pressing Congress to allow them to fine minors for giving false ages. But lawmakers did the opposite, in effect making it easier for parents to retrieve their children. On September 28, 1850, in the wake of an incident in which a father failed to retrieve a son who had enlisted and been taken out of state, Congress made it obligatory for the secretary of war to release anyone below the age of twenty-one whose parent or guardian could provide proof of minority and lack of consent.[38] Thwarted by legislators and the courts, military officials could only reiterate their complaints in what must have felt like an increasingly pointless exercise.

After being appointed secretary of war in 1853, Jefferson Davis took up the thankless task of trying to rein in the problem of minority enlistment. In his annual report of 1856, he complained that the 1850 law unjustly rewarded the youth who succeeded in this deception with an administrative discharge and transportation home at government expense.[39] He argued that the law should be revised so that enlisting offers could require suspected minors to take a binding oath affirming that they had reached their majority. "The very numerous applications for the discharge of minors—so many of which have succeeded with the past year," he explained to the chair of the Senate Committee for Military Affairs, "render it necessary that some steps should be taken to check the growing evil and the serious expense to which the Government is thereby subjected." Davis tried to address the problem again in 1858, this time in his role as the junior senator from Mississippi, but the House defeated his proposed legislation. Ironically, during the Civil War, the United States would adopt Davis's idea of a binding oath, but the Confederacy never approved such a measure.[40]

Though Congress clearly found it safer to appease constituents than to satisfy the War Department, the military's arguments against minor enlistees did make some headway with the public in the decade and a half preceding the Civil War, at least if press coverage accurately reflected popular attitudes. By the late 1840s, a new critical tone emerged in articles reporting on underage recruits released on habeas petitions, which ran under headlines like: "Defrauding the United States."[41] The New York press was particularly scathing. In that state, reporters suddenly began referring to writs filed on the basis of minority as "pleading the baby act"—an expression clearly meant to shame those who had taken on a man's role only to relinquish its responsibilities.[42] Mocking a young enlistee whose mother demanded his discharge in 1853, the New York Daily Times noted that the "judge looked at the papers and the proofs of babyhood" and ordered the soldier released, "inasmuch as he was only an infant."[43] By using this designation as an insult, the article ignored the fact that "infancy" was a formal term that registered a minor's peculiar standing in law; it was not an identity that recruits could necessarily shrug off. In fact, minors could not launch habeas petitions themselves: cases had to be initiated by parents, masters, or guardians. When petitioners succeeded, it was often over the objections of the enlistees themselves, who would have preferred to remain in service. Regardless, New York reporters continued to heap scorn on those discharged on the basis of minority. "The Baby Act. Extraordinary Case," ran a headline the following year, describing an instance of a minor who had served an enlistment out-of-state and then faced a habeas petition on his return to New York after attempting to re-enlist. With a heavy dose of sarcasm, the reporter concluded: "The Judge ordered the baby to be discharged and he went home with his mother."[44] Congress might have ignored military officers' arguments in favor of holding minors to service, but at least some reporters seemed to be on their side.

The actions of several New York courts in the early 1850s also suggest that, although most lower courts continued discharging underage enlistees, they were not immune to arguments in favor of holding them to account for lying or granting the federal government supremacy over enlistment decisions. Several judges released young men from service only to turn them over to the military to be prosecuted for obtaining government subsistence, clothing, and pay under false pretenses.[45] A judge in Philadelphia in 1852 declared that the enlistment of minors in the navy was valid, being governed by English, rather than American, common law.[46] And a Supreme Court judge in New York refused to release a fifteen-year-old enlistee in 1859, expressing "great doubts of his jurisdiction," and feeling that "the boy was much better off than he could be if discharged."[47] The legal landscape continued to tilt toward supporting parental rights and concurrent jurisdiction throughout this decade, but military officers could take some solace that the winds of change seemed to be moving in their direction. The fact that there had been no resolution to the question of how to deal with underage enlistees in the first half of the nineteenth century, however, ensured that this issue would continue to bedevil legislators, judges, and especially parents during the Civil War.

* * *

These struggles among parents, local and state court judges, and US officers over the fate of minor enlistees in the first half of the nineteenth century demonstrate a need to revise common assumptions about the decline of the state militias in the pre–Civil War era. It is well known that compulsory militia duty had become something of a joke in many areas by the 1840s, with men showing up for muster days dressed in ridiculous uniforms, blowing tin horns or carrying cornstalk weapons, burlesquing any officer foolish enough to take the event seriously. Instead of keeping the peace, militiamen were just as likely to start drunken brawls and riots.[48]

If the idea of compelling men to show up and drill in the town square was no longer taken seriously, however, the same cannot be said for the principles underlying the division between state militias and the US military. Even as support for compulsory militia duty broke down, most judges continued to uphold a legal distinction between service in the militia and service in the regulars, underscoring their belief that these were two very different kinds of obligations—one in defense of local and community interests, and the other, far more onerous, on behalf of a potentially overbearing federal government. Sustaining parental rights absent specific laws allowing for underage enlistment, they registered an ongoing belief that ordinary people required protection at the state and local level against centralized power—the basic idea on which America's dual military system was premised. Social commentators might scoff at militiamen, but the threat of military overreach remained no laughing matter.

3

Underdeveloped Bodies

Calculating the Ideal Enlistment Age

Not long after sixteen-year-old Edward Edes enlisted in the 33rd Massachusetts Infantry, he sent a letter to his parents that registered a widely shared notion: that underage enlistees were particularly prone to illness and therefore a drain on scarce military resources. Wavering between acknowledging this belief and seeking to disprove it, he assured his parents in November 1862 that he was "getting a little rugged again" after a recent period of feeling unwell. "I get very low spirited, sometimes, thinking of home, but I try to keep a stiff upper lip although as yet my youth does not allow much stiffening to grow there. I don't want it to be said that I am one of those that went too young & are filling up the hospitals." Edes vowed to defy the stereotype of the delicate boy who spent more time in hospital than in camp, even as he seemed to concede that he could not be expected to maintain the fortitude of his older comrades. Before closing, he circled back to the topic of health and sought to allay any anxiety his letter may have provoked. Affirming that he felt "first rate today," he spelled out his prescription for continued good health: "Plenty of letters, plenty of grub & plenty of sleep make a fellow feel hale, hearty & good humored."[1]

These brief lines capture a number of medical assumptions that had come to the fore by the outbreak of the Civil War. Most obviously, Edes' letter indicates a belief that age was intrinsically connected to health, leaving those who went to war "too young" especially vulnerable. Perhaps less obvious is his understanding of the relationship between illness, age, and emotional resilience. Edes knew that youths, unable to fully master their emotions, were more likely to become "low spirited" and thus more apt to give way to homesickness or nostalgia—believed to be a potentially fatal malady at this time, and one to which the young were particularly susceptible.[2] To remain "good humored" was therefore not just a moral but also a physical imperative. Receiving missives from home, being well nourished and rested, and keeping in good cheer all helped to ward off sickness and disease, with mind and body working in tandem to maintain a robust system.[3]

The specter of the feeble and ailing young soldier made it difficult for Edes to convince himself that his own health would hold out. In January 1863, he wrote home professing to feel "well, never better," adding cockily, "if they do say the boys between sixteen & twenty fill the hospitals, in this regt they are most all first platoon men & old at that."[4] But fears of illness continued to haunt him. He had been in the service for a year when his father wrote to him of a young soldier from the community who had sickened and died. It was a typical Civil War death: for every soldier felled by battlefield injuries, two succumbed to illness, usually due to infectious diseases like dysentery, typhoid, pneumonia, smallpox, and measles.[5] "[D]eath in an army hospital, by a lingering disease, has peculiar terrors to me," Edes wrote to his father in response to the sorrowful news. "I can hardly imagine a more mournful death than to die away from home, among strangers, with miserable nursing, & still worse—in many cases—medical attendance." His mind immediately turned to a soldier roughly his own age, "a boy in our company . . . about seventeen years old & a stranger to all of the company" who had suffered just such a death.[6] Sadly, Edward's anxieties proved prescient. He died of typhoid the following year, and the officious announcement sent to his parents offered little assurance that he had been tenderly cared for at the end.[7]

When Edes worried about young enlistees succumbing to illness and filling up hospitals, he gave voice to a relatively new understanding of age, albeit one widespread enough to make him self-conscious about his youth. Prior to the mid-nineteenth century, people rarely voiced concerns that those below a given age were intrinsically unqualified to serve. During the Revolutionary War, military commanders who complained about young soldiers focused on those who seemed to lack strength. What vexed them was the presence of boys too small and frail to withstand army life, not "stout" and "rugged" youths of the same age.[8] During the War of 1812, critics who opposed the unauthorized enlistment of minors between the ages of eighteen and twenty-one mustered every argument they could think of, but they never questioned the physical capacities or stamina of this age cohort. Nor did judges emphasize a lack of bodily development or a propensity toward illness among underage recruits when they upheld parental rights in subsequent decades. In other words, many people opposed youth enlistment and derided the enlistment of self-evidently weak soldiers. But until the mid-nineteenth century, they would not have assumed that age-specific weaknesses lurked within the bodies of healthy-looking youths or that those below a specific age were in-herently unsuited for military life.

This lack of concern reflected the fact that there was no yardstick for meas-uring age-related physical capacities in the first decades of the new republic's existence. In the political and legal sphere, the age of twenty-one had gained enhanced significance, at least for white males, as state governments removed property and residency requirements for voting but left age limits in place.[9] But in medicine, understandings of age remained vague, with medical texts rarely discussing the relationship between age and health or offering advice on optimal stages of mental or physical development. Scholars have there-fore typically dated the growth of age consciousness to the late-nineteenth century, with the emergence of medical specialties like pediatrics and gov-ernment bureaucracies that increasingly used birthdates to categorize and identify individuals.[10]

This chronology overlooks the fact that the military had long been fixated on trying to better understand the relationship between age and health. By the mid-nineteenth century, European states had already spent many decades working to increase the efficiency of their armies by applying the latest scientific advances. Army physicians, who produced numerous studies that claimed to measure human growth precisely to determine the optimal enlistment age, were at the forefront of the new science of human measure-ment that linked chronological age to specific physiological states. As one of the few entities that instituted rigid age restrictions and the only one preoccupied with understanding the process of human growth, the military played a key role in revolutionizing how people thought about age, both in the United States and elsewhere. In fact, prior to the late nineteenth cen-tury, the military was the institution most responsible for pioneering age consciousness.

By the 1850s, research produced by army doctors had convinced many military professionals across the Anglo-European world that males in their teens or younger had no business in uniform. Instead of strengthening the nation's fighting capacity, their undeveloped bodies proved a hindrance, slowing an army's march and filling hospitals. Young musicians raised no great alarm: their numbers were comparatively small, and their youth was seen as a virtue since they freed up older men for battle. But enlisted men serving on the front lines were another matter. These views were reiterated in a spate of works on army strength and recruiting that appeared right be-fore and during the Civil War, written primarily by military men who played some part in examining the health of enlistees. Addressing fellow army physicians and recruiters, they insisted that military service was suited only to full-grown men. While most believed that human physiology mandated a minimum age of enlistment of twenty or twenty-one, some set the bar as high as twenty-five.

Yet if critics of youth enlistment were numerous and vocal, they lost out to those who believed in filling out the military's ranks by whatever means necessary. From the war's outset, the Confederacy allowed youths eighteen and older to volunteer without parental consent. The Union enacted such a policy in February 1862, sanctioning what was already common practice on the ground. Many recruiters knowingly enlisted younger boys as well, often to the consternation of their parents. In the end, hard-headed pragmatism, not the latest scientific studies showing the costs of youth enlistment, guided most government officials and military officers.

Yet if medical criticism of youth enlistment often went unheeded, its influence was nonetheless significant. In the United States, legislators accepted the warnings of military doctors and established twenty rather than eighteen as the minimum age for conscription. Parents frequently referred to the presumed physical incapacities of youth when seeking their children's discharge. So, too, did court martial panels when recommending leniency in cases involving underage soldiers, especially if defendants were charged with sleeping on post—a crime typically understood as a failure of physical stamina. Harder to gauge is the influence of such arguments on underage youths themselves. If Edes' correspondence is any indication, young soldiers were acutely aware that they often evoked skepticism or pity from observers. This sometimes led to a resoluteness borne of the desire to prove their detractors wrong. But it could also cause foreboding and regret.

Changes in Warfare and the Study of Aging

A focus on soldiers' age and the imposition of age-related enlistment restrictions can be traced back to what has sometimes been called the Military Enlightenment, a period beginning in the mid-seventeenth century and characterized by efforts to systematize various aspects of military life. Following the introduction of guns, a growing number of works illustrated the many steps to be followed in loading and firing them, as well as the procedures and commands required to maneuver armed men in the field.

At the same time, states across Europe began to form permanent standing armies made up of regularized units with prescribed hierarchies based on chain-of-command rather than personal fealty or social rank. They drew up articles of war to regulate the conduct of their military and naval forces and established military education systems for officers. And they began paying greater attention to the elements that supposedly made for efficient soldiers, including those that caused men to break down on the march or in battle.[11]

The rapid movement of troops assumed particular importance in the eighteenth century, as national armies ballooned in size and battlefield tactics grew increasingly complex. Soldiers had to be capable of marching in lockstep for long distances, carrying heavy weapons and packs that usually weighed more than sixty pounds—tasks that required strength and stamina.[12] In identifying factors that contributed to battlefield success, authors of military tomes took their cue from the natural sciences and emphasized the importance of empirical observation, drawing on examples from recent campaigns rather than ancient precedent, as they had in the past. By the early nineteenth century, their volumes were filled with instances of battles won by the speedy arrival of troops or lost by exhausted regiments outflanked by swifter enemies—outcomes that allegedly came down to soldiers' stride and pace in an era before mechanized transportation. A military theorist writing in 1840 cited the experiences of two renowned French generals who commanded armies in the eighteenth century to express what had by then become a truism: "War in modern times consists so much in the science of making men march for the purpose of striking an unexpected blow on the enemy that the efficiency of soldiers depends greatly on their capacity for executing long marches with comparative ease."[13]

These changes in warfare significantly enhanced the importance of musicians and thus the number of boys and young men in uniform. Although music had long been an integral part of soldiering and boys had historically filled the role of army musicians, the growing regimentation of warfare elevated the significance of this work. By the mid-eighteenth century, almost all actions that soldiers performed took place to the sound of a drum, fife, or bugle, and every regiment was accompanied by musicians. Musicians not only helped to keep the blues at bay in camp and to motivate men going into battle, but also telegraphed instructions on the field. Most importantly, they led armies on the march, determining the speed and, therefore, the distance that a regiment could travel. To free up adult men for service, an increasing number of boys—some as young as eight or nine—occupied positions in military bands.[14]

While the number of young musicians ballooned in the eighteenth century, so did a concern with limiting the enlistments of youths as privates to ensure that each soldier was hearty and tall enough to keep in step with his peers. In the past, age restrictions were not unknown, but they tended to lack consistency and enforcement. Up through the seventeenth century—before the spread of military academies and army schools—elites might send their sons into service at the age of eleven or twelve, and young boys could end up commanding much older men. Nobleman Claude Alexandre, Comte de Bonneval, joined the French military in 1686 at the age of eleven, for instance, and was placed in charge of a regiment several years later.[15] By the following century, most European militaries had drawn up regulations that covered all recruits save for musicians. The criteria for enlistment varied between different branches of the service, with navies being most open to the recruitment of the young. But they typically included height and age restrictions and, less often, weight or chest girth. Enlistees also had to pass a medical inspection to ensure they were free from infirmity or disease.[16]

A new concern with standardizing troops' physical characteristics was one of several ways that the changing nature of warfare encouraged the study of aging and physical development. Throughout the eighteenth century near constant fighting and economic disruption across Europe had led rulers to prioritize the identification of every taxpayer who might fund future wars and every man who might be put into the ranks. States that had introduced centralized systems of national conscription had added incentive to count and measure the military-age population and to note distinguishing features that might identify deserters.[17] In addition, from the mid-eighteenth century onward, population studies undertaken in multiple countries revealed alarming levels of ill health and debility, which spurred interest in the question of precisely how the body developed and why growth rates varied between regions and countries.

Scientific investigations into physiology had been rare before this time, with interrogations of human growth remaining largely theoretical. Medical treatises typically linked physical growth and size to the body's internal balance, especially of heat and moisture (with children's markedly hot constitutions supposedly accounting for their more rapid growth).[18] Thinking began to change in the first half of the nineteenth century as physicians concerned with public health produced the first surveys based on the measurements of large numbers of people. Most famously, Louis-René Villermé in France, Lambert Quételet in Belgium, and Edwin Chadwick in England charted the dimensions of prisoners, asylum inmates, and industrial workers to expose the effects of poverty on human growth and mortality. Quantifying the shriveled frames, sunken chests, stunted organs, and early deaths of the poor, they put forward a new theory that emphasized environmental conditions such as climate, diet, exercise, and work regimes to account for differences in height, weight, or overall health.[19]

It was not industrial workers, however, but army and navy recruits who were most likely to have their measurements taken before mid-century.[20] Only a handful of scientists in this era had the independent means to conduct experimental research, and university professorships generally entailed full-time teaching. Physicians who worked in the military, however, had a guaranteed income, easy access to a large body of potential research subjects, and time on their hands.[21] Most also lived in isolated surroundings such as frontier posts, foreign locations, or aboard ships where diversions were few. Undertaking research helped to cement their professional status within the medical and scientific community and connected them to networks of likeminded researchers who shared their findings through publication, correspondence, and membership in professional associations. As a result, much of the initial research measuring human growth concentrated on the dimensions of those in uniform. These studies, in turn, became the primary evidence for authors tackling the problem of how to ensure a vigorous military.[22]

Henry Marshall was the first military physician who sought to address recruiting practices by compiling vital statistics on British soldiers. Born in Scotland in 1775 and educated at the University of Glasgow, Marshall served as a surgeon's mate in the Royal Navy, then as an assistant surgeon in the militia, followed by postings across the British Empire. He returned to the United Kingdom in the 1820s to oversee the medical inspection of recruits at the Dublin military depot and ended his career as the deputy inspector-general of army hospitals. Having spent most of his life scrutinizing the health of British soldiers and sailors, Marshall devoted his retirement to publishing advice for medical officers on ways to promote military strength by weeding out unfit recruits and retaining healthy ones.[23] Comparing his two major works in this vein reveals his growing sense of the importance of age as a factor in army health.

The first English-language work of its kind, Marshall's *Hints to Young Medical Officers of the Army on the Examination of Recruits* (1828) showed minimal interest in the topic of soldiers' age. In fact, Marshall urged medical officers not to worry too much about recruits' ages. He pointed out that standards varied widely between regiments and that recruits often lied about their birthdates. While physicians' training helped them to detect such lies, Marshall acknowledged that their assessments would inevitably be imperfect. "Changes of the physical character of man are so imperceptible, and the transition so little apparent, that no definite marks of any particular age can be assigned," he wrote. "Some lads of eighteen" might naturally look older than others of twenty-one, while other youths appeared prematurely aged due to immoral habits and disease. Medical officers could therefore only render their best guess as to an individual's fitness to serve.[24] In a work of over two hundred pages, only a few paragraphs, mostly relegated to the footnotes, addressed the topic of age.

Just a few years later, however, the age of enlistment had become one of Marshall's central preoccupations. Marshall was unambiguous on its critical importance, warning: "mortality arises in nearly an exact ratio with the age of individuals." The next manual he addressed to army doctors—*On the Enlisting, Discharging and Pensioning of Soldiers* (1832)—opened with the topic and then devoted a dozen pages to fleshing out its importance. It commenced with a discussion emphasizing the inability of young bodies to tolerate hard marches. "Long-protracted exertions" were guaranteed to "exhaust the frame . . . of young striplings," however brave they might be. Nor was the danger only to their own health, he warned. Given that troops ideally marched and fought "simultaneously," moving as a single body off the field and executing coordinated movements in battle, the weakness of some could prove fatal to all. Multiple pages of examples helped to drive this point home. In one, he compared a French force composed of seasoned troops above twenty-two years of age that marched "about 400 leagues," with almost no one dropping out along the way, and then fought successfully at the battle of Austerlitz, to a group of younger soldiers who marched a shorter distance during the campaign of 1809 and left "all the hospitals on the route . . . filled with sick," causing Napoleon to thunder: "*I must have grown men—boys serve only to fill the hospitals, and encumber the road-side.*" Achieving military success thus required that recruitment officers exercise utmost vigilance in rejecting anyone too young to serve. But what was too young, and how could age be known? Marshall quoted another army physician to the effect that members of his profession needed to be "intimately acquainted with the anatomy, physiology, and the diseases of the human body."[25] Aside from this general advice, he had little guidance to offer on the topic.

Around the same time, a range of additional voices had also begun to emphasize the importance of this question—most notably Adolphe Quételet's *A Treatise on Man and the Development of His Faculties* (1835). Instantly acclaimed and quickly translated into German and English, Quételet's work argued that age was the single biggest predictor of mortality.[26] Bemoaning the fact that no one had previously analyzed bodily changes with precision, Quételet drew together all existing studies of population measurements and added his own. He devoted one chapter to calculating the average height of individuals at different ages, another to analyzing individuals' typical weight gain year-by-year, and a third to assessing the relationship between strength and age.[27] Introducing the concept of a "normal distribution" or bell curve to data analysis, Quételet provided the analytical framework that informed all subsequent statistical work, as well as spawning countless imitators. By focusing on averages, he also transformed medical discussions relating to age from the nebulous concept described by Marshall to a set of average yearly alterations in height, weight, and strength that were specific and quantifiable.[28]

The growing interest in measuring age precisely in order to keep boys out of the army is perfectly illustrated by William Aitken's *On the Growth of the Recruit and Young Soldier* (1862). Aitken had held a teaching post as a demonstrator of anatomy at Glasgow University before heading to the Crimea in the mid-1850s to investigate the medical condition of British troops. On his return, he became a professor of pathology at the newly established army medical school at Chatham in Kent. His time overseas had convinced him that a lack of training in "physiological principles" among enlistment officers had played a key role in the military's spectacular public health disaster during that conflict. Written as a pair of introductory lectures for delivery at the Army Medical School, Aitken's volume minced no words: with the nation's wealth and military strength at stake, the armed forces could not afford to exercise less judgment in selecting and training recruits than that "which a gentleman thinks judicious and proper to bestow upon a useful dog or a valuable horse."[29]

This analogy suggested Aitken's main concern: the careful, scientific management of the nation's resources. To enlist and train a soldier cost money—£100 a year in his estimate—that would be squandered by putting those below a certain age into uniform. Worse, by excessively taxing a youth's growing body, military service virtually guaranteed that he would end up becoming a permanent burden on society "with one or more of his vital organs damaged for the remainder of his life." For Aitken, the issue was neither the military effectiveness of young soldiers, nor the impact of service on their minds or morals. He was dismayed by the improvidence of enlisting youths, which he believed willfully ignored the latest scientific evidence on human growth.

To ensure that army physicians mastered this topic, Aitken's lectures provided a physiological primer, charting the periodic alterations that took place in the bones, muscles, and sinews of the average male body. Beginning with the "normal growth" in weight and stature at different ages, Aitken's survey then moved on to describe age-based changes in the skeleton, organs, ribs, arm bones, leg bones, breast bones, and vital capacity, and the relationship between the growth of muscles and bones. Each discussion revolved around a simple point: anyone below the age of twenty should be disqualified from military service because their growth was incomplete. Before this age, the skeleton had not fully formed; the long bones in the arms and legs were still "in a soft, cartilaginous growing state"; the ribs incompletely developed; the bones only partly fused to their shafts, and so on. Etchings depicting each section of the skeleton illustrated Aitken's point. Age was now written on every body part, such that a "skillful anatomist" could assess a recruit with "considerable accuracy."[30] Of course, despite these confident assertions, military doctors could still not determine any individual enlistee's age with certainty; Aitken spoke of averages, while actual humans failed to line up so neatly. Nonetheless, his work was one of numerous studies in this era asserting that military physicians could greatly enhance military efficiency by using scientific principles to assess enlistees' ages.

Aitken's assumption that youths below age twenty were physically incapable of serving drew on the standard established by the Prussian and French militaries, both of which relied on universal conscription and only drafted those above this age.[31] As proof of his theory, he cited the many military authorities who claimed that the high percentage of youthful recruits significantly elevated the British army's mortality rate in the Crimea. Incapable of coping with harsh conditions, these "unformed" youths "fell victims to disease, and were swept away like flies."[32] George MacLeod, a lecturer on military surgery who worked in Sebastopol during the war and returned to publish *Notes on the Surgery of the War in the Crimea*, painted a similarly dim picture. He described the British ranks as a mass of "raw boys," many of them

(a)

(b)

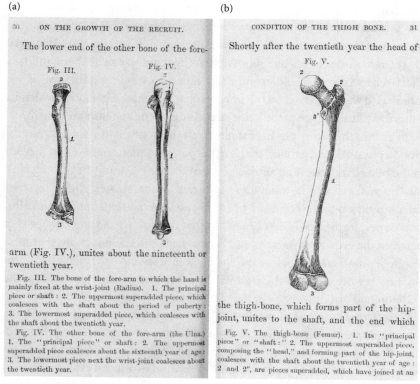

The lower end of the other bone of the fore-

Fig. III.

Fig. IV.

arm (Fig. IV.), unites about the nineteenth or twentieth year.

Fig. III. The bone of the fore-arm to which the hand is mainly fixed at the wrist-joint (Radius). 1. The principal piece or shaft : 2. The uppermost superadded piece, which coalesces with the shaft about the period of puberty : 3. The lowermost superadded piece, which coalesces with the shaft about the twentieth year.

Fig. IV. The other bone of the fore-arm (the Ulna.) 1. The "principal piece" or shaft : 2. The uppermost superadded piece coalesces about the sixteenth year of age : 3. The lowermost piece next the wrist-joint coalesces about the twentieth year.

Shortly after the twentieth year the head of

Fig. V.

the thigh-bone, which forms part of the hip-joint, unites to the shaft, and the end which

Fig. V. The thigh-bone (Femur). 1. Its "principal piece" or "shaft :" 2. The uppermost superadded piece, composing the "head," and forming part of the hip-joint, coalesces with the shaft about the twentieth year of age : 2 and 2″, are pieces superadded, which have joined at an

Figure 3.1 Pages from William Aitken's *On the Growth of the Recruit* (1862), which argued that anyone below the age of twenty should be disqualified from military service because their growth was incomplete. US physicians and sanitarians regularly cited this work during the Civil War, and its depiction of physical development influenced the decision by the US Congress to set the age of conscription at twenty rather than eighteen. Royal College of Physicians Edinburgh. Wellcome Collection.

"ill-conditioned, below the standard age, undeveloped in body, unconfirmed in constitution, and hence without stamina or powers of endurance."[33]

Aitken's endorsement of the French and Prussian example was never implemented in Britain or the United States, both of which relied on voluntary recruits rather than conscripts and accepted youths below the age of twenty. But the influence of European military medicine and its growing preoccupation with age-related disabilities can be seen in publications by US medical officers both immediately prior to and during the Civil War. In 1858, Charles

S. Tripler, who had served as an army surgeon in the Mexican American War and accompanied troops on a deadly expedition across Panama, published his *Manual of the Medical Officer of the Army of the United States*.[34] Initially, Tripler had planned simply to translate the official guide for the French army, *Aide Memoire de l'Officier de Sante*, which first appeared in 1842.[35] However, on finding it repetitive and not wholly appropriate for the American military system, he instead wrote his own book, while still relying heavily on the text and structure of the French model. Endorsed by the Department of War, Tripler's manual was quickly "accepted throughout the army as the authoritative last word on recruit requirements."[36] His work almost immediately addressed the issue of recruits' ages. The third page features a long passage from *Aide Memoire de l'Officier Sante* explaining why few "young men" made for good soldiers. The French authors rattled off a litany of potential problems—the "gastrointestinal mucous membrane" was "too readily over-excitable," the lungs were "too susceptible of morbid impressions," and the nervous system was "far" from fully developed. Tripler strongly seconded these objections "so forcibly urged against the enlistment of minors." Yet he did grudgingly concede that "so long as these enlistments are authorized," medical officers could not simply refuse them on the grounds of age alone.

Medical opinions published after the outbreak of the Civil War concurred with Tripler on the dangers of youth enlistment but urged a more proactive approach to keep still-growing boys out of the ranks by changing the enlistment age. The physicians, sanitarians, and clergymen who worked with the United States Sanitary Commission (USSC), for instance, early on emphasized the need to study the relationship between age and liability to sickness and death, "since this affects the question of the relative efficiency of men, as soldiers, at different ages."[37] They were of one mind when it came to youthful enlistment: every USSC writer who discussed this topic from a medical perspective suggested that setting the enlistment age at eighteen years was courting disaster. "A soldier should be a full-grown man, and not a boy," exclaimed Alfred Post and William Van Buren in a USSC pamphlet on military hygiene. "The most eligible age for a recruit is twenty to twenty-five years."[38] F. G. Smith and Alfred Stillé similarly warned that smallpox was most likely to threaten soldiers between the ages of fifteen and twenty-five.[39]

Most prominently, the Union army's top medical man, Surgeon General William Hammond, strongly endorsed the perspective that youth enlistment was ill advised—indeed, positively dangerous—and thus required alteration. In his annual report to the secretary of war in November 1862, he observed that "it was not uncommon" to find sixteen-year-olds in the ranks. Warning that such youths were "not developed" and could not long withstand "the fatigues and deprivations of the military life," he suggested an adjustment of the minimum age of enlistment to twenty was "imperatively demanded."[40] Hammond elaborated on this point in his *Treatise on Hygiene* (1863)—arguably the most influential medical text published during the Civil War. "Perhaps the subject of the age of the recruit is more important than any other," he wrote. Making liberal use of Aitken's volume and the European ones discussed above, Hammond reproduced their examples of hospitals filled with young enlistees and added anecdotes drawn from his own experience.[41] He reiterated Aitken's point about the costs of training and maintaining each recruit, stressing that it made no financial sense to enlist young men who would inevitably break down. Then, after quoting extensively from studies on human growth and physiology, he repeated his call to raise the enlistment age, this time suggesting that even age twenty might be too low. "Place it at twenty to twenty-two, and we shall find fewer inmates in our hospitals, and consequently more men in the field," he opined.[42]

In the end, the army's need for men trumped professional medical opinions about the ideal age for voluntary recruits. But such arguments undeniably shaped the Enrollment Act of 1863, which established twenty rather than eighteen as the minimum age at which a man could be drafted into the Union army. The initial bill, considered by the Senate in February of that year, proposed a system that followed the French model in establishing different classes of potential draftees: the first included men ages eighteen to thirty and all unmarried men between eighteen and forty-five; the second, married men between the ages of thirty and forty-five. After all of the men from the first class had been conscripted, those from the second class would be called up. In debating the plan, senators immediately raised questions as to whether the burden would fall unfairly upon the young. "It strikes me that a man thirty-one or thirty-two or thirty-five or forty years of age owes as much service to the Government as the man of eighteen, nineteen, or twenty," objected Senator James Nesmith, a Democrat from Oregon. In turn, Senator Henry Wilson of Massachusetts, who served as chairman of the Committee on Military Affairs and the Militia (later the Committee on Military Affairs), criticized the proposal on the grounds that men below age twenty were, "as a general rule," unfit to serve. "Go into the hospitals in the country," he urged, "and you will find that a very large portion of the sick consist of the young men under twenty years of age, or of men over forty years of age." Referring to the experience of the British, presumably during the Crimean War, Wilson argued that "the young men eighteen, nineteen, and twenty years of age" accounted for "an enormous percentage of the sick and dying," whereas "men above twenty or twenty-one years" fared much better, "having become matured."

Senator James A. McDougall, a War Democrat from California, supported Wilson's assessment, arguing that exempting the young from conscription was less a matter of "justice" than "sound policy." In sweeping terms, McDougall claimed that "The experience of the world . . . has shown that men do not acquire the hardiness that fits them for severe campaigning at an age much earlier than twenty-five, and that from twenty-five to forty-five is the period of life when men are best able to stand the fatigues of war. This is a simple, practical fact, the result of the experience of all military States, and, I think is not disputed." The problem with younger men was that "tendinous substance has not grown into bone and sinew," he continued, so they could not endure "the fatigues of a hard campaign" or "march with heavy weights, twenty, or thirty, or forty miles a day." If Congress was to adopt a policy of conscription, he concluded, "I say pick out those who are best capable of bearing arms," and "let the boys stay at home until their beards grow."

At this juncture in the debate, Republican Senator Samuel C. Pomeroy of Kansas interjected and moved to alter the proposed bill to make twenty rather than eighteen the minimum age for conscription. Several senators cried out from the floor, "Say twenty-one"—a suggestion to which he consented. Pomeroy's fellow senator from Kansas, abolitionist James Henry Lane, was the only senator to contest the proposal to exempt all males under twenty or twenty-one from conscription. Though he conceded that such youths might not "bear the fatigues of a campaign as well as older men," he argued that they were in fact "the most important element" in volunteer units. "They furnish the enthusiasm, the pluck, the adventure of a volunteer army," he argued. "If you call for volunteers for a dangerous expedition, nine out of ten of them will be under twenty years old." But in the end, Senator Wilson made the final call, urging that the minimum age be set at twenty—a proposal the other senators appeared to accept in deference to his status as the committee chair.[43] Clearly, understandings of the supposed physiological debilities of young soldiers had seeped into broader culture, allowing politicians without medical training to confidently assert that European experiences demonstrated the perils of enlisting the young.

Accounting for the Physical Limitations of Young Enlistees

Medical debates did little to curb youth enlistment, but they nevertheless shaped how military officers and civilians understood its effects. Court martial decisions in both the United States and the Confederacy, for example, reveal a strong tendency to show leniency "on account of youth."[44] This was especially evident in cases involving underage soldiers tried for sleeping on post—theoretically a capital offense, yet one that growing boys understandably found hard to avoid. Although some convicted soldiers were in fact sentenced to death for this very human crime, it seems that none actually paid the ultimate price. Nonetheless, rumors of impending executions circulated widely, often due to press reports of sentences that would later be commuted. In mid-1861, for instance, Confederate papers reported that two soldiers tried in Pensacola had been found guilty of sleeping on post; one had been sentenced to be shot the following day, while the other, "on account of extreme youth and inexperience," was to be drummed out of camp after a period of sixty days' imprisonment.[45] In the end, the older soldier was pardoned, but not before many had read of his presumed fate. Similarly, numerous northern newspapers reported in late 1861 that nearly fifty US soldiers convicted of capital offenses—the majority of them for sleeping on guard duty—were being held in Washington, their fate yet to be decided.[46]

Reports like these caused some parents of heavy-sleeping young soldiers to panic. William Gregg of Pennsylvania dispatched a flurry of frantic letters to Washington in late 1861 and 1862 regarding his fourteen-year-old son Oram, who had enlisted without his consent. "He can not stand guard and picket duty[,] for to sleep he will go and then death is certain," he wrote to Abraham Lincoln, explaining that his son would inevitably succumb to exhaustion "on account of his age." Had Gregg managed to get his letter before Lincoln, the president would almost certainly have released his son; the National Archives contain many similar petitions upon which Lincoln scrawled, "Let this boy be discharged," or "Let this boy be discharged on refund of any bounty received." But Gregg's petition was routed to the Adjutant General's Office, which summarily rejected his appeal. After pursuing several other avenues, the anxious father finally wrote to Secretary of War Edwin Stanton, begging that his son be relieved from sentry duty, or at the very least be exempted from punishment if he fell asleep while on guard duty. Should Oram end up being executed "for the nonperformance of duties because of his inability to perform them on account of his youth," he warned Stanton, "his Blood be upon your Head."[47]

In truth, Gregg need not have been quite so anxious, for court martial panels routinely took age into account and treated it as a mitigating factor. Officers, fellow soldiers, and military surgeons all underscored the disabilities of youth when summoned to submit evidence in cases of underage defendants. One Union surgeon, who testified on behalf of a soldier he judged to be between sixteen and eighteen years old, stated that the defendant was "not a fully matured and developed man" but rather "in that transition state when boys are more tender."[48] Another, asked to weigh in on the case of a sixteen-year-old convicted of sleeping while on duty, noted in his diary that he had urged "the mitigation or entire remission of any punishment that may have been awarded him." He hoped that his recommendation would "save the boy," for he hated "to see a delicate boy like him punished because he was not able to endure fatigue."[49]

Court martial panels also emphasized the physical limitations of young soldiers to justify lenient sentences, as did one that stated, "the court is satisfied from the general appearance of the prisoner that he is not more than sixteen years of age and of feeble constitution." In this case, the punishment administered for sleeping on post was not the loss of life, but the loss of $10 pay for four months, plus ten days of hard labor.[50] Not all young soldiers got off so easily: others suffered such punishments as a month's confinement on bread and water or having to stand on a barrel for several hours a day while wearing a placard reading "sleepy head." But an adult convicted of the same offense might be sent to prison for a year.

On rare occasion, court martial panels remitted punishments entirely in cases of underage soldiers, concluding that the real blame for a young defendant's offense lay with the officers who had overburdened him. Emphatically declining to "inflict any punishment" on a sixteen-year-old defendant, one panel explained that it did not "consider him as then or even now fit for the responsible duties of a sentry." Another recommended acquittal on the grounds that "the accused should not have been placed on guard" due to "his youth, physical condition, and evident want of mental capacity from sickness."[51] Henry Brown of the 3rd Alabama Infantry, Colored Troops, similarly escaped punishment after being arrested for sleeping on guard duty. Although witnesses testified that Brown was eighteen years old and had been fully briefed on his responsibilities, the panelists concluded that he was "evidently too young and ignorant for a soldier" and had been "but poorly instructed." They imposed a trifling sentence (to have his hands tied behind him and paraded in front of his company quarters for four hours over four days). The brigadier general who reviewed the case agreed. Declaring Brown a "mere boy" who had erred out of "ignorance instead of a disposition to shirk duty," he returned the youth to duty and disciplined his officers instead. He also ordered that the proceedings be published for the benefit of "Officers of Colored Troops," warning that future instances could lead to their discharge or loss of commission.[52]

The letters and petitions that parents sent to Washington in hopes of gaining their children's release also reflect the extent to which ordinary people regarded youth as a risk factor. Many who feared that their sons' enlistment would be a death sentence quite rationally dreaded the scourges of illness more than the dangers of the battlefield. Such anxieties come through clearly in Annette Hathaway's letter concerning her son William, who had enlisted at the age of sixteen, but "like a great many other foolish boys" had been "sick most of the time and in hospital for 2 or 3 month[s]." After rejoining his regiment, he wrote to her from Charleston, South Carolina, complaining that "it was so hot he must die." Whether William actually viewed the southern climate as potentially lethal, or whether he was simply grumbling about the weather, his mother believed the situation dire enough to warrant his release. With four sons in the army, she had already sacrificed much for the Union. As her youngest son wilted, so did she. "I must die if you dont releive me," she begged.[53]

Again and again, parents of underage soldiers evoked this image of a frail youth whose health was failing under the strain of military service. Appealing to the provost marshal general in 1864, one father noted that he had tried to prevent the enlistment of his seventeen-year-old son, believing him "too young to stand the service"—a conviction that proved "only too true" when the boy fell ill from yellow fever in Virginia.[54] A husband and wife wrote to Lincoln after hearing from their sixteen-year old son, who was so sick that he feared it might be the last letter he would ever write. "Our reason for [asking for] his return is his youth[.] he has not experience in hardships and will fall an easy prey to diseases or a southern son [sun]," they pleaded.[55] Similarly, a widow begged for the release of her only son on the grounds that "his health has failed." For over a year, he had earnestly tried to do his duty, she noted, but "a boy 17 years old is not fit for such hardships as they must undergo in the Army."[56] The same argument appears in one of the few letters written by a young soldier appealing for his own release. Apologizing for being "a very bad writer," he explained, "i am to young to be in the army and i am not 16 years of age. . . i am not able to march . . . i am not able to stand it."[57]

When confronted with pervasive doubts as to their physical capacities, along with the varied reactions that their presence elicited from older comrades—from protectiveness and sympathy to impatience and down-right disgust—most youths tried to put on a brave show. Thirteen-year-old drummer Corydon Foote had worked hard to learn his instrument, des-perate to join his older brother and a friend around his own age who were serving alongside the men of their community. After he fell ill, he was sent to the division hospital, where the nurses and the hospital surgeon treated him with special kindness. But when the surgeon proposed that he stay on as an orderly to keep out of harm's way, Corydon rebuffed the offer, declaring that he belonged with his regiment. In his memoir, he recalled how the doctor "growled something about the 'slaughter of the innocents' and the 'pigheaded presumption of upstart minors' and the 'criminal irresponsibility of those who were letting them into the army.'" But none of this dissuaded Corydon from returning to the comrades, who doted on him and called him "Little Foote." To abandon his regiment would have been tantamount to admitting that he did not belong in the army—that he was actually the weak youngster his doctor supposed him to be.[58] So like many other youths, he threw the dice, trusting that he would be among the lucky survivors.

Boys tried to dismiss the grim warnings that dogged them, but given the widespread assumptions about youth's greater frailties, not to mention the frequent deaths due to illness and disease that plagued military camps, they must have suffered doubts. Already eighteen when he enlisted, Robert J. Burdette's short stature made him appear considerably younger. When he went to sign up, the enlistment officer allowed the eager recruit to stand on tiptoe so that he could reach the requisite height of 5 feet, 3 inches, shaking his head in resignation. As Robert left the office, he overhead a sergeant's bleak prediction: "That child will serve most of his time in the hospital." Robert would go on to prove them wrong, at least according to his memoir. He claimed that he "never lost one day off duty on account of sickness" during three years of service and "never saw the inside of a hospital save on such occasions as I was detailed to nurse the grown men."[59] Still, the fact that he clearly recalled the sergeant's harsh words so many years later suggests that they had lodged in mind, surely a discomfiting way to go through the war.

Sixteen-year-old Nicholas B. Grant of Tennessee also endured the unsettling experience of being confronted with the perception of those who doubted his ability to survive, let alone fight. Standing just 5 feet, 1.5 inches, when he was mustered into service in April 1862, he overheard a man grousing about the "youngsters" who would soon be sent home "where we should be." This proved more or less true in Nicholas' case. After several un-eventful months in camp, he came down with a bad case of mumps, one of the dreaded diseases of childhood. His captain and the doctor urged him to concentrate on caring for himself, cautioning that it was a very "dangerous" disease. When his regiment relocated, Nicholas had to stay behind in a makeshift hospital, too ill to move. In mid-June 1862, a steward informed him and the other remaining patients that they needed to seek shelter in pri-vate homes, as the hospital would soon close. He managed to stagger the two miles to his aunt's house, but he became violently ill upon arrival and spent the next week in a state of fever-induced delirium. By the time he recovered his senses, all of his hair had fallen out, and he was so weak that he needed a walking stick to get around. Yet within two months, he was back with his regiment, enduring long marches with the enemy in close pursuit. During one particularly harrowing episode in Kentucky, he encountered a group of women fleeing from the rebels. One of them regarded him "mournfully" and cried out, "We shall all be killed. Law, look at that little boy!" To her mind, Nicholas' slight frame and gaunt visage signaled the Unionists' vulnerability. Fearing for her own safety, she also feared for his. Did he have a mother?, she pressed him. When he assured her that he did, she urged, "I would not go. You might get killed."[60]

In fact, Nicholas did not get killed. He lived to write a short account of his Civil War experiences at the age of eighty-one and died in a soldiers' home nine years later. His plainspoken memoir is a straightforward narrative of events, with little reflection and virtually no reproduced dialogue, which hints at the importance of the encounter in his memory. It is little wonder that he recalled the episode so clearly. At a very moment he must have been trying to summon all his strength and courage, a stranger reminded him of his frail boyishness, his debt to his mother, and his mortality. Young soldiers like Nicholas—especially those who looked the part—not only faced the dangers of the battlefield and the hospital, but also had to parry the fears and doubts of those who questioned whether they belonged in the army at all.

* * *

In an era when the relevance of subtle age gradations was still not evident in most areas of life, military officers and army doctors repeatedly stressed that such distinctions mattered. In one study after another, they argued that young enlistees could prove an Achilles heel that weakened the military as a whole. These warnings established a new sense that age was crucial to physical health, with immature bodies especially vulnerable to breakdown and disease. Such admonitions weighed less than the imperative to fill the ranks during the Civil War, but they did make their way into press commentary and Congressional debate. They informed conscription policy and determined how court martial panels judged and punished young offenders. And they came through in parents' anxious pleas for the discharge of young sons and in the writings of underage enlistees themselves.

Scholars have generally overlooked or dismissed mid-century assumptions about the frailties of young soldiers, assuming instead that they could endure the stress of campaigning and recover "more quickly from the shock of combat" than older troops.[61] But compilations of Civil War data make clear that soldiers who went to war at an early age often fared badly. Studies that rely on the Early Indicators Project (EIP)—a massive collection of sources relating to Union soldiers that includes enlistment records and pension files—show that the war had catastrophic effects on young bodies and minds.[62] One survey of EIP records notes that veterans who served below the age of eighteen were a whopping 93 percent more likely to experience physical and mental diseases than those who had enlisted at age thirty-one or older. "Mortality risk was significantly associated with age at entry into service," the authors conclude, with the youngest enlistees at "greatest risk for early death."[63] Another finds that Union soldiers taken prisoner at the age of thirty or above were much less likely to suffer mortality and morbidity compared to those imprisoned at younger ages, with the latter also faring worse in socioeconomic terms after the war.[64] Even the documentation contained in the EIP database probably undercounts the magnitude of the problem, given the number of young veterans who failed to apply for pensions or found their applications rejected.[65] In all likelihood, these veterans suffered comparable rates of physical and emotional distress, only with less financial support, than those who left medical records behind.

Over the past few decades, as modern wars have spotlighted the huge number of military personnel who return home physically or mentally wounded, historians have begun to re-examine the Civil War's long shadow on individual lives.[66] This work has not yet included an emphasis on young enlistees' distinctive experience, nor have historians grappled with the material contained in the EIP database. As it turns out, nineteenth-century

commentators who railed against youth enlistment understood something
that has eluded contemporary observers: the enlistment age mattered a great
deal not just for how soldiers fared during wartime but also to their postwar
experience. Among the multitude of seemingly hale and buoyant young
soldiers were a disproportionate number for whom wartime service would
spell an adulthood marred by chronic ill health and suffering.

PART II

THE SOCIAL AND CULTURAL ORIGINS OF UNDERAGE ENLISTMENT

4

Instructive Violence

Impressionable Minds and the Cultivation
of Courage in Boys

Nineteenth-century debates over youth enlistment in the political, legal, and medical realms focused mostly on older boys and young men whose labor power was vital to parents and the military. But thousands of boys in their early teens, and sometimes even younger, also went to war. From a modern perspective, it seems curious, if not downright immoral, that large numbers of children directly experienced such a vicious conflict. Even considering what scholars have revealed about the history of childhood in this period, parents' readiness to send boys into battle requires explanation. Children of poor, immigrant, and Black families may have faced unprecedented exploitation, but middle-class and elite youths are presumed to have gained new protections based on the concept of childhood as a special stage of life. This perspective cannot account for the fact that Americans of all classes and backgrounds waved off boys and youths to witness or participate in battle firsthand.

That parents across the country made such decisions suggests that we have been too quick to trace contemporary attitudes toward children and their emotional needs to the mid-nineteenth century. Take the actions of Edwin Hale Lincoln's father, a Unitarian minister, who allowed Edwin to enlist as a drummer in the 5th Massachusetts Infantry at the age of fourteen in September 1862. Very quickly, Edwin was detailed to work as a surgeon's assistant, service that exposed him to mangled bodies and acute agony. If either father or son were troubled by this fact, their misgivings are registered nowhere in the diary that Edwin kept during his enlistment.[1] Similarly, Henry Wharton's father did not consider fourteen too young to witness combat and its disturbing aftermath. When the battle of Cedar Mountain broke out just a few miles from his Virginia home, he left his daughters behind and took his son off to watch the fighting. Henry would later recall how they had returned the following day to the battlefield, where they found "hundreds of men lying in every position—the most of them dead, others wounded and dying." He did not mention the stifling heat, the smoke and dust that would have filled his eyes and mouth, the chilling screams of the wounded, or the reek of blood and death that surely surrounded them as they worked to aid the survivors. Nor did he question why his father had subjected him to this scene. He only noted that he found the killing "absolutely incomprehensible," and that it made an impression upon his mind that could "never be removed."[2] While Civil War–era Americans shared our present-day understandings of the young as uniquely impressionable, they most emphatically did not share our understanding of the influences required, or the dangers to be avoided, in order to raise a healthy child.

Histories of childhood have not shown much interest in how Victorian thinkers assessed the imaginative worlds of children—particularly how they conceived of the effects of exposure to scenes of violence on young minds. Analysis of children's literature from this period tends to focus on its political significance, asking how it shaped middle-class norms and values or reflected adults' ideas about childhood.[3] In turn, the scholarship on child-rearing and education emphasizes the changing techniques employed to train the young and how such ideas were applied to children differently based on race, sex, class, and ethnicity.[4] Comprehensive and often moving accounts exist of the working lives of children; the changing conditions of their schooling, socializing, and family relationships; the nature of childhood under slavery; and the experiences of civilian children during the Civil War.[5] But although the violence done to children has been frequently discussed, the way adults imagined the impact of violence on children has not.

An examination of the myriad forms of writing directed at the young in antebellum America, from juvenile literature to schoolbooks and spellers, shows that writers believed that brutal carnage was a topic appropriate for even the most immature readers. Alongside their wholesome moral messages, they filled their works with scenes of graphic violence. Authors believed that vivid depictions of violence served important pedagogical ends, cementing moral lessons in young minds and making them easier to recall. Similarly, adults who addressed children on the subject of the Civil War anticipated that they would find violent imagery both entertaining and enlightening. Rather than trying to shield children from the effects of war, they described in striking detail the way weapons tore bodies apart and left men shrieking in pain.

The pervasiveness of violence in children's literature and schoolbooks does not explain why so many youths enlisted during the Civil War. Parents made calculations based on numerous factors, ranging from the pragmatic to the patriotic, and many refused to grant consent or did so only with great reluctance. Nonetheless, it is surely relevant that adults in this period typically perceived violent imagery as more edifying than emotionally devastating for the young. The many thousands of parents who wrote to Union and Confederate officials demanding the return of underage boys often fretted about youths' physical and moral vulnerabilities, but they registered no fear that boys might be corrupted or traumatized by witnessing or perpetrating violence. If a belief in the educational value of violent imagery cannot fully account for the phenomenon of mass underage enlistment, it certainly helps to explain this curious lack of adult concern.

Despite the fact that masses of parents tried to retrieve youngsters who had run off to enlist without their consent, the material directed at children suggests that the culture as a whole broadly sanctioned young people's participation in war. Helping to prepare boys for battle, this material steeped them in martial exploits, instructed them in military nomenclature, and pictured them in uniform. If childhood innocence was prized by many, it was clearly a quality that did not preclude the cultivation of courage in boys or an intimate knowledge of violence.

The Imagined Impact of Violence on Children's Inner Lives

It is not easy to discern how adults in the first half of the nineteenth century thought about the imaginative worlds of children, and thus how images of violence, suffering, and death might affect them. The Victorians wrote a great deal about children, real and imagined, but they had no clear theory of children's inner lives. By the eighteenth century, new understandings had begun to emerge, conceiving of childhood as a crucial stage that provided the foundations for adulthood. Following philosopher Jean Jacques Rousseau's popular novel *Émile: or Treatise On Education* (1762), Romantic writers in the early nineteenth century elaborated on the notion that "childhood has its own ways of seeing, thinking and feeling."[6] For poets like William Blake, Samuel Coleridge, and William Wordsworth, the earliest years of life were a unique time of blithe innocence, freedom, and emotional spontaneity—a wellspring of authenticity from which adults could draw.[7] Although these writers emphasized the distinctiveness of childhood, the development of mental processes in actual children lay beyond their concern.

Scientific theories focusing on child development were also scant before mid-nineteenth century. Medical texts generally assumed that the young did not suffer the same nervous disorders and passions that afflicted adults, imagining, for instance, that since insanity entailed a loss of reason, children below the age of reason could not go insane.[8] But in general, physicians and scientists spent little time pondering whether the young might process emotions or experiences in their own ways. Nor did childrearing manuals or texts on domestic medicine consider the issue; until mid-century this writing concentrated on physical ailments and largely ignored psychological conditions such as night terrors or other disturbed states. As literary scholar Sally Shuttleworth notes, it was novelists rather than scientists who really prompted the public to think about children's inner lives. English writers like George Eliot, the Brontë sisters, and Charles Dickens led readers to assume the perspective of youthful protagonists who were finely attuned to their surroundings and often grasped far more than the adults around them acknowledged. Pointing to the interplay between the scientific and literary realms, Shuttleworth argues that this work helped to spur the rise of child psychology as a distinct medical specialty—a development that did not occur in the United States until several decades after the Civil War.[9]

In the first half of the nineteenth century, educators came closest to discussing the nature of children's internal worlds. Most of their work drew heavily on John Locke's *Thoughts Concerning Education* (1690), which emphasized both children's inherent malleability and capacity to reason. Locke argued that corporal punishment should be used only as a last resort, since severe punishment impeded rather than facilitated learning. Instead, he counselled parents on the strategic use of emotional manipulation, urging them to begin deploying praise and censure as early as possible. The ultimate objective was to instill self-control and internalized moral standards, as children came to understand that good behavior promoted esteem while bad conduct led to condemnation.

The balancing act that Locke recommended also required that parents develop a "brawniness . . . of mind" in children, such that they would not bend under the weight of adverse circumstances. He believed that children needed to feel fear so that they would not rush headlong into danger, but he warned parents about its potentially dire effects on timid and oversensitive youngsters. From the time children learned to speak, parents should cultivate "courage" and prevent them from crying unless they were actually injured. They should then begin "inuring Children gently to suffer some Degrees of Pain without shrinking." Slowly at first, in a spirit of affection and play, parents were to inflict pain so that the child "by Degrees be accustom'd to bear very painful and rough Usage from you without flinching or complaining." Fretful youngsters especially stood in need of such treatment, Locke explained. "The softer you find your child is, the more you are to seek Occasions, at fit times, thus to harden him."[10]

This concern about how to avoid fear and instill courage was based on a model that held that sensory experience was translated into representations in the mind and then linked to additional mental states. If a child developed a specific fear, then parents needed to ensure that this state did not become fixed through a train of associations. In order to promote courage, on the other hand, they were supposed to connect frightening and painful stimuli to pleasant experiences—like a playful whack given out by an affectionate father. No concern need be had that children would thereby come to desire pain, for as Locke concluded: "What our Minds yield not to makes but a slight Impression, and does us but very little Harm"[11] Potentially frightening concepts, thoughts, or experiences, and even physical suffering—provided none were impressed too deeply—were thus essential to toughen children so they could bear life's inevitable shocks and setbacks.

Lockean ideas about childrearing were widely accepted by the early nineteenth century, permeating moralistic children's literature and juvenile textbooks. As historians Peter Stearns and Timothy Hagerty point out, this writing revealed a marked shift from earlier traditions that had used fear to warn children away from strangers and other perils. Children were no longer supposed to be scared into doing the right thing, either by the threat of beating, sermons evoking hellfire, or folk stories promising violent consequences for wrongdoing. At the same time, authors "urged an active confrontation with fear," filling their texts with intrepid youngsters who faced down difficult circumstances. Ideally, both boys and girls were supposed to be fearless, though boldness and bravery were seen as especially crucial for boys who would have to compete in a dynamic market economy.[12]

To inoculate children against fear, writers used copious images and stories featuring violence, suffering, and death. Children's storybooks and textbooks from the first half of the nineteenth century are filled with blood-soaked scenes, from settlers being scalped by Indians and soldiers bayonetting their enemies, to women and children being murdered, and enslaved people contorting in agony while being whipped. Far from living in peace and safety, young protagonists regularly face the death of parents or siblings, sudden plunges into poverty, or ill treatment by cruel and intemperate adults. Writers relieved these grim scenes by offering clear moral messages and happy endings, but the regular inclusion of gruesome imagery suggests that they saw a purpose in exposing the young, early and often, to particular forms of adult brutality. This promiscuous use of violence is particularly notable when viewed in tandem with another key feature of juvenile literature from this era—its censorship of references to sexuality.[13] Such starkly differing attitudes toward the appropriateness of violence and sex are especially evident in early nineteenth-century editions of folk tales and fairy stories; even as authors and publishers went to great lengths to expunge scatological and ribald humor, they heightened the violence present in earlier fables.[14]

To appreciate the level of bloodshed that writers of children's literature embraced, consider a story published in the *Juvenile Miscellany*, one of America's first children's magazines, founded by Lydia Maria Child in 1826 to provide subscribers, mainly genteel Bostonians, with games, anecdotes, and moralistic tales.[15] Creating an alter ego known as "Aunt Maria" who addressed children as if they were seated in her lap, Child penned a gory tale in 1830 titled "The St. Domingo Orphans" set in the Haitian Revolution. The fictitious aunt describes the terror of two white sisters, ages six and ten, as they lay in their beds listening to the "shrieks and groans of those who were butchered." Trying to flee the following day, the girls are captured by rebel soldiers who kill their father before turning on their mother. As she begged for the lives of her children, "a ferocious soldier came behind her, and cut the head from her body so suddenly, that her blood flew all over her unfortunate daughters."[16] Unlike the violence contained in religious material or folktales of an earlier era, there was no warning here for children to heed; they were simply confronted with the full weight of adult depravity. Yet Child clearly saw nothing amiss with conjuring up an image of petrified children soaked in their mother's blood for her young middle-class subscribers.[17]

The earliest American textbooks produced for juvenile readers—work penned by Connecticut publisher Samuel Griswold Goodrich under the name Peter Parley—also contain notable levels of carnage. In *Parley's Common School History* (1837), one slaughter follows another in an endless procession of conquerors and shifting boundaries of empire. According to Goodrich, details of "human passions" were essential to capture the interests of the young. Complaining that previous histories written for children consisted of little more than a tedious recitation of dates and events, he sought to lay "hold of the sympathy of children and youth" with "lively narratives of the enterprises, adventures, dangers, trials, successes and failures of mankind." Graphic detail and striking visual imagery were essential to this task. Goodrich's work included a wealth of etchings, he explained, for the purpose of "fixing certain ideas permanently in the memory of the pupil."[18] In this he was not alone. By the 1830s, other writers of school textbooks—most notably Emma Willard—had also come to see visual aids as an essential way to train children's memories. Understanding vision as a medium of instruction, they believed that children remembered best if they could physically visit, or at least evoke in their mind's eye, particular places. Such physical conceptions of memory coincided with the rise of materialist understandings of the mind, evident in sciences like phrenology, which held that memories resided in particular locations in the brain. Emphasizing children's "concrete and observable" responses to learning rather than abstract instruction, childhood education took a decidedly bodily turn in the antebellum era.[19]

Judging by the etchings that Goodrich included in his work, he imagined scenes of violence and catastrophe as especially essential for young readers. In his *First Book of History; for Children and Youth* (1836), designed for pupils between the ages of nine to sixteen, Goodrich interspersed disturbing images of natural and human-made disasters amid lessons on geography and historical vignettes. One early etching depicts an avalanche about to bury a family alive, their fleeing figures captured in the moment before giant boulders rained down on them. Overleaf, another family is threatened with annihilation by a collapsing riverbank. Then, a few chapters later, readers are invited to visualize the "slaughter in Schenectady" during King William's War, when French and Indian forces attacked a settlement in the dead of night. To help the young picture the frenzied and terrifying scene, an etching shows a woman and her children cowering in the foreground, their arms raised in surrender as Indian and French warriors loom above with tomahawks poised to strike. Off to the side, a dead woman lays weltering in a pool of blood, while figures in the background run from their burning homes.[20] For Goodrich, this continuous recounting of distressing episodes helped not only to reinforce geographical details and events in children's memories, but also to steel them against any frightful circumstances they might confront in future, inuring them to fear and toughening their minds.

For both Locke and the writers who followed him, courage had a crucial moral component. Teaching children to use rationality to distinguish
between right and wrong would raise fearlessness above the level of mere
"Pride, Vain-glory, or Rage," as Locke put it. He therefore followed his discussion of courage in children with one directed toward preventing the
young from tormenting less powerful creatures or taking delight in others'
pain. This same task was one that writers of juvenile fiction readily adopted
in the first half of the nineteenth century.[21] In one novel after another, young
characters—often boys aged around ten or eleven—learned to resist temptation and tame wicked urges. Coming to understand the benefits of per-
severance, industry, generosity, and compassion, they mastered perilous
situations and firmly confronted naysayers' scorn, in the end finally reaping
the rewards of their forbearance.

While the didactic quality of Victorian children's literature or textbooks
has been analyzed, the question of how its violent content reflected adult
assumptions about the nature of children has remained unexplored.
According to one line of argument, the relentless moralizing of children's
literature aimed to instill the character traits that would allow the young
to succeed in a newly competitive economy, while preventing republican
democracy from collapsing due to selfishness and vice.[22] Another line
stresses the way these works encoded broader messages about the superi-
ority of Anglo-Saxon civilization and the naturalness of hierarchies based
on race, sex, and class by projecting irrationality and violence onto dark-
skinned others, while reserving principled heroism mostly for white male
characters.[23] Both arguments are convincing. But focusing on the violent
content of this writing can also reveal adult perceptions of children's inner
lives. In producing and purchasing this material for the young, writers and
parents were making assumptions about the type and nature of imagery suitable for children and how they might respond to such material.

Very few commentators in antebellum America cautioned that violent imagery might be unsuitable for children or that it could disturb and corrupt
young minds, concerns voiced loudly from the 1870s on. Ironically, pacifist
texts provide the best illustration of this point. Produced by the small and
marginalized contingent of anti-war activists, these works denounced militarism and its effects on children, as did one author who hoped to "commit to
the flames the military toys of children, and blot out the false glory of battles
and victories from their lessons in the school-book."[24] But their critiques
targeted the glorification of war and militarism, not children's exposure

violence or violent imagery per se. In fact, pacifist literature for children described the horrors of war in gruesome detail. Often drawing images and stories directly from works written for adults, authors simply added moral messages, explaining that, although violence tended to be glorified, it actually led to tremendous pain. Far from conceiving of depictions of bloodshed as inherently damaging, these writers readily appropriated them, because they believed that arresting and horrific accounts would impress upon children's minds the true costs and wickedness of war.[25]

Abolitionists similarly aimed to reach the young by dramatizing the tremendous violence at the heart of slavery. Anti-slavery activists pioneered the use of graphic imagery and testimony of slave suffering as a way of appealing to adult sympathies, strategies that were also widely deployed to shape children's perspectives.[26] The American Anti-Slavery Society's juvenile magazine, *The Slave's Friend* (1836–1838), for instance, plainly described the cruelty meted out to enslaved people in successive issues. Likewise, their *Anti-Slavery Alphabet* book (1847) introduced young readers to their letters by depicting Black children torn from their mothers' arms, along with slaves whipped until bloody and forced to work night and day to provide the sugar for treats that child readers enjoyed.[27] As historian Rebecca De Schweinitz argues, abolitionists addressed their material to children precisely because they were children and thus supposedly free from the prejudices of adulthood.[28] Lacking the bigotry of their elders and not yet hardened to the world, the young were imagined to share a natural affinity with slaves—themselves imagined as perpetual children—and thus to empathize with the suffering depicted in these texts. Abolitionists did not imagine child readers as powerless or weak; on the contrary, they told them that they were partly responsible for perpetuating slavery and thus had a duty to become politically active. "You are very young, 'tis true, But there's much that you can do," advised the *Anti-Slavery Alphabet*. "Even you can plead with men That they buy not slaves again."[29] Just as schoolbooks and juvenile literature asked children to feel compassion for victims while confronting brutal violence with fearless resolve, abolitionist literature taught that only those who could look pain and suffering in the eye could develop the inner resources that would support moral behavior. Much like Locke's injunction for parents to build moral courage early on, abolitionists expected children to begin this process from the moment they could read.

These views informed anti-slavery texts classified today as adult fiction, much of which was actually written for both adult and child readers.[30] The first audience for the most famous abolitionist work—Harriet Beecher Stowe's *Uncle Tom's Cabin*—included the author's own children, who at the time ranged in age from infancy to fifteen. According to Stowe's youngest son and biographer, before the novel was published in serialized form in the *National Era*, his mother gathered the family around her and read the agonizing scene in which Uncle Tom's cruel owner whips him to death. "Her two little ones of ten and twelve years of age broke into convulsions of weeping, one of them saying between sobs, 'oh, mamma! Slavery is the most cruel thing in the world.'"[31] This was exactly the reaction Stowe aimed to provoke. At the end of the final installment, she directly addressed her imagined readers—the "pleasant family circles" who had been sharing her tale week by week. "In particular, the dear little children who have followed her story have her warmest love," she closed, exhorting them to take inspiration from her work and "Never, if you can help it, let a colored child be shut out of school, or treated with neglect and contempt, because of his color."[32] Guaranteed to respond empathetically, the young were Stowe's ideal readers. With the shocking details of slavery permanently etched in their minds, they would be steeled to confront whatever evils they encountered in the real world.

Authors of antebellum children's literature used violent imagery to teach children to battle their own internal demons as well as external ones. As ABC books and primers published for preliterate children make clear, no reader was deemed too young to bear this message. John Ely's *The Child's Instructor*, first published in the 1790s and reprinted throughout the first half of the nineteenth century, for instance, is filled with lessons designed to train children to "love God, and to obey his parents" and instill middle-class virtues ranging from cleanliness, diligence, politeness and honesty, to benevolence toward lesser creatures or classes. In many ways, Ely's book is about as tame as one can imagine, particularly given its repeated emphasis on children being kind to animals and having tender regard for one another. Nonetheless, the essential words children needed to learn include "kill," "murder," "maul," "rack (to torture)," and "sword (a weapon)." Ely could apparently conceive of nothing more effective in helping them learn their ABCs than images relating to violent conflict. In one lesson, he invited children to imagine each letter of the alphabet as a potential soldier in a force commanded by letter "A." The supreme general presiding "over the commonwealth of Letters," it was A's job to "summon all the members to prepare for war." Each letter appeared, representing a particular type of character, most of whom were quickly rejected (Mr. C for coxcomb and coward, Mr. D for dunce and drunkard;

Mr. G a gambler; and Mr. K seeking to be king, "intoxicated with ambition, insensible to the cries of the distressed, and for grasping all power and riches into his own hand.") Only a few letters eventually make their way into Ely's imagined army—characters that his readers were obviously supposed to em- ulate if they, too, hoped to enlist: Mr. L, a "lover of learning" and "lively com- panion," and Mr. W, "a wise man, constant, benevolent, and industrious."[33]

These letters were notably peaceable—their attributes of bookishness, con- stancy, and hard work seeming more appropriate for, say, a student, book- keeper, or lawyer than a soldier. But that was no doubt Ely's point. Writing not long after the Revolution, he imagined the ideal soldier as a militiaman who had temporarily taken up arms, motivated by selfless patriotism and kept in line by his own wisdom and industry. He was not glorifying war or urging boys to join the regular army. But he was promoting the idea that shrinking from danger, like the coward Mr. C, was beyond the pale, for they would all be expected to engage in war, at the very least in the battle of life. Those cast out of Ely's alphabet army—overcome by their weakness for alcohol, glory, easy money, or power—had already lost the struggle against their own desires, making them useless to either the nation or their fellow men.

The notion of a world full of temptations that could lure the unwary from the path of virtue was the most formulaic of Victorian tropes. Educators like Ely saw it as their duty to prepare children to confront this world. At least in many northeastern states, the transition from a predominantly agricul- tural society of close-knit communities to one increasingly characterized by tremendous population mobility, industrialization, and anonymous eco- nomic exchange led many Americans to feel that the path to morally virtuous adulthood had grown more treacherous, especially for young men. The belief that children had to conquer their own urges and develop strong inner re- sources to deal with this new reality was thus central to a wide range of works directed toward the young, from religious sermons and temperance tracts to schoolbooks. No one seems to have thought it wise to attempt to shield chil- dren from the true brutality of the world, which would only have left them vulnerable to fears or enticements later on.

From Imagined Violence to Involvement in War

Once the Civil War broke out, the fictional battles of children's literature merged seamlessly into depictions of actual battle. From the outset, northern publishers assumed that violent images of war could be effective learning aids for even the youngest readers. The New York publishing firm McLoughlin Brothers, formed in 1858 and specializing in children's books, puzzles, board games, and paper soldiers and dolls, was at the forefront of this trend. The company produced a number of cheap alphabet books that illustrated letters with images of boys in military uniforms. One portrays the letter "D" with a drum being beaten by a boy dressed in Union blue who appears to be around five or six years old. "G" features a miniature grenadier with his gun, while "H" stands for Harry, a small, uniformed boy, as does "O" for Oliver, another youngster "armed for a fight." Too young to actually enlist, these characters were playing at war. But subsequent letters portray an easy transition between amusement and combat, picturing "S" as a young sailor "all trimmed for the fight," and "V" for volunteer, a boy around the age of twelve who is formally enlisted. (By contrast, girls are shown reading, eating cake, and being "gentle and fair.")[34] Given that McLoughlin Brothers also specialized in cheap storybooks about prepubescent boys who entered military service, it is no exaggeration to say that their output reflected and helped to normalize the enlistment of the young.[35]

ABC books could also be remarkably candid about the details of war, especially given the age of their intended readers—presumably preliterate boys and girls around the age of four to six. *Little Pet's Picture Alphabet*, for instance, illustrates the letter "V" with the image of a one-legged veteran sitting on a bench, his stump clearly visible above his peg leg. This picture is preceded by a soldier boy about the readers' own age—"U for Union Boy"— waving a flag that almost dwarfs his small frame. On the next page, "Y is for Youth" shows a slightly older sailor, cigar in hand, leaning over to retch against a wall after his first ill-advised attempt at smoking.[36] Apparently, it was never too soon to warn children of the perils of cigars or the costs of war, nor to invite them to imagine joining in the struggle.

Far more explicit is *The Union ABC*, an alphabet book published in Boston that consists of almost nothing but martial imagery. The page on "B" for battle portrays a Union soldier wielding a sword above his head in a desperate attempt to prevent an enemy from bayoneting a comrade; nearby, another soldier lies dead, blood seeping from his head. Even more grisly scenes follow. "T" pictures a traitorous officer's limp body swinging from a palm tree, while "W" stands for war, represented by a post-battle landscape littered with wounded and dead men, their faces contorted in horror and pain. Explaining the reasons for this carnage are two images of African Americans, shown celebrating the struggle and reaping its rewards rather than as active participants. In one, several "contrabands" dance a jig, while in the other, a white Union soldier strikes the shackles off a grateful slave. Clearly more concerned with the need to produce young patriots than the risk of provoking nightmares, the authors of this ABC book invited white children to see themselves in the role of a combatant, picturing "D" as a Union drummer boy, around age ten, and "Y" as a "Youth, who a soldier would go."[37] The very first books that some children read during the Civil War, in other words, brimmed with violence—imagery that sought to instruct and enlighten by dramatizing the deadly consequences of treason and slaveholding.

Such graphic violence is not as evident in material produced for children in the Confederacy, although there was far less of this material in general, making comparisons tenuous. From the beginning of the conflict, southern educators denounced northern publishers' domination of book production and printing, which supposedly allowed them to infiltrate the Confederacy with pro-Union or anti-slavery messages. Publishers therefore quickly began producing material with a Confederate imprint, determined to create an original literature suitable for white youngsters. Shortages of every kind, from a lack of paper and ink to a dearth of printers and graphic artists, hampered their efforts.[38] Nonetheless, historian Michael Bernath notes that high demand made works for children "one of the fastest growing segments of Confederate print culture" by the middle of the war, with schoolbooks, printers, and spelling books selling in the tens of thousands.[39]

Some war-related imagery did make its way into Confederate works written for children.[40] "Would you like to go into battle and have your head cut off?" asked one primer. "No; but God will punish [our enemies] for their crimes, and all wicked people like them."[41] The author of The Dixie Primer put a risky anti-war message into the mouth of a young narrator, who pulled no punches in describing war's devastating impact. "My papa went, and died in the army. My big brother went too and got shot. A bomb shel[l] took off his head," he told readers. "My aunt had three sons, and all died in the army. Now she and the girls have to work for bread."[42] Yet whereas death and suffering were occasionally present in Confederate works, the imagery tended to be far less prolific and less visually arresting. Unlike northern publishers who were able to produce material with original artwork, Confederate publishers usually relied on crude woodblocks of war imagery, such as toy soldiers, canons, or flags, that were apparently in their existing stocks. Whereas northern children's literature was commercially produced and thus directed toward entertainment as much as enlightenment, most Confederate material was created to educate youths and inculcate Confederate nationalism.

As a result, instructing the young via the use of violent scenes does not seem to have been particularly high on Confederate educators' agenda. *The First Reader, for Southern Schools* (1863) contained lessons similar to those promoted in texts like Ely's, reminding children to be good Christians, respect parents, avoid swearing, and keep themselves neat. Only one lesson out of fifty-nine mentioned the war: "That man's arm has been cut off. It was shot off by a gun. Oh! What a sad thing war is!" Printed on cheap paper and without illustration, this lament seems tepid in comparison to the striking colored images offered to children in the United States. Far more common was the pro-slavery language used in another lesson, which baldly argued: "It is not a sin to own slaves. It is right. God wills that some men should be slaves, and some masters. It is a sin to treat a servant ill. He is a man and Christ died for him. It is not best to set him free, but to keep him and be kind to him."[43] In the midst of a conflict fought on their own doorsteps, perhaps Confederate educators felt little need for lessons steeped in bloodshed. Instructing children on the justice of slaveholding, by contrast, formed the central rationale for creating a distinct literature for the new nation's young.[44]

When Confederate soldiers addressed children about the nature of war, on the other hand, they evoked violent scenes just as readily as their US counterparts. Fathers included all manner of detail in letters to their children, from their daily fare to the look and sound of battle and its aftermath. One Texan soldier wrote his four-year-old son about his participation in the battle of Gettysburg. During one attack, he explained, a "poor fellow had his head knocked off in a few feet of me, and I felt all the time as if I would never see you and little sister again." After being grazed by a bullet, he went past a hospital filled with "mangled and bruised" soldiers, "some with their eyes shot out, some with their arms, or hands, or fingers, or feet or legs shot off, and all seeming to suffer a great deal." Appearing to acknowledge that this description might not be appropriate for such a young child, he added a note to his wife, explaining that his letter was a keepsake that their son "could read when he was a big boy."[45] While he may have had second thoughts about sharing such details with a four-year-old, he still imagined that his son would read the letter during his childhood, and that what was most important to communicate were the dreadful aftereffects of battle.

Letters by Union soldiers display this same willingness to share details of wartime violence with young readers. On Christmas Eve, 1862, John

B. Kent of the 44th Massachusetts Infantry wrote a letter to be read to the students of the Hasret Sabbath School in Boston, likely children under the age of thirteen.[46] He described many run-of-the-mill facets of army life—soldiers' standard rations and pay, their foraging expeditions, the experience of sleeping on the frozen ground, along with the rheumatism that followed. But he neither downplayed the costs nor sugar-coated the brutality of war. "I have had a man killed <u>beside me</u> & one wounded, the other, at the same time," Kent wrote, noting that thirteen men in his regiment had been killed and another thirty-two injured. Even more remarkable is his forthright account of combat. "I felt myself in the midst of Death, but the fear is all felt while moving <u>to the field</u> & not <u>after you are engaged</u>," he explained. "Then excitement takes the place of thought." Kent clearly felt no compunction in exposing students to the harsh realities of war and the intense and conflicting emotions that it aroused.[47] In virtually every respect—from his detailed descriptions of camp life, to the manner in which he itemized the dead and wounded, to his unvarnished account of battle—his letter resembles those that Civil War–era soldiers sent to adult friends and relatives.

Around the same time, a captain in the 5th Iowa Cavalry engaged in a very similar exchange with another group of young children. Stationed outside St. Louis, Charles C. Nott had been passing a dreary New Year's Day in 1863 when he received a box from the children of New York's North Moore Street School. The letters and compositions transported him back to a happier time. A trustee of the public schools in New York City, Nott responded with a series of letters intended to be passed around or read aloud at the school. The first consisted of lengthy account of a "young and handsome" soldier who died "neglected and deserted" in the "cheerless wards of a public hospital." He wrote of going to pay his respects in the "dead room," where the corpse's frozen stare and gaping mouth had confronted him with a "ghastly sight." In subsequent correspondence, Nott related the assault on Fort Donelson, describing the sound and the feel of battle and praising the heroism of a "poor boy" whose foot "dangled horribly from his limb by a piece of skin." To help the students accurately visualize the morbid scene that he surveyed the following morning, he used reference points the children were sure to understand: "Here was one [corpse] close to me; about the width of a class-room beyond was another; a little further on two had fallen, side by side."

When Nott published his letters as a book, with the profits benefiting disabled soldiers, he included a preface that took up the question of whether such graphic material was appropriate for child readers. Addressing an adult audience, Nott explained that he had "carefully avoided that 'baby talk' which some people think simplicity, and that paltriness of subject which by many is thought to be alone within the grasp and comprehension of the child." Instead, he had selected the same incidents and topics for his child readers that he would have chosen for their parents, "only endeavouring, with greater strictness, to blend in the narration simplicity with elegance."[48] Children needed straightforward, uncomplicated prose, Nott believed, but they did not differ fundamentally from adults in terms of the type of content that engaged them, nor did they require sanitized versions that expunged shocking or horrifying material.

The same conviction regarding children's interests and emotional fortitude is evident in much of the work produced for the young during the Civil War, from plays and stories to novels and works of history. Designed to satisfy children's presumed curiosity about warfare and their hunger for war-related narratives, this literature conveys a belief that the young could handle not only disturbing representations of bloodshed, but also mind-numbing details about weaponry and battlefield tactics. William Thayer's phenomenally popular four-volume *Youth's History of the Rebellion*, first published between 1864 and 1866, is a case in point. Each volume is around 350 pages long and written in the form of a catechism, with a group of cousins pictured sitting at the feet of an uncle who answers their questions about the current war. The four boys and two girls span the ages of eight to fifteen—presumably mirroring the age range of Thayer's imagined audience. Into their mouths, he put all kinds of questions, from the number of pieces of artillery in a battery, to the different type of bullets that soldiers used. The intent was to educate young readers about war—to help them visualize forts, gunboats, and battlefields; to teach them the steps involved in flanking an enemy's position or launching a cavalry charge; and to school them on the meaning of terms like "grape shot."[49]

Yet what seems most notable about Thayer's volumes is the lack of any juvenile content, apart from a greater focus on underage soldiers and more regular didactic asides than might be found in the average adult history. They tended toward graphic descriptions of military clashes, such as this passage on the Battle of Bull Run:

> Shells shrieked in mad defiance, making the place hideous with their wild tumult and death. Men dropped from the ranks, and weltered in their blood. Horses fell with their valiant riders, torn, mangled, dead. Groans and

cries of agony pierced the air. The earth was covered with broken carriages, disabled guns, slaughtered horses, dead and dying men, in one indiscriminate, bloodstained mass. // Still the battle raged. The dead and dying were trampled beneath the feet of prancing steeds and advancing columns.

Page after page of similar descriptions follow, recounting limbs severed from bodies, children with their heads caved in, battlefields covered in blood. Thayer drew this material directly from newspapers, magazines, and histories written for adults, without the slightest alteration. Operating with a commercial objective in mind, he seemed unconcerned that parents might consider his work too explicit. He subscribed to the common belief that what young readers needed and wanted were the grisliest details.[50] Emphasizing in his preface that he aimed to educate children on the costs of preserving the Union, Thayer included this content not just to excite readers or to balance out the tedious recounting of military detail, but to instill patriotism through what he saw as the most effective means possible: arresting images of violence and death.

It is hard to know what children made of the representations of carnage that permeated their books, or how exposure to such imagery shaped their attitudes toward the Civil War. But it is clear that the adults who produced children's literature and the parents who purchased it believed that violence was instructive—that it made deep impressions upon children's minds and served both educational and moral ends. Graphic images of cruelty and bloodshed held children's attention and facilitated memorization by fixing certain information in their minds; such images also drove home critical moral and political lessons by stirring children's emotions and appealing to their sympathies. Thus, in an era when actual violence against children was increasingly condemned by educators and reformers as immoral and ineffective, parents continued to believe that children would benefit from being exposed to the harsh realities of violence outside the home.

Children's literature produced during the Civil War also demonstrated that parents assumed that even very young children would be interested in the bloody events that preoccupied their parents and other adults. They believed that children ought to know not only why the United States and the Confederacy were at war, but also how the military was structured, the kinds of weapons being used, and to what effect. Whether inadvertently or not, this literature helped to prepare boys to go to war. Many of those who served when still below military age would later recall how, prior to enlisting, they had spent hours poring over military manuals like Winfield Scott's *Infantry Tactics*. What they do not say, but was surely true for some, is that they had been primed to pick up these very grown-up books by reading children's literature that covered some of the same information.

* * *

When Ulysses S. Grant assumed command of the 21st Illinois Infantry, his eldest son Fred was eleven years old. Deeply attached to his family, Grant wanted his son by his side, and Fred immediately took a liking to camp life. "The soldiers and officers call him Colonel," Grant wrote to his wife Julia, "and he seems to be quite a favorite."[51] But when the regiment departed for Missouri, Grant overruled his son's objections and sent him home, even though the boy had to make it back to Galena on his own. "I did not telegraph," Grant wrote to Julia after dispatching Fred, "because I thought you would be in a perfect stew until he arrived. He did not want to go at all and I felt loath at sending him but now that we are in the enemy's country I thought you would be alarmed if he was with me."[52] Grant misjudged Julia's response, however, for she seemed to fear the thought of Fred traveling alone more than the thought of him under fire alongside his father. She quickly dashed off a note urging, "Do keep him with you," and reminding her husband that Alexander the Great had been no older than Fred when he accompanied his father, Philip II of Macedon, into battle. Although Fred had already departed, Grant delighted in his wife's reply.[53] Their son would "make a good general someday," he told her, suggesting that she "pack his valise and start him on now."[54]

Though he never enlisted, Fred would spend much of the next four years in camps with his father, staying with him throughout the siege of Vicksburg and the fighting that followed. In his memoir, Grant wrote proudly of his son's independence and fortitude: "He looked after himself and was in every battle of the campaign. His age then, not quite thirteen, enabled him to take in all that he saw and to retain a recollection of it that would not be possible in more mature years."[55] The passage marks the distance between their past and our present: because Fred was so young and impressionable, the scenes he witnessed would always remain vivid in his mind—and that, his father believed, was a good thing.

Fred's own recollections of his wartime experiences are not so sanguine. After the siege ended, Grant had left him sleeping on the deck of a ship docked in the Mississippi River, giving strict orders that he should not be allowed to go ashore. But Fred escaped his confinement and headed to the battlefield. As the Confederates retreated, he stumbled forward, overwhelmed by the hellish landscape. For a while he tagged along with a detachment collecting bodies for burial, but after "sickening at the sights," he joined another group charged with carrying the wounded to a makeshift hospital. "Here were scenes so terrible that I became faint," he remembered, "and making my way to a tree, sat down, the most woebegone twelve-year-old lad in America."[56] If Fred's presence at Vicksburg caused his father "no anxiety"—as Grant rather implausibly claimed—the same cannot be said of the boy himself.

In the end, Fred suffered only a minor flesh wound to his thigh. The greater risk to his life came from the diseases that felled so many full-grown soldiers. By the end of the Vicksburg campaign, he later related, "dysentery had pulled me down from one hundred and ten to sixty-eight pounds, and I had a toothache as well."[57] It took nearly five months before he had recovered enough to rejoin his father in camp. He then fell ill again, succumbing to what Julia called "camp dysentery and typhoid fever."[58] This time the boy sank so low that his family feared he would die; Grant rushed to his sick bed "hardly expecting to find him alive on my arrival."[59] Yet even after this serious bout of illness, Fred returned to his father's side. In June 1864, Grant informed Julia that their son had been "suffering intensely for several days with rheumatism," to the point that he was "unable to turn himself" in the ambulance wagon. Still, Grant blithely predicted that he would recover "in a day or two."[60]

Today, Ulysses and Julia Grant seem wildly irresponsible in the risks they allowed their son to take. Yet they were by no means negligent parents; on the contrary, they doted on their children. The numerous paintings, lithographs, and *cartes de visite* of the Grants from this period depict them as the quintessential Victorian family, happily ensconced in domesticity, though the two eldest boys are typically shown wearing uniforms. Like William Tecumseh Sherman, who delighted in his son Willie's presence in camp until, to his horror and regret, the nine-year-old sickened and died, Grant relished Fred's embrace of military life and took pleasure in watching him interact with his troops.

This acceptance of children venturing into military camps or even formally enlisting was not some peculiarity limited to military men and their families. Americans of all classes shared the belief that witnessing war would either be good for young boys, or at least not detrimental. In fact, middle-class parents who espoused Victorian ideals were those most likely to believe

Figure 4.1 General Ulysses S. Grant and his family in a typical Victorian family portrait. The boy standing in the center is Frederick Dent Grant (1850–1912), who entered West Point soon after the war and went on to have a successful military career. Like the Grants and the Lincolns, many middle-class families dressed sons too young to enlist in uniforms during the Civil War. Engraved *carte de visite* portraying General Ulysses S. Grant and his family, circa 1862–1864. Wisconsin Historical Society.

that male youth could benefit from exposure to this conflict. Violent scenes were useful for impressionable minds, because boys like Fred would require excesses of courage in the modern world. Watching a battle or witnessing its aftermath, they would never forget the sacrifices required to maintain their system of government—a system that supposedly left them free to prosper, provided they could develop inner resources to avoid the pitfalls they would face at every turn.

5

Pride of the Nation

The Iconography of Child Soldiers and Drummer Boys

Images of child soldiers and drummer boys suffused the Union war effort. Lithographs of youthful volunteers hung on the walls of homes and businesses. Oil paintings produced by renowned artists of young boys leaving home, rallying the troops, or lying dead in a battle's aftermath were displayed in fine art galleries and then transformed into *cartes de visite* to raise money for the troops. Poems, songs, and stories featuring the admirable deaths of young musicians were shared in family parlors and among friends. And patriotic stationery and envelopes decorated with plucky youths beating drums or heading into battle were used to convey letters to and from the field. Depicted as "The Spirit of the North," the boy soldier or musician became a popular wartime icon that could condense and convey a series of lessons about the struggle.

This popularity drew from a broader interest in child figures evident throughout the first half of the nineteenth century. For Victorian artists, poets, writers, and social commentators, no symbolism was more compelling than that which related to childhood. The best-loved novelists of the period left behind a particularly memorable cast of child characters—from Dickens's Oliver Twist and Little Nell to Harriet Beecher Stowe's Eva St. Clare—while countless lesser-known authors depicted innocent children as a means of inspiring readers and imparting moral lessons, or victimized youngsters as a way of pondering social relations. Drawing from the same well, graphic artists, painters, poets, and song writers populated their works with a range of youngsters to symbolize various aspects of society, politics, or social change.[1]

Children captured so much interest at this time because childhood had become freighted with especially heavy meaning. In the revolutionary era with its emphasis on human equality, children's lack of reason and experience had become an important rationale for denying a range of basic rights to those below a certain age or to anyone defined as childlike, including women and so-called lesser races. Conversely, the romantics' veneration of childhood as a unique stage of life and of the young as uniquely pure and innocent had made childhood a perfect vehicle for lamenting a vanishing past in a rapidly changing world.[2] Childhood generated a wide range of meanings, which were all the more powerful given their rootedness in the universal facts of aging and growth: an irrationality in need of regulation, a weakness requiring protection, a naivete worth celebrating, or an embryonic stage presaging inevitable transformation and progress. All these meanings were mobilized during the Civil War.

The few scholars who have discussed the outpouring of material depicting underage enlistees have concentrated on texts written for juvenile readers. Examining wartime poems and stories about dying drummer boys, Sean Scott suggests that these were mostly aimed at getting children to think about the meaning of death.[3] Looking at a broader range of juvenile literature, Alice Fahs notes that wartime adventures supplemented conventional tales of drummer boys' redemptive deaths during the Civil War. In these stories, battle served as an exciting backdrop for the derring-do of young males, she argues, allowing boys in particular to be active participants rather than passive victims in the national struggle.[4] As persuasive as these arguments are, they do not deal with the broad scope of material featuring child soldiers and musicians, which included a wealth of visual imagery addressed to Americans of all ages.

Considering the varying representations of uniformed children and comparing this material to other wartime representations of child figures in graphic and fine art, literature, music, and the press more broadly, it is clear that the iconic child soldier or drummer boy was typically designed to be inspirational. Pure of heart and ardently committed to the Union war effort, he led troops into battle and died without regret, exhibiting the kind of stalwart patriotism that adults were supposed to emulate. His young age suggested the purity of his motives, and his ability to remain morally unsullied amid war's butchery underscored the legitimacy of Unionism. By drawing forth tender feelings from his comrades, the boy soldier or musician also offered assurance that the conflict had not corrupted the nation's men.[5]

It is important to acknowledge that this figure was produced at a time when hundreds of thousands of boys and youths had entered the military. In reality, many parents fretted that young sons would become ill or degraded and tried desperately to get them discharged. Military physicians, politicians, and social commentators worried that underdeveloped bodies would give out and become a drain on the army. Yet these prevalent concerns are non-existent in popular depictions of child soldiers. In fictional representations, families did not decry the enlistment of boys but waved them off to war instead. And if these children died, they were usually in the thick of the struggle, not lying sick in a hospital. Despite being engaged in the roughest of all adult occupations, child soldiers were pictured as ideal children—frail, unspoiled, and angelic.

Perhaps most importantly, these inspirational figures were always white. Although Union camps were full of Black boys serving as cooks and servants, or as musicians or soldiers in United States Colored Troops (USCT) regiments, young African Americans only appeared in popular culture as victims of slavery, menial laborers, or comic relief, never as iconic figures who could rally the troops because they embodied the Union. Similarly, enslaved people and slavery rarely featured in writing or imagery focusing on white child soldiers or musicians. If depictions of inspirational child soldiers offered a fantasy in which males retained their innocence amid the fighting, it was also one in which whiteness remained uncorrupted and racial politics had no overt place. In a war that was won by the enlistment of hundreds of thousands of African American men and the steady erosion of slavery, proliferating images of martyred children re-imagined the preservation of the Union in terms of innocent white suffering.

The absence of similar narratives or imagery in the Confederacy draws attention to the iconic nature of this figure in the United States. Confederate partisans sometimes lauded boys who joined in the struggle, but their celebration of inspirational boy soldiers and musicians was notably mute. This disparity can only be partly explained by the paucity of Confederate art and literature or the comparatively small number of musicians in the Confederate ranks. The image of the young drummer boy or soldier simply did not lend itself as a symbol for the kind of nation Confederates hoped to build. At the core of Confederate nationalism were notions of tradition, bloodline, and vertical order: Confederate leaders emphasized a vision of family life and social order in which slaves, wives, and children existed in an organic hierarchy overseen by benevolent patriarchs. Celebrating the agency of the young undermined this agenda.

The United States' use of child figures during the Civil War accords with similar practices in Europe and Latin America. Since the late eighteenth century, nations based on republican or democratic systems of government have claimed political legitimacy through myths of heroic children

sacrificing themselves for the larger good. In fact, much of the American imagery related to child soldiers and drummer boys can be traced to the French
Revolution, when the deeds of child martyrs had been widely celebrated. In
contrast, regimes based on aristocratic or hereditary claims to power have
rarely evoked the constellation of meanings attached to childhood—from
newness and originality to innocence and future promise. The iconography
of child soldiers and musicians in the Civil War United States, then, says little
about the reality of youth enlistment but much about Unionists' emotional
needs and political vision.

Leading the Charge: Inspirational Drummer Boys

Americans' visual landscape underwent a stunning transformation in the
decades before the Civil War. Advances in print technology and the invention of photography and chromolithography allowed artists to replace a
monochrome world of print with a dazzling array of lavishly colored, eye-
catching material.[6] With the outbreak of war, northeastern cities—home to
most of the nation's leading printers, publishers, and illustrators—saw a veritable explosion of military-themed picture books, board games, stationery,
lithographs, and song sheets. This output fundamentally transformed the
look and feel of war for civilians. Participating in the conflict through their
consumption and display of this work, Unionists dressed children in miniature uniforms and ornamented shops, homes, and businesses with patriotic
decorations, infusing even the most mundane aspects of daily life with martial imagery. Through this new vivid world of goods, the public quickly met a
small army of child soldiers.

They mostly encountered these children through the graphic arts.
Photographers could not yet capture battles in progress or bodies in mo-
tion, nor replicate their images in the press; the public could only view
their work by visiting their studios and exhibitions or purchasing a ster-
eopticon viewer. But most people could afford to buy lithographs and lavishly engraved newspapers. *Frank Leslie's Illustrated Newspaper* had begun
publication just a few years before the Civil War began, followed shortly by
Harper's Weekly. Modelled on the tremendously popular *Illustrated London
News*, both were quarto-sized publications filled with highly detailed black
and white etchings—all for a nickel. Editors sent "special artists" to accompany armies in the field or to other locations so that they could sketch

war-related subjects with accuracy and immediacy. Hawked by newspaper boys on street corners and railroad cars and distributed through the mail, illustrated newspapers reached millions of Union soldiers and civilians, as did the colored lithographs, envelopes, and illustrated song sheets that could be purchased for a few cents either from stationery stores, travelling salesmen, or mail catalogues.[7]

These newspapers helped to spread stories about drummer boys and young soldiers by picturing them in the midst of war scenes and through incidents purportedly taken from real life. From the war's earliest months, *Harper's Weekly* carried images of drummers learning their new trade or plying it by drumming up recruits.[8] Typecast from the outset as beardless youths, they were typically portrayed as fighters rather than onlookers in battle. In *Harper's Weekly*, a double-page spread in June 1861 showed the Fifth New York Infantry charging into battle in perfect formation with their young drummer at the forefront, his face toward the enemy.[9] Both the diminutive size of the drummer boy figure and his position in the thick of the fight would become standard over the course of the war, despite the reality that many musicians were grown men, and drummer boys tended to be sent to the rear or designated as stretcher bearers once fighting began.[10]

Two of war's most famous artists—Winslow Homer and Thomas Nast—promoted this image of the brave yet childlike drummer boy in their work for *Harper's Weekly*. For one November 1861 issue, Homer produced a full-page drawing titled "The Songs of the War," which he divided into panels that illustrated popular wartime tunes. The first of these, labelled "The bold soldier boy," showed a young drummer in the act of leading an attack.[11] In another large-scale image published the following year, Homer pictured a bayonet charge that placed viewers in the midst of the contending armies. At the center of this arresting scene is a young drummer who has been shot and is pitching forward just before the two armies clash in hand-to-hand combat.[12] In both of Homer's depictions, the drummer boy is at the head of the troops, inspiring older men as they join the fray. In a similar vein, one of Thomas Nast's full-page illustrations for *Harper's*, titled "The Drummer Boy of Our Regiment," features panels representing scenes in the life of a boy who appears around ten years old. Images in each corner of the page show the young drummer engaged in mundane aspects of camp life such as washing, eating, and writing letters. A slightly larger panel at the top of the image, titled "the favorite in camp," depicts the boy sitting on the knee of an adult comrade, surrounded by a group of older men who are paying him court, while, below, the drummer appears "in action," beating his drum with a look of fierce resolve as he prepares to meet the enemy.[13] Drummer boys might be doted on by grown-up comrades, these depictions emphasized, but they were also directly engaged in soldiering.

The fact that artists pictured drummer boys leading troops was key to this figure's appeal. These were not just children who happened to be at war; they were inspirational figures whose ardent patriotism drove them to enlist. When it came time for battle, they rejected calls to stay out of the fray, instead taking a leading position on the front lines. This was the story behind much of the work of northern painters and poets who represented child soldiers or musicians. In Eastman Johnson's painting "The Wounded Drummer Boy," a small child, perhaps ten years old, is carried into battle on the shoulder of an adult comrade. His leg is bandaged; he could have been in hospital. But despite his injury, he has asked to be brought back into the fight to help rally the troops.[14] Popular illustrator Felix O. C. Darley portrayed the same scene in an 1864 etching that accompanied a selection of war lyrics.[15] Depicted as a small child hoisted up by a square-jawed soldier, the drummer's youth and innocence are conveyed by his soft face, wide-eyed gaze, full lips, and curling hair. Americans viewing these images would have known how the story ended: oblivious to the wounded bodies strewn on the ground and the enemy bullets whizzing through the air, the drummer boy's brave actions turn the tide of battle, as wavering troops find inspiration in his heroism. In some versions of this story, the drummer dies in the end, but his death is a glorious martyrdom that assures his place in heaven and increases devotion to the Union cause.

Johnson and Darley depicted only one moment of this story, but viewers knew the rest because it had been told so often, in so many different forms. Johnson's painting was modelled on an incident that purportedly took place during the battle of Antietam in September 1862. Just over a month later, the words to Albert Fleming's "The Drummer Boy of Antietam" appeared in newspapers, picturing the hero as a "fragile figure" beating out his "thrilling rat-tat-too," while "thousands fell like cattle at the butchers red employ."[16] At the end of Fleming's ballad, the drummer boy is dead, and his comrades gather at his grave to mourn his loss, even as they recognize that his "patriot blood" will act as "fertilizing dew" for national renewal.[17] The lyrics of the song that accompanied Darley's image offer a happier ending. Ignoring his injury and begging to be taken back into battle, the "little drummer" survives the hail of bullets and charging men, beating out an advance that

Figure 5.1 Eastman Johnson's *The Wounded Drummer Boy* (1871). Widely admired studies of this painting appeared during the war. They showed a small boy sporting a resolute expression, held aloft by a Union soldier so that he can continue rallying the troops despite the wound to his leg. Images like this one emphasized the heroism of the boy soldier, whose brave actions often turned the tide of battle. Held in private collection. Reproduced in Patricia Hills and Abigael MacGibney, "The Wounded Drummer Boy, an incident of the late War, 1871 (Hills no. 10.0.21)." Eastman Johnson Catalogue Raisonné.

Figure 5.2 Popular illustrator Felix O. C. Darley portrayed the same scene in an etching, "The Little Drummer," that accompanied a selection of war lyrics published in 1864. Darley accentuated the drummer's youthfulness, contrasting the boy's soft, wide-eyed gaze, and full lips to his adult assistant's angular visage and expression of fierce determination. R. H. Stoddard, *War Pictures: A Selection of War Lyrics with Illustrations on Wood by F.O.C. Darley* (New York: James G. Gregory, 1864), 17. Wikimedia Commons.

urges Union soldiers on to victory. Cheered and blessed by the wounded for his undaunted courage, he falls asleep once his work is done.[18] Whether the drummer lived or died, he was pictured as the bravest of the brave, spurred on by a patriotism so guileless that it overrode fear and galvanized adults into action.

These ballads were followed by dozens of other poems and songs depicting the deaths of drummer boys over the course of the war, not all of which ended on such a triumphant note. Among the hundreds of slipsheets and ballads offered by the publishing firm of Henry De Marsan in New York was a song titled "The Drummer of Antietam," which pictured the lonely death of a young musician. Although the song venerated those "cut off in their bloom" as "true martyrs of justice and sweet liberty," the drummer's grim passing was unrelieved by the presence on onlookers—a fact that would have been particularly disturbing for Victorian audiences, given the importance at this time of death bed rituals emphasizing the last words and comfort that family members and friends offered at the end of life.[19] A comparably desolate scene appeared in Connecticut composer Henry Clay Work's "Little Major" in 1862. His "noble drummer boy, the pride of all his regiment," lay in a pool of his own blood all night after a battle, begging for water, but his "dying prayer" was refused by Union troops with the callous assertion that he was "nothing but a wounded drummer" and should thus be left on the field. Forsaken and alone at the ballad's end, "he felt his keenest anguish/When at morn, he gasped and died."[20] Over subsequent years, a spate of new songs appeared, narrating the last words of dying drummers as they called on absent mothers.[21] Each of these songs bemoaned deaths that seemed devoid of any larger meaning, with no reference made to either patriotic motives or the positive effects of boys' anonymous deaths.

Scholars have interpreted this outpouring of material centered on children who went to war and ended up dying alone in several ways. Some hold that this focus allowed wartime audiences to mourn the loss of male youth in general, and perhaps even the loss of national innocence—an argument that seems credible in a context of a devastating war in which most Union soldiers were young men.[22] Others go further in suggesting that these were "anti-war songs" that reflected a larger critique of the Union war effort.[23] This interpretation is less convincing, given that none of the authors above even obliquely queried why children had been allowed to enlist in the first place, or questioned the necessity of the war. These songs and poems lamented individual deaths and offered a vehicle to mourn the kind of slaughter that cut down even fledgling innocents. But they consistently skirted wartime politics, never mentioning slavery and only discussing drummer boys' patriotism as a vague sentiment unmoored from the issues of the day.

There is a further reason not to interpret the trope of the dying drummer boy as a critique of the war: these dirges circulated in a culture in which children's deaths typically had notable symbolic import. For every story of a boy dying alone, there were a dozen in which a drummer boy's actions affected the course of events on the battlefield or, more regularly, the sentiments of adult witnesses. In this work, scenes of lonely battlefield deaths were designed to melt the hearts of the cynical and open them to moral teachings.

Wartime writers typically did emphasize the piety of the dying child, but they did not necessarily need to do so to produce this affect, since northern readers were already steeped in the conventions that made explicit the link between young deaths and religious faith.

The use of child deaths to promote conversion or increase piety long pre-dated the Civil War, providing the framework through which wartime child deaths would have been interpreted. Throughout medieval Christendom child martyrs were said to have performed miraculous deeds or remained steadfast to God in the face of agonizing torments. Their piety, understood as a gift from God, was meant to serve as a lesson for the larger Christian community in overcoming doubt and facing down disbelievers.[24] During the seventeenth and eighteenth centuries, James Janeway's *A Token for Children* (1671) was the most widely read work of juvenile literature in both England and the American colonies. Reprinted in abridged form by New England preacher Cotton Mather in 1700, it consists of vignettes recounting the conversions and exemplary deaths of children between the ages of two to fourteen. Calm and peaceful on their deathbeds, confident in their salvation, their unwavering faith offered witnesses a visible sign of the workings of God's grace.

As historian Diana Pasulka explains, this work provided a formula that numerous authors adopted and expanded on in the nineteenth century.[25] In fact, she notes that by 1850, "the memoir of the dying child could rightly be considered a distinct literary genre."[26] Spurred on by the proliferation of religious tract societies, rising literacy rates, and a publishing revolution that dramatically increased the availability of cheap printed material, writers churned out one tale after another focusing on children's deathbed scenes. The most popular of these works was, of course, *Uncle Tom's Cabin* (1852), which features the inspirational death of Little Eva as its centerpiece. Stowe's work combines romanticism's veneration of the lowly, a sentimental belief that social change had to spring from individual hearts, and a conviction that childhood marked a time of special purity and innocence. In her text, the act of observing a young child's goodness and piety at the point of death held far more power to transform social relations than rational arguments or attempts to alter laws and legislation. Through her pious demise, Little Eva demonstrated God's power and elevated the emotions of those left behind, thereby effecting social change.[27]

Most of those who portrayed the deaths of drummer boys no doubt hoped that their work would have a similar impact. Reminding audiences that death was ever-present, these images were designed to rouse a moral sense that extended beyond the loss of a pure-hearted youngster. At the same time, child deaths were turned to new purpose, directed not just at proselytizing to jaded adults but also emphasizing the innate justice of Unionism and holding up an unflattering mirror to wavering volunteers. Reflecting the wartime politicization of religion, tract societies, composers, and poets turned out a steady stream of work that imagined drummer boys facing injury and death with both piety and patriotism.[28]

Many of the war's major battles gave rise to stories of brave boys who sacrifice their lives for the cause and are blessed as a result. In the song "Drummer Boy's Farewell," John Ross Dix imagined a boy named Charlie dying on the field, telling his mother, sister, and brother that, with his "duty" done, "'Tis for our beloved *Union*/My life I gladly yield." A final verse confirms that angels now keep watch "o'er the little Drummer's grave."[29] P. De Greer's "Drummer Boy of Vicksburg" similarly tells of a young boy shot "while contending for the right." Unselfish to the last, he gives water to a wounded comrade before "his spirit took flight" into "the arms of his Saviour."[30] In an almost identical vein, Robert Johnson's "The Drummer Boy of Nashville" pictures a high-principled boy, "his conscience . . .pure as the sky," who lives by the motto "forward and never despair." First into battle, "never laying behind or shunning the fray," he is wounded while crying out: "Men! Rush to the Fight" and dies while struggling to keep drumming to rally the troops.[31]

If Union soldiers failed to get the message so clearly telegraphed in these songs, then decorative envelopes and letterhead helped drive the point home by picturing stalwart child soldiers juxtaposed with an infantile enemy in need of a good spanking. Thousands of different designs appeared on patriotic stationery during the war, with more than a hundred printers and lithographers involved in their creation and distribution, the vast majority operating in cities like New York and Philadelphia.[32] Embossed, printed, or engraved, they featured images that were either rendered in single shades of ink or hand-tinted in color. Alongside depictions of flags, eagles, camp scenes, and military leaders, printers offered a range of designs that emphasized the heroism of Union boy soldiers and poked fun at the puerility of their enemies. "Death or Victory," proclaimed one envelope, below the image of a young boy in a uniform, holding a flag aloft in one hand with a sword at the ready in the other. "When thus our hosts go proudly forth, Let foes beware the Spirit of the North!" declared another featuring a boy dressed in a Zouave uniform who is looking backward, presumably at the

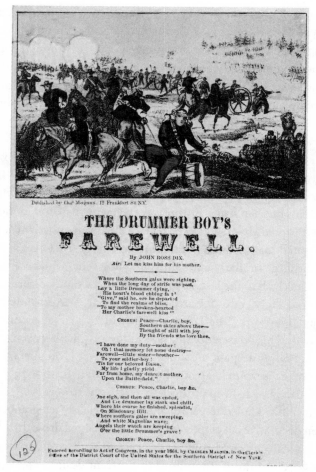

Figure 5.3 John Ross Dix, "The Drummer Boy's Farewell" (New York: Charles Magnus, 1864). Hand-tinted songsheets like this one, picturing young drummer boys dying "for our beloved *Union*" while crying out for their mothers, were standard fare in the United States, but not in the Confederacy. Library Company of Philadelphia, American Song Sheets, Slip Ballads and Poetical Broadsides Collection, 1850–1870.

troops behind him, while ignoring of the exploding shells to his left.[33] In contrast to these resolute Union children, Confederates often appeared on envelopes as unruly boys who lacked the impulse control and common sense of well-bred northerners. One design titled "Young America" featured two young boys, labelled "North" and "South." While the northern boy is busy examining technical instruments and machinery, taking instruction from a young mechanic dressed in a workman's smock, the southern boy rests lazily on a keg of alcohol, smoking a cigar and carrying a riding crop. The message was instantly clear: the industrial strength of the northern states could be traced to a system that taught youngsters the virtues of honest labor and education, while slavery in the southern states allowed children to grow up in indolence and vice.

Even more pointed, Union envelopes critiqued Confederates as akin to naughty children, too immature to take responsibility for their actions, and too ignorant and green to create a proper nation. One envelope, titled "Little 'Jeff' in a tight place," featured the Confederate president as a tiny baby, clutched firmly in the grip of a union soldier. Another portrayed him as a sickly boy addressing the Guardian of Liberty. "Please ma'am, my big brother won't let me alone," he whines. "Well it serves you right," Columbia fires back, "why don't you mind your Uncle Abe. Just wait until McClellan comes in contact with you, he will give you such a sound thrashing, you'll never complain again." Continuing the same theme, envelopes represented Confederate diplomats as squabbling youngsters vying for the attention of a decrepit Europe, or the Confederate army as a group of children playing on

When thus our hosts go proudly forth,
Let foes beware the Spirit of the North !

Figure 5.4 Patriotic stationery and envelopes were ubiquitous in the United States during the Civil War. Here, an envelope features a boy dressed in a Zouave uniform looking backward, presumably to rally the troops behind him, while shells explode nearby. Civil War Envelopes Collection, Box 1, American Antiquarian Society, Worcester, Massachusetts.

toy instruments and wearing paper hats.[34] Coupled with the many designs
that emphasized white southerners' lack of self-control—their love of horse-
racing, drinking, and sexual vice—these decorative envelopes and stationery
suggested that even the youngest Unionists approached the war with seriousness of purpose, while the Confederate war effort was little more than "the
drunken dreams of an overgrown boy, accustomed to wallowing in sin and
having his own way, unwilling to relinquish his petty tyrannies and become a
productive member of society."[35]

The fictional Union children pictured on envelope designs and in songs
and poems complemented stories in the northern press that celebrated
the brave deeds of actual boy soldiers and musicians. In fact, these various
representations—in newspaper accounts, poems, songs, and artwork—were
often linked, following a similar trajectory in their elaboration. Usually,
a letter to the press would convey an incident relating to a boy soldier or
drummer, written by someone claiming to have witnessed the event. This incident would then be reprinted by papers across the country. Within months,
poems or songs would retell the same event, distributed as sheet music or
as single-sided lithographs adorned with decorative borders. The boy in
question might then be feted, his image circulated in the form of a *carte
de visite*. This is how the tale of the "Drummer Boy of the Rappahannock"
spread. Starting as a rumor sent to the press, then amplified in subsequent
stories, the tale of this drummer boy—identified as Henry Hendershot—
was transformed into poetry, newspaper columns, a photograph taken by
Matthew Brady, and, finally, a biography that placed Hendershot in a long
line of selfless patriots that stretched back to the founders.

Child Soldiers as National Symbols

Unionists embraced these varying representations of child soldiers and
drummers because the war posed a profound challenge to democratic republicanism. Since the nation's founding, American commentators had favorably contrasted their peace-loving republic with the conflict-ridden Old
World, where rival states constantly warred for power and prestige. This version of US history was always aspirational; it conveniently overlooked the
fact that the country had been at war almost continuously—first with the
British, then with Mexico, and always with Native Americans. But with its
stunning casualty rates, the Civil War threatened to unravel the narrative

Figure 5.5 *Carte de visite* of a photograph by Mathew Brady of Robert Henry Hendershot, who claimed to be the celebrated "Drummer Boy of Rappahannock." He spent the rest of his life capitalizing on his wartime fame, but the Pension Bureau rejected his claims for an invalid veteran's pension. Congress finally awarded him a pension by a special act in 1924. Wikimedia Commons.

entirely. In the eyes of European critics, the conflict exposed the fundamental flaw at the heart of the American experiment: democracies, even those anchored in a republican structure, were inherently unstable and inevitably degenerated into vicious mob rule. Recognizing the power of this critique, Abraham Lincoln often reminded his countrymen that Union soldiers bore the fate of republican democracy upon their shoulders, not just in America but "in the world, for all future time."[36] As he told his private secretary in 1861, "We must settle this question now, whether in a free government the minority have the right to break up the government whenever they choose. If we fail it will go far to prove the incapability of the people to govern themselves."[37] In a conflict publicized around the world as a barbaric bloodbath, depictions of patriotic white children reassured Americans that their government continued to be guided by laudable ideals. With even the youngest children flocking to defend the cause, the nation surely remained a beacon for the world's oppressed.[38]

Multiplying images of children in uniform could, of course, have worked in a very different way, evoking a nightmarish vision of a completely militarized society. Perhaps this is why child soldiers and drummers are often pictured heading into battle, and sometimes even capturing enemy soldiers, but never actually killing or wounding anyone.[39] Typically, they are the ones who end up dead, with older comrades gathered around to mourn their loss, and a national audience paying homage by viewing, singing, or reading about their fate. In reality, the Civil War did lead to the mobilization of much of the population, as large numbers of underage boys took up arms, and women and children engaged in voluntary activities, dressed in military outfits, and visited military encampments. Tales of innocent white children who sacrificed freely for the Union acted to quell anxieties about what military mobilization on this scale portended for the republic. For if children could maintain their innocence while surrounded by such carnage, then clearly the war had not destroyed Unionists' finer feelings. The figure of the pure child as representative of the nation, in short, provided a perfect foil to claims that the United States, by engaging in a vindictive and brutal war, was destroying itself.

This use of martyred children as symbols of the nation can be credited to French revolutionaries, who firmly established the trope of the heroic drummer boy in the late eighteenth and early nineteenth centuries. At a particularly perilous moment for the republican cause in France—a "time of the greatest terror, of violence and dreadful purges carried out in the name of virtue"—revolutionary leader Maximillian Robespierre latched on to the stories of two dead youngsters, Joseph Bara (also Barra) and Joseph-Agricola Viala (also Joseph Agricol Viala), to cast the Revolution in a positive light.[40] Bara had joined the republican army as a drummer around the age of twelve and been killed by counter-revolutionary insurgents in 1793, allegedly for refusing to surrender the horses he

Figure 5.6 Newspapers sometimes recounted tales of drummer boys committing violence, but even in cases like that of Johnny Clem—alleged to have shot a Confederate officer—the act itself is not depicted. P. S. Duval & Son, Lithographer, "John Clem, a drummer boy of 12 years of age who shot a Rebel colonel upon the battle field of Chickamauga, Ga., Sept. 20th 1863" (Philadelphia: P. S. Duval & Son, c. 1863). Library of Congress Prints and Photographs Division, LC-DIG-pga-10345.

was leading. After a French general wrote an account of his actions, Robespierre transformed the boy into a heroic figure. He spun a tale in which Bara rebuffed an offer to spare his life if he pledged loyalty to the king, choosing instead to die while shouting *"Vive la République."* That

THE LAST CALL .

Figure 5.7 A Union drummer rallies the troops who appear behind him, oblivious to the cannonball that will shortly land at his feet and take his life. "The Last Call" (Boston: J.H. Bufford & Co., publisher, 1861), American Antiquarian Society, Worcester, Massachusetts.

same year, twelve-year-old Viala was mythologized in an almost identical manner. Having attached himself to the National Guards from Avignon, he had been killed while trying to delay the advance of anti-revolutionary forces by severing the ropes holding up a bridge. In Robespierre's retelling of his story, Viala used his last breath to cry out: "I die for liberty!" Cases of young boys getting caught up in war and dying—episodes that once drew little attention—were now reconceived as symbolic of both the spirit of the republic and the virtue of its supporters, who recognized and properly honored such sacrifice.

The French Assembly voted to inter Bara and Viala in the Panthéon and to hold a festival in their honor. Well-known artist Jacques-Louis David was commissioned to organize this event and to produce a work depicting Bara as an "embodiment of those concepts of virtue, incorruptibility, consolation, generosity and self-sacrifice." The arresting painting that he produced—showing the young drummer lying naked on the ground, clutching a tricolor cockade and a letter to his chest, his curly hair, feminine features, and softly curved prepubescent body emphasizing his childish innocence—was supposed to supplement other paintings of Bara to be carried on banners by a procession of children and mothers.[41] Although the planned celebration never occurred, its date coinciding with Robespierre's overthrow, Bara's and Viala's fame only grew in the years ahead. In 1794, the French navy named a ship in honor of each boy. Over the following decades, lithographs, songs, operas, plays, and biographies depicted them as ideal children who had worked to support their poor widowed mothers and gladly gave their lives for the republic. Etchings of the boys were also hung in classrooms to inspire similar patriotism in schoolchildren.[42] At a moment when revolutionaries sought to "dampen the spirit of faction, to find a symbol of unity, [and] to honor a hero who was outside politics," young boys without formal political affiliations or experience and capable of invoking the purity attached to childhood were perfectly suited for such ends.[43] Thus, when Napoleon Bonaparte faced enemies seeking to restore aristocratic power in France, he also transformed a young drummer, André Estienne, into a symbol for his cause.[44]

Using the constellation of meanings attached to childhood to symbolize the nation was especially appealing to those in the nineteenth century who rejected imperial or aristocratic claims to power.[45] Evoking freshness and purity, forward-looking zeal, and innocence of purpose, the figure of the martyred child helped to justify and naturalize the tremendous violence required to uphold new systems of governance. In contrast, this figure held far less appeal in societies that were not seeking to upturn their political order. The British Empire could boast large numbers of young musicians and soldiers, for instance, several of whom were known to have performed brave deeds during the Crimean War of 1853–1856 and the Indian Rebellion of 1857. But their heroism was not widely celebrated at the time. No outpouring of printed material or public mourning declared them to be national symbols, and no monuments were raised in their memory until the late nineteenth century. Nor did heroic children capture the attention of British artists, poets, or composers.[46]

The way child figures were depicted in British art, histories, and literature highlights the difference. According to historian Holly Furneaux, mid-century Britain was flooded with depictions of rough soldiers caring for children. By this time, an older model of aristocratic manhood emphasizing martial and chivalric values was on the back foot, challenged by the rise of humanitarianism and the spread of evangelical Christianity. In this context, work picturing British soldiers as protectors of the young rather than perpetrators of violence emphasized the army's essential humanity and undercut arguments about military service as intrinsically barbarous. Constructing the "military man of feeling," who found spiritual and moral redemption through the protection of a helpless child, British artists and writers helped to "reconcile a declining investment in physical violence with the need to produce soldiers and empire builders," Furneaux concludes.[47] The fact that images of powerless children were used so readily to demonstrate the morality of the British army underscores the lack of any similar celebration of martyred children. British boy soldiers and drummers were plentiful enough in numbers and brave deeds, but representations of the qualities that they conjured were superfluous to British nationalism at this time.

The same might be said for the Confederacy. In the modern era, virtually everyone who discusses the celebration of drummer boys and young soldiers during the Civil War assumes that both sides were equally compelled by these figures.[48] The strongest evidence in support of this contention lies in the publication of the "Drummer Boy of Shiloh," a song that circulated in both the Union and the Confederacy, as did a number of other wartime tunes. The original sheet music was printed in 1862 by D. P. Faulds of Louisville, Kentucky, a firm that took advantage of its position in a border state to publish pro-Union and pro-Confederate material. William S. Hays, who penned the song's original lyrics, also regularly addressed tunes to partisans on both sides. Initially, Faulds clearly had a Union audience in mind: the first version of the song was dedicated to a "Miss Annie Cannon of Louisville, Kentucky," who appears to have been either a Unionist or at least non-partisan.[49] And the sheet music was decorated with the lithographed image of figures dressed in Union blue. At the forefront is a young boy, held in the arms of an older soldier so that he can pray, the battle raging in the background temporarily forgotten. Around the pair, injured soldiers lie scattered, with one man on bended knee covering his face, overcome by emotion as he contemplates the drummer boy's pious death.[50] In promoting the sheet-music, Faulds placed numerous announcements in the northern press, including regular advertisements in the *Chicago Daily Tribune* and the *Daily Evansville Journal* in Illinois between December 1862 and March 1863. But the firm placed no similar notices in extant newspapers within the Confederacy.[51]

When the "Drummer Boy of Shiloh" was released, it joined a growing body of northern work that depicted similar tales. Hays's lyrics focused on the boy's abiding faith and patriotism and the effects of his innocent purity on adult witnesses, as did most of this work. In his original song, "a wounded soldier held . . . up" the drummer as he clasped his hands in prayer, begging God to have mercy on the "sinful souls" of the dying, and calling on his dead mother to "Look down from Heaven" and "take me home to thee." The penultimate verse emphasized the boy's patriotism, as he confirmed: "I've loved my country as my God; to serve them both I've tried./He smiled, shook hands—death seized the boy/Who prayed before he died." The song ended with a final verse, placing singers in the position of mourners, repeating the boy's prayer for "angels 'round the Throne of Grace," to "Look down upon the braves.[52]

Several notable changes were made to Hays's song when it was reprinted in the Confederacy.[53] First, the work was re-dedicated to "Mr. Harry B. Macarthy," a popular composer of Confederate ballads. More importantly, a new image appeared on the southern sheet music, featuring a much older drummer—still a youth but now sporting a moustache and beard, with a visible wound on his chest. The drum that sits beside his feet is full-sized, unlike the tiny instrument depicted on the Union sheet music. And the soldiers who appear in the scene are wearing light colored uniforms, meant to indicate Confederate gray. To complement the drummer's elevation to manhood, Hays's lyrics were slightly altered by E. Clarke Ilsley, who appears on southern versions as a co-author. Instead of being "held up" by a Union soldier, the drummer now simply "clasped his hands and raised his eyes" before dying. Ilsey did not need to change much else, since Union versions of the sheet music mentioned the drummer dying for a "cause" that receives no further elaboration. But he did remove the final verse, which lamented the "many homes made desolate" by the struggle, and the "many, like that drummer boy. Who prayed before they died!" The exclusion of this verse with its emphasis on continuous mourning, along with the new illustration that pictured soldiers only as background figures, no longer watching the boy's prayer or crying in sympathy, effectively undercut some of its inspirational potential, presenting the drummer as a young man cut off in his prime, but not as an exceptional youngster connected to a long history of child martyrs.

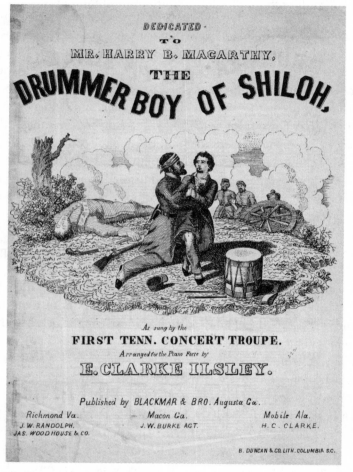

Figure 5.8 The original version of this song sheet pictured a small Union drummer, whose suffering inspires nearby comrades. In this version, produced for a Confederate audience, the drummer is pictured with facial hair and a full-sized drum. E. Clarke Ilsley also took out a final verse that emphasized the inspirational potential of the drummer boy's death. Will S. Hays, "The Drummer Boy of Shiloh," Augusta, Ga: Blackmar & Bro., c.1863. Civil War Sheet Music Collection, Library Company of Philadelphia.

This song clearly circulated on both sides during the war. In the United States, its wide appeal was obvious: advertisements mentioned the sheet music's "tremendous sale," multiple editions were released over the course of the war, and the press identified several Union drummer boys as the song's inspiration.[54] In the Confederacy, its popularity is less clear. It went unadvertised and unremarked in the press, and no young Confederates came forward to claim the title. More importantly, it failed to engender any imitations in the Confederate states. The two most popular southern periodicals during the war—the *Southern Illustrated News* and the *Magnolia Weekly*—contain scant references to heroic drummer boys. A handful of Confederate children's books included a young soldier or musician.[55] But artists, playwrights, authors, and composers produced nothing similar for adult readers.[56]

A disparity in the volume of popular material produced by the two sides cannot account for this absence. Confederate publishers might have lacked skilled artists and supplies, but they still managed to publish a great deal of work mirroring northern preoccupations, including dozens of sentimental poems focusing on mothers who lost sons in the struggle.[57] Other explanations rooted in the nature of Confederate nationalism are more likely. Despite their role in starting the war, Confederates portrayed themselves as victims seeking only to throw off a brutal adversary. They had no need for the symbolism attached to childhood innocence, given their inferior numbers and the presence of war on their doorstep. Children also represent the freshness of the new and the inevitability of change, looking toward the future rather than the past. These were hardly qualities that reinforced Confederate nationalism, which was by nature conservative and antidemocratic.[58] Thus while young Confederate enlistees were often lauded as proof of Confederate unity, they did not become symbols of the nation itself.

Having long described the enslaved as perpetual children, childishness also carried strong racial overtones in the Confederacy that may also have limited interest in the iconography of the heroic child. Racism knew no regional boundary, of course, and white commentators in Union states were just as likely to characterize African Americans as childlike. But since they vastly outnumbered the free Black people in their midst, white Unionists were in less danger than their southern counterparts of being tainted by association. Quite different stakes were involved in employing the metaphor of childhood in a society so heavily invested in justifying slavery by infantilizing African Americans. Confederate soldiers were themselves often cast by their enemies as immature, irresponsible, and undisciplined, as the decorative envelopes cited above make clear. They fired back with images of a venal, mongrelized north, but they did not condemn Union soldiers as childlike. As the death tolls increased, Unionists also developed a new stereotype of the Confederate military as brimming with decrepit old men and frail youngsters.[59] Given these realities, any equation between the Confederacy and childhood threatened to evoke Unionist critiques of southern puerility and powerlessness, or stereotypes of Black weakness, rather than the more positive associations attached to childhood.

Racial Politics and the Inspirational Child Soldier

Outside the Confederacy, representations of Black children in the press as weak, laughable, or pathetic worked to ensure that these positive associations attached only to white child soldiers. The first depictions of Black boys marching or beating drums appeared long before African Americans could legally enlist in the Union army. Instead, they aimed to poke fun at Confederate mobilization efforts. One etching in *Harper's Weekly* in June 1861, titled "Drumming Up Recruits for the Confederate Army," pictured a Black man wielding a huge drum, his striped pants, bowtie, and top hat resembling a minstrel costume. Alongside him, a small, scruffy Black boy marches barefoot, accompanied by a white fiddler, a small white drummer boy, and a crowd of apathetic-looking spectators. Portrayed with thick lips, a broad nose, and a mass of wiry curls, this boy is also rendered through the conventions of minstrelsy: shouldering a broom instead of a gun, his imitation of marching conjures the many performances in which actors in blackface lampooned African American efforts to mimic white manners.[60] Emphasizing the irreducibility of racial difference, minstrel performances told audiences that Blacks could never succeed in the serious business of war. Whereas the white boy at least looks the part, despite his sour expression, his Black imitator appears foolish and absurd. Designed to depict Confederate recruitment as hopelessly amateurish, this cartoon was followed by others that similarly pictured marching Black children as comical figures whose efforts at soldiering could only provoke laughter or contempt.[61]

More positive images of Black boys and men were also produced during the war. As historian Kate Masur points out, northern artists consistently addressed the future of slavery and race relations by portraying newly freed slaves. Their representations fell on a spectrum: on one end were racist caricatures that stressed irreducible difference and inferiority; on the other were more hopeful portrayals of freedpeople as harmless or exotic, perhaps pathetic in their dependency but nonetheless capable of improvement.[62] The same spectrum characterized representations of young Black soldiers and drummer boys. After the enlistment of African American soldiers began, the New York lithography firm of Currier and Ives released a lithograph titled "The Colored Volunteer," which showed a rosy-cheeked Black enlistee standing tall in his spotless uniform. Despite his boyishness, he looks ready to head off to war, his shiny metal belt buckle proudly declaring him a US soldier, and the gun and knapsack he shoulders suggesting an imminent departure.[63] Similarly, a front page of *Harper's Weekly* in early 1863 showed a white officer teaching a group of "negro recruits" how to use their weapons.[64] A small Black drummer with an instrument strapped to his back stands beside the men, drumsticks in hand. He is scruffy, his pants rolled up unevenly, but he looks resolute and attentive. By positioning the drummer in front of a group of newly minted Black soldiers, this image hints that he might one day lead them in battle. But much like the positive lithograph of "The Colored Volunteer," the promise is latent; both figures remain passive, still waiting to be tested in battle.

Cartoonist Thomas Nast produced his own, far more derisive version of "The Colored Volunteer" in 1863. Rather than a potentially brave youth, he depicted a ragged Black child marching with a broom, his wide-eyed stare suggesting simple-minded brutishness.[65] Unlike positive depictions of white drummer boys and soldiers that drew on familiar tropes of childhood innocence by picturing delicate features or soft expressions, there was no evocation of purity or goodness here. The boy's gleeful grin instead echoed the stereotype of the willful, unmanageable slave child, while his unkempt appearance and lack of any weapon were clearly supposed to produce laughter at such a feeble attempt even to play at soldiering. Reproduced and fixed to a *carte de visite* mount in 1863, indicating some popularity or at least commercial appeal, Nast's image provided a counterpoint to the heroic drummer boy, replacing the pure and angelic white child with a coarse and pitiful Black one.

It is difficult not to read Nast's etching as a direct response to images that portrayed Black volunteers as the vanguard of a new future in race relations. In addition to the lithograph mentioned above, a member of the 54th Massachusetts Infantry (the best known of the USCT regiments) also wrote a marching song called "The Colored Volunteer," to remind northern whites of their distinct dependence on Black enlistees:

THE COLORED VOLUNTEER
MARCHING INTO DIXIE.

Figure 5.9 This lithograph of a proud Black volunteer "marching into Dixie" emphasized its subject's youth by picturing his beardless face and rosy cheeks. "The Colored Volunteer," New York: Currier & Ives, c. 1863. Library Company of Philadelphia.

Colored Volunteer

Figure 5.10 Cartoonist Thomas Nast produced his own version of "The Colored Volunteer," shown in this 1863 photographic print on a *carte de visite* mount. Instead of a dignified and promising youth, he depicted a ragged Black child marching with a broom, his wide-eyed, vacant stare suggesting amusing coarseness. Thomas Nast, "The Colored Volunteer," Liljenquist Family Collection of Civil War Photographs, Library of Congress Prints and Photographs Division, ppmsca 74258.

McClellan went to Richmond with two hundred thousand braves;
He said, 'keep back the niggers,' and the Union he would save.
Little Mac he had his way—still the Union is in tears—
Now they call for the help of the colored volunteers.

. . . .

So rally, boys, rally, let us never mind the past;
We had a hard road to travel, but our day is coming fast,
For God is for the right, and we have no need to fear, —
The Union must be saved by the *colored volunteer*.[66]

Demanding recognition of their crucial part in the war, this song looked forward to a day when African American men would finally be welcomed as equal citizens for their role in preserving the Union. As if to neutralize such hopefulness, images of Black males as brutish and absurd promised white audiences that African Americans would never measure up.

Prevalent depictions of heroic drummer boys apparently also required a negative referent to emphasize this figure's whiteness and enhance its appeal. Will S. Hays, who penned the words to "Drummer Boy of Shiloh," perhaps the war's most popular song about a heroic white child, played a crucial role in cementing Nast's depiction of aspiring Black child soldiers as laughable rather than inspiring. In 1867, Hays released the minstrel tune "Little Sam" about a "happy little darkey, all the way from Alabam," who left his family to "find the happy land." As in many minstrel tunes, Hay's lyrics allowed some recognition of its Black character's humanity, imagining a boy who loves his family, works hard, sends his pay home, and desires freedom above all else. But Little Sam's dialect sharply telegraphs his racial distinctiveness, as does the lithograph that accompanied Hays's song. The image is almost a direct replica of Nast's etching, the only difference being that Little Sam holds his broom in the opposite hand while clutching a top hat, underscoring the absurdity of his self-important posturing. All the other elements—from the boy's unruly hair and untidy clothes to his almost fiendish expression—appear unchanged.[67]

The whiteness of the child soldier or drummer legitimized this racism and upheld racial hierarchy. Representations of white child soldiers and drummer boys stood entirely apart from discussions of slavery or the role of African Americans in the war. At the same time, northern artists and writers consistently pictured the many Black children who went to war as cheerful bootblacks or comedic figures—useful for emphasizing white paternalism or casting Black children as outlandish and amusing, but nothing like the inspirational white children who rallied the troops or embodied the Union. Citing the work of race theorists, Robin Bernstein recently observed that whiteness derives its power from being unremarked; it is everywhere and nowhere, and its nowhereness is its "deep cover." The fiction of childhood innocence has played a central role in creating that cover, she argues, crafting the pure white child through reference to its opposite: the cheerful Black pickaninny who is supposedly immune from pain.[68] Holding true for wartime images of white and Black children in general, this argument is especially relevant for depictions of child soldiers and drummers. Always merry and smiling, Black children were never shown suffering or dying for the Union cause. In a war that was quite literally fought over the future of Black children, the figure of the heroic white child soldier or drummer boy helped to ensure that white martyrdom would hold center stage.

* * *

In 1862, artist William Morris Hunt produced an oil painting of a drummer boy beating out a call to arms while standing on a pedestal marked "U.S. Volunteers!" A photographic print of this work was reproduced for sale that same year as a *carte de visite*, with the addition of a new heading "To Arms! Freemen to Arms!" lest anyone miss the young drummer's purpose.[69] In his youth, Hunt had studied in Paris under French painter Thomas Courture, so it is no wonder that his work mirrored the conventions of the heroic drummer boy that the French had earlier established. Indeed, Hunt's first drummer boy painting echoed one of Courture's own works.[70] He drew from French precedents again in 1862 to produce a second painting of a young drummer laying prone beside his drum, a reddish-yellow glow on the horizon intimating a battle still in progress.[71] Using symbolism pioneered by the French, Hunt was one of many well-known artists to see drummer boys as a fitting embodiment of the Union war effort and an ideal symbol to encourage enlistments.

Eastman Johnson's *The Wounded Drummer Boy* made the biggest splash among art critics of the time. "Everybody familiar with this painting . . .will remember the spirit and grace of the picture," enthused *Appletons' Journal* in 1874, a decade after Johnson first showed his initial canvas of a small boy held aloft by a Union soldier, heading into battle heedless of the wound to his leg. "Unlike Mr. Johnson's quiet genre pictures, this was one of the most animated war-scenes that any of our artists had delineated."[72] A few years earlier,

TO ARMS! FREEMEN TO ARMS!

Entered according to Act of Congress in the year 1862, by W. M. Hunt, in the Clerk's Office of the District Court of Mass.

Figure 5.11 Reproducing William Morris Hunt's painting "The Drummer Boy," this photographic print on *carte de visite* mount resembles the work of the French artists who first popularized the drummer boy figure as a symbol of republican purity and heroism. William Morris Hunt, "To Arms! Freemen to Arms!" Library of Congress Prints and Photographs Division, LC-DIG-ppmsca-11276.

the same publication had declared the painting "excellent," complimenting Johnson on his depiction of a boy "full of life ... vigorously drumming away," although owning that so many similar images of drummer boys existed that "one can hardly have a fresh emotion in seeing them."[73] Johnson was one of America's most widely respected artists by this point. Now remembered mainly for his sympathetic portraits of African American life, it was his retelling of a popular wartime myth that most enthused the Civil War–era public.[74]

The fact that the nation's best-known painters joined with cartoonists, journalists, lithographers, songwriters, and poets in taking up the topic of the heroic child soldier or drummer is telling. Taken together, this work represents more than a generic mourning for the deaths of so many young males. Depictions of uniformed children dying alone or in battle circulated in a culture in which child death had long been recognized as a powerful means of promoting religious faith. By the early nineteenth century, French revolutionaries had yoked this religious imagery to a secular cause, holding up drummer boys as the embodiment of the pure republican ardor that would allow their new political system to thrive. In the Civil War, the most popular depictions of child soldiers and drummers also placed these figures in the army's vanguard. As in Eastman Johnson's painting, young boys inspired others with their zeal and purity of purpose, symbolizing a spotless white heroism and epitomizing the virtuous Union cause.

6

Paths to Enlistment

Work, Politics, and School

Theodore Upson's political education began well before he enlisted in the Union army at the age of seventeen. In 1858, the thirteen-year-old farm boy from northern Indiana began a diary that shows him already attuned to the debates that would splinter the nation.[1] When relatives from Mississippi came to visit, he grilled his younger cousin about slavery. They argued about the veracity of *Uncle Tom's Cabin* and nearly came to blows when Theodore asked the boy if his father ever whipped their family's slaves. "Father heard about our fuss and asked me about it," he wrote in his diary. "I told him and he said boys should not quarrel about such things. It was bad enough for men to do so." Sure enough, the community's adults were getting into rows over slavery, too. A social at a minister's house turned ugly when a guest denounced the "abolitionist crowd" and stormed out with his family in tow. An altercation at the local bookstore led to one man calling another "a damned black Republican." Theodore noted it all in his diary. Sectional tensions loomed large even in the make-believe games that he and his friends played that winter, as they built snow forts and waged "great battles" in which northerners attacked southerners and liberated their slaves, sending them off to Canada.[2]

As the political situation further deteriorated over the next three years, Theodore grew into a capable youth. He still attended school when it was in session, but the census taker who stopped by in June 1860, a month after he turned fifteen, recorded his occupation as "farm laborer." His political consciousness was maturing as well. That summer he visited abolitionist relatives in Michigan, where he went to "a political meeting of some sort" almost every day. On one memorable evening, he joined a group of Wide Awakes—a militantly pro-Lincoln organization of mostly young men—as they marched through town brandishing torches and singing "John Brown's Body."[3] Convinced that "Lincoln is the man," he regretted being too young to vote in the November election.[4]

In April 1861, father and son were husking corn when a neighbor came bounding across the field with news of the firing on Fort Sumter. In the following months, Theodore attended numerous war meetings at the schoolhouse, placed his name on an enrollment list, and even drilled and camped out with a newly formed company of local recruits. His father humored him, thinking "it would not hurt me to play soldier for a while," but he underestimated his son's seriousness of purpose. When it came time for the company to depart and the captain patiently explained to the overeager sixteen-year-old that he could not accompany them without his father's consent, he "bawled" like the child he still partly was.[5]

Theodore's preoccupation with enlisting only grew as the seasons passed. "Well it is winter and school again," he wrote in early 1862, adding that he doubted he would "learn much" since his schoolmates spoke only of the war. At the end of term, he took part in an exhibition featuring patriotic songs and recitations. For the dramatic finale, the students staged a tableau featuring a mock execution of Jefferson Davis—complete with guards, gallows, and "colored fire"—apparently believing that Davis needed to be both hung and burned at the stake. Delighted, the audience responded by spontaneously bursting into song, pledging, "We Will Hang Jeff Davis to a Sour Apple Tree."[6]

That fall, Theodore again tried to enlist, and again his father vowed to have his name struck from the list. But Mr. Upson's resolve weakened after his mother-in-law advised, "'You might just as well let the boy go . . . you cannot blame him for wanting to go—the other boys he knows are going or gone.'" When Theodore next returned to the schoolhouse for a war meeting, he did so triumphantly, with his father at his side.[7] In September 1862, he was mustered into the army. By then, Congress had barred the enlistment of youths under eighteen, so the consent that he obtained from his father was essentially permission to lie about his age.

It took Theodore over a year to wear down his father's resistance, but the path that led him into the army had been cleared well before the war's outbreak. By the time he enlisted, he was strong enough to serve as a full hand on the farm. Having participated in numerous political events, he felt deeply invested in the national drama and considered himself a loyal Republican. He had even acquired a rudimentary military education by drilling with a local company. Then there was the fact that many of his friends and schoolmates had already joined the fight. Given all this, it is hardly surprising that Theodore believed his rightful place was in the Union army. The real wonder is not that he managed to get himself mustered in soon after his seventeenth birthday, but that his father succeeded in keeping him home for so long.

Boys in many times and places have found the prospect of war alluring. But distinctive features of antebellum society explain why such large numbers of underage youths ended up fighting in this particular war, and why so many adults reluctantly condoned or even facilitated their enlistment. Whether working, studying, or engaging in the social and political lives of their communities, boys below military age constantly rubbed elbows with youths above eighteen and full-grown men. This dynamic is best captured in the memoirs, diaries, and correspondence written by Union and Confederate veterans. Illuminating the daily lives of Civil War–era Americans, these sources bring to life the factors that allowed underage enlistment to occur on such a massive scale.

Consider the issue of labor. In the mid-nineteenth century, white males came of age in a culture that defined manhood in terms of individual striving, independence, and free will. Often saddled with serious duties from a young age and frequently sent to work outside their parents' homes, boys and youths were eagerly pushed toward maturity, even as they continued to be defined as legal dependents. In shops as well as fields, the young usually worked alongside adults, and particular tasks tended to be assigned according to skill, strength, and experience rather than numerical age.[8] Parents and guardians often opted to give older children their "time" before they attained the age of majority, allowing them to negotiate their own employment arrangements and to retain some or all of their wages.[9] Yet legally, parents and guardians could dictate the form and the terms of their boys' labor, while also laying claim to their full wages, until they reached the age of twenty one. This proved a recipe for underage enlistment, but not just for the obvious reason that boys and youths hoped to escape oppressive working conditions. More important still was the palpable disparity between their legal subordination and the feelings of competency and importance they often derived from working. Accustomed to performing demanding and sometimes dangerous tasks alongside adult men, many youths simply rejected the notion that they were too young to be of service to the military. It was an assumption belied by their everyday experience.[10]

Just as the world of work encompassed young people, so, too, did the political culture of antebellum America. "Politics" was not cordoned off as an adult preoccupation, and boys played a surprisingly central role in the era's notoriously raucous campaign events, as historian Jon Grinspan has shown.

Political operatives relied on energetic boys and youths to run messages, distribute handbills, and perform other campaign-related grunt work. More broadly, they welcomed the young with open arms, often "designing their events 'to catch the eye of a boy of nine years of age.' "[11] Boys and young men repaid this attention by flocking to parades, rallies, stump speeches, and other political events. They did so in part because spectacles and diversions of any sort were in short supply in the small towns and rural areas where most people lived. But they also gravitated to such events for more serious reasons. As even young boys readily grasped, politics was a proving ground for men-in-the-making.

The frequent intermingling of boys and young men is also paramount for understanding how schools inadvertently fostered underage enlistment. Prior to the Civil War, neither common schools nor academies and colleges rigidly stratified students into separate grades or classes according to age. Youths in their late teens and even early twenties attended common schools, while boys as young as thirteen or fourteen enrolled in colleges and universities.[12] As a result, boys in their mid-teens routinely studied and socialized with young men of military age, a social reality that had enormous implications for underage enlistment. When friends or college students headed off to enlist together, the youngest boys in the cohort often accompanied them, swept up in the excitement and feelings of camaraderie. Some youths even presented themselves to enlistment officers as a group, refusing to sign up unless all were accepted, with no one individual scrutinized too closely.[13]

The experiences that drew youths to enlist in the militaries of the United States and the Confederacy were in some ways remarkably similar. While their political convictions may have differed sharply, memoirs written by Confederate and Union veterans echo one another in describing how they came into political consciousness and how schools functioned as veritable feeding organizations for the military. But on the subject of labor, the sources point to notable differences. Nearly all of the underage Confederates who later wrote about their experiences came from affluent, slave-owning families and were students at the war's outset. Very few of these memoirists recounted performing significant labor, either paid or unpaid, before entering military service. In contrast, the ranks of the Union memoirists include those who had been working as farmers, clerks, newsboys, river workers, printers, and shoemakers, among other occupations, when they enlisted underage. This disparity is indicative of the much lower rates of literacy and greater barriers to social mobility in the Confederate states; white southerners who labored from a young age often lacked the literacy necessary to commit their life stories to paper.[14] Nonetheless, the same factors that led many working youths to believe themselves capable of serving in the Union army were almost certainly operative when it came to some portion of poor Confederates, even if their stories are harder to recover.[15]

In both southern and northern states, virtually everything about mid-nineteenth century American society militated against attempts to draw a firm line between those above and below the age of eighteen. The phenomenon of underage enlistment emerged from a social and political order in which males of different generations often shared spaces and interacted outside the confines of the family. This deceptively simple fact goes a long way toward explaining why so many boys and youths tried to finagle their way into the service—to lie and dissemble, run away from home, stand on tiptoe in examining rooms, or purchase concoctions that promised to make them sprout beards. For those who were used to being where the men were, the imposition of an arbitrary line seemed all but an invitation to defy it.

Labor and the Demonstration of Manly Competence

In 1927, at the age of eighty-one, Wisconsinite Elisha Stockwell finally yielded to his family's imploring and sat down to write the story of his Civil War experiences. He began as follows: "In the summer of 1861 I was fifteen years old, could rake and bind and keep up with the men. (They cut the grain with cradles then.) I got fifty cents a day and a man one dollar, but my father collected my wages as he was a very poor man." In a few plainspoken sentences, Elisha identified the labor conditions that led him and thousands of other poor and working-class youths to enlist. Though he toiled like a man alongside other men, he was neither treated nor paid like one.[16]

There was nothing new about children and youth working for little or no monetary compensation. Prior to the nineteenth century, those bound out as apprentices often worked in exchange for training, along with room and board and rudimentary education. But the economic transformations in the first half of the nineteenth century altered the nature and meaning of children's labor. With the rise of waged labor and a cash-based economy, the idea that children should honor their parents' financial and emotional support with obedience and hard work gradually came to seem less like the natural order of things. At the same time, the decline of indentured servitude and apprenticeships meant that bound labor became all but synonymous with the singular status of the enslaved. Especially when parents "rented out" their children, the distinction between minor children and the enslaved could seem vanishingly slim. Legally, parents owned their children's labor, not the children themselves. But to unhappy youths chafing under parental control or subject to corporal punishment, this may have felt like a distinction without a difference.

The war provided new opportunities for male youths who wanted to resist their subordination. In September 1861, Elisha Stockwell attended a war meeting at the log schoolhouse in his hometown of Alma, Wisconsin; when volunteers were called for, he stepped forward with his close friend, sixteen-year-old Edgar Houghton. But to Elisha's mortification, his father demanded that his name be struck from the list. Back home, his sister dressed him down as a "little snotty boy" for acting so foolishly, to which he snapped back, "I'll go and show you I am not the little boy you think I am." Eventually, Elisha calmed down and negotiated a compromise: he would remain at home so long as he could attend school that winter. But winter found him camping out near a coal pit with his father, who had taken a job burning charcoal for blacksmiths. In February, Mr. Stockwell ordered his son, who could handle their oxen team "as well as a man," to travel the 15 miles back to Alma to fetch supplies. Once home, Elisha learned that his friend's father, who had enlisted alongside his son, was home on furlough. Seizing his chance, Elisha paid the older man a visit and explained that he wanted to accompany him back to the military camp but needed help covering the train fare. At first Mr. Houghton demurred, warning him that minors had to obtain parental consent. But when Elisha made clear that he intended to join the army even if he had to walk the 200 miles to reach the camp, Mr. Houghton relented. Soon thereafter, Elisha was mustered into the 14th Wisconsin Volunteer Infantry.[17]

In both a positive and negative sense, Elisha's experiences as an unpaid laborer propelled his enlistment. Although he wanted to attend school, he instead had to work at a dirty and unpleasant outdoor job in the frigid Wisconsin winter. And though he had demonstrated a grown man's competence in meeting the responsibilities thrust upon him, he remained under his father's thumb. Such arrangements, in which parents expected sons to shoulder heavy loads, even as they denied them the fruits of their labor, inevitably fostered frustration and resentment. But they also equipped youths to act upon such feelings, for it was through their labor that many came to understand their own value and strength. Had Elisha not already proven that he could keep up with the men, he probably would not have spoken to Edgar's father so audaciously, nor would Mr. Houghton have been willing to hear him out and help facilitate his enlistment. Elisha's rebellion also points to the ways in which the war eroded parental authority. Perhaps he felt justified in running off because his father had reneged on the promise to allow him to attend school. But even the fact that the two had negotiated such an arrangement as the price that Mr. Stockwell would have to pay to keep his son home points to the attenuated nature of his authority. The war did not lessen families' economic reliance on their children's labor, but it made it easier and more socially acceptable for youths to free themselves from parental control.

Similar experience paved the way for Arthur J. Robinson, another Wisconsin boy, to enlist in the Union army at the age of sixteen or seventeen. As the first-born child, Arthur began to help his father when he was still quite young. In the late 1850s, Mr. Robinson rented a farm to earn extra income, and, as Arthur explained in his memoir, "I, a boy of 13 years of age, was made a full hand and did the greater part of the spring work, while father worked at his trade." Later, his father rented him out as a hired hand. Once the war began, Mr. Robinson enlisted and charged his oldest son with acting as "the mainstay of the family," but he soon fell ill and returned home. Arthur then proposed that they switch places: his father could resume his role as head of the household, while he represented the family in the military. Given how much Mr. Robinson had relied upon him in the past, it would have strained credulity had he tried to insist that Arthur was too young to take up arms. In any case, he had a compelling reason to consent, for in the meantime his second-born son, just fourteen years old but large for his age, had run off and joined the army. Mr. Robinson had already retrieved the boy once, only to see him repeat the offense. Concluding that it would be impossible to hold him back, the exasperated but anxious father made a calculated decision: he allowed his responsible eldest son to enlist and tasked him with watching over the free-spirited younger one.[18]

As the Robinsons' story indicates, the work duties and military obligations shouldered by fathers and their teenage sons sometimes proved interchangeable, especially in rural areas.[19] Especially after the draft was instituted, many families made decisions about who should stay home and who should enlist based on their collective needs and individual members' perceived hardiness, paying little heed to official age restrictions. John Allan Wyeth's father, for instance, convinced his sixteen-year-old son to delay enlisting in the

Confederate Army for a year by arguing that he was still "small of stature." Instead, Mr. Wyeth himself enlisted, leaving John to act as "the man of the family" in their home in Huntsville, Alabama. But in the end, John would prove the more robust of the two; like Mr. Robinson, Mr. Wyeth soon succumbed to illness and returned home, and in August 1862, his seventeen-year-old son took his place in the ranks.[20]

The closer a youth came to self-sufficiency, the stronger his case for making his own decisions in regard to military service. In the eyes of the law, those who fully supported themselves and no longer lived under the parental roof were fully emancipated.[21] But more typically, youths below the age of eighteen lived away from home for just part of the year or part of the week, remaining under their fathers' control to a greater or lesser extent.[22] Seventeen-year-old Elbridge Copp lived in this state of semi-dependence when attending school and working for his older brothers at their bookstore in Nashua, New Hampshire. Most nights he slept in an attic room above the store, but he sometimes returned to the family home in the countryside when school was not in session. After Elbridge decided to enlist, he first convinced an officer who was raising a company—and initially judged him "rather young and rather small for a soldier"—that he could be of service as a clerk. Only after devising this plan did he speak to his father. Mr. Copp reluctantly consented to the enlistment, with "the understanding that I was not to be in the ranks in the event of a battle." Yet he did consent. Had his son been more reliant on him for shelter and subsistence, Mr. Copp may have felt more empowered to forbid his enlistment outright. And had Elbridge been living a less independent life, he perhaps would not have felt so emboldened as to approach an officer and plead his case, especially prior to consulting his father. But because social custom and the law alike recognized separate residency and self-support as signaling emancipation from minority, Elbridge was in a stronger position to negotiate than many underage youths. In the end, he did not uphold his part of the bargain with his father: by June 1862, he had fought in his first battle, and in January 1863, he became a commissioned officer at the age of eighteen years and five months.[23]

The story of John H. Crowder, who did not survive the war to detail his youthful feats, is even more remarkable. At the age of sixteen, John became a commissioned officer in the 1st Louisiana Native Guards, a longstanding militia of free Blacks in New Orleans that was called into federal service after the city fell to Union control in the summer of 1862. Unlike the later-established USCT, Native Guard units were commanded by Black company officers who from the outset earned the same wages as white officers of equal rank.[24] John's salary of $105 a month was a far cry from the $5 a month he had earned when he first began working as a steamboat cabin boy at the age of eight. It was also a huge step up from the position he had held at the beginning of the war as a porter for a jewelry store, which earned him $25 a month. His mother, understandably proud, appears to have boasted of his success, leading John to anxiously reprove her: "never from this day tell any one my *age* under no circumstances . . . if you do you ruin me." Still, he clearly shared her pride, as he went on to muse, "If Abraham Lincoln Knew that a colored Lad of my age, could command a company, what would he say. [N]one would believe my exact age." What allowed John to become an officer was his unusual education; at an early age, a minister who discerned his promise singled him out for tutoring. But what allowed him to command men with confidence when still so young was at least in part a product of the self-reliance he acquired while working to provide for his mother.[25]

Like John, some of those who served underage recounted a degree of youthful pluck and initiative that would be hard to credit were it not for the idiosyncratic details they relate, along with collaborating census data and military records. George Ulmer, for example, described himself as a fourteen-year-old "midget of a newsboy" hawking papers on the streets of New York when the war began. That fall, his mother died, and his father, believing in the salutary influence of country life, purchased a farm in Maine and sent his four sons to live there. Under the charge of two hired men, the boys were tasked with clearing the heavily wooded land and building a house and barn. George detested the work and soon determined to become a drummer. When rejected by the enlisting officers as too small, he simply moved on to the neighboring town to try again, a strategy he could pursue only because he had raised enough money cutting down and selling hoop poles to purchase an old horse and rig. An irritated officer finally ordered enlistment papers drawn up so that "the young devil" could "go and get killed." Outfitted with a much-too-large uniform, George looked ridiculous, as he later acknowledged in his memoir. But it easy to see how a boy who had yelled out headlines on street corners and haggled with grown men might think himself capable of withstanding the hardships of military life.[26]

Seventeen-year-old Enos B. Vail, who joined a New York militia regiment at the war's outset, had also learned self-reliance on the job prior to his enlistment. In the winter of 1860–1861, Enos hauled hemlock bark to tanneries located some 12 to 14 miles away, boarding with a farm family to be closer to the woods. His memoir opens with a description of his typical workday. Braving the frigid cold, he rose at 5 a.m. to feed and harness a pair of horses that pulled his sleigh. Some ten hours later, he had completed his journey and returned to the hemlock stands, where he loaded up once more to prepare for an early start the following morning. His work required strength, stolidity in the face of trying weather conditions, and the ability to cope with unexpected adversity, as when one of the horses suddenly dropped dead, or his sleigh toppled over. Enos does not explain why, in a book that otherwise focuses almost entirely on his time in the military, he opens by describing these experiences, but the reason is not hard to fathom. Like many other memoirists who detailed the labor they performed as youths, he clearly saw this period of his life as an important prequel to the story of his enlistment and military service—one that in some sense prepared him for the hardships he would face as a soldier.[27]

This tendency to associate the capacity for labor with a fitness for military service was memorably expressed by a father whose twelve-year-old son, Stanton P. Allen, pestered him for permission to enlist. Mr. Allen did not tell him, "You are too young," although he surely thought so; what he said was, "They don't take boys who can't hoe a man's row." The following year, a cousin who had been wounded at Shiloh came to convalesce at the family's farmstead in eastern New York. Stanton sat by the soldier's bedside and listened, completely rapt, as he told battlefield stories and sang popular patriotic songs. Soon the thirteen-year-old's war fever had soared to "one hundred and twenty degrees in the shade." He ran off and enlisted, only to have his father retrieve him with a writ of habeas corpus—an incident written up as a humorous vignette in the local paper.[28] Another year brought yet another relapse. This time, Stanton understood that he would need to travel farther afield to avoid detection. Teaming up with some local friends, one of whom was also underage, he crossed the state line to join a Massachusetts cavalry company being formed by some Williams College students. In November 1863, he was mustered into service at the age of fourteen years, nine months. Incredibly, his military records show that he somehow passed himself off as a twenty-one-year-old.[29]

Given his chutzpah, it is fair to assume that Stanton would have tried to enlist no matter what his father said. But it is worth stressing that Mr. Allen had left the door to underage enlistment ever-so-slightly ajar by suggesting that the ability to work, not age, was what qualified a youth for military service. After all, what about boys who *could* hoe a man's row? By late 1863, with two years of "vigorous training in farm work" behind him, Stanton probably believed that he met that criteria, and indeed he may well have.[30] Such confidence borne of experience, whether misplaced or not, is what gave so many youths the wherewithal to put themselves forward—to march into an enlistment office "like a young Napoleon," as George Ulmer amusedly described his former self—and stare down a skeptical officer if pressed.[31]

By the time veterans wrote their memoirs, a celebration of Civil War era boy soldiers had been underway for several decades. To varying degrees, memoirists would have been conscious of this cultural construct and how it might shape the expectations that readers brought to their works. Thus, when Elisha Stockwell opened his memoir by immediately divulging his age, he was responding in part to relatives in the present day who, impressed that he had served while so young, urged him to record his recollections. But what came next—his assertation that he "could rake and bind and keep up with the men," along with a parenthetical explanation, "They cut the grain with cradles then"—carries readers back to the time of his childhood. In an era before mechanical reapers, when physical strength and stamina were in great demand, the youth who could keep up with the men was no longer a "small boy," whatever his numerical age. He could venture a claim—not to manhood exactly, but to a certain level of self-determination—that enlistment officers and society more broadly were inclined to recognize, regardless of the dictates of the law.

A Youth-Oriented Political Culture

Just as many boys and youths worked side-by-side with adults, so they inhabited the same political world as their elders. Audiences at political speeches and events almost always included substantial numbers of children and youth, as evidenced by lithographs and other illustrations from the period. In part, these portrayals simply reflected demography: those below age twenty constituted over half the population. The sheer prevalence of young people underlay the era's distinctive "youth-oriented" political culture, in which campaigners vied for the attention of even young schoolboys.[32] Without understanding this aspect of nineteenth-century democratic politics, it is impossible to fully grasp the phenomenon of youth enlistment during the Civil War. For many underage soldiers in both the United States and the Confederacy, enlistment represented the logical, almost inescapable consequence of a political culture that assiduously courted the young.

For political operatives, the flashy attractions that seemed to target children were simply gateways to a far more extensive process of education and acculturation. A short memoir by James Sullivan of Carlisle, Pennsylvania, who unsuccessfully tried to enlist at the age of thirteen, shows how boys' coming of age tended to be inextricably linked with the dawning of political consciousness. From his "earliest years," James recalled overhearing adults arguing about slavery and its potential expansion into the western territories. In 1856, the "four months' season of hot politics" preceding the election initiated the eight-year-old into "the rituals of party parading, banner raising, badge wearing, and boys' electioneering by fisticuffs." By the 1860 election, the twelve-year-old had matured enough to take an interest in the political speeches. And four years after that, the sixteen-year-old agonized over whether to remain a loyal Democrat, as his beloved older brother had been, or to "turn Republican" and support Lincoln's re-election. Torn between conflicting impulses, he found himself "continually in a fever of uncertainty as to my political duty."[33] In short, James' political development progressed through a series of stages over a period of eight years: as a mere boy, he reveled in the spectacle of all; as an older boy, he began to contemplate the issues; and as a stripling who longed to be in the army, he considered his party affiliation a matter of the utmost gravity, though it would be five more years before he could actually cast a ballot.

Boys came into political awareness early because they were so often present in the spaces where men discussed the news of the day. James Henry Hammock of Rockingham, Virginia (now West Virginia), offhandedly acknowledged this mingling of generations when he noted that newspapers could be found "in the stores, post offices, blacksmith shops, shoe shops and wherever men and boys would congregate to hear the news and discuss questions at issue."[34] One such site was a shoe and boot store in Knox County, Missouri, where sixteen-year-old James K. P. DeBord worked alongside his father. A subscriber to several papers, Mr. DeBord was "well posted on the issues of the war" and often debated "the political out-look" with customers as his son listened in.[35] Even schoolboys too young for serious work lurked in the spaces where adult men congregated and listened as their elders read aloud from the newspaper. President William B. McKinley, who enlisted at age eighteen, frequented a tannery in his hometown of Poland, Ohio, from the time he was a "mere boy," engaging in "warm controversies on the slavery question."[36] And when Theodore Upson's father forbade him from hanging out at the town bookstore, where he habitually went after school, he complained in his diary that he hated having to come straight home, "for I like hear the talk."[37] So long as boys were old enough not be a nuisance, men accepted their presence and sometimes even allowed them to partake in their conversations.

In the southern states, adults also encouraged boys and youth to join the broader political culture, though this dynamic seems to have played out within more narrow class parameters. David E. Johnston of Monroe County, Virginia (now West Virginia), who joined the Confederate army at age sixteen, began his memoir by situating himself in relation to the brewing political conflict: "As a boy, but little more than fifteen years of age, I heard and learned much of the pre-election news [in 1860], as well as read the newspapers." The prospect of secession and war dominated "everyday conversation" among David's schoolmates, many of whom "talked learnedly" on political issues. Following Lincoln's election, the school formed a debating society that zeroed in on the question foremost in everyone's minds: "Shall Virginia Secede from the Union?"[38] The fact that prominent men from the community attended the debates and served as judges suggests how seriously the elite took these "would-be statesmen." As a seventeen-year-old student, Josiah Staunton Moore of Jefferson Male Academy in Richmond, Virginia, also evinced "great interest in public debates." Prominent planter Williams C. Wickham, who would serve as a Confederate general in the Civil War, "kindly gave" the youth a visitor's ticket to Virginia's Secession Convention, which he regularly attended to hear the "exciting debates." When word of the fall of Fort Sumter reached the city on the night of April 13, Josiah joined the throng gathered outside the state capitol for a "grand illumination and torch-light parade" that occurred amid "great rejoicing and speech-making."[39]

Because boys' interest in politics drew them into actual public squares, they were often on hand to witness such momentous events. They experienced not only the memorable celebrations that marked the war's outset, but also the scenes of horror and bloodshed that soon followed. Fifteen-year-old Philip Stephenson and his schoolmates, for example, survived the Camp Jackson Affair—a bloody street clash in St. Louis involving federal troops, the pro-Confederate Missouri State Guard, and civilians that left twenty-eight dead and nearly one hundred wounded. Prior to the killings, Philip had resisted the pull of secession; like many border-state residents, he supported John Bell and the Constitutional Union Party in the 1860s election, and in early

1861, he presented a school essay railing against both northern abolitionists and southern fire-eaters. The Camp Jackson Affair, however, cemented his allegiance to the Confederacy and left him "in a fever to get away." The fact that many of his peers were either enlisting in the Union army or slipping out of the city to join the Confederates, as he and his older brother would in August 1861, only intensified his impatience.[40]

A closer look at Philip Stephenson's narrative illuminates yet another reason why he and thousands of youths like him became so fixated on joining the army: their ability to observe troops at close range. In his memoir, Philip initially implies that he and his friends had simply found themselves in the wrong place at the wrong time. But it soon becomes clear that they had actually been going to the camp every day after school, sneaking past the guards to watch the men train and to visit their friends and relatives. Unimaginable today, this permeability between military and civilian life, rooted in the tradition of community-based militia, played a key role in stoking youths' war fever. Take the case of Will B. Smith, "a wiry lad of thirteen" in the summer of 1861, when Col. Ulysses Grant and the 21st Illinois Infantry Regiment briefly set up shop outside his hometown of Naples, Illinois. Drawn to the "attractive drilling and maneuvering of the regiment by its gallant commander," Will soon befriended Grant's son, eleven-year-old Fred. When not otherwise engaged in exploring the camp and its surroundings, the two boys were "often about" the colonel's tent. Because of these experiences, Will entered a familiar realm, not a forbidding adult institution, when he enlisted two years later at the age of fifteen.[41]

Even before the war, Americans in both regions of the country encouraged boys' passion for militarism. The mid-to-late 1850s witnessed something of a craze for boys' military companies, which suddenly seemed to spring up everywhere. There was some precedent for this development; many antebellum militia companies had boys' auxiliaries, and antebellum fire companies typically included "volunteer aides" as young as ten years old. But the companies that emerged in the years immediately preceding the war reflected growing sectional tensions. John Wise, whose father served as governor of Virginia between 1856 and 1860, recalled how his older brother and another young man had decided to establish a "boys' soldier company" of youths ages twelve to sixteen. Governor Wise supported the plan and ordered that a hundred old muskets in the armory be cut down to a size that boys could handle. Outfitted in neat, gray uniforms and designated the "Guard of the Metropolis," the company became "one of the most striking institutions of

Richmond," according to Wise. (Too young at age nine to carry even a modified musket, John served as the flag bearer.)[42] The company's first public
performance attracted "hundreds of ladies and gentlemen," according to the
Richmond Dispatch, which praised the boys' "martial bearing and soldiery
decorum while going through a variety of military maneuvers."[43] In other
words, even quite young boys won praise and garnered public attention for
presenting themselves as soldiers-in-training.

Although a particularly marked streak of militarism has been attributed
to the antebellum southern states, similar boy companies existed throughout
the north as well. In 1858, for instance, fifteen-year-old Robert Lincoln
joined an organization called the Springfield Cadets, a military company
"whose primary purpose was to march in parades, such as the annual
event celebrating George Washington's birthday."[44] Boys and youth also
flocked to the Wide Awakes, a pro-Lincoln voluntary association that wore
uniforms, practiced drills, and organized themselves along military lines.[45]
Pascal Gilmore described how the Wide Awakes of Dedham, Maine, spent
the summer and fall of 1860 drilling and pursuing other kinds of military
"training." They dutifully studied the work of Winfield Scott, most likely his
popular *Infantry Tactics*, which Pascal claimed gave him a solid foundation
to build on when he subsequently enlisted at the age of sixteen.[46]

Given the prevalence of junior military organizations, including those
that welcomed boys barely in their teens, it is no surprise that children and
youths clamored to offer their services as the political crisis escalated. Still, it
is striking to view signatures reflecting the painstaking efforts of very young
children on a letter to Alabama's Governor A. B. Moore that was written soon
after the state seceded in January 1861. The signatories—twenty-one boys,
ranging in age from eight to fourteen, who called themselves the Canebrake
Cadets—solemnly offered up their services to the state. They acknowledged
being too young to take to the field with regular troops, but they believed they
could be of assistance should the state be invaded and asked to be supplied
with "suitable arms."[47]

As all of this suggests, for most underage soldiers who served during the
Civil War, joining the army represented the final stage of a process of politicization and militarization that had begun months if not years before. In ret-
rospect, veterans themselves identified their prewar engagement in partisan
politics and military companies as important factors that prepared them to
enlist. They also recognized how distant the world of their youth had come
to seem by the late nineteenth and early twentieth centuries. "The boys of my

age were . . . in good part educated in American political life. Some of them could already talk their party principles just like their fathers!," wrote James Sullivan, the exclamation point underscoring the chasm between past and present.[48] Likewise, John Wise anticipated and sought to pre-empt readers' skepticism concerning his childhood engagement with political questions. "I hear you exclaim, 'Now what possible interest could a presidential election possess for a boy ten years old?'" he wrote. "You ask that question because you do not know the society I am describing."[49] These memoirists strained to evoke the bygone social and political culture of the 1850s and early 1860s, because they believed that younger readers would need that context to understand the powerful forces that led them to defy parents or guardians, swear a false oath, and violate military policy.

To say that Civil War era youths' political interests and activities paved the way to their enlistment is not, however, to claim that all of them enlisted due to ideological beliefs. Some clearly did act on deeply held convictions, but most boys were influenced by society in more nebulous ways. Because mid-nineteenth-century American political cultural was so age-inclusive, native-born white boys early on imbibed the notion that they had a role to play in the public life of their communities. Already primed to respond to the drama of political campaigns, they refused to be shunted to the sidelines as the nation careened toward war and the militarized politics of the late 1850s morphed into actual military mobilization.

Schools and the Facilitation of Youth Enlistment

Burdened with the name Andrew Jackson Andrews, "Jack" grew up steeped in the nation's political and military history. His father had served with distinction as a captain of artillery in the War of 1812, and his grandfather commanded troops at the Battle of Yorktown. Given what he himself called his "pedigree," the native Virginian surprised no one when he enlisted to the fight the Yankees in June 1861 at the age of eighteen. But his memoir dates the beginning of his "military career" several years earlier, when he served proudly as a first lieutenant of the Cappahoosie Military Academy cadet corps. His revered teacher and commander, a graduate of the Virginia Military Institute, taught him and his fellow cadets to appreciate the importance of "neatness" and diligently put them through their paces. Their "gallant little corps," Andrews boasted, would have rivaled the US Army's best regiments in its mastery of drills and military maneuvers.[50] Although he went on to attend another school and had started a clerkship before the outbreak of the war, Andrews drew a direct line between his experiences as a military school cadet and his enlistment in the Confederate army.

For many Civil War–era boys and youth, schools played a key role in sparking or fueling their desire to enlist.[51] Boys enrolled in military academies, where students wore uniforms and the institutional structure mimicked the military's hierarchy, no doubt felt especially compelled by the mobilization for war.[52] But common schools were also sites of politicization and militarization.[53] The proverbial one-room schoolhouse encouraged "the kind of social mixing on which popular politics thrived," while drawing together children and youths of all ages, from "uninformed toddlers" to "virgin voters."[54] Aside from churches, schools were also among the only gathering sites in many small towns. Communities often held war meetings at the local schoolhouse, and newly enlisted troops frequently drilled on school grounds before reporting to more distant camps. A boy might therefore enlist under the same roof where he had recently delivered a patriotic recitation at the annual Exhibition Day, or learn to drill on the same grounds where he had recently played at recess.

Even before the war began, schools emerged as hotbeds of political enthusiasm, particularly in the future Confederate states, where students often voiced pro-secessionist sentiments while administrators, teachers, and professors counselled restraint.[55] During the 1860 presidential campaign, the cadets at the recently established North Carolina Military Institute in Charlotte were gripped by "so much excitement" that they made "very little advancement" in their studies, according to James Dinkins, a fifteen-year-old Mississippian who had enrolled that fall. After Lincoln's election, "All kinds of stories of insurrection" circulated around the school, including one alleging that local Black residents were plotting to seize the arsenal that the cadets were charged with guarding.[56] Students at William and Mary also reacted to the election with alarm, immediately requesting permission to form a college militia.[57] Meanwhile, in Loudoun County, Virginia, a mere 12 miles from the site of John Brown's raid, Luther W. Hopkins and his schoolmates were constantly "gathering in groups at noon and recess, on the way to and from school, and talking war" even before Virginia's secession conference convened.[58]

As soon as the fighting began, one Confederate would later recall, "every university, college, and common school in the South" became a site for "converting their pupils into soldiers."[59] In July 1861, the Confederate Congress authorized the enlistment of the entire student body of the state-supported North Carolina Military Institute, specifying only that the cadets had to obtain parental consent. This unusual move came several months after the governor granted the school's president, Daniel H. Hill, permission to form a regiment, which became the 1st North Carolina Volunteers, and charged him with organizing a military training camp in Raleigh. Hill thereupon announced that the school would temporarily close and instructed all cadets who wanted to serve as drill masters to obtain their parents' consent to enlist. James Dinkins, who still secretly cried at night because he so desperately missed his mother, knew his parents would never agree to his enlistment. But older cadets egged him on, until he finally determined "to risk all" by allowing one of them to forge a telegram from his father granting consent. Soon thereafter, James and the other cadets were in the state capital putting grown men through their paces.[60]

It is easy enough to see how cadets at state military academies ended up in the army, but even schools like Spring Hills College in Mobile, Alabama— a Catholic boarding school where Confederate elites sent boys as young as nine in hopes of preventing their enlistment—had trouble holding on to students.[61] Records left by its Jesuit administrators help to explain why. The school celebrated the taking of Fort Sumter as "a great holiday" at which senior cadets performed drills and shot off "little Boys' guns." When word that Virginia had seceded reached the school, the students were granted an extra half hour of recreation and served punch at supper, during which two boys, emotionally roused by the occasion, delivered impromptu speeches. That July, when the Confederates trounced Union troops at Bull Run, the school gave the student body the entire day off to bask in the victory. Did administrators purposely seek to foster boys' commitment to the war effort, or were they simply mirroring or bowing to the sentiments of the community and the boys themselves? Whatever the case, the school log reveals the results: multiple entries make note of students running off to join the army or to return home in hope of gaining parental approval to enlist.[62]

War fever swept through common schools and private academies in the United States as well, leading to the formation of all manner of drill clubs and military companies. Here again, wartime developments amplified preexisting trends. Pedagogues like the Episcopalian priest N. W. Taylor Root championed the benefits of military training for both public and private schools during the 1850s, parrying "the many objections" raised by both

THE LITTLE CONFEDERATE.

Figure 6.1 Sixteen-year old James Dinkins (1845–1939) of Canton, Mississippi, attended the North Carolina Military Institute and is shown here in his cadet uniform. In the early days of the war, it was common to see Confederate youths of his age leading adult men in drills. Reproduced in *1861 to 1865, by an Old Johnnie. Personal Recollections and Experiences in the Confederate Army* (Cincinnati: R. Clarke Co., 1897). Retrieved from Internet Archive.

parents and teachers. In 1857, he published *School Amusements; or, How to Make the School Interesting*—essentially a revised version of Winfield Scott's *Infantry Tactics* that promised to make "Every Teacher His Own Drill Master." The war all but silenced anti-militarist opposition to such schemes; when Root published a very similar work in 1863, he gave it the far less euphemistic title, *Infantry Tactics for Schools: Explained and Illustrated for the Use of Teachers and Scholars.*[63]

Schools that did not already boast their own companies quickly acquired them once the war began.[64] As Jesse Bowman Young recalled, news of Fort Sumter "set the boys" at his Pennsylvania boarding school "clean crazy with

Figure 6.2 Frontispiece from N. W. Taylor Root's *Infantry Tactics for Schools: Explained and Illustrated for the Use of Teachers and Scholars* (New York: A.S. Barnes and Burr, 1863). Addressing the "Boy-Soldiers" he hoped to instruct, Root urged them to "BE MANLY! Neither laugh at others, nor make others laugh at you. Talk and laugh at other times, but at drill, leave *play* to the *children*." Retrieved from Hathitrust Digital Library.

patriotic excitement," prompting them to establish the Seminary Cadets.[65] High school students in Providence, Rhode Island, formed the Ellsworth Phalanx and engaged an aged veteran to teach them how to drill.[66] These school-affiliated companies not only taught boys rudimentary skills and stoked their desire to enlist, but also created rich veins that could be tapped by military recruiters. The Ellsworth Phalanx, for example, became what was essentially a feeder organization for the Union army, with Company B of the 10th Rhode Island Infantry regiment drawn "almost entirely from the ranks of the High School and [Brown] University companies."[67]

Some boys were even recruited by former teachers who had left their positions to serve in the military. Just as parents entrusted underage sons to the care of older brothers or other relatives in the army, so they hoped that former schoolteachers would protect their boys from both the dangers of the battlefield and the corruption of camp life. When Harry Kieffer's father reluctantly allowed him to enlist, he did so in part because his son assured him that he would be "in a company commanded by my own school-teacher, and composed of acquaintances who would look after me."[68] Thirteen-year-old Charles Howard Gardner employed similar reasoning to conquer his mother's objections to his enlistment as a drummer boy. A posthumous account celebrated the "ardent attachment" between Gardner and his company commander and former teacher, Simon C. Guild, who "guarded Charlie like a father." But of course, promises of protection counted for little in the context of war: Guild was eventually killed in battle, leaving his young charge to fend for himself, and some months later Charlie was struck by a stray bullet and died before reaching home.[69]

In the end, schools may have proven most effective at mobilizing underage youth simply by reminding those who remained that they had been left behind. Seventeen-year-old Nimrod Bramham Hamner felt bereft upon returning to the University of Virginia after a brief stint in the Confederate army, which had given him a medical discharge due to his poor health. "True I am not 18—True I am not perfectly healthy—and true a good many things," he wrote to his mother, beseeching her to allow him to re-enlist. "But . . . I can not study—All of my acquaintances (that are alive) are in the army."[70] Even the prospect of death, here parenthetically acknowledged, did not dampen youths' powerful desire to be among peers. When Harry Kieffer's company was preparing to leave town, they encountered his best friend and fellow classmate heading to school. A level-headed boy, Andy had repeatedly dismissed his more excitable friend's obsession with enlisting. But when he beheld his schoolmates and acquaintances on the verge of departing, Kieffer later recounted, "what did he do but run across the streets to an undertaker's shop, cram his schoolbooks through the broken window, and take his place in the line."[71] Seventeen-year-old C. Henry Barney of Rhode Island responded with similar alacrity when he chanced upon a former schoolmate sporting the Union army's distinctive blue greatcoat. Henry had resigned himself to civilian life after his parents twice stymied his attempts to enlist, but a half hour's conversation with his schoolmate reignited his desire. The very next day, he appeared at the camp where his friend was temporarily stationed and, with "a little finesse," got himself mustered into service.[72] The desire to join peers and the fear of being left behind were powerful motivators, capable of causing even serious students and dutiful sons to turn on a dime.

In both the United States and the Confederacy, schools were incubators of patriotic sentiment, social hubs for their communities, and sites where boys might receive basic military training. But above all, schools were places where young people congregated and formed relationships with one another that were not bound by specific ages or grade levels. Ties with older youths heightened underage boys' desires to enlist and provided them with critical information to act on those desires, such as the name of a recruiter who might willingly turn a blind eye to their age. Whether the setting be a New England common school, a Pennsylvania private academy, or a southern military school, neither parental resistance nor legal restrictions offered an effective check against war fever and the lure of youthful camaraderie.

* * *

In mid-nineteenth-century America, boys expected to serve a kind of informal apprenticeship on their way to independent manhood—to be among adult men, listening in to their political discussions, and to be directed toward jobs commensurate with their physical abilities. The fact that so many boys believed that they belonged in the army should not be taken to mean that they saw themselves as men. Rather, it shows that they did not see military service as a realm exclusive to adult males. As in the case of workplaces, they assumed that there was a role for them to play—a subordinate role, but a role nonetheless.

They were of course right about this. Today, when people view eighteen as marking a youth's entrée into adulthood, the importance of that threshold is reinforced by the alignment of the ages of legal emancipation, voting, and military service. People often bristle at laws that establish a higher age for certain activities, as in states with a minimum drinking age of twenty-one, protesting that someone old enough to bear arms should be treated as an adult in all respects. Nineteenth-century Americans did not think this way. Army physicians and parents may have lamented the enlistment of those in their late teens or even early twenties, but Americans had long expected boys and youths to bear arms before they could exercise the legal and political prerogatives of adulthood, just as they had long required them to perform taxing and difficult labor.

Historians have typically portrayed Union and Confederate soldiers as unmarried, young adult men who fought "for cause and comrades."[73] But the armies' ranks also included sixteen-year-olds Edward Spangler, who weighed in at ninety-two pounds on enlistment, and Edward Burgess Peirce, who asked his mother to send him copies of *Youth's Companion*.[74] Also present were seventeen-year-old Frank Millet, who recorded a diary entry noting, "Tonight we made a blanket elephant and had fun," and seventeen-year-old William Sallada, who joined friends in creating a makeshift bowling alley and playing with "spherical case shells" until one exploded, frightening them badly enough to abandon the game.[75] Conceptions of Civil War armies must be broad enough to take into account the presence of boys who could not carry heavy packs and still liked to play and romp.

If the social and cultural norms of the mid-nineteenth century propelled underage youths into the military, however, it also equipped people to deal with their presence. Individual boys often formed close relationships with older males who offered them a degree of protection and assistance. William Ellis wrote to his mother that he had been relieved of guard duty and that his only job at present was to cook for the captain and a lieutenant, explaining: "Davis got me this place sow it would not be sow hard for me."[76] Other sources point to more collective attempts to protect the youngest and weakest from the most strenuous or dangerous duties. Asked to comment on an appeal for the discharge of a fifteen-year-old boy in July 1863, a Confederate officer supported the request but conceded that he could not in good conscience claim that the boy suffered from any age-related "disability," since "by the common consent of the company he has never been required to perform the more arduous duties of the camp."[77] Certainly not all youths benefited from such protections. But for many enlistees, the same paths that led them to enlist meant that older relatives and neighbors would be present to oversee their behavior and ease their burdens when necessary.

PART III

MALE YOUTH AND MILITARY SERVICE DURING THE CIVIL WAR

7

Contrary to All Law

Debating Underage Service in the United States

A few months before the outbreak of the Civil War, leading abolitionist Richard Henry Dana gave a speech making clear that although Republicans wanted to prevent the spread of slavery, they had no interest in undermining the institution itself, since "domestic relations" were naturally outside the purview of federal regulation. "It is a fundamental principle of our government that all the domestic relations are matters of State control," he explained. This principle was "bound up, indissoluably, with all the domestic relations of every State,—with those of husband and wife, parent and child, master and servant, master and apprentice, and all the laws regulating labor, education, internal police, and the tenure and descent of property." The insulation of private households from distant authorities seemed so obvious to Dana that he could no more imagine the federal government seizing slaves than he could foresee household heads losing control of wives, children, or other dependents.[1]

Dana's assumption turned out to be wrong. Most Unionists would eventually come to accept that national survival hinged on eradicating slavery and that the federal government therefore had a compelling reason to reach into slaveholders' households and emancipate their bondspeople. In far less spectacular fashion, families across the United States faced major disruption, as hundreds of thousands of males below the age of majority enlisted in the military and thereby gained independence from parental control. Their newfound autonomy was not just physical but also legal: in the eyes of the law, a boy or youth who left his parents' home and struck out on his own became "emancipated," empowered to control his own movements and entitled to the fruits of his labor. By the 1860s, the rise of more sentimental conceptions of childhood had rendered the analogy between children and slaves distasteful, and aggrieved parents no longer overtly likened themselves to slaveholders as they had done during the War of 1812. Nonetheless, the analogy was not entirely hollow, for the labor of minors, like that of the enslaved, continued to be defined as property. When parents lost control of boys and youths to military service, many interpreted the federal government's refusal to return their children as an outrageous intrusion that robbed them of a valuable—and for some, essential—asset.

The erosion of parental rights for white Americans is among the less noted outcomes of the Civil War. It was bound up with two other historical shifts that have similarly received little attention but were even more momentous in the long run: the transformation of America's dual military system and the federalization of habeas corpus. Wartime mobilization all but obliterated the ideological division between militia duty and service in the regulars, rooted in an understanding of the former as radically distinct from the latter, geared toward local defense and justified as a counterweight to federal military power. Parents experienced this change most immediately, because the wartime transformation of militia laws theoretically mobilized all males above the age of eighteen into a national army. At the same time, federal officials responded to parents' lawsuits for the discharge of minors by advocating for a highly contentious legal transformation that would deprive local and state courts of their longstanding power to grant habeas relief to federal detainees. During the war, these efforts were unsuccessful, with the suspension of habeas corpus only temporarily halting state and local courts from supporting parents' efforts to reclaim underage soldiers. But in 1872, the US Supreme Court referred to wartime disruptions caused by enlisted minors as the rationale for federalizing habeas corpus—a centralizing process that, much like the consolidation of military power, turned out to be permanent. Establishing the legal basis that enabled the US military to expand, these twin shifts had implications that extend to the present.

Histories of mobilization during the Civil War have little to say about underage enlistment. They tend to focus on soldiers' motivations, draft riots, and desertion, or on the stunning social transformation brought about by Black enlistment.[2] The assumption seems to be that questions around age were straightforward, with males above eighteen immediately allowed to enlist and only a few below that age signing up as musicians or using subterfuge to sneak into the ranks. In truth, the issue of underage enlistment was extraordinarily contentious. A constant stream of parents badgered military and political authorities for the release of their children, either in person or by letter, while lawsuits demanding the discharge of underage soldiers clogged state and local court dockets. Indeed, parental appeals consumed so much administrative and military attention and caused so much legal strife that they were one of the main grounds for the nationwide suspension of habeas corpus.

The push-and-pull between parents and federal officials over underage enlistees was so enduring because young males had enormous value to those on both sides. The government could have followed the antebellum precedent and simply discharged all youths whose parents or guardians offered convincing proof that they were underage and had enlisted without consent. Instead, they supported contradictory policies that made a difficult issue increasingly intractable. The likeliest reason for the government's contortions is the simplest one—the sheer number of underage enlistees. As the calculations laid out in the appendices suggest, around 10 percent of Union soldiers were below the age of eighteen when they entered the service; releasing this volume of soldiers threatened to wreak havoc on military strength and morale. But if officials were unwilling to hand out discharges on demand, they were equally reluctant to advocate for a lower enlistment age—a proposal that would have met with widespread and impassioned resistance. After all, parents who demanded the return of minor enlistees acted not only out of concern that their particular child was ill-suited to military life, but also because they relied so heavily on young men's labor and earnings. The struggles over this valuable cohort thus spotlight the challenge that centralizing military power posed to parental rights, while also illuminating one of the war's most enduring yet least often noted transformations—the federalization of habeas corpus and the corresponding loss of local oversight over the US military.

Confronting an "Epidemic" of Young Enlistees

Throughout the nineteenth century, military authorities had grappled with the problem of underage recruits, lawsuits demanding their discharge, and congressional aversion to siding with military officials over parents. These problems grew infinitely worse amid the rapid and chaotic mobilization for war. At the conflict's outset, the regular army and navy were minuscule, poorly equipped, and governed by "ancient bureaucratic routine." Even more dysfunctional was the state-based militia system designed to supplement the regulars, which limped along with debilities accrued over decades of fiscal and administrative neglect.[3] On April 15, 1861, just days after the firing on Fort Sumter, President Lincoln called 75,000 militiamen between the ages of eighteen and forty-five into federal service for three-month terms—the maximum length of time he could request under the Militia Act of 1795. Then in May, Lincoln requested that states raise an additional 60,000 volunteers to supplement the regular army's 16,000 enlistees, bypassing the constitutional mandate that granted only Congress the power to raise troops. When Congress reconvened in July, it not only retrospectively endorsed the president's action but also voted to dramatically expand the call to 500,000 volunteers. Meanwhile, states had begun raising volunteer regiments based on either one-, two-, or three-year enlistments, calling on civilian associations to help fund and equip the rapidly assembling force. By the time the Union army took to the field at Bull Run, it therefore encompassed both regulars who signed up for five years and volunteers and militiamen who had signed up for terms ranging between three months and three years. These men had received wildly diverse amounts of training, carried all manner of equipment, and dressed in a plethora of different uniforms, looking somewhat like "a circus on parade."[4]

Among this motley crew were many thousands of minors who took advantage of the highly decentralized mobilization process to finagle their way into the ranks. Since the War Department lacked a legal mandate to expand the regulars and the bureaucratic infrastructure to mobilize troops directly, the government largely depended on states to oversee this process. In turn, the disarray of state militia systems meant that the states looked to men of means or influence who expected to become officers in volunteer regiments. Delivering rousing speeches and often underwriting the expense of equipping a company or regiment, these self-appointed leaders would gather the requisite number of men and then present their ready-formed unit to the governor for approval. Competing with one another to organize companies and regiments, communities initially paid little heed to army regulations. At the war's outset, regulations stated that all volunteers below the age of twenty-one required the consent of a parent, guardian, or master, who were to sign the recruit's enlistment papers. Regulations also stipulated that every recruit had to be between the ages of eighteen and thirty-five (or above age twelve for musicians), at least 5 feet, 4.5 inches tall, of sound mind and morals, and an English speaker. Recruiters were sternly warned to be "very particular in ascertaining the true age of the recruit."[5]

Although the rules were clear, those tasked with building a gigantic army overnight regularly disregarded them. Across the military hierarchy, countless individuals facilitated the enlistment of boys and underage youths, ignoring the evidence before their eyes or neglecting to investigate in cases of genuine uncertainty. Medical examinations that might have uncovered information about age tended to be cursory at best, as the clandestine enlistment of hundreds of women demonstrates.[6] Delavan Miller later claimed that he was never examined before being mustered into service in March 1862 at the age of thirteen; he and other new recruits were simply "merged into the company without any formalities" at all.[7] Sixteen-year-old Robert Goldthwaite Carter was rejected "on account of an honest confession of his true age" when he tried to enlist in a Massachusetts regiment in the summer of 1862. Three weeks later, he tried again, claiming to have "gained *two years* in that period," and the very same enlisting officer "eagerly accepted" him into service.[8]

The scruples of military surgeons varied just as widely as those of recruiters. At sixteen, Edward Spangler stood five feet, two inches tall and weighed ninety-two pounds as he stood naked facing an army surgeon, who informed him that he did not meet the height regulation. Spangler immediately raised himself on tiptoe and urged, "Try it again," whereupon the surgeon gave him a wink and obliged.[9] Without the complicity of such individuals, underage enlistment in the Union army could never have occurred on such a mass scale. Even as enlistment and mustering practices became more streamlined over time, many recruiters and surgeons continued to look the other way when it came to beardless youths claiming to be orphans or above the legal age. Motivated by declining volunteerism, the need to fill enlistment quotas, and sometimes by bribes, they set aside whatever reservations they may have entertained.[10]

If some officials were willing to waive underage youths into the ranks, however, many parents were unwilling to let them go. From the war's earliest months, angry and distraught parents inundated the government with letters demanding the discharge of their sons. Constituting more than a quarter of the correspondence that flowed between civilians and the War Department in the war's first two years, parental appeals were far too numerous and impassioned to be dismissed.[11] Equally impossible to discount were the many who tried to plead their case in person, often travelling for miles to implore the president to release a young son, or appearing at a son's army camp and demanding the right to take him home.[12] Masses of parents also besieged local courts, requesting writs of habeas corpus in such numbers as to overwhelm the judicial system. Just a few days after the first Battle of Bull Run, Judge Joseph Allison of Philadelphia complained that his time was "now occupied solely by the hearing of writs of *habeas corpus* in cases of minors."[13]

The following month, the *New York Times* described "The Plea of Infancy" in courtrooms as "An Epidemic."[14] By the end of 1861, local courts in some areas were daily releasing multiple underage enlistees; such cases were so routine that the press usually did not even report them.[15]

Whether they petitioned the War Department or sought recourse through the courts, most parents initially assumed they would achieve their objective.[16] As one father wrote to Secretary of War Simon Cameron, "I have been assured that an application to your honr will ensure his Emediate discharge."[17] Throughout the spring and summer of 1861, those who followed proper procedures and submitted official affidavits did often succeed in recovering their children, including young men between the ages of eighteen and twenty-one. In fact, some parents felt so assured of their prerogatives that they actually allowed war-crazed sons who ran off and joined locally raised regiments to stay and train with them while stationed in the general vicinity, confident that they could pull them out the moment the troops were ordered south. Elijah and Mary Boyers displayed such reasoning in a letter addressed to President Lincoln concerning their sixteen-year-old son Alden. When the boy first absconded in 1862 and joined a regiment stationed in Buffalo, his father retrieved him, gaining the mustering officer's assurance that, should Alden return, he would reject him. But when Alden did come back, he was instead promptly mustered into service. This time, the Boyers explained to Lincoln, "his Father thought best to let him stay a while till his war fever had left him," since rumor held that the soldiers would not be leaving Buffalo. Upon learning that the regiment had in fact removed to Washington, the Boyers grew frantic.[18] Because they had never formally consented, they apparently believed they could allow Alden to experience military life while still retaining their control. Like many other parents of underage enlistees, they would discover that they had overestimated the strength of parental rights in relation to the newly empowered federal government.

In light of prewar precedents, the Boyers' expectations were not unreasonable. They probably viewed their son's actions in the context of the nation's militia tradition, in which young males joined older ones in training without ever leaving the state or severing connections to home and family. The Boyers certainly had no reason to suppose that a contract signed by their young son, rather than themselves, would carry weight, since common-law traditions typically imbued parents with substantial authority over children below the age of majority. This reality helps to account for how some parents framed their appeals. One father who sent a sworn affidavit to the War Department advanced a carefully constructed legal argument to explain why his son could not be considered emancipated. Prior to his son's enlistment, he explained, "I hired him out, took charge of his wages, attended to his purchases, settled his Bills up to the time of his enlistment, and his School Bill after he left, & in all things have regarded him only as subject to my own proper Guardianship & control."[19] Another petitioner—"a poor widow woman advanced in age"—put the matter even more bluntly: "Wm Abby is a minor I therefore consider him my property."[20] In petition after petition, parents portrayed the military's refusal to return their offspring as an unjust and illegal confiscation of a valuable resource, using terms like "theft," "fraud," or "kidnapping" to describe their loss.[21] In advancing such claims, ordinary Americans demonstrated both their strong sense of entitlement to minor children's labor and their deep familiarity with the law, which they experienced as a central feature of local governance.[22]

In parents' petitions, legal claims to property in children thus coexisted with sentimental representations of familial ties. Writers moved seamlessly between bald-faced assertions of ownership and expressions of love and solicitude, as in the case of a boot fitter who "depended in a great measure" upon his nineteen-year-old son's assistance. Thoroughly conflating his son's emotional and material value, he submitted a signed affidavit stating that he feared "further exposure would result in his son's permanent sickness if not death"—"an irreparable loss" that "would deprive him at once of his son and his valuable services."[23] Rather than demonstrating a lack of affection, references to children's material worth reflected the very substantial contributions that boys and youths made to family survival: in many cases, household independence rested quite literally on parents' ownership of their children's labor and wages. As a self-described "poor" and "lame" widow explained in August 1862, she was "intirely dependent" on her nineteen-year-old son George P. Blood, who had been "makeing Me a comfortable Home" prior to his enlistment. Demanding his release, she wrote, "He is all my dependance for support i claim him therefore."[24] Similarly desperate, a father who had already lost four older children to consumption and suffered from severe rheumatism begged, "Discharge him for me for I dont know what under the heavens to do. . . . I am scarcely able to dress and undress myself. . . . i am a contiencious man and I think i am acounted for my son as he is a Minor."[25] Suggesting the intimate connection between economic stability and general wellbeing, these parents' sense of entitlement to their children cannot be separated from their dependence upon their offspring, not just for economic, but also for emotional and even physical support.

Unfortunately for parents, the value of male children as wage earners, laborers, or household helpers peaked at precisely the age at which they were most likely to leave home and enlist. Even if sons vowed to send a portion of their army wages back to struggling families, nothing but a sense of duty compelled them to do so. Away from home and suffering from deprivations of their own, soldiers typically used their pay to supplement bland rations, purchase warm clothes, or alleviate camp boredom. What little remained could hardly compensate parents for the loss of a strong field hand or a full wage packet each month. Nor could the scattered local relief committees tasked with caring for soldiers' families make up the difference. Doling out small sums to the neediest, these organizations did not take on the mundane but essential tasks that older boys performed, like caring for younger siblings, helping an ailing parent, or harvesting a crop. Parents who wrote to government officials often insisted that the discharge of a single underage child would have a negligible impact on the Union war effort but a profound effect on their own family's very survival.

Legally compelled to deal with an unceasing flow of parents' letters, the secretary of war—first Simon Cameron and then the much more hardnosed Edwin Stanton—sought legislative changes. Already by the summer of 1861, Cameron was urging Congress to repeal the section of the 1850 law requiring the War Department to discharge any soldier under twenty-one who could be shown to have enlisted without parental consent. Debating the proposed change in mid-July 1861, Senator Henry Wilson of New Hampshire tried to persuade his colleagues to act, stressing that the War Department was "overburdened with applications to have minors discharged"—including, he alleged, many based on false claims.[26] Opponents did not deny the magnitude of problem; Representative Roscoe Conkling of New York admitted that he knew of some cases himself. But given that adult men were volunteering "in such numbers that it is impossible to accept them all," Conkling saw little justification in mid-1861 for repealing the only statute that protected parents' right to recover minor sons from the military.[27] For the moment, the arguments in defense of parental rights prevailed, and the proposed change was voted down.

Within days of this debate, Union troops suffered a disastrous defeat at Bull Run, and the calculus began to shift. Six weeks later, on September 7, 1861, the War Department imposed by decree the action that Congress had failed to legislate. General Order No. 73 tersely declared, "Hereafter, no discharges will be granted to volunteers in the service of the United States on the grounds of minority."[28] Soon, parents found their requests denied no matter what documentation they submitted.[29] This was the case for Eli McCalley of Indiana, who had already "given" two older sons to the army when in November 1862 he sought the release of sixteen-year-old Thomas McCalley. The War Department explained that it had been overburdened by requests from parents and that the release of minor enlistees had a "demoralizing effect" on the troops. This unsatisfactory response only fueled McCalley's indignation, leading him to write to US Representative James A. Cravens, denouncing "this system of kidnapping my minor children and carrying them all over the country . . . contrary to all law or usage." He also asked Cravens to convey a letter to President Lincoln, in which he challenged the "manifest injustice" of the War Department's policy. "I am willing to admit that perhaps many applications may have made of a similar nature and perhaps not predicated on facts," he wrote, "but is that to prove a bar against Justice in my case[?]"[30] The hard answer to this father's question would prove to be "yes." Although the army's general order contravened existing law, the War Department adopted a rigid stance in dealing with such cases.[31] Young Thomas would serve his full three-year term.[32]

General Order No. 73 did more than announce a change in departmental and military policy that undercut congressional authority; it also tried to usurp the power of the judiciary. By insisting that "no discharges will be granted on the grounds of minority," the order signaled that parents were barred from appealing not only to the War Department, but the courts as well. Some saw this power grab for what it was—an attempt to subject locally-raised volunteers to uniform, army-wide rules. After nineteen-year-old James Orson West enlisted in June 1861, his father James S. West, a machinist by trade, first wrote to the youth's commanding officer (he received no reply), then went to the regiment's camp to retrieve his son (the officer "refused to give him up"), and finally appealed to the adjutant general of Indiana (who informed him that his son's minority "would not avail me"). Aware that both army regulations and legal precedent affirmed his right to claim his namesake, West finally wrote to the secretary of war. Quoting a passage of the Massachusetts Supreme Court ruling in the 1814 case *Commonwealth v. Cushing*, he emphasized that militia duty was performed "at home under officers generally deriving their commissions from popular elections." In contrast, service in the regulars required the enlistee to enter into a contractual relationship with an entity not bound by local control and to endure "hardships and dangers unknown to the militia service."[33] This father clearly understood that the federal government was now asserting authority over all minors in the Union army—a new and, to his mind, ominous expansion of military power.

Attempts to reclaim minors—especially young men between the ages of eighteen and twenty-one—posed a serious threat to military strength, given the large percentage of males who enlisted in this age range. In February 1862, Congress finally passed legislation that lowered the age of enlistment without consent to eighteen for those joining either the volunteers or the regulars, thereby legalizing the practice that the military had already imposed.[34] In addition, the army could no longer enlist anyone below eighteen, save for a small number of musicians. Congress thereby tried to dispense with the entire question of parental consent: youths eighteen and older no longer needed it, and youths younger than eighteen could not enlist as soldiers even if they obtained it. Yet the law also rendered this new minimum age for enlistment toothless by decreeing, "the oath of enlistment taken by the recruit shall be conclusive of his age."[35] If a recruit under the age of eighteen lied his way into service, in other words, whatever age he swore to be became definitive and binding. As the Assistant Attorney General E. D. Townsend later complained, the new legislation "made it legal perjury for a man to swear falsely to his age," because whatever age he provided became true in the eyes of the law.[36] Since nearly all underage enlistees lied about their age, the law had the practical effect of strengthening the military's hold on all minors, even as it declared youths below the age of eighteen off limits.

By this point, the military situation in the Union was dire. In contrast to what occurred during the War of 1812, no one in Congress publicly asserted that parents' claims to minors aged eighteen or above should supersede those of the military. But some congressmen did push back against the stipulation that made enlistees' oaths legally binding, because it left parents with no means of recovering those below eighteen. As in previous conflicts, lawmakers' concerns centered more on the aggrieved parents than enlisted youths themselves. Democratic Senator Lazarus Powell of Kentucky worried that the law enticed "indiscreet and wild young men . . . to commit perjury for the purpose of getting clear of paternal influence." Republican Senator John Hale of New Hampshire agreed with the principle that minors who lied about their ages should be held to service, yet he questioned whether their fathers, having played no part in the deception, should also "be bound." Could not a father justly claim, "my rights have been violated; you took my son against my will and without my knowledge" and demand his return?[37] These objections failed to sway the majority, since most congressmen at this juncture were more worried about military efficacy than the difficulties parents might face in retrieving underage enlistees. Siding with the War Department, which hoped to dispense with the vexed issue once and for all, Congress approved the new legislation that effectively transformed minors into adults the moment they signed fictitious contracts.

Transforming the Militia System

As of February 1862, the age limit for those who enlisted in either volunteer regiments or the US regulars was consistent, with both under the control of the War Department and no one allowed to escape, no matter his actual age. But what about those units raised under the old militia system, which still remained under state jurisdiction? Civil War scholars have paid minimal attention to the wartime organization of militiamen, since few US citizens served in state militias, and their actions did not substantially affect the conflict's outcome. Union soldiers overwhelmingly signed up as volunteers or regulars, with militia units mostly active in local areas far removed from the fighting.[38] Yet in gauging the Civil War's long-term impact, it is critical to wade through the particularities of militia reorganization, because it produced a lasting shift in the ability of states, local communities, and ordinary people to counteract federal military power.

In order to raise yet more troops, Congress took up the Militia Draft Act in July 1862. With enlistment rates plummeting and contracts for one-year volunteers set to expire, there was no time to waste. Pushed through within a week, the legislation rewrote the nation's militia laws by allowing the president to call for an unlimited number of militiamen for up to nine months. All states were required to enroll every able-bodied male citizen between the ages of eighteen and forty-five and to provide, at the president's request, a designated number of recruits to be organized along the same lines as volunteer units.[39] On its face, this reorganization simply extended to the militia the existing Congressional approval of eighteen as the age of enlistment without parental consent. But, in fact, it did much more, transforming the nation's dual military system by shifting power away from the states while helping to consolidate the president's authority as commander in chief.

Permanently altering the dispersal of military strength in America, the legislation converted a system specifically designed to prevent the centralization
of power into a fully federalized structure, where state militias increasingly
came under federal government control, their efforts geared toward national
defense.[40]

Almost no one at the time or since registered the enormity of this change.[41]
When the Militia Draft Act is remembered today, it is because it also opened
the door to the enlistment of Black troops—an epic change recognized by
contemporaries as having the potential to "elevate" African American men
"to political rights," as one outraged Democrat put it.[42] The broader effects of
this new law only become evident when considering its impact from the perspective of parental rights, because parents were the group most immediately
affected. In the past, youths had been bound to perform militia duty after
reaching the age of eighteen, but since that duty was restricted and short-
term, it did not curtail parental rights or disrupt the mutual dependency of
parents and older sons. The Militia Act of 1862 transformed militia duty into
a very different type of service. Even though few parents felt this change directly, given that their sons typically served as volunteers, considering the
law's theoretical impact on parental rights helps expose the importance of
this shift on the nation's military organization.

Senators Jacob Collamer and Lyman Trumbull were among the only
congressmen to recognize how radically the Militia Draft Act law departed
from past practices. Collamer, the "Green Mountain Socrates," who had
served as a militia officer during the War of 1812 and an associate judge on the
Vermont Supreme Court, was widely known as the best lawyer in the Senate.
During the debate on the Militia Draft Act, he gently pointed out that "some
confusion has come over us in regard to volunteers and militia." Throughout
the nation's history, militia service had been locally bounded and temporary,
he reminded his colleagues. Under the Constitution, the federal government
could call militia units into national service during emergencies, but these
units retained their own forms of organization and command hierarchy.
They were not entirely subsumed into a regular force, and the president
could not reorganize them at will. The confusion stemmed from the fact that,
during the Mexican War and again in the first year of the current conflict, the
president had bypassed the militia structure to raise volunteers, blurring the
distinction between volunteers and militia in the process.[43]

What troubled Collamer and Trumbull was that the new law permanently
institutionalized this conflation between volunteers and militiamen. It was

"entirely a new thing" to allow the president to call out an unlimited number of militiamen for a lengthy period and to determine the organization and command of militia units.[44] Senator Lyman Trumbull of Illinois laid out the alarming implications for parents. "Under this bill . . . a young white man eighteen years of age will be mustered into the service of the United States," he explained, despite the fact that "the laws of every State of the Union" recognized parents' rightful claims "to the service of their sons until they are twenty-one." Did the government, he wondered, propose to "pay the parents for their service"? Quickly backing away from the enormous implications of the question he had raised, he remarked that there would be "time enough" for Congress to sort out the details "hereafter."[45]

In reality, hereafter never came; the idea of compensating parents for the loss of children's labor was never seriously considered. By July 1862, most Congressional Republicans recognized the need to prosecute the war to the hilt, even if that meant riding roughshod over formerly sacrosanct rights. Around the same time the Militia Act was passed, Congress ratified the Second Confiscation Act, which authorized Union officials to punish "traitors" by seizing their property, including slaves, who would thereafter "be deemed captives of war" and "forever free."[46] Yet even as congressmen endorsed this intrusion into Confederates' households, the idea of subjecting loyal US citizens to the same treatment remained contentious. Amid this debate, President Lincoln presented slaveholders in the border states with a policy for compensated emancipation if they agreed to liberate their enslaved workers. The plan ultimately failed in the face of enslavers' intransigence, but it raised a key question that echoed the debates in the War of 1812: why should enslavers expect payment for the loss of their bondsmen, while parents went uncompensated for the sacrifice of children's labor and wages? Congressmen pointed to this very inconsistency when responding to border state representatives who protested that the Militia Act would lead to the enlistment of Black men and thereby deprive slaveholders of valuable labor. When Senator Willard Saulsbury of Delaware declared such an action unconstitutional, his colleague John Sherman of Ohio retorted that Congress could raise and support armies by whatever means necessary, including by enlisting the enslaved or depriving "a father of his right to the labor of his son." The two were comparable, he implied, and if one deserved compensation, so did the other.[47]

William Whiting, solicitor for the War Department, likewise found it impossible to discuss emancipation without simultaneously defending the federal government's claim to minor children. In his influential *War Powers Under the Constitution of the United States*, first published as a pamphlet in spring 1862, he asserted, "The right to use the services of the minor, the apprentice, and the slave, for public benefit, belongs to the United States," adding that no other claim, "whether by local law, or by common law, or by indentures," could supersede that of the federal government. Whiting acknowledged that the question of whether the United States needed to compensate those forced to relinquish the services of their subordinates remained unsettled. But given that minor children, apprentices, and slaves were all "persons held to labor or service," he suggested that "any sound principle" would seemingly dictate that masters, slaveholders, and parents be treated alike.[48]

Given the fast-moving situation on the ground, it makes sense that the Lincoln administration embraced Whiting's sweeping defense of the federal government's wartime powers, including the authority to confiscate and liberate the enslaved, just as it had earlier found it necessary to dispense with parental consent when it came to enlisting youths of eighteen and older. Yet the government's resolve to hang on to boys who enlisted below the age of eighteen remains puzzling. After all, Lincoln handled border state slaveholders gingerly, offering to compensate them for emancipation to keep them on the Union's side. Yet his administration was prepared to risk upsetting large number of parents who merely sought the return of youngsters who should never have been enlisted in the first place. Granted, aggrieved parents were scattered throughout the country, not concentrated in a geographically strategic area that required appeasement. Nonetheless, their cases seemed designed to tug at the heartstrings of every citizen, evoking the specter of a tyrannical government willing to mollify enslavers even as it trampled on free laborers' dearest held rights. How could the benefits of such a policy outweigh the risk to civilians' wartime morale?

This was the question asked by some parents who went to tremendous effort and expense to retrieve young sons, only to come up empty-handed. William Gregg, a papermaker from Pennsylvania, endured a particularly frustrating ordeal when seeking to recover his son Oram, who enlisted at age fourteen. As soon as he learned of the boy's enlistment, Gregg hurriedly wrote to Oram's captain, hoping to intercept the company before it left Philadelphia, but he received no reply. Over the next six months, he wrote to President Lincoln, travelled to Washington to plead his case, and hired an agent to lobby on his behalf, all to no avail. The agent did manage to gain an audience with several high-ranking officials, but they stated that the matter had to be pursued in the courts. So, Gregg expended still more money to obtain a writ, only to be told that the courts could no longer hear such cases because the president had suspended habeas corpus.

By February 1862, Oram had been in the service for six months. It is impossible to tell whether or not Gregg knew that Congress had just passed legislation stating that boys like his son would be held to service based on their enlistment oaths. If he was aware of this new law, it surely contributed to the rage that he voiced in a letter written some ten days after its passage. Addressing himself to Secretary Stanton, he demanded, "Why will you not release him[?] Legally you have no right to hold him—as I have no doubt you are aware [—] but in the exercise of an arbitrary power you restrain him. . . . Pray tell me what is the difference between impressment and in this way robbing me of my children contrary to all law and to all necessity[?]" To drive the point home, Gregg postulated a scenario in which his hypothetical ten-year-old son joined the army. "[W]hat safeguard" did he now possess through which he could "be protected in my rights?" he asked, answering, "None whatever."

As this distraught father vented on the page, he cycled through a range of emotions—fury, helplessness, anxiety, despair. But for one brief moment, as if coming up for air, he moved beyond the distressing particulars of his own situation and paused to ask what it meant that he could not secure the release of his now fifteen-year-old son. "You will not release him for fear that you must do so to all those in like circumstances," he charged. The notion must have seemed outlandish, even after all Gregg had been through, because he went on to ask, "Can it be possible that there is such a vast number in the army only 15 years of age that . . . their release would prove such a serious loss[?]"[49]

In truth, the army could have withstood the loss of those age fifteen and younger without a serious decline in military efficacy.[50] Only about 20 percent of underage enlistees fell into this category.[51] Whether the army could have afforded to part with the other 80 percent—the sixteen- and seventeen-year-olds—is an entirely different matter. Eventually, the government would tip its hand as to its view of their value when responding to the growing number of parents who, barred from seeking relief from the War Department, turned to the courts to reclaim their sons.

Parental Appeals and the Suspension of Habeas Corpus

The administrative decision to hold underage enlistees to service regardless of their actual age did not solve the problem of what to do with angry parents; it simply shifted the locus of the struggle from the political and military sphere to state and local courts. Rebuffed by Congress and the War Department, parents increasingly filed writs of habeas corpus, hoping that judges would release their sons on the grounds of fraudulent enlistment. Wartime debates over habeas corpus are currently associated with attempts to repress free speech or detain political enemies without trial.[52] But most habeas petitioners in the loyal states were actually parents seeking the discharge of underage enlistees.[53] Unlike citizens condemned for antiwar activity who typically lived in border areas, parents who filed these writs were embedded in thousands of communities, and most had other sons or relatives in military service; they could not simply be dismissed as disloyal.[54] Federal officials trying to hold on to underage soldiers thus had to contest parents' legal suits in the face of widespread public and judicial opposition.

Each habeas case that a parent filed brought civil courts into direct conflict with military authority, raising the question of whether state courts held the power to rule on the legality of federal enlistments. In the prewar era, the principle of concurrent jurisdiction over habeas cases was widely accepted, ensuring petitioners the right to appeal to courts in their local areas and thereby avoid the trouble and expense of petitioning a distant federal court judge.[55] State and local courts had routinely decided these cases in parents' favor, expressing their opinion that attenuating parental rights would pose a serious threat to social stability. Despite the war's outbreak, many judges refused to cede their long-held role in preventing federal forces from overriding the rights of states and localities to intervene in the federal military. In their minds, this was no trivial issue, for the founders had charged the judiciary with responsibility for safeguarding civilian authority against the centralization of military power.[56]

Hoping to preempt parents' legal claims, the War Department cited case law that supposedly placed individuals detained by federal authorities, including soldiers in the Union army, beyond the reach of state and local courts. In other words, they claimed that judges could not issue writs of habeas corpus on behalf of parents seeking to recover underage sons.[57] Some judges at the local and state level accepted these arguments, but many did not. This meant that petitioners faced an unpredictable situation in the conflict's early years. In some areas, judges consistently ruled in parents' favor, and military commanders readily handed over minor enlistees. In others, courts dismissed parents' habeas petitions, and army commanders assertively rebuffed civilians and their judicial allies, leading to outraged charges of military despotism.

In printed versions of the law, the messy situation on the ground is largely erased. Ignoring the social context in which legal decisions are made, law reports give the appearance of judges ruling dispassionately on the basis of precedent-setting cases. In reality, they often faced packed courtrooms filled with petitioners' friends and family members. Cognizant of local opinion and the need for public support in their re-elections, judges ignored higher court rulings, defied seemingly clear-cut Congressional legislation, or handed down rulings that were blatantly contradictory. In October 1861, for instance, New York Supreme Court Justice George G. Barnard asserted that his state's statutes allowed youths over eighteen to enlist without parental consent—a position that was then supported by neither Congressional legislation nor army regulations.[58] A year and a half later, Barnard had apparently changed his mind. By this stage, Congress had amended the age limit to support his earlier position, yet he released a twenty-year-old enlistee from service on the grounds that the youth had enlisted without his mother's consent.[59] What caused this change of heart is unknown. Given that Barnard was a Democrat, he may have been politically motivated, ruling in defiance of whatever policy the Lincoln administration supported.[60] But it is equally plausible that the deciding factor lay in the judge's empathy for one petitioner over another, the physical appearance of a particular enlistee, or some other consideration lost to the past.

New legislation, no matter how straightforward, also proved no bar to judicial interpretation or disagreement. The wording of the February 1862 law, which established the recruit's sworn age as definitive, seemed incontrovertible. But shortly after its passage, Judge Wilson McCandless of the federal circuit court for the Western District of Pennsylvania, a Democratic appointee, granted a writ to a mother seeking to retrieve her nineteen-year-old son from the army. McCandless acknowledged that Theodore Turner had officially sworn he was twenty-one and that Congress had declared such oaths to be "conclusive." But what did "conclusive" really mean, he pondered, and who had the right to decide on the appropriate enlistment age? Surely Congress intended only to compel mustering officers to accept such oaths, leaving judges free to inquire into the truth of the matter and rule accordingly.

Acting on this novel interpretation, McCandless released Turner into his mother's care. To add insult to injury, he ignored the fact that the youth had deserted—though prewar legal precedents made plain that minors should not be released if they were facing court martial proceedings—blithely declaring, "there can be no criminal desertion if the enlistment was illegal."[61]

State judges elsewhere similarly found ways to navigate around federal legislation that mandated the binding nature of an enlistee's oath. The Supreme Court of Wisconsin did so by upholding a commonsense notion of who should or should not serve in the military, regardless of the actual statute. Reviewing a case involving a seventeen-year-old on appeal from a county circuit court in January 1863, Judge Orsamus Cole, a former Whig, dismissed the idea that Congress could possibly have meant to retain every underage soldier. Surely the government "wants no such persons in the service," he wrote, for those below the age of eighteen "have not constitutions sufficiently matured to enable them to endure the fatigue, hardships and trials of the service." Blaming the recruitment officer for having "seduced a boy from his home, and the control of his parents," the judge confidently assumed that any person of good sense would support the youth's discharge.[62]

Parents and guardians from New York who sought to reclaim minor enlistees likewise found a willing ally in City Judge John McCunn, a Tammany Hall Democrat. In December 1862, he cited an Indiana Supreme Court decision to support his position that those between the ages of eighteen and twenty-one needed parental consent to enlist.[63] Since common law, statutes, and "innumerable authorities" had all fixed the age of majority for boys at twenty-one years, he reasoned, "Congress cannot pass any act which destroys that relationship, and deprives the parent or guardian or master, against their consent of the services and control of such minor."[64] Six months later, a writer for the *New York Times* claimed—no doubt with some hyperbole—that the judge had released "more than two full regiments of soldiers, on one pretext or another," earning himself the nickname "Habeas Corpus MCCUNN."[65]

Like judges, military officers responded in varying ways to the conundrums posed by habeas petitions. In cases of alleged underage enlistees, writs were delivered to a commanding officer; if that individual refused to comply or did so in a way deemed inadequate, state habeas corpus laws allowed judges to levy substantial fines or call for a *posse comitatus* to assist local sheriffs in enforcing the court's will. Even though Congress eventually passed legislation that shielded Union officials from these penalties, the potential for showdowns between civil and military authorities remained high, especially in areas characterized by lukewarm support for the war effort.[66] Officers who received a writ thus had to decide if it was more prudent to reject the petition and thereby potentially incite community resentment and unrest or to abide by the court's demand and appear with the boy in tow. Much as law reports omit complex circumstances that shaped judicial rulings, military orders and reports do not show the way officers took local conditions into account when making such calls.

By the fall of 1862, Lincoln had suspended the privilege of applying for a writ numerous times in different regions. That September, he finally issued a proclamation suspending habeas corpus across the entire country. Long after this point, however, many high-ranking officers continued bending to the will of state courts when it came to underage soldiers. In early December 1862, for example, Major General Nathaniel P. Banks went to great lengths to appease Judge McCunn after receiving a writ for an alleged minor. Apologizing for being unable to produce the youth, who was on board a ship that had just left port, Banks promised to have the vessel "overhauled and searched before his fleet went out of the Narrows," allowing the boy to be "found, and discharged and set on shore." Pleased with this response, McCunn publicly praised the general for behaving "like a patriotic citizen and an able and high-toned general, showing that he was willing to respect the civil law."[67] Whether Banks acted out of sympathy for parental rights, support for civilian law, an ingrained deference to local courts, his own reading of the president's recent suspension order, or a simple desire to avoid conflict is unclear. Regardless, his solicitousness seems remarkable: amid preparations to leave with some 20,000 troops to assume command of New Orleans, he paused to honor a writ issued by a city judge.[68]

Officers elsewhere in the nation also hesitated to refuse all writs flat-out, though the president's nationwide suspension ordered them to do precisely that. In early 1863, "an old resident" of Racine, Wisconsin, sent an attorney to the nearby camp of the 31st Wisconsin Volunteer Infantry to discuss his son's release with Colonel Isaac Messmore, the regiment's commander. "[A]s a matter of favour," the colonel asked that "no Habeas Corpus should be issued in the matter," because his regiment included "many boys . . . who could not be legally holden, being under the age of legal enlistment." Fearful of starting a flood of petitions, he instead agreed to a half measure: he would "quietly discharge the boy" if the request came "through or from the Governor and not from the Courts." By the time he received the governor's appeal, however, Colonel Messmore was having second thoughts. According to the frustrated attorney, only a "long conversation . . . implicating the honor of the colonel" led to a satisfactory resolution of case. A few days later, the attorney resurfaced; just as Messmore had feared, another "well known citizen" of Racine suddenly felt emboldened to seek the discharge of his underage son. This time, the colonel purportedly dissembled. Claiming that the enlistee was not in his custody, he allowed the youth to escape rather than bowing again to a civilian authority.

It bears emphasizing that this all played out in the press, with Colonel Messmore charging that members of his regiment had been "spirited away" by a lawyer's "villainies," and the lawyer in turn portraying the colonel as dishonorable and imperious. A politician and successful lawyer himself before the war, Messmore would have known that his actions in such cases might affect his postwar career. The War Department and the president may have decreed his right to retain enlisted minors regardless of age, but Messmore had to consider how people might regard his decision either to defy parents' wishes or submit to bringing his troops to the local courthouse.[69] In these cases at least, he appears to have tacitly sided with the "well-known" fathers and allowed their children to return home, discreetly avoiding a public clash with civilian authorities.

How many officers followed his lead is impossible to say. But press coverage suggests that the number who continued to release underage enlistees was substantial. Military acquiescence was certainly the experience of Judge Allison of the Court of Oyer and Terminer in Philadelphia, who in July 1863 claimed that habeas cases involving minors were "so numerous as to form the principle [sic] feature of the day's work."[70] A fellow judge made the same observation a month later, mystified that officers kept accepting underage youths when "it is well understood that they will be discharged the moment their cases are brought to the attention of the court."[71] Such remarks indicate that officers continued appearing before this court and discharging enlistees at its behest until at least August 1863.

Further evidence that officers responded to writs long after the first nationwide suspension of habeas corpus can be found in newspapers. In every US state, the press included brief items that hinted at larger stories: of officers releasing boys and youths rather than incur fines or tangle with obstinate judges; of crowds cheering outside courthouses as young enlistees were discharged from service; of soldiers clashing with sheriffs who tried to serve writs relating to their underage comrades.[72] In a war largely reliant on volunteers who venerated "the Great Writ," military officers discerned the benefits of yielding to local communities' demands in certain cases rather than strictly imposing federal prerogatives.

Officers' abilities to exercise such latitude, however, diminished over the course of 1863 as the Lincoln Administration cracked down on judicial resistance. By this time, state judges were issuing writs not only for minors but also for those accused of draft evasion or antiwar activities. Indeed, the rulings of some state courts amounted to a virtual declaration of war between civil and military authorities.[73] Judges in Indiana—a state plagued by fierce partisan battles between the Republican governor and the Democratic-controlled legislature—were particularly vocal in denouncing wartime measures. Topping off a series of decisions that challenged the military's right to hold underage enlistees, Indiana Supreme Court Justice and Democratic Party loyalist Samuel Perkins issued a ruling that denied the president the power to institute martial law or suspend habeas corpus in areas where civil courts remained open.[74] As one Republican editor fumed in September 1863, seeking to shield minors from service was bad enough, but rulings like these threatened to turn the country into "a mess of warring factions—each State Court making its own construction of law and every state Government running its own hook."[75]

In the end, it took a nationwide imposition of military law and multiple explicit orders to finally stop judges from supporting parents' claims and discharging underage enlistees. On September 15, 1863, Lincoln issued another proclamation suspending habeas corpus across the entire country and directing "all magistrates, attorneys, and other civil officers" to take "distinct notice of this suspension and to give it full effect."[76] The War Department reinforced the proclamation by ordering officers to ignore all writs for the release of federal detainees.[77] At least for a time, this proclamation would prove effective.[78]

The fact that officials went to such lengths to keep cases relating to enlisted minors out of the courts again begs the question of why the military adopted such a rigid approach, insisting that every single writ should be ignored and every single enlistee retained. After all, there was an obvious rationale to punishing anti-war activists, holding conscripts or draft dodgers to service, and imprisoning treasonous speakers in a war for national survival. It is less clear why the government sought to deny a judge the right to examine an enlistee and allow parents to reclaim him if he was below the enlistment age.

Although officials were loath to admit it, the sheer volume of underage soldiers provides the likeliest answer. Renowned jurist Francis Lieber admitted as much soon after the war. Looking back, he noted that courts had early on "granted writs of habeas corpus in favor of volunteer soldiers to such an extent as to imperil military movements and strength." Lieber did not spell out that he was referring to soldiers below military age, but since the vast majority of writs concerned alleged minors, the implication was clear. Considered singularly, such cases did not affect the war's conduct; it was rather "the frequency of the proceedings that gave them importance, and which gave rise to the necessity of adopting a general rule to counteract them, viz. the suspension of the privileges of the writ."[79] In his usual succinct way, Lieber got to the heart of the matter: there were simply too many writs, and the parents who filed most of them wasted the military's precious time and depleted its ranks. Collectively, these cases posed a risk significant enough to warrant the drastic step of a blanket suspension.

Underage Enlistees and the Centralization of US Military Power

The War Department undoubtedly hoped that the president's suspension order and firm instructions to military officers would put an end to the vexed issue of underage soldiers. With the courts muzzled, parents could only appeal to Secretary Stanton, who continued to reject almost all requests for discharge on the basis on minority.[80] The matter might have rested there were it not for the press, sympathetic judges, and especially parents themselves, who clamored to recover their sons. Parents complained so bitterly and persistently, in fact, that Congress ultimately acted to re-open an administrative path through which underage recruits could be discharged. Likewise, many state and local judges refused to accept their loss of jurisdiction in this area. Some continued to issue writs throughout the conflict, even while knowing they would be ignored, while others reasserted their right to do so the moment the fighting ceased. The tug-of-war over underage enlistees, in other words, was never truly resolved during the war. It continued to exasperate both those who sought to free the US military from outside interference and those who viewed local control over enlistment decisions as a guarantee against military overreach. Ultimately, the Supreme Court would weigh in, with striking consequences not just for parents of underage enlistees but for the nation as a whole.

From the moment Lincoln issued his second nationwide suspension of habeas corpus in September 1863, critics across the political spectrum denounced its effects on parents of underage enlistees. Democratic newspapers like the *New York World* howled in protest, decrying it as "high-handed" and absurd—another display of the Republicans' "insolent pettishness"—that the order should encompass minor enlistees, whose discharge could not "seriously diminish the efficiency of our armies."[81] The Republican press also expressed misgiving with the order's sweeping nature. "Surely the Lincoln administration cannot expect to put a *stop* to all judicial proceedings in matters so vitally interesting to the people," the editor of the *National Intelligencer* ventured. After all, such a misguided policy would grant "every petit Provost Marshal or subaltern officer" the power to violate any "municipal or national law" at will.[82] Even some military officers warned of the political price the Lincoln Administration would pay for maintaining such a hardnosed stance. In October 1863, a New York provost marshal complained that the refusal to allow parents to access habeas relief had become a public relations nightmare, threatening recruitment efforts "a thousand times" more than any benefit the army could possibly derive from retaining young enlistees.[83]

Given Secretary Stanton's stubborn refusal to release underage soldiers, it is fair to assume that the War Department did not share this dismissive view of their military value. In February 1864, Congress responded to pressure from constituents and revised the law so that parents and guardians could once again appeal to the War Department to recover minors under the age of eighteen. Release would be considered if the petitioner submitted a certified affidavit attesting to the soldier's age and repaid any bounty money that he had received.[84] Final decisions, however, remained "subject to the . . . discretion" of Secretary Stanton, who was loathe to let anyone out unless it was in his political interest to do so.[85] This held true even in pitiable cases like that of Richard McClung, a drummer boy who enlisted in August 1862 at the age of fifteen following the deaths of two of his brothers. When yet another brother was killed in early March 1864, New York Representative J. B. Steele hand-delivered a petition from Richard's father to the War Department seeking his discharge, only to be told, "the discharge is not recommended by the Secretary of War and the request cannot therefore be granted."[86] Accounts of similar cases appeared in the press, including one of a widow whose only son, barely sixteen years old, had been swindled into the service by an unscrupulous broker. The distressed mother traveled all the way to Washington to seek his release, according to one news report, but "Mr. Stanton turned her off with scarcely a sentence of concern or reply."[87]

Such brusque dismissal of desperate parents, particularly those who had already sacrificed much for the war effort, outraged not just petitioners, but friends, neighbors, and relatives who sympathized with their plight. This group included congressmen who tried to intercede on constituents' behalf, only to receive the same cold shoulder. Senator Thomas A. Hendricks of Indiana described how Stanton had rebuffed his personal appeal to release a fifteen-year-old, stating simply that he "would not discharge anyone." Likewise, Senator Lyman Trumbull recounted the profound disappointment of a father who had traveled all the way from Illinois to Washington yet still "could not gain redress," because Stanton "refused to act."[88] Outraged by this recalcitrance, Congress revised the law yet again in July 1864, this time to clarify that "the Secretary of War *shall* discharge minors" when petitioning parents or guardians met the stipulated conditions.[89] By depriving Stanton of his discretionary power, this legislative change significantly enhanced parents' ability to recover underage enlistees, although the repayment of bounty money remained an insurmountable obstacle for many poor and working-class Americans.[90]

One parent to benefit from the change was Reverend Peter Van Winkle of Michigan, whose seventeen-year-old son Virgil ran away from school in February 1864 and enlisted in a Michigan regiment. Van Winkle immediately appealed to the provost marshal "with all confidence" that Virgil would be discharged as soon as "the facts" were made clear. To his great shock, he found that his son was already "beyond my reach"—that the only option was to appeal to Secretary Stanton, who "paid no attention to such matters." Virgil went on to fight in the Battles of the Wilderness and Spotsylvania before finally collapsing from "disease and exhaustion" at Cold Harbor. Granted a thirty-day furlough to recover, he arrived home emaciated and losing clumps of hair—"scarcely the semblance of the child he was when he left us." Yet at the end of his furlough, the Van Winkles had to send their son back. In the meantime, however, Congress enacted the law that compelled the Secretary of War to discharge minors if parents met its conditions. Van Winkle quickly secured the necessary affidavits and repaid the bounty, and on November 6, 1864, Virgil was discharged, even though he had by then turned eighteen. His release is all the more notable for the fact that an assistant surgeon, instructed to provide a report, described him as "a well built and able-bodied man capable of performing all the duties of a soldier."[91] Prior to Congress's intervention on behalf of distraught parents, such a petition would almost certainly have been denied.

While wresting discretionary authority away from the secretary of war, legislators also imposed stiff new penalties on negligent or corrupt recruiting and mustering officers. Those who "knowingly" enlisted minors under age sixteen would be dishonorably discharged and forfeit all due pay, in addition to whatever sentence the court martial imposed.[92] Seemingly designed to enforce age restrictions, the new measure actually undermined existing limits, since recruiting officers faced discipline only if they purposely signed up boys below age sixteen. This two-year gap—between the legal age of enlistment and what legislators were willing to accept as a de facto enlistment age—is telling. All were willing to throw the book at unscrupulous recruiters who signed up boys aged fifteen and younger, but some legislators, including Senator Henry Wilson, feared that the army was too dependent on sixteen- and seventeen-year-olds to risk a severe crackdown on the men who enlisted them.

At first, Wilson argued that the proposed law would lead to "a clamor for the dismissal of men," causing the army to lose "many men twenty-two or twenty-three years." When skeptical colleagues pointed out that "[t]he age of a person can be established almost invariably," he acknowledged what was likely his real concern—that the proposed legislation would force the army to discharge underage soldiers whose parents had consented to their enlistment. The question, according to Senator James W. Grimes of Iowa, "is whether we . . . are prepared to throw discord. . . into the Army by declaring that . . . every person who is below the age [of 18] shall be immediately discharged." Currently enlisted minors had "shown that they are capable of enduring the hardships of a campaign," he argued, and it would "not be wise" to allow them all "to leave the Army at this time."[93] Although other legislators disagreed, concerns over manpower ultimately carried the day.[94] In the end, the new measure signaled to recruiting officers that they could enlist those aged sixteen and above without fear of reprisal.[95]

Clearly, many in Congress and the military were aware of the large number of underage soldiers, and thus their importance to the army's overall strength. This value did not entirely diminish when the fighting stopped. As late as 1872, Secretary of War William W. Belknap reported having received nearly a thousand applications in the preceding calendar year for discharges from the US army. Given the minuscule size of army, which by this point had been reduced to around 30,000, this volume of petitioners suggests the extent to which underage enlistment remained a problem. Indeed, it underestimates the scale of the problem, since the War Department figures did not account for petitioners who sought writs from local judges. Frustrated with the constant hassle and expense of dealing with these cases, Belknap supported legislation that would pre-empt the issue by forbidding anyone from enlisting before age twenty-one, regardless of consent.[96] Congress did not go quite that far, but after receiving Belknap's counsel, it did amend the law so as to require parental consent from recruits between ages eighteen and twenty-one, thereby re-establishing the prewar status quo.[97] In the post-war era, underage enlistees might have continued to plague the military, but they were sufficiently expendable that a premium could once again be placed on parental rights.

A different situation prevailed in relation to the question of whether state courts had the right to oversee federal enlistments. To the chagrin of military officers, the moment the guns fell silent, local and state court judges reasserted their traditional right to issue writs for the recovery of underage enlistees, arguing that the suspension of habeas corpus had ended with the cessation of hostilities.[98] Others took the opportunity to express disgust with the wartime law that disallowed the enlistment of those below age eighteen, while simultaneously asserting the military's right to retain underage recruits. "To deprive the parent of the services of his child while the statute also secures to the parent the control of the child if under eighteen years of age," exclaimed a New York Supreme Court justice in December 1866, was to enable "a recruiting officer to perpetuate great frauds on the rights of parents and their children." According to this ruling, it was the role of state courts to protect citizens from abuse by powerful forces beyond their local areas.[99]

Incensed by the continuing flood of habeas petitions, high-ranking military officers fought to retain the power and autonomy they had gained during the war. Refusing to hand over young enlistees, their rejections of court summons led to dramatic standoffs with civilian authorities, press reports prophesying violence in the streets, and judicial pronouncements against military tyranny delivered in front of packed courtrooms. One notable incidence in Philadelphia in 1867 involved the Commodore of the Philadelphia Navy Yards rebuffing an attempt to serve a writ for the release of a seventeen-year-old enlistee. After an exchange of heated insults, the state's district attorney threatened to have the officer arrested. In reply, the secretary of the navy rushed to his subordinate's defense, advising him to establish a guard of marines and defend himself with force if necessary.[100] Only the intervention of the new attorney general, Henry Stanbery, defused the threat of violence. Pointing out that under Pennsylvania habeas corpus laws, state judges were required to issue writs on proper application and to send sheriffs to arrest officers who refused to cooperate, Stanberry concluded that it was up to the Supreme Court to prevent an "imminent collision between State and Federal authorities."[101]

As one case followed another, federal officials pressed for an unambiguous ruling from the highest court in the land that would finally prevent local courts from intervening in decisions relating to the US military. In the midst of a very public showdown in New York between a federal district court judge who sought to release an underage soldier, the US district attorney made his position clear: "Nothing could be more dangerous than this assumption and usurpation of jurisdiction in matters purely military and confined solely to the federal government." To allow unruly judges the capacity to determine the validity of enlistments was to "surrender the military power of the government . . . into the hands of the State Judges." If they could discharge one soldier, he asked, what prevented them from discharging men "by the hundred and by the thousand?"[102]

Here, the US district attorney inverted the enduring association between standing armies and the loss of liberty. He instead portrayed state and local judges as the country's potential oppressors in that they threatened to undermine the US military—the one institution that could safeguard national unity. Earlier in the century, the lawmakers who wrote state-level habeas corpus statutes and the judges who interpreted them believed that it was imperative to prevent the establishment of an oppressive state operating outside the bounds of local community oversight. They imagined that no organization required more oversight than the military, given its authoritarian structure and its dubious history of coercive recruitment methods. But the Civil War went far toward blunting Americans' deep-rooted antithesis to centralized military power, for it was the government's ability to mobilize a massive and consolidated military force that had ultimately preserved the Union.[103]

When the US Supreme Court finally ruled in the case of an underage enlistee in 1872, *Tarble's Case*, it firmly sided with those who charged that allowing state courts to decide habeas cases relating to federal detention or military enlistment dangerously undermined the central government. Declaring that local and state courts could never award habeas relief to individuals in federal custody, Supreme Court Justice Stephen Field referred back to the war. "The experience of the late rebellion has shown us that, in times of great popular excitement, there may be found in every State large numbers ready and anxious to embarrass the operations of the government, and easily persuaded to believe every step taken for the enforcement of its authority illegal and void," he explained. Allowing such individuals to issue writs for the discharge of soldiers would threaten the "efficacy and value" of the national government, he warned, "to the great detriment of the public service." Untroubled by the notion that restricting the reach of the state courts in such a manner potentially endangered citizens' liberty, Field asserted that the United States was "as much interested in protecting the citizen from illegal restraint" as were the individual states and "no more likely to tolerate any oppression." With this benign assessment of federal power, the justice dismissed the deep and longstanding suspicion of centralized authority and standing armies that had shaped the nation since its founding.[104] Henceforth, habeas corpus would come to be used primarily as an instrument of federal oversight into state court decision-making—a shift that one scholar has characterized as among "the greatest reversals in the history of American federalism."[105]

* * *

By the twentieth century, it would be hard to fathom how local authorities had once viewed it as their right and indeed their duty to protect citizens from the overreach of centralized military power. As the tug-of-war over underage soldiers shows, the Civil War put an end to such assumptions. The world in which parents, judges, and sheriffs saw fit to show up at military camps and demand the discharge of recruits, in which military officers ceded authority by handing them over, and in which courts felt empowered to decide the legality of enlistment in the US army receded so quickly and completely that it soon appeared inconceivable.

Virtually every account of the Union army depicts its mobilization as the culmination of a robust citizen-soldier tradition established during the American Revolution. Raised and outfitted locally, soldiers marched off in state-based regiments that remained closely tied to their home communities. What generally fails to be noted is that, even if most soldiers continued serving in locally raised units, the war irrevocably altered the meaning and conditions of their service. With the federalization of habeas corpus, local courts and communities lost the ability to inquire into enlistment decisions. As militia laws were rewritten, states lost much of their power to govern their own military forces. Reimagined as a means to defend the nation, state militias in the postwar years were increasingly used to support the interests of social and economic elites and to strengthen, rather than offset the power of the US military—a shift aptly symbolized by their new designation as the National Guard.[106]

These shifts are most evident in wartime disputes over underage enlistees because clashes between federal officials and parents were so intense and persistent, and because the enlistment of boys between the ages of fifteen or sixteen and eighteen—a group that had historically played a role in local militias—became more problematic as volunteers fell under central control and became more like regular forces. Military and political leaders recognized that young soldiers were too numerous and therefore too valuable to release. Local and state judges respected parental rights as the foundation of social order and community cohesion and thus tried to prevent boys from evading parents' control. And parents viewed the government's refusal to discharge young offspring as a gratuitous violation of sacrosanct rights and the theft of a valuable resource essential for supporting family economies. Only the enormity and longevity of this issue explains why Congress and the War Department were willing to brave public condemnation and legal resistance to reject parental demands.

In the long run, the struggle to hold on to underage enlistees led to the federalization of habeas corpus, redefining the relationship between citizens and the government, and weakening the ability of local communities to exercise any authority over the US military. For parents whose underage sons entered the military, the result was more direct: once their boys left home, they were released from parental control. Even those who did not understand the legal ramifications of enlistment could not remain oblivious to the way military service affected their sons, for they returned from war as veterans, used to the independence that came from living in a largely masculine sphere and the status derived from taking up adult responsibilities.

In early 1866, one father queried whether there was a way for parents to resume control over boys who were discharged from the military before reaching the legal age of majority. Writing to the Chief Justice of the US Salmon Chase, Allen Dunn of Kansas asked if an enlistment meant that he could no longer claim his child's "services"? Dodging the question with a touch of wit, Chase replied that so far as he was aware, "The fifth commandment [to honor one's parents] and Sabbath . . . remain unrepealed." But the control of minors was no laughing matter in Dunn's small town, prompting him to write again, this time to the secretary of war. "[S]ome of our military officials now returned from the army insist that a minor of 16, or 17 years of age owes no service to their parents, by reason of their service in the army," he explained, "and in my opinion are doing vast mischief, both to parents and the morals of some three or four boys in the neighborhood, none of whom are yet seventeen." The unsatisfactory response from the War Department simply echoed the chief justice in noting that the fifth commandment was "the only law known at this office on the subject."[107]

As these disingenuous replies suggest, officials tried to avoid acknowledging the war's repercussions on familial ties. But Dunn clearly understood that the relationship between parents and children was governed not just by belief but also by law. Appealing to one of the nation's top legal authorities, he posed a straightforward legal question: did the law recognize parental rights over veterans who had not yet reached their majority? The chief justice would have known the answer: military service irrevocably transformed minors' status and released them from parental control.[108] Seeking to restore the question to the domain of morality, government officials registered discomfort with wartime policies that had, in fact, weakened parental rights.[109]

8

Preserving the Seed Corn

Youth Enlistment and Demographic Anxiety in the Confederacy

The Virginia Military Institute cadets who fought at the Battle of New Market are the stuff of Confederate lore. On May 15, 1864, a force commanded by General Major John C. Breckinridge, former vice president of the United States, repelled a Union invasion near the town of Staunton, Virginia. Facing a break in his lines, Breckinridge reluctantly issued his famous command: "Put the boys in, and may God forgive me the order!" Union troops were then met by what historian James McPherson describes as "a spirited charge of 247 VMI cadets aged fifteen to seventeen, who were ever after immortalized in southern legend."[1] Dramatized in books and movies, the cadets' much-retold story has contributed to the widely shared perception that the Confederacy, being badly outnumbered, relied far more than the United States on underage soldiers.

This perception obscures the profound anxiety around underage enlistment that existed in the Confederacy and the concerted attempts to shield the young from regular military service. In truth, the ages of the VMI cadets ranged from fifteen to twenty-five, and of the ten who died, six were between the ages of eighteen and twenty—in other words, above the age of conscription.[2] Further mudding the waters is the fact that the Union side also counted boy soldiers among its ranks, including former inmates of the Massachusetts Reform School who had been released early on the condition that they enlist.[3] The mythology surrounding the Battle of New Market has thus obscured two unsavory truths. The first, addressed in the following chapter, is that the Union army enlisted boy soldiers who had been subjected to coercive enlistment practices. The second, taken up here, is that many elite families tried to prevent or delay their sons' enlistment into the Confederate army by enrolling them in schools and military academies. These inconvenient facts call into question the narrative that portrays the Confederacy as distinctive from the United States in that it enlisted from "cradle to grave"

In fact, what is surprising about the situation in the Confederacy is not that large numbers of underage boys and youths performed military service, but the comparative ease with which parents recovered them, and the government's staunch refusal to lower the official enlistment age for regular service. In April 1862, a full year before the United States instituted its far more limited draft, the Confederacy's acute need for soldiers led it to adopt universal conscription for men between the ages of eighteen and thirty-five.[4] Yet legislators resisted reducing the age of conscription to seventeen until February 1864, by which time the Confederate war effort was in dire straits. Even then, the War Department held that seventeen-year-olds could only be conscripted to serve as reserve troops in their home states, not as regular Confederate soldiers—a critical distinction that mattered greatly to people at the time.[5] During the war's final weeks, the Confederate Congress went so far as to enact legislation allowing for the arming of slaves, but the conscription of boys younger than eighteen for field service remained a step beyond the pale.[6] That politicians could countenance the once-unthinkable proposition of Black enlistment, while refusing to consider the full incorporation of those below age eighteen into the Confederate army, speaks to the nation's intense desire to preserve the next generation of white males.

Considering the increasingly desperate military situation, this unwillingness to fully mobilize youth calls for explanation, especially since boys of sixteen and seventeen often served in militias both before and during the war. At least three factors were at play. First is the simple reality that many underage youths had already enlisted. While the Confederate Congress early on established the proper military age as ranging from eighteen to thirty-five, it never barred those below eighteen from enlisting as soldiers, provided they had parental consent—a step the Union army took in February 1862. Even without consent, many young southerners joined the ranks with relative ease. If the Union army was often lax when it came to enforcing age restrictions, the Confederate army seems to have been positively cavalier.[7] Military and political leaders understood this and therefore knew that lowering the conscription age would not open up an untapped pool of potential soldiers.

Still more important was the fact that large numbers of underage youths were already performing other kinds of military service in their home communities. Like Unionists, Confederates began the war believing that service in the militia and the regular army differed markedly, and that it was appropriate for youths below eighteen to join the former but not the latter. They tasked boys and youths, along with the aged but not yet decrepit, with a crucial role in the war effort: while able-bodied men took to the field, the young and the old would tend farms, govern families, and oversee the enslaved population, taking up arms to defend the homefront when necessary. In the war's earliest stages, boys rushed to form voluntary units and junior military companies, and starting in 1862, some states drafted youths between the ages of sixteen and eighteen to serve in state-controlled home guard or reserve units.[8] As the war progressed, governors grew increasingly resentful of the central government's insatiable demand for conscripts, which they believed left their states unable to adequately defend themselves. Conscripting boys below the age of eighteen into the Confederate army would have exacerbated these tensions, further alienating powerful political figures.

Perhaps above all, what seems to have stopped Confederate leaders from lowering the conscription age for field service was the conviction that to do so would be to "grind up the seed corn"—to allow the urgent demands of the moment to dictate actions that would doom the nation in the long run. Elite southerners had long kept a wary eye on population trends in relation to both their northern neighbors and the Black population (both enslaved and free), but the war made anxieties about being outnumbered even more acute.[9] Concerns predictably centered on the military implications of the population disparity between the two sides, but Confederate leaders also expressed a kind of existential anxiety about the elite's ability to reproduce itself. Just as seed corn had to be protected through the winter, they argued, so the new nation needed to hold back its most promising youths to ensure future prosperity. This metaphor circulated widely in the Confederacy but not the United States—a telling difference that cannot be chalked up to the former's rural character, given that most communities outside the Confederacy were also still predominately agricultural at this time. Rather, the image of youth as carefully husbanded seed corn resonated because it tapped into the ruling class's longstanding fears of a population deficit and its wartime anxieties about perpetuating itself in a context of mass enlistment and rampant death. Present from the outset, these fears grew even more pronounced as schools and colleges shuttered and the war's human and material costs mounted.

The history of underage military service in the Confederacy, then, is murkier and in some respects even more contradictory than what occurred in the United States. The Union army officially barred youths under the age of eighteen, while refusing to release those who nonetheless found their way into service. In the Confederacy, requests to discharge minors met with less uniform resistance, and political and military leaders repeatedly voiced their commitment to protecting youth from service in the regular forces. But this stance coexisted with—and was likely a reaction to—widespread disregard for age restrictions on the ground. These differences speak to the broader significance that underage enlistment held for each side. Parents came into the war holding similar beliefs about youth and military service, and they had similar clashes with officers and government officials and similar experiences appealing to local and state courts. But in the United States, minority enlistment came to be framed largely as a question of parental rights—one bound up with centralizing processes that enhanced the power of a federalized military, while diminishing the reach of state courts. The high stakes involved in these transformations help to explain why the US federal government was so intent on holding underage youths to service. In contrast, the Confederate army failed to tighten its vise over underage enlistees to the same degree as the Union army, meaning that legal battles over minority enlistment never acquired the same significance. As a result, debates over minority enlistment were less likely to become conduits for fundamental disputes over the centralization of power in the Confederacy than in the United States.

In the Confederate states, minority enlistment tended to be portrayed less as a legal issue, and more as a social phenomenon with distressing implications for the new nation's future. As the situation deteriorated in 1864 and 1865, some die-hard Confederates continued to insist that boys in uniform revealed the nation's indomitable spirit. But for the majority, young soldiers would ultimately come to signify something quite different: the shameful failure of Confederate leaders, and southern men more broadly, to achieve victory while protecting their women and children.

Youth Enlistment before the Conscription Act of April 1862

In the early months of the war, newspapers across the Confederacy predicted a mass uprising of men, women, and children that would compensate for its smaller population. Some seemed almost eager for the coming devastation, breathlessly envisioning how even the youngest would abet the slaughter. After the seizure of Fort Sumter, the editor of Richmond's *Daily Dispatch* proclaimed that "every man and boy in the South" was prepared to march to the border "to kill or be killed." A few days later, the paper assured readers that the Confederacy held the upper hand, because the fighting would occur "on its own threshold," with "every man, woman and boy" taking part.[10] Throughout May and June, the *Dispatch* urged men, women, and children not to rely wholly on state units, but to form themselves instead into "guerrilla bands" composed of anyone old enough to hold a weapon.[11] Striking a similarly fervent note, Alabama's *Mobile Advertiser* exhorted all those capable of bearing arms to head "to the field" and form companies of "lancers, pikemen, swordmen, or knifemen" if rifles and shotguns were lacking.[12] Even an evangelical tract penned by "a Young Lady of Virginia" in 1861 insisted that God "counts none over military age, none unfit for service, who are willing to enlist." Praising the "fair-haired boy" who "left his mother's arms to rush to the battle-field," she told readers that "the military age is from the cradle to the grave."[13]

Actually, there was a more precise military age—one set by policy, not God. Like the US procedures from which it was derived, the Confederate *Regulations* ordered recruiters to accept "any free white male person" from age eighteen to thirty-five, with those below age twenty-one requiring the consent of a parent, guardian, or master.[14] Whether these requirements were heeded is another matter. There is little evidence that youths above age eighteen ever had to provide evidence of parental permission to enlist in the Confederate army, and there is plenty of evidence that companies regularly accepted youths below that age, with and without the consent of parents or guardians. Newspaper announcements concerning the raising of new companies and regiments often did not bother to include information on age limits, and stories in the press celebrated parents who allowed underage sons to enlist. In the spring of 1861, the *Dispatch* lauded a "Virginia Mother" who offered up her "beardless boy of 17 summer" and praised a "Patriotic Mechanic" who urged all his sons to join the army, including the youngest, then just fifteen years old.[15] One father, apparently worried that his consent would not suffice, requested "special dispensation" from the secretary of war to allow his sixteen-year-old son to enlist alongside him. The boy weighed 165 pounds, he boasted, and "rides like a Comanche and shoots as did the men of Misipippi when commanded by Jefferson Davis at Buena Vista."[16] The relaxed approach to the age limits that existed early in the war only grew over time. "They were more, yes, much more particular at that [early] period than later," recalled John Wickersham, who joined a locally raised company in Missouri in August 1861 at the age of fourteen or fifteen. "Any boy could join the State troops, but to be a government soldier one must be over the age limit."[17]

Indeed, most parents assumed that boys under eighteen would serve in home guard companies, not the Confederate army.[18] Unlike in the United States, where the vast majority of underage recruits enlisted in a federally controlled force, most youths in the rebelling states served in these state- or locally controlled units, a distinction scholarship on the Confederacy sometimes fails to make. Yet in a material and legal sense, the difference between these forms of service was typically vast. Those who joined state or local units usually remained at home with their families while not on active duty. They provided their own equipment and received neither food nor wages from the Confederate government, and they were not called on to operate beyond state borders. Although technically subject to army regulations while under arms, they did not face the harsh strictures of military discipline, since they served under men they knew and spent part of their time living as civilians. Most importantly, unlike the average Confederate private, those who joined local- or state-based units were often relatively safe. Performing roles like guarding infrastructure, keeping the peace, or catching deserters, many never saw combat.

Whereas youth in the United States formed similar companies, the assumption that Confederate boys would help to protect their communities from invasion lent more gravity to their efforts. Southern newspapers ran stories reporting on the establishment of juvenile units alongside the raising of Confederate companies or adult home guard units, signaling to readers how seriously they took boys' efforts. The Richmond *Daily Dispatch* reported in May 1861 that Danville, Virginia, had contributed 250 men to the Confederate army, while some fifty boys ages ten to twelve had formed a Young Guards unit that would soon elect its own officers.[19] A few weeks later, the paper noted that Roanoke boasted two home guard units—one consisting of men over fifty, the other of boys between the ages of twelve and eighteen.[20] "Let nobody criticise this thing of the boys forming themselves into military companies," declared the *New Orleans Crescent* after praising the performances of two such companies in a street parade in May 1861. "They have the same feeling as grown-up soldiers, and if they can't go to war now, they are preparing themselves to be capital soldiers when they get bigger."[21]

Confederate commentators enthusiastically applauded boys' martial impulses and their organization of home guard units, but they expressed alarm about the underaged making their way into the regular army.[22] President Jefferson Davis shared these concerns, especially when it came to youths privileged enough to be enrolled in secondary schools and colleges. In September 1861, a Mississippi newspaper claimed to "have it from good authority" that the president had ordered the discharge of some young volunteers whose parents wanted them to return to school. Davis had allegedly stated that the boys "ought never to have been mustered into the service" and pledged that he would "gladly" release any underage youth upon request. "Indeed," the article continued, "he said that, by enlisting those below eighteen, we are grinding our seed corn." This story of president's intervention on behalf of distraught parents was reported by newspapers throughout the Confederacy, sometimes accompanied by editorials critiquing youth enlistment.[23] In October 1861, for instance, a North Carolina paper complained that the Confederacy had "too many youths in the army," especially since there were plenty of men "over 20 years of age to fight our battles." That same month, the *Richmond Enquirer* denounced the enlistment of boys under eighteen as "the very worst policy we can adopt," since it would lead to the "suspension" of schools.[24]

In fact, many schools and colleges had by then already closed their doors. As early as July 1861, the *Fayetteville Weekly Observer* decried "the abandonment of our Schools" as "one of the most direful results of the war."[25] Some schools and tutors tried to stay afloat by enrolling younger boys. A. C. Lindsey's School in North Carolina, for instance, ran an advertisement explaining that "Many of our pupils have left for the war. It would be gratifying to have their places filled by those too young for soldiers."[26] So widespread was the trend toward shuttering schools that the University of North Carolina—among southern universities, second in size only to the University of Virginia—issued a statement in August 1861 "to correct the erroneous impression" that classes had been suspended.[27] Although the university remained open throughout the war, it limped along with a mere fraction of the students it had previously enrolled. By the end of September 1861, the prewar enrollment of 450 had fallen to ninety-one, and by the time the war ended, only a dozen students remained. Similarly, the student body at the University of Virginia, which numbered around 600 students in 1860–1861, plummeted to sixty-six in 1861–1862 and reached its low point of forty-six students in 1862–1863.[28]

Among the University of Virginia students left behind was Robert E. Lee, Jr. As soon as the war began, the seventeen-year-old and his classmates had formed two military companies and requested permission to be mustered into service—a request that the governor firmly denied. Soon thereafter, Rob sought his father's consent to enlist. As General Robert E. Lee related to his wife, he explained to their son that he could not "take boys from their schools and young men from their colleges and put them in the ranks at the beginning of a war, when they are not wanted and there were men enough for that purpose."[29] Rob reluctantly finished out the year and returned to school in the fall.[30] But in September 1861, with his eighteenth birthday fast approaching, he appealed to his father again. This time, Lee equivocated. He preferred for Rob to continue with his studies, but since the boy was nearly of military age, he explained to his wife, "I am unable to judge for him, & he must decide for himself." Rob, who found it "impossible" to go against the wishes of his imposing father, stayed in school until March 1862, when he finally left to enlist. By then, he was already eighteen, but Lee apparently still hoped to keep his son out of service, for he informed Rob—mistakenly, as it turned out—that college students would be granted exemptions under the conscription law that everyone knew was imminent.[31] "As I have done all in the matter that seems proper & right, I must now leave the rest in the hands of our merciful God," he wrote to his wife.[32]

The phenomenon of underage enlistment exposed both the power and the limitations of patriarchy within a wartime context that valorized self-sacrifice and honor.[33] At first glance, elite southern fathers would seem to have been particularly well equipped to exert authority over young sons. Compared to their northern counterparts, white youths in the antebellum era remained more firmly under their fathers' control, just as wives remained more subject to their husbands' authority.[34] The persistence of a more undiluted form of patriarchal authority in white southern households helps to explain why the Confederate government proved so reluctant to undercut parents' legal claims to their children. Unlike its US equivalent, the Confederate War Department never decreed an end to further discharges on the grounds of minority, and some individual officers continued to release minors upon direct appeal. All of this suggests that Confederate fathers—or at least those with resources—ought to have been more successful in keeping underage sons out of the war. But if anything, the reverse held true: they appear to have been less able to resist the imploring of underage sons who wanted to enlist and less intent upon recovering those who already had. Confederate fathers might have the law on their side, but their authority tended to dissolve amid the pressure to display patriotism and uphold familial honor. This reality constrained their ability to control their sons, even as it empowered underage youths to assert their autonomy.

As in the United States, Confederate fathers sometimes granted young sons' wishes to serve but insisted on determining the form that service would take. When fifteen-year-old Thomas Duncan of northern Mississippi enlisted in an infantry company at the war's outset, his father objected due to his youth and urged him to transfer to a cavalry company in which his older brother served. As Thomas recounted in his memoir, he reluctantly complied, because he was still "subject to parental rule." But when his former unit was called up first, he yearned to accompany his friends. Alert to this danger, Mr. Duncan "earnestly counseled" his son not to run off, warning him that "if I did not obey him I would not go to war at all." On the other hand, if he remained with the cavalry, Mr. Duncan promised that he would "offer no objection" to his son's service on the grounds of age, meaning that he would not attempt to reclaim him. This, according to Thomas, finally "settled my obedience to his will." Reflecting on these events from the vantage point of the 1920s, an era synonymous with youthful rebellion, the aged veteran felt compelled to explain, "Such things were different in those days than they are to-day. The average boy, however, high-spirited, was careful to heed a father's command."[35] Mr. Duncan, a wealthy merchant and enslaver who presided over a large family, no doubt exercised substantial power over his dependents. Nonetheless, perhaps because he did not want to risk his son's defiance, he chose to channel rather than squelch the boy's military fervor.

General Henry Wise, former governor of Virginia, also had to contend with an underage son who, though mindful of his filial duty, desperately wanted to enlist. Before he reached sixteen, John Wise had already written to his father more than once about the matter, pointing out that "many youths of my age were in the army." But the general sternly refused his requests. As the months passed, John grew "mannish and rebellious," much to the alarm of an older brother who feared that he would run off and enlist on his own. This brother wrote to their father and urged him to send John to the Virginia Military Institute (VMI), where he "would be under restraint, and receive instruction." Just as Mr. Duncan had negotiated with his son, so Wise accepted that he could no longer entirely suppress John's desire for some kind of military role. By arranging for him to enroll as a cadet at VMI, he tried to stave off a rebellion against his authority, appeasing his son's war fever while still keeping him out of the field.[36]

Figure 8.1 John S. Wise (1846–1913) ultimately got a taste of war when he and fellow VMI cadets participated in the famous Battle of New Market on May 15, 1864. John's father later saw that he was given a cushy assignment as a drill master. John S. Wise, 2nd Lt. Confederate Reserves, 1865, VMI Archives Photographs Collection, Virginia Military Institute, Lexington, Virginia.

A few Confederate memoirists did run off to enlist, but even their narratives testify to the power of patriarchal authority in southern households. To a greater extent than their US counterparts, these authors reflected on the trepidation they felt defying their parents, especially their fathers. This likely points to factors that shaped the pool of veterans who left memoirs; these former Confederates tended to come from elite backgrounds and had fathers who wielded considerable authority both within and outside their households. Yet it also suggests that Confederate youth had been less able to reap cultural and even psychological support from the widespread celebration of enterprising and independent lads, which by the 1850s had become so closely linked to free labor ideals. Confederate memoirists typically did not present the decision to enlist without consent as an act of plucky self-making. On the contrary, many described feeling unmoored by their defiance and relieved and empowered once consent was granted retroactively.

When John Wickersham of Missouri begged to be allowed to follow his older brothers to war, his father, a wealthy store owner, first tried to convince him that the idea was preposterous. He was "not yet fifteen," Mr. Wickersham argued, and would likely be run out of the camp. Undeterred, John stole away from home that very night, lifting an old rifle that rested on a pair of mounted deer horns in the hallway. His father soon followed him to the camp. But instead of demanding John's return, he bestowed upon him "the most beautiful little gun" the boy had "ever seen" and taught him how to load it. In his memoir, John portrays the consent that this gift implied as transformative: "Half an hour before I had been a runaway boy, but now I was a man going with my father's blessing to defend my State, and in my arms was the rifle he had given me."[37]

Parental consent also loomed large for James Dinkins of Canton, Mississippi. A student at the North Carolina Military Institute when the war began, James had followed his classmates into service at the age of sixteen, knowing full well that his parents would never have approved. After six months, he finally wrote home following a battle in which many of his comrades had been killed. His very wealthy father, at last apprised of his son's whereabouts, traveled to visit him in camp, bringing in tow an enslaved "body servant" to care for James so long as he remained at war. In his memoir, James recalled feeling overcome with gratitude and relief. "Not a word was said about running away," he wrote, "and no regrets were expressed."[38] While James's memoir is unusual even by Confederate standards in the degree to which the author depicts his younger self as emotionally dependent upon his family, it is worth underscoring the striking difference in tone from memoirs penned by Union veterans. That James's father brought an older enslaved man to serve him may have represented an attempt to restore his son to elite status, since James had enlisted as a regular private. But it was also evidence that Mr. Dinkins doubted his son's ability to care for himself amid the hardships of military service.

If Confederate parents found it difficult to deny sons who wanted to serve, they were also mindful of the judgment of their neighbors, including those who commanded the regiments their sons joined. Here, too, the question of regional differences can be overstated: families in the United States, especially in Republican-leaning areas, also felt considerable community pressure to show their patriotism by sending sons to war. But the case of sixteen-year-old George Boardman Battle of North Carolina, who followed an older brother into the service early in the war, is distinctively Confederate. In late July 1861, George sent his parents a sober letter after he witnessed the aftermath of battle for the first time. He described the ghoulish sights he had taken in—a death-blackened hand jutting out from the earth, worms consuming the face of a corpse. In response, his mother must have urged him to seek a discharge, for in his next letter home, George batted away the suggestion. He specifically refuted President Davis's recent and widely reported criticism of youth enlistment, which his mother may have referenced. "Concerning what Jeff Davis says, I don't think I shall take any notice of it at all," he wrote in October 1861. There were already "too many healthy young men skulking around home," and in any case, he could never endure "the disgrace of leaving the army because I was not eighteen years old." Shortly thereafter, George's parents learned that several men in their son's company had been killed and that a neighbor had managed to get his own underage son discharged. Taking matters into their own hands, they wrote to George's captain, J. S. Barnes, the son of a wealthy planter in their home county, asking for their son's release.[39]

Barnes's response, a study in equivocation, illustrates the social pressure that Confederate parents could face when attempting to assert their right to reclaim underage sons. The captain assured George's father that he was of course entitled to his son's discharge and would no doubt attain his objective if he appealed to the proper authorities at the War Department. But Barnes also communicated his disapproval, noting that he had understood Mr. Battle to have "fully and determinedly" consented to his son's enlistment for the duration of the war. He further pointed out that George wanted to remain with the company and had proven himself to be "a strong, athletic and good soldier." Barnes even enclosed a letter from George himself, who was plainly mortified by his parents' attempts to have him discharged. Insisting that "in size and strength" he was fully capable of performing military service, George appealed to his parents' patriotism, comparing the Confederate cause to the American Revolution. Besides, he added plaintively, "all the boys wish me to

stay." Confronted with their son's heartfelt pleading, and no doubt reluctant
to alienate a respected member of their community, George's parents chose
not to press the case. It was a decision they had cause to regret seven months
later, when he died from wounds sustained at the Battle of Seven Pines.[40]

Like these parents, many others who sought the return of underage sons
first appealed to the boys' military commanders, a strategy that generally
proved more effective in the Confederacy than in the United States. When
it failed, petitioners typically wrote to the War Department, President Davis,
or their state governors.[41] Parents and guardians who had read or heard of
Davis's opposition to youth enlistment often assumed that they would be
able to recover their sons without difficulty. Some very pointedly referenced
the president's statements or actions when presenting their case. One father, for instance, requested his son's discharge so that he could "accomplish
his Education," since "[a]s you knows our countrys heighest good" lay in
preparing the next generation.[42] Another, who complained to the secretary
of war that a commanding officer had refused to release his sixteen-year-old
son, even enclosed a newspaper clipping of an article entitled "Grinding Our
Seed Corn" that quoted Davis's pledge to discharge underage youths upon
request.[43]

Such attempts to hold the administration to account were typically successful during the war's first two years.[44] In fact, even when multiple factors
seemed to militate against a youth's discharge, Confederate authorities
often opted to release him. Edward Strother enlisted in April 1861 at the
age of fourteen, signing up along with an older brother, Corporal Edgar
Ferneyhough, who at seventeen years old was himself underage. By August,
Edgar was urging their father to have Edward discharged, first because he
was ill, and once he recovered "jest to get him out & let him go to school while
he is young."[45] But it was Mrs. Ferneyhough rather than her husband who
in September 1861 petitioned for the boy's release on the grounds that he
had enlisted without consent and was "unfit" for service. When Confederate
officials contacted Strother's captain, he objected to this assessment, arguing
that the Edward was "a remarkably strong & abled-bodied man" who wanted
to remain in service. He also pointed out that Mr. Ferneyhough had visited
the camp and expressed "satisfaction at his [son's] course," and that the request for a discharge came solely from Strother's mother, who acted "<u>without
the co-operation of his Father.</u>"

Had Confederate authorities been so inclined, they could have pointed to
numerous reasons to reject Mrs. Ferneyhough's appeal: it came many months

after Strother's initial enlistment, there was strong evidence of at least implicit parental consent on the part of the father, and the commanding officer opposed the discharge. Yet the secretary of war overruled the officer and ordered Strother's release, stating that the boy was "entirely too young to be kept in the army without his mother's consent and must be discharged."[46] Recall that around this same time, the US War Department began to deny nearly all requests for discharge on the basis of minority. In contrast, the Confederate disapprobation of minority enlistment remained powerful enough to allow a mother's appeal to prevail over not only the desires of a Confederate officer, but possibly even those of her husband.[47]

By the spring of 1862, however, Union victories in Tennessee, combined with McClellan's mobilization of his enormous Army of the Potomac, led some observers to question the Confederacy's commitment to withholding youths from field service. In mid-March of 1862, Mary Boykin Chesnut listened as her husband, head of South Carolina's newly established Department of the Military, grumbled about being besieged with requests to exempt students from the conscription policy that their state was preparing to implement.[48] In her diary, she approvingly noted his pithy retort: "Wait until you have saved your country to make preachers and scholars." A few days later, Boykin Chesnut recorded her exasperation after reading yet another newspaper article condemning youth enlistment as "grinding the seed corn." "How about preserving land wherein to plant your corn?" she wrote. "You need boys, even women's broomsticks, when the foe is pulling down your snake fences." At this juncture, Boykin Chesnut took heart knowing that "the boys will go"—that they would spurn any and all attempts to shield them from service.[49] But if this vision of armed youths lifted spirits and inspired confidence in 1861 and 1862, it would evoke quite different sentiments before the fighting ceased.

Conscription, Habeas Corpus, and the Courts

In March 1862, nearly a year had passed since the war began, and the Confederate government found itself at a crossroads. Many of the initial volunteers had signed up for terms of just twelve months, soon due to expire. Unable to risk a significant decline in manpower, President Jefferson Davis called for the conscription of all male citizens between the ages of eighteen and thirty-five. This was a radical move, given that the US federal government had never drafted citizens, relying instead on a state-based militia system and volunteers. Reluctant to acknowledge the need for compulsion, Davis tried to spin the proposal as a way to streamline a needlessly complex system, maintaining that the public had exhibited "a spirit of resistance so resolute, and so self-sacrificing, that it requires rather to be regulated than to be stimulated."[50] But no one was fooled. Conscription would prove deeply unpopular, even as it found grudging acceptance among those who had come to recognize its necessity.

In calling for a draft, Davis set clear parameters as to which men he believed should shoulder the burden of regular military service. Addressing Congress, he argued that it would be neither "wise" nor "judicious" for the Confederate army to accept those outside the age range of eighteen to thirty-five. "Youths under the age of 18 years require further instruction," he stated, while "men of matured experience are needed for maintaining order and good government at home, and in supervising preparations for rendering efficient the armies in the field." Davis envisioned both of these groups as "the proper reserve for home defence, ready to be called out in case of emergency, and to be kept in the field only while the emergency exists." Although he later called for conscripting men up to the age of forty-five for field service, Davis never repudiated the notion that it would be foolish and counterproductive to require boys below eighteen to perform regular service.[51]

The Confederate Congress answered Davis's call for a draft in April 1862, enacting legislation compelling males between eighteen and thirty-five to serve for three years. Whereas the United States placed the names of all eligible men on an enrollment list but called up only a select portion, the Confederate system was thoroughgoing. It not only conscripted the entire male population between certain ages, but also converted the terms of those already in service to continue for three years from their original date of enlistment. (Thus, enlistees who had signed up for one year in April 1861 had to serve an additional two years.) Healthy men could avoid service in one of two ways. If they held a job deemed essential to the war effort, they could claim an exemption based on their occupational status. Those without grounds for exemption could hire a substitute, but the prohibitively high cost of doing so meant that this option was available only to the prosperous.[52] Even then, finding a substitute was difficult, given that all white men between eighteen and thirty-five were either exempt or liable for service. This meant that substitutes could only be drawn from the small pool of "undomiciled foreigners" who had never declared their intention of becoming naturalized citizens, or from those above or below military age, the latter requiring the approval of parent or guardian.[53]

As a result, conscription immediately created a market for underage male youths (and older men) to serve in another's stead. This was not what the Confederate Congress had intended. In fact, the original conscription law contained a provision designed to ensure that the Confederate army consisted only of men aged over eighteen and under thirty-five. But its wording left enough wiggle room to allow for willful misreading. The law also stated that current enlistees who were not of proper military age would be discharged after "ninety days, unless their places can be sooner supplied by other recruits not now in service." While this proviso seems clear enough, Confederate officials, anxious to retain manpower, engaged in tortuous arguments over its meaning. Did it imply that all soldiers younger than eighteen and older than thirty-five would be released, whether they wanted to remain in service or not? And did the ninety days refer to the date on which the act was passed, or to the date on which a volunteer's enlistment contract expired?[54] In June and July 1862, the army issued two general orders that sought to clarify matters by decreeing that those who had enlisted for a year or less would be discharged, while those who had signed on for longer terms of service would not. Attorney General Thomas H. Watts concurred with this reading of the law, but Secretary of War George Randolph protested that the military should instead adopt a uniform approach—one that would compel everyone outside the ages of eighteen and thirty-five to serve only for ninety days beyond their term of enlistment. In the end, the attorney general's position prevailed, but the key point is that both Watts and Randolph proposed to retain underage youths (and overage men) who had signed on for more than a year. In other words, neither official supported the law's most obvious meaning: that all such individuals should simply be discharged within ninety days.

In response to what could rightly have been considered a clear attempt by the military and the attorney general's office to thwart Congress's intent, the House in August 1862 considered a bill that would have released any soldier under the age of eighteen "on the application of himself, his parents, guardian, or next of kin, to the colonel of the regiment to which such soldier belongs," if satisfactory evidence of age was presented.[55] Ultimately, this measure was voted down, for the simple reason that the majority of congressmen rejected the notion that no one below eighteen should serve. Representative Jeremiah Clapp of Mississippi, for instance, wanted to retain enlistees who had presented written parental consent, while his fellow statesman Otho Singleton opposed the discharge of underage youths who had enlisted as substitutes. John Crockett of Kentucky wanted boys from his state to be allowed to serve from the time they turned sixteen, so long as "proper authorities" judged them fit. For his part, Lucius Gartrell of Georgia argued that "disloyal persons" ought not be allowed to recover underage sons who had enlisted in the Confederate army. In short, the bill raised a series of contentious questions: What about the sanctity of written contracts, whether between a parent and the military, or between an underage enlistee and the principal who had paid him to serve? And did the government really want to ban everyone below eighteen from serving in the Confederate army? What about hearty Kentuckians "capable of performing military service" or underage sons of Unionist parents desperate to demonstrate their loyalty?[56] Concerned that discharging underage soldiers en masse would negatively affect the military, those who had hired them as substitutes, or the youths themselves, the Confederate Congress ultimately balked at approving such a blanket policy. By contrast, the US Congress never even considered legislation that would simply have discharged all underage enlistees.

As legislators debated how to parse the law and whether to pass a new one, parents anxious to recover their sons did not wait. On July 4, 1862, a man from New Bern, North Carolina, wrote to his son to convey the "good news" that he had a "right" to return home. "We have examined your age," he reported, "and find you was born on the 18th of July 1844," meaning he was still under the age of eighteen. "[C]onsequently, the conscript law won't catch you," the father continued, urging his son to "show the enclosed certificate of your age to your colonel." Reflecting his understanding of the conscription law, he added, "They say they have [im]pressed all [enlisted men] over and under the conscript age for ninety days longer. When that is out, come home, for you have as good a right to come as any of the rest."[57] Clearly believing that his son would greet the new law as welcome news, this father was likely addressing a youth who followed the familiar path of marching off to war with great enthusiasm, only to discover the reality of camp life far less alluring than his fantasies. If so, he was hardly alone. As the Confederacy's enlistment policy tacitly acknowledged, war fever had burned itself out, and coercion was now required to fill the ranks.

While Confederate politicians debated the question of whether or when to release those outside the designated enlistment age, a group of almost a thousand soldiers below the age of eighteen and above the age of thirty-five petitioned Congress for their immediate release. Claiming that they had enlisted under "the cherished principle of State sovereignty and individual free will," the petitioners condemned the conscription law as an "imperious" measure that smacked of despotism.[58] They appealed for release not on the grounds that their age should render them exempt—they had volunteered, after all—but rather on what they regarded as their outrageous and illegal treatment by the central government. Once Congress had enacted the conscription law, they argued, the military was duty-bound to obey it, meaning that they should all be discharged. But this petition appears to have gone nowhere. As in the United States, when it came to the release of younger and older enlistees, the military was loath to implement the law, rightly fearing that it would lead to the loss of good soldiers. The Adjutant General's Office finally clarified matters in August 1862 when it issued General Order No 57, mandating that "all soldiers under eighteen and over thirty-five years of age will be discharged at the expiration of the term for which they have engaged to serve."[59]

Even as the Confederacy took steps to retain underage youths who had already enlisted, it also sought to prevent those who remained civilians from entering the military as substitutes: on September 8, 1862, an additional order appeared prohibiting the "reception of substitutes under eighteen years of age."[60] An Arkansas newspaper applauded the decision as a kind of insurance policy that would guarantee that the Confederacy would not run out of sturdy soldiers down the road. "If we are to have a long war the boys are the hope and the dependence of the country," the paper argued, "and the best care should be taken of them until they develop and grow into hardy manhood."[61] In practice, however, the order against accepting substitutes below the age of eighteen was regularly ignored. Records from Halifax County, Virginia, for instance, indicate that many residents liable for conscription hired substitutes between the ages of fifteen and seventeen in 1862 and 1863.[62] And newspapers continued to run classified advertisements, such as one declaring that "a young man, just 16, healthy and well grown, having his father's consent" would willingly serve as a substitute in a heavy artillery unit for $3,500.[63]

Similarly, the Confederate War Department, unlike its US counterpart, never issued a blanket statement forbidding further discharges on the basis of minority.[64] Particular officers sometimes refused to release youths, but these were individual actions, not a reflection of top-down policymaking. Petitions from parents did face greater scrutiny after conscription was enacted, as Confederate officials increasingly looked for reasons to be able to hold onto enlistees. Still, whether a parent or guardian had granted permission remained the critical factor in determining whether or not an appeal would succeed.[65] As late as October 1864, the secretary of war granted a mother's request for the discharge of her son who had run off and joined a Virginia cavalry unit, even though he had already served for nine months. Many years later, when this youth applied for a veteran's pension from the state of Virginia, questions arose about his discharge, leading him to relate his story in a single, breathless sentence: "I was 14 years old and runaway from home and went in the army and got sick and was sent to hospital at Petersberg and my brother found me there and informed my mother where I was and she got the Sectary of War to discharge me without my consent."[66] Whereas this Virginia mother succeeded in recovering her son because she had never consented to his enlistment, a Georgia minister who forthrightly admitted that a "misguided patriotism" had "induced" him to allow his seventeen-year-old son to join the army faced a brick wall when he tried to rectify his mistake. After the War Department informed him that his son could not be released, he appealed to Vice President Alexander Stephens, who regretfully confirmed that the military would discharge only those youths who had volunteered in defiance of their parents' or guardians' will. "I think it wrong," Stephens explained, adding that he had tried his "utmost" but could not convince Secretary of War Seddon to adopt a policy of releasing all youths under military age at their own request or that of parents or guardians. Incredibly, Stephens then advised this father to perjure himself before a justice of the peace by swearing that his son had enlisted without his consent, so strongly did he object to the Confederacy's stance on the issue.[67]

The only other option for parents of underage enlistees was to turn to the courts. Theoretically, the suspension of habeas corpus could have closed off this avenue of recourse, as it did in the United States after September 1863. But in the Confederacy, suspension of the writ was less consistently applied and comprehensively enforced. At first this was a point of pride: in Jefferson Davis's message to Congress in November 1861, the president favorably contrasted the Confederate states to the United States by pointing to Lincoln's (initially unilateral) suspension of habeas corpus. "Our people now look with contemptuous astonishment on those with whom they had been so recently associated," he proclaimed. "When they see a President making war without the assent of Congress, when they behold judges threatened because they maintain the writ of habeas corpus so sacred to freemen; when they see justice and law trampled under the armed heel of military

authority. . . they believe that there must be some radical incompatibility between such a people and themselves."[68] Within a matter of months, though,
these pronouncements rang hollow. After the Confederacy resorted to conscription, Davis felt compelled to ask Congress for the power he had so recently disparaged. In February 1862 and October 1862, legislators approved
time-limited authorizations that allowed the president to suspend the writ
"in such towns, cities, and military districts as shall, in his judgment, be in
such danger of attack by the enemy." But they declined to renew this author-
ization in February 1863. A full year passed before Congress, in response
to Davis's imploring, finally enacted a sweeping suspension act in February
1864. (That same month, the military's acute need for manpower led to the
passage of a new conscription law.) Then in November 1864, legislators once
again denied the president's request for an extension.[69] For much of the war,
Davis thus lacked the critical power that Lincoln had seized early on and
wielded with increasing effectiveness over time.

More important still is the fact that, even when the writ of habeas corpus
was suspended, state judges throughout the Confederacy continued to review
cases of alleged illegal detention by the military, including those involving
enlisted minors.[70] While state judges in the United States sometimes sided
with federal authorities during the war, arguing that they lacked jurisdiction to issue writs to those in federal custody, Confederate state judges
were all but unanimous in defending their jurisdictional prerogatives. The
supreme courts of North Carolina, Georgia, and Alabama all upheld states
courts' constitutional right to hear habeas cases in 1863, with only a single
justice across all three cases dissenting. According to Winthrop Rutherfurd,
these justices understood the ability to issue writs to conscription officers as
a critical "procedural check" on potential abuses of federal power, viewing
the habeas process as "the vehicle to ensure the integrity of state sovereignty
amidst national military centralization." In fact, Rutherfurd contends that
the justices' willingness to uphold the constitutionality of conscription was
contingent upon their retention of this power.[71]

Disputes over access to the writ proved especially intractable in Georgia
and North Carolina, the two states most resistant to the Confederate
government's efforts to centralize power. Even the Southern District Court of
Georgia, a federal court, released all three cases of underage enlistment that
came before it in August 1862.[72] In November 1862, the Georgia Supreme
Court overturned a lower court decision and released a sixteen-year-old,
arguing that he was "incapable of contracting" and that his widowed mother

was "entitled to his services."[73] Likewise, the Georgia Supreme Court in 1863 unanimously ruled in *Mims v. Wimberly* that state judges had the authority to issue writs and rule on cases involving men held to service by the Confederate military.[74]

Conflict was similarly intense in North Carolina, where the white population was bitterly divided and resentment over federal conscription especially pronounced. North Carolinians feared that conscription would entirely destroy the state's militia and thus leave the state unable to defend itself against the encroaching Union army or slave uprisings.[75] In January 1863, William H. C. Whiting, then commander of the military district of Wilmington, North Carolina, wrote to Governor Vance, complaining about the many writs of habeas corpus that obliged his officers "to bring . . . minors before courts in distant parts of the State." Civilians had no cause to launch such legal proceedings, he argued, given that applications to military authorities were generally sufficient to secure an underage enlistee's discharge. Whiting's counterpart in Goldsboro, North Carolina, Major General S. G. French, seconded his request. If "parents show clearly that the enlistment was without their knowledge or consent and swear to the age," he argued, underage soldiers were "always discharged," for there was simply "no disposition on the part of the military authorities to prevent such discharges." But Governor Vance appeared uninterested in sparing military officers the trouble and expense of a court appearance. Having publicly condemned Confederate authorities for trampling on civilian law on numerous occasions, he could hardly turn around and meddle with the judiciary's functioning. "The writ of habeas corpus is the common right of every man," Vance's aide tersely replied to Whiting, "and he has neither the power or inclination to prevent the issuing of such process."[76]

It is impossible to know how many boys and men managed to gain release from the Confederate army through the habeas process. But critics warned that discharges by the judiciary threatened to sap military strength. In December 1863, the Commandant of Conscripts for the Trans-Mississippi Department reported to his superior that some Texas judges had "seriously obstructed the execution of the laws of conscription" by discharging men willy-nilly, with potentially "disastrous" results. He warned that these judges, although few in number, had the "power to do much harm," because people throughout the state knew of their propensities and appealed to them specifically.[77] That same month, an editorial in a North Carolina paper decried another pattern of abuse involving the writ, in which conscripts secretly plotted with friendly or corrupt militia officers and then pursued writs from judges outside their home communities. Returning officers in habeas cases almost always defended the military's right to hold the soldier in question, but in these cases, the compromised militia officers backed up the men's stories, leading the judge, who lacked contravening evidence, to order them discharged. To address the situation, the writer argued that habeas cases involving the military should be referred "to the county whence they came," where their claims could be more easily checked.[78]

When Confederate officers condemned courts for depleting military strength, however, they rarely singled out claims of minority as particularly problematic in the same way that Union officers did. The sheer reach of conscription in the Confederacy left countless families in such desperate straits that when they made recourse to the courts, they more typically sought to recover husbands and fathers, not underage sons. As a result, the debate surrounding the uses and abuses of habeas corpus in the Confederacy focused primarily on adult men who sought to be released from service for reasons other than minority.[79]

On the ground, age limits might have been ignored more often than enforced, yet they had the support of Confederate leaders, including the president and vice president. The Confederacy never forbade discharges on account of minority, and southern courts continued to release minors throughout the conflict. But would these same policies hold in the face of the Confederacy's imminent collapse? Remarkably, given the desperate situation facing its armies in the war's last year, the answer is yes.

From the Conscription Act of February 1864 to the Confederacy's Defeat

By the end of 1863, anxiety over dwindling Confederate manpower led to calls for a more robust approach to military mobilization. In December, under the guidance of Lieut. Gen. William J. Hardee, over two dozen high-ranking officers from the Army of Tennessee took the unprecedented step of publicly requesting changes to Confederate conscription policies. They wanted to place all white males between the ages of eighteen and fifty "able to perform any military duty" into service; either abolish or severely limit substitutions, exemptions, details, discharges, leaves, and furloughs; employ African Americans, both "bond and free," in non-combat positions in the army; and enroll all boys aged fifteen to eighteen, along with men aged fifty to sixty, for potential service "at the discretion of the President." While all twenty-nine signatories agreed on the dire need to increase the number of men in uniform, eight officers disclaimed the proposal to enroll boys and older men for potential service, believing that such individuals "would be of more service to the country at home." In other words, the petitioners as a whole were sufficiently alarmed about the military situation to appeal directly to Congress, but they declined to support the immediate conscription of youths below eighteen for field service—leaving their deployment to the president's discretion—and a significant minority opposed even enrolling such youths so that they might be summoned in case of emergency.[80]

President Davis also rejected the notion of expanding conscription to such an extent. So, too, did Congress, but not before considering similar proposals. Senator Louis Wigfall of Texas suggested drafting all white men between the ages of sixteen and sixty, leaving the particularities of their service to be determined the president, while Senator Albert Gallatin Brown of Mississippi called for a "levy en masse" of all white boys and men deemed capable of serving. Likewise, a bill put forward by the Senate Military Committee on December 14, 1863, would have drafted all men between the ages of sixteen and sixty, while stipulating that those under eighteen and over forty-five would serve in local defense units.[81] The press closely followed these debates, with the vast majority of editorialists arguing that military strength should be bolstered by other means. "Is not the obvious remedy to bring back the straggler, absentees, and deserters, and make them perform their duty?" asked the *Dispatch* on December 17.[82] Two weeks later, the paper proposed that the army instead replace white soldiers assigned to drive supply wagons with African Americans and able-bodied men assigned to non-combat positions with disabled soldiers, insisting, "The only effective military service that men outside the conscript age can render is in home organizations against raids."[83] As Congress debated possible amendments to the bill in January 1864, yet more editorials appeared in the *Dispatch*. One proclaimed it "the height of folly" to "compel schoolboys and gray-headed men to take the places of stalwart deserters," since it would be read as "a proclamation that the Confederacy is on its last legs and is compelled to play its last card."[84] Another expressed support for retaining the "present limits," warning that "Any other measure ought to be entitled, 'An act for filling up Confederate hospitals and exterminating old men and boys.'"[85]

Public opposition to expanding the age of conscription is not hard to fathom. Communities already stripped of military aged men badly need to retain boys and older males to remain productive, and women who had lost so much increasingly balked at calls to sacrifice still more.[86] But something had to be done to reinforce the Confederate army. In early 1864, Congress passed several new laws designed to compel more men to serve on the frontlines, transforming the Confederacy into what one high-ranking clerk approvingly called "a military nation."[87] In January, it banned the much-resented practice of substitution and made all principals—men who had previously hired substitutes—liable for conscription. The following month, legislators enacted a new military bill stipulating that all resident white males between the ages of seventeen and fifty "shall be in the military service of the Confederate States for the war." Seventeen-year-olds and men between the ages of forty-five and fifty, however, would serve in reserve units in their home states, not in the Confederate army. In addition to creating this new reserve force, the law sharply limited classes of exemptions and allowed for the employment of 20,000 free and enslaved African Americans "for special work connected with the army." Although this legislation did lower the age of conscription by a year, its "fundamental purpose" was not to extend the burden of field service to younger boys and older men, but rather "to release the able-bodied between 18 and 45 for action on the main battlefields."[88]

Anecdotal reports, however, suggest that growing numbers of boys below age eighteen were finding their way into the Confederate army, often with the encouragement of military authorities and political leaders.[89] In January 1864, the *Nashville Daily Union* published a letter from a citizen who had observed "a large number of boys from fifteen to eighteen summers" among the prisoners and deserters recently brought into the city. "It would seem from this that Jeff has been compelled to grind his 'seed corn,'" the writer lamented. "In a year more, he will have nothing to grind."[90] The *Staunton Spectator* leveled similar criticism at General John D. Imboden, who responded to General Franz Sigel's advance in the Shenandoah Valley in May 1864 by announcing that boys of seventeen and eighteen would be called up "immediately," while men over forty-five would be summoned in case of "great emergency." Appropriating Davis's oft-used analogy, the paper concluded, "It would seem that the 'seed corn' of this section is to be sent immediately to the mill."[91]

White southerners were not alone in observing an increasing number of underage youths in Confederate ranks. "The Rebels have now in their ranks their last man," General Grant famously wrote in August 1864 to Rep. Elihu Wasburne. "The little boys and old men are guarding prisoners, guarding railroad bridges, and forming a good part of their garrisons for intrenched positions. A man lost by them cannot be replaced. They have robbed alike the cradle and grave to get their present force."[92] Intended for public consumption, Grant's letter was liberally quoted in both southern and northern newspapers; one scholar has claimed that it "became famous as a [Republican] campaign document" during the 1864 presidential election.[93] It also inspired numerous satirical representations of the Confederacy in the US press. Confronted with Grant's devastating but clear-eyed appraisal, some Confederates doubled down, spinning the enlistment of old and young as a sign of unwavering patriotism rather than a portent of defeat. In September 1864, the *Richmond Examiner* predicted that, once the public fully grasped the situation that Atlanta faced under Sherman, there would be neither "men too old" nor "boys too young" to join the fray. "Let [Gen. Grant] see that the 'cradle and the grave' are not to be sneered."[94] That same month, a company of militiamen in Jackson County, Florida, hastily organized to confront a Union incursion, thumbed their noses at northern critiques by declaring themselves the "Cradle and Grave Company."[95]

The government's contradictory impulses on the matter of youth enlistment can be glimpsed in the treatment of certain individuals scooped up by provost guards who scoured trains and city streets looking for those suspected of evading conscription or desertion. Richard Evans, a seventeen-year-old refugee, was arrested on such charges in Richmond in the fall of 1864.[96] He claimed that he had traveled to the capital to join a particular artillery battery in which some friends were serving, only to be apprehended before he could do so. Placed in the reserves due to his age, he petitioned to be transferred to the unit that he had originally hoped to join. Told that he needed parental consent, he got his father, a captain in the Confederate navy, to send a letter endorsing his request. Yet officials still hesitated, sending the matter up the chain of command all the way to secretary of war. Not only did Secretary Seddon reject this particular petition, he also decreed that "young men between the ages of 17 & 18 must not be transferred to the active service." Only after a high-ranking War Department official interceded and sought a personal interview with Seddon did Richard attain his objective.[97] This case seems to exemplify the Confederacy's profound ambivalence toward underage soldiers, especially during the last two years of the conflict. The desperate need for men meant that any civilian youth who looked like he

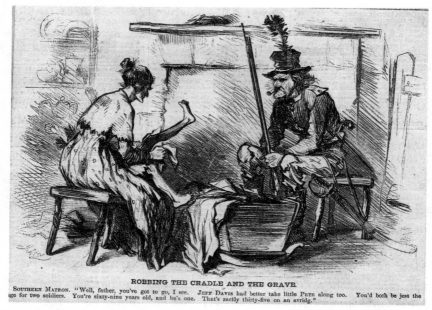

ROBBING THE CRADLE AND THE GRAVE.
Southern Matron. "Well, father, you're got to go, I see.   Jeff Davis had better take little Pete along too.   You'd both be jest the age for two soldiers. You're sixty-nine years old, and he's one. That's zactly thirty-five on an avridg."

Figure 8.2 Satirizing the Confederacy's desperate need to replenish their armies, a woman changing her baby's diaper addresses her wizened husband: "Well, father, you've got to go, I see. Jeff Davis had better take little Pete along too. You'd both be jest the age for two soldiers. You're sixty-nine, and he's one. That's zactly thirty-five on an avridg." During the last phase of the war, the Union press often claimed that the Confederate army had resorted to enlisting both the very aged and the very young. In fact, the Confederacy never conscripted those below age eighteen for field service. John McLenan, "Robbing the Cradle and the Grave," *Harper's Weekly*, December 17, 1864. GettDigital: Civil War Era Collection, Special Collections and College Archives, Gettysburg College, Gettysburg, Pennsylvania.

might plausibly have reached the age of conscription was liable to be seized and arrested.[98] But the desire to shield the young from frontline service apparently remained strong enough that Confederate officials refused to condone sending seventeen-year-olds into the field, no matter how badly the army needed them.[99]

Officials well understood the public opprobrium they faced if they attempted to fully mobilize youths below age eighteen because of what they heard from constituents. An irate mother who wrote to the governor of North Carolina in October 1864 related how two officers had recently appeared at her home, unannounced and in a "drenching rain." She claimed that they had proceeded to carry off her oldest child—"a lad just turned 16, small and undergrown for that age"—to have him enrolled "for the defence of our country." This preliminary step toward her son's conscription sent her into an emotional tailspin. "Sir, I would give up our last negro, last dollar, last foot of land for our country, and will cheerfully give up my sons and daughters too, if the duties required of them are commensurate with their strength of mind and body," she wrote. "But it will break my heart to see my little children led off to corrupt camps to be ruined in morals and then marched to the battlefield to be mangled, slain, or put into a comfortless prison." Begging the governor to place her son and his younger brother in clerkships or other positions that would exempt them from regular military service, she raged against the conscription of seventeen-year-olds—boys "too immature in mind, morals and body" to be taken from their homes. Although clearly an enslaver herself, and evidently a well-educated one, she laid the blame for the Confederacy's failures squarely at the feet of the selfish "gentry." They secured exemptions for themselves, she charged, while "leading off the little boys 'to guard bridges,' they say, but in fact to suffer and die in their stead."[100]

This distraught mother was right to worry, especially as a resident of North Carolina, which created a particularly well-organized junior reserve composed of youths below the age of eighteen. For most of 1864, the reserve troops were in fact assigned to guard bridges and serve in other non-combat roles, but as she suspected, that had begun to change. In December, several battalions of junior reserves volunteered to board trains that carried them to fight in Virginia, even though they were not supposed to be sent beyond state lines. One man wrote to interrogate his son about "a report here that all you boys had volunteered to go to Petersburgh or Richmond." He demanded to know "if that is a fact," adding sternly, "I wrote to you not to volunteer."[101] This father clearly hoped to maintain a line between reserve and regular forces that the deteriorating military situation increasingly threatened to blur. Once these youth returned to North Carolina, having sustained losses before even reaching the battlefield, they would be sent to fight in a number of different battles up until the war's end.[102]

In the face of impending defeat, even Jefferson Davis seemed to waver in his opposition to youth enlistment during the war's final phase. In late 1864, he pinned his hopes on Lincoln's defeat in the upcoming US election. A show of force at this critical juncture, he believed, could lead war-weary Unionists to elect Democrat George McClellan, who opposed emancipation and was generally more sympathetic to Confederates. "Now is the good and accepted time for every man to rally to the standard of his country, and crush the invader upon her soil," Davis exhorted an audience in Columbia, South Carolina, a month before the election. Though he did not explicitly encourage boys under seventeen to report for duty, he came close. Urging his fellow citizens to emulate the generation that had secured American independence, when boys "grew to manhood" amid the revolutionary struggle, he asked, "May not your country claim similar services from the youth of the present day?"[103] That Davis framed his appeal as a question rather than an assertion is telling, but he had undoubtedly traveled a long distance since 1861 and 1862, when he had so adamantly condemned the notion of "grinding the seed corn."

If Confederate leaders wavered in their opposition to enlisting those below age eighteen for field service, they never reversed course. This fact stands in contrast to the debate over whether to arm the enslaved. Witnessing the Confederacy's desperate plight, editors, politicians, and military leaders weighed the pros and cons of slave enlistment throughout 1864. In March 1865, Congress finally passed legislation to enlist enslaved men, though it stopped short of including emancipation as a reward for service.[104] In the end, the Confederacy's leaders chose a policy destined to destroy the slave system they had gone to war to defend, but they declined to force more white youths into the ranks.

In early April 1865, after Richmond was hurriedly evacuated, President Davis took refuge at the estate of William T. Sutherlin in Danville, Virginia. Over the course of several days, while waiting impatiently for news of Lee's forces, Davis and his host engaged in a series of wide-ranging conversations. At one point, according to Sutherlin, Davis confided to him, "I often discuss the matter in my own mind as to the propriety of taking boys and young men under serviceable age, whose enthusiasm might have been of service in the army." Yet he had never been able to bring himself to promote such a policy, since the young represented "the chief hope of the country in the future."[105]

It is hard to know how much to credit Sutherlin, given that he was recounting conversations that had occurred nearly thirty years earlier. Then again, Sutherlin would have known at the time that the Confederate president's views, voiced as the country was collapsing, were of historic value. He likely retained vivid memories of those dramatic days and may even have written down what transpired. But whether accurate or not, the remarks that Sutherlin attributed to Davis ring true, because the president, like other leading Confederates, clearly did feel conflicted on the issue of youth enlistment.

Only when the myth of the Lost Cause took root did memories of this ambivalence fade, as former Confederates told themselves that they had sacrificed everything to the war effort, including their young. In the late nineteenth century, many Americans would come to share the belief that the Confederate army included significantly more underage soldiers, and that those who enlisted in the Union army served primarily as drummer boys. For different reasons, this narrative appealed to both southerners and northerners. But it overwrote Confederate elites' profound uneasiness with youth enlistment and their refusal to fully exploit youths sixteen to eighteen years old, many of whom were already performing home guard and reserve duties in their respective states. At the very end, Confederate leaders were desperate enough to place arms in the hands of the enslaved, but even in the face of defeat, they were loath to force boys below military age into the field.

* * *

As 1864 drew to a close, Mary Boykin Chesnut expressed her growing despair. "We have lost nearly all of our men," she wrote in her diary on November 28, "and we have no money, and it looks as if we had taught the Yankees how to fight since Manassas. Our best and bravest are under the sod; we shall have to wait til another generation grow up." Soon thereafter, a large Union force landed at Coosawhatchie in the southernmost part of South Carolina. "Our troops down there are raw militia, old men and boys never under fire before; some college cadets, in all a mere handful," she fretted. Back in early 1862, the military fervor of her state's white youths had reassured Boykin Chesnut that all would be well, however much the grownups squabbled over the details of governance. Now, she lamented that the country's fate had come to rest on such narrow shoulders, along with the stooped frames of old men.[106]

Less than a week after Boykin Chesnut recorded these diary entries, Abraham Lincoln would deliver his annual Message to Congress. With the uncertainty of the election behind him, the president adopted a determined, even cocksure tone when reflecting on the current status of the war. Although he allowed that it was "melancholy to reflect that the war has filled so many graves and carried mourning to so many hearts," Lincoln asserted that Americans could find "some relief" in the knowledge that, "compared with the surviving, the fallen have been so few." The "important fact" was that "we do not approach exhaustion in the most important branch of national resources, that of living men." Remarkably, after three and a half years of fighting, the United States boasted more men than when the war began: the country was "gaining strength," the president reported, and could "if need be maintain the contest indefinitely."[107]

These chilling assertions are difficult to reconcile with the dominant view of Lincoln as the humane consoler-in-chief, who even before the war's end would speak of the need to "bind up the nation's wounds." How could he assert to a war-weary and grief-stricken people that the prolonged and bloody conflict had produced "so few" casualties? And why would he propose with such equanimity that the Union possessed the human resources to pursue the fight "indefinitely"? To modern ears, the passage conveys a startling callousness. But Lincoln's words read differently if one assumes that they were not really addressed to the legislators seated before him, nor even to his loyal countrymen. Instead, he was speaking directly to the adversary, whose psychology he understood well. Playing upon white southerners' longstanding fears of demographic decline, he was saying, in essence: Your recurring nightmare has come to pass. Our sheer numbers give us an advantage that you cannot possibly match. Even as you grow weaker, we grow stronger. It is time to give up the fight.

It was a boast well calculated to cause Confederates to despair, as southern families and communities reckoned with what seemed to Boykin Chesnut the loss of an entire generation of male youth. For decades preceding the war, southern elites had fretted over the rapidly expanding population in the non-slaveholding states and speculated about its political and social ramifications. Such concerns had helped to fuel the secession movement and the creation of the Confederacy. But even when independence still seemed within reach, Confederate leaders feared that the price that they would have to pay in young male lives would prove so high that their nation would be handicapped from its founding, drained of the human and social capital necessary for building a prosperous and well-governed society. After nearly four years, those fears seemed realized. Celebrated as evidence of Confederate unity and determination early in the war, the military service of the young reeked of desperation and impending social collapse by its end.

9

Forced into Service

Enslaved and Unfree Youth in the Union and Confederate Armies

When Morris Cohen found himself facing a court martial panel in October 1863 on charges of desertion, his only defense was to recount a troubling story about his enlistment. A seventeen-year-old orphan, he had left his Brooklyn home to seek work as a cigarmaker in Albany. As he wandered the streets, almost out of funds, he ran into a broker who offered him the princely sum of $450 if he signed up as a substitute. All he had to do was accompany the broker until they found a willing enlistment officer, and he would instantly have nearly as much cash in hand as he might earn in a year working at his trade. Boarding an eastbound train, the pair stopped first at a town in Massachusetts, but the provost marshal rejected Morris as too young and too small (he was 5 feet, 1 inch). Next, they travelled to Portsmouth, New Hampshire, only to meet with the same dismissal. As they journeyed on to Maine, the broker urged Cohen to give his age as twenty-one. Fearing he might otherwise be ejected from the carriage and left stranded, he reluctantly agreed. This time, they met with success; the enlistment officer simply asked Cohen for his age and height and took him at his word.

Having passed this initial hurdle, Cohen was furious to receive a mere $100 of the promised bounty. Throwing the money on the floor, he went in search of the broker but discovered that both he and the enlistment officer had disappeared. The local provost marshal could only offer vague promises to investigate the matter. Trapped in a regiment that would soon be heading off to war, Cohen bribed a sergeant to accompany him to a local dance, where he tried to escape by jumping out the window. But a passing policeman arrested him as soon as he hit the ground and took him to jail, where he spent several months awaiting military trial. In the end, his tale failed to sway the court martial panel, which found him guilty of desertion and sentenced him to hard labor for three years, along with the forfeiture of all pay and allowances.[1]

Was Cohen really a duped innocent or a scheming bounty jumper finally caught in the act? His behavior might just as well have fallen between
these extremes—less a matter of explicit planning than a series of impul-
sive decisions culminating in an attempt to flee as the harsh reality of the
situation finally hit home. Whatever the facts in this case, elements of his
tale ring true. It was indeed perilous for young white males to wander the
streets of northern cities during the last two years of the war; thousands of
stories similar to Cohen's can be found in court martial transcripts, newspaper articles, and letters and petitions sent to officials demanding the discharge of young soldiers. They told of boys and youths accosted on the street
and lured into service by older men, plied with alcohol or drugs, or forced to
enlist by unscrupulous guardians. In rarer cases, they narrated tales of outright kidnapping and violent restraint. Brokers and runners were waiting
at the docks and railway stations, ready to importune new immigrants or
rural boys. Even young Canadians living close to the northern border of the
United States found themselves prey to those seeking an easy mark.

The exploitation of boys and youths grew significantly as the price of
substitutes skyrocketed. The vast sums that Union substitutes commanded
by 1864 ensured that the temptation to exploit them outweighed the risks.
By this point, boys and youths were the largest untapped pool of potential enlistees, and the most vulnerable—easy prey for conmen and their
accomplices in the military who sought to take advantage of their situation.
It might take a few attempts, but there were always enlistment officers, provost marshals, examining surgeons, and military commanders willing to
defy orders to reject underage recruits if the price was right. The young males
who fell victim to these schemes were also often, like Cohen, angry or scared
enough to run off, feeling that the theft of money owed to them negated any
promise made to enlist, or simply ignorant of the seriousness of desertion.
A fortunate few met with sympathy, their sentences mitigated on account of
their youth, but such outcomes were rare. Without parents or guardians who
could demand their release and afford to repay all their stolen bounty money,
most ended up trapped in the military.

The situation that young Black males faced was even more precarious. The
first contact that many fleeing slaves had with the Union army was marked
by brutality and exploitation. Regardless of age, they might be scooped up
by recruiters looking to fill the ranks, or by officers searching for laborers to
load and unload supplies, build fortifications, bury the dead, or engage in
any of the hundreds of other tasks necessary to maintain an enormous army.

Freedpeople's position at the very bottom of the social hierarchy ensured that they had few means to correct injustices. Even the poorest white citizens could file a habeas corpus petition before a local judge or appeal to a local or state politician for aid. Without money, literacy, or social status, formerly enslaved people lacked even those meager protections. Their obvious powerlessness left them open to abuse and easy prey for recruiters who were paid for every enlistee they signed up.

In the Confederacy, age also provided little protection for Black boys and youths. Free and enslaved males of all ages were impressed into situations that were grueling and sometimes terrifying. When it came to the labor of free white boys and youths, the situation was different. Contrary to what one might suppose given the two sides' relative strength, white males below military age were more likely to be subject to coercive enlistment in the United States than the Confederacy. In Union-held areas, a labor market in underage substitutes emerged that was more organized, hazardous, and widespread than anything found in the Confederacy—not least because the ability to buy one's way out of service by hiring a substitute existed there for a limited time. In contrast, the ever-rising price commanded by substitutes to serve in the Union army ensured that middlemen continued to profit off the fraudulent enlistment of both Black and white youths until the fighting ceased.

Most young enlistees, of course, were not tricked or strong-armed into service. They went willingly, choosing to brave the hazards of service for the chance of large bounties and a regular wage. As the value of military labor increased in the Union, growing numbers seized the opportunity to turn a profit. Many of the youngest enlistees were utterly destitute and turned to the army as a kind of social welfare organization, enlisting as a survival strategy and to help their struggling families. Others—perhaps Cohen among them—turned youth itself into a valuable commodity, participating in schemes to entrap their peers or engaging in bounty jumping, while relying on their age and size to allay suspicion.

The degree to which underage substitutes acted of their own accord is difficult to assess. Most of what is known about young soldiers comes from the writing of those who signed up eagerly and looked back fondly on their time in uniform. Reluctant substitutes, coerced recruits, unscrupulous youths, and those who had few pleasant memories to recall were least likely to reminisce about their past. Evidence of them comes second hand—through letters that parents wrote to government officials, newspaper accounts of frauds committed by bounty brokers, court martial transcripts, or official reports

and congressional testimony dealing with the problem of underage enlistment. These sources make clear that a significant number of minors who
found their way into the ranks exercised very little if any free will in the
matter, while many others turned to the military for employment, seeking a
place where their labor could command the highest value.

Few Civil War historians have focused on the importance of the market
in military labor, and even fewer on the place of youth within that market.[2]
The emphasis has instead been on the question of men's motivations, with
debate concentrating on the varying impulses that led them to volunteer or
the question of whether this conflict was a "rich man's war but a poor man's
fight."[3] Treating war as an exceptional moment and enlistment as a singular act falling outside people's everyday calculus of survival, scholars have
tended to examine the extent of each side's commitment to fight, rather than
looking at the way the war opened up new avenues for employment or new
means to turn the labor of others into profit.

Focusing on motivation not only obscures the degrees of coercion or pragmatism that impelled males of all ages into military service, but also eclipses
questions about the conditions of military employment. Curiously, military
service has not, until recently, been examined as a distinctive form of work.
Like slaves and wives, soldiers lacked a range of basic rights, with enlistment
contracts entailing more brutal and restrictive conditions than virtually any
other form of paid work.[4] Similarly, the hundreds of thousands of boys and
youth who served in uniform are marginalized in histories of child labor, despite the fact that boys and youths had long turned to the army and navy for
employment.[5] They often signed up without any knowledge of the conditions
they would face, and once mustered in, they had no chance to leave (save for
serious injury, illness, or death) until their contracts expired; they yielded
to whatever commands were given or risked the harsh rigors of military
discipline.[6]

In reality, the US government became the largest single employer of child
labor in the Civil War era. In the Union army, a particularly high percentage
of those who signed up as substitutes and gave their age as eighteen or above
were actually younger. Much like adult men, boys and youths were bound to
military labor once they signed an enlistment contract. It did not matter if
their romantic illusions of wartime were quickly quashed, if they fell sick, or
if they grew terrified amid the chaos of battle. The act of putting on a uniform
and signing an enlistment contract indelibly altered their legal status: emancipated from parents' control, they were firmly under the military's yoke.

Underage Service and the Conditions of Military Labor

Most of the young males who gravitated to the military would already have been engaged in paid or unpaid work before signing up. Entry into the labor force generally occurred somewhere between age seven and fifteen in rural, working-class, and immigrant families, while enslaved children were also put to work from the age of five or six upward.[7] In antebellum America, tens of thousands of poor boys earned meager sums for sweeping sidewalks, blacking boots, hawking newspapers, delivering packages, and scavenging.[8] Hazardous jobs like cleaning chimneys fell to African American youths, while the breakdown of the artisanal system saw masses of parents send their children into textile mills or factories.[9] In the absence of well-paying jobs for the young, and with large swathes of the population living hand to mouth and poor children frequently succumbing to disease or illness before reaching adulthood, military service no doubt looked appealing to many young workers.[10]

Whatever its dangers, enlistment offered regular wages, medical care, food, camaraderie, and bounties. In the Union, privates received $13 a month, rising to $16 by war's end—a sum that might not have been generous for older men, but must have seemed lavish to those unaccustomed to receiving the same wages as adults, if they received wages at all.[11] A private in Confederate service earned a comparable sum in a dollar sense, although the value of his pay depreciated quickly due to runaway inflation. Bounties were lower in the Confederacy, too, and shortages meant that provisions for soldiers were less reliable. Nonetheless, there were freedoms to be found in military service for at least a portion of young enlistees on both sides. Some underage soldiers who published memoirs in later life looked back with satisfaction, remembering their pride in donning a uniform, their newfound friendships, interesting surroundings, or the growing self-esteem they felt in their new roles. That they found pleasure in the trying circumstances of wartime underscores the hardships of their lives in peacetime.

Given the nostalgic tenor of these memoirs, it is understandable that studies of underage enlistees tend to focus on comings-of-age during wartime. But when read alongside official sources, this material can be used to think not only about individual experience but also to consider the kinds of military labor performed by the young, and to ask why so many officials welcomed, or at least tolerated, boys and youths in camp and seemed so reluctant to let them escape, even in the face of enormous parental resistance.

In reality, the military needed young workers, just like their parents did. Children and youth performed vital labor in an age when armies lacked support staff like cooks, hostlers, grave-diggers, and professional nurses. Musicians were essential too, not just to enliven camp but also to transmit instructions on the field, mark time as soldiers marched, and telegraph orders in camp. As officers understood quite well, every boy who signed up to perform these crucial roles freed up an older male for battlefield service.

Since enlistment contracts allowed workers no control over the terms or conditions of their labor, there was no guarantee that a youth would remain in the role he had signed up to perform. The line between musician and soldier, for instance, was nowhere near as clear as Civil War imagery suggests. Some who started out serving in bands willingly chose to take up arms. Ten months after enlisting as a drummer at the age of sixteen, Edward Burgess Peirce informed his mother that he had entered the ranks after his drum "got bursted."[12] Other musicians found themselves pressured or ordered to take up arms against their will.[13] Fifteen-year-old Cyrus Hanks, a machinist who had signed up as a musician, abandoned his unit after being "compelled to serve as a private." Hauled before a court martial panel and charged with desertion, he was forced to return to his company and subsequently killed by friendly fire.[14] Another headstrong boy, sixteen-year-old Robert Irwin, adamantly refused his commanding officer's order to carry a gun as punishment for goofing off and marching out of ranks. A court martial partially exonerated him, finding that the order was "an unlawful one." But the reviewing authority, Brig. Gen. A. A. Humphreys, set the record straight. "[N]o law, regulation or custom sustains such a decision or prevents musicians being armed with fire arms, and being made to use them," he stated.[15] Just like older enlistees, boys and youths had to obey their officers, regardless of whether they were ordered to perform life-threatening acts they considered outside their job descriptions.[16]

Even if they managed to avoid being sent into battle, the young often faced work that was scarcely less frightening, dangerous, or dreadful. C. W. Bardeen, a young musician in the 1st Massachusetts, was sent to work as a hospital orderly during the battle of Fredericksburg, a grisly but common detail for the young. At first, he was tasked with holding down limbs as the surgeon sawed them off. Once the operations were complete, he was transferred to the division hospital to look after several insane soldiers and empty the bedpans of a half-dozen others suffering from dysentery, no doubt lucky to escape this affliction himself.[17] George Ulmer, who had been rejected as too

Figure 9.1 Sixteen-year-old Edward Burgess Peirce, who enlisted as a drummer in Company F of the 2nd Massachusetts Heavy Artillery Regiment, later wrote home, "I have left off drumming and taken a musket. I shall get three dollars more a month and I like it first rate so far." The line between Civil War drummers and soldiers could be very fluid; while some youths like Peirce officially "joined the ranks," others simply acted as soldiers in the heat of the moment. Locket containing the tintype portrait of Edward Burgess Peirce, c. 1863, Collections Online, Massachusetts Historical Society.

small four times before managing to enlist, was sent to help gather the dead during his first battle. Having completed this noxious task, he was assigned to help a surgeon by administering ether during amputations and carting out the severed limbs for burial when the pile by the table grew too large.[18] When they enlisted, these youths probably had no notion that they would be forced to perform such tasks, yet they had virtually no choice in the roles they filled. The focus on soldiers' motivations tends to sideline the inescapable reality that, unlike other forms of labor, military employment was fundamentally coercive. Once in uniform, an enlistee's choice was irrelevant.

Enlistment contracts were virtually impossible to annul, particularly if a parent had initially allowed a son to go to war. Just as most enlistees signed up without knowing what their jobs would entail, parents often had no comprehension of how officials would construe their consent. Those who had disposed of their children's labor freely before the war were used to having some say over the conditions under which sons worked, so many were shocked to discover that their wishes and demands were entirely disregarded once their sons were in uniform. Others were dismayed to learn how narrowly officials defined their authority. On both sides, if a parent demanded a child's discharge on the basis that a son had gone against their wishes, officials sent out inquiries to assess the truth of his claims. Had he talked to a commanding officer or accepted a portion of his son's pay? Did he regularly correspond with his son, and how long had he known of his enlistment? Any evidence that a parent had acknowledged an enlistment, no matter how reluctantly, was grounds to dismiss a claim, at least in the Union. Once that acknowledgment or acceptance had taken place, moreover, it was considered absolute: parental consent could not be rescinded any more than an enlistment contract could be abandoned once signed. In this respect, military enlistment resembled a marriage, which altered the parties' legal status and proved extraordinarily difficult to end, no matter whether the parties came to regret their decision, and regardless of their age.[19]

Most underage enlistees probably had no desire to escape their enlistment contracts, not least because military service promised financial independence. In the vast majority of cases, underage enlistees could claim their own wages. They were legally entitled to do so, since service in the army emancipated them. When fathers and underage sons enlisted in the same unit, however, engrained traditions sometimes proved more powerful than legal dogma, frustrating youths who chafed at parental claims and control. This was the experience of Melzar B. Strong, who found himself before a court martial panel following a dispute with his father over his army pay. In late 1862, father and son had together enlisted in the Michigan Provost Infantry. Claiming to be fifteen years old (though he was likely just thirteen), Melzar signed on as a drummer, while his father became a corporal. When the paymaster first visited the regiment, Corp. Strong stepped forward to receive both his own and his son's wages. As Melzar explained at his court martial hearing, he did not protest, nor did he speak out when his next pay packet disappeared the same way. But when his father for a third time sought to commandeer his wages, he insisted on being paid directly. His captain, however, sided with his father, leaving the boy empty-handed once more. Having labored for many months without pay, Melzar decided to abscond with a friend. Crossing the nearby Canadian border, he stayed away for several weeks, no doubt hoping to punish his father. But when he voluntarily rejoined his unit, it was Melzar who paid the price. After spending several months in confinement awaiting trial, he was found guilty of desertion and sentenced to a further six months in prison at hard labor, along with the loss of all pay and allowances.[20]

The panel's harsh treatment must have come as a shock to Melzar. He had called no witnesses at his trial and pled guilty, only introducing a statement explaining that he had served many months without reward. Stressing that he had surrendered himself willingly and desired to remain in service, he defended his actions by suggesting that the army had failed to honor its side of the bargain. Like other enlistees who made similar arguments before court martial panels—claiming the right to leave their military employment due to unpaid wages, harsh conditions, or unjust treatment—Melzar discovered that a military contract went only one way: he was compelled to abide by its conditions, but the War Department was under no similar constraint. If wages were not forthcoming, food was scanty, or conditions intolerable, such were the trials of war.

Putting Youth to Work in the Confederacy

At least those in uniform could grumble to their officers or petition officials for redress. Young Black slaves who worked as impressed laborers for the Confederacy had virtually nothing in the way of protection. From the beginning of the conflict, Confederate officials requisitioned enslaved workers to labor on fortifications or in war-related industries or activities.[21] The enslaved understood that a certain value adhered in their bodies as property, which they could use to negotiate with masters by manipulating their physical appearance, feigning illness, or using self-mutilation in a bid to improve their conditions.[22] They lost even this meager power when they came under the control of army officers.[23] Confederate commanders had no direct financial incentive to ensure that enslaved laborers remained fit or healthy, for a new requisition could always be issued if an enslaved worker sickened or died. Enslavers often bitterly complained that the military had appropriated their valuable laborers only to work them to death or return them emaciated

Figure 9.2 Numerous fathers enlisted alongside their underage sons. Sometimes the father reluctantly followed an overeager son into the service, hoping that he could continue to protect and oversee his boy. In other cases, the father decided to enlist, and the son eventually convinced his father to allow him to join as well. Two unidentified soldiers, possibly father and son, in Union uniforms and US belt buckles with bayoneted muskets, c. 1861–1865. Liljenquist Family Collection, Library of Congress Prints and Photograph Division, LC-DIG-ppmsca-67835.

or crippled. Vexing for them, the situation for the enslaved often surpassed the horrors of the battlefield, particularly if they ended up caught between Union bombardments and Confederate commanders who viewed them as expendable.

The terrifying experiences recounted by Jacob Stroyer, who was forced to labor on Confederate fortifications at the age of thirteen, make this point clearly. In a memoir written decades after the event, Stroyer described growing up on Kensington Plantation in Eastover, South Carolina, one of 465 slaves of whom more than a dozen were requisitioned by the Confederate War Department each year. Jacob's turn came in the summer of 1863. Taken from familiar surroundings, he was thrust into a group of thousands of enslaved males drawn from plantations across the state and sent to points near Charleston, where they waited for boats to ferry them to the fortified islands off the coast. Looking out across the channel, he could see the row of union gunboats "like a flock of black sheep feeding on a plane of grass," the men on deck visible as they paced back and forth. Stroyer and a group of fellow enslaved workers were taken to Sullivan's Island to repair forts damaged by the Union bombardment and to build batteries on which to mount heavy guns to keep the Union navy at bay. While the older men performed these tasks, the younger ones like Stroyer carried water, ferried messages, or did Confederate officers' bidding. Stroyer recounts the two months that he spent in this situation with mixed feelings: the shells from the nearby Union gunboats were not especially deadly, and he received better treatment and more freedom than he had ever known before. Recalling a young boy's delight at gaining experience of the world beyond the slave cabins, the only dark spot in his memory lay in the horror of witnessing a Confederate officer summarily murdering a youth like himself who had been serving as a body servant. But if his first bout of impressed labor was punctuated only by a few terrible incidents, the same could not be said for the situation in which Stroyer found himself the following year as he was again forced to work for the Confederate war effort, this time at Fort Sumter.

Taken once more to Charleston, he was carried across the harbor with 360 other enslaved workers of various ages, first by steamboat to John's Island and then by rowboat to the fort. The first part of the trip was harrowing as Stroyer's vessel navigated around the floating torpedo mines laid by the Union navy. After transferring to a rowboat, he came under fire from Union sharpshooters stationed on nearby Morris Island. Many died on the journey, including a young boy from Stroyer's plantation who was killed disembarking. From that point on, the fear was unremitting. Every few minutes, shells rained down on the fort as the enslaved workers tried to repair the resulting damage. In the daylight, sharp shooters picked off anyone within range of their guns, so Black laborers mostly worked at night, scrambling to avoid the constant shelling. Since they were close to Union lines with every incentive to escape, they were kept during the day in what Stroyer called the "rat-hole," a sweat box that was "so hot and close" that even exposure to shells was preferable. Lacking any source of fresh water, the enslaved had only whiskey to wash down their twice-daily rations of hard-tack and salt pork.[24]

Confederate officers, however, inflicted the greatest terror. As the enslaved dodged falling shells, an overseer named Duburgh drove them back to their positions with the swing of an iron bar, dealing indiscriminate death blows as he called for those he murdered to be removed. A Confederate captain was just as "harsh and cruel," seeking "every opportunity to expose the negroes to as much danger as he dared," seeming to hate the enslaved as much as he despised his Union enemies. The "very atmosphere wore the pall of death," Stroyer recounts, as the men worked on ground covered by the mutilated body parts of their fellow laborers, mingled with pieces of fallen shell and splintered timber that covered the sodden landscape. At one point, Stroyer was taken to the hospital tent where he watched, terrified and appalled, as the doctors threw injured men on to a table "as one would a piece of beef." He claimed that only forty of the 360 enslaved workers who accompanied him to the fort made it out alive. For the next fifty years, he would relive one near-death moment when he sought shelter from the falling shells, only to find himself almost suffocated below a stampede of bodies. "Their weight was so heavy that I cried out as for life. The sense of that crush I feel at certain times even now."[25] Not all impressed Black laborers shared the same terrifying ordeals, but many came under fire, and most did backbreaking work under appalling conditions.

The percentage of enslaved young males forced to work on behalf of the Confederate war effort can never be known. All the various impressment laws passed at the state and federal level specified an age range, typically obligating owners to relinquish a specified number of male slaves between seventeen or eighteen and fifty years old.[26] Enslavers, however, chose which of their bondspeople to hand over. Since they knew that transferring them to military officers would likely to result in their injury or death, they had a powerful incentive to retain their strongest hands and instead give up those deemed too young or too old to labor at the rate of full-grown adults.

Military records only identify the number of people submitted for service, either ignoring workers' ages or providing information given by enslavers who had every reason to lie. Yet Stroyer's master sent him off at the age of thirteen and again at the age of fourteen, along with at least one other boy around his age, rather than the adult workers requested. Undoubtedly many others did the same.

In addition to relying on press gangs made up of the enslaved, Confederate officers required free Black males to perform menial work in camp and participate in war-related employment or industry. Free African American families living in the Confederate states were in an unenviable position during the war. They had long been subject to white fear and distrust given their anomalous position in a slave-based society, but the conflict significantly magnified their threat. Ineligible for service in the ranks, free Black families were seen as a fifth column that could undermine the struggle from within—which, indeed, they did.[27] Initially, Confederate authorities tried to encourage free Black males to labor for wages, much as they tried to get enslavers to voluntarily contribute their bondspeople to the war effort. But when those calls went unmet, some states impressed free Blacks into service, just as they impressed enslaved people. In Virginia, for instance, the legislature passed a measure in February 1862 to register all free African American men between the ages of eighteen and fifty with local courts. When a commanding officer required laborers to build entrenchments or fortifications, pave roads, or repair rail lines, he sent a requisition and the courts supplied a certain number of workers, who were required to serve for up to six months in exchange for minimal wages and army rations.[28]

Most of the free Black males impressed in this manner were probably above the requisite age, given that no one under eighteen was compelled to register with authorities. The same cannot be said for those who were snatched up by foraging parties. When Confederate officers scoured communities to find workers to labor on fortifications or in camps, they seized anyone who might prove useful, regardless of age.[29] The experience of a free Black family in North Carolina's Piedmont region, where Unionists clashed with secessionists throughout the war, was probably typical. Confederate recruiters abducted this family's two sons, leaving behind their sick father, a mother, and several small children without means of support. In this case, the family appealed to local white authorities in Davies County, who in turn petitioned the North Carolina governor in August 1861. The twenty-seven signatories to this petition knew who had taken the children. They named the soldiers' company, specified that it was raised in a neighboring county, and identified its current location, suggesting that the parties were known to each other before the war. This might have been a random kidnapping, or the soldiers might have had personal scores to settle, as many in divided southern communities pursued old grudges under the cover of war.[30] Whatever the case, the petitioners sought to allay any concern that this particular family shared the Unionist leanings of many local residents by emphasizing that the parents had already contributed two relatives to the Confederate war effort— a "son and a son in law who volunteered to go with the military companies from this county."[31] Ironically, some members of this family might well have "volunteered" to serve, since it could be safer and more profitable for free Black males to work in army camps than to remain at home, subject to the depredations of marauding soldiers from both armies and constant impressment demands.[32] Equally likely, soldiers had arrived to demand their service, just as they had now seized the family's remaining sons. Either way, parents had little chance of retrieving their relatives until war's end. There is no evidence that the governor responded to their community's petition.

That same month, another group of Confederate troops searched for Black boys to commandeer for military service in Orange County, North Carolina. Some men from a volunteer company forming nearby had come by the home of seventy-one-year-old Gerry Day and his wife "to look at" two boys, "about 14 and 15 years of age." They announced that they would soon "take them away." This led Day to seek assistance from whites in the community, who petitioned the governor on his behalf. Describing him as a "respectable free man of colour," the petitioners warned that these youths were "bound" to Day and "able to work and help support the family." The relationship between these youths and the Days, however, appears to have been more that of parent-child than master-servant: Day and his wife had taken in four orphaned nephews and nieces, including two still too young to "render service." Having the youths bound to him by the county was likely a strategy for keeping the family together. Yet at the same time, the elderly Day and his wife probably did rely upon these two young nephews to get by. Tellingly, in making the case for why the Days should be allowed to retain their nephews, the white petitioners said nothing about the boys' ages, presumably because no one would have seen their youth as a problem. Instead, they made two points: the Days had five older sons who were working for the Confederate army, and the family would "become a charge on the county" if the youths were taken.[33] With white authorities who could speak on their behalf, this family might have managed to retain their charges, but many other free Black families doubtless had no such assistance and thus no way to prevent the seizure and exploitation of their children.

Free white families in the Confederacy faced less peril, but as the war dragged on, they were not completely immune to the kidnapping or coercion of underage boys. Scattered reports indicate that enrollment officers sometimes swept up boys well below the enlistment age, particularly as the Confederacy grew more desperate for recruits. Certain communities appear to have been especially vulnerable, including German immigrants in Texas, who feared that Confederate officials would deal with them harshly, since most German immigrants supported the Union. "Our thoughts were bound up in the one word 'conscription,' and our one answer was the hope of escape, which meant not to be caught at home," recalled Charles Nagel, who was just twelve years old at the war's outset. As the conflict grew "closer and closer," Charles's parents finally determined that he and his father should flee to Mexico, which they did in November 1863.[34] Though their son was just fourteen, the Nagels feared that he would not escape the clutches of Confederate conscriptors. Their concern that their underage son would be forced into service was no doubt shared in Unionist areas throughout the Confederacy, given the widespread denial of civil liberties that such communities suffered.[35]

Similarly, although those below the enlistment age were forbidden from serving as substitutes in the Confederacy, this rule seems to have been ignored or misunderstood more often than observed. Indeed, some individuals and substitute brokers who placed advertisements in southern newspapers actively solicited youths below military age. "Wanted, a substitute for the war—must be either under 18 or over 35 years of age," read one such notice in *Alabama Beacon* in May 1862.[36] The widespread acceptance of underage youths as substitutes seems to have fostered uncertainty on the part of officials. In August 1862, the clonel of the 18th Mississippi Infantry inquired of his state's adjutant and inspector general whether he could legally accept "a boy under 18 years of age" to serve in place of a conscript, suggesting that he was unsure of the rules.[37] Likewise, a provost marshal from North Carolina inquired of the secretary of war whether it "lawful" that people in his home region were hiring substitutes "about 16 years of age." Did the practice not amount to "Swindling the government out of the 'Seed corn' of the Army?"[38] Likely because of such queries, the Confederate War Department published an order the following month confirming that the "reception of substitutes under eighteen years of age" was prohibited.[39] Still, some officers remained oblivious or chose to ignore the order. In November 1862, a private in a Virginia infantry regiment who wanted out of the army wrote to his brother, "Our Captain wont except none [as substitutes] but boys from sixteen to seventeen or good men born in the South unless the Colonel is agreed." Noting that he was willing to pay up to fifteen hundred dollars for an acceptable substitute, he warned his brother that the colonel had already rejected a comrade's request to take a "foreigner" in his stead.[40] At least for this officer, young native-born males below the official enlistment age were desirable substitutes, while foreign-born males of legal age were not.

A lack of reliable records makes it difficult to assess how the Confederacy's substitution policies worked on the ground. Estimates of the number of Confederate substitutes range from 50,000 to 150,000, with no trustworthy approximation of substitutes' ages at enlistment.[41] It is clear, though, that the policy of allowing conscripts to hire substitutes quickly generated flourishing markets in some southern cities where substitutes sold their services to the highest bidder, usually with the aid of brokers and agents.[42] In August 1862, one outraged commentator who had just returned from Calhoun, a town roughly 8 miles north of Atlanta, reported on the "organized system of buying and selling substitutes" in that location. Condemning the business as "nothing more nor less than a traffic in white human flesh," he vented his outrage at the poor men forced to offer themselves as substitutes, the brokers who profited from their desperation, and the plethora of able-bodied men allegedly seeking to evade service. Brokers, he explained, were scouring the countryside for substitutes and then bringing them to Calhoun, where unwilling conscripts bought their way out of service for amounts that were "rarely under and frequently over $2000!"[43]

In response to the press outcry that this report provoked, the Confederate government immediately sought to shut down the brokerage system, passing an order later that month stating that any agent who took money from a substitute or his principal would find his fees confiscated and all parties to the transaction immediately impressed into service.[44] Henceforth, those looking to buy their way out of service had to find their own proxies, which usually meant advertising in the press. Nonetheless, the price of substitutes continued to climb. By the latter part of 1862, anxious conscripts were regularly posting ads that offered thousands of dollars to anyone willing to enlist in their stead.[45]

The fact that the pool of potential substitutes in the Confederacy was so small ensured that the price for their service would remain high, with or without the brokerage system. With all military-age males already conscripted and only a small number of foreign residents, that left only those outside the eighteen to forty-five age range. Most substitutes were probably over age forty-five given the embargo against underage enlistment, yet in a context in which some officers were clearly willing to bend the rules, it is probable that many below the enlistment age were also drawn to the possibility of turning a quick profit, perhaps supported by parents who hoped to provide for desperate families. Whatever the case, the market for young substitutes in the Confederacy was ultimately checked by the policy's short duration: conscripts could only hire a surrogate between April 1862 and December 1863, when a tremendous public backlash against the practice led the Confederate Congress to abolish substitutions entirely.[46]

The irony of a war to protect property rights in Black bodies developing into one in which white males were forced to sell themselves to the highest bidder was not lost on southern commentators. The writer who detailed the situation in Calhoun sarcastically referred to middlemen's conversion of white bodies into cash as a "delectable traffic," evoking the lust for domination and tantalizing promise of riches that characterized the slave trade. By the time the substitution policy had ended, ironies had been heaped upon ironies in the Confederacy, as a war for states' rights and the preservation of slavery had transmuted into an increasingly centralized effort where the enslaved refused to act as chattel and the government coopted enslavers' property, where masses of white parents lost control over boys and youths, and where all white males were conscripted into service for the duration, whether they liked it or not.[47] Perhaps the one irony that Confederate supporters would actually have appreciated is that, in some ways at least, the exploitation of young males in the Union was equally dire and the market for "flesh" there even greater.

Exploiting Boys and Youths in the United States

The Union's recruitment policies ensured that northerners saw a much more extensive, organized, and profitable trade in young military recruits and substitutes. In March 1863, almost a year after the Confederacy began conscripting troops, the US government passed the Enrollment Act, which required that all male citizens aged between twenty and forty-five be placed on draft rolls. Every state was divided into districts, each of which had an enlistment quota to meet. If they failed to achieve these quotas through voluntary enlistments, the district then held a lottery. Those whose names were drawn had two means to avoid the draft: they could pay a $300 commutation fee or hire a substitute.[48] The former provision was designed to keep the price of substitutes from spinning out of control by offering draftees a way to buy themselves out of service for $300. Regardless, those hoping to capitalize on the wartime market in military labor found other ways to turn the recruitment process to their advantage.

As soon as the Enrollment Act came into effect, districts began vying with one another to attract volunteers. Their aim was to avoid holding a draft, which ran the risk of provoking backlash in local communities whose members were unwilling to offer up their sons under duress. On top of the promise of $100 in federal bounty paid to recruits at the end of service, local and state governments thus raised extra funds to entice willing recruits, which were often paid in cash. In some areas, those who volunteered received upward of $1,000 in federal, state, and local bounties—more than three years' wages for a common laborer in the 1860s. Unsurprisingly, such immense sums invited fraud, which quickly spread to alarming proportions in the form of bounty jumping—a term that referred to the practice of signing up, collecting bounties, and then bolting at the earliest chance to repeat the process elsewhere.[49] In short order, bounty jumping had become a professional operation with groups of six to a dozen men travelling from city to city. Some would enlist, while the rest aided in escapes by bribing officials or creating distractions so jumpers could flee. By the war's last year, between 3,000 to 5,000 bounty jumpers were reportedly operating in New York City alone, living the high life in "well known hotels" between brief stints in uniform.[50]

With every enlistment officer and provost marshal on the lookout for deserters, bounty jumping was extremely risky. It also usually meant working in a group or paying kickbacks to officials, and thus splitting the profits. Many unscrupulous operators who sought equal rewards with less risk turned instead to brokerage so they could convince someone else to volunteer—preferably someone as guileless and frail as possible—and then take their cut of the soldier's bounty money or steal the whole. Although historians have noted the vast extent of enlistment fraud in the Civil War, they have not explored the particular impact of Union recruitment policies on young males, whose size and inexperience made them easy to scam or coerce. Even before the Enrollment Act came into effect, boys had already become a favored target for swindlers. The story told by Charles W. L. Hayward's father in a letter seeking his son's release was typical. The fifteen-year-old had run away from their home in Weymouth, Massachusetts, and enlisted in Navy in early 1863, but after he arrived in Boston to be mustered in, an examining physician dutifully rejected the boy for being "too light." That should have been the end of his misadventure, but a Mr. Stevenson was lurking to seize upon just such an opportunity. According to Hayward's father, Stevenson promptly took his son to an army recruiter, had him sworn in, and made off with his bounty.[51]

As bounties climbed, so too did the incentive to exploit the most vulnerable population, particularly by brokers who sought out likely enlistees and presented them to recruiters. Whereas bounty jumping was a criminal activity, it was perfectly legal to act as a bounty broker in the United States throughout the war. Union officials were willing to tolerate these middlemen because they brought in much-needed troops and helped local recruitment committees and volunteers to navigate an unfamiliar bureaucracy. For their efforts, brokers received a fee (upwards of $15 per enlistee, although fees varied by state or district).[52] But the sums scammed off recruits could be much larger. Many volunteers signed without much knowledge of enlistment procedures and ignorant of the bounties they could obtain. Brokers could profit from their inexperience by promising recruits a fee amounting to far less than their entitlement and then pocketing the difference. Or, if they were less scrupulous, they might pay nothing at all, simply waiting until a green recruit had been mustered and then organizing to have him beaten or drugged and his pockets turned out.[53]

Situated near recruiting depots and provost marshal's headquarters, brokerage offices sent runners out to haunt train stations, wharves, and hotels, and posted billboards and newspaper ads announcing their ability to secure the highest bounties for enlistees. Stories in the press and correspondence sent to officials expose the various methods they used to entrap the unwary, from spinning clever lies to physical intimidation. In mid-1863, for instance, three youths aged between fifteen and seventeen who had been brought up on charges of desertion claimed that they had taken off because, as one put it, they had been "fooled into the service and found it different from what it was represented." Having been told that there would be "no knapsacks and guns to carry and no picket duty to do," only guard work away from the front lines, they were shocked to discover that they had been enlisted in an artillery battery about to be sent to the front.[54] With equal credulity, large numbers of young enlistees apparently trusted brokers enough to turn over most of their bounty, either to hold for them or to send on to family members, as more than one parent lamented to Colonel Lafayette C. Baker, head of the War Department's National Detective Bureau, which looked into cases of enlistment fraud. One mother, for instance, explained to Baker that her seventeen-year-old son had entrusted roughly $1,200 to his broker to send on to her many months before, but the family had only received $50. To buttress her case, she enclosed a letter from her son, who claimed to have been enlisted against his will.[55]

Were these youths really so innocent as to hand over large sums of money to strangers, or to enlist believing they would escape the fighting once in uniform?[56] Countless charges along these lines appear in the historical record, but it is impossible to establish their truth since those who wrote to officials or appeared before court martial panels had strong reason to present themselves as innocent boys. The ability to look the part, not chronological age, usually determined whether they would get a sympathetic hearing.[57] In the case of the three boys who claimed to have enlisted with no expectation of danger or drudgery, for instance, an initial sentence of hard labor for three years was commuted to a few months' loss of pay based on the panel's recommendation after all three emphasized their gullibility. Others of similar age were not so fortunate. Court martial panels might seek leniency on behalf of those in their early twenties on account of "extreme youth," while delivering harsh rulings for boys barely out of short pants, depending on whether they identified, and thus empathized, with the defendants. Particular youths— especially those with appearances marked by grinding poverty or self-reliance—struggled to stoke officials' concern, although few would have been oblivious of the need to do so.

This is not to say that everyone claiming to be victimized by brokers was lying, but instead to note that all parties were operating in the novel marketplace created by the war, where vast sums could be made through enlistments. Young males traded in this market, too, knowing that their best chance of making quick money or escaping parental control lay in a military enlistment, where planning and savvy could determine the amount of bounty received and where monthly wages were established through military rank rather than age or experience. To survive in this market, they used whatever resources they had, and youth could be one of these resources. Much like older men, young ones looked to the military for complex reasons, lofty and self-interested, but in an economy of high inflation and limited opportunities to make a decent living, few could afford to ignore financial considerations entirely. They sought out the best deals, throwing in their lot with whatever broker seemed to offer the highest bounties and the best opportunities. Some must have calculated that bounty jumping was worth the risk, and others surely hoped to use their youth to shield them from the battlefield even if they remained in the service. With constant talk of fabulous bounties, even the merest boys knew where the money lay. According to one newspaper story originally printed in Kansas, a "lad of about ten years of age, representing himself as a substitute broker" had appeared at a recruiting office with three other boys between the ages of eight and twelve in tow, "whom he desired to 'sell' for two hundred dollars apiece." Meeting only with laughter, he told the recruiter that he would take the boys to Boston "where he could do better."[58]

From the beginning of the war, youth could be either an asset or a liability in this marketplace, but the balance between opportunity and hazard shifted considerably over time as the price paid for substitutes rose. Initially, the cost of substitutes was in effect capped due to the commutation provision. But commutation also generated tremendous class resentment among those who saw it as a measure that favored the rich and held down the price substitutes could command.[59] In response to public sentiment, Congress decided to revoke the ability to buy one's way out of service in July 1864, and the prices paid for substitutes immediately skyrocketed.

This development affected youths in particular ways. Since the draft covered men between the ages of twenty and thirty-five, this left eighteen- and nineteen-year-olds as the largest pool of legal substitutes. But most in this group who were willing to enlist had already done so, and although more reached the enlistment age each year, their numbers did not match the vast quantity of troops wanted.[60] This meant that anyone seeking to tap into the lucrative trade in substitutes had to turn their attention elsewhere—to older males and especially to younger boys. To make matters worse, as the government became more desperate for troops, the War Department clamped down on discharges of all kinds, ensuring that those lured or impressed into service found it increasingly hard to escape, regardless of their circumstances.

The exploitation of young males in the United States thus rose along with the cost of volunteers and substitutes, at times extending into outright kidnapping.[61] Accounts in the press and letters sent to officials reveal that brokers were not the only ones seeking to exploit youths. Parents wrote to officials complaining of neighbors who had enlisted their children and made off with their bounties, or of hiring out young sons only to find that they had ended up in the military with nothing to show for it.[62] One brother sold his younger sibling into service and kept the proceeds, but found himself in court in 1868 charged with various wartime forgery schemes.[63] And, in New York, the press accused the city's police force of rounding up "vagrant" boys, filling out false guardianship papers, and enlisting them for profit.[64] Similar cases of devious individuals claiming the right to dispose of boys' labor grew so pervasive that the city temporarily stopped issuing letters of guardianship over minor children midway through 1864.[65]

Throughout this year, stories proliferated of boys who had been forced into service or had their bounties stolen. In August, the press reported on two brokers arrested for kidnapping three youths, the oldest of whom was sixteen, and taking them from Vermont to Poughkeepsie to sell as substitutes. Their plans went awry after one of their targets—a sixteen-year-old from a prominent Vermont family—refused to go along with their scheme to lie about his age. His captors kept him confined for several days, plied him with liquor, and took him to a brothel, but they were eventually forced to release him. With a powerful father on his side, he managed to get the brokers charged with kidnapping and suborning perjury, although he lost his case when a faulty warrant led to the brokers' release.[66] Others simply vanished, leaving families to surmise that they had been lured into service. In January, the *New York Daily Herald* ran an ad offering a $5 reward for information concerning the whereabouts of fourteen-year-old Peter Hudson, "supposed to have been enticed to enlist in the United State Army."[67] Fourteen-year-old James Henry Crawford went missing in December, leading his parents to offer a "liberal reward" for his return.[68] A few months later, a soldier in the 25th Iowa Infantry posted an ad searching for his twelve-year-old son, apparently plucked off the streets of Iowa City.[69] No further information on these missing children appeared, but they signaled a larger issue with youth vulnerability in an economy that allowed previously unheard of sums to be made by those trafficking in the young.

For those seeking relatively defenseless youths, institutions housing children became promising hunting grounds. Homes for newsboys in Philadelphia, New York, and Washington, DC, all lost residents as boys joined the army.[70] The New York House of Refuge, widely viewed as a model for other juvenile reformatories, sent several hundred boys directly from the reformatory to the military.[71] Because such institutions routinely indentured out older boys to work on farms and in trades, overseeing or negotiating enlistment contracts probably did not seem like much of a departure from the norm. But as the costs of running schools rose steeply amid wartime inflation, and the bounties offered to enlistees shot up, some institutions even facilitated the enlistment of underage boys in the face of parental opposition.

The superintendent of the Providence School of Reform in Rhode Island, for instance, began to funnel inmates to a particular provost marshal in 1863, appropriating the lion's share of their bounties. Most of these youths were children of Irish immigrants or African Americans. One mother, whose son had been enlisted after she expressly stated that she did not want him joining the army, filed a complaint that led the state legislature to investigate the matter. Testifying before the committee, the superintendent acknowledged that several boys had been enlisted "against their will" but asserted that he and the trustees could legally act as the youths' guardians. Apparently, the provost marshal had communicated that he could enlist all youth aged sixteen to eighteen, so long as the superintendent gave his consent. Existing law in fact forbade the enlistment of those below age eighteen, but when Congress strengthened penalties against wayward recruiting officers in 1864, it decided to penalize only those who recruited youths below age sixteen. This opened the door further for institutions like reform schools that sought to use enlistment to raise funds or dispense with difficult inmates.[72] In the end, the Rhode Island Senate Committee concluded that the school had overstepped its bounds and engaged in an unlawful practice, depriving parents of their minor children and "of the control of those children's earnings."[73]

Indian reservations were similarly vulnerable to intrusions by unscrupulous brokers. Many Native Americans signed up as substitutes, attracted by the promise of high bounties, only to regret their decision. By 1864, as many as forty-three Iroquois, primarily of the Seneca Nation, had asked to be discharged from New York regiments in which they served. They claimed to be younger than eighteen, to have never received their bounty, or both. Chief Samuel George, an honorary brevet general who served as their designated spokesman, met with President Lincoln to discuss the situation in November 1863. George urged Lincoln to prevent recruiters from signing up underage Indian youths and reminded him that drafting of Native Americans could not occur legally without tribal consent. Lincoln followed up with the secretary of war, leading to the discharge of thirteen enlistees. But George struggled to get others released, including those who had already received and spent their bounty money.[74]

Recently arrived immigrants were another vulnerable group who found themselves in brokers' sights. Despite the extent of battlefield losses, the United States saw population growth during the war, largely because of the more than 800,000 newcomers who had been driven from Europe, Britain, and Ireland by low wages and lean harvests, military conflict, or lack of opportunities. Almost all entered northern states, where they were welcomed by employers, government officials, and the press as a way to replenish the workforce. Indeed, the US government enticed migrants by advertising in the foreign press, passing laws granting expedited citizenship to immigrants who volunteered for service, and offering free land under the Homestead Act of 1862.[75] Many of these new arrivals were young, and an unknown number, though almost certainly in the thousands, were forced into uniform against their will.[76]

A constant stream of foreign minors alleged to have been impressed into service were brought to the State Department's attention. British Ambassador Lord Lyons presented Secretary of State William Seward with at least 235 instances of underage Britons whose parents had petitioned for their release, in some cases writing to him themselves. His French counterpart sought the release of an additional fifty boys, while similar appeals numbering in their dozens arrived from representatives of the Scandinavian, German, and Italian governments.[77] In a few instances, parents pursued children who had enlisted willingly, albeit illegally. But other petitioners told of minors being tricked, held hostage, or enlisted under duress. Many ended up serving out their time, finding it impossible to prove their charges or simply facing long bureaucratic delays.

When it came to the impressment of those born outside the United States, the Canadian government had the greatest cause for complaint. By 1864, substitute brokers were regularly crossing the Canadian border looking for targets to strongarm into service. The thousands of British soldiers in garrisoned towns along the border proved the most common victims, but young Canadians also had cause to beware.[78] In July 1864, a fifteen-year-old named John Allison recounted walking home one evening in Niagara Falls after supper and waking up some time later on the other side of the border to find himself facing a three-year enlistment in the US Navy. In the meantime, his relatives had launched a frantic search, placing ads in the local press and convincing the police to drag the Niagara River to hunt for his body. When they finally heard from Allison, he was in Ohio aboard a US gunboat. The British Consul, stationed in Buffalo, New York, reported this incident to Lord

Lyons, writing on July 25, "How many of these are drugged and brought over to this side it is impossible to say. But a regular system is now organized by which men are passed over the frontier and kept stupefied with liquor until they enlist. I have no doubt whatsoever."[79]

Almost identical cases also regularly found their way to Canadian Governor-General Charles Monck. In April the same year, he received a petition from Michael Boyle, who stated that his son, "under age, delicate in health and of consumptive habits," had been "seduced and taken away from his school by some of the American private recruiting agents."[80] Shortly thereafter, a group of six French-Canadians appealed to Monck regarding a sixteen-year-old named Alfred Boissoit. They claimed the youth had been plied with liquor by a recruiting agent in Montreal, swindled out of his bounty, and made to sign a receipt for a vast sum of money that he never received.[81] To counteract this trade, Canada created a secret police force in 1864 headed by Commissioner Gilbert McMicken. Placing spies in border towns and major railway junctions to watch for bounty jumpers and brokers, McMicken had agents check trains and monitor steamboats for suspicious activities, but his small and underpaid force could only do so much.[82] In the war's final year, larger fines for recruiters and longer prison sentences for deserters demonstrated Canada's ongoing concern with the trade in illegal substitutes and the enticements offered by Union bounties.[83]

Other examples of foreigners who found themselves in the ranks similarly cry out for scrutiny. While most suspect enlistments date from the latter part of the war, one of the few Chinese immigrants known to have served in the Union army signed up under dubious circumstances in May of 1861. John Tomney or Tommy—his Chinese name remains unknown—endured a stint as a prisoner of war and died of wounds sustained in the Battle of Gettysburg.[84] But how had he come to join the army in the first place? According to one widely printed account, Tommy arrived in the United States soon after the war began and "was induced" to enlist in Daniel Sickle's brigade, then in the process of being raised. Given that he was "a mere lad, entirely ignorant of our language" at the time of his enlistment, it is reasonable to wonder what form that inducement took.[85]

US officials exhibited a distinct lack of urgency in looking into instances of foreigners—some mere boys—being tricked or forced into uniform. On receiving a charge, they usually wrote to commanding and enrollment officers asking for details about individual recruits. But when word came back that an enlistment was above board, officers were invariably taken at their word. One recent study of fraudulent enlistment practices at naval recruitment stations notes that the Naval Department launched only a single full-scale inquiry into such a charge during the war—a court of inquiry at the Boston Navy Yard which concerned a British subject born in Nova Scotia who claimed to have been enlisted in a drunken stupor. Even though naval officials knew their rendezvous were swarming with crimps and runners, they nonetheless sided with officers who swore that the recruit had been sober. Like virtually everyone who made a similar charge, this enlistee was therefore compelled to perform the service he was probably coerced to contract.[86]

By July 1862, young African American males had joined immigrants, asylum inmates, and unprotected white youths as a group wide open to be exploited for toil or profit.[87] That month, Congress passed the Militia Act, which allowed for the enrollment of Black laborers and soldiers, though the recruitment of African Americans had already begun in some Union-held areas. In the coastal regions of South Carolina, General David Hunter started raising Black regiments in May, simply decreeing that officers should send to his headquarters "under a guard, all the able-bodied negroes capable of bearing arms." According to one account, this measure "terrified the ex-slaves and convinced them that such efforts preceded a return to bondage."[88] A policy of impressing Black males as soldiers or workers continued in this area under Hunter's successor, Rufus Saxton, while federal recruiters in Maryland likewise conducted "vigorous" campaigns that included forcing the enslaved into uniform.[89]

One of the few accounts left by a Union recruiter—a diary written by James Ayers—suggests that the official enlistment age of eighteen to thirty-five was irrelevant to men in his position. Ayers, who entered the Union army in his late fifties after lying about his own age, had been sent to Nashville and put in charge of recruiting for Black regiments in that state. In his diary, he described travelling from one planation to another throughout 1864, explaining the Emancipation Proclamation to Black inhabitants and endeavoring to sign up all "able bodied Negroes" who volunteered to enlist. Although he would certainly have known of the army's age requirements, Ayers' diary suggests that a visual inspection rather than evidence of birth was the only criteria he used.[90] This also seems likely given that many of the enslaved did not know their precise birthdates, leaving it up to recruiters to decide on their eligibility.[91]

Few were as conscientious as Ayers in accepting only willing enlistees. Faced with an especially powerless population, recruiters often signed up

Black boys and older men via threats and coercion, knowing that documentation was difficult for the formerly enslaved to produce and easy for officers to discount where it did exist. One veteran of the 104th Infantry US Colored Troops, a regiment mostly made up of former bondspeople from the coastal low country of South Carolina, told pension officials that he was sixteen years old in 1865, the year federal recruiters forced him into uniform. "My pa went to my owner and got my age, and I remember it well," he explained. "While we were located at Beaufort, S.C., my pa brought a writing from my owner showing that I was 16 and tried to get me out of the army. I was then nothing but a lad . . . and anyone could see that I was not over 16." But this verbal appeal and the word of a former master were not enough. Robert Moses continued in service despite his youth, which also failed to shield him from his white officers' wrath. His pension request was partly based on a wound "caused by a punch the captain gave me with his sword" when he fell out of line on the march. According to his application, this wound grew progressively larger and increasingly painful over the years.[92]

The impressment of enslaved males into the Union army became particularly widespread after July 1864, when both state and federal governments began vying for Black enlistees. Before this point, businessmen in Massachusetts—the most industrialized state in the Union—had begun lobbying Congress to allow it to recruit outside the state. Alarmed by the evaporation of their white labor force into the ranks and the rising cost of new workers, they hoped that enlisting former slaves would allow the state to meet its quotas, while preserving their workforce and thereby keeping wages low. Western senators opposed the move, rightly interpreting it as a way for northeasterners to shirk their responsibilities under the draft, but their opposition was not enough to prevent Congressional approval. In short order, the Massachusetts governor chose Boston entrepreneur John Murray Forbes to raise funds for out-of-state recruiting. He, in turn, created a businessmen's committee comprised of leading industrialists to help him. Once this committee had raised the necessary capital to employ agents, it sent them southward in a bid to add as many African American names to the state's enlistment rolls as possible.[93]

According to commentators at the time, these agents were ruthless—threatening, cajoling, and outright kidnapping enslaved and free Black boys and men into service. Albert G. Brown, who had served as a secretary to Governor Andrew before becoming a Treasury Department agent in South Carolina and Georgia, told his former employer that he found "the whole system. . . . damnable. I can conceive nothing worse on the coast of Africa." Former slaves, he charged, "have been hunted like wild beasts, dragged from their families," and given "only a fraction of the money promised them, with agents pocketing the rest." In a similar vein, a Massachusetts officer wrote home in early 1865 decrying the "traffic of New England towns in the bodies of wretched negroes, bidding against each other for these miserable beings who are deluded, and if some affidavits that I have in my office are true, tortured into service."[94]

The recruiting situation was especially dire in Kentucky, a border state with an enslaved population that remained technically unaffected by the Emancipation Proclamation. In February 1865, President Lincoln rebuked one recruiter, noting: "complaint is being made to me that you are forcing negroes into the military service and even torturing them . . . to extort their consent. . . . You must not force Negroes any more than white men."[95] The following month, Senator Garrett Davis of Kentucky gave a lengthy speech in Congress describing the many "wrongs and outrages" allegedly perpetrated upon the state in previous years. His most detailed complaints focused on the way recruiting officers had swept across the area, first inducing a handful of enslaved men to join them, and then using these recruits as "effective agents of their work . . . invading every household, workshop, or field . . . beguiling, constraining, and forcibly dragging away . . . all men and half-grown boys." He failed to note that many went willingly, no doubt keen to swap their unpaid toil for a soldier's wages and the promise of freedom. But he was not wrong in asserting that recruiters carried off males of all ages—"many who were over age, who were physically incompetent, who were under age, [some] as low as ten or twelve years," only to sell "these living chattels as substitutes, both in and out of the State, making enormous profits."[96]

Black boys and youths were exploited not just as soldiers but also as servants and laborers in Union camps and on the front lines, often for minimal compensation. One young soldier in the 10th Rhode Island talked about a thirteen-year-old "contraband" named Abraham Douglass who was paid $2.50 a month to clean soldiers' dishes and clothing and provide their entertainment. "Cheap enough, isn't it," he wrote in his diary. "The boys enjoy the singing very much and call Little Abe out every night."[97] What Douglass made of his situation is anyone's guess. Dependent on the goodwill of those he served, it was his lot to put on a cheerful show whatever his true feelings.

African American youths were similarly obliged to provide low-cost military labor on Roanoke Island, an area under Union command since 1862.

Figure 9.3 Wherever Union army camps were established, Black children sought refuge there, sometimes with parents or other relatives, sometimes on their own. These boys are all wearing Union army uniforms—note the turned-up cuffs on the youngest boy's jacket—but they were probably not on the army payroll. Instead, they had likely been given or purchased the clothes in exchange for working as servants to the officers. Captain Beriah S. Brown of Co. H, 2nd Rhode Island Infantry Regiment, Captain John P. Shaw of 1st Rhode Island Infantry Regiment and Co. F, 2nd Rhode Island Infantry Regiment, and Lieutenant T. Fry with three African American boys at Camp Brightwood, Washington, DC, c. 1861-63. Liljenquist Family Collection, Library of Congress Prints and Photograph Division, LC-DIG-ppmsca-67835.

Here, parents who hoped to keep boys in school so they could gain the literacy denied them under slavery clashed with Union officials who sought to limit costs by sending youths into the workforce. Seeking to force the issue, officials denied rations to boys above age fourteen. When that strategy failed, they were not above using trickery to meet their goal. In one instance, white officials told a group of twenty teenage boys that they could collect rations

Figure 9.4 A photographer employed by Matthew Brady, James F. Gibson, took some of the best-known photographs of African American refugees who had fled slavery. Those pictured here—the small boy with bandaged foot, nestled between the legs of a Union soldier, and the older Black man crouched behind—likely made their way to Union lines when the army took over parts of southeastern Virginia in 1862. They were probably recent escapees and may have been posed by Gibson with this group of men. The child's body language and downturned face, half hidden by the soldier's newspaper, speak poignantly to his desperate need for shelter. James F. Gibson, "Cumberland Landing, Virginia. Group at Mr. Foller's farm," May 1862. Library of Congress Prints and Photographic Division, LC-DIG-cwpb-00288.

at the superintendent's headquarters. But when the youths reached this location they were placed under guard, forced onto a nearby ship, and sent to New Bern to perform menial labor.[98] Viewing African American parents as unfit to govern their offspring, Union officials established a pattern of interfering in Black family life that would only expand after the war, as military officials across the former Confederacy stepped in to negotiate apprenticeship contracts, settle disputes between freedmen and women, and establish guidelines governing relationships between freedpeople's families and former enslavers.[99]

Free Black families in the northern states were less subject to intrusion, but they also faced the loss of their children as reports began surfacing of a trade in African American substitutes. A Pennsylvania paper, the *Wyoming Democrat*, noted in July 1864 that "Negroes are brought north by the car-load, and sold to persons who have been drafted, or who fear the draft, at from $300 to $600 each." While the recruits received "only a small part of this amount," the report noted, "the dealer makes a handsome thing of it."[100] Young Black boys, suffering the powerlessness of both age and racial status, seem to have been especially common prey for brokers. Reverend Henry Highland Garnett, a well-known orator and anti-slavery activist who was active in recruiting Black soldiers and ministered to USCT regiments stationed on Riker's Island before being sent to the field, later recalled how brokers had hampered his recruiting efforts. "The runners kidnapped boys and old men, cripples and maimed, and by collusion with the proper officers, forced them to Riker's Island," he noted.[101] Nor did they operate only in large eastern cities. Willis Butcher of Wathena, Kansas, sent a telegram to the district provost marshal in March 1865, stating that he "forbid" the enlistment of his seventeen-year-old son, Henry. According to his account, the boy had been "abducted" in order to be "used as a substitute" for an older white youth who lived in the same county.[102] In every state, runners were on the lookout for African Americans, young or old, who might be coerced to enlist and forced to hand over their bounties.[103]

Union officers and soldiers joined those seeking quick money by preying on Black males, operating with an impunity that can be seen in an affidavit that John Alexander provided to Colonel Lafayette Baker at the end of 1863. Employed with the 20th US Colored Troops, then stationed in New York City, he was walking up Broadway one afternoon when he saw a "colored man, apparently a sailor" in conversation with several white soldiers. The man looked scared, and Alexander feared that he was about to be taken to a nearby "pen" and impressed into service, so he followed to see "how much of his bounty he received." Judging by the form and substance of his testimony, Alexander was an experienced older man, and certainly a brave one, for he was about to disrupt the kidnapping of more than half a dozen Black males held in this pen, in a city that had recently seen hundreds of African Americans beaten or killed in the streets. As he looked inside the pen to scrutinize the proceedings, Alexander was dragged inside by a white officer who taunted: "You damned nigger you've got to stay here now." Probably nervous at being caught in the act or enraged at having his authority challenged, the officer then told Alexander that he would force him to enlist and kill him if he tried to leave. He was clearly shaken when his victim countered with a threat of his own. Referring to his white colonel, Alexander warned his captor that he "could go out and would make trouble for him." As the officer and his men held a whispered conference, Alexander discovered that his fellow captives had all been snatched off the streets, and some showed signs of a beating. Alexander was eventually released, his jailers no doubt deciding that it was riskier to coerce a defiant adult with a powerful sponsor than to go through with their plans. But although he immediately took his tale to his superior officers, the pen containing the Black prisoners was still there when Alexander returned a few days later. At this point, he was either sent to Colonel Baker to investigate further or chose to go on his own.[104]

There is no indication whether Alexander's courageous snooping paid off, but it shows the thriving underground market the war had created in Black male bodies, which could quickly be turned into cash by individuals working in either official or unofficial capacities, and in which the unscrupulous did not seem overly worried about being caught. As Alexander noted in his affidavit, he initially followed the frightened man because he had heard about a nearby pen where African Americans were being impressed; the business he disrupted was obviously an open secret. And the soldiers involved left their victims in place despite his threat to "make trouble," suggesting they calculated that the potential rewards outweighed the risk of punishment.

Gambles like these took place in a labor market where the stakes for corrupt recruiters and officers were minimized by the nature of enlistment contracts and military justice and borne unequally by enlistees. Thousands of brokers must have been involved in fleecing unwary recruits, but only a handful ever appeared in court. Union officers were still less likely to be punished for enlistment violations. Even if they were caught and tried, officers knew they would only face dismissal from the service and public shame, not jail time or penury.[105] Above all, corrupt recruiters and officials knew that their dealings were relatively safe because enlistment contracts were fundamentally coercive. In a civilian labor market, the only real power that workers had was the ability to move between jobs in search of better wages or conditions. As soon as that worker's name went down on a muster roll, he instantly lost that right, regardless of whether he had contracted freely or received the promised compensation for doing so.

When a recruit claimed to have been strong-armed into service or fallen victim to fraud, the War Department followed up on the claim, but these investigations rarely resulted in a discharge, except in cases of underage recruits who had clearly lacked parental consent. Even then, policies forbade the release of anyone unable to pay back the costs of bounties and equipment, and most families did not have large sums of ready cash to meet such contingencies. As a lawyer for Henry Clay Pritchard's father explained to the War Department, a substitute broker had plied his seventeen-year-old son with alcohol and left the boy with just $150 of the bounty money he had received. Explaining that his client was "very poor" and unable to raise the stolen money immediately, the lawyer asked whether Pritchard could be discharged prior to repayment. To this and many similar queries, the government responded negatively.[106] The same implacable rule applied regardless of whether the enlistee himself had ever possessed the bounty. Near the end of the war, a Philadelphia newspaper reported on a case in which some dishonest brokers had pursued a "villainous scheme" to enlist a young boy with the help of an "abandoned woman" who agreed to impersonate his mother. After collecting the boy's bounty money, the woman's accomplices were arrested and taken into service themselves. Still, military authorities refused to release the young recruit until the money listed under his name had been refunded, even though he had received nothing at all.[107] Unscrupulous brokers, recruiters, and officers, in other words, could be fairly certain that those they scammed would be far away at the front, powerless to escape the deals made in their names and unable to testify against them in person.

* * *

By the war's final year, the exploitation of male youths by brokers, recruiters, and sometimes even parents had grown so extensive that it became fodder for the anti-war press. Earlier, pro-Union editors had accused Confederate parents of cheerfully selling young sons into service—placing "a higher estimate on [their] slaves than they did upon their boys."[108] Once the Confederacy banned brokers and then scrapped the substitution policy altogether, however, accusations of a traffic in white children were directed mainly at the United States. Anti-war Democrats used tales of children sold into service as a cudgel against their opponents, drawing on the well-honed claim that white workers were the real slaves. Picturing a treacherous system in which the poor fought and toiled while others reaped the rewards, they accused the most avid Unionists of sitting out the war by selling their own children into service or "coaxing little boys to go as substitutes in their stead!"[109] "Let us hear no more of the barbarism of slavery," declared the *Bedford*

Gazette, when loyal men sold "half grown, ill-shaped boys," and "loud-mouthed" abolitionists bargained to buy them.[110]

These accounts of "little boys" led like lambs to slaughter contained plenty of hyperbole. The emotive power of imagery related to innocent child victims was clearly useful for pro- and anti-war commentators, just as it could be useful for boys and youths in seeking to evade adult responsibilities. Yet the war did in fact lead to the increased victimization of young males. On both sides, it created a market in which free white and Black children could be sold for profit and forced into harsh labor, placing them, at least temporarily, on the same level as the enslaved. In the Confederacy, enslaved youths and those from free Black families were impressed into service, joining a smaller number of white youths coerced into the ranks. An even greater number of young white and African American males who served the Union were reduced to pawns in others' money-making schemes or exploited as a low-cost workforce, their vulnerability increasing exponentially as volunteering declined and the costs of hiring a substitute shot upward.

Still, the distinction between constraint and free will seems somewhat redundant when it comes to boys' and youths' enlistment decisions. The majority enlisted without the need for physical compulsion. But they did so in a labor market that required all family members to work to support their households, while providing youths with only the narrowest opportunities to earn a living. In this economic climate, a military wage offered the best—sometimes the only—chance for a boy or youth to get ahead. To seize that chance did not mean grasping what it meant. Almost no one who entered the bottom ranks of the military hierarchy had any experience of war. Once in uniform, enlistees performed whatever tasks they were assigned, even if these were not the tasks they thought they had contracted to do. Choice became irrelevant the moment an enlistment contract was signed, for there was little scope for bargaining and almost no chance of escape—a situation designed to compound the widespread victimization of the young.

The wartime market for military labor confronted boys and youths with unique pitfalls and opportunities. They might be kidnapped and exploited, or they might receive unprecedented benefits, ranging from high bounties and a regular adult wage to the legal right to keep whatever they made and free land if they managed to survive. The published reminiscences of those who enlisted underage show that some relished the experience, seeing war as a golden opportunity to learn, profit, and mature. Growing up in the military evidently offered a potent psychological boost to a lucky cohort: former boy soldiers were well over-represented in leadership roles in the post-bellum years. More than twenty-five underage Union enlistees, and an even larger number who fought for the Confederacy eventually served in the US Congress. Countless others achieved success in local or state politics, government, or business. While no one has attempted to quantify the state legislators, governors, or captains of industry who parlayed an underage enlistment into postwar prestige, anyone searching for a boy soldier who went on to a prominent career will not have to look far.[111]

As both sides began to celebrate boy soldiers in the decades ahead, the stories of those who emerged from war unscathed in body and mind would come to dominate the historical record, while tales of boys and youths who experienced the greatest exploitation went largely unrecorded. In reality, the latter were in the majority. Rather than a collective coming-of-age for the young, the Civil War proved to be a crucible: some emerged stronger, but most bent or broke under the strain, their plight known only by friends and family.

Epilogue
A War Fought by Boys

Reimagining Boyhood and Underage Soldiers after the Civil War

Between the end of the Civil War and the start of World War I, the idea of actively encouraging boys to enlist in the military became unthinkable in American culture. Ironically, this shift took place at the same moment when adventurous boyhood became a celebrated phenomenon—an antidote for those concerned with rising immigration, the perils of over-civilization, and the growing visibility of women in schools and workplaces. Cultural anxiety focused particularly on male adolescence. With manhood and womanhood defined in increasingly oppositional terms, masculinity came to be understood as something that boys needed to attain. The risk was too high to let them develop unaided, for according to new ideas about social evolution, nothing less than the future of civilization was at stake. Setting up a range of artificial structures, from rifle clubs to the Boy Scouts, adult men sought to ensure that white American boys would achieve the right mix of competitiveness, strength, and toughness. Celebrating the brave boy soldiers of America's past became a common way to train a new generation in the daring and hardiness of male forebears, even as the paths that would have allowed boys in the present to follow in their footsteps narrowed.

No longer allowed to enlist for war, American boys were instead urged to emulate their heroic ancestors by participating in military drill in their schoolyards. This was a far cry from either militia training or military enlistment. Even if such training made boys more likely to consider soldiering, there was no direct relationship between this form of military preparedness and going to war. Marching alongside those of similar age under the guidance of an adult man, boys no longer mingled as peers with males of all ages. By the late nineteenth century, many Americans frowned on even this indirect association between childhood and military service, believing that the young had no business wearing any kind of military uniform before reaching the age of eighteen. A new generation of experts had reconceptualized the years between birth and adulthood by this point, transforming childhood into a medical issue, a psychological field, and a social problem. Avidly debating the issue of military drill in schools, no one even bothered to consider the merits or pitfalls of enlisting boys below eighteen into the US military. That issue was now closed.

As underage enlistment became a distant phenomenon, no longer conceivable in the present, the Civil War's boy soldiers became quaint symbols of a lost world. Interest in their service peaked in the lead-up to World War I, as Civil War veterans died off in large numbers. In the 1910s, a myth took hold throughout the nation that boy soldiers had not just fought in the war but constituted the majority of armed participants. Fabricated records claiming that there were over a million underage enlistees in the Union army alone spread like wildfire, reported in the press, amplified in Congress, and reprinted in books and memoirs. Valuable for those who sought to use the past to reflect on the present, these exaggerations would ultimately lead to the whole topic of boy soldiers being dismissed as an over-hyped curiosity fit only for popular histories and children's books.

Celebrating Boy Soldiers

The first celebrations of underage enlistment in the Civil War began in the 1880s amid a wave of enthusiasm for wartime reminiscing.[1] Initially, age itself was the focus. As former officers began releasing eyewitness accounts of battles, and as participation in veterans' organizations spiked after the economic downturn of the 1870s, several widely read newspapers ran competitions to discover the Union's "youngest veteran."[2] Printing letters from claimants, sometimes with biographical details attached, the newspapers implied that youth enlistment was an honorable accomplishment in and of itself.

By suggesting that "youngest veteran" was a distinction worth holding, the press unleashed a deluge of correspondence. The editor of Chicago's staunchly Republican *Inter Ocean* had to concede that he had bitten off more than he could chew, and that the paper would no longer publish the claims of anyone who had enlisted after reaching the age of fifteen.[3] Still, the letters kept coming. Squabbles broke out as veterans accused each other of egotism or lying. Thomas Hubler had to defend his claim in 1881 after another young veteran went to the trouble of checking the muster rolls in Washington and accused him of inconsistencies. Declaring his detractor a "little bit tainted with jealousy," Hubler produced his family Bible and baptismal certificate to verify his claim. If the paper saw fit "to scratch me from their list and put . . . any other egotistical man, or boy, in my place, all well and good," he huffed, "for wrangling over soldier business now does not bring in any bread and butter."[4] Despite such protestations, securing a place on the *Inter Ocean*'s "Roll of Honor" of "Young Heroes of the Late War" clearly did matter to Hubler and many others. Thereafter, claimants began to list their age not just in years but also in months and days. Many also tacitly compared their service to that of others by noting the length of their enlistment, the number of battles they fought in, or the fact that they served in the ranks rather than as musicians.[5]

The whole issue took on the feel of a horse race as successive newspapers claimed to have discovered the youngest veteran. In fact, so many hundreds of veterans made these assertions that the discovery of "the youngest soldier" became a regular punchline by the turn of the century. One paper joked that, "The most beautiful woman in the world is about as numerous as the youngest soldier in the Civil War."[6] Another printed a humorous exchange: "Well, no man has to die more than once, anyway." "I don't know about that. How about 'the youngest soldier to enlist in the civil war?' He dies regularly every year or so."[7] Taking the jest to absurd extremes, an Iowa paper finally gave the title of "youngest veteran" to a baby who had been born in a Union camp in December 1863 and "formally" mustered into the regiment at ten days old.[8]

The southern press also carried stories about the "youngest Confederate soldier," but they appeared roughly a decade later and not in such volume. In April 1891, the *Richmond Dispatch* pointed to a recent claim made about the youngest Union enlistee and asked readers to send details to identify his Confederate counterpart, including "how long he *served in the field*."[9] Over subsequent weeks, dozens of letter writers obliged. More came forward to claim the title in 1906, when the same paper offered a bejeweled medal to the youngest and oldest Confederate veterans still living. The paper ran a full-page spread on the winner in the first category—William F. Hopkins, described as "a soldier, carrying a musket when but a little more than eleven years old."[10]

The tenor of discussions around underage enlistees had shifted noticeably by this point. Much as they had during the war, writers invariably pictured young soldiers who were white and eager to enlist. But they had become much more warlike over time. In place of references to golden curls, childlike innocence, or love of God and mother, young soldiers increasingly carried weapons and threw themselves into battle, killing enemies rather than dying inspirational deaths. Drummer boys became older, too, indistinguishable from young soldiers who engaged in daring acts, hairbreadth escapes, and amusing antics. Addressing readers across the entire country, writers frequently discussed white Union and Confederate enlistees in the same breath, stressing their identical bravery.[11] Writing for the *Youth's Companion* in 1893, Wilbur Hinman told young readers that "the boy soldier was as brave as a lion" in battle. "He knew no fear; if he did, he was too proud to allow it to get the mastery." He had personally witnessed "boys of sixteen years charge with flashing bayonets into deadly fire," he claimed. Having served as an officer during the war before publishing a popular memoir in the late 1880s, Hinman wrote with conviction, describing masses of boy soldiers on both sides who cheerfully weathered privation and laughed in the face of death. "Scores and hundreds went down before the blast, but those who were spared kept on, leading the way for those who were less eager to fling themselves upon the enemy."[12]

The promotion of bravery and daring in boys was widely seen as a matter of vital importance by the 1890s. This was an anxious decade for many, bookended by the Census Bureau's announcement that no tracts of unsettled land remained in the West and ending in war in the Philippines. In the years between, a devastating economic depression; mass immigration from central, eastern, and southern Europe; and rapid industrialization combined to produce a sense of seismic rupture. A rising tide of agrarian and labor radicals, anti-lynching campaigners, and women's rights activists was also challenging established elites' hold on power. As social Darwinists fretted that "over-civilization" was rendering middle-class white Americans incapable of competing against lesser races and classes, social commentators increasingly worried about the leadership capacity of white males.[13] Had the next generation of boys grown soft and flabby, they wondered, with women presiding over homes, churches, and schools, the three main arenas of childhood socialization? How would boys learn the rugged skills of their forebears living in cities or towns and destined for work behind desks, counters, or production lines?[14] Images of young white enlistees who were fearless and militant were perfectly suited to capture this milieu. "War," Hinman argued, was "a stern, hard school for the lads, North and South, but all were obeying the command of duty as they saw it, and the experience made them men years before they could have reached that stage of life in the usual pursuits of peace."[15]

Hinman referred to "lads, North and South," but the heroic boy soldiers that he and others celebrated were all white. Although large numbers of young Black males had also fought for the Union or been compelled to perform military labor for both sides, interest in youth enlistment in the 1890s was a noticeably white phenomenon. There are very few memoirs written by Black Union veterans, and even fewer written by any who served underage, so there were not as many published stories to draw upon. Still, using a boy soldier as a representative figure never had much appeal to African American authors or artists, given racist stereotypes of black infantilization and savagery. During the Civil War, military service had been a way for Black males to demonstrate manhood and to claim the rights of adult men.[16] When African American communities commemorated the Civil War, they remembered the coming of freedom, the heroism of Black troops, their contribution to saving the Union, and resilience in the face of ongoing oppression.[17]

Yet if boy soldier had negligible appeal in Black communities, the figure gained new purchase elsewhere in the late nineteenth century, along with new characteristics. During the Civil War, patriotic white drummer boys usefully personified republican virtue, signaling national innocence amid violent struggle. In the 1890s, their appeal was more generic, communicating traits that all white boys—not just republican ones—were supposed to embody. This is evident in the fact that statues and paintings of white drummer boys or young soldiers began appearing not just in former Union states but in those that had supported the Confederacy, as well as in Britain, where little interest was previously apparent.[18] It was also obvious in the updated qualities of the boy soldier figures popping up at this point: no longer signifying guileless purity, statues and images of drummer boys and boy soldiers by the late nineteenth century typically pictured hardy, fearless youths of the kind that Hinman praised.

Tales of young warriors had not entirely superseded sentimental depictions of drummer boys who inspired with their sacrificial deaths by this point. At least outside the south, the most widely performed play of the postwar era was Samuel Muscroft's *The Drummer Boy: or the Battle-field of Shiloh* (1868), the centerpiece of which was a young drummer boy's death in Andersonville prison—a scene reminiscent of Little Eva's demise in *Uncle Tom's Cabin*. In this work, though, it was a redemptive drummer boy who roused onlookers as he called on his mother, expressed his willingness to die to his country, and then ascended to heaven dressed in white robes, accompanied by guardian angels.[19] Year after year, veterans who formed Grand Army of the Republic (GAR) posts across the country raised money by staging Muscroft's work, depicted in the press as the war's "most popular military drama."[20] While writers in the 1890s were busy updating tales of boy soldiers and drummers to present them as fearless fighters no matter their side, Muscroft's work kept older narratives alive.

Still, in other forms of popular entertainment marketed to the young, drummer boys were spirited fighters rather than innocent victims. In the 1890s, major companies that marketed children's toys all started selling boardgames featuring young drummers or soldiers, most of which asked boys to imagine themselves in active roles on the path to military leadership. In 1889, for instance, Parker Brothers of Salem, Massachusetts, released a boardgame called "The Game of the Soldier Boy," where players enlisted at a recruiting office and then advanced through concentric circles until the lead player became commander in chief. Over the next decade, the firm produced "The Drummer Boy," which placed competitors on a track with squares featuring obstacles on their path toward the rank of colonel, along with a number of similar board games with titles like "The Game of War," "Following the Flag," and "The Little Corporal."[21] Older children appear to have played similar board games during the Civil War; it was their volume and popularity, not their content, that had changed by the late nineteenth century.[22]

The immensely popular juvenile fiction about the Civil War that appeared in the 1880s and 1890s also registered the dramatic social and political changes that had occurred since the conflict's end. As historian Alice Fahs has shown, the emphasis on adventure that had been a "trend" in Civil War juvenilia had become "the *sine qua non* of boys' fiction" by the late nineteenth century. Comparing Oliver Optic's wartime series with his popular Blue and Gray novels, which began appearing in 1888, Fahs highlights telling differences: in the later books, the fictional fathers emerged as more central and manly characters, while the formerly revered mothers descended into overbearing nags. While reimaging the war with the "markedly masculinist ethos" of the late nineteenth century, Optic also abandoned his earlier emphasis on the potentially corrupting influence of wealth while incorporating a whitewashed, romanticized view of slavery.[23]

A spate of memoirs released by former boy soldiers around the turn of the century likewise contributed to an emphasis on war as a salutary experience for the young. Since those with happy memories had the most incentive to reminisce, most of these memoirs were upbeat. They tended to portray the war as a coming of age, often harrowing but ultimately character-building, following the lead of popular writers like Stephen Crane—whose *Red Badge of Courage* (1898) famously told of a naïve youth who emerged from war chastened but wiser, transformed from a boy into a man. This emphasis indelibly shaped understandings of youth enlistment in the Civil War, crowding out the experience of most boy soldiers, who never wrote about their lives, and for whom enlistment led not to beneficial growth but to prolonged suffering, reduced capacity for work, and lives cut short.

Former boy soldiers with fond memories also found their voices significantly amplified as they outlived older peers to become the last living links to the war. As militant boyhood became a source of pride, they were in high demand as Memorial Day orators, school visitors, and commentators.[24] They were equally prominent in the GAR: A full thirty of the last fifty-one men to head this organization appear to have enlisted underage, a number widely out of proportion to their share of the veteran population overall.[25] By the late nineteenth century, having served underage had become a powerful boast, demonstrating an audacity that was prized in an increasingly cutthroat economy, or an innate patriotism useful for political office seekers.

Age Consciousness and the Social Transformation of Boyhood

If the figure of the boy soldier had changed significantly in writing addressed to juvenile and adult readers by the 1890s, an even more substantial shift is evident in the literature aimed at very young children. During the war years, books written for children contained simpler language than material directed at adults, but identical—in fact, often heightened—amounts of bloodshed. Even work for preliterate youngsters featured battlefields strewn with the dead. McLaughlin's output during the Civil War, for instance, included ABC books that employed violent imagery to teach children their letters, picturing "B" for battle and "W" for war, alongside graphic images.

PRIVATE FORAKER,
Co. A. 89th O. V. I.
Campaign Picture, 1883.

Figure E.1 Joseph B. Foraker (1846–1917) enlisted in the army at sixteen. He went on to have a successful political career, serving as Ohio's governor and a US senator in the 1880s and 1890s. His campaigns made great hay of his wartime service, recognizing that his reputation as a "boy soldier" earned him political capital. This image of Foraker circulated during his 1883 campaign for governor. From Joseph Benson Foraker, *Notes from a Busy Life*, vol. 1 (Cincinnati: Stewart & Kidd Company, 1916). Retrieved from Hathitrust Digital Library.

By the late nineteenth century, this was no longer the case. Children's books registered a new sense that the very young required quite different fare from their older siblings. A McLaughlin's catalogue from the mid-1890s includes hundreds of alphabet books, lithographed blocks, and works for early readers, all purged of violent imagery. Only one book—"Little Soldier's ABC"—depicts boy soldiers, featuring on its cover a regiment of youths around fifteen years old dressed in pristine blue uniforms, marching with rifles shouldered. Yet the scene is bucolic: in place of war, there is a cloudless sky and a peaceful country lane surrounded by greenery and all the bloodshed has been expunged, with "B" now symbolized by an adult bugler, and "W" by a wagon. All the other ABC books this company marketed in the late nineteenth century feature children wearing paper hats, playing at war rather than participating in war.[26]

This transformation in the material directed at pre-literate children points to a new concern with protecting young readers from violent content in literature. In the 1870s, American physicians had first started identifying children's exposure to violence as a problem, particularly in relation to the new genre of dime novels, which were phenomenally popular among boys. Because the rise of cheap printing allowed publishers to charge so little, large numbers of children for the first time began to purchase books directly, often without their parents' awareness. Librarians expressed similar concerns in 1870s and 1880s and sought to direct boys toward less "violent and vulgar" works.[27]

Marketing distinct content to readers of different age ranges likewise registered a new preoccupation with stages in childhood. By the end of the century, virtually every institution in which the young participated had come to be organized on the basis of chronological age. Whereas children and youths of varying ages had once sat in the same classrooms, read from the same primers, and joined social clubs containing members who ranged widely in age, they were now far more likely to enter schools rigidly divided into age groupings, to read textbooks designated for learners of a specified age range, and to join clubs or social groups with those very close in age. The growing professionalization of groups like fire companies or volunteer militia also effectively barred younger boys from participating in organizations that had once welcomed their presence. Demographic realities underlay these shifts. With birth rates declining and families growing smaller, the space between siblings shrank and the proportion of children in the population declined. Between 1840 and 1900, the percentage of adults aged between forty-five and sixty-five in America almost doubled. Having once constituted a sizeable majority of the population, those aged below eighteen years had become a minority by the turn of the century.[28]

Growing age consciousness was both cause and consequence of the new scientific interest directed at the young from the 1870s onward. At mid-century, much of the scientific literature linking age, growth, and health relied on measuring those in uniform and focused on ensuring military or industrial efficiency. Several decades later, attention had shifted to school children and college students. In fact, the American Civil War marked the highwater mark in military measurements, capped off by the publication of Benjamin Apthorp Gould's *Investigations in the Military and Anthropological Statistics of American Soldiers* (1869). Having completed that study, the USSC donated its measuring equipment to educational institutions. From this point until World War I, anthropometric research was mostly performed by American physical educators, school superintendents, and medical inspectors working with schoolchildren. Driven by fears that industrialism was leading to physical degeneration and the conviction that calculating an average or "ideal" body would aid in social advancement, they produced a flood of data by the turn of the century.[29]

This material formed the basis for the work of pioneering psychologist G. Stanley Hall. He had developed the child study movement in the 1880s, dedicated to understanding patterns of growth and learning in the young. A subsequent generation of scientists would concentrate on infants and toddlers, but adolescent children, particularly middle-class white boys, were Hall's main interest. He defined adolescence as the early to mid-teens—a developmental stage that began with the onset of puberty and was considerably more specific than the older term "youth," which had once applied to those ranging from the age of six to twenty-six. Like many of his contemporaries, Hall viewed the topic through the lens of social evolutionary theory. In articles and then his two-volume study *Adolescence* (1904), Hall popularized recapitulation theory—the notion that each individual repeated the evolutionary stages of their "race" over the course of development. Explaining that "the child and the race are keys to the other," Hall argued that children were little savages who should ideally be allowed to go through a "wild, undomesticated stage." Unfortunately, the rapid pace of urban life, with its "temptations, prematurities, sedentary occupations, and passive stimuli," was robbing youth of the ability to evolve through the necessary stages and thus achieve their highest potential.[30]

For Hall, adolescence was a time of great peril but also immense potential—the "bud of promise for the race."[31] To nurture this promise, educators, parents, and others who worked with children needed to accept and embrace the "primitive vitality" of white male adolescents—to welcome, rather than repress, their savage instincts. Much could go wrong if they failed. Hall's work is replete with anxious descriptions of adolescents dropping "limp and exhausted in body and soul."[32] He devoted entire chapters to the mental and physical diseases to which boys were allegedly subject at the onset of puberty—"the birthday of the imagination"—when ideas flowed rapidly but could easily be channeled in ways that threatened "decomposition of the personality."[33] As numerous scholars observe, Hall's work contained an ambiguous brew of optimism and dread, liberalism and authoritarianism, that at once urged adults to allow boys wide scope for independent development, yet simultaneously advised them to rigidly control and regulate boys' leisure time so as to shepherd them through the dangerous adolescent years and onward to maturity.[34]

Hall's unease in relation to shoring up maleness and his re-evaluation of boyhood were both hallmarks of the late nineteenth century. With growing numbers of women challenging male privileges—entering male-dominated professions and institutions, demanding voting rights, attacking male vices—middle-class men fixated on distinguishing themselves from women. Embracing competitive sports, adventure novels, wilderness adventures, body building, or leisure activities like boxing that had once been reserved for the working class, they turned away from promoting the kind of moral, self-restrained characters that marked their difference from those of other races and classes and instead championed traits that all men supposedly shared. "The obsessions of male writing about manhood in the late nineteenth and early twentieth century—competition, battle, physical aggression, bodily strength, primitive virtues, manly passions—all were inversions of 'feminized' Victorian civilization," notes historian Anthony Rotundo.[35]

This obsession fundamentally transformed the relationship between younger and older males. Having once thought of themselves as the opposite of boys—their acquisition of adulthood requiring them to overcome childish impulses—men were urged to embrace the "boy inside"; to recapture the spontaneity and vigor of boyhood as a means to protect themselves from the effeminizing tendencies of modern life.[36] Increasingly, adult men took on the role of organizing and leading boys' leisure activities, both to guide them through the perilous adolescent years and to recapture their own youth by association. By the late nineteenth century, the Young Men's Christian Association (YMCA) had shifted its focus from middle class men in their late teens and early twenties toward adolescent boys of all classes, promoting muscular Christianity through the establishment of summer camps and competitive sports teams. A group of wealthy New Yorkers that included Theodore Roosevelt had set up the Boone and Crockett Club to transport urban boys into the wilds of Montana for hunting and marksmanship training. The National Rifle Association (an organization founded by Union veterans) had begun sponsoring competitive shooting programs for teenagers, and after 1910, American boys could also join the Boy Scouts, a group that originated in Britain a few years prior, based on a centrally managed and promoted program that taught wilderness skills to young males.[37]

Lecturing the next generation about their Civil War experiences became another common way for older men to train younger ones in the 1890s. In this decade, veterans shifted from discussing boy soldiers as an exceptional cohort to portraying them as one of the war's defining features. Speaking to a GAR group in 1892, veteran John C. Black opened by claiming that well over a million boys had enrolled in the Union army at or before their eighteenth birthdays. Was it any wonder, then, that the Civil War was so filled with dash and valor? "Age is cautious; it treads dangerous ways with tentative steps . . . and pauses on the perilous edge." "But youth! . . .it launches its speedy attack upon the foe; who shall picture its daring, its rushing, splendid, exuberant advance." It was boys who furnished "many of the war's heroes," Black argued, and youth with their fervent energy and high spirits who kept the faith when older, more jaded men might have given up. "Boys of the twentieth century, this is what the Boys of the nineteenth century, through their sacrifices and wounds and holy death, will leave you," he told his audience. "We charge you, as you are the sons of our strength. See that no harm befalls the Republic."[38]

Despite such exhortation, boys were no longer supposed to fulfill this weighty responsibility by joining the US military or participating in state militia companies. Instead, men like Black concentrated on promoting patriotism and military drill in schools. For different reasons, veterans and fraternal organizations in all parts of the country turned to children's education as an important battleground in the 1890s. Across the northeast and midwest, in particular, as new arrivals streamed into cities and as workers and farmers joined together to protest political corruption and advocate for economic reforms, these organizations worked to promote respect for national symbols and to foster discipline and order. Along with campaigns to ensure that schools flew the American flag and sang the national anthem, the

GAR's Committee on Patriotism and its Committee on the Systematic Plan of Teaching Lessons of Loyalty to Our Country scoured textbooks to ensure that they depicted the Union victory as a noble effort to end slavery and secure the nation's future. Every year on Memorial Day, the organization sent veterans into schools to discuss their experiences and give patriotic speeches. At the GAR's National Encampment in 1892, the organization agreed to promote the introduction of military instruction across "all the schools in the land," a plan they furthered by lobbying legislatures, school officials, and teachers' gatherings.[39]

Part of the motivation for these efforts came from the success of pro-Confederate organizations, which were engaged in many of the same activities across the south. In these same years, the United Confederate Veterans worked alongside the United Daughters of the Confederacy (UDC) to ensure that the subsequent generations of white southerners would be steeped in the myth of the Lost Cause.[40] While veterans' organizations sent members into schools to tell children about their service, UDC members raised money to make sure that an image of Robert E. Lee or Jefferson Davis hung in every classroom.[41] They created children's auxiliaries, funded scholarships, and donated books to libraries. Under their watchful eyes, any textbook that failed to sufficiently glorify Confederate heroism, emphasize states' rights, or depict slavery as benign was soon expunged from school reading lists.[42]

As was the case in former Union states, Confederate veterans also promoted military drill in schools. Re-establishing military colleges that had been damaged or destroyed during the war and adding to their number, state legislatures largely relied on federal government land grants to fund this "rebirth of military education in the South." A handful of Black schools in the south—notably Hampton Institute in Virginia—also adopted military programs, but since military accoutrements were expensive and arming Black males controversial, this tended to be a white effort. Living in barracks, dressing in uniforms, learning how to drill and follow orders, generations of young white southern males learned to revere Confederate leaders and follow in their footsteps. Much like veterans' organizations in the other parts of the country, elite white southerners tended to view the "discipline and subordination of youth to authority" as essential in a time of labor strife, racial violence, and rapid economic change.[43]

In many ways, these efforts to promote military drill across all parts of the country paralleled the adult take-over of boys' leisure time: even as they promoted qualities like bravery, competition, and aggression, plans to drill male youth subordinated them in adult structures designed around uniformity and order, as did groups like the Boy Scouts. Perhaps this is not surprising given the transformation of the postbellum US economy. For as much as middle-class white adults agonized over how to raise white men who were fit to compete in the struggle of life, they also recognized that most would not become independent leaders but cogs that kept the machinery of industry turning.[44] Paeans to the vast number of brave youths in the Civil War urged boys to live up to a heroic past while also letting them know them that their forebears did not just play at war by marching around a school yard, but actually shouldered weapons and went into battle. Drilling boys, often under the instruction of former veterans, was a far cry from putting them in harm's way. Metaphorically gathering at the feet of an older generation, they were to passively consume, not actively emulate, their ancestors' acts of youthful daring.

Enthusiasm for military drill generated little dissent among social commentators or students themselves in the former Confederate states but met with considerable resistance elsewhere. At universities in the Midwest, students protested attempts to introduce military drill, arguing that American tradition opposed such displays of militarism. In the 1880s, those at the University of Wisconsin broke into the armory and sabotaged hundreds of muskets, while students at the University of Illinois forced several of the college's presidents to resign over the issue.[45] Similarly, the GAR's campaign to drill schoolboys garnered praise from some (including G. Stanley Hall and Theodore Roosevelt), but also howls of protest. Populists and labor unions were convinced that a militarized population would be used against ordinary people, no doubt based on their experience with the government's use of militia units to violently suppress labor strikes. Conversely, some conservative commentators worried that arming the "children of the masses" might end up endangering "the property of the country," while many others simply rejected the notion that it was morally sound to immerse youngsters in the study of war. Receiving the GAR's plan to introduce military instruction in his district, one school superintendent replied: "the men who put guns into the hands of children and train them for a life of warfare are traitors and should receive the contents of the guns if ever ordered to kill human beings."[46]

Peace activists, progressives, and anti-imperialists were similarly active in critiquing war mongering in the late nineteenth century. When it came to children and youth, they not only pushed back against military drill but also managed to pass a slew of laws banning the sale or use of weapons, guns, or explosive devices to children. At the same time as the NRA was sponsoring boys' rifle clubs, and gun and ammunition manufacturers were aggressively marketing their products as a way for youths to get into the great outdoors and sharpen physical and mental fitness, the danger of arming the young was drawing increased scrutiny and concern. Between 1870 and World War I, states and cities across the country passed laws to regulate the sale or use of weapons based on age—both actual guns and toy weapons, which, while not designed to kill, often contained explosive material that could cause injury. For instance, in 1875 Indiana barred the sale, gift, or bartering of any "deadly weapons or ammunition" to minors under the age of twenty-one, imposing a fine of between $5 and $50, for instance. More typically, prohibitions against selling, trading, or gifting real or toy weapons covered those under the age of fifteen or sixteen, with fines ranging from $50 to $200 and terms of imprisonment of thirty to sixty days.[47]

Interestingly, few of these new laws mentioned the use of guns in military drill. Their concern instead appears to have been prompted by a new phenomenon: the mass marketing of real and toy weaponry to boys and the widespread press reportage of the resulting deaths, injuries, and mayhem.[48] With the price of guns decreasing (the Toronto department store Eaton's offered a .22 caliber rifle for only two dollars in its mail order catalogue in 1899), boys could now buy weapons without parents' knowledge or consent, much as they could sneak off and consume cheap sensational literature. The effectiveness of these laws is unclear: like the dime novel scare, which apparently had little impact on either the sale or content of popular fiction, legislation aimed at keeping real and toy guns out of children's hands did little to restrain popular demand.[49]

There was clearly a wide range of views regarding whether military drill or gun ownership was appropriate for the young. For GAR members or NRA spokesmen who favored military preparedness and teaching boys how to wield weapons and hit targets, it was important for older males to teach younger ones how to become fearless, hardy men. For those protesting these developments, children required shielding from such knowledge and responsibilities. Yet for all their differences, both groups agreed that putting guns into children's hands was a distinct act—either for good or ill—that required careful adult supervision. Neither side debated the question of whether those under the age of eighteen had a role to fill in actual military service, for they all understood that the activities appropriate for boys differed substantially from those of men.

Childhood Vulnerability in Law and Medicine

Despite all the concern with promoting strenuous boyhood, changes in the legal, medical, and social realms had transformed attitudes toward children by this time, such that youth enlistment became a distant phenomenon, no longer conceivable on a large scale. In an inexorable shift that was still far from complete by the end of World War I, children gradually came to be seen as vulnerable dependents, deserving of political and legal protection. In principle, patriarchal rights remained enshrined in law well into the twentieth century, technically rendering children's labor the property of their fathers. But, in practice, judges and legislators increasingly reached into the household to direct children's lives. In the Gilded Age and Progressive Era, numerous laws aimed at regulating childhood, sexuality, marriage, and morals were enacted, the majority at the state and local level.[50] When it came to issues like custody rights or child labor laws, working-class, Black, and Native American families felt the impact of these changes most profoundly. They lost the ability to send children into the labor market below a certain age and sometimes lost their children entirely through court-appointed apprenticeship and guardianship and enforced boarding-out arrangements.[51] But in other areas, such as compulsory schooling and public health, lawmakers chipped away at the concept of paternal authority in ways that affected all families, not just those without wealth and power.

Like most historical change, this one was gradual and uneven. It was well underway by the time James Schouler published the third edition of his *Treatise on the Law of Domestic Relations* (1882), the most influential work dealing with family law in the second half of the nineteenth century. On the question of whether children owed service and labor to parents, Schouler repeatedly hemmed and hawed. Contrasting Blackstone's confident pronouncements of absolute patriarchal rights under English law with the ambiguous situation that prevailed in the United States, he explained: "In America, the question of [w]hether this right remains absolute in the father until the child has attained full age is apparently a matter of doubt." As slavery ended and the principle of free labor spread nationwide, the legal situation of older children—much like that of wives—had come to seem anomalous. Commenting that the "duties and rights of parents are limited," Schouler suggested that once a father had obliged a child "to support himself, our courts are reluctant to admit his right to the child's services." He cited a New Hampshire ruling on this point, which held: "Under such circumstances, 'there is no principle but that of slavery which continues his right to receive the earnings of his child's labor.' "[52] The slavery analogy had earlier served to shore up patriarchal claims to children's labor and wages, but after the Civil War, it was mustered to discredit such claims.

The mass enlistment of minors in the Civil War played some role in shaping the legal understanding of children as autonomous beings with individual rights, but not in any straightforward way. On the one hand, young enlistees provided judges with examples of boys who earned an adult wage, bore adult responsibilities, and thus deserved adult rights. When Schouler reached for examples of children who no longer owed parents their wages, he mostly cited legal cases relating to underage enlistees.[53] Similarly, when children's right to liberty came up in the 1870s in a case testing Illinois's policy of housing abused and neglected children in reformatories, the reality of underage enlistment helped convince the state's highest court that the young should have independent legal standing. In response to the charge that children could not sign a valid contract or represent themselves in court and thus had no liberty to lose, the opposition pointed to the copious minors who had "endured the hardships and privations of a soldier's life in defense of the constitution and laws." The enslaved had once had no liberty, the opposition noted, but the Civil War had overturned that notion, opening a new chapter in American history in which both freedpeople and children possessed civil rights. The court agreed, maintaining that to confine a boy to a reformatory would make him little better than a slave. Thereafter, according to legal historian David Tanenhaus, only children tried and convicted of a crime were accepted in Illinois' reformatories, as well as other states where similar cases were heard.[54] In these instances, the reality of underage enlistment supported minors' rights to retain their wages or claim due process protections.[55]

On the other hand, the overall trajectory of legal decision-making in relation to children's rights in postbellum America did not emphasize their strength and capacity, but rather their weakness and dependency. Many legal histories have shown how judges gradually adopted the principle of the "best interest of the child" to determine guardianship and custody cases, while lawmakers increasingly drew on the doctrine of *parens patriae* (the right of the state to protect children's welfare) to shape legislation aimed at constraining parents' right to manage and oversee children.[56] In establishing juvenile courts, expanding compulsory schooling, and enacting laws in relation to children's labor or health, lawmakers challenged the concept of the private family, transforming fathers' custody power over offspring "from a property right to a trust tied to his responsibilities as a guardian."[57] Rather than guaranteeing individual rights for children, this shift enhanced the role of experts and the state in child protection and, ironically, shored up patriarchal power as children were cast as vulnerable charges.[58] A new generation of "child savers" had emerged by this time, made up of scientific experts, philanthropists, reformers, and ministers who were dedicated to improving the education, health, and welfare of the young.[59] Examining their efforts, scholar Susan Pearson points out that helplessness and dependency, once grounds for denying rights, came to be understood as the basis for granting legal protections, albeit with state regulators and experts acting on children's behalf.[60]

Buttressing these legal trends, older medical ideas of children's minds as tough and resilient also made way in the early twentieth century to a heightened recognition of children's psychological frailty. This new focus is abundantly evident in medical texts, child-rearing manuals, prescriptive literature, and children's books, according to historian Peter Stearns, especially in the way this material recommended managing children's fear. In the nineteenth century, boys had been urged to overcome their fear through direct confrontation, with courage understood as a "staple of a boy's identity." By the 1920s, parents were cautioned that forcing children into frightening situations could cause lasting damage. Either punishing fearful children or trying to repress their anxieties risked cementing or worsening the problem, turning childhood apprehensions into full-blown adult neurosis. "Avoidance, not mastery, of fear was the central goal, and it was open to males and females alike," writes Stearns. This objective obviously made the idea of sending young boys off to war seem irresponsible at best, if not catastrophically harmful.[61] Working in tandem with the legal emphasis on childhood dependency, this focus on children's physiological and psychological frailty would eventually lead to the kinds of debates over the enlistment age that dominate contemporary discussions.

World War I and the Myth of an Infant Army

The celebration of hardy boyhood in the late nineteenth century, coupled with new legal and medical understandings of vulnerable childhood, rendered underage soldiering in the Civil War simultaneously appealing and anachronistic—a phenomenon worth celebrating but relegated to the past. This topic drew new interest in the lead-up to World War I, as newspapers and social commentators began trying to put a figure on the number of boys who had fought in the Civil War. The discussion appears to have started around 1890, as legislators debated the cost of providing pensions to all disabled Union veterans. To calculate the cost of potential changes to the pension law, Congress asked the War Department to provide an estimate of ages at enlistment. Captain F. C. Ainsworth, assistant surgeon, responded with a memorandum that pointed to the impossibility of providing reliable figures. He noted total Union enlistees of 2,213,365, and then estimated survivors at various ages by relying on Benjamin Gould's 1866 study, which concluded that roughly 1 percent of all Union enlistees signed up before reaching the age of eighteen. Ainsworth did not dispute this claim.[62] However, at some point in the decade after his testimony, a rumor began circulating that over a million youths had enlisted at or below the age of seventeen. The origins of this allegation are obscure; the press reported that it came from the Senate Pension Committee, but no such discussion seems to exist. What is evident is the speed with which these false numbers spread and the extent to which they were accepted.

In the first decade and a half of the twentieth century, hundreds of newspaper articles carried titles like "Civil War Soldiers Mostly Boys" or "Boys of '61 were Real Boys."[63] Writers gave a range of different figures, but all contended that underage enlistees constituted somewhere between a third to a half of all fighters. In 1908, for instance, Confederate veteran Luther W. Hopkins published a popular memoir that cited the following figures for Union enlistees, without attribution:

At the age of 11 and under 63
At the age of 13 and under 525
At the age of 15 and under 100,512
At the age of 17 and under 1,075,942
At the age of 18 and under 1,151,538
At the age of 21 and under 2,159,798

At the age of 22 and older   618,511
At the age of 25 and older   46,625
At the age of 44 and over   16,071[64]

A few years later, on the fiftieth anniversary of the conflict's outbreak, historian Francis Trevelyan Miller added underage Confederates into the mix. In a full-page feature appearing in several newspapers, he breathlessly proclaimed that a "board of researchers" had just made the startling discovery that "two million schoolboys" had fought in the Civil War. Schoolhouses and workshops had been "emptied onto the battlefields," as children as young as nine and ten marched "to the front with guns and swords to battle for their country." Inviting his audience to stand on a nearby street corner and imagine "a quarter-million newsboys" marching past, or to witness "school-boys as they flood from the schoolhouses tomorrow noon" and envision them "going not to their homes—but to war," he declared that America had raised "the greatest army of boys that the world has ever witnessed."[65] Entered into the Congressional Record, repeated in the memoirs of well-known military figures, recited by teachers and Memorial Day speakers, the myth of an infant army exhibited an appeal that defied common sense.[66]

It is not as if these claims went unchallenged. Journalist William Ghent laughed at tables like the ones Hopkins reprinted, marveling that so many "excellent persons" had missed "the inherent absurdity of the thing": first, the ridiculousness of great armies "composed so largely of fledglings," and second, the notion that a single War Department employee could have combed through millions of records to come up with such precise accounting. No one with even a "small knowledge of history" or any "sense of figures" could believe this hoax, he chortled.[67] A few years later, historian William Gist tried to set things straight. As well as making his own calculations based on the rosters of several Iowa regiments, he made inquiries to the War Department. They replied that no comprehensive study of soldiers' ages existed, nor did they have the capacity to produce one. They had sent out thousands of letters "to correct these false figures, but without avail." Gist concluded that even "a very little investigation will show how absurd these figures are."[68]

Writing in 1913 in the looming shadow of the Great War, Ghent attributed the public's credulousness to a "deep human need" to prove that wars specifically devastated the young.[69] His argument assumed that commentary typically disapproved the alleged extent of youth enlistment in the past. This was true in some cases—including that of one Kansan who cited inflated figures to argue that the "barbarism" of war would cease immediately without "hot-headed unsophisticated youths" since the "masters could not maintain themselves a year if they appealed to those who understood the game."[70] More commonly, though, writers in this period relied on Civil War precedent to celebrate youth enlistment.

The national preparedness movement was in full swing by the time the press began its most relentless publicity in relation to the extent of underage enlistment in America's past. As fighting broke out in Europe, two organizations—the National Security League and the American Defense Society—began campaigns to strengthen national security by introducing universal military training for males aged eighteen and above and building up the US army and navy. Comprised mostly of Northeastern lawyers, politicians, businessmen, and military professionals, these groups joined a host of others in urging the Wilson administration to prepare for war.[71] Many of those involved in this movement had long believed that such preparations should start with boys; now they urged the wholesale introduction of military drill across the public school system.

As had been the case in earlier decades, their plans were derailed, this time by a revitalized peace movement comprised of temperance advocates, women's rights activists, socialists, trade unionists, and religious pacifists. Public school teachers, many of them women, were also particularly vocal in speaking out against military drill.[72] By the time the United States entered the war in Europe in April 1917, proposals to introduce military drill in public schools had been defeated in every state except New York. Yet, as historian Susan Zeiger notes, peace advocacy came at a cost. As soon as America entered the war, educators faced intimidation, loyalty tests, and dismissal, in a prelude to the more vicious red baiting that would erupt at war's end. Likewise, the Wilson administration, anxious at the strength of pacifist sentiment and fearful of a backlash against the draft, seized on the movement's rhetoric of women's innate peacefulness and turned it back against female activists. Launching a smear campaign that mobilized powerful gendered imagery, war managers heaped praise on "good mothers" who did their patriotic duty by tearfully waving sons off to war while virulently condemning "bad mothers" who clung to their boys out of selfish and unnaturally excessive attachment. Traitorous, domineering, and hysterical, bad mothers were "a danger to American men and, by extension, a detriment to the struggle against fascism."[73] In films, books, and war propaganda, their pathologies were reflected in their sons. Drawing on social and clinical understandings of "normal" male development that began taking shape in the 1890s, popular culture depicted sons who refused to enlist as failed men, too timid to cut the apron strings—"cowards, sissies, Milquetoasts, and mollycoddles."[74]

The gigantic number of boy soldiers in the Civil War was another stick used to beat reluctant enlistees, useful both in debates over the conscription age and to imply that males of the present had fallen sadly below standards set in the past. American men had given a collective shrug when offered the choice of enlisting to fight in a distant war, forcing the Wilson administration to turn to conscription. The Selective Service Act, signed into law in May 1917, initially compelled unmarried males aged between twenty-one and thirty-one to register for the draft. Samuel Young, commander-in-chief of the Loyal Legion (a fraternal organization composed of former Civil War officers), was one of many to express outrage over the "menacing" number of husbands relying on the new law's exemption provisions to escape service. "There can be but one answer: the young unmarried men must save this country, even as they saved it in the civil war." Citing figures to prove that underage enlistees constituted a huge percentage of total fighters in that war, he held that "the greatest army the world had ever known to that time was composed of men 22 years old and under, exactly that class which has been omitted in the otherwise very comprehensive provisions of the draft law."[75] Former President Theodore Roosevelt amplified his point by citing the same statistics to buttress his argument that the draft age should be set at nineteen, as did many others.[76] "The Civil War, it is clear, was a boys' war," wrote one, "fought in large part by youngsters whom today we could consider children." It was therefore only "natural," that the nation should look to youths aged between eighteen and twenty-two for "the dash and spirit and resiliency that makes the ideal soldier."[77]

Congress eventually agreed and in August 1918 expanded the draft to include males between the ages of eighteen and forty-five, but not because they were persuaded by the claims regarding Civil War armies. In the initial discussion about setting the conscription age at nineteen, several congressmen argued for a conscription age of eighteen by pointing to Civil War precedent, including Senator Irvin Lenroot of Wisconsin. Representative James Byrnes, a Democrat from South Carolina, pushed back by mocking the evidence Lenroot had presented to Congress the previous day. "I looked at [Lenroot's] figures and do you know what they show? They show that there were 1,183,130 men under 18" in the Union army. Given the overall number of enlistees, "Who believes it?" he asked. He certainly did not. Having called the Adjutant General's Office and the Legislative Reference Bureau to discover the truth of the matter, he pronounced the figures bogus.[78]

Noteworthy in these discussions is the fact that no one—not even the war's most avid supporters—pointed to the value of enlisting anyone below age eighteen, though at this point males could still enlist in the army at sixteen, provided they had their parents' consent. Men like Roosevelt and Lenroot used the prevalence of underage enlistment in a distant war to press for a lower conscription age, but they did not advocate for conscripting those below eighteen or encouraging their voluntary enlistment. Debate instead focused on whether younger men should shoulder the burdens of war. Representative Byrnes went from panning colleagues' claims about youth enlistment in the Civil War to deriding the notion that those above age twenty-six should be exempt from the draft. Warning that this policy would likely fuel antiwar sentiment, he urged lawmakers to put themselves in the shoes of a mother who would certainly curse "the statesmanship that so framed a law as to leave all the men and take her boy to fight their battles."[79] This was an entirely different debate to the ones that took place during the Civil War, then. At that time, arguments had focused on the capacity of younger males, not the patriotism of older or married ones.

The transformation of the nation's dual military system during and after the Civil War contributed to this shifting debate by rendering irrelevant the key issue at the heart of long-running concerns over underage enlistment: namely, the distinction between militia service and service in the US military. Antebellum debates had focused on the age at which a boy could enlist in the regulars without parental consent. People did not protest boys fighting in militia units or entering military service with parental consent, because the issue at stake was not children's right to be free from danger, but parents' right to utilize and direct minor children's labor. Across the Union, parents and their allies in state and local courts routinely distinguished between militia service and a military enlistment contract and assumed the right to intervene in enlistment decisions. With the federalization of habeas corpus, they lost that right. At the same time, the War Department turned to the militia system as a way of raising troops for a national army, further centralizing military power.

Developments in the post-war years reinforced these trends. In many parts of the country, state militias either disbanded or became inoperative after

1865. This situation changed substantially in 1877, as the last federal troops withdrew from former Confederate states and labor unrest spread nationwide. Once so-called Redeemer governments came to power in the South, they quickly sought to remake state militias as white-only forces dedicated to preserving the racial status quo.[80] State governments across the country also called up militiamen to crush striking workers and protect private property. Believing these forces to be insufficiently organized and equipped, a group of militia officers met in 1879 to form the National Guard Association to lobby for federal appropriations to reform state militias. Business leaders, conservative newspaper editors, and middle-class spokespeople supported these efforts, viewing militiamen as the best means to preserve "law and order" and protect private property in the absence of professionalized police forces.[81]

Already by the 1870s, many state militia units had started calling themselves National Guards, indicating their sense that their main role lay in national service. But state militias only became fully federalized in the early twentieth century. In 1903, a new Militia Act (known as the Dick Act) granted federal funding to train and equip state militias and provided for joint army–National Guard encampments. Subsequent amendments to this act allowed the president to call up National Guardsmen directly and to employ them in service beyond the nation's borders. Finally, the National Defense Act of 1916 expanded National Guard units and placed them completely under federal control by authorizing their use in wartime without state approval, allowing their mobilization for unlimited periods and placing their funding and organization under the direction of the Militia Bureau.[82] Henceforth, the National Guard would act as a subordinate arm of the US military.

Contemporary scholarship exploring the reformulation of the nation's dual military system typically focuses either on the last decades of the nineteenth century or the expansion of America's overseas empire at the turn of the twentieth century.[83] Only recently—as National Guardsmen became pivotal to fighting America's so-called global war on terror—have studies begun to explore the ramifications of this shift, pointing to the way it has led to an unchecked expansion of centralized military power.[84] But in the late nineteenth century, commentators like Provost Marshal General Enoch Crowder—the official responsible for implementing the draft in World War I—still recalled when and how this shift had actually occurred. He looked back to the Civil War to locate "the first wide departure from the old theory of citizenship," when "men's liability for military service" had been transferred "from their state to the nation."[85]

It is perhaps unsurprising that both the Civil War's victors and subsequent generations of historians chose to celebrate this conflict as the culmination, rather than the death-knell, of the citizen-soldier tradition. In former Union states, it had been the war's losers—anti-war Democrats—who most loudly protested military overreach. Few were inclined to heed their warnings once victory was achieved, especially since that outcome had clearly resulted from a centralized military force. At the same time, the rapid demobilization of the Union army created the illusion that changes to the military system had been temporary. Once the US army had contracted almost to its pre-war size, concerns over military power waned, at least outside the former Confederacy. Most importantly, the US army played a key role in democratizing former Confederate states and protecting Black civil rights during Reconstruction, and the main critics of this situation were Lost Cause proponents and white supremacists. As a result, modern scholars—particularly those writing in the shadow of the Civil Rights movement—have tended to defend the US military and the Lincoln administration from charges of federal overreach. Anything less risked feeding into a powerful strain of victimhood and griev- ance nursed by Confederate apologists. It is only recently that the Lost Cause myth has been sufficiently discredited so that arguments no longer had to be built around a defense of the Union war effort.

Retrieving the original concerns that people had in relation to underage enlistment offers a new way to think about how the Civil War altered mili- tary power, as well as a new angle from which to view wartime critiques of this shift. The purpose of adopting such a perspective is not to second guess wartime policy makers, but rather to give a more complete accounting of the war's unintended and sometimes ironic consequences. Chief among these is the fact that parents' attempts to reclaim their underage sons played a pivotal role in transforming the dual military system established by the Founders: in response to those who challenged the army's right to hold their children, authorities came down firmly on the side of centralized power. Faced with such an acute need for military manpower, the federal government was willing to violate longstanding legal and social norms and risk alienating loyal citizens to retain underage enlistees. In the process, the war effort undermined the localism embodied by the militia tradition—the very aspect of the wartime mobilization that has been so widely celebrated, both then and now. Although at the time this reality went largely unacknowledged— save for the rare, exasperated outburst from a straight-talking officer who balked at releasing an underaged boy—policy decisions and actions at both the executive and legislative levels make clear that it was widely understood.

Yet after a period in which the numbers and importance of underage soldiers in the Civil War were wildly exaggerated, that fundamental insight was lost. Overhyped as the majority of combatants prior to World War I, underage soldiers as a group would subsequently be dismissed as a tiny fraction of enlistees, especially on the Union side. As individuals, the boy soldiers and drummers captured in tintypes and ambrotypes would be reduced to quaint or poignant curiosities. Today they mark the distance between our own, supposedly more humane present and an unenlightened past that tolerated small children in the ranks. Boy soldiers in the Civil War, however, were neither omnipresent nor vanishingly rare, their enlistment neither accepted without a second thought nor rejected out of hand. Indeed, it was precisely because they were at once present in large numbers and seen as problematic that the contests over their fate proved to be so consequential.

Counting Underage Soldiers

Henry C. Houston's story resembles that of many underage Union enlistees who appear in this book. Born in Portland, Maine, he was just fourteen when the war began. Twice, he tried to enlist, only to be rejected by the examining physicians. Finally accepted at the age of sixteen, he served for a year before being badly wounded in the thigh—an injury that likely helped him to secure the government posts he held after the war, first as a register of deeds and later as a pension agent. An active member of the GAR, he devoted his free time to researching and writing the history and compiling a roster of his regiment, a task that took fifteen years to complete.[1] In this regimental history, Houston points to something fishy about Union soldiers' stated ages of enlistment: while only "one or two musicians" had a recorded age lower than eighteen, "it is at once curious and suggestive to glance over the rolls and observe how many of the enlisted men had just reached . . . the exact age at which the Government would accept their services." To the uninitiated, this "preponderance of eighteen-year olds" might have been perplexing. But as Houston knew from his own experience, many of these youths had simply lied—or, as he more delicately put it, "borrowed time."[2]

The leading scholarship on the Civil War has not always adopted such a healthy skepticism of official documents. The first modern history of Union soldiers, Bell Irvin Wiley's *The Life of Billy Yank* (1952), argued that only around 1.6 percent of Union enlistees signed up before reaching their eighteenth birthdays, a figure based on information extracted from muster rolls.[3] Wiley compared his findings to data initially collected during the war by the United States Sanitary Commission's Statistical Bureau. In September 1863, that organization published the first survey of Union soldiers' "physiological characteristics." Based on anthropometric measurements, such as height, weight, chest circumference, and strength, this work organized soldiers into age clusters and determined a mean for the measurements of those in each cluster, and then compared this data to similar studies compiled for various, mostly European, populations. Despite identifying subjects by age, this study did not attempt to identify birthdates accurately. Nor was this a concern for Benjamin Gould, who took over the USSC's Statistical Bureau at the end of the war. Extending and expanding this work, Gould hoped to intervene in long-running debates over so-called national characteristics; to identify average measurements for "American" soldiers (by which they meant white Union volunteers) to show their superior development in relation to foreign populations. This objective determined the questions he asked, the data he collected, and hence his conclusions.[4]

Focusing on white volunteers, Gould extracted data from muster roles relating to roughly a million Union enlistees. He determined that, excluding musicians, only around 1 percent of Union soldiers were below the age of eighteen on enlistment. When Wiley set out to test these findings in the 1940s, he did so by looking at the descriptive lists of more than 14,000 men. Although he arrived at a slightly higher figure of underage enlistees (1.6 percent versus 1.06 percent), he concluded that Gould's percentages were basically trustworthy, representing "with reason able accuracy the age pattern of the Union army."[5]

Because both men relied on official documents, it is unsurprising that their findings largely agreed.

By the time Wiley wrote his book, however, radically different claims had been made about the percentage of boys who served in the Union army. Whereas Gould assumed in 1866 that somewhere between 10,000 and 30,000 enlistees were below the age of eighteen, numerous commentators writing several decades after the war asserted that over a third of all Union soldiers were sixteen or seventeen on enlistment. Modern Civil War scholars have ignored these obviously exaggerated figures and instead accepted Wiley's far more conservative estimate. The exceptions are works focusing exclusively on "boy soldiers" or "child soldiers," which tend to elevate the number of young recruits. In the 1990s, for instance, Jim Murphy's *The Boy's War* informed juvenile readers that "between 10 and 20 percent of all soldiers" who fought in the Civil War enlisted underage, or "approximately 250,000 to 420,000 boys."[6] More recently, David M. Rosen speculated that as many as a million underage enlistees may have served, though he concluded there is no way to be sure.[7]

In fact, it is possible to determine the extent of inaccuracies in official records with some precision through a painstaking process of comparing the ages provided by each soldier in a given regiment to census data and other records. If a recruit provided one age upon enlistment, when he had an incentive to meet a certain age threshold, but another on records filled out before and after the war, when he had no such incentive, then we can assume his military record is incorrect. We conducted such a study of all the self-reported eighteen-year-olds in the 64th New York Volunteer Infantry. We chose a New York regiment because the state conducted its own census in 1855, 1865, and 1875, as well as in 1892, thus providing multiple data points for determining soldiers' actual ages. In addition to state and federal census data, we consulted the following collections, available on Ancestry.com: New York, Civil War Muster Roll Abstracts, 1861–1900; New York, Registers of Officers and Enlisted Men Mustered into Federal Service, 1861–1865; and New York, Town Clerks' Registers of Men Who Served in the Civil War, circa 1861–1865. Additionally, we used findagrave.com and family genealogies when available.

Of the 1,758 men in the 64th New York, only eight enlistees (.45 percent) stated that they were younger than eighteen when they enlisted, whereas 266 claimed to be eighteen years old. We were able to determine with a high degree of certainty that half of the latter group—134 individuals, or 50.3 percent—misreported their actual age. Of this number, just six were older than eighteen, whereas 128 were younger, an imbalance that shows why such inaccuracies cannot be chalked up to the possibility that youths did not know their precise age. What this means is that a minimum of 7.67 percent of the men in the 64th New York Infantry Volunteers were not yet eighteen when they enlisted. But for two reasons, the actual percentage of underage enlistees is almost certainly closer to 10 percent. First, we were unable to determine with any degree of certainty the age of sixty-one individuals who claimed to be eighteen years old upon enlistment; if the enlistees in this group lied at the same rate as the youths whom we could trace, then about 164 individuals, or 9.32 percent of the total, were underage when they enlisted. In addition, we did not scrutinize those who claimed to be nineteen years old or older, but a small number of these enlistees were undoubtedly also underage. We therefore conservatively estimate that 9.5 percent of soldiers in this regiment were below age eighteen on enlistment.

The age distribution of the 134 who lied or misstated their age (along with the two who *may* have misstated their age) is as follows:

- o 2 were 13 years old
- o 9 were 14 years old
- o 7 were 15 years old
- o 8 were either 15 or 16 years old
- o 45 were 16 years old
- o 14 were either 16 or 17 years old
- o 52 were 17 years old
- o 2 were either 17 or 18 years old

    - o We did not include these two cases in our total of those who misstated or lied about their ages.

- o 4 were 19 years old
- o 1 was 20 years old
- o 1 was either 20 or 21 years old

It is worth underscoring that the large majority of those who joined the 64th New York when underage—111 out of 134, or 82.28 percent—did so at the ages of sixteen or seventeen years. (In another eight cases, we could determine only that the youths in question were either fifteen or sixteen). This supports our explanation for why the federal government fought so hard to hold underage youths to service: the vast majority were old enough to be performing valuable service.

Though we could not conduct another full regimental study, we also analyzed Company A of the Minnesota 2nd Infantry to see if a regiment from one of the newer states contained an even higher proportion of underage soldiers. Out of 177 men, twenty-four enlistees, or 13.5 percent, can be shown to have enlisted when underage. In this case, four enlistees claimed to be seventeen years old when they signed up; all four were in fact even younger, and all enlisted as substitutes near the end of the war. Of the twenty-nine enlistees who gave their age as eighteen, a full twenty, or 69 percent, were actually younger, ranging in age from fifteen to seventeen years and ten months.

The data presented in Appendix B, however, suggests that the newer western states overall did not have higher rates of underage enlistment. Conducted by mathematician Christopher Roudiez, this study relies on the Early Indicators of Later Work Levels, Disease, and Death database initiated by economic historian Robert W. Fogel in the 1980s. The largest and most extensive resource for conducting quantitative studies on Union soldiers and veterans, the Early Indicators database encompasses information drawn from the military service records, medical records, and pension records of nearly 40,000 white Union soldiers, 6,000 African American soldiers, and 10,000 men who were rejected from service. As Earl Hess points out, Civil War historians have been slow to appreciate the potential of this database, which has so far been utilized primarily by scholars in fields that offer training in statistics and prepare them to navigate large databases.[8] To make use of this resource, we turned to Roudiez for assistance. Suffice it to say here that his conclusions are roughly congruent with our study of the 64th New York: he found that half of white soldiers who claimed to be eighteen upon enlistment were in fact younger, and that 11 percent of all white soldiers in the Union army were underage when they enlisted.

A number of studies that focus on specific communities or regiments have arrived at similar conclusions. Directly after the war, several counties either canvassed local veterans or sent out questionnaires for the purpose of documenting an area's wartime contributions. Two such surveys asked veterans to list their age at enlistment or to provide their date of birth and date of enlistment. In Quincy, Massachusetts, sixty-five of the 583 veterans living in the town in 1866 (approximately 11 percent) reported that they had enlisted before reaching the age of eighteen.[9] Similarly, fifty-nine of the 468 questionnaires (or 12.6 percent) completed by the veteran population in O'Brien County, Iowa, in the early twentieth century indicated that the enlistee had signed up before his eighteenth birthday.[10]

Additional evidence comes from social histories published in the recent past. Drawing on "The Valley of the Shadow: Two Communities in the American Civil War" database, along with Samuel P. Bates's *History of Pennsylvania Volunteers*, Kathleen Shaw finds that almost 9 percent of Franklin County boys who were between the ages of ten and seventeen in 1860 served in the military over the course of the war. She reports that the percentage of underage enlistees constituted over 10 percent of total county enlistment in 1861 and 9 percent in 1862 but declined from 1863 to 1865. According to Shaw's data, of the nearly 3,000 males from Franklin County who served over the course of the war, 178 (about 6 percent) were underage on enlistment.[11]

Several recently conducted regimental or company histories have arrived at estimates closer to our own. An analysis of the 19th Indiana Volunteer Infantry found that although only 1 percent of its members claimed to be underage, 12 percent of those who could be located on the 1860 census appear to have been mustered in before reaching the legal enlistment age.[12] Due to well-known problems with census data, however, including misspelled names and other abundant errors, the author could identify only 23 percent of the 1,246 members of the regiment with certainty. Other studies are more complete. Research on the 48th Pennsylvania Infantry that matched descriptive lists with census records found that, of the 657 enlistees who could be located in the 1860 census, 84 (or roughly 12.8 percent) were underage.[13] Dennis Brandt's examination of the 87th Pennsylvania Volunteer Infantry compares soldiers' enlistment data with every other available record for this cohort. He finds that just five recruits who enlisted in 1861 reported that they were underage, whereas in reality 133 recruits (13 percent) had yet to turn eighteen.[14] Researching the 13th New Jersey Volunteer Infantry Regiment, Jim Sundman has likewise confirmed that at least fifty-one boys and youths, constituting over 6 percent of the regiment, lied about their ages, including boys ages fourteen through sixteen who claimed to be nineteen, twenty, or twenty-one years old. (This figure exclude musicians and the small number who were accepted as seventeen-year-olds.)[15] Finally, Hugh Dubrulle, who has exhaustively researched 540 members of the 5th New Hampshire Volunteer Infantry, has determined that a minimum of 10 percent of volunteers enlisted when under the age of eighteen.[16] In sum, our conclusion that roughly 10 percent of all Union enlistees signed up before reaching the legal enlistment age is based not only on our own research, but on a range of other studies that have relied on census data and other records to check the accuracy of enlistees' stated ages.

Assessing the percentage of underage youth who served in the Confederate Army is even more difficult. Confederate soldiers' compiled service records often do not include a recorded age of enlistment, inflated or otherwise. One of the earliest demographic studies, still frequently cited, is Bell Irvin Wiley's examination of 11,000 Confederates, most of whom enlisted in 1861–1862. Wiley found that 5 percent of enlistees were below the age of eighteen, but he also argued that "the ratio of men above 45 and boys below 18 was probably higher in 1861 and early 1862" than later in the war. This led him to conclude,

"There is apparently little foundation for the charge . . . that the Confederacy was robbing the cradle and the grave to sustain its forces." Wiley did not attempt to verify ages, however, and the fact that the eighteen-year-olds constituted the largest age cohort (9 percent of all enlistees) is a red flag. In addition, the fact that Wiley excluded from his sample those who served in the militia and other state-controlled forces suggests that the percentage of Confederate youth who served underage was in fact higher.[17]

This supposition finds support in the work of Edmund Drago, who has studied the wartime experiences of children and youth in South Carolina. Drago defines "boy soldiers" as youths who took up arms at age sixteen or younger, including those who served in the militia and local and state reserve units. Conceding that number is "almost impossible to determine," Drago ventures that "it did not exceed five thousand." Using his estimate of 65,000 as the total number of South Carolinians who served during the war, this would mean that 7 to 8 percent were sixteen or younger when they enlisted. But as Drago cautions, the sources allow for only "educated guesses."[18]

The most reliable statistical analysis of Confederate soldiers is Joseph Glatthaar's study of the Army of Northern Virginia (ANV), based on a careful sampling of 600 soldiers who served in the infantry, cavalry, and artillery. Glatthaar notes that one in every seven enlistees (around 14 percent) was eighteen years old or younger in 1861. Of those who joined in the final months of 1862, nearly half were twenty-one years old or younger, including "many" who had just come of age. In subsequent work, Glatthaar reports that 9.5 percent of the men who would go on to serve in Lee's army were seventeen or younger when the war began in April 1861.[19] But of this group, 37.3 percent joined the ANV in 1863 or 1864, by which time many had undoubtedly turned eighteen. Although Glatthaar does not give the percentage of soldiers in his sample who were underage on enlistment, his data suggests that it was probably no more than 6 percent. Considering that Lee was loath to enlist boys below military age, this is not surprising.[20]

Finally, it is worth stressing that several factors make a statistical comparison of white underage youth who served the United States and the Confederate armies a difficult enterprise. Confederate records are less likely to include an enlistment age, but if there is a recorded age, it is probably more reliable than Union records in cases of underage enlistees. This is because the Confederacy was less intent on enforcing age restrictions and never forbade youths below eighteen from enlisting if they had the consent of parents or guardians. Moreover, "military age" did not always mean the same thing for the two sides. Until February 1862, the age of enlistment without consent in the Union army was twenty-one, whereas it was eighteen from the start of the war in the Confederacy and dropped to seventeen for reserve service in February 1864. Also critical is the fact that the dual military system persisted to a greater degree in the Confederacy, whereas the vast majority of boys and youth who fought for the United States did so as part of a federalized force. Because this was a significant qualitative difference, as this book has shown, even if we could say with some precision how many underage youths served on each side, the meaning attached to this label would not be same.

Finally, it is impossible to determine the percentage of USCT troops who enlisted underage with any degree of certainty, in large part because many freedmen did not know their precise ages. But even outside the slaveholding states, recruiters and mustering officers tended to be especially cavalier when it came to filling USCT regiments. Kathleen Shaw's study of Franklin County, Pennsylvania, for instance, suggests a striking willingness to openly flout age restrictions in these cases. Although the total number of underage African American recruits from the county is tiny—just thirteen in total—more than

50 percent of them actually reported being younger than eighteen but were still mustered into service. In contrast, only 20 percent of the underage enlistees overall from Franklin County acknowledged being younger than eighteen years old. This difference is especially notable given that, by the time African Americans could enroll, the War Department had banned enlistment below eighteen, save for musicians; in contrast, at least some of the white soldiers aged seventeen or younger had enlisted with their parents' consent earlier in the war.

Other evidence also makes clear that the USCT had significant numbers of young enlistees, even if accurate estimates remain elusive. One data set, for instance, comes from an existing register of patients for Louverture Hospital in Alexandria, which opened in February 1864 to care for African American soldiers and civilians. Taking only those patients who were soldiers and for whom an age is recorded, a total of 6 percent of hospital patients consisted of soldiers ages seventeen and younger, including a thirteen-year-old enlisted as a private.[21] This dataset is problematic for a range for reasons: ages were recorded at the date of hospitalization, not enlistment, and the group is probably not representative of the USCT overall, since the youngest soldiers may have been either more or less likely to end up hospitalized. Still, it suggests that the percentage of UCST soldiers who enlisted underage probably reached at least 5 percent.

In some Black regiments, the percentage was significantly higher, because recruiters, who were clearly following orders, signed up youths as young as thirteen or fourteen, recording their ages as such. Officials apparently decided that enlistees in these regiments did not need to meet age restrictions because they would not be sent into battle, but would instead perform garrison or guard duty or engage in military labor. In such cases, the standard language on enlistment contracts was altered. Recruiting officers usually had to attest that "to the best of my judgment and belief [the recruit] is of lawful age" and "duly qualified to perform the duties of an able-bodied soldier." On some USCT contracts, however, recruiters would cross out "able-bodied soldier" and insert "a soldier in this regiment" by hand.[22] This practice was likely related to the fact that contraband camps tended to judge residents as "able-bodied" by age fourteen. More research is needed to determine the extent to which USCT routinely and knowingly enlisted youths below the age of eighteen.

Using the *Early Indicators of Later Work Levels, Disease, and Death* Database to Determine Age of Enlistment in the Union Army

Christopher Roudiez

While studies of individual regiments and companies discussed in Appendix A provide ample evidence of widespread underage enlistment in the Union army, they could reflect regional biases. The best means of arriving at a clearer view of underage enlistment for the Union army as a whole is to rely on the *Early Indicators of Later Work Levels, Disease, and Death* database, available online at uadata.org.

Sample

In the *Early Indicators* dataset, there are approximately 39,000 white soldiers from 328 companies, and 21,000 USCT soldiers from 169 companies, that are representative samples of Union army companies. The dataset includes information from the soldiers' military records, linked census manuscripts, and pension files (for those who received pensions). Their pension data often contains the exact birthdate for the veterans, possibly from a birth certificate, family records, a Pension Bureau investigation, or other sources.

Methods

To estimate the actual age distribution of Union army enlistees, I used the soldiers' reported enlistment age and date of enlistment and, when available, the exact birthdate. Using either source on its own would lead to inaccurate estimates.

The reported enlistment age alone would dramatically underestimate the proportion of underage enlistees. Underage enlistees had strong incentives to report being eighteen or older when enlisting. Only 1.9 percent of white soldiers in the Union army sample claimed to be underage at enlistment.

Comparing the enlistment date with the exact birthdate from the pension gives a reliable age of enlistment for any given individual soldier. Using the exact birthdate from the pension and date of enlistment to determine the distribution of age of enlistment, however, would lead to an overestimation of the proportion of underage enlistees. This is because soldiers who enlisted at younger ages were more likely to survive and be in the pension system by the time the Pension Bureau began verifying veterans' ages. For example, 44 percent of enlistees who claimed to be eighteen years old at enlistment have exact dates of birth in the pension data, compared to just 23 percent of those who reported that they were thirty years old at enlistment.

I used pension-derived enlistment ages when available and estimated the enlistment ages for those soldiers who lacked an exact pension birthdate. I based on these estimates on the pension-derived enlistment ages of soldiers with the same reported enlistment age: for each reported enlistment age, I multiplied the number of soldiers without an exact birthdate by the fraction of soldiers with a given pension-derived enlistment age.

It is helpful to look at two examples: soldiers who reported their age as eighteen at the time of enlistment and those who reported their age as thirty. These examples are explained in the following section and illustrated in Tables A and B.

Table A Pension-Derived Enlistment Age Distribution for Union Army Data Example Soldiers

	Pension-Derived Enlistment Age							
Reported Enlistment Age	15 or younger	16	17	18	19 or older	Have Exact Birth Date	No Exact Birth Date	Total
18	8.6%	14.5%	27.1%	37.9%	11.9%	2,476	3,143	5,619
30	0.7%	0.0%	0.4%	0.7%	98.2%	275	873	1,148

Table B Estimated Enlistment Age Counts for Union Army Data Example Soldiers

		Pension-Derived Enlistment Age				
Reported Enlistment Age		15 or younger	16	17	18	19 or older
18	Have exact birth date	213	359	671	938	295
	Estimates for those without exact birth date	8.6% X 3143=270	14.5% X 3143=456	27.1% X 3143=852	37.9% X 3143=1191	11.9% X 3143=374
	Total estimates	483	815	1523	2130	669
30	Have exact birth date	2	0	1	2	270
	Estimates for those without exact birth date	0.7% X 873=6	0% X 873=0	0.4% X 873=4	0.7% X 873=6	98.2% X 873=857
	Total estimates	8	0	5	8	1127

There are 2,476 white soldiers who claimed to be eighteen years old when enlisting and who have exact birthdates in their pension data. According to their pension birthdates, their actual ages at enlistment break down as follows:

- 9% were 15 years old or younger
- 15% were 16 years old
- 27% were 17 years old
- 38% were 18 years old
- 12% were 19 years old or older

I apply these same percentages to the 3,143 soldiers who claimed to be eighteen years old when enlisting and do not have an exact birthdate in their pension data. This gives an estimate of:

- 270 were 15 years old or younger (9% of 3,143)
- 456 were 16 years old (15% of 3,143)
- 852 were 17 years old (27% of 3,143)
- 1,191 were 18 years old (38% of 3,143)
- 374 were 19 years old or older (12% of 3,143)

Adding these estimates to the soldiers with exact pension birthdates yields the following:

- 483 were 15 years old or younger
- 815 were 16 years old
- 1,523 were 17 years old
- 2,130 were 18 years old
- 669 were 19 years old or older

For comparison, there are 275 white soldiers who claimed to be thirty years old when enlisting and who have exact birthdates in their pension data. According to their pension birthdates:

- 0.7% were 15 years old or younger
- 0% were 16 years old
- 0.4% were 17 years old
- 0.7% were 18 years old
- 98.2% were 19 years old or older

Applying these percentages to the 873 white soldiers who claimed to be thirty years old and do not have exact birthdates gives estimates of:

- 6 were 15 years old or younger
- 0 were 16 years old
- 3 were 17 years old
- 6 were 18 years old
- 857 were 19 years old or older

Adding this to the soldiers with exact pension birthdates yields:

- 8 were 15 years old or younger
- 0 were 16 years old
- 5 were 17 years old
- 8 were 18 years old
- 1,127 were 19 years old or older

This is equivalent to using a weighted average of the pension-derived enlistment age, where soldiers with higher enlistment ages are given more weight. Soldiers with higher enlistment ages are given more weight because they had a lower probability of surviving to get an exact pension birthdate. As the above examples show, soldiers with exact birthdates who have a reported enlistment age of thirty are given around twice the weight of those with reported enlistment age of eighteen. Every soldier with an exact birthdate and reported enlistment age of thirty is used to represent approximately four soldiers—the soldier himself and three soldiers without exact birthdates. Every soldier with an exact birthdate and reported enlistment age of eighteen is used to represent approximately two soldiers—the soldier himself and one other soldier without an exact birthdate.

Table C Final Estimates for Union Army Data Samples

Estimated Enlistment Age	Subsample			
	White Soldiers	USCT	Western States	Substitutes
13 or younger	0.2%	0.3%	0.3%	0.3%
	[0.10,0.22]	[0.13,0.48]	[0.05,0.38]	[0,0.58]
14	0.5%	0.6%	0.3%	0.5%
	[0.42,0.65]	[0.34,0.80]	[0.05,0.38]	[0.01,1.25]
15	1.5%	0.9%	1.4%	2.2%
	[1.32,1.69]	[0.63,1.23]	[0.79,1.53]	[1.66,4.44]
16	3.3%	2.6%	3.3%	5.7%
	[3.03,3.60]	[2.05,3.19]	[2.15,3.27]	[5.48,9.70]
17	5.5%	4.0%	5.6%	6.3%
	[5.18,5.90]	[3.37,4.58]	[3.77,5.25]	[6.70,11.2]
Underage (17 or less)	11.1%	8.4%	10.9%	14.9%
	[10.56,11.57]	[7.49,9.33]	[9.65,12.11]	[12.08,17.79]
18	8.5%	9.5%	9.1%	12.5%
	[8.09,8.98]	[8.25,10.8]	[6.42,8.32]	[14.0,20.5]
19 or older	80.4%	82.1%	80.1%	72.6%
	[79.7,81.1]	[80.5,83.6]	[82.4,85.2]	[57.8,66.8]
Number of soldiers with exact pension birthdate	11,934	3,188	2,147	519
Total number of soldiers	38,502	20,778	5,166	2,315

95% confidence intervals in brackets

Subsamples

I performed this analysis on the full samples of white soldiers and African American soldiers. In addition, I performed the analysis on a subsample of 2,147 white soldiers with exact birthdates (out of 5,166 overall) who enlisted in four newly admitted western states: Kansas, Iowa, Minnesota, and Wisconsin to determine if they were unusually lax when it came to enforcing age restrictions. I also performed the analysis on a subsample of 519 white soldiers who enlisted as substitutes, because anecdotal evidence suggested that many substitutes were underage.

Results

The estimates for the age distribution of each subsample are shown in Table C. The estimated fraction of underage enlistments is much higher than the official enlistment records show. The subsample of white soldiers is estimated to include 11.1 percent who were underage at the time of enlistment. The fraction of underage white soldiers from new western states is 10.9 percent, which is not significantly different from the full sample of white soldiers. The fraction of substitutes who were underage is significantly higher than the full sample of white soldiers at 14.9 percent. It should be noted that this estimate is based on a small sample; of the soldiers marked as substitutes in the dataset, only 519 soldiers have exact birthdates in the pension data. Overall, substitutes also tended to skew much younger than non-substitutes. For example, we estimate that 12.5 percent of all substitutes were actually 18 years old at enlistment, as compared to 8.5 percent of the full sample.

The estimates for USCT soldiers should be viewed with much less confidence than those for white soldiers. Only 8.4 percent of USCT soldiers are estimated to be underage at enlistment, which is significantly less than the white soldiers. But there are numerous reasons to question this finding. Many African American enlistees, especially those newly emancipated from slavery, did not know their exact ages, and white enlisting officers often made little effort to arrive at even approximate ages when dealing with African Americans. Moreover, USCT veterans were half as likely to have an exact birthdate in their pension data as the white soldiers. This is due to lower survival rates, less reliable age documentation, and lower rates of pension approval. Any of these factors could bias the estimates for the USCT soldiers.

Notes

Introduction

1. Carolyn Leffler and Sue Jones, "Livingston County in the Civil War," Livingston County Library, http://www.livingstoncountylibrary.org/history_civilwar.htm
2. According to his tombstone, Julian was born December 26, 1846. In surviving records, the family surname is sometimes spelled "Gudgel," and Julian's first name appears as "Julien." We adopt the spelling that he used consistently in later life, except in the notes to identify documents where it appears differently.
3. Julien M. Gudgel, complied service record, https://www.fold3.com/image/231552395.
4. John Gudgel to Hon. F.P. Blair, May 15, 1862, Addison Files, 1848-62, Letters Received Relating to Soldiers, Entry 416, Box 49, Record Group 94, National Archives and Records Administration, Washington, DC (hereafter Addison Files).
5. "Missouri Legislature," *Daily Missouri Republican* (St. Louis, MO), December 29, 1862, 2.
6. Capt. F. M. Bell to L.[orenzo] Thomas, Adjutant General of the US Army, December 7, 1862, Box 49, Addison Files.
7. James M. McPherson, *Battle Cry of Freedom: The Civil War Era* (New York: Oxford University Press, 1988), 322.
8. As William R. Scaife and William Harris Bragg detail in *Joe Brown's Pets: The Georgia Militia* (Macon, GA: Mercer University Press, 2004), Governor Joseph Brown of Georgia was especially determined to hold back enough men to maintain an independent militia, much to the frustration of Confederate officials. In December 1863, he signed into law an act reorganizing the militia that enrolled all white males from ages sixteen through sixty, although the sixteen-year-olds and those aged fifty and above were classified "Militia Reserve."
9. Musicians were exempted from height restrictions and allowed to enlist from the age of twelve, provided they had parental consent. For estimates of the number of musicians enlisted on both sides, see Christian McWhirter, *Battle Hymns: The Power and Popularity of Music in the Civil War* (Chapel Hill: University of North Carolina Press, 2012), chap. 5; Francis A. Lord and Arthur Wise, *Bands and Drummer Boys of the Civil War* (South Brunswick, NJ: A. S. Barnes, 1966), 30; and Kenneth E. Olson, *Music and Musket, Bands and Bandsmen of the American Civil War* (Westport, CT: Greenwood Press, 1981), 72.
10. Bell I. Wiley, *The Life of Billy Yank: The Common Soldier of the Union* (New York: Book of the Month Club, [1953] 1994), 299, 303.
11. We discuss these works in Appendix A.

12. See, for instance, the entry for "Child Soldiers," on Encyclopedia.com, https://www.encyclopedia.com/history/applied-and-social-sciences-magazines/child-soldiers.

13. The US navy almost certainly included a higher percentage of youths under the age of eighteen. We occasionally draw on sources relating to naval enlistees, but our book deals only with the army, since many more served in its ranks, and each service branch had its own rules and regulations, command structure, and justice system.

14. This case, detailed in Susan C. Reneau, *The Adventures of Moccasin Joe: The True Life Story of Sgt. George S. Howard* (Missoula, MT: Blue Mountain Publishing, 1994), 1, exemplifies how hard it can be to unravel the fabrications in military records.

15. Scholars often state that the average age at enlistment for all Union soldiers was 25.8, and the mean age 23.5, implying enough confidence in the data to warrant the decimal points. See, for example, James M. McPherson, *For Causes and Comrades: Why Men Fought in the Civil War* (New York: Oxford University Press, 1997), viii.

16. On the Confederacy's appropriation of George Washington as an authorizing symbol, see Drew Gilpin Faust, *The Creation of Confederate Nationalism: Ideology and Identity in the Civil War South* (Baton Rouge: Louisiana State University Press, 1989), 14, 24–25; and François Furstenberg, *In the Name of the Father: Washington's Legacy, Slavery, and the Making of a Nation* (New York: Penguin Books, 2007), 100.

17. In "Invading the Home: Children, State Power, and the Gendered Origins of Modern Conservatism, 1865–1933" (PhD diss., Rutgers University, 2018), Julia Bowes argues that the governance of the child "became a key litmus test in demarcating the very boundaries of state power." She shows how a set of ideas about "paternal sovereignty" coalesced after the Civil War that opposed the expansion of power at the local, state, and federal levels, viewing it as a threat to the family and paternal rights. *Of Age* suggests that the dynamic she traces had roots in the Civil War experience. During the war, however, the anti-statism expressed in defense of paternal rights focused more exclusively on the federal government.

18. On the legal issues that plagued the Confederacy, see Mark E. Neely, Jr., *Southern Rights: Political Prisoners and the Myth of Confederate Constitutionalism* (Charlottesville: University of Virginia Press, 1999); and G. Edward White, "Recovering the Legal History of the Confederacy," *Washington and Lee Law Review* 467 (2011): 467–554.

19. George C. Rable, *Civil Wars: Women and the Crisis of Southern Nationalism* (Urbana: University of Illinois Press, 1989), 81.

20. "Loyal Citizens of Livingston" to Maj. Gen. Dodge, April 21, 1865; and Brig. Gen. Isaac V. Pratt to Maj. Gen. Dodge, April 21, 1865, in Julien M. Gudgel, complied service record.

21. Charles Sheldon Sargeant, *Personal Recollections of the 18th Missouri Infantry in the War for the Union* (Unionville, MO: Stille and Lincoln, 1891).

22. Mark A. Drumbl, "Child Soldiers and Clicktivism: Justice, Myths, and Prevention," *Journal of Human Rights Practice* 4:3 (2012): 481–485 (482). See also Drumbl's *Reimagining Child Soldiers in International Law and Policy* (New York: Oxford University Press, 2012).

23. For the prehistory of the concept of children's rights, see Susan J. Pearson, *The Rights of the Defenseless: Protecting Animals and Children in Gilded Age America* (Chicago: University of Chicago Press, 2011).

24. The contrasts between representations of contemporary children and their historical counterparts are drawn most effectively by anthropologist David Rosen, *Child Soldiers in the Western Imagination: From Patriots to Victims* (New Brunswick, NJ: Rutgers University Press, 2015), x–xi. He argues that the present-day construction of the child soldier is based on an understanding of a "universal child" whose "most striking features" are "its mobility, transferability, and disconnectedness from history." In using history as a foil for thinking more critically about the present, however, Rosen downplays the extent to which people in the past *did* view young enlistees as problematic—just not for the same reasons that people object to child soldiers today.

25. Charles A. Kimball, "Luther C. Ladd," *Harper's Weekly* 5:231 (June 1, 1861): 341; and *Life of Luther C. Ladd: The First Martyr that Fell a Sacrifice to His Country* (Belfast, ME: J.W. Dickinson, 1862).

26. Letter from W. T. Sherman to E. M. Stanton, August 18, 1863, reprinted in "A Brave Drummer Boy," *The Soldier's Journal* (Alexandria, VA), May 11, 1864, 7, among many other places.

27. Dennis M. Keese, *Too Young to Die: Boy Soldiers of the Union Army, 1861-1865* (Huntington, WV: Blue Acorn Press, 2001); Eleanor C. Bishop, *Ponies, Patriots and Powder Monkeys: A History of Children in America's Armed Forces, 1776-1916* (Del Mar, CA: The Bishop Press; 1982); and Allan C. Stover, *Underage and Under Fire: Accounts of the Youngest Americans in Military Service* (Jefferson, NC: McFarland & Co., 2014).

28. Susan R. Hull's *Boy Soldiers of the Confederacy* (New York: Neale Publishing, 1905); A. J. Schenkman, *Unexpected Bravery: Women and Children of the Civil War* (Guilford, CT: Globe Pequot, 2021); and Anne Palagruto, *Babes in Arms: Boy Soldiers in the Civil War* (n.p.: privately printed, 2010). The literature aimed at young readers is too extensive to cite, but two widely cited works are Jim Murphy, *The Boys' War: Confederate and Union Soldiers Talk about the Civil War* (New York: Clarion Books, 1990); and Mary Louise Clifford, *Drummer Boy of Company C: Coming of Age in the Civil War* (Alexandria, VA: Cypress Communications, 2013).

29. Exceptions include Edmund Drago, who discusses Confederate boy soldiers (whom he defines as below the age of seventeen) in *Confederate Phoenix: Rebel Children and Their Families in South Carolina* (New York: Fordham University Press, 2008), chap. 2; and Kathleen Shaw, "'Johnny Has Gone for a Soldier': Youth Enlistment in a Northern County," *Pennsylvania Magazine of History* 135:4 (October 2001): 419–446. Mark E. Neely, Jr., addresses the legal aspects of underage enlistment in *Lincoln and the Triumph of the Nation: Constitutional Conflict in the Civil War* (Chapel Hill: University of North Carolina Press, 2011), chap. 4, and "Legalities in Wartime: The Myth of the Writ of Habeas Corpus," in Stephen D. Engle, ed., *The War Worth Fighting: Abraham Lincoln's Presidency and Civil War America* (Gainesville: University of Florida Press, 2015), 110–126. James G. Mendez, *A Great Sacrifice: Northern Black Soldiers, Their Families, and the Experience of Civil War* (New York: Fordham University Press,

2019), 121–129, discusses cases in which Black parents sought the discharge of underage sons. See also Caroline Cox's study of boy soldiers (whom she defines as below age sixteen) in the Revolutionary War, *Boy Soldiers of the American Revolution* (Chapel Hill: University of North Carolina Press, 2016).

30. Our book answers historian Sarah Maza's call to focus less on the "history of children" and instead pursue history "through children." Maza especially praises works that "use children as a way of finding fresh approaches to classic issues in the historical repertoire—questions about the nature of status, rights, and consent that are closely linked to questions of political inclusion." Sarah Maza, "The Kids Aren't All Right: Historians and the Problem of Childhood," *American Historical Review* 125:4 (October 2020): 1261–1285.

31. By way of comparison, the median age is nearly twice as high today, and children and teens account for only one quarter of the total population. US Census Bureau, "Median Age of Population, 1820-2000," https://www2.census.gov/programs-surv eys/decennial/2000/phc/phc-t-09/tab07.pdf; and "Age and Sex Composition in the United States, 2019," https://www.census.gov/data/tables/2019/demo/age-and-sex/ 2019-age-sex-composition.html.

32. Common law, based on ancient precedents, defined the legal age of puberty as fourteen in boys and twelve in girls, prior to which children could not marry. But evidence indicates that the biological markers of puberty arrived significantly later in eighteenth- and nineteenth-century Europe. Most of these studies focus on girls, for whom there are more comprehensive records, and indicate that the average age of first menstruation was between fifteen and seventeen. (In the United States today it is twelve.) Edward Shorter, *Women's Bodies: A Social History of Women's Encounters with Health, Ill-Health, and Medicine* (New Brunswick, NJ: Transaction, 1991), 18–19. But one fascinating study, which looks at detailed records of schoolboy choristers who performed in Johann Sebastian Bach's male choirs in Leipzig in the first half of the eighteenth century, suggests a higher age of puberty for boys as well. These records indicate that boys' voices began to change between sixteen and a half and eighteen years old. S. F. Daw, "Age of Boys' Puberty in Leipzig, 1727-49, as Indicated by Voice Breaking in J.S. Bach's Choir Members," *Human Biology* 42:1 (February 1970): 87–89.

33. Jon Grinspan, *The Virgin Vote: How Young Americans Made Democracy Social, Politics Personal, and Voting Popular in the Nineteenth Century* (Chapel Hill: University of North Carolina Press, 2016).

34. The question of when Americans became more 'age conscious' is a matter of some debate. Howard P. Chudacoff, *How Old Are You? Age Consciousness in American Culture* (Princeton, NJ: Princeton University Press, 1989); Joseph F. Kett, *Rites of Passage: Adolescence in America, 1790 to the Present* (New York: Basic Books, 1977); and Susan J. Pearson, "'Age Ought to Be a Fact': The Campaign against Child Labor and the Rise of the Birth Certificate," *Journal of American History* 101:4 (March 2015): 1144–1165, point to the late nineteenth and early twentieth centuries, which saw the proliferation of age-graded schools, the rise of pediatrics as a medical specialty, and the growth of government bureaucracies that categorized people by birthdates. But according to Nicholas L. Syrett and Corinne T. Field, "Chronological

Age: A Useful Category of Historical Analysis," *American Historical Review* 125:2 (April 2020): 371–384 (quotation, 377), recent scholarship shows that attention to chronological age "has been fundamental to the growth of both democratic and colonial institutions since at least the seventeenth century." Holly N. S. White in "Negotiating American Youth: Legal and Social Perceptions of Age in the Early Republic" (PhD diss., College of William and Mary, 2017), for instance, demonstrates that many Americans were "age conscious" in the late eighteenth and early nineteenth centuries.

35. Jon Grinspan, "A Birthday Like None Other: Turning Twenty-One in the Age of Popular Politics," in Field and Syrett, eds., *Age in America*, 86–102, illustrates the emotional and psychological significance of turning twenty-one for white males, for whom it marked an "unambiguous passage into adulthood." Corinne T. Field, "Are Women . . . All Minors? Woman's Rights and the Politics of Aging in the Antebellum United States," *Journal of Women's History* 12:4 (Winter 2001) 113–137, shows how state conventions in the decades after 1820 rendered age twenty-one newly salient for white males, but not for women or African Americans. The singling out of the number twenty-one can be traced all the way back to ancient and medieval philosophers, according to Philippe Ariès, *Centuries of Childhood: A Social History of Family Life*, trans. Robert Baldick (New York: Vintage, [1960] 1962), 19–21.

36. Kett, *Rites of Passage*, chap. 1.

37. Richard H. Steckel, "The Age at Leaving Home in the United States," *Social Science History* 20:4 (Winter 1996): 507–532, estimates that the median age at which children left home in 1850 was twenty-six for males and twenty-five for females. He found significant regional variations: males stayed at home longest in the northeast, where the median age of home leaving was nearly twenty-nine, and left earliest on the frontier, between twenty-four and twenty-five years old. See also Mary Ryan, *Cradle of the Middle Class: The Family in Oneida County, New York, 1790-1865* (Boston, MA: Cambridge University Press, 1981), 168.

38. The expectation that youths would be working by age sixteen had a precedent in poll or "head" taxes that dated back to the colonial period. Both Massachusetts and Connecticut levied a head tax on all men over the age of sixteen. Because the labor of minor children and apprentices profited fathers and masters or employers, however, they (rather that the minors themselves) were held liable. Jane Fiegen Green, "The Boundaries of Youth: Labor, Maturity, and Coming of Age in Early Nineteenth-Century New England, 1790-1850" (PhD diss., Washington University in St. Louis, 2014), 286–296.

39. In British common law, the age of majority was twenty-one for both males and females, but as Nicholas L. Syrett has shown in *American Child Bride: A History of Minors and Marriage in the United States* (Chapel Hill: University of North Carolina Press, 2016), 34–38, most states lowered the age of majority for women to eighteen over the course of the nineteenth century, bringing it into alignment with the age at which they could marry without parental consent.

40. Michael Burlingame, *The Inner World of Abraham Lincoln* (Champagne-Urbana: University of Illinois Press, 1994), 36–37, argues that the experience of being

forced to work as his father dictated and without compensation strongly informed Lincoln's critique of slavery. Sidney Blumenthal's *Self-Made Man: The Political Life of Abraham Lincoln, vol. 1., 1809-1849* (New York: Simon and Schuster, 2017), 1–20, likewise sees the core of Lincoln's political philosophy as rooted in these unhappy years. Emancipation before age twenty-one could occur in one of several ways: a father might choose to gift a son his "time" or grant him the right to marry, or he might lose his paternal rights by neglecting his offspring and forcing them to shift for themselves. James D. Schmidt, "'Restless Movements Characteristic of Childhood: The Legal Construction of Child Labor in Nineteenth-Century Massachusetts," *Law and History Review* 23:2 (2005): 315–350, has shown how the concept of "implied consent" allowed minors to enter into non-binding labor contracts and thereby facilitated the transition to a wage-labor economy.

41. Mary Ann Mason, *From Father's Property to Children's Rights: The History of Child Custody in the United States* (New York: Columbia University, 1994), 50.

42. Michael Grossberg, "Who Gets the Child? Custody, Guardianship, and the Rise of a Judicial Patriarchy in Nineteenth-Century America," *Feminist Studies* 9:2 (Summer, 1983): 235–260. Grossberg expands this argument in *Governing the Hearth: Law and the Family in Nineteenth Century America* (Chapel Hill: University of North Carolina Press, 1985). In contrast, Dennis E. Suttles, "'For the Well-Being of the Child': The Law and Childhood," in Daniel W. Stowell, ed., *In Tender Consideration: Women, Families, and the Law in Abraham Lincoln's Illinois* (Urbana: University of Illinois Press, 2002), 46–68, argues that even as mothers occasionally gained custody over infants and judges began imagining themselves as guardians of the vulnerable, the law resolutely upheld parents' and guardians' rights to children's labor until late in the nineteenth century. More broadly, scholars like Reva B. Siegel, "'The Rule of Love': Wife Beating as Prerogative and Privacy," *Yale Law Review* 105 (1996): 2117–2207, and Barbara Young Welke, *Law and the Borders of Belonging in the Long Nineteenth Century United States* (New York: Cambridge University Press, 2010), point out that the sentimental elevation of mothers and children reformulated rather than overturned patriarchalism.

43. The 1850 Fugitive Slave Law attempted to make it easier for enslavers to recapture freedom-seeking runaways, in large part by preventing state and local courts in northern states from interfering in the process. It placed the decision as to whether to return an alleged runaway in the hands of a federal judge or commissioner. Critics pointed out that the law was unconstitutional because it in effect suspended the writ of habeas corpus. R. J. M. Blackett, *The Captive's Quest for Freedom: Fugitive Slaves, the 1850 Fugitive Slave Law, and the Politics of Slavery* (New York: Cambridge University Press, 2018), 11–12; and Steven Lubet, *Fugitive Justice: Runaways, Rescuers, and Slavery on Trial* (Cambridge, MA: Harvard University Press, 2010). The Supreme Court upheld the law's constitutionality in *Ableman v. Booth*, an 1859 case that would be cited during the Civil War as grounds for denying state and local judges the power to issue writs in cases involving enlisted minors.

44. As Laura F. Edwards argues in "Sarah Allingham's Sheet and Other Lessons from Legal History," *Journal of the Early Republic* 38:1 (Spring 2018): 121–147 (quotation,

146), "[P]eople between the Revolution and the Civil War did not see law as something abstract, arcane, and inaccessible. Instead, law infused all aspects of life, even the lives of those without resources and with tenuous claims on rights." She develops this argument more even fully in Laura F. Edwards, *The People and Their Peace: Legal Culture and the Transformation of Inequality in the Post-Revolutionary South* (Chapel Hill: University of North Carolina Press, 2009).

45. In "Age Ought to be a Fact," Pearson looks at how the affidavit system of confirming children's ages so that they could legally work was replaced by birth certificates and other state-produced "documentary evidence" during the first four decades of the twentieth century. She argues that "Birth registration not only made age absolute but it also shifted epistemological authority from families to documents and from oral to written forms of knowledge," resulting in the loss of parental "autonomy over their children." Her analysis of this change and its effects is highly persuasive, but we question her relegation of affidavits to the "before" side of the story. The affidavits that parents of minor enlistees submitted to the US War Department were something in-between oral testimony offered in court and official state documents. On the one hand, the testimony—someone's word—was itself the evidence. On the other, as notarized statements, affidavits took on a degree of authority as documentary evidence. They were sent to Washington, DC, and assessed absent of any face-to-face contact between the petitioner and the person with authority to grant or deny the request. The epistemological shift and concomitant loss of parental authority that Pearson charts, in other words, were already underway during the Civil War.

46. Prior to this point, Americans did have the experience of speaking to census enumerators, but the census did not record specific ages. It instead lumped people into various age groupings. In fact, the first census, completed in 1790, noted only the ages of free white men, who were divided into two broad groups: those above and below the age of sixteen. Over time, the census slotted other categories of people into increasingly specific age ranges, but the level of precision continued to vary according to one's status. Only in 1850 did the census begin to record all people's ages, including those of the enslaved, who were not even identified by name. On the history of the census, see Margo Anderson, *The American Census: A Social History*, 2nd ed. (New Haven: Yale University Press, 2015).

47. Charles Gooding to Secretary of War Simon Cameron, November 26, 1861, in C. W. Holbrook, November 1, 1861, Addison Files, Box 47.

48. It was not necessarily easy to establish one's birthdate at this time. Based on his examination of antebellum voting practices, which required men to testify as to their age and allowed others to challenge their testimony, Richard Franklin Bensel, *The American Ballot Box in the Mid-Nineteenth Century* (New York: Cambridge University Press, 2004), estimates that roughly 10 percent of voters in this period did not know their own age. While most native-born, white Union enlistees knew their date of birth, a lack of such knowledge was more common in the Confederacy and likely widespread among the formerly enslaved. Official age documentation lagged far behind official age restrictions. In most states, birth registration did not become a routine, legally mandated practice until the late nineteenth or early twentieth century, according to

Susan J. Pearson, *The Birth Certificate: An American History* (Chapel Hill: University of North Carolina Press, 2021). Prior to this time, some churches documented births, and Protestants often inscribed each new birth on the flyleaves of family Bibles—a record that common law tradition deemed admissible in court. Shane Landrum, "From Family Bibles to Birth Certificates: Young People, Proof of Age, and American Political Cultures, 1820-1915," in Field and Syrett, eds., *Age in America*, 124–147. In the absence of written records, judges had to rely on communal knowledge, oral testimony, and the authority of local elites.

49. Leander Stillwell, *The Story of a Common Soldier of Army Life in the Civil War, 1861-1865* (Erie, KS: Press of the Erie Record, 1917), 13.

50. Mrs. Mary Ward to "My Most Worthy Magistrate," April 2, 1862, Addison Files, Box 51.

51. As Stephen Berry notes, "In 1860, most Americans still lived in houses, irreducible loci of production and reproduction, economic units as much as familial ones." But the war helped to deliver "a devastating blow to the household as the constituent unit of American life" by placing the "sanctity of the individual (a legal entity) ahead of the sanctity of the household (as an 'organic' economic and patriarchal entity)." The struggle over underage soldiers reveals this process in action, as parents struggled to retain the integrity of households as economic and affective realms. "From Household to Personhood in America," in Lisa Tendrich Frank and LeeAnn Whites, eds., *Household War: How Americans Lived and Fought the Civil War* (Athens: University of Georgia Press, 2021), 287–292 (quotations 288, 290).

52. Eugene C. Murdock, *One Million Men: The Civil War Draft in the North* (Madison: State Historical Society of Wisconsin, 1971), 5.

53. For instance, Louis Fisher, *Military Tribunals and Presidential Power: American Revolution to the War on Terrorism* (Lawrence: University Press of Kansas, 2005).

54. Paralleling the legal breakdown of the dual military system was a growing disillusionment with volunteer soldiering at the grassroots level. On this point, see Andrew F. Lang, *In the Wake of War: Military Occupation, Emancipation, and Civil War America* (Baton Rouge: Louisiana State University Press, 2017).

55. *The Statutes Relating to the Army of the United States, as Revised, Simplified, Arranged, and Consolidated* (Washington, DC: Government Printing Office, 1868), 2–3, 48–49. Congress apparently never voted to change the July 1862 law establishing age eighteen as the minimum age of enlistment. However, because it later enacted laws that seemed to use age sixteen as that threshold—for instance, stipulating punishments for recruiting officers who enlisted youths only below age sixteen, not eighteen—the committee charged with "revising" and "consolidating" laws governing the army simply changed the minimum age to sixteen, where it remained until the end of the century.

56. Calls to make the voting age and the age of majority consistent with the draft age were also heard during World War II. In fact, two states—Georgia and Kentucky—reduced the age of majority to eighteen in the 1940s and 1950s, respectively. However, widespread support for such a shift arose only during the Vietnam War, as detailed in Jennifer Frost, *"Let Us Vote!" Youth Voting and the Twenty-Sixth Amendment*

(New York: New York University Press, 2022). The Twenty-Sixth Amendment, ratified in 1971, prohibits states from barring those eighteen and older from voting. Today, only three states—Alabama, Nebraska, and Mississippi—set the age of majority above eighteen.

57. Seventeen-year-olds can also enlist in all US military branches, but only with parental consent. For a legal history that criticizes contemporary standards, see Wayne Barnes, "Arrested Development: Rethinking the Contract Age of Majority for the Twenty-First Century Adolescent," *Maryland Law Review* 76 (2017): 405–448.

58. C. S. Barton to "Sec Stanton," December 14, 1862, RG 94, Office of the Adjutant General, Records of the Enlisted Branch, Letters Received, 1862-1889, entry 409, Box 1.

59. "Obituary: Joseph Warren Barton," *The Dakota Huronite* (Huron, SD), February 20, 1908, 6.

60. Joseph W. Barton, National Archives and Records Administration. *U.S., Civil War Pension Index: General Index to Pension Files, 1861-1934* [database on-line], Provo, UT, Ancestry.com Operations Inc, 2000.

61. Laura F. Edwards argues in *A Legal History of the Civil War and Reconstruction: A Nation of Rights* (New York: Cambridge University Press, 2015) that historical assessments should move beyond frameworks that see expanded federal authority as either "a perversion of the country's basic principles" or "as a means of achieving them." She advocates a more nuanced view, noting that the centralization of power effected by the Civil War "led in multiple, contradictory directions in matters of political participation, civil rights, and even opportunities for economic advancement. The one clear outcome was the transformation of the people's relationship to the federal government and, consequently, to the nation's legal order" (15). Similarly, we do not portray the diminution of parental rights as a positive or negative development, but instead seek to understand the forces that propelled it and what it meant for ordinary Americans.

Chapter 1

1. Richard D. Blackmon, *The Creek War, 1813-1814* (Washington, DC: Center of Military History, 2014); and Howard T. Weir III, *A Paradise of Blood: The Creek War of 1813-14* (Yardley, PA: Westholme, 2016).

2. The lawyers here paraphrased the preeminent legal authority Sir William Blackstone, *Commentaries of the Laws of England*, book 1 (New York: Harper & Brothers, 1852 [1765]), 453, who argued, "For to those, who gave us existence, we naturally owe subjection and obedience during our minority, and honor and reverence ever after; they, who protected the weakness of our infancy, are entitled to our protection in the infirmity of their age; they who by sustenance and education have enable their offspring to prosper, ought in return to be supported by that offspring in case they stand in need of assistance." W. G. Gilbert and B. Sherrod, "The Case of Nicholas Flint," *Washington*

Monitor (Washington, GA), October 13, 1813, 3. The spelling of the family surname is actually Flynt, according to a family genealogy. http://freepages.rootsweb.com/~flynt/genealogy/p27.htm#i7885.

3. Alexander Pope, "Communication," *Washington Monitor*, October 13, 1813, 3.

4. [No title], *Pennsylvania Republican* (York), December 5, 1812, 3.

5. On the importance of domestic partisanship as a driving force in this conflict, see Alan Taylor, *The Internal Enemy: Slavery and War in Virginia, 1772-1832* (New York: W.W. Norton, 2013), 132; and Richard van Wyck Buel, Jr., *America on the Brink: How the Political Struggle over the War of 1812 almost Destroyed the Young Republic* (New York: St. Martin's Press, 2005), 1.

6. Corinne Field argues in *The Struggle for Equal Adulthood: Gender, Race, Age, and the Fight for Citizenship in Antebellum America* (Chapel Hill: North Carolina University Press, 2014), 29–30, 33–34, 56–57, legislators in colonial Massachusetts created an "intermediary" form of citizenship for male youths over the age of sixteen: as workers they were subject to a poll tax, but it was paid by their fathers or guardians; as able-bodied males they had to perform militia duty, but they were not responsible for the cost of outfitting themselves. During the Revolution, some Americans argued that serving in the militia should ensure the right to vote, and Pennsylvania even briefly enacted a law to that effect. But attempts to tie citizenship rights to military service did not prevail. Instead, age became one of the central categories through which the political legitimacy of the independent, white, male citizen was established.

7. These stories can be found in Caroline Cox, *Boy Soldiers of the American Revolution* (Chapel Hill: University of North Carolina Press, 2016); and Emmy E. Werner, *In Pursuit of Liberty: Coming of Age in the American Revolution* (Westport, CT: Praeger, 2006).

8. Nicole Eustace, *1812: War and the Passions of Patriotism* (New York: Philadelphia: University of Pennsylvania Press, 2012), x, notes that militiamen constituted the vast majority of those who fought in the War of 1812. Many "served very brief terms, often contributed services that were more ceremonial than actual, and frequently refused to cross state lines to render assistance any place where it was actually needed."

9. Blackstone: "He may indeed have the benefit of his children's labor while they live with him, and are maintained by him: but this is no more than he is entitled to from his apprentices or servants. The legal power of a father (for a mother, as such, is entitled to no power, but only to reverence and respect) the power of a father, I say, over the persons of his children ceases at the age of twenty-one: for they are then enfranchised by arriving at years of discretion, or that point which the law has established (as some must necessarily be established) when the empire of the father, or other guardian, gives place to the empire of reason."

10. Holly Brewer, *By Birth or Consent: Children, Law, and the Anglo-American Revolution in Authority* (Chapel Hill: University of North Carolina Press, 2005), 1–6.

11. Rosemarie Zagarri, "Morals, Manners, and the Republican Mother," *American Quarterly* 44:2 (June 1992): 192–215. The elevation of motherhood did not lessen women's subordination. On the contrary, as Carole Pateman's *The Sexual Contract* (Oxford: Polity Press, 1988) argues, the rise of governments based on social contract

theory—in which legitimacy derives from consent of free citizens—is inherently gendered masculine; the "social contract" is in fact based on a pre-existing "sexual contract," meaning that the independence of the rights-bearing citizen was premised on the dependence of women.

12. Daniel Scott Smith, "Parental Power and Marriage Patterns: An Analysis of Historical Trends in Hingham, Massachusetts," *Journal of Marriage and the Family* 35 (1973): 31–35; Daniel Scott Smith and Michael S. Hindus, "Premarital Pregnancy in America, 1640-1971: An Overview and Interpretation," *Journal of Interdisciplinary History* 5 (Spring 1975): 560–564; and Ruth H. Bloch, "Changing Conceptions of Sexuality and Romance in Eighteenth-Century America," *William and Mary Quarterly* 60:1 (January 2003): 13–42.

13. In colonial times, sons often worked their natal families' land after they reached their majority, sometimes even after they married. Daniel Vickers, *Farmers and Fishermen: Two Centuries of Work in Essex County, Massachusetts, 1630-1850* (Chapel Hill: University of North Carolina Press, 1994), kindle loc. 1234.

14. Vickers, *Farmers and Fishermen*, kindle loc. 4420.

15. Referring to the period immediately preceding the Civil War, Stephanie McCurry, *Masters of Small Worlds: Yeoman Households, Gender Relations, and the Political Culture of the Antebellum South Carolina Low Country* (New York: Oxford University Press, 1995), 60, has shown how the economic fortunes of yeoman farmers in South Carolina closely tracked stage of life and family size, noting, "The most prosperous farmers, those who cultivated the most land, had the greatest number of children and the oldest ones." This likely held true in earlier decades as well. According to probate records, at his death in 1820, John Benjamin Flynt bequeathed "one Negro woman Lydia and her child Ned" to his son Augustus, and "the Negro woman Julia" to his wife. Notably, he stipulated that any remaining money after settling his debts should be evenly distributed among his children, "Nicholas Flynt excepted." *Georgia, Wills and Probate Records, 1742-1992* [database on-line]. Provo, UT, USA: Ancestry.com Operations, Inc., 2015.

16. On slavery and emancipation in the northern states, see, among other works, Leon F. Litwack, *North of Slavery: The Negro in the Free States, 1790-1860* (Chicago: University of Chicago Press, 1967); Joanne Pope Melish, *Disowning Slavery, Gradual Emancipation and 'Race' in New England, 1780-1860* (Ithaca: Cornell University Press, 2016); Manisha Sinha, *The Slave's Cause: A History of Abolition* (New Haven: Yale University Press, 2016); and Patrick Rael, *Eighty-Eight Years: The Long Death of Slavery in the United States* (Athens: University of Georgia Press, 2015).

17. Leading scholarship on free labor ideology, such as Jonathan H. Earle, *Jacksonian Antislavery and the Politics of Free Soil, 1824-1854* (Chapel Hill: University of North Carolina Press, 2004); Robert J. Steinfeld, *The Invention of Free Labor: The Employment Relation in English and American Law and Culture, 1350-1870* (Chapel Hill: University of North Carolina Press, 1991); and Eric Foner, *Free Soil, Free Labor, Free Men: The Ideology of the Republican Party before the Civil War* (New York: Oxford University Press, 1970), does not address the topic of minor children's labor.

18. *United States v. Bainbridge*, 24 F. Cas. 946 (No. 14,497) (C.C.D. Mass 1816).

19. Marcus Cunliffe, *Soldiers and Civilians: The Martial Spirit in America, 1775-1865* (London: Eyre & Spottiswoode, 1968), 21.

20. On the history of the militia during and prior to the Revolution, see Kyle F. Zelner, *A Rabble in Arms: Massachusetts Towns and Militiamen in King Philip's War* (New York: New York University Press, 2009); Fred Anderson, *A People's Army: Massachusetts Soldiers and Society in the Seven Years' War* (Chapel Hill: University of North Carolina Press, 2012); Ronald L. Boucher, "The Colonial Militia As a Social Institution: Salem, Massachusetts 1764-1775," *The Journal of Military History* 37:4 (1973): 125–130; and John Shy, *A People Numerous and Armed: Reflections on the Military Struggle for American Independence* (New York: Oxford University Press, 1976), chap. 2. In rare cases African American males also participated in the militia, but their service did not generally translate into political rights. Kenneth R. Alakson discusses the revealing case of the free colored militia in New Orleans *in Making Race in the Courtroom: The Legal Construction of Three Races in Early New Orleans* (New York: New York University Press, 2014), 67–97.

21. Zelner, *A Rabble in Arms*, 52–53. On the diversity of the colonial militia experience, see John W. Shy, "A New Look at Colonial Militia," *William and Mary Quarterly* 20 (1963): 175–185. Scholars use the term "militia" variously. On the one hand, the label refers to the formal system in which authorities enrolled eligible men and organized them for training (sometimes called the "standing militia"). On the other, it might refer to groups selected from this standing militia and organized in various ways. Those who could afford to buy their own uniforms and specialist equipment, for instance, sometimes formed elite "volunteer" militia units of rangers, artillerymen, or cavalry. Alternatively, less elite companies made up of militiamen who agreed to serve for bounties, wages, or other inducements might be called up for a limited time to achieve a particular purpose. Finally, when colonial governments issued troop levies, militiamen could be conscripted or impressed to serve in a militia unit to satisfy their area's quota.

22. Michael A. McDonnell, "Class War? Class Struggles during the American Revolution in Virginia," *William and Mary Quarterly* 63:2 (2006): 305–344.

23. Paul David Nelson, "Citizen Soldiers or Regulars: The Views of American General Officers on the Military Establishment, 1775-1781," *Military Affairs* 43:3 (1979): 126–132.

24. Samuel Adams to James Warren, November 4, 1775, reprinted in *The Writings of Samuel Adams*, ed. Harry Alonzo Cushing, 4 vols. (G.P. Putnam's Sons, 1907), 3:236.

25. See Const., art. 1, sec. 8

26. U.S. Const., art. 1, sec. 8 and art. II, sec. 2.

27. U.S. Const., amend., art. II. On the long-running debate over the meaning of the Second Amendment and its relationship to the militia clause, see Lawrence Delbert Cress, "An Armed Community: The Origins and Meaning of the Right to Bear Arms," *Journal of American History* 71:1 (1984): 22–42.

28. Terry Bouton, *Taming Democracy: "The People," the Founders, and the Troubled Ending of the American Revolution* (New York: Oxford University Press, 2007); Woody Holton, *Unruly Americans and the Origins of the Constitution* (New York: Hill

and Wang, 2008); and Saul Cornell, *The Other Founders: Anti-Federalism and the Dissenting Tradition in America, 1788-1828* (Chapel Hill, N.C.: University of North Carolina Press, 1999).

29. "An Act to provide for calling forth the Militia to execute the laws of the Union, suppress insurrections, and repel invasions," 1 *Stat.* 264, ch. 28, approved May 2, 1792; and "An Act more effectually to provide for the National Defence by establishing an Uniform Militia throughout the United States," 1 *Stat.* 271, ch. 33, approved May 8, 1792.

30. "An Act to provide for calling forth the Militia to execute the laws of the Union, suppress insurrections, and repel invasions, and to repeal the Act now in force for those purposes," 1 *Stat.* 424, ch. 36, approved March 2, 1795. Legislation to bring militia units simultaneously under presidential and state controls had bipartisan support. As Joshua M. Smith, "The Yankee Soldier's Might: The District of Maine and the Reputation of the Massachusetts Militia, 1800-1812," *New England Quarterly* 84:2 (June 2011), 234–264, notes, political elites of all persuasions saw the militia as a means to discipline a diverse populace and sought to use it for partisan advantage. In thinking about the federalism in this era, Gregory Ablavsky, "Empire States: The Coming of Dual Federalism," *Yale Law Journal* 128 (2018): 1792–1868 is insightful. The purpose of a federal system, he argues, was not to diffuse power but "to bolster federal authority in order to *protect* state authority, especially against internal competitors" (p. 1796). A similar argument can be made in relation to the federalization of the militia system. That is, the Militia Acts of the 1790s did not augment the federal government's power at the expense of the states but, rather, allowed both federal and state governments to exert greater control over the militia system.

31. Christopher Alan Bray, "Disobedience, Discipline, and the Contest for Order in the Early National New England Militia" (PhD diss., University of California, Los Angeles, 2012). Quotes on 4, 12. Bray mostly deals with how militia officers understood their service, but other scholarship suggests that his point can be extrapolated to the men they led.

32. This also held true in the case of military discipline: militiamen could only be court martialled by their own officers and were precluded from certain forms of punishment, like whipping. "An Act to authorize a detachment from the Militia of the United States," 2 *Stat.* 705, ch. 56, approved April 10, 1812.

33. On the importance of European military heritage to US regulars, see Earl J. Hess, *Civil War Infantry Tactics: Training, Combat, and Small-Unit Effectiveness* (Baton Rouge: Louisiana State University Press, 2015), chap. 1; and Coffman, *The Old Army*, 97–98. Militia officers might have relied on drill manuals similar or identical to the ones used by officers in the regulars, but most had little formal military training. Elected by their men and reliant on their goodwill to a large extent, most were unwilling to exert the kind of discipline that characterized the regulars.

34. Service in the US military was governed by the Articles of War, first passed by Congress in 1806. Lifted almost wholesale from English precedents, these articles laid down the rules and practices of military justice. To flesh them out, Congress approved general guidelines for both branches of the service (known respectively as *The*

Regulations for the Army of the United States, and the *Articles for the Government of the United States Navy*), which were revised from time to time. Major revisions to US military law only occurred when Congress adopted the Uniform Code of Military Justice after World War II. Walter T. Cox, "The Army, the Courts, and the Constitution: The Evolution of Military Justice," *Military Law Review* 118 (1987): 1–30.

35. Gilbert and Sherrod, "The Case of Nicholas Flint," 3.

36. Paul A. Gilje, *Free Trade and Sailors' Rights in the War of 1812* (New York: Cambridge University Press, 2013).

37. Donald R. Hickey, *The War of 1812: A Forgotten Conflict* (Urbana: University of Illinois Press, 1989), 255. Additional overviews include J.C.A. Stagg, *The War of 1812: Conflict for a Continent* (New York: Cambridge University Press, 2012); Alan Taylor, *The Civil War of 1812: American Citizens, British Subjects, Irish Rebels, & Indian Allies* (New York: Alfred A. Knopf, 2010); and Jeremy Black, *The War of 1812 in the Age of Napoleon* (Norman: University of Oklahoma Press, 2009). See also C. Edward Skeen, *Citizen Soldiers in the War of 1812* (Lexington: University Press of Kentucky, 1999).

38. The debates that follow are contained in *Annals of Congress*, 12th Cong., 2nd sess., November 20–21, 1812, 581–592. Reported in slightly different form, they also appear in the *Congressional Reporter*, 12th Cong., 2nd sess., November 20–21, 1812, 8–27.

39. *Annals of Congress*, 12th Cong., 2nd sess., November 20, 1812, 582–583.

40. Stow's reference is to U.S. Const. amend. V, which provides that private property shall not be "taken for public use, without just compensation," and Art. 1, sec. 10, clause 1, which forbids states from passing laws "impairing the Obligation of Contracts." Although the latter clause says nothing about the federal government, everyone who spoke against the bill argued that it violated both provisions.

41. John Kyle Day, "The Federalist Press in the Age of Jefferson," *Historian* 65:6 (Winter 2003): 1303–1329.

42. *Congressional Reporter*, 12th Cong., 2nd sess., November 21, 1812, 17.

43. Quincy's speech was applauded by editors who opposed the war and either condemned or ignored by the bill's supporters. The latter included *National Intelligencer* (Washington, DC), December 1, 1812, 2 and "Mr Quincy's Speech," *National Aegis* (Worcester, MA), December 9, 1812, 3, while the former included the *Portland Gazette and Maine Advertiser*, December 2, 1817, 3; and Rhode Island's *Providence Gazette and Country Journal*, December 5, 1812, 3.

44. On the increasing number of young, single men in cities of the early Republic, see Howard P. Chudacoff, *The Age of the Bachelor: Creating an American Subculture* (Princeton: Princeton University Press, 1999), 28–35; and Mary Ryan, *Cradle of the Middle Class: The Family in Oneida County, New York, 1790-1865* (Boston, MA: Cambridge University Press, 1981), chap. 1.

45. Claudia Goldin and Kenneth Sokoloff, "Women, Children, and Industrialization in the Early Republic: Evidence from the Manufacturing Censuses," *Journal of Economic History* 42:4 (December 1982): 741–774.

46. W. J. Rorabaugh, *The Craft Apprentice: From Franklin to the Industrial Age* (New York: Oxford University Press, 1986), chaps. 1–2.

47. Edgar P. Richardson, "The Athens of America, 1800-1825," in Russell F. Weigley, Nicholas B. Wainwright, and Edwin Wolf, *Philadelphia: A 300 Year History* (New York: W.W. Norton & Co., 1982), 208–257.

48. In early 1775, Rhode Island allowed apprentices to enlist and retain their enlistment bounty, stipulating that half their military pay would go to their masters. Because bounties were large compared to military pay, this in effect encouraged apprentices to enlist. The Continental Congress, mindful of masters' growing complaints, considered the issue in 1776 and agreed that apprentices from Pennsylvania, Delaware, New Jersey, and Maryland could enlist only if they obtained masters' written consent. Rorabaugh, *The Craft Apprentice*, 20–21.

49. See, for instance, Steven Mintz, *Huck's Raft: A History of American Childhood* (Cambridge: Harvard University Press, 2004); and N. Ray Hiner and Joseph M. Hawes, *Growing Up in America: Children in Historical Perspective* (Urbana: University of Illinois Press, 1985).

50. *Annals of Congress*, 12th Cong., 2nd sess., November 20, 1812, 582, 585.

51. In *Pricing the Priceless Child: The Changing Social Value of Children* (NY: Basic Books, 1985), 3, Viviana A. Zelizer argues that between 1870 and 1930, society witnessed a major shift, in which children came to be reconceptualized as "economically 'worthless' but emotionally 'priceless.'" While the overall trajectory she traces is no doubt correct, the situation in the early republic looked considerably different.

52. *Annals of Congress*, 12th Cong., 2nd sess., November 21, 1812, 585–587.

53. Fears concerning young males being "enticed" away from home and young women being "seduced" were widespread at this time. The presumed risks were different (seduction suggested hopeless enthrallment and irreversible corruption for females, while enticement implied boys' agency and potential for restoration), but both represented a threat to paternal authority that could result in claims for legal redress. Since stories of female seduction took the form of sensational novels, however, scholars have tended to focus solely on this theme. See, for instance, Cathy N. Davidson, *Revolution and the Word: The Rise of the Novel in America* (New York: Oxford University Press, 1986); and Elizabeth Barnes, *States of Sympathy: Seduction and Democracy in the American Novel* (New York: Columbia University Press, 1997).

54. *Annals of Congress*, 12th Cong., 2nd sess., November 21, 1812, 589.

55. "Extract of a letter from a citizen of Massachusetts to a Member of Congress," *The Sun* (Pittsfield, MA), December 24, 1812, 3. Emphasis in original.

56. *Annals of Congress*, 12th Cong., 2nd sess., November 21, 1812, 591–592. No debate entered the Congressional Record, but declining support for the war, as well as the outrage voiced by opponents of the legislation in the House and in the press, undoubtedly played a role in the bill's defeat.

57. Hickey, *The War of 1812*, chap. 5.

58. *Congressional Reporter* 12th Cong., 2nd sess., November 21, 1812, 17.

59. Quoted in Michael A. Scully, "The Triumph of the Capitol," *The Public Interest* 74 (Winter 1984): 99–115 (quotation, 102).

60. Merry Ellen Scofield, "Yea or Nay to Removing the Seat of Government: Dolley Madison and the Realities of 1814 Politics," *The Historian* 74 (2012): 449–466.

61. These bills are discussed in Skeen, *Citizen Soldiers in the War of 1812*, 31–38; and Hickey, *The War of 1812*, 243–244.

62. The full House debate on the second enlistment bill can be found in *Annals of Congress*, 13th Congress, 3rd sess., December 4–6, 1814, 720–756. Quotes from King's speech 728, and from Grosvenor's speech on 733.

63. "Half a Cent Reward," *Virginia Argus* (Richmond), February 18, 1813, 4.

64. See, for example, "Notice," *Milledgeville Georgia Journal*, December 7, 1814, 12; and "Stop the Runaways!!" *Lancaster Intelligencer* (PA), July 16, 1814, 2.

65. *Annals of Congress*, 13th Congress, 3rd sess., December 4–6, 1814, 720–756. Quotes from King's speech, 728, and from Grosvenor's speech, 733. Tellingly, Webster declined to publish his speech, perhaps fearing his comments might make him vulnerable to charges of fomenting "servile insurrection." For a discussion of these debates and Webster's unpublished speech, see Skeen, *Citizen Soldiers in the War of 1812*, 31–32, 189.

66. "Enlistment of Minors," *Weekly Messenger* (Boston, MA), December 23, 1814, 3, Reprinted in the *Dedham Gazette*, December 30, 1814, 1.

67. First raised by George Washington, the notion of classifying the militia had been bandied about since the nation's founding. According to Pitcavage, "An Equitable Burden," 66–67, Washington's stance set the "terms of the debate for years to come," ensuring that militia reform became "associated with increased federal control of the state militias and with classification." By 1807, however, even Thomas Jefferson had come around to supporting classification. Robert L. Kerby, "The Militia System and the State Militias in the War of 1812," *Indiana Magazine of History* 73:2 (June 1977): 102–124.

68. The "main corps" of men, age twenty-one to forty-five years old, would train for just four days a year at state expense, while the reserve corps of older men would simply appear for muster twice a year. Kerby, "The Militia System and the State Militias in the War of 1812," 109–110, portrays Knox's plan as a "radical reorganization of the militia." The scheme "of organization by age rather than by territory and the virtual nationalization of militiamen for training purposes," he argues, "threatened to make state autonomy meaningless."

69. Daniel Webster, "Speech on the Conscription Bill," December 9, 1814, *The Writings and Speeches of Daniel Webster*, 18 vols. (Boston: Little, Brown & Co., 1903), 14:55–69.

70. Morris Miller's speech is in *Annals of Congress*, 13th Congress, 3rd sess., December 8, 1814, 784–799, quotes, 784, 799.

71. "Report and Resolutions of the Hartford Convention," reprinted in *Public Documents, Containing Proceedings of the Hartford Convention of Delegates* (Boston: Published by order of the [Mass.] Senate, 1815), 8. Theodore Dwight acted as the convention's secretary and subsequently authored *History of the Hartford Convention; with a Review of the Policy of the United States Government, which led to the War of 1812* (New York: N.J. White, 1833), 335–336.

72. Taylor, *Internal Enemy*, 334–335.

73. Jack Allen Clark, "Thomas Sidney Jesup: Military Observer at the Hartford Convention," *New England Quarterly* 29:3 (September 1956): 393–399.

74. Van Wyck Buel, Jr., *America on the Brink*, 220–221.

75. Quoted in John C. Frederiksen, ed., *The War of 1812: U.S. War Department Correspondence, 1812-1815* (Jefferson, NC: McFarland and Co., 2016), 173, 214–215.

76. "An Act to Secure the Rights of Parents, Masters and Guardians," *The Public Statute Laws of the State of Connecticut*, book 2 (Hartford: Hudson and Godwin, 1808), 189–190. Massachusetts enacted a similar law on February 27, 1815. *The General Laws of Massachusetts*, 4 vols. (Boston: Wells & Lilly and Cummings & Hillard, 1823), 2:371–72.

77. "145,000," *American Mercury* (Hartford, CT), February 4, 1817, 3. Emphasis in original.

78. In early July 1815, the Division of the South ordered that "All minors and apprentices who may have enlisted without the consent of their parents or guardians, on application by the same, shall be discharged and not form part of the peace establishment." Quoted in "Peace Establishment," *Weekly Franklin Repository* (Chambersburg, PA), September 12, 1815, 1.

Chapter 2

1. *Commonwealth v. Cushing*, 11 Mass. (1814), 67–71.

2. Rollin C. Hurd, *A Treatise on the Right of Personal Liberty, and on the Writ of Habeas Corpus and the Practice Connected with It* (Albany: W.C. Little, 1858), 166. Hurd was reiterating a position put forward several decades before by influential jurist James Kent, *Commentaries on American Law*, 2 vols. (New York: O. Halsted, 1826), 1:375–376.

3. Benjamin L. Oliver, *Rights of an American Citizen; with a Commentary on State Rights, and on the Constitution and Policy of the United States* (Boston: Marsh, Capen & Lyon, 1832), 321–322, 335–338.

4. Compulsory militia service was not universally despised. As Paul Foos, *A Short, Offhand Killing Affair: Soldiers and Social Conflict during the Mexican-American War* (Chapel Hill: University of North Carolina Press, 2002), 24–29, suggests, some labor organizations and radical Democrats fought to reform rather than abandon the system, recognizing that the only alternative was to allow elites to wield military power.

5. Exemptions from militia duty varied by state but typically covered only middle-class occupations. For those who could not afford to equip themselves for militia service, most state laws specified that a certificate testifying to this fact should be obtained from an overseer of the poor. Given the dishonor entailed in making such a public declaration of poverty, few would have taken advantage of this offer.

6. "Injustice of Requiring Minors to do Military Duty," *Citizen Soldier*, December 11, 1840, 1541–1542.

7. Judges routinely ruled against parents who tried to have this obligation waived for sons below age twenty-one. For instance, *Commonwealth v. Frost*, 13 Mass. 491; and *Stevens v. Foss*, 18 Maine, 19; *Porter v. Sherburne*, 21 Maine, 258.

8. Mandatory militia duty was first abolished by Delaware in 1831, with numerous other states following suit in subsequent decades. Scholars differ on the reason for the decline of the compulsory militia system. Richard Kohn, *Eagle and Sword: The Federalists and the Creation of the Military Establishment in America, 1783-1802* (New York: Macmillan, 1975), emphasizes the failure of Congress to provide legislation adequate to build a robust system. Mark Pitcavage, "An Equitable Burden: The Decline of the State Militias, 1783-1858" (PhD diss., Ohio State University, 1995), focuses on the difficulties in trying to distribute the burdens of military defense equitably, while Marcus Cunliffe, *Soldiers and Civilians: The Martial Spirit in America, 1775-1865* (London: Eyre & Spottiswoode, 1968), 177–212, and John K. Mahon, *History of the Militia and the National Guard* (New York: Macmillan, 1983), 80–83, point to broad changes in Jacksonian America, from rapid population shifts to disgust over the militia's inefficiency and unequally spread costs. As Mary Ellen Rowe argues in *Bulwark of the Republic: The American Militia in the Antebellum West* (Westport, CT: Praeger, 2003), militias in Kentucky, Missouri, and Washington Territory remained strong into the 1850s.

9. The peace movement failed to attract widespread support, despite its extensive publishing efforts. See Merle E. Curti, *The American Peace Crusade, 1815-1860* (Durham, NC: Duke University Press, 1929); and Valarie H. Ziegler, *The Advocates of Peace in Antebellum America* (Bloomington: Indiana University Press, 1992).

10. Lorri Glover, *Southern Sons: Becoming Men in the New Nation* (Baltimore: Johns Hopkins University Press, 2007), 155–156, points to the fact that "southern gentlemen" distinguished between militia service and a career in the regulars, regarding the latter as "insufficiently exclusive." Joining the US military, she notes, also "required a level of discipline and submission to authority that ran counter to the culture of southern men."

11. Cunliffe, *Soldiers and Civilians*, chap. 7, deals with volunteer military companies, as does Patrick J. Jung, "The Volunteer Military Companies of Antebellum Milwaukee," *Midwest Review* 14 (1992): 1–22. On the militia's important role in binding communities, see also Harry S. Laver, "Rethinking the Social Role of the Militia: Community-Building in Antebellum Kentucky," *Journal of Southern History* 68:4 (November 2002), 777–816.

12. Cunliffe, *Soldiers and Civilians*, 234.

13. Jon Grinspan, *The Virgin Vote: How Young Americans made Democracy Social, Politics Personal, and Voting Popular in the Nineteenth Century* (Chapel Hill: University of North Carolina Press, 2016), chap. 1.

14. Among those who have questioned the tendency to associate contractual labor relation with the growth of individual freedom, see Karen Orren, *Belated Feudalism: Labor, the Law, and Liberal Development in the United States* (New York: Cambridge University Press, 1991); Christopher Tomlins, *Law, Labor, and Ideology in the Early American Republic* (New York: Cambridge University Press, 1993) and *Freedom*

Bound, Law, Labor, and Civic Identity in Colonizing English America, 1580-1865 (Cambridge: Cambridge University Press, 2010); and Robert J. Steinfeld, *Coercion, Contract, and Free Labor in the Nineteenth Century* (Cambridge: Cambridge University Press, 2001).

15. Foos, *A Short, Offhand, Killing Affair*, 15.

16. Cunliffe, *Soldiers and Civilians*, 112. On the number of newly arrived immigrants in the ranks, see Foos, *A Short, Offhand Killing Affair*, 22.

17. Edward M. Coffman, *The Old Army: A Portrait of the American Army in Peacetime, 1784-1898* (New York: Oxford University Press, 1986), 137.

18. Coffman, *The Old Army*, 42. Matthew Karp, *This Vast Southern Empire: Slaveholders at the Helm of American Foreign Policy* (Cambridge, MA: Harvard University Press, 2016), notes that in the 1840s and 1850s, southern Democrats sought to use the federal government to prevent the spread of anti-slavery sentiment both at home and abroad. Part of this mission involved bolstering US military forces. Despite opposition, their efforts saw success in the mid to late 1850s, with rising military budgets and troop levels.

19. William E. Birkhimer, review of *Digest of the Opinions of Judge Advocate General, Journal of the Military Service Institution of the United States* 29 (1901): 22–23, 454.

20. "Damages for Enlisting a Minor," *American State Papers: Military Affairs*, 7 vols. (Washington: Gales and Seaton, 1832), 1:669.

21. *Emanuel Roberts*, 2d Hall's L.J., (1809), 192.

22. *United States v. Bainbridge*, 24 F. Cas. 946 (No. 14,497) (C.C.D. Mass 1816).

23. Because appellate courts decide on points of law rather than considerations of facts and evidence, law reports rarely included granular details of cases. Instead, they generally focus on an examination of relevant laws and legal precedent.

24. *Commonwealth v. Downes*, 41 Mass. (1836), 227.

25. *Commonwealth ex. rel. Webster v. Fox*, 7 Penn. L.J. (1847), 227. The court here ignored the fact that army regulations did, in fact, exclude musicians from the age restrictions relating to soldiers.

26. "An Act for the Protection of the Personal Liberty of the Citizens, and for other Purposes," *Laws of the State of Maine*, 2 vols. (Kennebec, ME: Hallowell, 1830), 1:90–92. Passed February 24, 1821.

27. "An Act Concerning the Acquisition, the Enjoyment, and the Transmission of Property, Real and Personal, the Domestic Relations, and Other Matters Connected with Private Rights," *Revised Statutes of the State of Indiana* (Indianapolis: John Dowling and R. Cold, 1843), 620.

28. On the way early laws to protect citizens from various threats to personal liberty evolved into antislavery measures by the 1840s and 1850s, see H. Robert Baker, *Prigg v. Pennsylvania: Slavery, the Supreme Court, and the Ambivalent Constitution* (Lawrence, KS: University Press of Kansas, 2012); and Thomas D. Morris, *Free Men All: The Personal Liberty Laws of the North, 1780-1861* (Baltimore, MD: Johns Hopkins University Press, 1974).

29. J. K. Paulding, "Report from the Secretary of the Navy," November 30, 1839, *Public Documents of the U.S. Senate*, vol. 1, 1st Sess., 26th Cong. (Washington: Blair and Rives, 1840), 531–539.

30. "Important Decision," *Daily Madisonian* (Washington, DC), June 10, 1843, 2, dealing with the case of *United States v. Geo. Cottingham*.

31. "California Regiment," *New York Daily Tribune*, August 24, 1846, 4.

32. "Superior Court," *New York Daily Tribune*, August 27, 1846, 3.

33. "Law Courts," *New York Daily Tribune*, August 28, 1846, 4.

34. "Habeas Corpus Case," *Alexandria Gazette* (Alexandria, VA), February 1, 1847.

35. *United States v. Blakeney* 44 Va. (3 Gratt) (1847), 405, 411–413.

36. *Commonwealth v. Archer*, 9 Monthly L. Rep. (847), 465.

37. "Report of the Adjutant General," *The Republic* (Washington, DC), December 16, 1850, 1.

38. Virginia Democrat Richard Meade proposed the measure, explaining that the Judiciary Committee had asked him to draw up a joint resolution after hearing from a Pennsylvania citizen whose young son had joined the army. This father had trouble securing a writ because his son had been sent to the Texas frontier. Meade suggested that compelling the secretary of war to release minors would present "a better mode of relief." Only a basic summary of the debate preceding this measure made its way into the Congressional Record. *Cong. Globe* 31st Cong., 1st Sess. 124 (1850).

39. Jefferson Davis to Franklin Pierce, December 1, 1856, Lynda Lasswell Crist and Mary Seaton Dix, eds., *The Papers of Jefferson Davis*, 14 vols. (Baton Rouge: Louisiana State University Press, 1971-2015), 6:62–91.

40. Jefferson Davis to Sen. John B. Weller, March 17, 1856, Crist and Dix, eds. *The Papers of Jefferson Davis*, 6:15–17. On the continuing vexation over failure to hold minor enlistees to account for giving false ages, see "Report of the Secretary of War," S. Doc. No. 1, 37th Cong., 2d Sess. (1861), 10.

41. "Defrauding the United States," *Daily National Intelligencer* (Washington, DC) February 22, 1847, 1.

42. This expression appears to have first been used in relation to parents' petitioning for the release of underage recruits stationed in New York during the Mexican American War. As these troops were about to head south, several correspondents wished them success and assured them that they were well rid of those who had been discharged "by pleading the baby act," for they had been replaced by "*choice* men." "To the Editor of the Union," *The Daily Union* (Washington, DC), August 29, 1846, 3. The New York press continued using this term over the next decade, although it does not seem to have been popular elsewhere.

43. "Superior Court Chambers. Before Judge Bosworth—The Baby Act Again," *New York Daily Times*, February 5, 1853, 6.

44. "Superior Court—Chambers—Before Judge Emmet The Baby Act Extraordinary Case," *New York Daly Times*, August 27, 1853, 6. Likewise, see "Supreme Court at Chambers—Before Judge Mitchell," *New York Daily Times*, October 3, 1851, 1; "In *Re. Adam Noland, alias M'Clennand*," *New York Daily Times*, May 29, 1852, 3; "Supreme Court—Chambers. Before Judge Roosevelt—The Baby Act Case," *New York Daily*

Times, July 2, 1853, 6; "A Recruit," *New York Daily Times*, June 16, 1854, 6; "Court of Common Pleas—Chambers. Before Judge Daly. The Baby Act," *New York Herald*, August 22, 1855, 5.

45. "Superior Court—Chambers—Before Judge Duer," *New York Tribune*, October 30, 1851, 1; "U.S. Commissioner's Office—Before Mr. Commissioner Nelson," *New York Times*, October 8, 1852, 2.

46. [No Title], *New York Daily Times*, July 29, 1852, 3.

47. "Can the State Courts Release United States Recruits?" *New York Times*, June 24, 1859, 3. In 1854, the attorney general weighed in the question of underage aliens, determining that they could be legally enlisted provided they spoke fluent English, and that consent was unnecessary if they had no parent or guardian living in the country. Attorney General's Opinion to Secretary of War, August 28, 1854, General Order No 14, Orders and Circulars, 1797-1910, Entry 44, Office of the Adjutant General, RG 94, National Archives and Records Administration, Washington, DC. See also "Opinion of the Attorney General—Enlistment of Alien Minors," *New York Times*, September 22, 1854, 1.

48. On the militia's role in riots and revelry, see Richard Stott, *Jolly Fellows: Male Milieus in Nineteenth Century America* (Baltimore, MD: Johns Hopkins University Press, 2009), 26–27; Susan Davis, *Parades and Power: Street Theatre in Nineteenth-Century Philadelphia* (Philadelphia: Temple University Press, 1986), 77–84, 93–103, 160–161; and Mahon, *History of the Militia*, 81–86.

Chapter 3

1. Edes to his parents, November 24, 1862. This letter is contained in a notebook created by Edes' father after his death, titled "E.L, Edes, extracts of letters, 1862-1864," (hereafter Edes Letters). Other letters cited below are contained in "Memoriam of Edward Louis Edes," (hereafter Edes Memoriam). Both are housed in the Edes Family Papers, Ms. N-1159, Massachusetts Historical Society, Boston, MA.

2. On December 28, 1862, Edes Letters, he indicates his particular fear of homesickness, writing: "If it were not for letters I don't know what I should do unless it was get homesick, a disease I have kept clear of." On this point, see Frances M. Clarke, "So Lonesome I Could Die: Nostalgia and Debates over Emotional Control in the Civil War North," *Journal of Social History* 41 (2007): 253–282.

3. On soldiers' understanding of the "interconnectivity of nature, health, morale, and behavior" and their preemptive efforts to ward off illness, see Kathryn Shively Meier, *Nature's Civil War: Common Soldiers and the Environment in 1862 Virginia* (Chapel Hill: University North Carolina, 2013).

4. Letter dated January 4, 1863, Edes Memoriam.

5. Margaret Humphreys, *Marrow of Tragedy: The Health Crisis of the American Civil War* (Baltimore: Johns Hopkins University Press, 2013), 77.

6. Letter dated August 12, 1863, Edes Memoriam.

7. Telegraph dated July 15, 1864, contained in Robert Edes' Diary, Edes Family Papers.
8. General George Washington expressed such concerns in 1776, for instance, as did Lord Barrington, the British secretary of war, who thought "young boys" so useless that recruiting them amounted to a "fraud on the public." Quoted in Caroline Cox, *Boy Soldiers of the American Revolution* (Chapel Hill: University of North Carolina Press, 2016), 30.
9. Corinne T. Field, *The Struggle for Equal Adulthood: Gender, Race, Age, and the Fight for Citizenship in Antebellum America* (Chapel Hill: University of North Carolina Press, 2014), chap. 2.
10. For scholarship on this question, see introduction, fn. 34.
11. John A. Lynn, *Battle: A History of Combat and Culture from Ancient Greece to Modern America* (Cambridge, MA: Westview Press, 2004), chap. 4; Andrew N. Liaropoulos, "Revolutions in Warfare: Theoretical Paradigms and Historical Evidence," in Gary Sheffield, ed., *War Studies Reader: From the Seventeenth Century to the Present Day and Beyond* (New York: Continuum, 2010), 129–157; and Geoffrey Parker, "Military Revolutions, Past and Present," *Historically Speaking* 4:4 (2003): 2–14.
12. Earl J. Hess, *Civil War Infantry Tactics: Training, Combat, and Small-Unit Effectiveness* (Baton Rouge: Louisiana University Press, 2015), charts the system of linear tactics developed in seventeenth-century Europe and modified in the following century before being imported to the United States.
13. Henry Marshall, *On the Enlisting, Discharging and Pensioning of Soldiers*, 2nd ed. (Philadelphia: A. Waldie, 1840), 12.
14. William H. McNeill, *Keeping Together in Time: Dance and Drill in Human History* (Cambridge, MA: Harvard University Press, 1995,) chap. 5, points out that rhythmic movement held an important role in warfare over many centuries. But as John Norris, *Marching to the Drums: A History of Military Drums and Drummers* (Stroud: Spellmount, 2012), explains, the changing nature of warfare significantly elevated the role of military musicians over time.
15. Philippe Ariès, *Centuries of Childhood: A Social History of Family Life*, trans. Robert Baldick (New York: Vintage, 1962), 193.
16. A complete survey of the changing age and height restrictions for the US army between 1790 and 1874 can be found in J. H. Baxter, *Statistics, Medical and Anthropological, of the Provost-Marshal-General's Bureau Derived from Records of the Examination for Military Service in the Armies of the United States During the Late War of the Rebellion of Over a Million Recruits, Drafted Men, Substitutes, and Enrolled Men*, 2 vols. (Washington, DC: Government Printing Office, 1875), 1:xlix. Military physicians showed much less concern with the age of naval enlistees, who did not have to endure long marches with heavy equipment. Naval service was also understood as akin to a skilled trade that boys needed to enter while young in order to 'learn the ropes' from older men.
17. J. M. Turner, *A History of the Study of Human Growth* (Cambridge, UK: Cambridge University Press, 1981), 142. Ian Hacking, *The Taming of Chance* (Cambridge, UK: Cambridge University Press, 1990), 2, observes that governing elites had enumerated populations for the purposes of military recruitment or taxation long

before this point, but such data was published only in the late eighteenth century. Beginning in the eighteenth century and focusing on continental Europe, Heinrich Hartmann's *The Body Populace: Military Statistics and Demography in Europe before the First World War* (Cambridge, MA: MIT Press, 2019) traces the growing reliance on statistical methods to assess potential soldiers.

18. Turner, *A History of the Study of Human Growth*, chap. 2.

19. A. Quetelet, *Sur l'homme et la Développement de ses facultés, ou Essai de Physique Sociale*, 2 vols. (Paris: Bachelier, 1835); Louis René Villermé, *Tableau de l'état Physique et Moral des Ouvriers Employés dans les Manufactures de Coton, de laine et de Soie* (Paris: J. Renouard, 1840); and Edwin Chadwick, *Report on the Sanitary Condition of the Labouring Population of Great Britain* (London: R. Clowes & Sons 1843).

20. Turner, *History of the Study of Human Growth*, 50–65.

21. W. Bruce Rye, "Why a Physiologist?—The Case of Henry P. Bowditch," *Bulletin of the History of Medicine* 56 (1982): 19–29, looks at how positions for full-time medical scientists and clinical faculty members emerged in the United States after the Civil War. On the development of physiology before this time, as well as the role of military physicians in the field, see John Warner, "Physiology," in Ronald L. Numbers, ed., *The Education of American Physicians: Historical Essays* (Oakland, CA: University of California Press, 1980), 48–71.

22. Turner, *History of the Study of Human Growth*, chap 5.

23. Richard L. Blanco, "Henry Marshall (1775-1851) and the Health of the British Army," *Medical History* 14 (1970): 260–276; and *Edinburgh Medical and Surgical Journal* 76 (1851): 489–492.

24. Henry Marshall, *Hints to Young Medical Officers of the Army on the Examination of Recruits, and Respecting the Feigned Disabilities of Soldiers* (London: Burges & Hill, 1828), 11, 58–59.

25. Henry Marshall, *On the Enlisting, the Discharging, and the Pensioning of Soldiers: with the Official Documents on these Branches of Military Duty* (London: Egerton, 1832), 11, 37. This work went through at least five editions between its initial release and 1889. We draw from the second US edition, published in Philadelphia in 1840 by A. Waldie.

26. We draw here from the first English translation of this work, M. A. Quételet, *A Treatise on Man and the Development of His Faculties* (Edinburgh: W. and R. Chambers, 1842), 57.

27. Quételet, *A Treatise on Man*, 57–70.

28. Works of this nature contributed to what philosopher Ian Hacking, *The Taming of Chance*, chap. 2, has described as the "avalanche of printed numbers" in the first decades of the nineteenth century. By this point, statistics had come to hold a privileged position among scientists and physicians, based on a growing belief that "quantities were more exact than qualities . . . less subject to the uncertainty and caprice of personal judgment." See also Mary Poovey, *A History of the Modern Fact: Problems of Knowledge in the Sciences of Wealth and Society* (Chicago: University of Chicago Press, 1998); and Patricia Cline Cohen, *A Calculating People: The Spread of Numeracy in Early America* (Chicago: University of Chicago Press, 1982), 219.

29. William Aitken, *On the Growth of the Recruit and Young Soldier, with a view to a Judicious Selection of 'Growing Lads' for the Army, and a Regulated System of Training for Recruits* (London: Griffin, Bohn, and Company, 1862). This work was issued at least six times between 1862 and 1887, x. On Aiken's background, see: J. B. Nias, "Aitken, Sir William (1825-1892)," *Oxford Dictionary of National Biography*, Oxford University Press, 2004, http://www.oxforddnb.com/view/article/257.

30. Aitken, *On the Growth of the Recruit*, vii–ix, 25, 35.

31. Marshall, *Hints to Young Medical Officers*, 30–54, includes enlistment procedures for French and Prussian recruits.

32. Aitken, *On the Growth of the Recruit*, 24.

33. George H. B. Macleod, *Notes on the Surgery of the War in the Crimea* (London: Churchill, 1858), 11.

34. Charles S. Tripler, *Manual of the Medical Officer of the Army of the United States: Part 1, Recruiting and Inspection of Recruits* (Cincinnati, OH: Wrightson & Co., 1858).

35. François Clement Maillot and Jean Antoine Aimé Edmond Puel, *Aide-mémoire médico-légal de l'officier de santé de l'armée de terre* (Paris: J.-B. Baillière... [et al.], 1842).

36. On Tripler's life and influence, see James M. Phalen, "Obituaries: Charles S. Tripler," *The Army Medical Bulletin* no. 61 (April 1942): 176–81.

37. US Sanitary Commission, *A Report to the Secretary of War of the Operations of the Sanitary Commission, and upon the Sanitary Condition of the Volunteer Army* (Washington, DC: McGill & Witherow, December, 1861), 14.

38. Alfred Post and William H. VanBuren, "Military Hygiene and Therapeutics," in William A. Hammond, ed., *Military Medical and Surgical Essays prepared for the United States Sanitary Commission* (Philadelphia: J.B. Lippincott & Co., 1864), 41–42.

39. F. G. Smith and Alfred Stillé, "Vaccination in Armies," in William A. Hammond, ed., *Military Medical and Surgical Essays prepared for the United States Sanitary Commission* (Philadelphia: J.B. Lippincott & Co., 1864), 134.

40. William A. Hammond, "Annual Report of the Surgeon General, U.S.A.," November 10, 1862, reprinted in *Boston Medical and Surgical Journal* 67:22 (January 1, 1863): 437–443 (quotation, 442).

41. William A. Hammond, *A Treatise on Hygiene with special Reference to the Military Service* (Philadelphia: J.B. Lippincott & Co., 1863), 19; see also 18–100.

42. Hammond, *Treatise on Hygiene*, 25. Manuals of instructions for Union recruiters were equally adamant on this point. For instance, John Ordronaux, *Manual of Instructions for Military Surgeons on the Examination of Recruits and Discharge of Soldiers* (New York: D. Van Nostrand, 1863), 14; and Roberts Bartholow, *A Manual of Instructions for Enlisting and Discharging Soldiers* (Philadelphia: J.B. Lippincott & Co., 1864), 38.

43. *Cong. Globe*, 38th Cong., 1st sess., 3379–3381.

44. Very few transcripts of Confederate court martial cases survived, so it is impossible to fully compare the sentences passed by Union and Confederate court martial panels. But printed general orders in relation to Confederate court martials frequently make similar references to youth.

45. "Military Law," *Fayetteville Semi-Weekly Observer* (Fayetteville, NC), August 29, 1861, 3

46. "Punishable by Death," *Daily Milwaukee News*, December 19, 1861, 1.

47. William L. Gregg to Abraham Lincoln, October 14, 1861; and William L. Gregg to Edwin Stanton, February 23, 1862, AGO Letters Received, Addison Files, RG 94, Box 47. G. Oram Gregg ended up serving his entire three-year term before being mustered out at the rank of sergeant. Census records show that he was still under the age of enlistment when discharged in August 1864.

48. Court martial hearing of John McKusker [McCusker], September 8, 1862, # KK463, Record Group 153, National Archives and Records Administration, Washington, DC. All general court martial files for Union soldiers are contained in this record group, filed under a single number preceded by two letters. Hereafter, we cite only the file number.

49. Cyrus Bacon, Diary, Archives of Michigan, MS22, box 1, folder 22, Lansing, Michigan. For online transcript, see: https://drive.google.com/file/d/1S1dREcJ7tM120TVVR a5cD_Fjj4QTuBIv/view .

50. Court martial hearing of James H. Scott, August 19, 1862, #KK628.

51. Court Martial hearing of Charles Hendrickson, March 6, 1862, #II806.

52. Court martial hearing of Henry Brown, April 2, 1864, #LL1908 and #NN1795.

53. Annette Hathaway to President Abraham Lincoln, [n.d.], AGO Letters Received, Enlisted Branch, Box 21.

54. John O'Connor to Provost Marshal General James B. Fry, November 15, 1864, AGO Letters Received, Enlisted Branch, Box 200. This father was ultimately able to secure his son's discharge in January 1865 after he returned the $238 his son had received in bounty money and advance pay.

55. Elijah and Mary Boyers to President Abraham Lincoln, April 15, 1862, AGO Letters Received, Addison Files, Box 49. They were not able to legally secure their son's release, and he deserted in August 1862.

56. Sophia Allen to President Abraham Lincoln, November 14, 1863, AGO Letters Received, Enlisted Branch, Box 1. Her request was denied, and her son served until the end of the war.

57. William Young to the War Department, April [1864], AGO Letters Received, Enlisted Branch, Box 260. Young's request was denied, and he served out his full term.

58. Corydon Edward Foote, *With Sherman to the Sea: A Drummer's Story of the Civil War* (New York: The John Day Company, 1960), 54, 60.

59. Robert J. Burdette, *Drums of the 47*th (Indianapolis: Bobbs-Merrill Co., 1919), 12.

60. Nicholas B. Grant, "The Life of a Common Soldier, 1862-1865," LaFollette, TN: LaFollette Press, [1927], US Army Military History Institute, Carlisle, PA, 10–12, 14.

61. Earl Hess, *The Union Soldier in Battle: Enduring the Ordeal of Combat* (Lawrence: University Press of Kansas, 1997), 144–145, followed Bell Irvin Wiley in making this claim, but did so before the EIP database became available.

62. Larry T. Wimmer, "Reflections on the Early Indicators Project: A Partial History," https://www.nber.org/system/files/chapters/c9626/c9626.pdf.

63. Judith Pizarro, Roxane Cohen Silver, and JoAnn Prause, "Physical and Mental Health Costs of Traumatic War Experiences Among Civil War Veterans," *Archive of General Psychiatry* 63:2 (2006): 193–200.

64. Dora L. Costa and Matthew E. Kahn. "Surviving Andersonville: The Benefits of Social Networks in POW camps," *American Economic Review* 97:4 (2007): 1467–1487.

65. According to Ashley Elizabeth Bowen-Murphy, "'All Broke Down': Negotiating the Meaning and Management of Civil War Trauma" (PhD diss., Brown University, 2017), 93, pension office employees who reviewed soldiers' service histories and medical records understood the relationship between age of enlistment and disability, applying a "lower burden of proof" for applicants who had enlisted while still in their teens. But young veterans were sometimes wary of submitting applications in the first place. For instance, Anon., *Opium Eating: An Autobiographical Sketch* (Philadelphia: Claxton, Remsen & Haffelfinger, 1876), 13, 54; and W. B. Smith, *On Wheels, and How I Came There: A Real Story for Real Boys and Girls, Giving the Personal Experiences and Observations of a Fifteen-year-old Yankee Boy as Soldier and Prisoner in the American Civil War*, ed. Joseph Gatch Bonnell (New York: Hunt & Eaton, 1892), 334–335. Black veterans and their families also faced significant hurdles in filing successful applications, a topic canvassed most recently by Brandi Clay Brimmer, *Claiming Union Widowhood: Race, Respectability, and Poverty in the Post-Emancipation South* (Durham: Duke University Press, 2020); and Larry M. Logue and Peter Blanck, *Race, Ethnicity, and Disability: Veterans and Benefits in Post-Civil War America* (Cambridge, UK: Cambridge University Press, 2010).

66. The growing scholarship addressing the cost of war for Civil War veterans includes: Holly A. Pinheiro Jr., *The Families' Civil War: Black Soldiers and the Fight for Racial Justice* (Athens: University of Georgia Press, 2022); Sarah Handley Cousins, *Bodies in Blue: Disability in the Civil War North* (Athens: University of Georgia Press, 2019); Diane Miller Somerville, *Aberration of Mind: Suicide and Suffering in the Civil War Era South* (Chapel Hill: University of North Carolina Press, 2018); Matthew Jordan, *Marching Home: Union Veterans and Their Unending War* (New York: Liveright Publishing, 2015); James Marten, *Sing Not War: The Lives of Union and Confederate Veterans in Gilded Age America* (Chapel Hill: University of North Carolina Press, 2014); Larry M. Logue and Peter Blanck, *Heavy Laden: Union Veterans, Psychological Illness, and Suicide* (Cambridge, UK: Cambridge University Press, 2012); and Donald Robert Shaffer, *Marching On: African-American Civil War Veterans in Postbellum America, 1865-1951* (College Park: University of Maryland, 1996).

Chapter 4

1. Edwin Hale Lincoln, *Drummer Boy: The Civil War Diary of Edwin Hale Lincoln*, eds. Karl Marty and Lee C. Drinkamer (Raleigh, NC: Ivy House Publishing, 2005).

2. H. M. (Henry Marvin) Wharton, *War Songs and Poems of the Confederacy, 1861-1865. . . with Personal Reminiscences of the War* (Philadelphia: American Book and Bible House, 1904).

3. Scholarship examining the way children's literature helped to construct class, gender, and race relations and middle-class subjectivities includes: Paul B. Ringel, *Commercializing Childhood: Children's Magazines, Urban Gentility, and the Ideal of the Child Consumer in the United States, 1823-1918* (Amherst: University of Massachusetts Press, 2015); Robin Bernstein, *Racial Innocence: Performing American Childhood* (New York: New York University Press, 2011); Barbara Hochman, *Uncle Tom's Cabin and the Reading Revolution: Race, Literacy, Childhood, and Fiction, 1851-1911* (Amherst: University of Massachusetts Press, 2011); Anna Mae Duane, *Suffering Childhood: Violence, Race, and the Making of the Child Victim* (Athens: University of Georgia Press, 2010); Michelle H. Martin, *Brown Gold: Milestones of African American Children's Picture Books, 1845-2002* (New York: Routledge, 2004); Deborah C. De Rosa, *Domestic Abolitionism and Juvenile Literature, 1830-1865* (New York: State University of New York Press, 2003); Patricia Crain, *The Story of A: The Alphabetization of America from the New England Primer to the Scarlet Letter* (Stanford, CA: Stanford University Press, 2000); Gail Schmunk Murray, *American Children's Literature and the Construction of Childhood* (New York: Twayne, 1998); Anne Scott MacLeod, *A Moral Tale: Children's Fiction and American Culture, 1820-1860* (Connecticut: Archon, 1975); and Monica Kiefer, *American Children Through Their Books, 1700-1835* (Philadelphia: University of Pennsylvania Press, 1948).

4. On the varying experiences and conceptions of children in the nineteenth century, see Steven Minz, *Huck's Raft: A History of American Childhood* (Cambridge, MA: Belknap, 2004); Joseph E. Illick, *American Childhoods* (Philadelphia: University of Pennsylvania Press, 2002); Paula Fass and Mary Ann Mason, eds., *Childhood in America* (New York: New York University Press, 2000); Harvey J. Graff, *Conflicting Paths: Growing Up in America* (Cambridge, MA: Harvard University Press, 1995); Elliot West and Paula Petrik, eds. *Small Worlds: Children and Adolescents in America, 1850-1950* (Lawrence: University of Kansas Press, 1992); and Joseph Kett, *Rites of Passage: Adolescence in America, 1790 to the Present* (New York: Basic Books, 1977). On children's working lives see: Pamela Riney-Kehrberg, *Childhood on the Farm: Work, Play, and Coming of Age in the Midwest* (Lawrence: University Press of Kansas, 2005); Karen L. Zipf, *Labor of Innocents: Forced Apprenticeship in North Carolina, 1715-1919* (Baton Rouge: Louisiana State University Press, 2005); Ruth Wallis Herndon and John E. Murray, eds., *Children Bound to Labor: The Pauper Apprentice System in Early America* (Ithaca: Cornell University Press, 2009); and Pricilla Ferguson Clement, *Growing Pains: Children in the Industrial Age, 1850-1890* (New York: Twayne, 1997).

5. Marie Jenkins Schwartz, *Born in Bondage: Growing Up Enslaved in the Antebellum South* (Cambridge, MA: Harvard University Press, 2000); Brenda Stevenson, *Life in Black and White: Family and Community in the Slave South* (New York: Oxford University Press, 1992); and Wilma King, *Stolen Childhood: Slave Youth in Nineteenth-Century America* (Bloomington: Indiana University Press, 1995); examine the lives of enslaved children, while the following studies analyze childhood in the Civil War: William McGovern, "Street Children: St. Louis and the Transformation of American Reform, 1832-1904" (PhD diss., University of California, San Diego, 2016);

Catherine A. Jones, *Intimate Reconstructions: Children in Emancipation Virginia* (Charlottesville: University of Virginia, 2015); James Marten, ed., *Children and Youth during the Civil War Era* (New York: New York University Press, 2012); Anya Jabour, *Topsy-Turvy: How the Civil War Turned the World Upside Down for Southern Children* (New York: Ivan R. Dee, 2011); James Marten, *Children and Youth in a New Nation* (New York: New York University Press, 2009); Edmund L. Drago, *Confederate Phoenix: Rebel Children and their Families in South Carolina* (New York: Fordham University Press, 2008); James Marten, *Children for the Union: The War Spirit on the Northern Home Front* (Chicago, Ivan R. Dee, 2004); and James Marten, *The Children's Civil War* (Chapel Hill: University of North Carolina Press, 1998).

6. Jean Jacque Rousseau, *Émile; or Treatise on Education*, trans. William H. Payne (New York: D. Appleton and Company, 1918), 54.

7. On Romantic writers' and artists' conceptions of childhood, see Colin Heywood, *A History of Childhood* (Cambridge, UK: Polity Press, 2001), Kindle location 1215–1278. Philippe Ariès, *Centuries of Childhood: A Social History of Family Life*, trans. Robert Baldick (New York: Vintage, [1960] 1962), and Lawrence Stone, *The Family, Sex and Marriage in England, 1500-1800* (London: Weidenfeld and Nicholson, 1977), were among the first to trace changing conceptions of childhood. More recent work is canvassed in Peter N. Stearns, *Childhood in World History* (New York: Routledge, 2006); Jean Mills and Richard Mills, eds., *Childhood Studies: A Reader in Perspectives of Childhood* (New York: Routledge, 2000); Colin Heywood, *A History of Childhood: Children and Childhood in the West from Medieval to Modern Times* (Cambridge: Polity, 2001); and Hugh Cunningham, *Children and Childhood in Western Society since 1500* (New York: Longham, 1995).

8. On domestic advice manuals' neglect of childhood fears in the first half of the nineteenth century, see Peter N. Stearns and Timothy Haggerty, "The Role of Fear: Transitions in American Emotional Standards for Children, 1850-1950," *American Historical Review* 96:1 (1991): 63–94.

9. Sally Shuttleworth, *The Mind of the Child: Child Development in Literature, Science, and Medicine, 1840-1900* (New York: Oxford University Press, 2010), chaps. 1–2. Work that examines the emergence of child psychology and psychiatry as distinct fields includes Dorothy Ross, *G. Stanley Hall: The Psychology as Prophet* (Chicago: University of Chicago Press, 1972); and Stephen Kern, "Freud and the Birth of Child Psychiatry," *Journal of the History of the Behavioral Sciences* 9:4 (1973): 360–368.

10. John Locke, *Some Thoughts Concerning Education*, 2nd ed. (London: Cambridge University Press, 1889), quotes from sec. 50, 46, 113, 115.

11. Locke, *Some Thoughts Concerning Education*, sec. 113.

12. Stearns and Haggerty, "The Role of Fear," 67.

13. Whereas authors were "happy to regale their [young] readers with scenes of torture, violent death, and general mayhem, all set out in gory detail," they "flinched from the remotest sexual allusion," according to Anthony Kearney, "Savage and Barbaric Themes in Victorian Children's Writing," *Children's Literature in Education* 17:4 (1986): 233.

14. Maria Tatar, *Off with Their Heads! Fairy Tales and the Culture of Childhood* (Princeton, NJ: Princeton University Press, 1992), 5–7.

15. Quoted in Etsuko Takentani, "The 'Omnipresent Aunt' and the Social Child: Lydia Maria Child's *Juvenile Miscellany*, *Children's Literature* 27 (1999): 22.

16. Lydia Maria Child, "The St. Domingo Orphans," *Juvenile Miscellany* 5 (September 1830): 82, 85–86. Sarah N. Roth, *Gender and Race in Antebellum Popular Culture* (New York: Cambridge University Press, 2014), chap. 2, examines this story, albeit without commenting on the violence of its imagery.

17. Carolyn L. Karcher, "Rape, Murder and Revenge in 'Slavery's Pleasant Home': Lydia Maria Child's Antislavery Fiction and the Limits of Genre," *Women's Studies International Forum* 9:4 (1986): 323–324.

18. Samuel G. Goodrich, *The First Book of History; for Children and Youth* (Boston: Charles J. Hendee, 1836), preface, iii–iv.

19. Keith Beutler, "Emma Willard's 'True Mnemonic History': America's First Textbooks, Proto-Feminism, and the Memory of the Revolution," in Michael A. McDonnell, Clare Corbould, Frances M. Clarke, and W. Fitzhugh Brundage, eds., *Remembering Revolution: Memory, History, and Nation Making from Independence to the Civil War* (Amherst: University of Massachusetts Press, 2013), 152–167. On learning theories in antebellum America, see also Barry Joyce, *The First U.S. History Textbooks: Constructing and Disseminating the American Tale in the Nineteenth Century* (Lanham: Lexington Books, 2015), chap. 3.

20. Goodrich, *First Book of History*, 14, 16, 53.

21. Locke, *Some Thoughts Concerning Education*, sec. 115–117.

22. Anne Scott MacLeod, *A Moral Tale: Children's Fiction and American Culture 1820-1860* (Hamden, CT: Archon Books, 1975).

23. See work cited in fn. 3.

24. "Training Children for War," *The Calumet* (New York), March 1, 1834, 568–570 (quotation 569).

25. Anon, *Charles Ashton; The Boy that Would be a Soldier* (Boston: N.S. & J. Simpkins, 1823), exemplifies this point.

26. Elizabeth B. Clark, "The Sacred Rights of the Weak:" Pain, Sympathy, and the Culture of Individual Rights in Antebellum America," *Journal of American History* 82:2 (September 1995): 463–493.

27. *The Anti-Slavery Alphabet* (Philadelphia: Merrihew & Thompson, 1847).

28. Rebecca de Schweinitz, "'Waked Up to Feel': Defining Childhood, Debating Slavery in Antebellum America," in Marten, ed., *Children and Youth during the Civil War Era*, 13–28; and Elizabeth Kuebler-Wolf, "'Train Up a Child in the Way He Should Go': The Image of Idealized Childhood in the Slavery Debate, 1850-1870," in *ibid.*, 29–45.

29. *The Anti-Slavery Alphabet*, preface.

30. Beverly Lyon Clark, *Kiddie Lit: The Cultural Construction of Children's Literature in America* (Baltimore, MD: Johns Hopkins University Press, 2003).

31. Charles Edward Stowe, *The Life of Harriet Beecher Stowe* (Boston: Houghton, Mifflin and Company, 1890), 148–149.

32. Stowe, *Life of Harriet Beecher*.

33. [John Ely], *The Child's Instructor; Consisting of Easy Lessons for Children* 3rd ed. (Bridgeport, CN: J.B. and L. Baldwin, 1833), 76–81.

34. *Picture Alphabet* (New York: McLoughlin Bros, [c. 1861–1870]).

35. *Little Sailor Boy* (New York: McLaughlin Bros., [c. 1859–1862]); and *The Little Drummer* (New York: McLaughlin Bros., [c. 1863–1866]).

36. *Little Pet's Picture Alphabet* (New York: McLoughlin Bros. Manufacturers, [c. 1861–1865])

37. *The Union A B C* ([Boston]: Degen, Estes & Company, [c. 1865–1866]).

38. Mark E. Neely, Jr., Harold Holzer, and Gabor S. Boritt, *The Confederate Image: Prints of the Lost Cause* (Chapel Hill: University of North Carolina Press, 1987), 3–7.

39. Michael T. Bernath, *Confederate Minds: The Struggle for Intellectual Independence in the Civil War South* (Chapel Hill: University of North Carolina Press, 2010), 195–120 (quote 195).

40. Laura Elizabeth Kopp, "Teaching the Confederacy: Textbooks in the Civil War South" (MA thesis, University of Maryland, College Park, 2009), 68.

41. *Bourke's Picture Primer* (Macon, GA: Burke, Boykin & Co., 1864), 47.

42. Mrs. M. B. Moore, *The Dixie Speller* (Raleigh, NC: Branson & Farrar, 1864), 23. On Confederate schoolbooks, see also Marten, *The Children's Civil War*, 52–61. He notes that this example of pacifism was unique among the more than one hundred similar Confederate schoolbooks published during the war.

43. *The First Reader, for Southern Schools* (Raleigh, NC: Christian Advocate, 1864), 12, 17.

44. Bernath, *Confederate Minds*, 200. Even when Confederate spelling books did use wartime imagery to help children learn their letters, the images tended to be patriotic rather than violent. See, for instance, A Lady of Savannah, *For the Little Ones* (Savannah, GA: John M. Cooper & Co., [1861]); A. de V. Chaudron, *Chaudron's Spelling Book* (Mobile: S.H. Goetzel, 1865); or Marinda Branson Moore, *The Dixie Primer*, 3rd ed. (Raleigh, NC: Branson & Farrar, 1863).

45. Cited in James Marten, "Fatherhood in the Confederacy: Southern Soldiers and Their Children," *Journal of Southern History* 63:2 (May 1997): 269–292 (quotation, 282).

46. On typical Sabbath school classes, see Anne M. Boylan, *Sunday School: The Formation of an American Institution, 1790-1880* (New Haven: Yale University Press, 1988).

47. John H. B. Kent to "Mr. Baxter, Teachers, & members of the Hasret Place Sabbath School," reprinted in *Yankee Correspondence: Civil War Era Correspondence between New England Soldiers and the Home Front*, eds. Nina Silber and Mary Beth Sievens (Charlottesville: University of Virginia Press, 1996), 41–42.

48. Charles C. Nott, *Sketches of the War: A Series of Letters to the North Moore Street School of New York*, 4th ed. (New York: Anson D. F. Randolph, [1863] 1865), quotes 11, 14, 34, viii.

49. William Makepeace Thayer, *A Youth's History of the Rebellion*, 4 vols. (New York: James Miller, 1864–1865). The original publisher released five editions of this work in 1864 alone, and seven additional publishers in Boston and New York picked up the series, which was reprinted continuously until 1900.

50. Thayer, *A Youth's History of the Rebellion*, 1:196, 167–200.

51. Ulysses S. Grant to Julia Dent Grant, July 7, 1861, *The Papers of Ulysses S. Grant*, vol. 2, *April-September 1861*, ed. John Y. Simon (Carbondale: Southern Illinois University Press, 1969), 59.

52. Ulysses S. Grant to Julia Dent Grant, July 13, 1861, *The Papers of Ulysses S. Grant*, 2:70.

53. Julia Dent Grant, *Personal Memoirs of Julia Dent Grant (Mrs. Ulysses S. Grant)*, ed. John Y. Simon (Carbondale: Southern Illinois University Press, 1975), 92.

54. Ulysses S. Grant to Julia Dent Grant, August 3, 1861, *The Papers of Ulysses S. Grant*, 2:82.

55. Ulysses S. Grant, *Personal Memoirs*, ed. Caleb Carr (New York: Random House, 1999 [orig. 1885]), 259.

56. Frederick Dent Grant, "With Grant at Vicksburg," *Outlook* 59 (July 2, 1898): 533–543(quotation, 534).

57. A.E. Watrous, "Grant as His Son Saw Him: An Interview with Colonel Frederick D. Grant about His Father," *McClure's Magazine* 2:6 (May 1894): 515–519 (quotation, 517).

58. Dent Grant, *Personal Memoirs*, 126.

59. Grant, *Personal Memoirs*, 365.

60. Ulysses S. Grant to Julia Dent Grant, June 1, 1864, *The Papers of Ulysses S. Grant, Vol. 11: June 1-August 15, 1864*, ed. John Y. Simon (Carbondale: Southern Illinois University Press, 1984), 5.

Chapter 5

1. Claire Perry, *Young America: Childhood in 19th Century Art and Culture* (New Haven: Yale University Press, 2006).

2. On metaphors relating to childhood and youth in in early America, see Anna Mae Duane, *Suffering Childhood in Early America: Violence, Race, and the Making of the Child Victim* (Athens: University of Georgia Press, 2010); Holly Brewer, *By Birth or Consent: Children, Law and the Anglo-American Revolution in Authority* (Chapel Hill: University of North Carolina Press, 2005); and Jay Fliegelman, *Prodigals and Pilgrims: The American Revolution Against Patriarchal Authority, 1750-1800* (New York: Cambridge University Press, 1982). For the nineteenth century, see also Robin Bernstein, *Racial Innocence: Performing American Childhood from Slavery to Civil Rights* (New York: New York University Press, 2011); and Karen Sanchez-Eppler, *Dependent States: The Child's Part in Nineteenth-Century American Culture* (Chicago: University of Chicago Press, 2005).

3. Sean A. Scott, "'Good Children Die Happy': Confronting Death During the Civil War," in James Marten, ed., *Children and Youth During the Civil War Era* (New York: New York University Press, 2012), 92–109.

4. Alice Fahs, *The Imagined Civil War: Popular Literature of the North & South, 1861-1865* (Chapel Hill: University of North Carolina Press, 2001), 260.

5. Fahs, *Imagined Civil War*, 259, makes a similar point.

6. Bryan R. Le Beau, *Currier & Ives: America Imagined* (Washington, DC: Smithsonian Institution Press, 2001); Mark E. Neely Jr. and Harold Holzer, *The Union Image: Popular Prints of the Civil War North* (Chapel Hill: University of North Carolina Press, 2000); and Clive Ashwin, "Graphic Imagery 1837-1901: A Victorian Revolution," *Art History* 1:3 (1978): 360–370.

7. Andrea G. Pearson, "*Frank Leslie's Illustrated Newspaper* and *Harper's Weekly*: Innovation and Imitation in Nineteenth Century Pictorial Reporting," *Journal of Popular Culture* 23:4 (Spring 1990): 81–111.

8. For instance, "Middies Learning the Ropes," *Harper's Weekly*, May 11, 1861, 295, and "Recruiting in the Park," *Harper's Weekly*, September 7, 1861, 566.

9. "Charge of Duryee's Zouaves," *Harper's Weekly*, June 29, 1861, 409.

10. Looking back from the perspective of old age, one former Union army drummer who enlisted at the age of fourteen scoffed at Thomas Nast's etchings of a young musician leading a charge. "Fighting isn't done that way," he explained; charges were rare and drummers were usually hiding in the rear, trying to avoid getting shot. C. W. Bardeen, *A Little Fifer's War Diary* (Syracuse, NY: priv. printed, 1910), 127. On the work performed by musicians, see also Francis A. Lord and Arthur Wise, *Bands and Drummer Boys of the Civil War* (South Brunswick, NJ: A. S. Barnes, 1966), chap. 7.

11. [Winslow Homer], "The Songs of the War," *Harper's Weekly*, November 23, 1861, 744.

12. [Winslow Homer], "The War for the Union, Bayonet Charge," *Harper's Weekly*, July 12, 1862, 440–441.

13. Thomas Nast "The Drummer Boy of Our Regiment," *Harper's Weekly*, December 19, 1863, 805.

14. Eastman Johnson created a preparatory study for this oil painting that was exhibited in 1864, with proceeds from the exhibition going to the Union war effort. The finished painting was not completed until 1871. The Brooklyn Museum holds Johnson's early efforts, which can be viewed online at https://www.brooklynmuseum.org/opencollection/objects/1185.

15. F.[elix] O. C. Darley, *A Selection of War Lyrics* (New York: James G. Gregory, 1864), 17.

16. "The Drummer Boy of Antietam," *Bradford Reporter* (Towanda, PA), October 30, 1862, 3.

17. Albert Fleming, "Drummer Boy of Antietam, A War Ballad," (Louisville, KY: D.P. Faulds, 1863).

18. Darley, *A Selection of War Lyrics*, 14–18.

19. "The Drummer of Antietam," (New York: H. De Marsan, Publisher, n.d.). On the importance of deathbed rituals in Victorian America, see Mark S. Schantz, *Awaiting the Heavenly Country: The Civil War and America's Culture of Death* (Ithaca: Cornell University Press, 2008), chap. 1.

20. Henry C. Work, "Little Major," (Chicago: Root & Cady, 1862).

21. For instance, Comp. L. Grube, lyrics by J. C. Koch, "The Dying Drummer Boy," (Brooklyn: Louis Grube, Publisher, 1863); C. A. Shaw, "If I Sleep Will Mother Come?" (Boston: Oliver Ditson & Co., 1864); and Mary A. Lathbury, "The Dying Drummer Boy" (New York: William A. Pond & Co, 1864).

22. Fahs, *Imagined Civil War*, chap. 3. Marten, *Children for the Union*, chap. 5, points to the way such imagery reflected the militarization of childhood in the north.

23. Steven H. Cornelius, *Music of the Civil War Era* (Westport, CT: Greenwood Press, 2004), 62; Albert Boime, "Thomas Couture's Drummer Boy Beating a Path to Glory," *Bulletin of the Detroit Institute of Arts* 56:2 (1978), 125.

24. Patricia Healy Wasyliw, *Martyrdom, Murder, and Magic: Child Saints and Their Cults in Medieval Europe*, vol. 2. (New York: Peter Lang, 2008), chaps. 2–3. Comparable instances of children venerated for remarkable devoutness exist in the Judaic, Islamic, and numerous other religious traditions. Philippe Ariès, *Centuries of Childhood: A Social History of Family Life*, trans. Robert Baldick (New York: Vintage Books, 1962), 112.

25. Diana Pasulka, "A Somber Pedagogy—A History of the Child Death Bed Scene in Early American Children's Religious Literature, 1674-1840," *Journal of the History of Childhood and Youth* 2:2 (Spring 2009), 117–197 (quote 177).

26. Pasulka, "A Somber Pedagogy," 185.

27. Jane P. Tompkins, *Sensational Designs: The Cultural Work of American Fiction, 1790-1860* (New York: Oxford University Press, 1985), chap. 5; and Richard H. Brodhead, *Cultures of Letters: Scenes of Reading and Writing in Nineteenth-Century America* (Chicago: University of Chicago Press, 1993), 38–42.

28. *Charlie the Drummer Boy* (New York: American Tract Society, 1863) is one example. On the wartime politicization of religion, see also James H. Moorhead, *American Apocalypse: Yankee Protestants and the Civil War, 1860-1869* (New Haven: Yale University Press, 1978), 1–22; and Ernest Lee Tuveson, *Redeemer Nation: The Idea of America's Millennial Role* (Chicago: University of Chicago Press, 1968), 187–214.

29. John Ross Dix, "The Drummer Boy's Farewell" (New York, Charles Magnus, [1864]). Emphasis in original.

30. P. De Greer, "Drummer Boy of Vicksburg, or, Let Him Sleep" (Philadelphia: J. Marsh, 1864).

31. Robert Johnston, "The Drummer Boy of Nashville" (New York: Chas. Mangus, 1864).

32. Stephen W. Berry, "When Mail was Armor: Envelopes of the Great Rebellion," *Southern Cultures* 4:3 (1998): 63–83. See also, James Brush Hatcher, "The Patriotic Envelope in Civil War Days," *American Collector* 12 (May 1943): 12–13, and Catharine S. Oveson, "Civil War Envelopes," *Antiques* 13 (June 1928): 490–492.

33. "Civil War Envelopes Collection," box 1, American Antiquarian Society, Worcester, Massachusetts (hereafter, AAS).

34. Copies of these envelopes are held in the "Civil War Envelopes Collection" at the AAS.

35. Berry, "When Mail was Armor," 68.

36. Abraham Lincoln, "Address in Independence Hall," Philadelphia, February 22, 1861, *Collected Works of Abraham Lincoln*, ed. Roy P. Basler, asst. eds. Marion Dolores Pratt, and Lloyd A. Dunlap, 8 vols. (New Brunswick, NJ: Rutgers University Press, 1953–1955), 4:241.

37. James M. McPherson, "'The Whole Family of Man': Lincoln and the Last Best Hope Abroad," in Robert E. May, ed., *The Union, the Confederacy, and the Atlantic Rim* (West Lafayette, IN: Purdue University Press, 1995): 131–158 (quote, 133).

38. Frances M. Clarke, *War Stories: Suffering and Sacrifice in the Civil War North* (Chicago: University of Chicago Press, 2012), chap. 5.

39. A few exceptions can be found in newspaper stories. See, for instance, "Our Youngest Soldier," *Harper's Weekly*, February 6, 1864, 85, which lauds John Clem for killing a Confederate Colonel.

40. Helen Weston, "Jacques-Louis David's 'La Mort de Joseph Bara': A Tale of Revolutionary Fantasies," *Paragraph* 19:3 (November 1996): 241.

41. Jacques-Louis David (1748–1825), *The Death of Young Bara* ("La Mort de Bara"), 1794.

42. Louis Emmanuel Jadin (1768–1853) staged his play *Agricol Viala, ou Le Jeune Héros de la Durance* ("Agricol Viala, or The Young Hero of the Durance") in Paris on July 1, 1794. Further accounts of the lionization of Bara and Viala include Lynn Hunt, *The Family Romance of the French Revolution* (Berkeley: University of California Press, 1992), 79; Weston, "A Tale of Revolutionary Fantasies': and Warren Roberts, *Jacques-Louis David, Revolutionary Artist: Art, Politics and the French Revolution* (Chapel Hill: University of North Carolina Press, 1989), 301. More broadly, Marilyn R. Brown, *The Gamin de Paris in Nineteenth-Century Visual Culture: Delacroix, Hugo, and the French Social Imaginary* (New York: Routledge, 2017), analyzes the symbolic appeal of boys who appeared in nineteenth-century French art.

43. Roberts, Jacques-Louis David, 301.

44. André Estienne would serve this role for Napoleon, even though he was already nineteen years old in 1796 when he led a charge during the battle of Arcole. Despite his relative maturity, he was widely portrayed as a small child. Like Bara and Viala, he was celebrated in a ceremony in the Panthéon and awarded the nation's highest military award. He appears on one of the six bas reliefs on Arc de Triomphe's façade as a small boy beating a drum and following Napoleon into battle. Michel Dillange, *The Arc de Triomphe and the Carrousel Arch*, trans. Angela Moyon (Paris: Ouest France, 1984), 13.

45. For instance, in the Italian wars of unification, *"Piccola vedetta Lombarda"* ("the little Lombard lookout") and *"Tamburino Sardo"* (the "Little Sardinian Drummer Boy") were both said to have been shot by Austrian forces while performing brave deeds. The first republic of Costa Rica also chose drummer boy Juan Santamaría as its national symbol.

46. A number of young British soldiers and drummer boys received commendations for bravery during wartime, but there was no public celebration of their service until the late nineteenth century. One exception is artist Richard Buckner's "Battle of Balaclava Drummer Boy" (1854). Unlike French and American representations, though, Buckner depicts his subject standing alone, posed for his portrait, not engaged in military action or suffering in its aftermath.

47. Holly Furneaux, "Children of the Regiment: Soldiers, Adoption, and Military Tenderness in Victorian Culture," *Victorian Review* 39:2 (Fall 2013): 79–96 (quote 85).

48. For instance, Fahs, *Imagined Civil War*, chap. 8, or E. Lawrence Abel, *Singing the New Nation: How Music Shaped the Confederacy, 1861-1865* (Mechanicsburg, PA: Stackpole Books, 2000), chap. 12.

49. Census records list only one woman by this name living in Kentucky in 1860. According to *American Ancestry*, vol. 11 (Albany, NY: Joel Munsell's Sons, 1898), 6, Annie Cannon of Louisville, Kentucky, married Chicagoan William Zearling in July 1864 but died two years later. We can find no further information on why she received this dedication.

50. Will S. Hays, "Drummer Boy of Shiloh" (Louisville, KY: D.P. Foulds, 1863). The lithographed version that circulated in the North is reproduced here: https://library.duke.edu/rubenstein/scriptorium/sheetmusic/b/b10/b1051/b1051-1-72dpi.html.

51. Complete copies of all southern newspapers for the Civil War era have not survived, but we have examined full runs in the original of major periodicals like the *Illustrated Southern News*, *Magnolia Weekly*, and the *Daily Dispatch* (Richmond, VA), as well as searching all available publications in databases such as *Chronicling America*, *ProQuest Historical Newspapers*, and *Accessible Archives*.

52. Will S. Hays, "Drummer Boy of Shiloh" (Louisville, KY: D.P. Foulds, 1863).

53. Will S. Hays, "Drummer Boy of Shiloh: as sung by the First Tenn. Concert Troupe" (Augusta, GA: Blackmar & Bro., 1863). Dozens of editions of this sheet music exist. Versions that circulated in the North included the names of northern publishers and lithographers on the title page, along with the aforementioned black-and-white lithograph featuring men in dark uniforms that are clearly meant to indicate Union blue. The southern versions list E. Clarke Ilsley as a co-author and a lithograph by the firm of B. Duncan & Co. of Columbia, South Carolina, as well as the names of additional publishers that operated in the south.

54. The quote is from *Louisville Daily Democrat* (Louisville, KY), January 21, 1863, 2 (a pro-Union publication).

55. For instance, William A. Campbell and William R. J. Dunn, *The Child's First Book* (Richmond: Ayres & Wade, 1864); and *Uncle Buddy's Gift Book, For the Holidays* (Augusta, GA: Blome & Tehan, Publishers, 1863).

56. Neither Marjorie Crandall, *Confederate Imprints: A Check List Based Principally on the Collection of the Boston Athenaeum*, vol. 2 (Boston: The Boston Athenaeum, 1955); E. Lawrence Abel, *Confederate Sheet Music* (Jefferson, NC: McFarland & Company, Inc., 2004); or any of the other archival collections we have examined contain further depictions of boy soldiers or drummers as Confederate icons.

57. For Confederate songs extolling mother love, see Abel, *Confederate Sheet Music*; and Allan, comp., *A Collection of Southern Patriotic Songs*.

58. For studies of Confederate nationalism, see references contained in Paul Quigley's *Shifting Grounds: Nationalism and the American South, 1848-1865* (New York: Oxford University Press, 2012).

59. For instance, the engraving titled "Jeff Davis's Last Appeal to Arms," *Harper's Weekly*, August 22, 1863, 544.

60. Eric Lott, *Love and Theft: Blackface Minstrelsy and the American Working Class* (New York: Oxford University Press, 1993); and Robert C. Toll, *Blacking Up: The Minstrel Show in Nineteenth Century America* (New York: Oxford University Press, 1974).

61. "Drumming Up Recruits for the Confederate Army," *Harper's Weekly*, June 1, 1861, 345; "Recruiting for the Confederate Army at Woodstock, Virginia," *Harper's Weekly*, October 5, 1861, 632.

62. Kate Masur, "'A Rare Phenomenon of Philological Vegetation': The Word 'Contraband' and the Meanings of Emancipation in the United States," *Journal of American History* 93:4 (March 2007): 1050–1084 (quotes 1057).

63. "The Colored Volunteer" (New York: Currier & Ives, c.1863), held at the Library Company of Philadelphia, Print Department, accession number: (9)1540.F.

64. "Teaching the Negro Recruits the Use of the Minie Rifle," *Harper's Weekly*, March 14, 1863.

65. Thomas Nast etching, "The Colored Volunteer," c. 1863, held by the Library Company of Philadelphia, 5780.F.51c McA-1257.

66. "A Negro Volunteer Song," *The Liberator*, June 19, 1863, 100.

67. Will S. Hays, "Little Sam," ([New York]: J.L. Peters & Brother, 1867).

68. Bernstein, *Racial Innocence*, 7–8.

69. William Morris Hunt, "The Drummer Boy," c. 1862, held in the Museum of Fine Arts, Boston. A copy of the photographic print or this work, headed "To Arms! Freemen to Arms!" is held at the Library of Congress, reproduced at: http://www.loc.gov/pictu res/item/2010647925/.

70. Thomas Couture, "The Drummer Boy" (1857), held at the Detroit Institute of Art, is reproduced at: https://commons.wikimedia.org/wiki/File:Drummer_Boy_1857_Thomas_Couture.jpg.

71. William Morris Hunt, "The Wounded Drummer Boy," c. 1862. Held at the Museum of Fine Arts Boston, is reproduced at: https://www.mfa.org/collections/object/the-wounded-drummer-boy-31723.

72. "Eastman Johnson," *Appletons' Journal: A Magazine of General Literature* 11:260 (March 14, 1874): 347.

73. "The Wounded Drummer Boy," *Appletons' Journal: A Magazine of General Literature* 7:165 (May 25, 1872): 579.

74. Gerry Souter, *American Realism* (New York: Parkstone Press, 2015), 17.

Chapter 6

1. The original manuscript, in Upson's hand, is actually a hybrid—part diary, part memoir. According to the editor of the published version, it was "rewritten from diaries, journals, and letters written by him before, during, and shortly after the Civil War." While "occasional interpolations . . . reveal postwar addenda," the journal was "largely transcribed from his original diaries and letters." Theodore F. Upson, *With Sherman to the Sea: The Civil War Diaries and Reminiscences of Theodore F. Upson*, ed. and intro. Oscar Osburn Winther (Bloomington: Indiana Press, 1958), xxvi–xxvii.

2. Upson, *With Sherman to the Sea*, 1–3.
3. On the Wide Awakes, see Jon Grinspan, "'Young Men for War': The Wide Awakes and Lincoln's 1860 Presidential Campaign," *Journal of American History* 96 (September 2009): 357–378.
4. Upson, *With Sherman to the Sea*, 7–8.
5. Upson, *With Sherman to the Sea*, 9–10, 12.
6. Upson, *With Sherman to the Sea*, 13–14.
7. Upson, *With Sherman to the Sea*, 16–17.
8. Howard P. Chudacoff, *How Old Are You? Age Consciousness in American Culture* (Princeton: NJ: Princeton University Press, 1989), 18–19.
9. James D. Schmidt, "'Restless Movements Characteristic of Childhood: The Legal Construction of Child Labor in Nineteenth-Century Massachusetts," *Law and History Review* 23:2 (2005): 315–350.
10. Although dealing with a slightly later period, Pamela Riney-Kehrberg's discussion of the rural children's labor in *Childhood on the Farm: Work, Play, and Coming of Age in the Midwest* (Kansas: University Press of Kansas, 2005) is relevant here; she argues that "work could be a self-affirming and positive experience for children, not just one of exploitation" (5).
11. Jon Grinspan, *The Virgin Vote: How Young Americans Made Democracy Social, Politics Personal, and Voting Popular in the Nineteenth Century* (Chapel Hill: University of North Carolina Press, 2016), 29. As Grinspan notes, politicians focused on first-time voters and those still ineligible to vote in part because it was hard to sway men who had already pledged their fealty to a particular party.
12. According to Joseph F. Kett, *Rites of Passage: Adolescence in America, 1790 to the Present* (New York: Basic Books, 1977), 5, "loosely structured academies containing young people between the ages of 10-25" declined over the course of the nineteenth century, replaced by schools that "exclusively served teenagers." Similarly, as Michael David Cohen explains in *Reconstructing the Campus: Higher Education and the American Civil War* (Charlottesville: University of Virginia Press, 2012), 8, the term "college" had a broader meaning in the antebellum period than it does today; it could refer to an institution that, in addition to a bachelor's program, offered primary and secondary curricula in a preparatory department. During the 1850s youths under the age of seventeen made up 23 and 15 percent, respectively, of those attending college in midwestern and northeastern states (145). Robert F. Pace claims in *Halls of Honor: College Men in the Old South* (Baton Rouge: Louisiana University Press, 2004) that the average age of a first-year college student in the antebellum south was just fifteen years old.
13. For instance, Stanton P. Allen, *Down in Dixie: Life in a Cavalry Regiment in the War Days, from the Wilderness to Appomattox* (Boston: D. Lothrop Co., 1893), 32–33.
14. Keri Leigh Merritt, *Masterless Men: Poor Whites and Slavery in the Antebellum Era* (Cambridge, UK: Cambridge University Press, 2017), chap. 5.

15. It is also likely that devotion to the Confederacy—the kind of devotion that would lead one to write a war memoir, despite having fought on the losing side—was more limited to the elite than its leaders wanted to believe.

16. Elisha Stockwell, Jr., *Private Elisha Stockwell, Jr., Sees the Civil War*, ed., Byron R. Abernethy (Norman: University of Oklahoma Press, 1958), 3–4.

17. Stockwell, Jr., *Private Elisha Stockwell*, 3–6.

18. Arthur J. Robinson, *Memorandum and Anecdotes of the Civil War, 1862 to 1865* (n.p.: priv. pub., 1912). This memoir claims he was born on March 25, 1845, but census records and his tombstone indicate that he was born in 1846. His younger brother Hiram was born October 22, 1848.

19. This pattern was at odds with the message of certain didactic stories and novels of the period, which suggested that youths in their mid-teens could best display their patriotism at home, by taking the place of adult men who left to fight. For instance, Horatio Alger, Jr.'s debut novel, *Frank's Campaign; or, What Boys Can do on the Farm for the Camp* (Boston, MA: Loring, 1864), features a sixteen-year-old boy who leaves school and takes charge of the family farm, freeing up his father to enlist.

20. Wyeth is one of the few Confederate memoirists to detail the work that he performed as a boy. The son of a Pennsylvanian who became a district judge in Alabama, he was taught to appreciate the dignity of labor and to eschew the prideful masculinity celebrated by many elite southerners. In this sense, he is the exception who proves the rule. John Allan Wyeth, *With Sabre and Scalpel: The Autobiography of a Soldier and Surgeon* (New York: Harper & Brothers, 1911), 106–176.

21. Such was the case for sixteen-year-old Charles Storke, who struck out on his own at the age of fourteen, leaving school and his widowed mother behind to take a printer's job in a different town. Charles Albert Storke, with Michael J. Phillips, "After the Bugles—the West!," box 2, vol. 4, Charles Albert Storke Papers, 1856–1936, Bancroft Library, University of California, Berkeley.

22. The point at which a parent or guardian surrendered legal control by allowing a minor child independence could be quite murky, since youths tended to use their parents' house as a kind of home base to which they often returned. Chudacoff, *How Old Are You?*, 14, notes that maturation was a long, drawn-out process during the mid-nineteenth century. Many middle-class sons lived at home until they were almost thirty.

23. Elbridge J. Copp would later promote his memoirs, *Reminiscences of the War of the Rebellion, 1861-1865* (Nashua, NH: Telegraph Publishing, 1911), 7, 11–16, as penned by "the youngest Commissioned Officer in the Union army who rose from the ranks." .

24. James G. Hollandsworth, Jr., *The Louisiana Native Guards: The Black Military Experience During the Civil War* (Baton Rouge: Louisiana State University Press, 1995).

25. Joseph T. Glatthaar and John H. Crowder, "The Civil War Through the Eyes of a Sixteen-Year Old Black Officer: The Letters of Lieutenant John H. Crowder of the 1st Louisiana Native Guards," *Louisiana History* 35:2 (spring 1994): 201–216 (quotation, 204–205, 213).

26. George T. Ulmer, *Adventures and Reminiscences of a Volunteer or a Drummer Boy from Maine* (n.p.: privately printed, 1892), 5–20.

27. Enos B. Vail, *Reminiscences of a Boy in the Civil War* (Brooklyn: priv. print., 1915).

28. The article "More Than He Bargained For," *Daily Times* (Troy, NY), September 1, 1863, is included in Allen, *Down in Dixie*, 13–14.

29. Allen, *Down in Dixie*, 14, 18, 41. Census records confirm that Allen was born in 1849.

30. Allen, *Down in Dixie*, 19–20.

31. Ulmer, *Adventures and Reminiscences*, 19.

32. Grinspan, *The Virgin Vote*. See also Kett, *Rites of Passage*, 39–43.

33. James W. Sullivan, *Boyhood Memories of the Civil War, 1861-1865: Invasion of Carlisle* (Carlisle, PA: Hamilton Library Association, 1933), 3–4.

34. John Henry Cammack, *Personal Recollections: A Soldier of the Confederacy, 1861-1865*, Huntington, WV: Paragon Printing and Publishing, 1920, 7.

35. James K. P. DeFord, *From 1861 to 1865: Civil War Record* (Kahoka, MO: R.L. Christy Job Print, 1905).

36. William H. Armstrong, *Major McKinley: William McKinley and the Civil War* (Kent, OH: Kent State University Press, 2000), 8.

37. Upson, *With Sherman to the Sea*, 3.

38. David E. Johnston, *Confederate Boy in the Civil War* (Portland, OR: Glass and Prudhomme, 1914), 4.

39. J.[osiah] Staunton Moore, *Reminiscences, Letters, Poetry and Miscellanies* (Richmond, VA: O.E. Flanhart Printing Co., 1903), 31–34.

40. Nathaniel Cheairs Hughes, Jr., ed., *The Civil War Memoir of Philip Daingerfield Stephenson* (Baton Rouge: Louisiana State University Press, 1995), 5.

41. W.[ill] B. Smith, *On Wheels, and How I Came There: A Real Story for Real Boys and Girls, Giving the Personal Experiences and Observations of a Fifteen-year-old Yankee Boy as Soldier and Prisoner in the American Civil War*, ed. Joseph Gatch Bonnell (New York: Hunt & Eaton, 1892), 16–19.

42. John Sergeant Wise, *End of an Era* (Boston: Houghton, Mifflin, and Co., 1899), 59–60.

43. "Guard of the Metropolis," *Richmond Dispatch*, May 26, 1856, 1.

44. Alan Manning, *Father Lincoln: The Untold Story of Abraham Lincoln and His Boys—Robert, Eddy, Willie, and Tad* (Guildford, CT: Rowman and Littlefield, 2016), 86.

45. At the very outset of his memoir, Will Smith describes himself as "the youngest member of the uniformed Lincoln Wide Awake company in Naples." Smith, *On Wheels, and How I Came There*, 15–16.

46. Pascal Pearl Gilmore, *Civil War Memories* (Bangor, ME: s.n., 1928), 17.

47. Letter from Marengo County boys to Governor A.B. Moore, January 19, 1861, Confederate Regimental History Files, Alabama Department of Archives and History, Montgomery, Alabama, http://digital.archives.alabama.gov/cdm/ref/collection/voices/id/2103. In 1860 Marengo County's enslaved population outnumbered the white population three to one. Tom Blake, "Marengo County, Alabama," 2001, rootsweb, ancestry.com. Support for secession was strongest in areas with similar demographics, and young men from such regions were often among the most impassioned "fire eaters."

48. Sullivan, *Boyhood Memories of the Civil War*, 3.

49. As the governor's son, Wise could possibly have been referring to his personal up-bringing. But given his discussions of political fights in the schoolyard and Richmond youths' engagement in the Guard of the Metropolis, it is fair to read his reference to "society" as extending beyond his own familial circumstances. Wise, *End of an Era*, 76.

50. Andrew Jackson Andrews, *A Sketch of Boyhood Days* (Richmond: Hermitage Press, 1905), 9. Born on August 18, 1842, Andrews enlisted in June 1861 at the age of nineteen.

51. Prior to 1870, "fewer than 50 percent of children aged between 5 and 17 attended school," and the average school year ran for just seventy-eight days—or about fifteen weeks. Samuel Bowles and Herbert Gintis, *Schooling in Capitalist America: Educational Reform and the Contradictions of Economic Life* (New York: Basic Books, 1976), 153.

52. In the southern states, nearly one hundred private and state-funded military academies opened their doors between 1839 and the Civil War. According to Jennifer Greene, *Military Education and the Emerging Middle Class in the Old South* (Cambridge: Cambridge University Press, 2008), these institutions generally served boys between the ages of thirteen and twenty-two who came from upwardly mobile, middle-class families rather than the planter elite. See also Rod Andrew, Jr., *Long Gray Lines: The Southern Military School Tradition, 1839-1915* (Chapel Hill: University of North Carolina Press, 2001); and Bruce Allardice, "West Points of the Confederacy: Southern Military Schools and the Confederate Army," *Civil War History* 43:4 (1997): 310–31. For military academies in the northern United States, see Lee Duemer, "The History of Antebellum Military Academies in the North: 1803-1865," *American Educational History Journal* 26:1 (1999): 128–33. Kurt A. Sanftleben, "A Different Drum: The Forgotten Tradition of the Military Academy in American Education" (PhD diss., College of William & Mary, 1993), discusses both regions.

53. Carl Kaestle, *Pillars of the Republic: Common Schools and American Society, 1780-1860* (New York: Hill and Wang, 2011); and Johann N. Neem, *Democracy's Schools: The Rise of Public Education in America* (Baltimore: Johns Hopkins University Press, 2017).

54. Grinspan, *Virgin Vote*, 24.

55. Sean Michael Heuvel and Lisa Heuvel, *The College of William and Mary in the Civil War* (Jefferson, NC: MarFarland, 2013), 27. See also Mary Elizabeth Massey, "The Civil War Comes to the Campus," in R. C. Simonini, Jr., ed., *Education in the South: Institute of Southern Culture Lectures* (Richmond, VA: Cavalier Press, 1959, 11–37).

56. James Dinkins, *1861 to 1865, by an Old Johnnie: Personal Recollections and Experiences in the Confederate Army* (Cincinnati, OH: The Robert Clarke Co., 1897), 22–27.

57. Heuvel and Heuvel, *The College of William and Mary in the Civil War*, 28. In the end, all but two students enrolled in the college in 1861 served in the Confederate Army.

58. Hopkins, *From Bull Run to Appomattox*, 21.

59. John Brown Gordon, *Reminiscences of the Civil War* (New York: Charles Scribner's Sons, 1904), 302.

60. Dinkins, *1861 to 1865, by an Old Johnnie*, 22–27.

61. According to Charles Stephen Padgett, the school's student roster "swelled with names like Semmes, Maury, Taylor, Beauregard, and Bullock, as high officers of the Confederacy tried to shelter sons who were approaching draft age. Boys sent to Spring Hill were often separated from their families for the war's duration." "Spring Hill College," *Encyclopedia of Alabama*, http://www.encyclopediaofalabama.org/article/ h-1029.

62. Anon., *A Civil War Diary: The Diary of Spring Hill College Between the Years 1860-1865*, Raymond H. Schandt and Josephine H. Schulte, eds. (Mobile, AL: Spring Hill College Press, 1982). This log is called "Vice President's Diary, from 1859-1887," but according to the editors, it is unclear who exactly made the entries.

63. N. W. Taylor Root, *School Amusements; or, How to Make the School Interesting* (New York: Jones and Denyse, 1857), xi, and *Infantry Tactics for Schools: Explained and Illustrated for the Use of Teachers and Scholars* (New York: A.S. Barnes and Burr, 1863).

64. A history of Philips Exeter Academy implies that this trend was all but universal, noting that students too young to join the army had, "in common with the youth of the entire North," established drill clubs to practice military maneuvers. Quoted in Axel Bundgaard, *Muscle and Manliness: The Rise of Sport in American Boarding Schools* (Syracuse, NY: Syracuse University Press, 2005), 58.

65. Jesse Bowman Young, *What a Boy Saw in the Army: A Story of Sight-Seeing and Adventure in the War for the Union* (New York: Hunt and Eaton, 1894), 18.

66. William Spicer, "The High School Boys of the Tenth Rhode Island Regiment," *Soldiers and Sailors Historical Society of Rhode Island: Personal Narratives of Events in the War of the Rebellion*, second series, no. 13. (Providence, RI: N. Bangs Williams & Company, 1882), 8–11.

67. Spicer, "The High School Boys of the Tenth Rhode Island Regiment," 11.

68. Kieffer, *Recollections of a Drummer Boy*, 23, 29.

69. Frank Moore included the story of "The Drummer Boy of the Eighth Michigan Infantry" in his famous compendium of wartime events, *The Rebellion Record: A Diary of American Events*, vol. 8 (New York: D. Van Norstrand, 1865), 29–30. See also Mary Livermore, *My Story of the War: A Woman's Narrative of Four Years Personal Experience as Nurse in the Union Army* (Hartford, CT: A.D. Worthington, 1890), 275–79.

70. Nimord Bramham Hamner Diary, Hamner Family Papers (Mss1H1845a), Virginia Historical Society, Richmond, Va.

71. Kieffer, *Recollections of a Drummer Boy*, 31–32. Kieffer's friend, referred to as "Andy" throughout the book, was Fisher Gutelius, who later became a minister, as did Kieffer himself. On the Pennsylvania muster rolls, Kieffer's age is recorded as seventeen and Gutelius's as nineteen, whereas they were actually sixteen and seventeen years old, respectively.

72. C. Henry Barney, *A Country Boy's First Three Months in the Army* (Providence, RI: N. Bangs Williams & Company, 1880), 7–8.

73. James M. McPherson, *For Cause and Comrades: Why Men Fought in the Civil War* (New York: Oxford University Press, 1997).

74. Edward W. Spangler, *My Little War Experience, with Historical Sketches and Memorabilia* (privately published, 1904), 17; and Edward Burgess Peirce to Mother [Mrs. J.N. Peirce], August 11, 1863, Edward Burgess Peirce Letters, Massachusetts Historical Society, Boston, MA.

75. Francis Davis Millet, "Civil War Diary," entry for July 15, 1864, Millet family papers, 1858–1984, Archives of American Art, https://www.aaa.si.edu/collections/francis-davis-millet-and-millet-family-papers-9048. Millet went on to become a famous painter and war correspondent before dying on the *Titanic*. William H. Sallada, *Silver Sheaves: Gathered through Clouds and Sunshine* (Des Moines, IA: priv. print., 1887), 77–78.

76. William P. Ellis to Mary Ellis, February 23, 1863, folder "William M. Ellis Correspondence," box 20, Norman Daniels Collection, Harrisburg Civil War Round Table Collection, U.S. Army War College Library and Archives, Carlisle, Pennsylvania.

77. Capt. A. M. Jones to Gen. Robert E. Lee, July 10, 1863, compiled service record for Benjamin H. Dennard, Ancestry.com, https://www.fold3.com/image/43376913.

Chapter 7

1. *Speech of Richard H. Dana, Jr. at Manchester, N.H. on Tuesday Evening, February 19, 1861* (Boston: Redding & Co, 1861), 11.

2. On draft riot and desertion see James W. Geary, *We Need Men: The Union Draft in the Civil War* (DeKalb: Northern Illinois University Press, 1991); and Eugene C. Murdock, *One Million Men: The Civil War Draft in the North* (Champaign: University of Illinois, 1971); on soldiers' motivations, James McPherson, *For Cause and Comrades: Why Men Fought in the Civil War* (New York: Oxford University Press, 1997); and on black enlistment: Ira Berlin, Joseph P. Reidy, and Leslie S. Rowland, eds., *Freedom's Soldiers: The Black Military Experience in the Civil War* (New York: Cambridge University Press, 1998).

3. James McPherson, *Battle Cry of Freedom: The Civil War Era* (New York: Oxford University Press, 1988), chap. 10 (quote 313).

4. McPherson, *Battle Cry of Freedom*, 323.

5. The army regulations for 1857 were operative until September 1861. They were superseded by *Revised United States Army Regulations of 1861* (Philadelphia: G.W. Childs, 1863), which left all these provisions in place save for the height restriction, which was lowered to five feet three inches. These regulations were amended again in February 1862 to allow males between the ages of eighteen and twenty-one to enlist without parental consent.

6. In the fall of 1861, the United States Sanitary Commission (USSC) surveyed two hundred newly organized volunteer regiments and concluded that in a full 58 percent "there had been no pretence of a thorough inspection of recruits on enlistment." Only 9 percent had undergone careful medical scrutiny. *A Report to the Secretary of War*

of the Operations of the Sanitary Commission, and upon the Sanitary Condition of the Volunteer Army (Washington, DC: McGill & Witherow, 1861), 12, 14–15.

7. Delavan S. Miller, *Drum Taps in Dixie: Memories of a Drummer Boy, 1861-1865* (Watertown, NY: Hungerford-Hobrook Co., 1905), 16.

8. Richard Goldthwaite Carter, *The Record of Military Service of First Lieutenant and Brevet Captain Robert Goldthwaite Carter, U.S. Army, 1862-1877* (Washington, DC: Gibson Bros, Printers and Bookbinders, 1904), 3.

9. Edward W. Spangler, *My Little War Experience, with Historical Sketches and Memorabilia* (privately published, 1904), 18.

10. Provost Marshal General James B. Fry's final report of March 17, 1866, describes the transformation of enlistment procedures during the war. *The War of the Rebellion: A Compilation of the Official Records of the Union and Confederate Armies*, 128 vols. (Washington, DC: Government Printing Office, 1880-1901), ser. III, vol. X, 855ff. Hereafter cited as *OR*.

11. Whether parents addressed President Lincoln, the secretary of war, or any other military official, their letters were sent to the Enlistment Branch of the Adjutant General's Office. This correspondence is held in two collections at NARA: RG 94: Office of the Adjutant General, Addison Files, 1848-62, Letters Received Relating to Soldiers, 1848-62, entry 416; and RG94: Office of the Adjutant General, Records of the Enlisted Branch, Letters Received, 1862-1889, entry 409 (hereafter AGO Letters Received, Addison Files; and AGO Letters Received, Enlisted Branch). There are roughly 900 boxes in these two record groups for the war years, each of which includes between 200 and 300 letters or cases. We examined all of the AGO Letters Received, Addison Files, and then sampled every twentieth box of the much larger collection of AGO Letters Received, Enlisted Branch. Because this sampling strategy involved examining thousands of cases, we were forced to stop at box 120. But to ensure that we took account of material received in 1864 and 1865, we also looked at a dozen boxes in the 200s and the 600s, having determined that the material after this point mostly consisted of descriptive lists and other records forwarded by regiments as they disbanded. In the boxes containing letters for 1861 and 1862, it was common to find a quarter or more of all the letters in a single box written by parents seeking the return of minors. Sampling boxes later in this collection made clear that such cases declined significantly over time as enlistment procedures hardened and the War Department became increasingly deaf to parents' appeals.

12. Matching every parent's letter with a government reply proved unfeasible, since correspondence and replies are filed in separate collections with no easy cross-referencing system. To understand the administrative response to the problem of minor enlistees, we therefore created a database of 145 cases for which we could determine an outcome—a process that replied on notations on the correspondence itself or by checking enlistees' compiled service records, pension files, Ancestry.com and Fold3.com. In what follows, we usually cite only the original archival collection used when we refer to individuals, and not the myriad sources we employed to track case outcomes or biographical details.

13. "Quarter Sessions," *Press* (Philadelphia, PA), July 25, 1861, 3.

14. "The Plea of Infancy," *New York Times*, August 27, 1861, 3.

15. See, for example, *Daily Ohio Statesman* (Columbus, OH), October 19 and 26 and November 2, 8, 9, and 16, 1861. This paper was one of the few that sent a court recorder to detail the results of cases in a single probate court; the press generally ignored legal cases heard in lower courts, as remains the case today.

16. Gregory P. Downs' analysis in *Declarations of Dependence: The Long Reconstruction of Popular Politics in the South, 1861-1908* (Chapel Hill: University of North Carolina Press, 2011) is useful for assessing the letters parents sent to Washington. Focusing on North Carolina, he shows how petitioners appealed to political leaders by using claims of dependence as "a strategy, a tool to mediate politics for their own benefit." Yet whereas Downs interprets appeals from North Carolinians as "innovative attempts to take advantage of new government powers," the letters cited here often angrily protested such powers, even as they used personal appeals to try and achieve their desired ends.

17. Matthew Green to Secretary Simon Cameron, August 1861, AGO Letters Received, Addison Files, Box 47.

18. Elijah and Mary Boyers wrote to Abraham Lincoln on July 7, 1862, and to Edwin M. Stanton on June 22, 1862, and July 7, 1862, AGO Letters Received, Addison Files, Box 49. Census records confirm that Alden, who enlisted under the name Byers, was sixteen years old when he signed up. His parents' appeal failed; according to his compiled service record, he deserted in August 1862 but later returned to his regiment, only to desert again in October 1863.

19. Benjamin Warren to the War Department, April 23, 1862, AGO Letters Received, Addison Files, Box 51. Emphasis in original.

20. Maria Abby to Abraham Lincoln, September 1, 1861, AGO Letters Received, Addison Files, Box 46.

21. For instance, Mary Kane, February 7, 1862; and Hiram Vail, March 15, 1862, AGO Letters Received, Addison Files, Box 49; Joseph W. Barton, December 14, 1862; and Thomas B. McCalley, December 22, 1862, AGO Letters Received, Enlisted Branch, Box 1; and Bridget Cunningham, n.d., AGO Letters Received, Enlisted Branch, Box 21.

22. Laura F. Edwards, *The People and Their Peace: Legal Culture and the Transformation of Inequality in the Post-Revolutionary South* (Chapel Hill: University of North Carolina Press, 2009).

23. John Archer to Simon Cameron, September 20, 1861, AGO Letters Received, Addison Files, Box 46.

24. This mother claimed that the boy's captain had promised him that the regiment would go no farther than Manchester, New Hampshire, about twenty miles from his home. George Blood was killed in action in May 1863; that same month, his mother filed for a pension. Eliza J. Stevens to "Honourable Sir," August 4, 1862, AGO Letters Received, Addison Files, Box 49.

25. John Mummert to Edward Stanton, October 7, 1863, AGO Letters Received, Addison Files, Box 46. This father was not exaggerating his family's losses. Records on Ancestry.com show that two daughters had died in 1857 and 1860 and two sons in

1862 and 1863. Although the boy he wanted released was his sole surviving son, his appeal was unsuccessful.

26. *Congressional Globe,* 37th Congress, 1st Session, July 17, 1861, 157. Secretary of War Simon Cameron also called for the law's repeal, citing its "injurious operations," in his annual report of the Secretary of War in late 1861.

27. That very month, in fact, Conkling intervened on behalf of a father whose son had enlisted at age seventeen under an alias; he wrote to the colonel of the boy's regiment multiple times and provided the father with a letter that he forwarded to the War Department, finally resulting in a discharge in September 1861. Letters relating to Thomas Bannagan [alias Charles Wilcox], AGO Letters Received, Addison Files, Box 47.

28. General Orders No. 73, Adjutant General's Office, September 7, 1861. Orders and Circulars, 1797-1910, Entry 44, National Archives and Records Administration, Washington, DC.

29. See, for example, documents relating to Samuel Johnson, AGO Letters Received, Addison Files, Box 47.

30. Eli McCalley to President Lincoln, December 11, 1862, AGO Letters Received, Enlisted Branch, Box 1.

31. In our aforementioned database of 145 cases, a total of twenty-six petitions are dated prior to September 7, 1861. Of these, sixteen were rejected, and ten were successful and resulted in discharge. Of the first twenty-six cases that *followed* September 7, 1861, twenty-three cases were rejected, and only three were accepted, one of whom was a British subject.

32. Eli McCalley to Abraham Lincoln, November 25, 1862.

33. James S. West, August 19, 1861, AGO Letters Received, Addison Files, Box 49.

34. As early as July 1861, Senator Henry Wilson of Massachusetts, chair of the Senate Committee on Military Affairs, urged his colleagues to act, explaining that the Secretary of War was "very anxious" to see the law changed. *Congressional Globe,* 37th Congress, 1st Session, July 17, 1861, 157. Secretary of War Simon Cameron shared his opinion on "the injurious operation of this law" in his annual report. "Report of the Secretary of War," December 1, 1861, 37th Congress, 2d session, Senate, Ex. Doc. No. 1.

35. "An Act making an appropriation for completing the defences of Washington, and for other purposes," February 13, 1862, *U.S. Statutes at Large* 12 (1859–1863), 339–340.

36. E.D. Townsend, undated note to N. T. Devin, October 30, 1863, AGO Letters Received, Enlisted Branch, Box 107. The administration interpreted the law to mean that, if a soldier had sworn to be eighteen, no court could hear "any evidence" challenging the legitimacy of his enlistment, whatever his actual age. Joseph Holt to Edwin Stanton, October 2, 1862, RG153, Entry 1, Office of the Judge Advocate General, Letters Sent: Record Books, 1842-1889, National Archives and Records Administration, Book 1, September 1862 (hereafter JAG Records). The predictable result, according to one provost marshal, was that enlisting officers felt new license to be "extremely careless" when it came to verifying recruits' ages W. Silvey Capt 1st Arty A.A. Provost Marshal General (Rhode Island) to Provost Marshal General James. B. Fry, November

12, 1863, contained in N. T. Devin, October 30, 1863, AGO Letters Received, Enlisted Branch, Box 107.

37. *Cong. Globe*, 37th Cong, 2nd sess., January 21, 1862, 409.

38. On northern militias see Thomas Bahde, "'Our Cause is a Common One': Home Guards, Union Leagues, and Republican Citizenship in Illinois, 1861-1863," *Civil War History* 56:1 (March 2010): 66–98; John Michael Foster, Jr., "'For the Good of the Cause and the Protection of the Border': The Service of the Indiana Legion in the Civil War, 181-1865," *Civil War History* 55:1 (March 2009): 31–55; and Robert S. Chamberlain, "The Northern State Militia," *Civil War History* 4:2 (June 1958): 105–118.

39. Militia Act of 1862, 12 *Stat.* 597, enacted July 17, 1862.

40. In 1861, the Militia Acts of 1792 and 1795 remained in force. Under these acts, the centralized control of the militia was specifically designed to be short-lived, and local authority over militiamen received unambiguous protection. The Militia Act of 1862 was quite different. This new law not only empowered the president to call forth an unlimited number of militiamen for up to nine months, but to make "all necessary rules and regulations" relating to militiamen, and to reorganize militia forces in line with volunteers. Thereafter, the federal executive—not the states—would determine how militia units in national service were organized, and militiamen—in addition to serving longer terms—came fully under the power of a centralized military justice system. This was the confusion to which Collamer referred, although this law muddled things still further, by simultaneously allowing the president to accept up to 100,000 volunteer infantrymen "for up to nine months." Militia service remained shorter than enlistment in the regulars or as a volunteer, but the new law obliterated the older sense that such service was transient and geared to home defense, with militiamen serving under local officers who remained embedded in their communities and held disciplinary power over their men. Conflating volunteers and militia, the 1862 law ensured the mandatory conscription of eighteen-year-old males as nine-month militiamen, adding to a law passed in February 1862 which allowed eighteen-year-olds to volunteer for service without parental consent.

41. Rachel A. Shelden, "Measures for a 'Speedy Conclusion': A Reexamination of Conscription and Civil War Federalism," *Civil War History* 55:4 (2009): 469–498, provides a valuable analysis of the Militia Act of 1862. Studying interactions between local, state, and national officials and the northern public, her work complicates the traditional narrative of wartime federalism, which assumes that conscription was an unwelcome imposition of centralized power on states and localities and understood by citizens as a major infringement of their constitutional rights. To the contrary, Sheldon argues, most northern politicians and citizens welcomed militia reorganization and recognized the need for the introduction of a draft as a means to raise troops and protect the union. The transformation of the dual military system may have been inevitable and widely supported, as Sheldon's work suggests. Nonetheless, it remains one of the war's most significant and least accredited outcomes.

42. The quote is from Senator Willard Saulsbury, a Democrat from the border state of Delaware. *Cong. Globe*, 37th Cong., 2nd sess., July 9, 1862, 3198–3199.

43. Militia laws at this point only allowed the President to call out militiamen in the event of invasion or insurrection. Since the Mexican American War was fought on foreign soil, the government was forced to rely on volunteers to supplement the regulars, establishing a precedent that would shape Civil War mobilization.

44. *Cong. Globe*, 37th Cong., 2nd sess., July 11, 1862, 3227–3228. No one responded directly to Collamer's critique, although the Militia Act of 1862 did limit the president's right to call out the militia to nine months, overriding an earlier plan to allow for their indefinite mobilization, suggesting that his arguments were not entirely ignored.

45. *Cong. Globe*, 37th Cong., 2nd sess., July 11, 1862, 3338.

46. "An Act to Suppress Insurrection, to Punish Treason and Rebellion, to Seize and Confiscate the Property of Rebels, and for Other Purposes," *U.S. Statutes at Large* 12 (1859–1863), 589.

47. *Cong. Globe*, 37th Cong., 2nd sess., July 9, 1862, 3198-99.

48. William Whiting, *The War Powers of the President: And the Legislative Powers of Congress in Relation to Rebellion, Treason and Slavery*, 2nd ed. (Boston: John L. Shorey, 1862), 22–23. According to John Fabian Witt, *Lincoln's Code: The Laws of War in American History* (New York: Simon and Schuster, 2012), 205, Whiting exaggerated his influence when he claimed that his work had been reprinted forty-three times (it was closer to ten). But Whiting won Lincoln's approval, and Mark Neely, Jr., *Lincoln and The Democrats: The Politics of Opposition in the Civil War* (New York: Cambridge University Press, 2017), 185, credits him "as the principal source of the far-reaching argument" that justified emancipation as an act of war by making recourse to international law.

49. William L. Gregg, February 23, 1862, AGO Letters Received, Addison Files, Box 47.

50. Oram Gregg proved to be a valuable recruit: he served his entire three-year term before being mustered out in August 1864 at the rank of sergeant–all prior to reaching the legal age of enlistment. In 1886, he spoke of his experiences to the YMCA. "A Boy's Cavalry Experiences," *Delaware County Daily Times* (Chester, Penn.), December 8, 1886, 3.

51. See our appendices.

52. Recent scholarship on the history of habeas corpus includes: Anthony Gregory, *The Power of Habeas Corpus in America: From the King's Prerogative to the War on Terror* (New York: Cambridge University Press, 2013); Justin J. Wert, *Habeas Corpus in America: The Politics of Individual Rights* (Lawrence: Kansas University Press, 2011); Paul D. Halliday, *Habeas Corpus: From England to Empire* (Cambridge, MA: Harvard University Press, 2010); Cary Federman, *The Body and the State: Habeas Corpus and American Jurisprudence* (Albany, NY: State University of New York Press, 2006); Eric M. Freedman, *Habeas Corpus: Rethinking the Great Writ of Liberty* (New York: New York University Press, 2001); and Amanda L Tyler, *Habeas Corpus in Wartime: From the Tower of London to Guantanamo Bay* (New York: Oxford University Press). On the use of habeas corpus during the Civil War, see: Robert O. Faith, "Public Necessity or Military Convenience? Reevaluating Lincoln's Suspensions of the Writ of Habeas Corpus," *Civil War History* 26 (2016): 284–320; Brian McGinty, *The Body of John Merryman: Abraham Lincoln and the Suspension of Habeas Corpus*

(Boston: Harvard University Press, 2011); Jonathan W. White, *Abraham Lincoln and Treason in the Civil War: The Trials of John Merryman* (Baton Rouge: Louisiana State University Press, 2011); and Mark E. Neely, Jr., *The Fate of Liberty: Abraham Lincoln and Civil Liberties* (New York: Oxford University Press, 1991).

53. Mark E. Neely, Jr., "Legalities in Wartime: The Myth of the Writ of Habeas Corpus," in Stephen D. Engle, ed., *The War Worth Fighting: Abraham Lincoln's Presidency and Civil War America* (Gainesville: University of Florida Press, 2015), 110–126.

54. Neely, *The Fate of Liberty*, 233–234, points out that although the volume of civilians jailed during the war was high, their arrests did not provoke mass protest because most detainees were not arrested for taking a principled political stance. They were "citizens of the Confederacy, blockade-runners, foreign nationals, returning Southern sea captains, and the like"—individuals caught up by "mere incidents or friction of war."

55. On concurrent jurisdiction, see chap. 2. This was a taken-for-granted position at the war's outset, as noted by US Attorney General Edward Bates. 10 *Op. Att'y Gen.* (1861), 146.

56. Our view of these dissenters is in keeping with legal historian Nicholas Mosvick's perspective on the judges and lawyers who questioned the constitutionality of the United States' conscription act; indeed, they were often one and the same. Because most of these judges were Democrats, scholars tend to read their objections as political resistance to the Lincoln administration's war efforts. Mosvick argues that we should instead regard them as "constitutional conservatives," whose commitment to limiting executive power was genuinely rooted in their understanding of the founders' vision of federalism. To grant that there were legitimate constitutional grounds for such objections is not, however, to affirm these judges' views or to argue that political considerations played no role in their thinking. Nicholas Matthew Mosvick, "Courtroom Wars: Constitutional Battles over Conscription in the Civil War North" (PhD diss., University of Mississippi, 2019).

57. Opinion of William Whiting, Solicitor of the War Department, printed as Circular No. 36, Provost Marshal General's Office, July 1, 1863, *OR*, ser. III, vol. III, 460–461. On the government's legal arguments, see Frances M. Clarke and Rebecca Jo Plant, "No Minor Matter: Underage Soldiers, Parents, and the Nationalization of Habeas Corpus in Civil War America," *Law and History Review* 35:4 (November 2017): 910–911.

58. *The People ex. rel. Mary Ann Allen vs. Daniel H. Burtness*, reported in *New York Times*, October 9, 1861, 2.

59. "Government Habeas Corpus Case," *New York Times*, June 23, 1863, 2.

60. Barnard was elected Justice of the Supreme Court of New York on a Tammany Hall ticket.

61. *United States ex rel. Turner v. Wright*, Circuit Court of the United States, Western District of Pennsylvania, reported in *Monthly Law Reporter* 25:8 (June 1863): 459. Judge McCandless, nominated to the US District Court by President Buchanan in 1859, discharged a string of soldiers on claims of minority and for various other reasons, as noted in "Drafting a Minor," *Pittsburgh Daily Gazette and Advertiser* (Pittsburgh, PA), October 24, 1862, 4; "Another Habeas Corpus," *Pittsburgh Daily*

Gazette and Advertiser, October 30, 1862, 3; and "A Writ of Habeas Corpus Issued," *Cleveland Morning Leader* (Cleveland, OH), December 13, 1862, 3.

62. *Re Higgins*, 16 Wis. 351 (1863).

63. "Important Decisions Respecting Recruits," *New York Times*, December 10, 1862, 3.

64. "Before John H. McCunn, City Judge," *New York Times*, December 8, 1862, 3.

65. "Judge McCunn and the Habeas Corpus," *New York Times*, July 26, 1863, 2. On his political affiliations see his obituary, *New York Times*, July 7, 1872, 1.

66. The Habeas Corpus Suspension Act, 12 Stat. 755, passed March 3, 1863, prevented military and civilian officials from being sued for alleged crimes relating to upholding Lincoln's suspension of habeas corpus. Jonathan W. White, *Abraham Lincoln and Treason in the Civil War: The Trials of John Merryman* (Baton Rouge: Louisiana State University Press, 2015), notes that this act began in the House as an indemnity bill and was primarily aimed at protecting officers acting on behalf of the US government.

67. "Gen. Banks is a Brick," *Boston Post* (Boston, MA), December 11, 1862, 1.

68. On November 9, 1862, President Lincoln ordered Major General Banks to New Orleans to relieve Benjamin F. Butler of his command over the Department of the Gulf.

69. Jared Thompson, Jr. "A Case to Be Looked Into," *Milwaukee Daily Sentinel* (Milwaukee, WI), March 2, 1863, 1.

70. "Court of Oyer and Terminer and Quarter Sessions—Judge Allison," *Press* (Philadelphia, PA), July 27, 1863, 4.

71. "Judge Ludlow--Habeas Corpus Cases," *Press*, August 12, 1863, 4.

72. On officers releasing alleged minors after Lincoln's first nationwide suspension of habeas corpus in September 1862 see, for example, "Discharged on Habeas Corpus," *Daily Ohio Statesman*, October 30, 1862, 3; and "Court of Oyer and Terminer and Quarter Sessions--Judge Ludlow," *Press*, August 24, 1863, 3. On cheering crowds, see "The Case of F.M. Lowe," *Cincinnati Daily Press* (Cincinnati, OH), January 8, 1862, 3. On a sheriff facing violence from soldiers as he tried to serve a writ relating to a minor, see "The Military and Civil Power in Conflict," *Daily Ohio Statesman*, December 28, 1861, 2.

73. In "*Dishon ex parte*. Habeas Corpus Before Judge Perkins," *Daily State Sentinel* (Indianapolis, IN), October 22, 1862, Perkins used considerable mental gymnastics to deny that Congress had repealed an earlier law stating that anyone below age twenty-one required written consent to enlist, essentially arguing that federal laws allowing for the enlistment of those above the age of eighteen only applied to volunteer forces. In another case, his fellow jurists decided that the enlistment contract of anyone below the age of eighteen was "void and inoperative." "Important Decision," *Daily State Sentinel*, December 3, 1862, 3. See also Emma Lou Thornbrough, "Judge Perkins, the Indiana Supreme Court, and the Civil War," *Indiana Magazine of History* 60 (March 1964),:79–96, and Frank L. Klement, *The Copperheads in the Middle West* (Chicago: Chicago University Press, 1960).

74. *Griffin v. Wilcox*, 21 Indiana 370 (1863). In this case, Perkins held that civilians could not be subjected to military orders, that the president could not institute martial law or suspend habeas corpus, and that civilians detained without charge could seek

restitution through damage suits—all matters disputed by congressional legislation and executive orders.

75. "State vs. National Authority," *Daily Evansville Journal* (Evansville, IN), September 5, 1863, 2.

76. Proclamation 103, "Suspending the Privileges of the Writ of Habeas Corpus Throughout the United States in Certain Specified Cases," *U.S. Statutes at Large* 13 (1863–1865), 734.

77. Abraham Lincoln, "A Proclamation," General Orders, No 315, War Department, Adjt. General's Office, September 7, 1863, *OR*, ser. III, vol. III, 817–818.

78. In January 1864, for instance, the Vermont Supreme Court's Chief Justice, Luke P. Poland, a Unionist who would eventually become a Republican senator, granted writs to the parents of several minors who had enlisted in a state regiment, arguing that such cases fell under Vermont laws, which prohibited the enlistment of minors without parental consent. Important Decision," *Green-Mountain Freeman* (Montpelier, VT), January 12, 1864. Judges in Vermont followed his lead and continued to release minors in 1864, according to *Ashland Union* (Ashland County, Ohio) April 6, 1864, 2. Similarly, Judge Tilden of Ohio's Probate Court reportedly released several minor enlistees the following month, accepting their lawyer's claim that the soldiers' "military service was properly due to the State, and not to the Federal Government." "Probate Court," *Cleveland Morning Leader* (Cleveland, OH), May 6, 1864, 4; and, in May 1865, Rufus Peckham, a widely respected justice on New York's Supreme Court, issued a writ for a minor enlistee, insisting that the government could not really have intended to suspend the writ in relation to Union soldiers. *The People, ex rel. Starkweather v. Gaul*, 44 Barb. 98 (1865). In general, however, even those most active in asserting judicial prerogatives desisted from issuing writs after the September 1863 proclamation. Judge Cadwalader, for example, issued a verbal opinion in which he stated that he would postpone all proceedings in cases of pending applications and accept no further applications for habeas corpus relief while the president's orders were in effect. "Habeas Corpus," *Daily National Intelligencer*, September 21, 1863, 1.

79. Francis Lieber and G. Norman Lieber, *To Save the Country: A Lost Treatise on Martial Law*, eds. Will Smiley and John Fabian Witt (New Haven: Yale University Press, 2019), 100.

80. In October 1863, the judge advocate general explained to a senior military officer that the secretary of war "uniformly" gave "a literal construction" to the law. Once a recruit had sworn that he was of age, "this declaration necessarily precludes any testimony to the contrary." Joseph Holt to Colonel W. H. Ludlow, October 20, 1863, JAG Records, Book 5.

81. "The Suspension of Habeas Corpus," *The World*, September 13, 1863, 4.

82. "The Last Proclamation," reprinted in *East Saginaw Courier* (East Saginaw, MI), September 20, 1863, 2. Emphasis in original.

83. A. S. Diven, Acting Asst. Provost-Marshal-General's Office, Western Division, State of New York, October 22, 1863 to Col. James B. Fry, Provost-Marshal-General, *OR*, ser. III, vol. III, 912.

84. "An Act to amend an Act entitled 'An Act for enrolling and calling out the National Forces, and for other Purposes," approved February 24, 1864, *U.S. Statutes at Large* 13 (1863–1865), 6. Congress rejected proposed solutions that would have restored power to discharge minors to the local level. Representative Francis William Kellogg, a Republican from Michigan, proposed an amendment to allow local enrollment boards to assume responsibility for assessing claims of minority and discharging youth in credible cases, claiming that the provost marshal general wanted Congress to enact such a measure. Similarly, Representative John Ganson, a New York War Democrat, suggested that the suspension of habeas corpus be revised to exempt cases of alleged minor enlistees. Without such a measure, he warned, the War Department would become inundated by requests from parents, and congressmen would find themselves reduced to glorified "errand boys," burdened with the job of ensuring that their constituents' affidavits and supporting materials reached the Secretary of War. *Cong. Globe*, 38th Cong., 1st Sess., 577–579.

85. A notorious micromanager, Stanton frequently concerned himself with individual inquiries, including those from parents of underage soldiers. Whereas "[c]ommon folk seeking the discharge of underage runaways met routine refusal, even if the family had already sacrificed sons in the war," Stanton proved more receptive to appeals from the rich and powerful. William Marvel, *Lincoln's Autocrat: The Life of Edwin Stanton* (Chapel Hill: University of North Carolina Press, 2015), 318.

86. Hon J. B. Steele, n.d., AGO Letters, Enlisted Branch, Box 220.

87. In both of these cases, the parents ultimately succeeded in getting their children released by gaining an audience with congressional representatives who in turn brought their cases to Lincoln's attention. Lincoln ordered discharges in virtually all cases of minority to reach his desk, although even he stipulated that bounties first had to be repaid. Hon J. B. Steele, n.d., AGO Letters, Enlisted Branch, Box 220; and "Enlistment of Minors," *Richmond Palladium*. See also an untitled article, reprinted from the Boston *Traveller*, that ran in the *Chicago Tribune* (Chicago, IL) on March 7, 1864, 2. "Enlistment of Minors," *Richmond Palladium* (Richmond, IN), March 30, 1864.

88. *Cong. Globe*, 38th Cong., 1st sess., 3379 and 3381.

89. "An Act further to regulate and provide for the enrolling and calling out the National Forces, and for other Purposes," *U.S. Statutes at Large* 13 (1863–1865), 380. Emphasis in original.

90. Of the twenty-one cases in our database that postdate the July 1864 change, all but three (one of whom was facing a court martial) were promised release contingent on repayment of bounties received. In several cases, however, families could not afford to repay the bounty money, and the youths remained in service.

91. Peter Van Winkle to Edwin Stanton, October 24, 1864, and Asst. Surgeon P. B. Rose to Adjutant J. F. McGinley, October 8, 1864, AGO Letters Received, Enlisted Branch, Box 240.

92. "An Act further to regulate and provide for the enrolling and calling out the National Forces, and for other Purposes," enacted July 4, 1864, *U.S. Statutes at Large* 13 (1863–1865), 380.

93. *Congressional Globe*, 38th Congress, 1st Session, 3379–3381. Congressmen also disagreed over whether minors should be immediately and unconditionally discharged, or whether their release should be contingent upon the repayment of bounties. When Senator Lafayette S. Foster of Connecticut moved to strike the phrase "unconditionally discharged" and insert "upon payment of the bounty received," Senator Howe vigorously protested, insisting that "the Government has no right to hold a person under the age of eighteen years, enlisted without the consent of the parent or guardian." Yet in the end, the bill signed into law required repayment of the bounty in full—a policy the government rigorously enforced.

94. *Cong. Globe*, 38th Cong., 1st sess., 3380.

95. *Cong. Globe*, 38th Cong., 1st sess., 3379–3381. Congress revisited the issue of underage enlistees once more in March 1865, to enact higher fines or penalties on those who recruited anyone younger than sixteen. "An act to amend several acts heretofore passed to provide for the enrolling and calling out of the national forces and for other purposes," enacted March 3, 1865, reprinted in *Acts and Resolutions of the Second Session of the Thirty-eighth Congress* (Washington, DC: Government Printing Office, 1865), 78.

96. William W. Belknap, "Letter from the Secretary of War relative to soldiers discharged for minority," February 1, 1872, 42nd Congress, 2d sess., Ex. Doc. No. 113.

97. "An Act to provide that Minors shall not be enlisted in the military service of the United States without the Consent of Parents or Guardians," May 15, 1872, *U.S. Statutes at Large* 17 (1872), 117–118.

98. Probate Judge Daniel R. Tilden, a former Whig who sat on the Common Pleas Court in Cleveland, Ohio, held this opinion. "Habeas Corpus—A Soldier Discharged by Order of Court," *Chicago Tribune*, July 12, 1865.

99. "The Courts—Supreme Court Chambers," *New York Herald*, December 27, 1866. Additional cases reported in the press in this year suggest that state court judges elsewhere tended to side with parents.

100. "How the 'Awful Majesty of the Law' is Preserved," *Evening Telegraph*, September 26, 1867; "The Conflict of Authority: Philadelphia vs. The United States of America," *Evening Telegraph*, September 28, 1867; "The Conflict of Authority Case--Opinion of General Holt," *Evening Telegraph*, September 28, 1867; "Conflict of Jurisdiction in Philadelphia," *The Sun* (New York, NY), September 28, 1867; "Secretary Welles and the Philadelphia Courts," *Commercial Advertiser* (New York, NY), September 30, 1867; "Inter-State Comity," *Evening Telegraph*, October 3, 1867; "The Selfridge-Gormley Case," *Evening Telegraph*, October 6, 1867; "The Writ of Habeas Corpus," *Daily National Intelligencer*, October 7, 1867.

101. Henry E. Wallace, *Philadelphia Reports Containing Decisions Published in the Legal Intelligencer during 1868, 1869, and 1870*, vol. 7 (Philadelphia: J.M Power Wallace, 1875), 76–81. See also Henry Stanbery to Gideon Welles, October 4, 1867, "Gormley's Case--Habeas Corpus," in J. Hugley Ashton, *Official Opinions of the Attorneys General of the United States*, 13 vols. (Washington, DC: W.H. & O.H. Morrison, 1870), 12:258–275.

102. "Conflict of Jurisdiction: The Case of General Neill Taken from the State to the Federal Courts," *New York Herald*, January 22, 1871; See also "Gen. Neill Released," *New York Tribune*, January 28, 1871.

103. "Federal and State Jurisdiction of the Courts," *New York Herald*, January 22, 1871.

104. *Tarble's Case*, 80 U.S. (13 Wall.) 397. For background on this case, see Ann Woolhandler and Michael G. Collins, "The Story of Tarble's Case: State Habeas and Federal Detention (August 11, 2003). *Federal Court Stories*, Vicki C. Jackson and Judith Resnik, eds., Thomson/West. Available at SSRN: http://ssrn.com/abstract= 1447422.

105. Gregory, *The Power of Habeas Corpus in America*, 108. Four years before this case stripped state courts of their power to review federal detentions, Congress passed legislation decisively expanding federal habeas review over state detentions. See William M. Wiecek, "The Great Writ and Reconstruction: The Habeas Corpus Act of 1867," *Journal of Southern History* 36:4 (1970): 530–548; and Todd E. Pettys, "State Habeas Relief for Federal Extrajudicial Detainees," *Minnesota Law Review* 92 (2007): 265–322.

106. One of the most potent manifestations of this shift is the role of militiamen in relation to federal government efforts to put down internal dissent. Through the first half of the nineteenth century, militia forces were famously independent and often refused to be used as tools to advance elite interests. But after serving for four years on behalf of a national effort, the role of state militias in the postbellum era lay predominantly in repressing protest movements and promoting "law and order"— from joining with federal troops to repress angry victims of the Chicago Fire in 1871, through to putting down striking workers in the 1880s and 90s. On this point see Carl Smith, *Urban Disorder and the Shape of Belief: The Great Chicago Fire, the Haymarket Bomb, and the Model Town of Pullman* (Chicago: University of Chicago Press, 1995).

107. Allen Dunn, February 21, 1866, AGO Letters, Enlisted Branch, Box 679.

108. See James Schouler, *A Treatise on the Law of Domestic Relations*, 3rd ed. (Boston: Little, Brown, and Company, [1870] 1882), 683–684. Recognition of the legally emancipatory nature of both marriage and military service is evident in the 1862 Homestead Act, which stipulated that individuals below age twenty-one could apply for a land grant if they were heads of household or had performed military service for at least fourteen days during a time of war. *U.S. Statutes at Large* 12 (1861–1862), 392.

109. Overall, the state played a mixed role in this period in relation to family stability and parental rights. By removing so many men from home, wartime mobilization proved extremely disruptive to many households. But as Megan J. McClintock, "Civil War Pensions and the Reconstruction of Union Families," *Journal of American History* 8 (1996): 456–480, points out, the government's generous pension system also helped sustain Union families' financial integrity. Similarly, whereas the nationalization of habeas cases sharply curtailed parental rights vis-à-vis the military, the federal government also championed the legalization of relationships between freedmen and women and typically supported their right to control minor children

against the claims of former masters. On this point, see Catherine A. Jones, *Intimate Reconstructions: Children in Postemancipation Virginia* (Charlottesville: University of Virginia Press, 2015), chap. 2. On the broader question of how to assess the legal changes brought about by the Civil War, see Laura F. Edwards, *A Nation of Rights: A Legal History of the Civil War and Reconstruction* (New York: Cambridge University Press, 2015), 10.

Chapter 8

1. James McPherson *Battle Cry of Freedom: The Civil War Era* (New York: Oxford University Press, 1988), 723–724.

2. Of the four underage youths who died, two were seventeen years old, and another two were sixteen. As Susan R. Hull, *Boy Soldiers of the Confederacy* (New York: Neale Publishing, 1905), 95–104, notes, not all the cadets were sent into battle; the "very young" boys were kept back to guard the Institute. For details on the those who fought, see https://www.vmi.edu/archives/manuscripts/new-market--vmi-in-the-civil-war/.

3. Brendan Hamilton, "Other Lost Shoes: The Forgotten Reform School Boys Who Fought the VMI Cadets at New Market," https://irishamericancivilwar.com/2020/05/21/other-lost-shoes-the-forgotten-reform-school-boys-who-fought-the-vmi-cadets-at-new-market/.

4. On Confederate conscription, see John Sacher, *Confederate Conscription and the Struggle for Southern Soldiers* (Baton Rouge: Louisiana State University Press, 2021); and Albert Burton Moore, *Conscription and Conflict in the Confederacy* (Columbia: University of South Carolina Press [1924] 1996). See also Richard Bensel, "Southern Leviathan: The Development of Central State Authority in the Confederate States of America," *Studies in American Political Development* 2 (Spring 1987): 68–136; Marc Kruman, "Dissent in the Confederacy: The North Carolina Experience," *Civil War History* 27:4 (1981): 293–312; David Carlson, "'The Distemper of the Time': Conscription, the Courts, and Planter Privilege in Civil War South Georgia," *Journal of Southwest Georgia History* 14 (Fall 1999): 1–24; and Robert D. Carlson, "'Breach of Faith: Conscription in Confederate Georgia" (PhD diss., Emory University, 2009).

5. Catherine A. Jones, *Intimate Reconstructions: Children in Emancipation Virginia* (Charlottesville: University of Virginia, 2015), 17, is one of the few scholars to stress that the Confederacy was "equivocal about [boys'] direct participation in military mobilization," preferring to recruit them for home defense.

6. In mid-March 1865, just a few weeks before the evacuation of Richmond, the Confederate Congress enacted a bill allowing for the arming of the enslaved. Bruce Levine, *Confederate Emancipation: Southern Plans to Free and Arm Slaves During the Civil War* (New York: Oxford University Press, 2006).

7. A cursory review of the compiled service records of the two sides reveals the Confederacy's comparative lack of age consciousness: whereas most records for Union soldiers include an age, whether accurate or not, many Confederate service records do not. Of those that list an age, a significant number indicate that the enlistee was below eighteen, suggesting that underage Confederate enlistees, compared to the US counterparts, felt less need to lie to be accepted. Differences in levels of age consciousness and in the enforcement of age restrictions can also be detected by comparing the memoirs of Confederate versus Union soldiers who enlisted underage. Union army veterans often dwelled at length on how they managed to evade the age restriction, recounting complex tales involving the multiple rejections that preceded their mustering in. Such stories are far less common in the Confederate memoirs. Also telling is the fact that underage Union enlistees were more likely than Confederates to self-identify as "boy soldiers."

8. Edmund Drago, *Confederate Phoenix: Rebel Children and Their Families in South Carolina* (New York: Fordham University Press, 2008), 6.

9. In the antebellum period, southern anxieties over the uneven rate of white population growth centered on the loss of political power in Congress. In his final address to the Senate in 1850, John C. Calhoun of South Carolina pointed to the widening population gap between slaveholding and non-slaveholding states as a threat to national unity. John C. Calhoun, "On the Slavery Question," March 4, 1850, in *The Works of John C. Calhoun*, vol. 4, ed. Richard Crallé (New York: D. Appleton, 1854), 542–573.

10. "The South To Arms!" April 17, 1861, 2; and "Blattertion," April 19, 1861, 2. *Daily Dispatch* (Richmond, VA).

11. "Spirit of 76," May 1, 1861, 1; and "Guerrilla Forces," May 8, 1861, 2. *Daily Dispatch*.

12. "To the Field," *Mobile Advertiser and Register* (Mobile, AL), November 10, 1861, 1.

13. [Anon.]. *Enlist! Enlist!!: An Appeal to Young Soldiers. By a Young Lady of Virginia* (Petersburg, VA: Evangelical Tract Society, 1861).

14. *Regulations for the Army of the Confederate States, as Adopted by Act of Congress, Approved March 6, 1861* (New Orleans: Henry P. Lathrop, 1861), 209–210. These regulations replicated those of the US army with a single variation: in 1861, the US version specified that enlistees had to be at least 5 feet, 3 inches tall, whereas the Confederate *Regulations*, mirroring the US edition published in 1857, mandated a height of 5 feet, 4 ½ inches.

15. "A Virginia Mother," April 29, 1861, 1; and "Patriotic Mechanic," *Daily Dispatch*, May 2, 1861, 1.

16. F.G. Skinner to His Excellency the President, June 23, 1861, #1788-1861, Reel 4, Record Group 109, M437, Letters Received by the Confederate Secretary of War, 1861–1865, (hereafter Letters Received by the Confederate Secretary of War).

17. John T. Wickersham, *The Gray and the Blue* (Berkeley, CA: privately published, 1915), 50. For a more recent edited version, see Kathleen Gorman, ed., *Boy Soldier of the Confederacy: The Memoir of John T. Wickersham* (Carbondale: Southern Illinois University Press, 2006). As Gorman explains, Wickersham was prone to embellishment, so we have used his memoir sparingly.

18. There were numerous types of local and state based military organizations in the Confederacy, organized along different lines and performing various roles. These are best laid out by Steven H. Newton, "The Confederate Home Guard: Forgotten Soldiers of the Lost Cause," *North and South* 6:1 (December 2002): 40–50.

19. "What Danville Is Doing," *Daily Dispatch*, May 4, 1861, 3.

20. "From Roanoke, Salem, Va." *Daily Dispatch*, May 27, 1861, 1; and "Correspondence of the Richmond Dispatch. From Roanoke," *Daily Dispatch*, June 1, 1861, 2.

21. "The Boy Soldiers," *New Orleans Crescent*, May 22, 1861, 1.

22. For instance, in Josiah Turner, Jr., "Showing His Faith by This Works," *Fayetteville Semi-Weekly Observer*, June 11, 1861, 2.

23. See, for instance, [untitled], *Sunday Delta* (New Orleans, LA), September 22, 1861, 1; [untitled], *Athens Post* (Athens, TN), September 27, 1861, 2; and [untitled], *Alabama Beacon* (Greensboro, AL), October 11, 1861, 1. According to these papers, the original article was published by the *Oxford Intelligencer*, apparently sometime in September 1861.

24. "Grinding the Seed Corn!" *Fayetteville Semi-Weekly Observer*, October 7, 1861, 4; and "Grinding the Seed Corn," *Richmond Enquirer*, October 1, 1861, 2.

25. "Our Schools," *Fayetteville Semi-Weekly Observer*, July 1, 1861, 1.

26. "A.C. Lindsey's School [McLeansville]," *Semi-Weekly Standard* (Raleigh, NC), July 3, 1861, 3.

27. "University of North Carolina," *Fayetteville Semi-Weekly Observer*, August 5, 1861, 3.

28. Ervin L. Jordan, Jr., "The University of Virginia during the Civil War," March 24, 2016, *Encyclopedia Virginia*. http://www.EncyclopediaVirginia.org/University_of_Virginia_During_the_Civil_War_The. Erika Lindemann, *True and Candid Compositions: The Lives and Writings of Antebellum Students at the University of North Carolina*, chap 6. https://docsouth.unc.edu/true/chapter/chp06-01/chp06-01.html.

29. Robert E. Lee to Mary Custis Lee, April 30, 1861, Clifford Dowdey, ed., *The Wartime Papers of Robert E. Lee* (Boston: Little, Brown and Co., 1961), 15.

30. Quoted in John William Jones, *Life and Letters of Robert E. Lee: Soldier and Man* (New York: Neale Publishing Co., 1906), 150.

31. In early 1863, Confederate Secretary of War James Seddon denied a request to exempt University of Virginia students from conscription. Jordan, Jr., "The University of Virginia during the Civil War." In October 1863, Governor David Lowry Swain of North Carolina had better luck when he appealed to Jefferson Davis to allow students enrolled at the University of North Carolina to complete their studies. When he renewed the request for exemptions in 1864, however, Seddon denied it. Lindemann, *True and Candid Compositions*, chap. 6.

32. Robert E. Lee to Mary Custis Lee, September 9, 1861, and March 15, 1862, Dowdey, ed., *Wartime Papers of Robert E. Lee*, 71, 129.

33. On the southern honor and manhood, see Bertram Wyatt-Brown, *Southern Honor: Ethics and Behavior in the Old South* (New York: Oxford University Press, 1982).

34. Peter Bardaglio, *Reconstructing the Household: Families, Sex and the Law in the Nineteenth-Century South* (Chapel Hill: University of North Carolina Press, 1995),

xii. On the distinctiveness of southern domestic relations, see also Elizabeth Fox-Genovese, *Within the Plantation Household: Black and White Women of the Old South* (Chapel Hill: University of North Carolina Press, 1988); and Stephanie McCurry, *Masters of Small Worlds* (New York: Oxford University Press, 1996).

35. Thomas D. Duncan, *Recollections of Thomas D. Duncan: A Confederate Soldier* (Nashville, TN: McQuiddy Printing Co., 1922), 10–11.

36. John S. Wise, *The End of an Era* (Boston: Houghton-Mifflin, 1899), 231.

37. Wickersham, *The Gray and the Blue*, 13. While Wickersham claimed to have enlisted at fourteen, census records suggest he was probably fifteen years old at the time.

38. James Dinkins, *1861 to 1865, by an Old Johnnie: Personal Recollections and Experiences in the Confederate Army* (Cincinnati: The Robert Clarke Co., 1897), 26–28. James would go on to become a commissioned officer in the Confederate cavalry before he turned eighteen.

39. George Boardman Battle to Mother, July 31, October 11, and October 24, 1861, in Laura Elizabeth Lee, *Forget-me-nots of the Civil War; A Romance, Containing Reminiscences and Original Letters of two Confederate Soldiers* (St. Louis, MO: A.R. Fleming Printing, 1909), 46–47, 50–52.

40. Letters from J. S. Barnes to Chas. W. Lee, November 2, 1861, and George Boardman Battle to Father, November 2, 1861, in Lee, *Forget-me-nots of the Civil War*, 53–55.

41. Donna Rebecca Krug, who sampled the hardship letters that people sent to the Confederate secretary of war, found that those concerning underage enlistees represented a significant percentage of the total during the first two years of the war—16.8 percent in 1861, and 11 percent in 1862—but that these requests declined markedly thereafter, constituting only 3.1 percent in 1863, .9 percent in 1864, and 0 percent in 1865. By way of explanation, Krug suggests that underage youths were more likely to enlist during the war's early months and that parents may have been less inclined to seek such discharges as the war progressed. Donna Rebecca Krug, "The Folks Back Home: The Confederate Home during the Civil War" (PhD diss., University of California, Irvine, 1990), 52. It is unclear, however, if this decline reflects a real decrease in the number of parents seeking to recover underage sons or simply changes in the filing system, because letters requesting discharges on the basis of minority can also be found in the records of the Office of the Confederate Adjutant and Inspector General, as well as in soldiers' compiled service records. Historian George C. Rable, *Civil Wars: Women and the Crisis of Southern Nationalism* (Urbana: University of Illinois Press, 1989), 81, compiled a sample of 536 letters by women who petitioned to have soldiers discharged that were sent either to the War Department or to the governors of Virginia, North Carolina, South Carolina, Georgia, Alabama, and Mississippi. In his sample, only "economic support" (75.4 percent) and "soldier's health" (36 percent) topped "soldier is underage" (25.6 percent) as reasons that women cited for requesting a soldier's release. (Most letters cited multiple reasons.) Even assuming that some women fudged their sons' ages, the frequency of these appeals suggests the prevalence of underage enlistment in the Confederate army.

42. Eli W. Cuthriell to Inspector General Benjamin Huger, October 10, 1861, M474, RG109, Confederate Letters, 1861–1865: Letters Received in the Office of the

Confederate Adjutant and Inspector General from April 1861 to April 1865, National Archives and Records Administration, Washington, DC, (hereafter Confederate Letters Received, Adjutant and Inspector General); William Duncan Buckels to Jefferson Davis, January 22, 1862, microfilm #10288-1861, Letters Received by the Confederate Secretary of War.

43. J. B. Gilbert petition dated January 24, 1862, and undated clipping from an unidentified newspaper, #10323-1861, Letters Received by the Confederate Secretary of War.

44. Rable *Civil Wars*, 75, states that appeals for the release of underage youths who enlisted without consent "occasionally" succeeded prior to the first conscription law in April 1862, but that "such paternalistic dispensations ended abruptly" thereafter. In contrast, we have found that such cases usually succeeded prior to the conscription law, and that some continued to meet with success thereafter.

45. Edgar M. Ferneyhough to Father, August 24, 1861, and September 12, 1861, Ferneyhough Family Papers, 1861–1866, Mss2F3954b, Virginia Historical Society, Richmond, Virginia.

46. Mrs. E. S. Ferneyhough to General Cooper, September 18, 1861; Capt. J. G. Griswold to Assistant Adjutant General Thomas Jordan, [n.d.]; and Note by J[udah]. P. B[enjamin], "Compiled Service Records of Confederate Soldiers Who Served in Organizations from the State of Virginia," [n.d.], misfiled under Edgar M. Ferneyhough, Confederate Letters Received, Adjutant and Inspector General. Although Strother appears to have been promptly discharged, he did not stay out the military for long; by March 1862, he had joined the Crenshaw Battery, a light artillery unit. He later claimed that he stayed with this unit until the war's end, but his service records show him serving in the Virginia Reserves in 1864.

47. See, for example, sixteen-year-old Oscar E. Phillips's Discharge, January 15, 1863, Accession 20751, Personal Papers Collection, Library of Virginia, Richmond, VA.

48. As Eric Andrew Lager, "Radical Politics in Revolutionary Times: The South Carolina Secession Convention and Executive Council of 1862" (PhD diss., Clemson University, 2008), has detailed, South Carolina promoted military centralization measures even before the Confederate government.

49. Diary entries for March 12 and 13, 1862, in C. Vann Woodward, ed., *Mary Boykin Chesnut's Civil War* (New Haven: Yale University Press, 1981), 305–306.

50. Jefferson Davis to the Hon. Speaker of the House of Representatives, March 28, 1862, ed. James D. Richardson, *A Compilation of the Messages and Papers of the Confederacy, Including the Diplomatic Correspondence, 1861-1865*, vol. 1 (Nashville: United States Publishing Co., 1906), 206.

51. See Jefferson Davis to Sen. John B. Weller, March 17, 1856, Lynda Lasswell Crist and Mary Seaton Dix, eds., *The Papers of Jefferson Davis, 1856-1860*, 14 vols. (Baton Rouge: Louisiana State University Press, 1971-2015), 6:15–17.

52. "An Act to Further Provide for the Public Defence," April 16, 1862, *The Statutes at Large of the Confederate States of America, Commencing with the First Session of the First Congress; 1862*, ed. James M. Matthews (Richmond: R.M. Smith, 1862), 29–32.

53. Initially, Confederate officials bowed to appeals from British and French consuls, who intervened when their countrymen were threatened with conscription. But as the

Confederacy's hopes of gaining diplomatic recognition waned, while its manpower needs grew, aliens found themselves in an increasingly precarious position. A new law in the summer of 1864 made the conscription of foreigners even easier. Paul Quigley, "Civil War Conscription and the International Boundaries of Citizenship," *Journal of the Civil War Era* 4:3 (September 2014): 373–397.

54. For evidence of the full extent of confusion concerning this stipulation, see "The Conscript Law," *Daily Selma Reporter* (AL), May 15, 1862, 3.

55. Tellingly, the proposed measure said nothing about men above the age of thirty-five, even though both age groups had been deemed important for home defense. This suggests that legislators and the public they represented were particularly anxious to secure the release of underage youths, rather than just trying to ensure that communities retained enough men to guarantee safety and subsistence.

56. August 29, 1862, *Journal of the Confederate Congress*, vol. 5, 325–328.

57. This soldier never made it home: the letter was found on his body at Antietam and printed in the newspaper because, according to the editor, "it shows the feeling of many in the South, and is worthy of all attention." "A Home View of Secession," *Newbern Weekly Progress* (Newbern, NC), October 18, 1862, 3.

58. The *Daily Dispatch* reported extensively on this petition, reprinting the text of Gilmer's correspondence with the Confederate Congress, the petition he wrote on behalf of a group (which he described as including almost a thousand Confederate enlistees from different states), and his follow-up letter to Congress in late September. See "Opinion of J.H. Gilmer on Conscription Act," July 12, 1862, 1; "The Petition of Certain Non-Conscripts, respectfully presented to the Confederate States Congress," August 11, 1862, 1; and "Congress and the Conscript Acts," *Daily Dispatch*, September 25, 1862, 1,

59. Compare General Orders, No 44, June 17, 1862; General Orders, No 46, July 1, 1862, and General Orders, No 57, August 14, 1862, *General Orders from Adjutant and Inspector-General's Office, Confederate States Army, from January, 1862, to December, 1863* (Columbia: Presses of Evans & Cogswell, 1864), 58–60, 71.

60. General Orders, No 65, September 8, 1862, *General Orders from Adjutant and Inspector-General's Office . . . from January, 1862*, 75–76.

61. [No title], *Weekly Arkansas Gazette* (Little Rock, AR), October 11, 1862, 2.

62. Mary Leigh Boisseau, *Abstractions of Exemptions from Military Service and etc., 1862-63: A Record of Halifax County Court House Halifax, Virginia* (Danville, VA: priv. printed, 1980). Other boards did not accept underage youths so readily. In Pittsylvania County, Virginia, those in charge of exemptions typically recorded substitutes' ages, yet among the hundreds of cases appearing before this board there is only one mention of a youth hired in this capacity before reaching age eighteen. Mary Leigh Bouisseau, *Pittsylvania County, Virginia Board of Exemptions Minutes* (s.l., priv. printed, 1994).

63. Soldiers in heavy artillery units, who served farther behind the frontlines, suffered lower casualty rates than those in the infantry. "Will Go as Substitute," *Daily Journal* (Wilmington, NC), August 29, 1863, 2.

64. The Confederate army does appear to have temporarily halted discharges on the basis of minority after the passage of the first conscription act. In response to a request that Assistant Secretary of War A. T. Bledsoe forwarded to him in June 1862, Gen. Robert E. Lee replied, "It is understood that no discharges on acct of age are to be made in the present crisis untill 17th July period prescribed by law except in cases of physical incapacity." (This date marked the end of the ninety-day period referred to in the conscription law.) Confederate Letters Received, Adjutant and Inspector General.

65. As Governor Vance's office explained when responding to a father in November 1862, if he had consented to the enlistment, the boy could "not be discharged," but if he had withheld consent, his son could be released "upon the proper application." S. Lack Suttels to Zebulon B. Vance, November 30, 1862, Zebulon B. Vance Correspondence, G.P. 160, Correspondence September 1, 1862 to November 30, 1862, North Carolina State Archives, Raleigh, NC.

66. Amusingly, in his pension application, this veteran tried to strengthen his claim to a pension by insisting that he had not consented to his own discharge. (Of course, as a minor, he was not legally in a position to grant or withhold his consent in regard to his enlistment.)

67. C5-1862, William J. Cotter to J. A. Seddon, December 10, 1862; and C48-1863, William J. Cotter to Vice President Alexander Stephens, petition for discharge of Sgt. H. Cotter, January 3, 1863; Alexander Stephens to William J. Cotter, January 12, 1863, Letters Received by the Confederate Secretary of War. In December 1861, Stephens had in fact tried to convince the War Department to alter its policy of underage enlistees. Interceding on behalf of another distraught father, he argued that "every minor under 18 years of age ought by general order to be immediately discharged." Their enlistment was illegal, he claimed, "and the policy of retaining them in service can but be injurious to the cause." 8698-1861, Alexander Stephens to J.P. Benjamin, December 22, 1861, Letters Received by the Confederate Secretary of War. An early critic of the Davis administration's handling of the war, Stephens saw the refusal to discharge underage youths as in keeping with other Confederate policies, including conscription, slave impressment, and martial law, that dangerously infringed on citizens' rights and liberties. Midway through the war, he was in open rebellion against Davis. Whether the father followed this advice is unclear, but a few months later his son was transferred to a local defense unit stationed closer to home, in which he served alongside other youths of age seventeen and sixteen, according to the compiled service record for Hal [F.] Cotter.

68. Jefferson Davis, Message to Congress, November 18, 1861, contained in US War Department. *The War of the Rebellion: A Compilation of the Official Records of the Union and Confederate Armies.* 128 vols. (Washington, DC: Government Printing Office, 1880–1901), ser. IV, vol. 1, 732–738, (hereafter *OR*).

69. In the Confederacy, the periods of suspension "amounted in aggregate to one year, five months, and two days," less than half of the war's total duration. Paul S. Hochstettler, "Suspension of the Writ of Habeas Corpus in the Confederacy during the Civil War" (MA thesis, Ohio State University, 1932), 51. On the history of habeas corpus and its suspension in the Confederate states, see Mark E. Neely, Jr., *Southern Rights: Political*

Prisoners and the Myth of Confederate Constitutionalism (Charlottesville: University of Virginia Press, 1999); 47–59, 153–167; John B. Robbins, "The Confederacy and the Writ of Habeas Corpus," *Georgia Historical Quarterly* 55:1 (1971): 83–101; and Stephen C. Neff, *Justice in Blue and Gray: A Legal History of the Civil War* (Cambridge: Harvard University Press, 2010).

70. For instance, just days after Congress suspended habeas corpus in February 1864, a father successfully sued to recover a sixteen-year-old youth who had enlisted in a Virginia infantry regiment. "Richmond Circuit Court," *Daily Dispatch*, February 22, 1864, 1.

71. None of these three cases involved minor enlistees; instead, they concerned adult men who claimed, for various reasons, that they should not have been conscripted. Winthrop Rutherfurd, "Drawing Lines of Sovereignty: State Habeas Doctrine and the Substance of States' Rights in Confederate Conscription Cases," *University of Richmond Law Review* 51:93 (2017): 93–132 (quotations 94 and 95).

72. "In District Court, Confederate States of America, for the Southern District of Georgia, April Term, 1862," *Weekly Sun* (Atlanta, GA), August 19, 1862, 3.

73. *Moncrief v. Jones*, in *Reports of Cases in Law and Equity Argued and Determined in the Supreme Court of Georgia*, vol. 33 (Macon, GA: J.W. Burke, 1870), 450–451.

74. Wilkes, Jr., "From Oglethorpe to the Overthrow of the Confederacy," 1061–1062.

75. Although North Carolina had been one of the first states to join the Confederacy, Unionism remained strong in coastal areas and in the mountainous west, where deserters and draft dodgers found refuge among the local population. Already by the summer of 1862, certain regions of North Carolina—especially those dominated by non-slaveholding yeoman farmers—faced food shortages due to the loss of farm labor. See, for example, Joshua McLaughlin, "'Few Were the Hearts . . . that did not Swell with Devotion': Community and Confederate Service in Rowan County, North Carolina, 1861-1862," *North Carolina Historical Review* 73:2 (April 1996): 156–183. By the end of 1862, the western counties of North Carolina had "ceased to be a contributing part of the Confederacy," according to historian Paul Escott. "Tax collections stopped, officials did not dare to enforce conscription, and opponents of the Confederate authorities overawed whatever loyal citizens remained in the regions." Paul D. Escott, *After Secession: Jefferson Davis and the Failure of Confederate Nationalism* (Baton Rouge: Louisiana State University Press, 1978), 133.

76. W. H. C. Whiting to Z. B. Vance, January 24, 1863, S. G. French to Maj. Genl. Smith, February 1, 1863, and undated response from David A. Barnes (Vance's aide-de-camp) to W. H. C. Whiting, Zebulon B. Vance Letterbooks, North Carolina State Archives, Raleigh, NC.

77. Brig. Gen. E. Greer to Brig. Gen. W. R. Boggs, December 7, 1863, *OR*, ser. 1, vol. 36, 493–495.

78. "Civio," *Fayetteville Weekly Observer* (Fayetteville, NC), December 21, 1863, 2.

79. Judge Halyburton of the Eastern District of Virginia, for instance, presided over habeas cases involving men who claimed to be over forty-five years old, "undomiciled foreigners," or exempt from conscription based on their current employment status, as well as cases involving underage youths.

80. Confederate States of America. Army of Tennessee, *Memorial*, December 17, 1863 (s.l., s.n. [1863]). According to Wiley Sword, "'Our Fireside in Ruins: Consequences of the 1863 Chattanooga Campaign," in Evan C. Jones and Wiley Sword, eds., *Gateway to the Confederacy: New Perspectives on the Chickamauga and Chattanooga Campaigns, 1862-1863* (Baton Rouge: Louisiana State University Press, 2014), 227–253, this document should be viewed as an important precursor to Maj. Gen. Patrick R. Cleburne's more famous proposal to arm the enslaved, which was circulated among a small group of officers just two weeks later, in early January 1864. Larry J. Daniel, *Conquered: Why the Army of Tennessee Failed* (Chapel Hill: University of North Carolina Press, 2019), takes a different view, arguing that the controversial aspect of Hardee's memorial was not its suggestion concerning the use of African Americans for military labor, a practice that was already widespread, but rather the proposal to expand the age range for conscription (269).

81. Wilfred Buck Yearns, *The Confederate Congress* (Athens: University of Georgia, 1960), 86–88.

82. "Stragglers, Deserters, and Absentees," *Daily Dispatch*, December 17, 1863, 2.

83. "Our Principal," *Daily Dispatch*, December 30, 1863, 2.

84. "The Stragglers," *Daily Dispatch*, January 4, 1864, 2.

85. "The Military Bill," *Daily Dispatch*, February 16, 1864, 2.

86. According to Drew Gilpin Faust, *Mothers of Invention: Women of the Slaveholding South in the American Civil War* (Chapel Hill: University of North Carolina Press, 2000), many elite women eventually repudiated the insistence on self-abnegation and sacrifice in the face of material and psychological deprivation.

87. J. B. Jones, *A Rebel War Clerk's Diary at the Confederate States Capital* (Philadelphia: J.B. Lippincott & Co., 1866), 138.

88. Moore, *Conscription and Conflict*, 309–310, rightly observes that "General Grant's remark that the Confederates were robbing the cradle and the grave to fill their armies did not give due weight" to the fact that the Military Law's "fundamental purpose" was "to release the able-bodied between 18 and 45 for action on the main battlefields." The General Order implementing the law used the threat of regular service as an enforcement mechanism, stipulating that those liable for reserve duty who did not report within thirty days would be "placed in service in the field of the war, in the same manner as though he were between the ages of eighteen and forty-five." General Orders, No 26, March 1, 1864, 252–253.

89. Many Confederate memoirs note the growing presence of youths in the ranks toward the end of the war. See, for instance, B. M. Zettler, *War Stories and School-Day Incidents for the Children* (New York: The Neale Publishing Co., 1912), 142.

90. [No title], *Nashville Daily Union*, January 14, 1864, 2.

91. "Grinding the Seed Corn," *Staunton Spectator*, May 3, 1864, 2. General Imboden also notified the Superintendent of VMI to hold the cadet corps there in reserve; on May 15, they would fight in the Battle of New Market.

92. Ulysses S. Grant to Rep. Elihu B. Washburne, August 10, 1864, in *U.S. Grant: Memoirs and Selected Letters*, ed. William F. McFeeley and Mary D. McFeeley (New York: Library of America, 1990), 1064–1065. For evidence of the circulation

of Grant's letter in both the US and the Confederacy, see "Gen. Grant's Letter," *Hillsdale Standard* (Hillsdale, MI), September 13, 1864, 2; "Letter of Gen. U.S. Grant," *Alexandria Gazette* (Alexandria, VA), September 9, 1864, 2; "Gossip from Washington," *Fayetteville Semi-Weekly Observer* (Fayetteville, NC), November 17, 1864, 2. On Grant's support for Lincoln's re-election, see John Y. Simon, "Grant, Lincoln, and Unconditional Surrender," in Gabor S. Borritt, ed., *Lincoln's Generals* (New York: Oxford University Press, 1994), 189–190. In his memoirs, Grant wrongly recollected the February 1864 Confederate conscription law as encompassing boys much younger (and men much older) than it actually did—"boys from fourteen to eighteen" for the junior reserves, and men "from forty-five to sixty" for the senior reserves. His mistake suggests the extent to which perceptions of the Confederate army as composed of boys and old men had taken hold by the time Grant wrote his memoirs in the 1880s. Ulysses S. Grant, *Personal Memoirs* (New York: Barnes and Noble, 2003; orig. 1885), 617–618.

93. Ella Lonn, *Desertion During the Civil War* (Lincoln: University of Nebraska Press, 1998; orig. 1928), 23.

94. "The Fall Campaign," *Weekly Conservative* (Raleigh, NC), September 21, 1864, 2. See also an article from the *Richmond Examiner* reprinted in the *Buffalo Courier*, September 22, 1864, 3.

95. The militia was composed mainly of boys under the age of sixteen and men above the age of fifty. Mark F. Boyd, "The Battle of Marianna," *Florida Historical Quarterly* 29:4 (April 1951): 225–242 (quotation, 231).

96. Throughout much of the war, the Confederate government imposed a domestic passport system that required every traveler to obtain official documents before embarking on their journey. Vividly depicted by Mark E. Neely, *Southern Rights: Political Prisoners and the Myth of Confederate Constitutionalism* (Charlottesville: University of Virginia Press, 1999), 2–6 (quotation, 2), it "affected all railroad travel for most of the war and imposed restrictions on other modes of travel in places far from the military front," causing delays and subjecting all citizens to "impertinent scrutiny."

97. Letters in file for Richard Evans, April–December 1864, Letters Received by the Confederate Adjutant and Inspector General's Office, RG109, War Department Collection of Confederate Records, National Archives and Records Administration, Washington D.C.

98. Government records contain many letters attesting to the fact that underage youths were vulnerable to such arrests. For example, B835-1863, T. G. J. K. Bryant to Secretary of War, November 23, 1863, Letters Received by the Confederate Secretary of War.

99. H. C. Lockhart, Lieutenant-Colonel and Commandant, Alabama, to Capt. R. H. Browne, Act. Asst. Adj. Gen., February 6, 1865, *OR*, ser. 4, vol. 3, 1059–1063.

100. This letter ended up being published in a local paper, [Anon.], "A Mother's Appeal," *Daily Conservative* (Raleigh, NC), October 10, 1864, 4.

101. Thomas M. Carr, Sr., to Thomas M. Carr, Jr., November 1864, Archive of 23 Letters to a Young Confederate Soldier Serving in the North Carolina Junior Reserves, sold

at auction, Between the Covers catalogue, https://www.betweenthecovers.com/ima ges/upload/btc-catalog-240.pdf.

102. Jordan Pearce, "'Grinding up the Seed Corn of the Confederacy': The North Carolina Junior Reserves," *Explorations* 11 (2016): 30–40. https://uncw.edu/csurf/ explorations/volume%20xi/pearce.pdf. According to Pearce, over 4,500 junior reserves served in North Carolina; he claims they constituted a ninth of all the state's soldiers who fought for the Confederacy. More work is needed to assess the impact of such forces on the Confederate war effort. Although young soldiers who fought in reserve forces were extravagantly lauded in the postwar era, official correspondence during the war casts some doubt on the value of their military contributions. For instance, Maj. Gen. W. H. C. Whiting complained to Secretary Seddon about the reserve troops sent to help protect Wilmington, North Carolina. "As to the Senior and Junior Reserves, I think they would rather interfere with than aid (sic)," he wrote. "The little boys are prostrate with all the diseases of children and too weak to bear arms. Their officers, made by election, are entirely ignorant. These are the facts and to you I see no use in disguising them." Maj. Gen. W. H. C. Whiting to Secretary of War James Seddon, September 8, 1864, OR, Series I, Vol. XLII, Part II-Correspondence, 716–717.

103. Jefferson Davis, "Ladies and Gentlemen of the Metropolis of South Carolina," October 4, 1864, in Lynda Lasswell Crist, Barbara J. Rozek, and Kenneth H. Williams, eds., *The Papers of Jefferson Davis: September 1864–May 1865*, vol. 11 (Baton Rouge: Louisiana State University Press, 2003), 81–91 (quotation 83–84). In this same speech, Davis implored audience members not to appeal for writs to gain release from the military, even if they had legitimate grounds. At the time, Congress had allowed the blanket suspension to lapse, and Davis clearly worried that the access to the habeas process was undermining military efficacy.

104. Levine, *Confederate Emancipation*.

105. William T. Sutherlin to the Editor, in "Prominent People Give Personal Recollections of Mr. Davis," *Daily Dispatch*, May 31, 1893, 5.

106. Diary entry for December 1, 1864, in Woodward, ed., *Mary Boykin Chesnut's Civil War*, 680.

107. Abraham Lincoln, "Annual Address to Congress," December 6, 1864, *Abraham Lincoln: Speeches and Writings, 1859-1865* (New York: The Library of America, 1989), 646–664 (quotation, 659).

Chapter 9

1. Morris Cohen, #LL1299, RG153, Records of the Office of the Judge Advocate General (Army), Court Martial Case Files, National Archives and Records Administration, Washington, DC (hereafter JAG Records).

2. Two notable exceptions are Russell L. Johnson's *Warriors into Workers: The Civil War and the Formation of Urban-Industrial Society in a Northern City* (New York: Fordham

University Press, 2003); and Brian P. Luskey's *Men Is Cheap: Exposing the Frauds of Free Labor in Civil War America* (Chapel Hill: University of North Carolina Press, 2020), which focuses on the fraudulent speculations and coercive schemes that turned wage earners into victims, making a mockery of free labor claims that character determined success. Luskey also discusses the market for substitutes that emerged in the last two years of the war and the fraud that surrounded it in "Special Marts: Intelligence Offices, Labor Commodification, and Emancipation in Nineteenth-Century America," *Journal of the Civil War Era* 3:3 (September 2013): 360–391.

3. The question of what motivated men to enlist and fight has long been one of the central preoccupations of Civil War historians. The latest salvo in this debate is William Marvel's *Lincoln's Mercenaries: Economic Motivation among Union Soldiers During the Civil War* (Baton Rouge: Louisiana State University Press, 2018). Relying on quantitative data, he suggests that even the Union's earliest recruits tended to be drawn from among the region's poorest households. Given a stagnant economy, high unemployment, and low wages, recruits in 1861 had a strong economic motivation to enlist, he argues, as did those who signed up in later years. Contrary positions can be traced through his footnotes.

4. As Paul Foos, *A Short, Offhand, Killing Affair: Soldiers and Social Conflict during the Mexican- American War* (Chapel Hill: University of North Carolina Press, 2003), points out, the failure to consider military work as labor is especially surprising given that those who entered the US military prior to the Civil War generally did so only when other opportunities dried up and typically spent most of their enlistments engaged in menial labor. Similarly, A. Hope McGrath, " 'A Slave in Uncle Sam's Service': Labor and Resistance in the U.S. Army, 1865-1890," *Labor: Studies in Working-Class History of the Americas* 13:3–4 (2016): 37–56, notes that those enlisting in the postbellum era were mostly tasked with clearing land, digging ditches, constructing housing, or other such grueling work. Although soldiering was interpreted as "a patriotic vocation rather than a job, service to one's country rather than servitude," a military enlistment entailed the work of a common laborer, but without even the modest protections offered by a free labor regime. (49) Although few historians of American history have followed their lead, there is a growing British and European scholarship that focuses on military service as work, including a special feature on "Labor and the Military," edited by Joshua B. Freeman and Geoffrey Field in *International Labor and Working-Class History* 80 (Fall 2011): 3–147; and a collection edited by Erik-Jan Zürcher, *Fighting for a Living: A Comparative History of Military Labour, 1500-2000* (Amsterdam: Amsterdam University Press, 2013).

5. The number of boys and youths in military employment in this era dwarfed those in other forms of paid work, yet they rarely feature in surveys of child labor. To cite the most recent example, Steven Mintz's *Huck's Raft: A History of American Childhood* (Cambridge, MA: Harvard University Press, 2004), chaps. 3, 6, and 7, covers children's experiences in the Revolution and the Civil War and includes a few boys who served in uniform, but the military is absent as an employer in a chapter related to laboring children. Works like Hugh D. Hindman, *Child Labor: An*

American History (Armonk, NY: M.E. Sharpe, 2002); and Viviana A. Zelizer, *Pricing the Priceless Child: The Changing Social Value of Children* (New York: Basic Books, 1985) contain no mention of young enlistees, while Priscilla Ferguson Clement, *Growing Pains: Children in the Industrial Age, 1850-1890* (New York: Twayne Publishers, 1997) and Chaim M. Rosenberg, *Child Labor in America: A History* (Jefferson, NC: McFarland & Co., 2013) touch on underage soldiers and sailors without detailing the conditions or nature of their work. The broadest survey on the topic of child labor around the world—a door stopper of roughly a thousand pages—devotes a seven-page chapter to youth in modern military service. Zoë Marriage, "Worst Forms of Child Labor: Children and War," in Hugh D. Hindman, ed., *The World of Child Labor: An Historical and Regional Survey* (Armonk, NY: M.E. Sharpe, 2009), pt. 1, sec. 3.

6. Luskey, "Commodification and the Cultural Economy of the Household," 7–8.

7. Joseph F. Kett, *Rites of Passage: Adolescence in America, 1790 to the Present* (New York: Basic Books, Inc., 1977), 16; Marie Jenkins Schwartz, *Born in Bondage: Growing up Enslaved in the Antebellum South* (Cambridge, MA: Harvard University Press, 2000), 14.

8. Timothy J. Gilfoyle, "Street-Rats and Gutter-Snipes: Child Pickpockets and Street Culture in New York City, 1850-1900," *Journal of Social History* 37:4 (2004): 834. According to Vincent DiGirolamo, "Newsboy Funerals: Tales of Sorrow and Solidarity in Urban America," *Journal of Social History* 36:1 (Autumn 2002): 7, there were five or six hundred newsboys in New York and Philadelphia when the Civil War broke out, most of them from poor Irish and German families and typically aged between six and fifteen.

9. Paul A. Gilje and Howard B. Rock, "'Sweep O! Sweep O!': African American Chimney Sweeps and Citizenship in the New Nation," *William and Mary Quarterly* 51:3 (July 1994): 509; Clement, *Growing Pains*, 15, argues that by war's end, children under age sixteen made up 13 percent of the workforce in Massachusetts textile mills and 22 percent of those in Pennsylvania.

10. For rates of infant and child mortality in Massachusetts in 1860, where more than 14 percent of children died in infancy and accidents accounted for 10 percent of children's deaths thereafter, see *Historical Statistics of the United States, Colonial Times to 1970*, pt. 1, Series B, 148.

11. *Army Paymaster's Manual. . . Revised to include June 30, 1864*, comp. by J. H. Eaton (Washington, DC: Government Printing Office, 1864). Company musicians were initially paid $1 less than privates, but their pay was equalized in 1864 at $16 a month. In recognition of music's crucial role in warfare at this time, leaders of brigade and regimental bands received the princely sum of $75 per month, almost triple the $26 paid to sergeant majors. The pay rate for privates was not especially generous compared to wages for non-military occupations: in New England in 1860, a farm laborer's monthly earnings with board averaged $14.73, for instance, while a common laborer working on the Erie Canal in 1864 typically made $1.50 per day. The average daily wage for skilled laborers like blacksmiths, carpenters, and machinists was $1.67 in 1861, rising to $2.50 by 1865. *Historical Statistics of the*

United States, Colonial Times to 1970, pt. 1, Series D, 705–714, 728–734. Then again, military pay was constant, whereas day laborers did not generally have year-round employment. Wartime inflation also massively increased the costs of the basic necessities like food, fuel, and shelter, which laborers had to buy but enlistees did not, and volunteers also often received sizeable bounties.

12. Edward Burgess Peirce to Mother [Mrs. J.N. Peirce], May 29, 1864, Edward Burgess Peirce Letters, Massachusetts Historical Society, Boston, MA.

13. The father of seventeen-year-old Wilson B. Hart complained to his US representative that his son had not been furnished with a drum for six months and that "every effort" was being made "to force him into the ranks to carry a musket." H. P. Hart to Hon. Wm. E. Lansing, February 12, 1863, Addison Files, Box 50.

14. Cyrus Hanks, #NN1647, JAG Records. The panel explained that its sentence— which simply required Hanks to serve the full period of his enlistment without pay—was unusually lenient due to "the extreme youth and apparent physical weakness of the prisoner."

15. Robert Irwin, #NN1594, JAG Records.

16. Military regulations specified that musicians "will be instructed as soldiers, and liable to serve in the ranks on any occasion." *Revised United States Army Regulations of 1861* (Washington, DC: Government Printing Office, 1863), 19.

17. C. W. Bardeen, *A Little Fifer's War Diary* (Syracuse, New York: privately printed, 1910), 122–123.

18. George T. Ulmer, *Adventures and Reminiscences of a Volunteer; or, a Drummer Boy from Maine* (n.p., privately printed, 1892), 40, 59.

19. Nicholas L. Syrett, *American Child Bride: A History of Minors and Marriage in the United States* (Chapel Hill: University of North Carolina Press, 2016).

20. Melzar B. Strong, #LL2232, JAG Records.

21. On the Confederate government's impressment of the enslaved and enslavers' pushback, see Stephanie McCurry, *Confederate Reckoning: Power and Politics in the Civil War South* (Cambridge, MA: Harvard University Press, 2010), chap. 7. Jaime Amanda Martinez, *Slave Impressment in the Upper South* (Chapel Hill: University of North Carolina Press, 2013) argues that impressment policies largely succeeded in the face of opposition. But as McCurry notes, impressment also challenged the Confederacy's *raison d'être*—support for states' rights and the protection of slavery—bringing the central tensions of the Confederate project to the surface in ways that ultimately undermined the war effort.

22. On enslaved men and women employing such power to shape their sales or bargain for better treatment, see Walter Johnson, *Soul by Soul: Life Inside the Antebellum Slave Market* (Cambridge, MA: Harvard University Press, 2001); and John Hope Franklin and Loren Schweninger, *Runaway Slaves: Rebels on the Plantation* (New York: Oxford University Press, 2000).

23. The Confederate government paid enslavers for the use of enslaved workers and provided compensation in cases of death or injury, but these costs were borne by the government rather than by individuals who had a personal stake in keeping enslaved people alive and healthy enough to labor.

24. Jacob Stroyer, *My Life in the South*, 4th ed. (Salem, MA: Newcomb & Gauss, 1898), chap. 3 (quote 98).

25. Stroyer, *My Life in the South*, 92, 95–96. Susanna Ashton, "'The Sense of That Crush I Feel at Certain Times Even Now': Jacob Stroyer and the Defense of Fort Sumter," *South Carolina Law Review* 46:2 (2014): 135–139, notes that Confederate military dispatches reported fewer deaths among the enslaved people at the fort than Stroyer claimed. But however many died, Stroyer's recollection is surely accurate in evoking the terrifying experiences of these impressed workers.

26. McCurry, *Confederate Reckoning*, 274–288.

27. Edna Greene Medford, "'I was always a union man': The Dilemma of Free Blacks in Confederate Virginia," *Slavery and Abolition* 15:3 (1994): 1–16.

28. Tinsley Lee Spraggins, "Mobilization of Negro Labor for the Department of Virginia and North Carolina, 1861-1865," *North Carolina Historical Review* 24:2 (April 1947): 171.

29. On the wartime impressment of free African Americans in North Carolina, see Warren E. Milteer, Jr., *North Carolina's Free People of Color, 1715-1885* (Baton Rouge: Louisiana State University Press, 2020).

30. On the intricate family ties within the county that neighbored this one, see William T. Auman, "Neighbor against Neighbor: The Inner Civil War in the Randolph County Area of Confederate North Carolina," *North Carolina Historical Review* 61:1 (1984): 59–92. Divided loyalties were even more common in the mountainous western regions of the state, a topic covered in Barton Myers, *Rebels against the Confederacy: North Carolina's Unionists* (New York: Cambridge University Press, 2014); and John C. Inscoe and Gordon B. McKinney, *The Heart of Confederate Appalachia: Western North Carolina in the Civil War* (Chapel Hill: University of North Carolina Press, 2003).

31. Petition to "His Excellency H.C. Clark [*sic*]," undated c. August 1861, Governor Henry T. Clark Papers, North Carolina State Archives, Raleigh, North Carolina (hereafter Clark Papers).

32. Medford, "'I was always a Union man,'" makes a similar point, while noting that wartime conditions elevated the value of free Black male labor, allowing a fortunate few to improve their conditions significantly.

33. Petition to "his excellency Governor Clarke [sic]" August 22, 1861, Clark Papers.

34. Charles Nagel, *A Boy's Civil War Story* (St. Louis, MO: Eden Publishing House, 1934), 220.

35. On this topic, see Myers, *Rebels against the Confederacy*.

36. See, for example, the advertisements for substitutes in the *Richmond Dispatch*, August 22, 1862, 2.

37. Col. W. E. Buckner to Jones S. Hamilton, August 12, 1862, reprinted in Jerry Causey, ed., "Selected Correspondence of the Adjutant General of Confederate Mississippi," *Journal of Mississippi History* 43:1 (1981): 47.

38. R. D. Jones to Jefferson Davis, May 21, 1862, J193-1862, reel 54, RG 109, M437, Letters Received by the Confederate Secretary of War, 1861–1865.

39. General Orders, No 65, September 8, 1862, *General Orders from Adjutant and Inspector-General's Office, Confederate States Army, from January, 1862, to December, 1863* (Columbia: Presses of Evans & Cogswell, 1864), 75–76.

40. Adam Wise Kersh to George P. Kersh, November 22, 1862, Personal Papers, Valley of the Shadow Project, University of Virginia, http://valley.lib.virginia.edu. At least some officers generally tried to follow Robert E. Lee's order to reject anyone below age eighteen, including substitutes. For instance, H. B. Tomlin, the commander in charge of militia forces in the town of West Point, Virginia, wrote to the governor asking for special permission to enlist a robust seventeen-year-old as a substitute for his more "delicate" older brother. The governor allowed the exception. Maj. H. B. Tomlin to Gov. John Letcher, July 26, 1862, Tomlin's Infantry Battalion Letterbook, 1861, Virginia Historical Society, Richmond, VA. On Lee's injunction to his commanders in relation to substitutes, see Joseph T. Glatthaar, "Everyman's War: A Rich and Poor Man's Fight in Lee's Army," *Civil War History* 54:3 (September 2008): 239.

41. John Sacher, "The Loyal Draft Dodger?: A Reexamination of Confederate Substitution," *Civil War History* 57:2 (June 2011): 154.

42. Patrick J. Doyle, "Replacement Rebels: Confederate Substitution and the Issue of Citizenship," *Journal of the Civil War Era* 8:1 (2018): 10.

43. "To the Editor of the Republican," August 15, 1862. Undated newspaper clipping contained in RG109, Letters Received by the Confederate Secretary of War, 1861–1865. This clipping has no accompanying letter. It is contained on microfilm M437, reel 30, following letter B942-1862.

44. "Substitute Brokers," *Memphis Daily Appeal*, August 28, 1862, 1.

45. Mary L. Wilson "Profiles in Evasion: Civil War Substitutes and the Men who Hired Them in Walker's Texas Division," *East Texas Historical Journal* 43:1 (2005): 25–38, discusses prices ranging from $1,500 to $6,000.

46. On the backlash against substitution, see Albert Burton Moore, *Conscription and Conflict in the Confederacy* (Columbia: University of South Carolina Press, [1924] 1996), chap. 3; and Paul D. Escott, *After Secession: Jefferson Davis and the Failure of Confederate Nationalism* (Baton Rouge: Louisiana State University Press, 1978), chap 4. Patrick J. Doyle, "Replacement Rebels," 3–31, argues that the policy of substitution was not initially seen as "incompatible with the duties of citizenship in the South," but public opinion had turned decidedly against the practice by mid-1863.

47. McCurry, *Confederate Reckoning*, chap. 7. Medford, "'I was always a Union man,'" 11, highlights an additional irony, noting that the shortage of labor gave some free Black workers unprecedented control over the terms of their employment.

48. On the way the draft functioned, see Eugene C. Murdock, *One Million Men: The Civil War Draft in the North* (Madison: State Historical Society of Wisconsin, 1971), chap. 1.

49. Ella Lonn, *Foreigners in the Union Army and Navy* (New York: Greenwood Press, 1951), 438–439. On the frauds associated with the draft, see also Samuel Negus, "'Conduct Unbecoming of an officer': Fraudulent Enlistment Practices at U.S. Navy Recruitment Rendezvous During the American Civil War," *The Northern Mariner/ le Marin du Nord* 22:1 (January 2012): 27–52; Michael Thomas Smith "The Most

Desperate Scoundrels Unhung: Bounty Jumpers and Recruitment Fraud in the Civil War North," *American Nineteenth Century History* 6:2 (June 2005): 149–172; Murdock, *One Million Men*, chaps. 9–13; Eugene Murdock, *Patriotism Limited, 1862-1865: The Civil War Draft and the Bounty System* (Kent, OH: Kent State University Press, 1967); and Fred A. Shannon, *The Organization and Administration of the Union Army, 1861-1865*, 2 vols. (Cleveland: Arthur H. Clark, 1928), 2:69–78.

50. Shannon, *Organization and Administration of the Union Army*, 2:72. See also *New York Tribune*, January 2, 1865.

51. M. Hayward, February 20, 1863, Record Group 94: Records of the Adjutant General's Office, Entry 409, Letters Received 1862-89, Box 20, National Archives and Records Administration, Washington, DC.

52. Lonn, *Foreigners in the Union Army and Navy*, 438, notes that the amount paid to any officer, soldier, or civilian who brought in a recruit differed by state and district. In Baltimore, it was fixed in May 1864 at $25 for a veteran and $15 for a new recruit. But advertisements in other cities suggest higher amounts: an ad in the *New York Herald*, August 23, 1864, 7, seeking volunteers or substitutes for the County of New York, for instance, offered brokers "hand money" of $20 for each two- or three-year recruit who passed muster, and $35 for each substitute. By March 27, 1865, a similar ad in the same paper promised $50 for each one-year recruit, $75 for each two-year recruit, and $100 for each three-year recruit.

53. Eugene C. Murdock, "New York's Civil War Bounty Brokers," *Journal of American History* 53:2 (September, 1966): 259–278.

54. James Overcash, #LL610, JAG Records. The same file number contains the cases of George Pensinger and Dallas Wasner.

55. Affidavit of Mary Ryan dated April 19, 1865, Colonel L.C. Bakers Papers, RG 110, Provost Marshal General's Bureau, National Archives and Records Administration, Washington, DC, Box 1, (hereafter Baker Papers).

56. Luskey, *Men Is Cheap*, 205, notes that most workers were not paid up front at this time, so it is unsurprising that "they fell for brokers' stories about future payments."

57. The same might be said of the family members who appealed to Baker or other Union officials for help. All would have known that claiming defenselessness and privation was their best, and usually their only, means of gaining assistance. Luskey, "Commodification and the Cultural Economy of the Household," 17.

58. "Young America," *Leavenworth Bulletin* (Leavenworth, KS), March 14, 1864, 1.

59. Shannon, *The Organization and Administration of the Union Army*, 2:22.

60. From the first Enrollment Act to the end of the war, the Lincoln administration made six additional calls for troops, requesting a total of more than one and a half million extra men.

61. Although some youths and their parents no doubt lied in hopes of gaining a discharge, stories about kidnapping should not be dismissed out of hand. After all, the nation had witnessed many forms of kidnapping over its history, including the kidnapping of free Blacks to be sold into slavery. Richard Bell argues that such kidnapping rings focused particularly on children and youth, who were easier to lure and to hold than grown adults. Professional kidnappers, he argues, "stole tens of thousands of free

black people in the first six decades of the century, many of them children who were under the age of eighteen." Richard Bell, *Stolen: Five Free Boys Kidnapped into Slavery and Their Astonishing Odyssey Home* (New York: Simon and Schuster, 2019). W. Caleb McDaniel, *Sweet Taste of Liberty: A True Story of Slavery and Restitution in America* (New York: Oxford University Press, 2019), 54–66, also discusses kidnapping gangs, some of which worked in concert with corrupt law enforcement. For the politicizing effects of kidnapping cases that ended up in court, see M. Scott Heerman, "'Reducing Free Men to Slavery': Black Kidnapping, the 'Slave Power,' and the Politics of Abolition in Antebellum Illinois, 1830-1860," *Journal of the Early Republic* 38:2 (Summer 2018): 261–291.

62. For instance, Elisabeth Tenfort to Colonel Baker, March 9, 1865, Baker Papers, Box 1; and "Arrest for Forgery," *Chicago Tribune*, February 9, 1865, 4.

63. "Forgeries of S.P. Stoddard in Massachusetts," *Alexandria Gazette* (Alexandria, VA), August 6, 1868, 1.

64. "Bounty Jumping in New York," *Appleton Crescent* (Appleton, WI), February 25, 1865, 1. Lafayette C. Baker, *The United States Secret Service in the Late War* (Philadelphia: John E. Potter & Company, 1867), 249, claimed that "the majority of the officers assigned to the recruiting service were guilty of great dereliction of duty," either because they looked the other way or actively connived with brokers. Baker might have been a chronic exaggerator, but his account echoed that of numerous Union officials.

65. "Miscellaneous," *New York Daily Herald*, April 3, 1864, 4.

66. "A Shocking Case of Kidnapping by Bounty Brokers," *New York Times*, August 7, 1864, 2; "End of the Kidnapping Case," *Rutland Weekly Herald* (Rutland, VT), August 18, 1864, 3; and "Substitute brokers," *Burlington Free Press* (Burlington, VT), August 26, 1864, 1. "Kidnapping of Substitutes," *The Grand Haven News* (Grand Haven, MI), September 7. 1864, 1.

67. *New York Daily Herald*, January 25, 1864, 8.

68. *Evening Star* (Washington, DC) December 20, 1864, 3.

69. *Sioux City Register*, February 18, 1865, 3; "Mysterious Disappearance," *New York Daily Herald*, April 3, 1865, 2.

70. According to Vincent DiGirolamo, *Crying the News: A History of America's Newsboys* (New York: Oxford University Press, 2019), 121, enlistments among its residents were so numerous that the Philadelphia Newsboys' Home closed its doors soon after the war began.

71. Peter R. Eisenstadt, *The Encyclopedia of New York State* (Syracuse: Syracuse University Press, 2005), 1088.

72. A close study of the Michigan Reform School suggests that, of the ten boys most frequently punished, five ended up being sent into service. Of these five, only one was over age eighteen, and two were as young as fourteen. Dennis Thavenet, "The Michigan Reform School and the Civil War: Officers and Inmates Mobilized for the Union Cause," *Michigan Historical Review* 13:1 (1987): 21–46. In March 1861, Michigan had enacted a state law permitting the enlistment of minors with parental consent; those without parents or guardians could be mustered on the consent of a

justice of the peace. A total of ninety-five students at the school gained early release on the condition that they enlist.

73. *Report Made to the Senate Relative to the Enlistment of Boys from the Reform School into the Army of the United States* (Providence: Hiram H. Thompson, 1865), 5. Although the committee recommended passage of a law that would clarify institutions' authority vis-à-vis parents, no such legislation was enacted. The war's most widely publicized case of a youth impressed into service similarly involved an asylum inmate. Cornelius Garvin's plight is charted in "A Hard Case—A Mother in Search of Her Son," *New York Herald*, May 21, 1864, 5. For a longer description of this incident, see Damian Shiels, "In Search of Con: The Remarkable Story of the Hunt for the 'Idiot' Boy Sold into Service," available at: https://irishamericancivilwar.com/2015/01/11/in-search-of-con-the-remarkable-story-of-the-hunt-for-the-idiot-boy-sold-into-service/.

74. Laurence M. Hauptman, *The Iroquois in the Civil War: From Battlefield to Reservation* (Syracuse, NY: Syracuse University Press, 1993), 108–110.

75. Eszter Szabó, "The Migration Factor in the American Civil War: The Impact of Voluntary Population Movements on the War Effort," *Americana: E-Journal of American Studies in Hungary* 12:1 (Spring 2016), available at: http://americanaejournal.hu/vol12no1/szabo. See also Mack Walker, "The Mercenaries," *New England Quarterly* 39 (September 1866): 390–398.

76. Michael Douma, Anders Bo Rasmussen, and Robert Faith, "The Impressment of Foreign-Born Soldiers in the Union Army," *Journal of American Ethnic History* 38:3 (Spring 2019): 76–106. Over a thousand claims alleging impressment were made before the Enrollment Act even took effect.

77. Lonn, *Foreigners in the Union Army and Navy*, 469–470.

78. In 1861, in the wake of the *Trent* affair, Britain had begun sending thousands of troops to Lower Canada, fearing the outbreak of war with the United States. By May, the British government had proclaimed a policy of neutrality in relation to the war, making it illegal for British subjects to enlist in either the US or Confederate forces or to induce others to do so. Nonetheless, attempts to lure British soldiers to desert often succeeded. According to Marguerite B. Hamer, "Luring Canadian Soldiers into Union Lines During the War Between the States," *Canadian Historical Review* 27:2 (June 1946): 150–162, these troops were "for the most part Irish boys from Belfast," many under the age of eighteen. In the garrison towns along the Canadian border, brokers and crimps scoured saloons and other places where soldiers congregated. Playing on Irish resentment against the Crown, boredom, homesickness, or discontent with pay and conditions, they promised soldiers huge sums to cross the border and sign up as substitutes.

79. Adam Mayers, "Stolen Soldiers," *Civil War Times Illustrated* 34 (June 1995): 56–59.

80. Cited in William F. Raney, "Recruiting and Crimping in Canada for the Northern Forces," *Mississippi Valley Historical Review* 10:1 (1923): 29.

81. Quoted in Raney, "Recruiting and Crimping in Canada," 29.

82. Cheryl MacDonald, "Canada's Secret Police," *Beaver* 71:3 (1991): 44–49.

83. Hamer, "Luring Canadian Soldiers," 158–159.

84. Ruthanne Lum McCunn, "Chinese in the Civil War: Ten Who Served," *Chinese America: History and Perspectives* 10 (1996): 149–181.

85. "China at Gettysburg," *New York Times*, July 12, 1863, 2.

86. Negus, "'Conduct Unbecoming of an Officer,'" 38.

87. Further detail on the exploitation of Black youth as workers can be found in Thavolia Glymph, *The Women's Fight: The Civil War's Battles for Home, Freedom, and Nation* (Chapel Hill: University of North Carolina Press, 2019), chap 7; and Luskey, *Men Is Cheap*, chap. 2. On the exploitation of young Black refugees, see also Abigail Cooper, "'Lord, Until I Reach My Home': Inside the Refugee Camps of the American Civil War," PhD diss., University of Pennsylvania, 2015; and Samantha Q. de Vera, "A Freedom No Greater than Bondage: Black Refugees and Unfree Labor at the Dawn of Mass Incarceration" (PhD diss., University of California, San Diego, 2022).

88. Richard Reid, "Raising the African Brigade: Early Black Recruitment in Civil War North Carolina," *North Carolina Historical Review* 70:3 (July 1993): 267.

89. John W. Blassingame, "The Recruitment of Colored Troops in Kentucky, Maryland and Missouri, 1863-1865," *The Historian* 29:4 (August 1967): 538.

90. John Hope Franklin, ed., *The Diary of James T. Ayers Civil War Recruiter* (Baton Rouge: Louisiana University Press, 1999).

91. Schwartz, *Born in Bondage*, 15. This point is confirmed by evidence contained in J. Raymond Gourdin, ed. and comp., *104th Infantry Regiment—USCT Colored Civil War Soldiers from South Carolina* (Berwyn Heights, MD: Heritage Books, Inc., 1997). He notes that 196 out of 592 pension applications from this regiment were rejected, mostly on the grounds of a lack of documentation relating to age or condition of servitude. The more than 80 biographical sketches contained in this work make clear that many Black veterans lacked a precise knowledge of their age upon enlistment.

92. See biographical sketch relating to Robert Moses (alias Robert Harven) in Gourdin, *104th Infantry Regiment*.

93. Richard H. Abbott, "Massachusetts and the Recruitment of Southern Negroes, 1863-1865," *Civil War History* 14:3 (September 1968): 197–210. See also Stephen D. Engle, *Gathering to Save a Nation: Lincoln and the Union's War Governors* (Chapel Hill: University of North Carolina Press, 2016), 410–411.

94. Quoted in Abbott, "Massachusetts and the Recruitment of Southern Negroes," 208.

95. Blassingame, "The Recruitment of Colored Troops," 539. Despite such tactics, state recruiters had minimal success. Dudley Taylor Cornish, *The Sable Arm: Black Troops in the Union Army, 1861-1865* (Lawrence: University Press of Kansas, 1956), 256, reports that northern states sent 1,045 agents to recruit in southern regions controlled by Union troops but netted a mere 5,042 African American enlistees. Following outraged reports of their activities, Congress repealed their authority to recruit by an act of March 3, 1865. See also William A. Dobak, *Freedom by the Sword: The U.S. Colored Troops, 1862-1867* (Washington, DC: Center of Military History, 2011).

96. Davis's speech before the US Senate was reprinted under the title "Gen. Burbridge's Administration of Affairs in Kentucky," *Cincinnati Enquirer*, March 15, 1865, 1.

97. William A. Spicer, "The High School Boys of the Tenth R.I. Regiment," *Soldiers and Sailors Historical Society of Rhode Island: Personal Narratives of Events in the War of the Rebellion*, second series, no. 13 (Providence: N. Bangs Williams & Company, 1882), 22–23.

98. Richard M. Reid, *Freedom for Themselves: North Carolina's Black Soldiers in the Civil War Era* (Chapel Hill: University of North Carolina Press, 2008), 244. See also Karin L. Zipf, *Labor of Innocents: Forced Apprenticeship in North Carolina, 1715-1919* (Baton Rouge: Louisiana State University Press, 2005), 47.

99. See, among other works, Catherine A. Jones, *Intimate Reconstructions: Children in Postemancipation Virginia* (Charlottesville: University of Virginia Press, 2015); Tera Hunter, *Bound in Wedlock: Slave and Free Black Marriage in the Nineteenth Century* (Cambridge, MA: Harvard University Press, 2017); Mary Niall Mitchell, *Raising Freedom's Child: Black Children and Visions of the Future After Slavery* (New York: New York University Press, 2008); and Karin L. Zipf, "Reconstructing 'Free Woman': African-American Women, Apprenticeship, and Custody Rights during Reconstruction," *Journal of Women's History* 12:1 (Spring 2000): 3–31.

100. "Trade in Substitutes," *Wyoming Democrat* (Tunkhannock, PA), July 20, 1864, 2.

101. James McCune Smith, "Sketch of the Life and Labors of Rev. Henry Highland Garnet," *Garnet, Memorial Discourse* 17 (1865): 57.

102. Register of Letters Received, Provost Marshal General's Bureau, Office of the Acting Assistant Provost Marshal for the Northern District of Kansas, RG110, National Archives and Records Administration, Kansas City, Missouri.

103. In 1868, some former brokers described their wartime business in St. Louis while testifying in a bankruptcy case. One noted that he "made more money on colored men than white men." Another noted that, as time went on, "the substitutes were mainly black." "The Substitute Broker Business—How it was Carried On," *Nashville Union*, July 1, 1868, 1.

104. Affidavit of John Alexander, December 29, 1863, Baker Papers, Box 5. Newspaperman George Stephens, a correspondent for the *Weekly Anglo-African* (the most widely read black newspaper of the 1860s), also discussed the case of a white officer who tried to sell a "free colored boy" into slavery. Stephens helped to mount a search party when this twelve-year-old, who had been travelling with the regiment, mysteriously disappeared. They eventually found the boy and extracted his harrowing story.

105. Because of the "widespread nature of the problem" of underage enlistment Judge Advocate General Holt argued that it was necessary to " 'make an example' " of First Lieutenant Cornelius Green after he was caught enlisting a fifteen-year-old. But what this meant for Green as a commissioned officer was a dishonorable discharge, not hard labor in a military prison. Cornelius Green, December 3, 1863, RG153, Entry 1, Office of the Judge Advocate General, Letters Sent: Record Books 1842-1889.

106. Isaac Van Winkle, August 22, 1864, AGO Letters, Enlisted Branch, Box 240.

107. [No title], *Press* (Philadelphia, PA), May 8, 1865.

108. "Selling White Boys South," *Burlington Weekly Hawk-Eye*, September 26, 1863, 8; and "Selling White Boys," *Knoxville Whig*, November 11, 1863.

109. "Query," *Star of the North*, March 2, 1864, 2; "Letter from Catspawton," *Dayton Daily Empire*, May 9, 1864, 1.

110. "The Slave Market Outdone," *Bedford Gazette* (Bedford, PA), July 1, 1864, 1. The same editor published a similar charge the year before: "Son Sold as Substitute," *Bedford Gazette*, November 20, 1863, 1.

111. Former boy soldiers often attributed their postwar success to military careers. See, for instance, Joseph Benson Foraker, *Notes of a Busy Life*, 2 vols. (Cincinnati: Stewart & Kidd Company, 1916), 1:122–123; and Stanton P. Allen, *Down in Dixie: Life in a Cavalry Regiment in the War Days from the Wilderness to Appomattox* (Boston: D. Lothrop Company, 1893), 144, 487. A comprehensive study of US congressmen who served in the late nineteenth and early twentieth centuries would show that an astonishing number had enlisted in the Union or Confederate army prior to reaching the age of eighteen. This research can be conducted by studying biographical data on congressmen available at https://bioguideretro.congress.gov and cross-referencing it with census data and military records. We have identified over fifty US congressmen who fit this description.

Epilogue

1. Among numerous important studies on this topic, see David W. Blight, *Race and Reunion: The Civil War in American Memory* (Cambridge, MA: Harvard University Press, 2001) and Caroline E. Janney, *Remembering the Civil War: Reunion and the Limits of Reconciliation* (Chapel Hill: University of North Carolina Press, 2013).

2. The discussion in the *National Tribune* can be seen in "The Youngest Soldier," May 1, 1881, 6, and constantly thereafter up through the 1890s. *Inter Ocean*'s discussion began around the same time and continued in successive issues, as did the *Globe*'s.

3. "The Boy Veterans," *Inter Ocean*, May 28, 1881, 9.

4. "The Boy Soldiers," *Inter Ocean*, June 18, 1881, 9

5. "Youngest Civil War Soldier," *Inter Ocean*, September 2, 1900, 20. On the enduring nature of these disputes, see: "Enjoys the Distinction of Being Youngest Soldier," *Washington Times*, March 5, 1905, 13.

6. "A Puzzle," *Daily News-Republican* (Lawton, OK), May 11, 1907, 2.

7. "Continuous Performance," *Minneapolis Journal*, October 12, 1901, 12.

8. Untitled article relating to Edward M. Roberts, *Daily City Gate* (Keokuk, IA), June 1, 1909, 8; "Youngest Real Soldier of the Civil War," *San Francisco Call*, June 13, 1909.

9. "Youngest Soldier," *Richmond Dispatch*, April 22, 1891, 2. Emphasis in original. The *Confederate Veteran* also got in on the action. See, for example, Charles Hay Carter, "About Another 'Youngest Soldier,'" *Confederate Veteran* 9:8 (1901): 352.

10. "Iron Cross to Confederate Soldiers," *Times Dispatch* (Richmond, VA), August 9, 1906, 12; and "William F. Hopkins is the Youngest Confederate Soldier," *Times Dispatch*, January 20, 1907, 5.

11. On the commercial imperatives that drove writers to sanitize the war see Janney, *Remembering the Civil War*, 166.

12. W. F. Hinman, "Boy Soldiers," *Youth's Companion*, May 25, 1893, 267. For a recent edition of Hinman's memoir, see *Corporal Si Klegg and His 'Pard'* (Lincoln: University of Nebraska Press, 2007; orig. 1887).

13. Richard White, *The Republic for Which it Stands: The United States during Reconstruction and the Gilded Age, 1865-1896* (New York: Oxford University Press, 2017) is the most recent survey of these changes.

14. On transformations in understandings of male identity and power in the nineteenth and early twentieth centuries, see: Anthony E. Rotundo, *American Manhood: Transformations in Masculinity from the Revolution to the Modern Era* (New York: Basic Books, 1993); Gail Bederman, *Manliness and Civilization: A Cultural History of Gender and Race in the United States, 1880-1917* (Chicago: University of Chicago Press, 2008); Julia Grant, *The Boy Problem: Educating Books in Urban America* (Baltimore: Johns Hopkins University Press, 2014); Kevin P. Murphy, *Political Manhood: Red Bloods, Mollycoddles, and the Politics of Progressive Era Reform* (New York: Columbia University Press, 2008); and Michael Kimmel, *Manhood in America* (New York: Oxford University Press, 2017); and Benjamin René Jordan, *Modern Manhood and the Boy Scouts of America: Citizenship, Race, and the Environment, 1910-1930* (Chapel Hill: University of North Carolina Press, 2016). On the changing advice literature directed at boys, see also Judy Hilkey, *Character Is Capital: Success Manuals and Manhood in Gilded Age America* (Chapel Hill: University of North Carolina Press, 1997).

15. Hinman, "Boy Soldiers," 267.

16. Carole Emberton, "'Only Murder Makes Men': Reconsidering the Black Military Experience," *Journal of the Civil War Era* 2:3 (2012): 369–393.

17. Janey, *Remembering the War*, 88-91, 115-120. Blight, *Race and Reunion*, chap. 9.

18. The drummer boy figure in Sir William Gascombe John's Memorial to the King's Liverpool regiment, erected in 1904, for instance, was so popular that a replica was created for the National Museum of Wales. https://museum.wales/collections/onl ine/object/be047d0a-939f-3e70-9a3b-1337952330d5/. In this decade, several other drummer boy monuments appeared in the United Kingdom., along with a handful in the former Confederate states.

19. *The Drummer Boy: or, the Battle-Field of Shiloh: A New Military Drama in Six Acts, and Accompanying Tableaux* (Detroit: Daily Post Book and Job Printing Establishment, 1868). At least seven additional printed versions of this play exist, published between 1868 and 1888.

20. "The Famous Military Allegory," *National Tribune*, June 19, 1884, 5. The official program of *The Drummer Boy, or, the Battle Field of Shiloh* (Worchester, MA: Blanchard & Co. Printers, [1891]), Massachusetts Historical Society, Boston, Box-L 1891, claimed that the play had been staged four thousand times across the country by this point. Several versions existed, allowing GAR posts to cater to the tastes of local audiences. As late as 1912, an Ohio newspaper was still reporting the play's upcoming season, promising "no history can furnish a better idea of the war or instil into the minds

of the young and the old a spirit of patriotism. . . . You will be a better citizen for having seen it." "The Drummer Boy of Shiloh, *Democratic Banner* (Mt. Vernon, OH), November 26, 1912, 5.

21. Edward Ryan, *Paper Soldiers: The Illustrated History of Printed Paper Armies of the 18th, 19th and 20th Centuries* (London: New Cavendish Books, 1995), 512–519, itemises these and similar games.

22. For the 1860s and 1870s, only the catalogue entries rather than the games themselves appear to exist. But according to Marisa Kayyem and Paul Sternberger, *Victorian Pleasures: American Board and Table Games of the Nineteenth Century from the Liman Collection* (New York: Miriam and Ira D. Wallach Art Gallery, Columbia University, 1991), 39, Milton Bradley, which opened in Springfield Massachusetts in 1860, released numerous board games "of war and patriotism" for older children, which they packaged and sold together in the mid-1870s as "The Union Games."

23. Alice Fahs, "Remembering the Civil War in Children's Literature of the 1880s and 1890s," in Alice Fahs and Joan Waugh, eds., *The Memory of the Civil War* (Chapel Hill: University of North Carolina Press, 2004), 79–93.

24. An identity as a former boy soldier was so valuable that some men exaggerated or outright fabricated their military service records. Thomas Fox, *Drummer Boy Willie McGee, Civil War Hero and Fraud* (Jefferson, NC: McFarland & Company, 2008) follows one such instance.

25. *Final Journal of the Grand Old Army of the Republic, 1866-1956* (Washington, DC: US Government Printing Office, 1957), 35–50. Their biographies can also be found in Frank L. Grzyb, *The Last Civil War Veterans: The Lives of the Final Survivors, State by State* (Jefferson, NC: McFarland and Company, 2016). This cohort likely experienced and recalled the war differently than older men: they were more likely to have received lenient treatment for disciplinary infractions and to have been doted on and protected by mature colleagues. They did not usually leave behind wives and children, established trades or professions, so going to war was far less likely to conjure anxiety about being able to protect and provide for dependents back home. It was perhaps more prone to induce survivors' guilt—a sense of indebtedness to men who had helped to care for and essentially raise them—many of whom had died. Given that they grew up amid the militant politics of the 1850s and then enlisted in their youth, it makes sense that they would uphold a vision of the Civil War as a paradigmatic moment of male heroism and cross-generational male bonding—precisely the version of the war that would become prominent by the late nineteenth century.

26. McLaughlin Bros. catalogues are held by the Antiquarian Society, Worcester, MA and available online at: https://www.americanantiquarian.org/mcloughlin-bros-catalogs-price-lists-and-order-forms.

27. Mark I. West, "Not to be Circulated: The Response of Children's Librarians to Dime Novels and Series Books," *Children's Literature Association Quarterly* 10:3 (Fall 1985): 137–139; and Dawn Keetley, "The Injuries of Reading: Jesse Pomeroy and the Dire Effects of Dime Novels," *Journal of American Studies* 47:3 (2013): 673–697.

28. Joseph F. Kett, *Rites of Passage: Adolescence in America, 1790 to the Present* (New York: Basic Books, Inc., 1977), 38–41. See also Steven Mintz, *Huck's Raft: A*

History of American Childhood (Cambridge, MA: Belknap Press of Harvard University Press, 2004), chap. 9.

29. Roberta J. Park, "'Taking Their Measure' in Play, Games, and Physical Training: The American Scene, 1870s to World War 1," *Journal of Sport History* 33:2 (Summer 2006): 193–217.

30. Quotations from G. Stanley Hall, *Adolescence; its Psychology and its Relations to Physiology, Anthropology, Sociology, Sex, Crime, Religion, and Education*, 2 vols. (New York: Appleton and Company [1904] 1919), 1:vii, xv, xiv. Studies focusing on Hall include Dorothy Ross, *G. Stanley Hall: The Psychologist as Prophet* (Chicago: University of Chicago Press, 1972), and Bederman, *Manliness and Civilization*, chap. 3.

31. Hall, *Adolescence*, 50.

32. Hall, *Adolescence*, 321.

33. Hall, *Adolescence*, chap x, quote from pp. 313, 269.

34. Kett, 217–219.

35. Rotundo, *American Manhood*, 253. See also Arnaldo Testi, "The Gender of Reform Politics: Theodore Roosevelt and the Culture of Masculinity," *Journal of American History* 81:4 (March 1995), 1509–1533.

36. Rotundo, chap. 11.

37. Jay Mechling, "Boy Scouts, the National Rifle Association, and the Domestication of Rifled Shooting," *American Studies* 53:1 (2014): 5–26. See also Jordan, *Modern Manhood and the Boy Scouts of America*; and David I. Mcleod, *Building Character in the American Boy: The Boys Scouts, YMCA, and Their Forerunners, 1887-1920* (Madison: University of Wisconsin Press, 1983).

38. John C. Black, "Our Boys in the War. Read June 9, 1892," in Military Order of the Loyal Legion of the United States, *Military Essays and Recollections: Papers Read before the Commandery of the State of Illinois*, 4 vols. (Chicago: Dial Press, 1891–1899), 2:443–456.

39. Grand Army of the Republic, *Journal of the Twenty-Sixth National Encampment 1892* (Albany, 1892), 82. Further details on this effort can be found in subsequent GAR's yearly journals and in Wallace Evan Davies, *Patriotism on Parade: The Story of Veterans' and Hereditary Organizations in America 1783-1900* (Cambridge, MA.: Harvard University Press, 1955), chaps. 10–13.

40. Key texts that chart the evolution of the lost cause myth include Charles Reagan Wilson, *Baptized in Blood: The Religion of the Lost Cause, 1865-1920* (Athens: University of Georgia Press, 1980); Gaines M. Foster, *Ghosts of the Confederacy: Defeat, the Lost Cause and the Emergence of the New South* (New York: Oxford University Press, 1987); Gary W. Gallagher and Alan T. Nolan, eds., *The Myth of the Lost Cause and Civil War History* (Bloomington: Indiana University Press, 2000); and Anne E. Marshall, *Creating a Confederate Kentucky: The Lost Cause and Civil War Memory in a Border State* (Chapel Hill: University of North Carolina Press, 2010).

41. Charles Reagan Wilson, "The Religion of the Lost Cause: Ritual and Organization of the Southern Civil Religion, 1865-1920," *Journal of Southern History* 46:2 (May, 1980): 223–224. Karen L. Cox, Dixie's *Daughters: The United Daughters of the*

Confederacy and the Preservation of Confederate Culture (Gainesville: University Press of Florida, 2003)

42. Fred Bailey, "The Textbooks of the 'Lost Cause': Censorship and the Creation of Southern State Histories," *Georgia Historical Quarterly* 75:2 (Summer 1991): 507–533.

43. Rod Andrew Jr., "Soldiers, Christians, and Patriots: The Lost Cause and Southern Military Schools, 1865-1915," *Journal of Southern History* 64:4 (November 1998), quotations, 685, 691.

44. *Rites of Passage*, 174.

45. Rodd, "Soldiers, Christians, and Patriots," 687–688.

46. Quotes from Davies, *Patriotism on Parade*, 341.

47. The Duke Center for Firearms Law has an online database that enables the searching of all American laws passed in relation to gun usage. Using the terms "minor," "child" "under the age," or "parent and guardian" brings up more than a hundred state and local laws along these lines, the vast majority enacted between 1890 and 1920. Age ranges vary widely as do penalties, with no apparent regional patterns.

48. Putting "toy pistol" or "boy" and "gun" into a newspaper database such as Chronicling America brings up hundreds of stories in the Progressive Era focused on boys firing toy cannons or pistols, placing explosive devices on train tracks, or holding up policemen or members of the public.

49. R. Blake Brown, "Every boy ought to learn to shoot and to obey orders': Guns, Boys, and the Law in English Canada from the late Nineteenth Century to the Great War," *Canadian Historical Review* 93:2 (June 2012): 196–225, suggests that this was the case in Canada.

50. On post–Civil War state-building and parental rights, see Julia Bowes, *Invading the Home: Children, State Power, and the Gendered Origins of Modern Conservatism, 1865-1933* (PhD diss., Rutgers University, 2018).

51. The rich scholarship on these topics includes Catherine Jones, *Intimate Reconstructions: Children in Postemancipation Virginia* (Charlottesville: University of Virginia Press, 2015); Mary Niall Mitchell, *Raising Freedom's Child: Black Children and Visions of the Future After Slavery* (New York: New York University Press, 2008); Karin L. Zipf, *Labor of Innocents: Forced Apprenticeship in North Carolina, 1715-1919* (Baton Rouge: Louisiana State University Press, 2005); Margaret D. Jacobs, *White Mother to a Dark Race: Settler Colonialism, Maternalism, and the Removal of Indigenous Children in the American West and Australia, 1880-1940* (Lincoln: University of Nebraska Press, 2009); and Marilyn Holt, *The Orphan Trains: Placing Out in America* (Lincoln: University of Nebraska Press, 1992).

52. James Schouler, *A Treatise on the Law of Domestic Relations*, 3rd ed. (Boston: Little, Brown, and Company, [1870] 1882), quotes 347, 348.

53. Schouler, *A Treatise on the Law of Domestic Relations*, 347–351, 597–598.

54. David Tanenhaus, "Between Dependency and Liberty: The Conundrum of Children's Rights in the Gilded Age," *Law and History Review* 351 (2005): 351–385. Quote 366.

55. James D. Schmidt, *Industrial Violence and the Legal Origins of Child* Labor (New York: Cambridge University Press, 2010), vividly depicts the increasing perils

that children endured in industrial workplaces, and the way legal rulings left them incapable of holding employers liable for workplace injuries.

56. Bowes, *Invading the Home*. See also Michael Grossberg, *Governing the Hearth: Law and the Family in Nineteenth-Century America* (Chapel Hill: University of North Carolina Press, 1988); Mary Ann Mason, *From Father's Property to Children's Rights: The History of Child Custody in the United States* (New York: Columbia University Press, 1994); and Viviana A. Zelizer, *Pricing the Priceless Child: The Changing Social Value of Children* (New York: Basic, 1985). Peter W. Bardaglio, *Reconstructing the Household: Families, Sex, and the Law in the Nineteenth-Century South* (Chapel Hill: University of North Carolina Press, 1995), notes that family law in the former Confederacy approximated the rest of the country after the Civil War.

57. Michael Grossberg, "Who Gets the Child? Custody, Guardianship, and the Rise of a Judicial Patriarchy in Nineteenth-Century America," *Feminist Studies* 9:2 (Summer, 1983): 239.

58. On the endurance of patriarchalism in the private sphere, see Evelyn Atkinson, "Out of the Household: Master-Servant Relations and Employer Liability Law," *Yale Journal of Law & the Humanities* 25 (2018): 205–270.

59. Steven Mintz, *Huck's Raft: A History of American Childhood* (Cambridge: The Belknap Press of Harvard University Press, 2004), chap. 8.

60. Susan J. Pearson, *The Rights of the Defenseless: Protecting Animals and Children in Gilded Age America* (Chicago: University of Chicago Press, 2011).

61. Peter Stearns, "Girls, Boys, and Emotions: Redefinitions and Historical Change," *Journal of American History* 81:1 (June 1993), 36–74, quotes 43, 56. Daniel Greenstone, "Frightened George: How the Pediatric Educational Complex Ruined the Curious George Series," *Journal of Social History* 39:1 (Fall 2005), 221–228. On the growing social scientific interest in children more broadly, see Alice Boardman Smuts, *Science in the Service of Children, 1893-1935* (New Haven, Yale University Press, 2006).

62. *Congressional Record—House*, vol. 21 (1890). The discussion can be found on 4031. Ainsworth's report constitutes an appendix at 93–96, later reprinted under the title *Memorandum Relative to the Probable Number and Ages of the Army and Navy Survivors of the Civil War* (War Dept, Government Printing Office, 1905).

63. "Civil War Soldiers Mostly Boys," *Fargo Forum and Daily Republican* (Fargo, ND), May 19, 1915, 9; "Boys of '61 were Real Boys," *Wausau Pilot* (Wausau, WI), September 4, 1917, 4.

64. Luther W. Hopkins, *From Bull Run to Appomattox: A Boy's View* (Baltimore: Press of Fleet McGinley Co., [1908] 1914).

65. Francis Trevelyan Miller, "Two Million Boys on the Battle Line in Civil War," *Times Dispatch* (Richmond, VA) December 3, 1911; reprinted as "2 Million Schoolboys in the Civil War," *San Francisco Call*, January 28, 1912, 3.

66. For instance, statements in relation to H.R. 15775 by House member M. E. Burke of Wisconsin, *Congressional Record* 53 (1916): 1323–1327; William Harding Carter, *The American Army* (Indianapolis: Bobbs-Merrill Company Publishers, 1915), 108–109; and "Youngest Veteran," *National Tribune* (Washington, DC), November 10, 1910,

5. For a discussion of the wide acceptance of these figures, see W. J. Ghent, "Some Popular Hoaxes," *The Independent* 75 (September 11, 1913), 617–618; and William Gist "The Ages of the Soldiers in the Civil War," *Iowa Journal of History and Politics*, (1918): 387–399.

67. Ghent, "Some Popular Hoaxes, 617–618.

68. Gist, "Ages of Soldiers," 388. The inflated claims about boy soldiers that alarmed Gist also led to the celebration of specific Confederate companies in ways that have been remarkably enduring. One former Confederate general, for instance, asserted that Virginia's Parker Battery, which he commanded at the Battle of Antietam, was "composed nearly entirely of beardless boys from 14 to 18." Gen. Stephen L. Lee, "The Seed Corn of the Confederacy," *Clarion-Ledger* (Jackson, MS), November 4, 1907, 9. Reprinted as "Seed Cover of the Confederacy: The Famous Boy Company of Richmond, Commanded by Capt. W.W. Parker," *Southern Historical Society Papers* 35 (1907): 102–107 (quotation, 102). Historian Douglas Southall Freeman, *Lee's Lieutenants: A Study in Command*, vol. 2 (New York: Scribner's and Co., 1943), 282, perpetuated this myth when he waxed poetic about "Capt. W.W. Parker's artillerists" in his trilogy published during World War II. "These were boys of 14 to 17," he wrote, quoting Lee's account of how he had rallied the troops by exhorting them, "You are boys, but you have this day gone where only men dare to go." But extant muster rolls show that just twenty-two of the 144 members for whom ages are available (or 15 percent) enlisted below the age of eighteen. Compared to the norm, this was likely a high percentage of underage youths, which is which explains the battery's reputation. But the notion that the company consisted *primarily* of underage youths is ridiculous.

69. Ghent, "Some Popular Hoaxes," 618.

70. "Fought by Boys," *Appeal to Reason* (Girard, KS), July 22, 1911, 1.

71. Manuel Franz, "Preparedness Revisited: Civilian Societies and the Campaign for American Defense, 1914-1920," *Journal of the Gilded Age and Progressive Era* 17 (2018): 671.

72. Susan Zeiger, "The Schoolhouse vs. the Armory: U.S. Teachers and the Campaign Against Militarism in the Schools 1914-1918," *Journal of Women's History* 15:2 (Summer 2003): 150–179.

73. Susan Zeiger, "She Didn't Raise Her Boy to Be a Slacker: Motherhood, Conscription, and the Culture of the First World War," *Feminist Studies* 22:1 (1996): 6–39, quote 35. See also Rebecca Jo Plant, *Mom: The Transformation of Motherhood in Modern America* (Chicago: University of Chicago Press, 2011), chap. 1.

74. Zeiger, "She Didn't Raise Her Boy," 24; on concerns with mothers raising effeminate sons, see also Kirsten Marie Delegard, *Battling Miss Bolsheviki: The Origins of Female Conservatism in the United States* (Philadelphia: University of Pennsylvania Press, 2012); Julia Grant, "A 'Real Boy' and Not a Sissy: Gender, Childhood, and Masculinity, 1890-1940," *Journal of Social History* 37:4 (Summer 2004): 829–851; and Kim E. Nielson, *Un-American Womanhood: Antiradicalism, Antifeminism, and the First Red Scare* (Columbus: Ohio State University Press. 2001).

75. "General Young Believes Young Men Should Undergo Military Training," *Tulsa Daily World*, August 28, 1917. Reprinted as "An Amendment to Draft Law is Proposed," *Arizona Republican*, August 29, 1917, 8.

76. "Draft of Youths of 19 Urged by Col. Roosevelt: Union Saved by Soldiers Most of Whom were Under 21, says Ex-President," *Harrisburg Telegraph* (Harrisburg, PA), October 16, 1917, 3.

77. "The Boys of Sixty One," *Lexington Intelligencer* (Lexington, MO), May 18, 1917, 3.

78. House debate April 25, 1917, *Congressional Record* 55 (1917), 1098–1099.

79. House debate April 25, 1917, *Congressional Record* 55 (1917), 1100

80. On Black militias in the post-Civil War era, see articles by Otis A. Singletary, Roger D. Cunningham, Alwyn Barr, Eleanor L. Hannah, and Beth Taylor Muskat in Bruce A. Glasrud, ed., *Brothers to the Buffalo Soldiers: Perspectives on the African American Militia and Volunteers, 1865-1917* (Columbia: University of Missouri Press, 2011), pt. 1. As Barr notes, some black militia companies managed to survive in the former Confederate states until the late nineteenth century, despite facing extra-legal violence and intimidation.

81. Jerry M. Cooper, "The Army as Strike-Breaker: The Railroad Strikes of 1877 and 1894," *Labor History* 18:2 (1977): 179–196.

82. John K. Mahon, *History of the Militia and the National Guard* (New York: Macmillan Publishing Company, 1983), chap. 10.

83. Most recently, Matthew Margis, "America's Progressive Army: How the National Guard Grew out of Progressive Era Reforms" (PhD diss., Iowa State University, 2016), argues that militia legislation grew out of Progressive Era reforms geared toward centralization and efficiency, while Christopher Capozzola, "Minutemen for the World: Empire, Citizenship, and the National Guard, 1903-1924," in Alfred W. McCoy and Francisco A. Scarano, eds., *Colonial Crucible: Empire in the Making of the Modern American State* (Madison: University of Wisconsin Press, 2009), 421–430, focuses on the shift toward empire building in the early twentieth century as a key moment in reconsidering the relationship between citizenship and military service. Broader studies of America's militia tradition chart a longer history, of course, but this work tends to treat the federalization of the militia as an inevitable process that went largely uncontested until militia units became a weapon used against ordinary people after 1877. For instance, James C. Bradford, "The Citizen Soldier in America: Militia, National Guard, and Reserves," in *A Companion to American Military History*, 2 vols. (Malden, MA: Blackwell Publishing Ltd., 2019), 1:472–496; Mahon, *History of the Militia*, chaps. 8–9; and Jerry Cooper, *The Rise of the National Guard: The Evolution of the American Militia, 1865-1920* (Lincoln: University of Nebraska Press, 1977).

84. Robert Leider, "Federalism and the Military Power of the United States," *Vanderbilt Law Review* 73:4 (May 2020): 989–1076; and Jonathan Turley, "The Military Pocket Republic, 97," *Northwestern University Law Review* 91:1 (2002): 1–134, note the lack of constitutional support for the unchecked expansion of centralized US military power in the modern era. Turley briefly traces this expansion back to the Civil War, but his main concern lies in the contemporary implications of this shift rather than its genesis.

85. Cited in William L. Shaw, "The Civil War Federal Conscription and Exemption System," *Judge Advocate Journal* 32 (1962): 27.

Appendix A

1. "Henry C. Houston, G.A.R. Vet of Portland, Dies," *Boston Sunday Globe*, March 26, 1922, 141.
2. Henry Clarence Houston, *Complete Roster of the Officers and Men of the Thirty-Second Maine Regiment* (Portland, ME: Press of Southworth Brothers, 1903), 45–46.
3. Bell Irvin Wiley, *The Life of Billy Yank: The Common Soldier of the Union* (New York: Book of the Month Club, [1952] 1994), 299, 303.
4. E. B. Elliott, *On the Military Statistics of the United States of America* (Berlin: R.V. Decker, 1863); Benjamin Apthorp Gould, *Ages of U.S. Volunteer Soldiery* (New York: Welch, Bigelow, & Co, 1866); and *Investigations in the Military and Anthropological Statistics of American Soldiers* (New York: Hurd and Houghton, 1869). On the racial implications of Gould's study, see Leslie A. Schwalm, "'A Body of Truly Scientific Work;' The U.S. Sanitary Commission and the Elaboration of Race in the Civil War Era, *Journal of the Civil War Era* 8:4 (2018): 647–676;
   Lundy Braun, "Spirometry, Measurement and Race in the Nineteenth Century," *Journal of the History of Medicine* 60 (2005): 135–169; and John S. Haller, "Civil War Anthropometry: The Making of a Racial Ideology," *Civil War History* 16 (1970): 309–324.
5. Wiley, *The Life of Billy Yank*, 299, 303.
6. Jim Murphy, *The Boys' War: Confederate and Union Soldiers Talk about the Civil War* (New York: Clarion Books, 1990), 2. The misleading statistics used in popular work focusing on underage enlistees in the Civil War continues to be widely cited online, often without attribution. "The Civil War Saga," website, for instance, claims that 20 percent of Union enlistees were below the age of eighteen: https://civilwarsaga. com/child-soldiers-in-the-civil-war/. The Wikipedia entry on "Child Soldiers in the American Civil War" likewise claims that well over 800,000 youths below the age of eighteen fought against the Confederacy: https://en.wikipedia.org/wiki/Child_soldiers_in_the_American_Civil_War.
7. David M. Rosen, *Child Soldiers: A Reference Handbook* (Santa Barbara, CA: ABC-Clio, 2012), 3, and *Child Soldiers in the Western Imagination: From Patriots to Victims* (New Brunswick, NJ: Rutgers University Press, 2015), chap. 2.
8. Earl J. Hess, "The Early Indicators Project: Using Massive Data and Statistical Analysis to Understand the Life Cycle of Civil War Soldiers, *Civil War History* 63:4 (December 2017): 377–399 (quotation, 381).
9. B. W. Underwood, *Rebellion Record of the Town of Quincy, an Alphabetically arranged Record of Each Resident of Quincy who has Served in the Army and Navy of the United States during the late Rebellion* (Boston: J.E. Farwell and Company, 1866).

10. George W. Schee and O. H. Montzheimer, *Biographical Data and Army Records of Old Soldiers who have lived in O'Brien County, Iowa* (Iowa: Primghar, 1909). The slightly higher percentage of underage enlistees found in this survey likely reflects the fact that the author sent out questionnaires more than forty years after the war's end, after older veterans had begun dying off.

11. Kathleen Shaw, "'Johnny Has Gone for a Soldier': Youth Enlistment in a Northern County," *Pennsylvania Magazine of History* 135:4 (October 2001): 419–446 (quotation, 444).

12. Jared Anthony Crocker, "An Average Regiment: A Re-Examination of the 19th Indiana Volunteer Infantry of the Iron Brigade" (MA thesis, Indiana University, 2016).

13. John David Hoptak, "The Influence of Socio-Economic Background on Union Soldiers During the American Civil War" (MA thesis, Lehigh University, 2003), 23. More than 70 percent of the soldiers in this regiment had been residing with parents or relatives in 1860, according to the US census, while slightly less than 30 percent were household heads.

14. Dennis W. Brandt, *From Home Guards to Heroes: The 87th Pennsylvania and Its Civil War Community* (Columbia, MO: University of Missouri Press, 2006), 44.

15. Jim Sundman, "And Your Age Is?" guest post on Emerging Civil War website, December 1, 2011, https://emergingcivilwar.com/2011/12/01/and-your-age-is/.

16. Hugh Dubrulle, blog post and comment, "How Should We Think about Civil War Numbers that Never Add up?" H-CivWar, May 27, 2022, https://networks.h-net.org/node/4113/blog/h-civwar-authors-blog/10313095/how-should-we-think-about-civil-war-numbers-never#reply-10375231.

17. Bell Irvin Wiley, *The Life of Johnny Reb: The Common Soldier of the Confederacy* (Baton Rouge: Louisiana State University Press, 1943), 330–331

18. Edmund Drago, *Confederate Phoenix: Rebel Children and Their Families in South Carolina* (New York: Fordham University Press, 2008), 14 and 146–147.

19. Joseph T. Glatthaar, *General Lee's Army: From Victory to Collapse* (New York: Free Press, 2008), 17–18, 204.

20. Joseph T. Glatthaar, *Soldiering in the Army of Northern Virginia: A Statistical Portrait of the Troops Who Served Under Robert E. Lee* (Chapel Hill: University of North Carolina Press, 2011), 115, 120.

21. The patient register for L'ouverture Hospital can be downloaded at https://civilwardc.org/data/.

22. See, for example, the enlistment contracts for those who served in the 42nd USCT. These appear toward the end of enlistees' compiled service records. Available at Fold3, https://www.fold3.com/browse/hQi_vJlC4YnhLbqLlkDPg4wXy.

Bibliography

Primary Sources

Manuscript Collections

Alabama Department of Archives and History, Montgomery, Alabama
Confederate Regimental History Files.

American Antiquarian Society, Worcester, Massachusetts
Amateur Newspaper Collection
Civil War Envelopes Collection

Bancroft Library, University of California, Berkeley, California
Charles Albert Storke Papers

Boston Athenaeum, Boston, Massachusetts
Confederate Imprints Collection
Orin S. Baker Letters

Boston Public Library, Rare Books and Manuscripts Department, Massachusetts
Horace Killam Correspondence
Samuel G. Bowdlear and Austin C. Wellington Correspondence
Records of the Recruiting Committee of Ward 9

Library Company of Philadelphia, Pennsylvania
McAllister Civil War Prints, Ephemera, and Scrapbooks
Nicholas B. Wainwright Lithograph Collection
Amateur Newspapers and Journals Collection
American Song Sheets, Slip Ballads, and Poetical Broadsides Collection
Civil War Graphics and Ephemera Collection

Massachusetts Historical Society, Boston
Civil War Patriotic Covers Collection
Edward Louis Edes Letters
Andrew R. Linscott Papers
Edward Burgess Peirce Letters
Henry J. Wardwell Diary

Michigan History Center Archives, Lansing, Michigan
Cyrus Bacon Diary

National Archives and Records Administration, Kansas City, Kansas
Record Group 110: Records of the Provost Marshal Generals Bureau. War Department.
    Division of Missouri. Department of Missouri. Office of the Chief Mustering Officer.
    Series 4209: Letters and Telegrams Sent, 1863-1869.
    Series 6500: Letters Sent, 1863-67.

RG110: Records of the Provost Marshal Generals Bureau. War Department. Provost Marshal General's Bureau. Office of the Acting Assistant Provost Marshal for Missouri. Draft Rendezvous and General Recruiting Depot, St. Louis.

Series 4425: Letters Received, 1864-65.

Series 4427: Proceedings of Board of Examination.

Series 4428: Telegrams Received and Descriptive List of Men Rejected, 1864-65.

RG110: Records of the Provost Marshal Generals Bureau. War Department. Office of the Acting Assistant Provost Marshal for Missouri. Office of the Superintendent of the Volunteer Recruiting Service.

Series 4199: Correspondence with Recruiting Officers and Special Orders, 1863-64.

RG110: Records of the Provost Marshal Generals Bureau. War Department. Office of the Acting Assistant Provost Marshal for Missouri.

Series 4183: Registers of Recruits Rejected at the General Recruiting Depot and Stoppages Against Provost Marshals and Surgeons for Rejected Recruits, 1863-64.

RG110: Records of the Provost Marshal Generals Bureau. War Department. Provost Marshal General's Bureau. Office of the Acting Assistant Provost Marshal for Missouri. 2nd District.

Series 4296: Medical Register of Examinations of Drafted Men, Recruits, and Substitutes, 1864-65.

RG110: Records of the Provost Marshal Generals Bureau. War Department. Provost Marshal General's Bureau. Office of the Acting Assistant Provost Marshal for Missouri. 3rd District.

Series 4316: Register of Medical Examinations of Drafted and Enrolled Men, Showing Rejections and Exemptions, 1864-65.

RG110: Records of the Provost Marshal Generals Bureau. War Department. Provost Marshal General's Bureau. Office of the Acting Assistant Provost Marshal for Missouri. 6th District.

Series 4371: Medical Register of Examinations of Enrolled Men, Drafted Men, Recruits, and Substitutes Showing Exemptions, 1864-65.

RG110: Records of the Provost Marshal Generals Bureau. War Department. Provost Marshal General's Bureau. Office of the Acting Assistant Provost Marshal for Missouri. Office of the Superintendent of the Volunteer Recruiting Service.

Series 4200: Endorsements Sent and Received, 1864-65.

RG110: Records of the Provost Marshal Generals Bureau. War Department. Provost Marshal General's Bureau. Office of the Acting Assistant Provost Marshal for the Northern District of Kansas.

Series 6545: Letters Sent, 1863-65

Series 6546: Register of Letters Received, 1863-65.

Series 6553: Medical Register of Examinations of Recruits and Substitutes, 1864-65.

RG110: Records of the Provost Marshal Generals Bureau. War Department. Provost Marshal General's Bureau. Office of the Acting Assistant Provost Marshal for Iowa. 1st District

Series 6396: Medical Register of Examinations of Enrolled Men, Recruits, and Substitutes, 1864-65.

RG110: Records of the Provost Marshal Generals Bureau. War Department. Provost Marshal General's Bureau. Office of the Acting Assistant Provost Marshal for Iowa. 3rd District

Series 6429: Descriptive Book of Drafted Men and Substitutes, 1864-65.

RG110: Records of the Provost Marshal Generals Bureau. War Department. Provost Marshal General's Bureau. Office of the Acting Assistant Provost Marshal for Iowa. 4th District

Series 6452: Medical Register of Examinations of Recruits and Substitutes, 1864-65.

RG110: Records of the Provost Marshal Generals Bureau. War Department. Provost Marshal General's Bureau. Office of the Acting Assistant Provost Marshal for Iowa. 5th District

Series 6464: Letters and Telegrams Received, 1863-65.

RG110: Records of the Provost Marshal Generals Bureau. War Department. Provost Marshal General's Bureau. Office of the Acting Assistant Provost Marshal General for Kansas, Nebraska, Colorado, and Dakota. Office of the Superintendent of the Volunteer Recruiting Service, and Chief Mustering and Disbursing Officer.

Series 6501: Letters Sent by the Superintendent of the Volunteer Recruiting Service and the Chief Mustering and Disbursing Officer, 1862-64.

Series 6502: Letters Sent to the Provost Marshal General, 1863-65.

Series 6504: Register of Letters Received, 1863-65.

Series 6505: Register of Letters Received and Endorsements Sent Relating to Districts, 1863-65.

National Archives and Records Administration, Washington, DC

RG107, Records of the Office of the Secretary of War.

Letters Received by the Secretary of War, Main Series, 1801-1870, M221.

Letters Received by the Secretary of War from the President, Executive Departments and the War Bureaus, 1862-1870, M494.

Letters Sent by the Secretary of War to the President and Executive Departments, 1863-1870. M421.

RG109, War Department Collection of Confederate Records

Letters Received by the Confederate Secretary of War, 1861-1865, M437.

Letters Received by the Confederate Adjutant and Inspector General's Office.

RG94, Records of the Adjutant General's Office

Letters Received by the Office of the Adjutant General (Main Series), 1861-1870. M666.

Letters Sent by the Office of the Adjutant General (Main Series), 1800-1890. M689

Letters Sent Relating to Soldiers, 1860-62 (Addison Files). Entry 415.

Letters Received Relating to Soldiers, 1860-62 (Addison Files). Entry 416.

Letters Sent by the Office of the Adjutant General (Enlisted Branch), 1863-1865. Entry 406.

Letters Received by the Office of the Adjutant General (Enlisted Branch), 1862-1889. Entry 409.

Orders and Circulars, 1797-1910. Entry 44.

Register of Letters Sent, Entry 406.

Endorsements and Memoranda, 1863-1870. Entry 408.

Subject Index to Letters Received, 1863-81. Entry 412.

Letters Sent, Recruiting Division, 1823-1882. Entry 467.

Letters Received, Recruiting Division, 1814-1913. Entry 471.

Register of Letters Received, Recruiting Division. Entry 472.

RG153, Records of the Office of the Judge Advocate General (Army)

Court-martial case files, 1809-1894.

Letters Sent; Record Books, 1842-1889. Entry 1.

Opinions of the Attorney General. 1834-1870. Entry 12.

RG110, Records of the Provost Marshal General's Bureau
    Papers of Colonel L.C. Baker

U.S. Army War College Library and Archives, Carlisle, Pennsylvania
William M. Ellis Correspondence, Norman Daniels Collection, Harrisburg Civil War
    Roundtable.

Virginia Historical Society, Richmond, Virginia
Nimrod Bramham Hamner Diary
Hamner Family Papers
Ferneyhough Family Papers
Tomlin's Infantry Battalion Letter book, 1861

North Carolina State Archives, Raleigh, North Carolina
Zebulon Baird Vance Letterbooks and Correspondence
Governor Henry Toole Clark Letterbooks and Correspondence
Edward Jones Hale Papers
William H.C. Whiting Papers

Library of Virginia, Richmond.
Personal Papers Collection.

Government Publications

Annals of Congress
Army Paymaster's Manual. . . Revised to include June 30, 1864. Comp. J.H. Eaton.
    Washington, DC: Government Printing Office, 1864.
*A Compilation of the Messages and Papers of the Confederacy, Including the Diplomatic
    Correspondence, 1861-1865,* vol. 1. Comp. James D. Richardson. Nashville: United
    States Publishing Co., 1906.
Confederate States of America. *General Orders from Adjutant and Inspector-General's
    Office, Confederate States Army, from January, 1862, to December, 1863,* 2 vols.
    Columbia: Presses of Evans & Cogswell, 1864.
Confederate States of America. *Journal of the Congress of the Confederate States of America,
    1861-1865.* 7 vols. Washington, DC: Government Printing Office, 1904–1905.
Congressional Globe
Congressional Reporter
Official Opinions of the Attorneys General of the United States. 12 vols. Washington, DC: R.
    Farnham, 1852–1870.
Public Documents of the U.S. Senate, vol. 1, 1st Sess., 26th Cong. Washington, DC: Blair
    and Rives, 1840.
*The Statutes at Large of the Confederate States of America, Commencing with the
    First Session of the First Congress; 1862.* Ed. James M. Matthews. Richmond: R.M.
    Smith, 1862.
Regulations for the Army of the United States, 1857. New York: Harper & Brothers, 1857.
Revised Regulations for the Army of the United States, 1861. Philadelphia: G.L. Brown,
    Printer, 1861.
Revised United States Army Regulations of 1861. Philadelphia: G.W. Childs, 1863.

Regulations for the Government of the Navy of the United States 1865. Washington, DC: Government Printing Office, 1865.

Regulations for the Army of the Confederate States, as Adopted by Act of Congress, Approved March 6, 1861. New Orleans: Henry P. Lathrop, 1861.

Statistical Report on the Sickness and Mortality in the Army of the United States. Washington, DC: Government Printing Office, 1840.

The Statutes Relating to the Army of the United States, as Revised, Simplified, Arranged, and Consolidated. Washington, DC: Government Printing Office, 1868.

US Bureau of the Census. *Historical Statistics of the United States, Colonial Times to 1970.* Washington, DC: Government Printing Office, 1975.

United States Congressional Serial Set

United States Statutes at Large

US War Department. *The War of the Rebellion: A Compilation of the Official Records of the Union and Confederate Armies.* 128 vols. Washington, DC: Government Printing Office, 1880–1901.

Periodicals

Annual Reports of the Navy Department (1860–1869)
Army & Navy Official Gazette (1863–1865)
Army & Navy Chronicle (1835)
Confederate Veteran (1901)
Military and Naval Magazine (1833–1836)
Naval Magazine (1836–1837)
New York Military Magazine (1841)
U.S. Service Magazine (1864–1864)
Youth's Companion (1893)

Newspapers

Alabama Beacon (Greensboro, AL).
Alexandria Gazette (Alexandria, VA).
American Mercury (Hartford, CT).
Appleton Crescent (Appleton, WI).
Athens Post (Athens, TN).
Bedford Gazette (Bedford, PA).
Boston Post (Boston, MA),
Boston Traveller (Boston, MA).
Boston Sunday Globe (Boston, MA).
Bradford Reporter (Towanda, PA).
Brooklyn Daily Eagle (Brooklyn, NY).
Burlington Free Press (Burlington, VT).
Burlington Weekly Hawk-Eye (Burlington, VT).
Chicago Tribune (Chicago, IL)
Daily Dispatch (Richmond, VA).
Daily Ohio Statesman (Columbus, OH).
Delaware County Daily Times (Chester, PA).
Chicago Tribune (Chicago IL).
Citizen Soldier (Philadelphia, PA).

Cincinnati Daily Press (Cincinnati, OH).
Cincinnati Enquirer (Cincinnati, OH).
Cleveland Morning Leader (Cleveland, OH).
Commercial Advertiser (New York, NY).
Daily Conservative (Raleigh, NC).
Daily Dispatch (Richmond, VA).
Daily Evansville Journal (Evansville, IN).
The Daily Exchange (Baltimore, MD).
Daily Journal (Wilmington, NC).
Daily Madisonian (Washington, DC).
Daily Milwaukee News (Milwaukee, WI).
Daily Missouri Republican (St. Louis, MO)
Daily National Intelligencer (Washington, DC).
Daily Ohio Statesman (Columbus, OH).
Daily Selma Reporter (Selma, AL).
Daily State Sentinel (Indianapolis, IN).
The Daily Union (Washington, DC).
The Dakota Huronite (Huron, SD)
Dayton Daily Empire (Dayton, OH).
East Saginaw Courier (East Saginaw, MI).
Evening Telegraph (Philadelphia, PA).
Evening Star (Washington, DC).
Fayetteville Semi-Weekly Observer (Fayetteville, NC).
Gallipolis Journal (Gallipolis, OH).
The Grand Haven News (Grand Haven, MI)
Green-Mountain Freeman (Montpelier, VT).
The Independent (New York, NY).
Frank Leslie's Illustrated Newspaper (New York, NY).
Harper's Weekly (New York, NY).
Southern Illustrated News (Richmond, VA).
Hillsdale Standard (Hillsdale, MI).
Knoxville Whig (Knoxville, TN).
Leavenworth Bulletin (Leavenworth, KS).
The Liberator (Boston, MA)
Louisville Daily Democrat (Louisville, KY).
Magnolia Weekly (Richmond, VA).
Memphis Daily Appeal (Memphis, TN).
Milwaukee Daily Sentinel (Milwaukee, WI).
Mobile Advertiser and Register (Mobile, AL).
Nashville Daily Union (Nashville, TN)
National Aegis (Worcester, MA).
National Tribune (Washington, DC)
Newbern Weekly Progress (Newbern, NC).
New-England Palladium (Boston, MA).
New York Sun (New York, NY).
New York Herald (New York, NY).
New York Daily Times (New York, NY).

New York Daily Tribune (New York, NY).
New York Morning Express (New York, NY).
The Ohio Democrat (Canal Dover, OH).
New Orleans Crescent (New Orleans, LA).
Pennsylvania Republican (York, PA).
Pittsburgh Daily Gazette and Advertiser (Pittsburgh, PA).
Portland Gazette and Maine Advertiser (Portland, ME).
Providence Gazette and Country Journal (Providence, RI).
Press (Philadelphia, PA).
The Republic (Washington, DC).
Richmond Dispatch (Richmond, VA).
Richmond Enquirer (Richmond, VA).
Richmond Palladium (Richmond, IN).
Richmond Times Dispatch (Richmond, VA).
Rutland Weekly Herald (Rutland, VT).
Semi-Weekly Standard (Raleigh, NC).
Sioux City Register (Sioux City, IA).
Staunton Spectator (Staunton, VA).
The Sun (Pittsfield, MA).
The Sun (New York, NY).
Sunday Delta (New Orleans, LA).
Virginia Abingdon (Abingdon, VA).
Virginia Argus (Richmond, VA).
Washington Monitor (Washington, GA).
Washington Times (Washington, DC).
Weekly Anglo-African (New York, NY).
Weekly Arkansas Gazette (Little Rock, AK).
Weekly Conservative (Raleigh, NC).
Weekly Franklin Repository (Chambersburg, PA).
Weekly Messenger (Boston, MA).
Weekly Sun (Atlanta, GA).
The World (New York, NY).
Wyoming Democrat (Tunkhannock, PA).

Legal Cases

Re Higgins, 16 Wis. 351.
The People, ex rel. Starkweather v. Gaul, 44 Barb. 98.
Commonwealth v. Cushing, 11 Mass. 67.
Commonwealth v. Frost, 13 Mass. 491.
Stevens v. Foss, 18 Maine, 19.
Porter v. Sherburne, 21 Maine, 258.
Emanuel Roberts, 2d Hall's L.J., 192.
United States v. Bainbridge, 24 F. Cas. 946 (No. 14,497).
Commonwealth v. Downes, 41 Mass., 227.
Commonwealth ex. rel. Webster v. Fox, 7 Penn. L.J., 227.
United States v. Blakeney 44 Va. (3 Gratt), 405, 411-413.
Commonwealth v. Archer, 9 Monthly L. Rep. 465.

Griffin v. Wilcox, 21 Indiana. 370.
United States v. Tarble, 80 U.S. (13 Wall.) 397

Sheet Music

De Greer, P. "Drummer Boy of Vicksburg, or, Let Him Sleep." Philadelphia: J. Marsh, 1864.
Dix, John Ross. "The Drummer Boy's Farewell." New York: Charles Magnus, [1864].
Dodge, William Sumner. *The Brave Drummer Boy of the Rappahannock*. Chicago: Church and Goodman, 1867.
Fleming, Albert. "Drummer Boy of Antietam, A War Ballad." Louisville, KY: D.P. Faulds, 1863.
Grube, L. comp., lyrics by J. C. Koch, "The Dying Drummer Boy." Brooklyn: Louis Grube, Publisher, 1863.
Hays, Will S. "Drummer Boy of Shiloh." Louisville, KY: D.P. Foulds, 1863.
Hays, Will S. "Drummer Boy of Shiloh: as sung by the First Tenn. Concert Troupe." Augusta, GA: Blackmar & Bro., 1863.
Hays, Will S. "Little Sam." [New York]: J.L. Peters & Brother, 1867.
Johnston, Robert. "The Drummer Boy of Nashville" New York: Chas. Magnus, 1864.
Lathbury, Mary A. "The Dying Drummer Boy" New York: William A. Pond & Co, 1864.
Martin, S. Wesley. "Little Harry the Drummer Boy." In *6 Beautiful Songs*. Chicago: H.M. Higgins, 1864.
Shaw, C.A. "If I Sleep Will Mother Come?" Boston: Oliver Ditson & Co., 1864.
Work, Henry C. "Little Major." Chicago: Root & Cady, 1862.

Articles, Pamphlets, Reports, Speeches, & Tracts

"An Act for the Protection of the Personal Liberty of the Citizens, and for Other Purposes." *Laws of the State of Maine*. 2 vols. Kennebec, ME: Hallowell, 1830, 1:90–92.
"An Act Concerning the Acquisition, the Enjoyment, and the Transmission of Property, Real and Personal, the Domestic Relations, and Other Matters Connected with Private Rights." *Revised Statutes of the State of Indiana*. Indianapolis: John Dowling and R. Cold, 1843, 620.
Callan, John F. *The Military Laws of the United States Relating to the Volunteers, Militia, and to Bounty Lands and Pensions, from the Foundation of the Government to the Year 1863*. Philadelphia: George W. Childs, 1863.
Causey, Jerry, ed. "Selected Correspondence of the Adjutant General of Confederate Mississippi." *Journal of Mississippi History* 43:1 (1981): 47.
Charlie the Drummer Boy. New York: American Tract Society, 1863.
Child, Lydia Maria. "The St. Domingo Orphans." *Juvenile Miscellany* 5 (September 1830): 82, 85–86.
"Damages for Enlisting a Minor," *American State Papers: Military Affairs*. 7 vols. Washington DC: Gales and Seaton, 1832, 1:669.
Downs, Annie Sawyer. "The Drummer-Boy of Marblehead." *The Volunteer* (New York), March 1, 1862, 43-45.
"The Drummer Boy." *The Highland Weekly News*, July 2, 1863, 1.
"Eastman Johnson." *Appletons' Journal: A Magazine of General Literature* 11:260 (March 14, 1874): 347.
Enlist! Enlist!!: An Appeal to Young Soldiers. By a Young Lady of Virginia. Petersburg, VA: Evangelical Tract Society, 1861.

"Enlistment Under Age." *Western Law Journal* 3:12 (September 1851): 567.

Glatthaar, Joseph T., and John H. Crowder. "The Civil War Through the Eyes of a Sixteen-Year Old Black Officer: The Letters of Lieutenant John H. Crowder of the 1st Louisiana Native Guards." *Louisiana History* 35:2 (Spring 1994): 201–216.

Hardee, William J., et al. *Memorial to the Congress of the Confederate States of America.* Mobile, AL: S.H. Goetzel, December 14, 1863.

Lance, E.H. comp. *The Soldier's Record of Jericho, Vermont.* Burlington, VT: R.S. Styles, 1868.

"Little Giffen," *The Land We Love: A Monthly Magazine Devoted to Literature* 4 (November–April 1867–1868), 7.

"Little Johnny Clem." In E.S.S. Rouse, editor, *The Bugle Blast, or, Spirit of the Conflict: Comprising Naval and Military Exploits, Dashing Raids, Heroic Deeds, Thrilling Incidents, Sketches, Anecdotes, etc.* Philadelphia: J. Challen & Son, 1864, 334–336.

"The Little Drummer Boy." *The Big Blue Union* (Marysville, KS), December 27, 1862, 2.

"On Popular Prejudices against Military Establishments." *Military and Naval Magazine* 1:5 (July 1833), 292–303.

"On the Necessities and Advantages of an Army and the Utility of War." *Military and Naval Magazine* 2:4 (December 1833), 210–213.

Post, Alfred, and William H. VanBuren. "Military Hygiene and Therapeutics." In William A. Hammond, ed., *Military Medical and Surgical Essays prepared for the United States Sanitary Commission.* Philadelphia: J.B. Lippincott & Co., 1864, 41–42.

Spicer, William. "The High School Boys of the Tenth Rhode Island Regiment." *Soldiers and Sailors Historical Society of Rhode Island: Personal Narratives of Events in the War of the Rebellion,* second series, no. 13. Providence: N. Bangs Williams & Company, 1882, 22-23.

Smith, James McCune. "Sketch of the Life and Labors of Rev. Henry Highland Garnet." *Garnet, Memorial Discourse* 17 (1865): 57.

A Record of the Soldiers of Southborough during the Rebellion from 1861 to 1866. Marlboro, MA: Mirror Steam Job Press, 1867.

Report Made to the Senate Relative to the Enlistment of Boys from the Reform School into the Army of the United States. Providence: Hiram H. Thompson, 1865.

Roe, Alfred S. "The Youth in the Rebellion: Address Given before Geo. H. Ward, Post 10 G.A.R. in Mechanics Hall, Worcester, June 1883." Worcester: Press of C. Hamilton, 1883.

Leland, Charles G. "The Draft—Recruiting and Enlistment." *United States Service Magazine* 4:2 (August 1865): 516.

Smith, F.G. and Alfred Stillé. "Vaccination in Armies." In William A. Hammond, ed., *Military Medical and Surgical Essays prepared for the United States Sanitary Commission.* Philadelphia: J.B. Lippincott & Co., 1864, 134.

Speech of Richard H. Dana, Jr. at Manchester, N.H. on Tuesday Evening, February 19, 1861. Boston: Redding & Co, 1861.

Stephens, Alexander H. *Speech delivered before delivered before the Georgia Legislature on March 16, 1864.* Atlanta, GA: Intelligencer Steam Power Presses, 1864.

"Training Children for War." *The Calumet* (New York), March 1, 1834, 568–570.

U.S. Sanitary Commission. *A Report to the Secretary of War of the Operations of the Sanitary Commission, and upon the Sanitary Condition of the Volunteer Army.* Washington, DC: McGill & Witherow, December, 1861.

Watrous, A. E. "Grant as His Son Saw Him: An Interview with Col. Frederick D. Grant about His Father." *McClure's Magazine* 2:6 (May 1894): 515–519.

"The Wounded Drummer Boy." *Appletons' Journal: A Magazine of General Literature*. 7:165 (May 25, 1872), 579.

Memoirs and Recollections of Underage Soldiers

Musicians, and Camp Followers (Union)

Aubery, Cullen B[ullard]. *Recollections of a Newsboy in the Army of the Potomac, 1861-1865: His Capture and Confinement in Libby Prison, After Being Paroled Sharing the Fortunes of the Famous Iron Brigade*. Milwaukee, WI: J.H. Yewdale & Sons Co., 1897.
April 1, 1846—February 1, 1908
Never officially enlisted, but went to war in June 1861 with Co. H, 2nd Vermont (age 14)

Allen, Stanton P. *Down in Dixie: Life in a Cavalry Regiment in the War Days from the Wilderness to Appomattox*. Boston: D. Lothrop Company, 1893.
February 20, 1849—December 5, 1901
Enlisted November 28, 1863, in Co. I, 3rd Battalion, 1st Massachusetts Cavalry (age 14)

Barney, C[aleb] Henry. "A Country Boy's First Three Months in the Army."
Providence: N. Bangs Williams & Company, 1880.
January 10, 1844–January 10, 1904
Enlisted December 14, 1861, in Co. A, 5th Rhode Island Heavy Artillery (age 17)

Bardeen, C[harles] W. *A Little Fifer's War Diary*. Intro. by Nicholas Murray Butler.
Syracuse, New York: privately printed, 1910.
August 28, 1847–August 19, 1924
Enlisted July 23, 1862, as a musician in Co. D, 1st Massachusetts Infantry (age almost 15)

Beneway, Almon. *Drummer Boy of Company C: Coming of Age during the Civil War*.
Cypress Communications, 2013.
January 1847–April 21, 1926
Went to war in August 1861 with Co. D, 19th Indiana Infantry as a "camp follower" (age 14); enlisted September 1, 1862, in Co. C, 75th Indiana Infantry (age 15)

Cole, Jacob H. *Under Five Commanders; or, A Boy's Experience with the Army of the Potomac*. Paterson, NJ: News Printing Co, 1906.
February 22, 1847–April 22, 1929
Enlisted September 21, 1861, in Co. A, 57th New York Infantry (age 14)

Copp, Elbridge J[ackson]. *Reminiscences of the War of the Rebellion, 1861-1865*. Nashua, NH: Telegraph Publishing Co., 1911.
July 22, 1844–August 3, 1923
Enlisted August 14, 1861, in Co. F, 3rd Infantry (age 17)

DeBord, James K. P. *From 1861 to 1865: Civil War Record*. Kahoka, MO: R.L. Christy Job Print, 1905.
January 1, 1846–October 1, 1924
Enlisted October 14, 1862, in Co. B, 3rd Missouri Cavalry (age 16)

Foote, Corydon Edward. *With Sherman to the Sea: A Drummer's Story of the Civil War*.
New York: The John Day Company, 1960.
January 9, 1849–January 10, 1944
Enlisted on January 16, 1862, as a musician in the 13th Michigan Infantry (age 13)

Foraker, Joseph Benson. *Notes of a Busy Life*, vol. 1, 3rd ed. Cincinnati: Steward and Kidd, 1917.
>   July 5, 1846–May 10, 1917
>   Enlisted July 14, 1862, in Co. A, 89th Ohio Volunteer Infantry (age 16)

Gilmore, Pascal Pearl. *Civil War Memories* (Bangor, Me.: s.n., 1928)
>   June 24, 1845–December 5, 1931
>   Went to war October 29, 1861, as a clerk with Co. G, 11th Maine Infantry Volunteers (age 16)
>   Enlisted September 5, 1863, in Co. E, 16th Maine Infantry as a substitute (age 18)

Grant, Nicholas B[iddle]. "The Life of a Common Soldier, 1862-1865." LaFollette, TN: LaFollette Press, [1927].
>   February 1846–September 1930
>   Enlisted April 20, 1862 in Co. F, 6th East Tennessee Infantry (age 16)

Kirkpatrick, George Morgan. *The Experiences of a Private Soldier of the Civil War* (n.p.: Reprinted by the Hoosier Bookshop, 1973.
>   January 5, 1846–March 26, 1931
>   Enlisted August 1861 in Co. A, 42nd Indiana Regiment (age 14)

Livermore, Thomas L[eonard]. *Days and Events, 1860-1866*. Boston: Houghton Mifflin Company, 1920.
>   February 7, 1844–January 9, 1918
>   Enlisted June 24, 1861 in Co. F, 1st New Hampshire Infantry (age 17)

Miller, Delavan S[amuel]. *Drum Taps in Dixie: Memories of a Drummer Boy, 1861-1865*. Watertown, NY: Hungerford-Hobrook Co., 1905.
>   January 1849–July 28, 1917
>   Enlisted April 5, 1862 as a musician in Co. H, 2nd New York Heavy Artillery (age 13)

Upson, Theodore F[relinghuysen]. *With Sherman to the Sea: The Civil War Diaries and Reminiscences of Theodore F. Upson*, ed. and intro. Oscar Osburn Winther. Bloomington: Indiana Press, 1958.
>   May 5, 1845–January 31, 1919
>   Enlisted August 15, 1862 in Co. C, 100th Indiana Infantry (age 17)

Robinson, Arthur J. *Memorandum and Anecdotes of the Civil War, 1862 to 1865*. Privately published, 1912.
>   March 25, 1846–May 8, 1930
>   Enlisted August 15, 1862 in Co. E, 33rd Wisconsin Infantry (age 16)

Sallada, William H. *Silver Sheaves: Gather through Clouds and Sunshine*. Des Moines, published by author, 1887.
>   July 12, 1846–May 1935
>   Enlisted March 10, 1864 in Co. B, 57th Pennsylvania Infantry (age 17)

Smith, W[ill] B. *On Wheels, and How I Came There: A Real Story for Real Boys and Girls, Giving the Personal Experiences and Observations of a Fifteen-year-old Yankee Boy as Soldier and Prisoner in the American Civil War*. Ed. Joseph Gatch Bonnell. New York: Hunt & Eaton, 1892.
>   1845–October 27, 1918
>   Enlisted December 21, 1863 in Co. K, 14th Illinois Infantry (age 15)

Spangler, Edward W[ebster]. *My Little War Experience, with Historical Sketches and Memorabilia*, privately published, 1904
>   February 12, 1846–April 22, 1907
>   Enlisted on August 4, 1862 in Co. K, 130th Pennsylvania Infantry Volunteers (age 16)

Storke, Charles Albert, with Michael J. Phillips. "After the Bugles—the West!" Box 2, vol. 4, Charles Albert Storke Papers, 1856-1936, Bancroft Library, University of California, Berkeley
    November 19, 1846–December 6, 1936
    Enlisted February 28, 1864 in Co. G, 36th Wisconsin Infantry (age 17)
Stockwell, Elisha, Jr. *Private Elisha Stockwell, Jr., Sees the Civil War*. Ed. Byron R. Abernethy. Norman: University of Oklahoma Press, 1958.
    June 28, 1846–December 29, 1935
    Enlisted February 25, 1862 in Co. I, 14th Wisconsin Infantry (age 15)
Ulmer, George T. *Adventures and Reminiscences of a Volunteer; or, a Drummer Boy from Maine*. Privately printed, 1892.
    1848–March 1, 1899
    Enlisted April 2, 1864 in Co. H, 8th Maine Infantry (age 16)
Vail, Enos B. *Reminiscences of a Boy in the Civil War*. Brooklyn: Printed by the author for private distribution, 1915.
    September 8, 1843–November 17, 1927
    Enlisted April 23, 1861 in Company E, 20th New York State Militia (age 17)
Wilkeson, Frank. *Turned Inside Out: Recollections of a Private Soldier in the Army of the Potomac*, ed. James McPherson. Lincoln: University of Nebraska Press, 1999, orig. 1887.
    March 8, 1848–April 1913.
    Enlisted March 26, 1864 in the 11th Battery of the NY Light Artillery (age almost 16)

Memoirs and Recollections of Underage Soldiers (Confederate)

Dinkins, James. *1861 to 1865, by an Old Johnnie: Personal Recollections and Experiences in the Confederate Army*. Cincinnati: R. Clarke Co., 1897.
    April 18, 1845—July 19, 1939
    Enlisted March 10, 1862, in Co. C, 18th Mississippi Regiment (age almost 17)
Duncan, Thomas D. *Recollections of Thomas D. Duncan: A Confederate Soldier*. Nashville, TN: McQuiddy Printing Co., 1922.
    June 30, 1846–September 19, 1931
    Enlisted February 20, 1861, in Co. D, Tishomingo Rangers, Mississippi (age 14)
Hopkins, Luther W. *From Bull Run to Appomattox: A Boy's View* (Baltimore, 1909)
    November 13, 1843–July 4, 1920
    Enlisted September 1, 1862, in Co. A, 6th Virginia Cavalry (age 19). His memoir discusses two younger brothers who enlisted underage.
Johnston, David E[mmons]. *Confederate Boy in the Civil War*. Portland, OR: Glass and Prudhomme Co, c. 1914.
    April 10, 1845–July 7, 1917
    Enlisted May 13, 1861, in Co. D, 7th Virginia Infantry Regiment (age 16)
Mixson, Frank M[aner]. *Reminiscences of a Private*. Columbia, SC: State Company, 1910.
    December 2, 1846–November 5, 1911
    Enlisted April 12, 1862, in Co. E., 1st South Carolina Volunteers (age 15)
Stephenson, Philip Daingerfield. *The Civil War Memoir of Philip Daingerfield Stephenson*, ed. Nathaniel Cheairs Hughes, Jr., ed. Baton Rouge: Louisiana State University Press, 1995.
    September 7, 1845–March 12, 1916
    Enlisted May 10, 1861, in Co. A, 13th Arkansas Artillery Regiment (age 15)

Staunton, Moore J.[osiah]. *Reminiscences, Letters, and Miscellanies.* Richmond, VA: O.E. Flanhart Printing Co., 1903.
June 18, 1843–May 3, 1913
Enlisted May 14, 1861, in the Co. B, 15th Virginia Infantry Regiment (age 17)

Robson, John S. *How a One-Legged Rebel Lives: Reminiscences of the Civil War.* Durham, NC: Educator Co., 1898.
March 26, 1844–June 6, 1920
Enlisted July 1861 in Co. D, 52nd Virginia Infantry Regiment (age 17)

Wickersham, John T. *Boy Soldier of the Confederacy: The Memoir of Johnnie T. Wickersham.* Ed. Kathleen Gorman. Carbondale: Southern Illinois University Press, 2006, orig. 1915.
February 1846–November 16, 1916
Never officially enlisted. Tagged along with older brothers, first in the 3rd Infantry Regiment of the 7th Division of the Missouri State Guards. Later seems to have joined his brother James T. Wickersham in 4th Missouri Infantry Regiment (probably age 15)

Wise, John Sergeant. *End of an Era.* Boston: Houghton, Mifflin, and Co., 1899.
December 27, 1846–May 12, 1913
Enrolled as a cadet at the Virginia Military Institute in September 1862 (age 15); fought in Battle of New Market (age 17); enlisted in the Confederate States Army as 2nd Lt. Drillmaster in September 1864 (age 17)

Wyeth, John Allan. *With Sabre and Scalpel: The Autobiography of a Soldier and Surgeon.* New York: Harper & Brothers Publishers, 1914.
May 26, 1845–May 23, 1922
Enlisted December 15, 1862, in Co. I, 4th Alabama Cavalry (age 17)

Books

The ABC in verse, for young Learners. New York: J.S. Redfield, 1846.

Adams, Samuel. *The Writings of Samuel Adams,* ed. Harry Alonzo Cushing, 4 vols. New York: G.P. Putnam's Sons, 1907.

Anon. *Charles Ashton; The Boy that Would be a Soldier.* Boston: N.S. & J. Simpkins, 1823.

Aitken, William. *On the Growth of the Recruit and Young Soldier, with a View to a Judicious Selection of "Growing Lads" for the Army, and a Regulated System of Training for Recruits.* London: Griffin, Bohn, and Company, 1862.

Ainsworth, F. C. *Memorandum Relative to the Probable Number and Ages of the Army and Navy Survivors of the Civil War.* War Dept, Government Printing Office, 1905.

Alger, Horatio. *Frank's Campaign; or, What Boys Can do on the Farm and the Camp.* Boston: Loring, 1864.

Allan, Frances D. comp. *A Collection of Southern Patriotic Songs, Made During Confederate Times.* Galverston, TX: J.D. Sawyer, Publisher, 1874.

Andrews, Andrew Jackson. *A Sketch of Boyhood Days.* Richmond: Hermitage Press, 1905.

The Anti-Slavery Alphabet. Philadelphia: Merrihew & Thompson, 1847.

Baker, Lafayette C. *The United States Secret Service in the Late War.* Philadelphia: John E. Potter & Company, 1867.

Bartholow, Roberts. *A Manual of Instructions for Enlisting and Discharging Soldiers.* Philadelphia: J.B. Lippincott & Co., 1864.

Baxter, J. H. *Statistics, Medical and Anthropological, of the Provost-Marshal-General's Bureau Derived from Records of the Examination for Military Service in the Armies of the United States During the Late War of the Rebellion of Over a Million Recruits,*

Drafted Men, Substitutes, and Enrolled Men. 2 vols. Washington: Government Printing Office, 1875.

Birkhimer, William E. Review of *Digest of the Opinions of Judge Advocate General, Journal of the Military Service Institution of the United States* 29 (1901): 22–23, 454.

Blackett, R. J. M., ed. *Thomas Morris Chester, Black Civil War Correspondent: His Dispatches from the Virginia Front.* Baton Rouge: Louisiana State University Press, 1989.

Blackstone, William. Commentaries of the Laws of England. *Book 1.* New York: Harper & Brothers, 1852 [1765].

The Bold Soldier Boy's Song Book. Richmond: West & Johnston, c. 1861–1865.

Bonnell, Joseph Gatch. *Soldier and Prisoner in the American Civil War.* New York: Hunt & Eaton, 1892.

Boisseau, Mary Leigh. *Abstractions of Exemptions from Military Service and Etc., 1862-63 A Record of Halifax County Court House Halifax, Virginia.* Danville, VA: priv. printed, 1980.

Boisseau, Mary Leigh. *Pittsylvania County, Virginia Board of Exemptions Minutes.* s.l., priv. printed, 1994.

Bourke's Picture Primer. Macon, GA: Burke, Boykin & Co., 1864.

Boys and Girls Stories of the War. Richmond: West & Johnston, 1863.

Burdette, Robert J. *Drums of the 47th* Indianapolis: Bobbs-Merrill Co., 1919.

Cammack, John Henry. *Personal Recollections: A Soldier of the Confederacy, 1861-1865.* Huntington, WV: Paragon Printing and Publishing, 1920.

Campbell, William A., and William R.J. Dunn, *The Child's First Book.* Richmond: Ayres & Wade, 1864.

Carter, Richard Goldthwaite. *The Record of Military Service of First Lieutenant and Brevet Captain Robert Goldthwaite Carter, U.S. Army, 1862-1877.* Washington, DC: Gibson Bros, Printers and Bookbinders, 1904.

Carter, William Harding. *The American Army.* Indianapolis: Bobbs-Merrill Company Publishers, 1915.

Chaudron, A. de V. *Chaudron's Spelling Book.* Mobile: S.H. Goetzel, 1865.

Chapman, Conrad Wise. *Ten Months in the "Orphan Brigade": Conrad Wise Chapman's Civil War Memoir,* ed. Ben L. Bassham. Kent, OH: Kent State University Press, 1999.

Crallé, Richard, ed. *The Works of John C. Calhoun,* 6 vols. New York: D. Appleton, 1854.

Crandall, Marjorie. *Confederate Imprints: A Check List Based Principally on the Collection of the Boston Athenaeum,* 2 vols. Boston: The Boston Athenaeum, 1955.

Crist, Lynda Lasswell, and Mary Seaton Dix, eds. *The Papers of Jefferson Davis, 1856-1860,* 14 vols. Baton Rouge: Louisiana State University Press, 1971–2015.

Davis, Charles E., Jr. *Three Years in the Army: The Story of the Thirteenth Massachusetts Volunteers.* Boston: Estes and Lauriat, 1894.

Davis, Jefferson. *The Papers of Jefferson Davis: September 1864-May 1865,* vol. 11., edited by Lynda Lasswell Crist, Barbara J. Rozek, and Kenneth H. Williams. Baton Rouge: Louisiana State University Press, 2003.

Dowdey, Clifford, ed. *The Wartime Papers of Robert E. Lee.* Boston: Little, Brown and Co., 1961.

Dwight, Theodore. *History of the Hartford Convention; with a Review of the Policy of the United States Government, which led to the War of 1812.* New York: N.J. White, 1833.

Elliott, Ezekiel B. *On the Military Statistics of the United States of America.* Berlin: R.V. Decker, 1863.

[Ely, John]. *The Child's Instructor; Consisting of Easy Lessons for Children* 3rd ed. Bridgeport, CN: J.B. and L. Baldwin, 1833.

The First Reader, for Southern Schools. Raleigh, NC: Christian Advocate, 1864.

Franklin, John Hope, ed. *The Diary of James T. Ayers Civil War Recruiter.* Baton Rouge: Louisiana University Press, 1999.

The General Laws of Massachusetts, 4 vols. Boston: Wells & Lilly and Cummings & Hillard, 1823.

Gerry, H.E. *Camp Fire Entertainment and True History of Robert Henry Hendershot.* Chicago: Hack & Anderson, 1910.

Ghent, W. J. "Some Popular Hoaxes." *The Independent* 75 (September 11, 1913), 617–618.

Gist, W. W. "The Ages of Soldiers in the Civil War," *Iowa Journal of History and Politics* 16 (1918): 387–399.

Goodrich, Samuel G. *The First Book of History; for Children and Youth.* Boston: Charles J. Hendee, 1836.

Gordon, John Brown. *Reminiscences of the Civil War.* New York: Charles Scribner's Sons, 1904.

Gould, Benjamin Apthorp. *Ages of U.S. Volunteer Soldiery.* New York: Welch, Bigelow, & Co., 1866.

Gould, Benjamin Apthorp. *Investigations in the Military and Anthropological Statistics of American Soldiers.* New York: Hurd and Houghton, 1869.

Gourdin, J. Raymond, ed. and comp., *104th Infantry Regiment—USCT Colored Civil War Soldiers from South Carolina.* Berwyn Heights, MD: Heritage Books, Inc., 1997.

Grant, Ulysses S. *Personal Memoirs.* New York: Barnes and Noble, [1885] 2003.

Grant, Ulysses S. *The Papers of Ulysses S. Grant*, ed. John Y. Simon, 32 vols. Carbondale: Southern Illinois University Press, 1969-2012.

Grant, Julia Dent. *Personal Memoirs of Julia Dent Grant*, ed. John Y. Simon. Carbondale: Southern Illinois University Press, 1975.

Hall, G. Stanley. *Adolescence; its Psychology and its Relations to Physiology, Anthropology, Sociology, Sex, Crime, Religion, and Education, 2 vols.* New York: Appleton and Company [1904] 1919.

Hammond, William A. *A Treatise on Hygiene with special Reference to the Military Service.* Philadelphia: J.B. Lippincott & Co., 1863.

Hinman, W.F. *Corporal Si Klegg and His 'Pard.'* Lincoln: University of Nebraska Press, [1887] 2007.

Houston, Henry Clarence. *Complete Roster of the Officers and Men of the Thirty-Second Maine Regiment.* Portland, ME: Press of Southworth Brothers, 1903.

Hull, Susan R. *Boy Soldiers of the Confederacy.* New York: Neale Publishing, 1905.

Hurd, Rollin C. *A Treatise on the Right of Personal Liberty, and on the Writ of Habeas Corpus and the Practice Connected with It.* Albany: W.C. Little, 1858.

Jones, John William. *Life and Letters of Robert E. Lee: Soldier and Man.* New York: Neale Publishing Co., 1906.

Jones, J. B. *A Rebel War Clerk's Diary at the Confederate States Capital*, 2 vols. Philadelphia: J.B. Lippincott & Co., 1866.

Kent, James. *Commentaries on American Law*, 2 vols. New York: O. Halsted, 1826.

Lawrence, Abel, E. *Confederate Sheet Music.* Jefferson, NC: McFarland & Company, Inc., 2004.

Kilmer, George Langdon. "Boys in the Union Army," *Century* 70 (June 1905): 269–275.

Lee, Laura Elizabeth. *Forget-me-nots of the Civil War; a Romance, Containing Reminiscences and Original Letters of two Confederate Soldiers.* St. Louis, MO: A.R. Fleming printing, 1909.

Lieber, Francis, and G. Norman Lieber. *To Save the Country: A Lost Treatise on Martial Law,* ed. Will Smiley and John Fabian Witt. New Haven: Yale University Press, 2019.

Lincoln, Abraham. *Abraham Lincoln: Speeches and Writings, 1859-1865.* New York: The Library of America, 1989.

Lincoln, Abraham. *Collected Works of Abraham Lincoln,* ed. Roy P. Basler, asst. ed. Marion Dolores Pratt, and Lloyd A. Dunlap, 8 vols. New Brunswick, NJ: Rutgers University Press, 1953–1955.

Lincoln, Edwin Hale. *Drummer Boy: The Civil War Diary of Edwin Hale Lincoln.* Karl Marty and Lee C. Drinkamer, eds. Raleigh, NC: Ivy House Publishing, 2005.

The Little Drummer. New York: McLaughlin Bros., c. 1863–1866.

Little Pet's Picture Alphabet. New York: McLoughlin Bros. Manufacturers [c. 1861–1865].

Little Sailor Boy. New York: McLaughlin Bros., [c. 1859–1862].

Livermore, Mary. *My Story of the War: A Woman's Narrative of Four Years Personal Experience as Nurse in the Union Army.* Hartford, Conn.: A.D. Worthington, 1890.

Locke, John. *Some Thoughts Concerning Education,* 2nd ed. London: Cambridge University Press, 1889.

McFeeley, William F., and Mary D. McFeeley, eds. *U.S. Grant: Memoirs and Selected Letters.* New York: Library of America, 1990.

McKenzie, Clarence D. *The Little Drummer Boy, The Child of the Thirteenth Regiment, N.Y.S.M. and the Child of the Mission Sunday School.* New York: Hosford & Ketcham, 1861.

Macleod, George H. B. *Notes on the Surgery of the War in the Crimea.* London: Churchill, 1858.

Marshall, Henry. *Hints to Young Medical Officers of the Army on the Examination of Recruits, and Respecting the Feigned Disabilities of Soldiers.* London: Burges & Hill, 1828.

Marshall, Henry. *On the Enlisting, Discharging and Pensioning of Soldiers,* 2nd ed. Philadelphia: A. Waldie, 1840.

Military Order of the Loyal Legion of the United States. Military Essays and Recollections: Papers Read before the Commandery of the State of Illinois, 4 vols. Chicago: Dial Press, 1891–1899.

Militia Laws of the United States and the Commonwealth of Massachusetts. Dedham, MA: Printed at the Gazette Office, 1815.

Moore, Frank. *Rebellion Record: A Diary of American Events,* 8 vols. New York: G.P. Putnam, 1861–1868.

Moore, Marinda Branson. *The Dixie Primer,* 3rd ed. Raleigh, NC: Branson & Farrar, 1863.

Moore, Mrs. M. B. *The Dixie Speller.* Raleigh, NC: Branson & Farrar, 1864.

[Muscroft, Samuel]. *The Drummer Boy: or, the Battlefield of Shiloh: A New Military Drama in Six Acts.* Detroit: Daily Post Book and Job Printing Est., 1868.

Nagel, Charles. *A Boy's Civil War Story.* St. Louis, MO: Eden Publishing House, 1934.

Nott, Charles C. *Sketches of the War: A Series of Letters to the North Moore Street School of New York,* 4th ed. New York: Anson D. F. Randolph, [1863] 1865.

Oliver, Benjamin L. *Rights of an American Citizen; with a Commentary on State Rights, and on the Constitution and Policy of the United States.* Boston: Marsh, Capen & Lyon, 1832.

Ordronaux, John. *Manual of Instructions for Military Surgeons on the Examination of Recruits and Discharge of Soldiers.* New York: D. Van Nostrand, 1863.

Picture Alphabet. New York: McLoughlin Bros, [c. 1861–1870].

Public Documents, Containing Proceedings of the Hartford Convention of Delegates. Boston: Published by order of the [Mass.] Senate, 1815.

The Public Statute Laws of the State of Connecticut, Book II. Hartford: Hudson and Godwin, 1808.

Quételet, M. A. *A Treatise on Man and the Development of His Faculties.* Edinburgh: W. and R. Chambers, 1842.

Reports of Cases in Law and Equity Argued and Determined in the Supreme Court of Georgia, vol. 33. Macon, GA: J.W. Burke, 1870.

Root, N. W. Taylor. *Infantry Tactics for Schools: Explained and Illustrated for the Use of Teachers and Scholars.* New York: A.S. Barnes and Burr, 1863.

Rousseau, Jean Jacque. *Émile; or Treatise on Education,* trans. William H. Payne. New York: D. Appleton and Company, [1762] 1918.

Savannah, A Lady of. *For the Little Ones.* Savannah, GA: John M. Cooper & Co., [186?].

Schandt, Raymond H., and Josephine H. Schulte, eds. *A Civil War Diary: The Diary of Spring Hill College Between the Years 1860-1865.* Mobile, AL: Spring Hill College Press, 1982.

Schee George W., and O. H. Montzheimer. *Biographical Data and Army Records of Old Soldiers who have lived in O'Brien County, Iowa.* Iowa: Primghar, 1909.

Schouler, James. *A Treatise on the Law of Domestic Relations,* 3rd ed. Boston: Little, Brown, and Company, [1870] 1882.

Stillwell, Leander. *The Story of a Common Soldier of Army Life in the Civil War, 1861-1865.* Erie, KS: Press of the Erie Record, 1917.

Stowe, Charles Edward. *The Life of Harriet Beecher Stowe.* Boston: Houghton, Mifflin and Company, 1890, 148–49.

Stroyer, Jacob. *My Life in the South,* 4th ed. Salem, MA: Newcomb & Gauss, 1898.

Sullivan, James W. *Boyhood Memoires of the Civil War, 1861-1865: Invasion of Carlisle.* Carlisle, PA: Hamilton Library Association, 1933.

Thayer, William Makepeace. *A Youth's History of the Rebellion,* 4 vols. New York: James Miller, 1864–1865.

Uncle Buddy's Gift Book, For the Holidays. Augusta, GA: Blome & Tehan, Publishers, 1863.

Underwood, E.W . *Rebellion Record of the Town of Quincy: An Alphabetically arranged Record of each Resident of Quincy who has served in the army and navy of the United States during the late rebellion.* Boston: J.E. Farwell, 1866.

The Union A B C. [Boston]: Degen, Estes & Company, [c. 1865–1866].

Van Woodward, C., ed. *Mary Boykin Chesnut's Civil War.* New Haven: Yale University Press, 1981.

Wallace, Henry E. *Philadelphia Reports Containing Decisions Published in the Legal Intelligencer during 1868, 1869, and 1870,* 7 vols. Philadelphia: J.M Power Wallace, 1875.

Webster, Daniel. *The Writings and Speeches of Daniel Webster,* 18 vols. Boston: Little, Brown & Co., 1903.

Wharton, H.M. *War Songs and Poems of the Confederacy, 1861-1865 . . . with Personal Reminiscences of the War.* Philadelphia: American Book and Bible House, 1904.

Young, Jesse Bowman. *What a Boy Saw in the Army: A Story of Sight-Seeing and Adventure in the War for the Union.* New York: Hunt and Eaton, 1894.

Secondary Sources

Books

Abel, E. Lawrence. *Singing the New Nation: How Music Shaped the Confederacy, 1861-1865*. Mechanicsburg, PA: Stackpole Books, 2000.

Alakson, Kenneth R. *Making Race in the Courtroom: The Legal Construction of Three Races in Early New Orleans*. New York: New York University Press, 2014.

Anderson, Fred. *A People's Army: Massachusetts Soldiers and Society in the Seven Years' War*. Chapel Hill: University of North Carolina Press, 2012.

Anderson, Margo. *The American Census: A Social History*, 2nd ed. New Haven: Yale University Press, 2015.

Andrew, Rod, Jr. *Long Gray Lines: The Southern Military School Tradition, 1839-1915*. Chapel Hill: University of North Carolina Press, 2001.

Ariès, Philippe. *Centuries of Childhood: A Social History of Family Life*, trans. Robert Baldick. New York: Vintage, 1962, orig. 1960.

Baker, H. Robert. *Prigg v. Pennsylvania: Slavery, the Supreme Court, and the Ambivalent Constitution*. Lawrence: University Press of Kansas, 2012.

Bardaglio, Peter W. *Reconstructing the Household: Families, Sex, and the Law in the Nineteenth-Century South*. Chapel Hill: University of North Carolina Press, 1995.

Barnes, Elizabeth. *States of Sympathy: Seduction and Democracy in the American Novel*. New York: Columbia University Press, 1997.

Bederman, Gail. *Manliness and Civilization: A Cultural History of Gender and Race in the United States, 1880-1917*. Chicago: University of Chicago Press, 2008.

Bell, Richard. *Stolen: Five Free Boys Kidnapped into Slavery and Their Astonishing Odyssey Home*. New York: Simon and Schuster, 2019.

Berlin, Ira, Joseph P. Reidy, and Leslie S. Rowland, eds. *Freedom's Soldiers: The Black Military Experience in the Civil War*. New York: Cambridge University Press, 1998.

Bernath, Michael T. *Confederate Minds: The Struggle for Intellectual Independence in the Civil War South*. Chapel Hill: University of North Carolina Press, 2010.

Bell, Richard. *Stolen: Five Free Boys Kidnapped into Slavery and Their Astonishing Odyssey Home*. New York: Simon and Schuster, 2019.

Bernstein, Robin. *Racial Innocence: Performing American Childhood from Slavery to Civil Rights*. New York: New York University Press, 2011.

Black, Jeremy. *The War of 1812 in the Age of Napoleon*. Norman, OK: University of Oklahoma Press, 2009.

Blackmon, Richard D. *The Creek War, 1813-1814*. Washington, DC: Center of Military History, 2014.

Blight, David W. *Race and Reunion: The Civil War in American Memory*. Cambridge, MA: Harvard University Press, 2001.

Blumenthal, Sidney. *Self-Made Man: The Political Life of Abraham Lincoln, vol. 1., 1809-1849*. New York: Simon and Schuster, 2017.

Bouton, Terry. *Taming Democracy: "The People," the Founders, and the Troubled Ending of the American Revolution*. New York: Oxford University Press, 2007.

Bowles, Samuel, and Herbert Gintis. *Schooling in Capitalist America: Educational Reform and the Contradictions of Economic Life*. New York: Basic Books, 1976.

Boydston, Jeanne. *Home and Work: Housework, Wages, and the Ideology of Labor in the Early Republic*. New York: Oxford University Press, 1990.

Boylan, Anne M. *Sunday School: The Formation of an American Institution, 1790-1880*. New Haven: Yale University Press, 1988.

Brandt, Dennis W. *From Home Guards to Heroes: The 87th Pennsylvania and Its Civil War Community*. Columbia, MO: University of Missouri Press, 2006.

Brewer, Holly. *By Birth or Consent: Children, Law and the Anglo-American Revolution in Authority*. Chapel Hill: University of North Carolina Press, 2005.

Brodhead, Richard H. *Cultures of Letters: Scenes of Reading and Writing in Nineteenth-Century America*. Chicago: University of Chicago Press, 1993.

Brown, Marilyn R. *The Gamin de Paris in Nineteenth-Century Visual Culture: Delacroix, Hugo, and the French Social Imaginary*. New York: Routledge, 2017.

Bundgaard, Axel. *Muscle and Manliness: The Rise of Sport in American Boarding Schools*. Syracuse, NY: Syracuse University Press, 2005.

Bunge, Marcia J., ed., *The Child in Christian Thought*. Grand Rapids, MI: William B. Eerdmans Publishing Company, 2001.

Burlingame, Michael. *The Inner World of Abraham Lincoln*. Urbana: University of Illinois Press, 1994.

Burlingame, Michael. *Abraham Lincoln: A Life*, 2 vols. Baltimore: Johns Hopkins University Press, 2008.

Bynum, Victoria E. *The Free State of Jones: Mississippi's Longest Civil War*. Chapel Hill: University of North Carolina Press, 2016, orig. 2001.

Chudacoff, Howard P. *The Age of the Bachelor: Creating an American Subculture*. Princeton: Princeton University Press, 1999.

Chudacoff, Howard P. *How Old Are You? Age Consciousness in American Culture*. Princeton: Princeton University Press, 1989.

Clark, Beverly Lyon. *Kiddie Lit: The Cultural Construction of Children's Literature in America*. Baltimore, MD: Johns Hopkins University Press, 2003.

Clarke, Frances M. *War Stories: Suffering and Sacrifice in the Civil War North*. Chicago: University of Chicago Press, 2012.

Clement, Priscilla Ferguson. *Growing Pains: Children in the Industrial Age: 1850-1890*. New York: Twayne Publishers, 1997.

Coffman, Edward M. *The Old Army: A Portrait of the American Army in Peacetime, 1784-1898*. New York: Oxford University Press, 1986.

Cohen, Michael David. *Reconstructing the Campus: Higher Education and the American Civil War*. Charlottesville: University of Virginia Press, 2012.

Cohen, Patricia Cline. *A Calculating People: The Spread of Numeracy in Early America*. Chicago: University of Chicago Press, 1982.

Cooper, Jerry. *The Rise of the National Guard: The Evolution of the American Militia, 1865-1920*. Lincoln: University of Nebraska Press, 1977.

Cornelius, Steven H. *Music of the Civil War Era*. Westport, CT: Greenwood Press, 2004.

Cornell, Saul. *The Other Founders: Anti-Federalism and the Dissenting Tradition in America, 1788-1828*. Chapel Hill, N.C.: University of North Carolina Press, 1999.

Cornish, Dudley Taylor. *The Sable Arm: Black Troops in the Union Army, 1861-1865*. Lawrence: University Press of Kansas, 1956.

Cox, Caroline. *Boy Soldiers of the American Revolution*. Chapel Hill: University of North Carolina Press, 2016.

Cox, Karen L. *Dixie's Daughters: The United Daughters of the Confederacy and the Preservation of Confederate Culture*. Gainesville: University Press of Florida, 2003.

Crain, Patricia. *The Story of A: The Alphabetization of America from the New England Primer to the Scarlet Letter*. Stanford, CA: Stanford University Press, 2000.

Cross, Gary. *Kids' Stuff: Toys and the Changing World of American Childhood*. Cambridge: Harvard University Press, 1997.

Cunliffe, Marcus. *Soldiers and Civilians: The Martial Spirit in America, 1775-1865*. London: Eyre & Spottiswoode, 1968.

Cunningham, Hugh. *Children and Childhood in Western Society since 1500*. New York: Longham, 1995.

Curti, Merle E. *The American Peace Crusade, 1815-1860*. Durham, NC: Duke University Press, 1929.

Daniel, Larry J. *Conquered: Why the Army of Tennessee Failed*. Chapel Hill: University of North Carolina Press, 2019.

Davidson, Cathy. *Revolution and the Word: The Rise of the Novel in America*. New York: Oxford University Press, 1986.

Davies, Wallace Evan. *Patriotism on Parade: The Story of Veterans' and Hereditary Organizations in America 1783-1900*. Cambridge, MA.: Harvard University Press, 1955.

Davis, Susan. *Parades and Power: Street Theatre in Nineteenth-Century Philadelphia*. Philadelphia: Temple University Press, 1986.

Delegard, Kirsten Marie. *Battling Miss Bolsheviki: The Origins of Female Conservatism in the United States*. Philadelphia: University of Pennsylvania Press, 2012.

De Rosa, Deborah. *Domestic Abolitionism and Juvenile Literature, 1830-1865*. New York: State University of New York Press, 2003.

Devine, Shauna. *Learning from the Wounded: The Civil War and the Rise of American Medical Science*. Chapel Hill: University of North Carolina Press, 2014.

DiGirolamo, Vincent. *Crying the News: A History of America's Newsboys*. New York: Oxford University Press, 2019.

Dillange, Michel. *The Arc de Triomphe and the Carrousel Arch*, trans. Angela Moyon. Paris: Ouest France, 1984.

Dobak, William A. *By the Sword: The U.S. Colored Troops, 1862-1867*. Washington, DC: Center of Military History, 2011.

Donald, David Herbert. *Lincoln*. New York: Simon and Schuster, 1995.

Downs, Gregory P. *After Appomattox: Military Occupation and the Ends of War*. Cambridge: Harvard University Press, 2015.

Downs, Gregory P. *Declarations of Dependence: The Long Reconstruction of Popular Politics in the South, 1861-1908*. Chapel Hill: University of North Carolina Press, 2011.

Drago, Edmund. *Confederate Phoenix: Rebel Children and Their Families in South Carolina*. New York: Fordham University Press, 2008.

Duane, Anna Mae. *Suffering Childhood: Violence, Race and the Making of the Child Victim*. Athens: University of Georgia Press, 2010.

Earle, Jonathan H. *Jacksonian Antislavery and the Politics of Free Soil, 1824-1854*. Chapel Hill: University of North Carolina Press, 2004.

Edwards, Laura F. *A Nation of Rights: A Legal History of the Civil War and Reconstruction*. New York: Cambridge University Press, 2015.

Edwards, Laura F. *The People and Their Peace: Legal Culture and the Transformation of Inequality in the Post-Revolutionary South*. Chapel Hill: University of North Carolina Press, 2009.

Engelman, Rose C., and Robert J. T. Joy. *200 Years of Military Medicine*. Fort Detrick, MD: Historical Unit of the U.S. Army Medical Department, 1975.

Escott, Paul D. *After Secession: Jefferson Davis and the Failure of Confederate Nationalism.* Baton Rouge: Louisiana State University Press, 1978.

Eustace, Nicole. *1812: War and the Passions of Patriotism.* New York: Philadelphia: University of Pennsylvania Press, 2012.

Fahs, Alice. *The Imagined Civil War: Popular Literature of the North & South, 1861-1865.* Chapel Hill: University of North Carolina Press, 2001.

Fass, Paula, and Mary Ann Mason, eds. *Childhood in America.* New York: New York University Press, 2000.

Federman, Cary. *The Body and the State: Habeas Corpus and American Jurisprudence.* Albany, NY: State University of New York Press, 2006.

Ferris, Marc. *Star-Spangled Banner: The Unlikely Story of America's National Anthem.* Baltimore: Johns Hopkins University Press, 2014.

Field, Corinne T. *The Struggle for Equal Adulthood: Gender, Race, Age, and the Fight for Citizenship in Antebellum America.* Chapel Hill: University of North Carolina Press, 2014.

Field, Corinne T., and Nicholas L. Syrett. *Age in America: The Colonial Era to the Present.* New York: New York University Press, 2015.

Fliegelman, Jay. *Prodigals and Pilgrims: The American Revolution Against Patriarchal Authority, 1750-1800.* New York: Cambridge University Press, 1982.

Foner, Eric. *Free Soil, Free Labor, Free Men: The Ideology of the Republican Party before the Civil War.* New York: Oxford University Press, 1970.

Foos, Paul A. *Short, Offhand, Killing Affair: Soldiers and Social Conflict during the Mexican-American War.* Chapel Hill: University of North Carolina Press, 2003.

Foster, Gaines M. *Ghosts of the Confederacy: Defeat, the Lost Cause and the Emergence of the New South.* New York: Oxford University Press, 1987.

Fox, Thomas. *Drummer Boy Willie McGee, Civil War Hero and Fraud.* Jefferson, NC: McFarland & Company, 2008.

Fox-Genovese, Elizabeth. *Within the Plantation Household: Black and White Women of the Old South.* Chapel Hill: University of North Carolina Press, 1988.

Franklin, John Hope, and Loren Schweninger. *Runaway Slaves: Rebels on the Plantation.* New York: Oxford University Press, 2000.

Frederiksen, John C. ed., *The War of 1812: U.S. War Department Correspondence, 1812-1815.* Jefferson, NC: McFarland and Co., 2016.

Freedman, Eric M. *Habeas Corpus: Rethinking the Great Writ of Liberty.* New York: New York University Press, 2001.

Furstenberg, François. *In the Name of the Father: Washington's Legacy, Slavery, and the Making of a Nation.* New York: Penguin Books, 2007.

Gallagher, Gary W. and Alan T. Nolan, eds. *The Myth of the Lost Cause and Civil War History.* Bloomington: Indiana University Press, 2000.

Geary, James W. *We Need Men: The Union Draft in the Civil War.* DeKalb: Northern Illinois University Press, 1991.

Gienapp, William E. *The Origins of the Republican Party, 1852-1856.* New York: Oxford University Press, 1987.

Gilje, Paul A. *Free Trade and Sailors' Rights in the War of 1812.* New York: Cambridge University Press, 2013.

Glasrud, Bruce A., ed., *Brothers to the Buffalo Soldiers: Perspectives on the African American Militia and Volunteers, 1865-1917.* Columbia: University of Missouri Press, 2011.

Glatthaar, Joseph T. *General Lee's Army: From Victory to Collapse.* New York: Free Press, 2008.

Glatthaar, Joseph T. *Soldiering in the Army of Northern Virginia: A Statistical Portrait of the Troops Who Served Under Robert E. Lee.* Chapel Hill: University of North Carolina Press, 2011.

Glymph, Thavolia. *The Women's Fight: The Civil War's Battles for Home, Freedom, and Nation.* (Chapel Hill: University of North Carolina Press, 2019).

Gourdin, J. Raymond, ed. and comp. *104th Infantry Regiment—USCT Colored Civil War Soldiers from South Carolina.* Berwyn Heights, MD: Heritage Books, Inc., 1997.

Graff, Harvey J. *Conflicting Paths: Growing Up in America.* Cambridge, MA: Harvard University Press, 1995.

Gregory, Anthony. *The Power of Habeas Corpus in America: From the King's Prerogative to the War on Terror.* Cambridge: Cambridge University Press, 2013.

Greene, Jennifer. *Military Education and the Emerging Middle Class in the Old South* Cambridge: Cambridge University Press, 2008.

Grinspan, Jon. *The Virgin Vote: How Young Americans Made Democracy Social, Politics Personal, and Voting Popular in the Nineteenth Century.* Chapel Hill: University of North Carolina Press, 2016.

Grossberg, Michael. *Governing the Hearth: Law and Family in Nineteenth Century America.* Chapel Hill: University of North Carolina Press, 2004.

Grossberg, Michael, and Christopher Tomlins, eds. *Cambridge History of Law in America,* 3 vols. New York: Cambridge University Press, 2008–2011.

Grzyb, Frank L. *The Last Civil War Veterans: The Lives of the Final Survivors, State by State.* Jefferson, NC: McFarland & Company, Inc., Publishers, 2016.

Hacking, Ian. *The Taming of Chance.* Cambridge: Cambridge University Press, 1990.

Halliday, Paul D. *Habeas Corpus: From England to Empire.* Cambridge, MA: Harvard University Press, 2010.

Heinrich Hartmann. *The Body Populace: Military Statistics and Demography in Europe before the First World War.* Cambridge, MA: MIT Press, 2019.

Hauptman, Laurence M. *The Iroquois in the Civil War: From Battlefield to Reservation.* Syracuse, NY: Syracuse University Press, 1993.

Herndon, Ruth Wallis, and John E. Murray, eds. *Children Bound to Labor: The Pauper Apprentice System in Early America.* Ithaca: Cornell University Press, 2009.

Hess, Earl J. *Civil War Infantry Tactics: Training, Combat, and Small-Unit Effectiveness.* Baton Rouge: Louisiana State University Press, 2015.

Heuvel, Sean Michael, and Lisa Heuvel. *The College of William and Mary in the Civil War.* Jefferson, NC: MarFarland, 2013.

Heywood, Colin. *A History of Childhood: Children and Childhood in the West from Medieval to Modern Times.* Cambridge: Polity, 2001.

Hickey, Donald R. *The War of 1812: A Forgotten Conflict.* Urbana: University of Illinois Press, 1989.

Hilkey, Judy. *Character Is Capital: Success Manuals and Manhood in Gilded Age America.* Chapel Hill: University of North Carolina Press, 1997.

Hindman, Hugh D. *Child Labor: An American History.* Armonk, NY: M.E. Sharpe, 2002.

Hiner, N. Ray, and Joseph M. Hawes. *Growing Up in America: Children in Historical Perspective.* Urbana: University of Illinois Press, 1985.

Hochman, Barbara. *Uncle Tom's Cabin and the Reading Revolution: Race, Literacy, Childhood and Fiction.* Amherst: University of Massachusetts Press, 2011.

Hockett, Homer Carey. *The Constitutional History of the United States, 1776-1826: A More Perfect Union.* New York: Macmillan Company, 1939.

Hollandsworth, James G., Jr. *The Louisiana Native Guards: The Black Military Experience During the Civil War.* Baton Rouge: Louisiana State University Press, 1995.

Holt, Marilyn. *The Orphan Trains: Placing Out in America.* Lincoln: University of Nebraska Press, 1992.

Holton, Woody. *Unruly Americans and the Origins of the Constitution.* New York: Hill and Wang, 2008.

Holzer, Harold, and the New York Historical Society. *The Civil War in 50 Objects.* New York: Viking, 2013.

Hunt, Lynn. *The Family Romance of the French Revolution.* Berkeley: University of California Press, 1992.

Illick, Joseph E. *American Childhoods.* Philadelphia: University of Pennsylvania Press, 2002.

Inscoe, John C., and Gordon B. McKinney, *The Heart of Confederate Appalachia: Western North Carolina in the Civil War.* Chapel Hill: University of North Carolina Press, 2003.

Jabour, Anya. *Topsy-Turvy: How the Civil War Turned the World Upside Down for Southern Children.* New York: Ivan R. Dee, 2011.

Jacobs, Margaret D. *White Mother to a Dark Race: Settler Colonialism, Maternalism, and the Removal of Indigenous Children in the American West and Australia, 1880-1940.* Lincoln: University of Nebraska Press, 2009.

Janney, Caroline E. *Remembering the Civil War: Reunion and the Limits of Reconciliation.* Chapel Hill: University of North Carolina Press, 2013.

Jenkins, Henry. ed., *The Children's Culture Reader.* New York: New York University Press, 1998.

Johnson, Russell L. *Warriors into Workers: The Civil War and the Formation of Urban-Industrial Society in a Northern City.* New York: Fordham University Press, 2003.

Johnson, Walter. *Soul by Soul: Life Inside the Antebellum Slave Market.* Cambridge, MA: Harvard University Press, 2001.

Jones, Catherine A. *Intimate Reconstructions: Children in Postemancipation Virginia.* Charlottesville: University of Virginia Press, 2015.

Jordan, Benjamin René. *Modern Manhood and the Boy Scouts of America: Citizenship, Race, and the Environment, 1910-1930.* Chapel Hill: University of North Carolina press, 2016.

Jordan, Winthrop D. *White Over Black: American Attitudes Toward the Negro, 1550-1812* Chapel Hill: University of North Carolina Press, 1968.

Joyce, Barry. *The First U.S. History Textbooks: Constructing and Disseminating the American Tale in the Nineteenth Century.* Lanham: Lexington Books, 2015.

Kammen, Michael. *A Season of Youth: The American Revolution and the Historical Imagination.* New York: Alfred A. Knopf, 1978.

Karp, Matthew. *This Vast Southern Empire: Slaveholders at the Helm of American Foreign Policy.* Cambridge, MA: Harvard University Press, 2016.

Kayyem, Marisa, and Paul Sternberger. *Victorian Pleasures: American Board and Table Games of the Nineteenth Century from the Liman Collection.* New York: Miriam and Ira D. Wallach Art Gallery, Columbia University, 1991.

Keese, Dennis M. *Too Young to Die: Boy Soldiers of the Union Army, 1861-1865.* Huntington, WV: Blue Acorn Press, 2001.

Kett, Joseph F. *Rites of Passage: Adolescence in America, 1790 to the Present*. New York: Basic Books, Inc., 1977.

Kiefer, Monica. *American Children Through their Books, 1700–1835*. Philadelphia: University of Pennsylvania Press, 1948.

Kimmel, Michael. *Manhood in America*. New York: Oxford University Press, 2017.

King, Wilma. *Stolen Childhood: Slave Youth in Nineteenth-Century America*. Bloomington: Indiana University Press, 1995.

Klement, Frank L. *The Copperheads in the Middle West*. Chicago: Chicago University Press, 1960.

Kohn, Richard. *Eagle and Sword: The Federalists and the Creation of the Military Establishment in America, 1783-1802*. New York: Macmillan, 1975.

Lang, Andrew F. *In the Wake of War: Military Occupation, Emancipation, and Civil War America*. Baton Rouge: Louisiana State University Press, 2017.

Le Beau, Bryan R. *Currier & Ives: America Imagined*. Washington, DC: Smithsonian Institution Press, 2001.

Levine, Bruce. *Confederate Emancipation: Southern Plans to Free and Arm Slaves during the Civil War*. New York: Oxford University Press, 2006.

Litwack, Leon F. *North of Slavery: The Negro in the Free States, 1790-1860*. Chicago: University of Chicago Press, 1967.

Lonn, Ella. *Foreigners in the Union Army and Navy*. New York: Greenwood Press, Publishers, 1951.

Lonn, Ella. *Desertion During the Civil War*. Lincoln: University of Nebraska Press, [1928] 1998.

Lord, Francis A., and Arthur Wise. *Bands and Drummer Boys of the Civil War*. South Brunswick, NJ: A. S. Barnes, 1966.

Lott, Eric. *Love and Theft: Blackface Minstrelsy and the American Working Class*. New York: Oxford University Press, 1993.

Lurie, Jonathan. *The Supreme Court and Military Justice*. Thousand Oaks: CQ Press, 2013.

Luskey, Brian P. *Men Is Cheap: Exposing the Frauds of Free Labor in Civil War America*. Chapel Hill: University of North Carolina Press, 2020.

Lynn, John A. *Battle: A History of Combat and Culture from Ancient Greece to Modern America*. Cambridge, MA: Westview Press, 2004.

McCurry, Stephanie. *Confederate Reckoning: Power and Politics in the Civil War South*. Cambridge, MA: Harvard University Press, 2010.

McCurry, Stephanie. *Masters of Small Worlds: Yeoman Households, Gender Relations, and the Political Culture of the Antebellum South Carolina Low Country*. New York: Oxford University Press, 1995.

McDaniel, W. Caleb. *Sweet Taste of Liberty: A True Story of Slavery and Restitution in America*. New York: Oxford University Press, 2019.

McGinty, Brian. *The Body of John Merryman: Abraham Lincoln and the Suspension of Habeas Corpus*. Boston: Harvard University Press, 2011.

MacLeod, Anne Scott. *A Moral Tale: Children's Fiction and American Culture 1820-1860*. Hamden, CT: Archon Books, 1975.

Mcleod, David I. *Building Character in the American Boy: The Boys Scouts, YMCA, and their Forerunners, 1887-1920*. Madison: University of Wisconsin Press, 1983.

McNeill, William H. *Keeping Together in Time: Dance and Drill in Human History* Cambridge, MA: Harvard University Press, 1995.

McPherson, James. *For Cause and Comrades: Why Men Fought in the Civil War.* New York: Oxford University Press, 1997.

McPherson, James. *Battle Cry of Freedom: The Civil War Era.* New York: Oxford University Press, 1988.

McWhirter, Christian. *Battle Hymns: The Power and Popularity of Music in the Civil War* Chapel Hill: University of North Carolina Press, 2012.

Mahon, John K. *History of the Militia and the National Guard.* New York: Macmillan, 1983.

Manning, Alan. *Father Lincoln: The Untold Story of Abraham Lincoln and His Boys— Robert, Eddy, Willie, and Tad.* Guildford, CT: Rowman and Littlefield, 2016.

Marshall, Anne E. *Creating a Confederate Kentucky: The Lost Cause and Civil War Memory in a Border State.* Chapel Hill: University of North Carolina Press, 2010.

Marten, James, ed. *Children and Youth During the Civil War Era.* New York: New York University Press, 2012.

Marten, James. *Children and Youth in a New Nation.* New York: New York University Press, 2009.

Marten, James. *Children for the Union: The War Spirit on the Northern Home Front.* Chicago: Ivan R. Dee, 2004.

Marten, James. *The Children's Civil War.* Chapel Hill: University of North Carolina Press, 1998.

Martin, Michelle H. *Brown Gold: Milestones of African-American Children's Picture Books, 1845-2002.* New York: Routledge, 2004.

Martinez, Jaime Amanda. *Slave Impressment in the Upper South.* Chapel Hill: University of North Carolina Press, 2013.

Marvel, William. *Lincoln's Autocrat: The Life of Edwin Stanton.* Chapel Hill: University of North Carolina Press, 2015.

Marvel, William. *Lincoln's Mercenaries: Economic Motivation among Union Soldiers during the Civil War.* Baton Rouge: Louisiana University Press, 2018.

Mason, Mary Ann. *From Father's Property to Children's Rights: The History of Child Custody in the United States.* New York: Columbia University Press, 1994.

Meier, Kathryn Shively. *Nature's Civil War: Common Soldiers and the Environment in 1862 Virginia.* Chapel Hill: University North Carolina, 2013.

Melish, Joanne Pope. *Disowning Slavery, Gradual Emancipation and 'Race' in New England, 1780-1860.* Ithaca: Cornell University Press, 2016.

Merritt, Keri Leigh. *Masterless Men: Poor Whites and Slavery in the Antebellum Era.* Cambridge: Cambridge University Press, 2017.

Mills, Jean, and Richard Mills, eds. *Childhood Studies: A Reader in Perspectives of Childhood.* New York: Routledge, 2000.

Milteer, Warren E., Jr. *North Carolina's Free People of Color, 1715-1885.* Baton Rouge: Louisiana State University Press, 2020.

Mintz, Steven. *Huck's Raft: A History of American Childhood.* Cambridge, MA: Harvard University Press, 2004.

Mitchell, Mary Niall. *Raising Freedom's Child: Black Children and Visions of the Future After Slavery.* New York: New York University Press, 2008.

Moore, Albert Burton. *Conscription and Conflict in the Confederacy.* Columbia: University of South Carolina Press, 1996, orig. 1924.

Moorhead, James H. *American Apocalypse: Yankee Protestants and the Civil War, 1860-1869.* New Haven: Yale University Press, 1978.

Morris, Thomas D. *Free Men All: The Personal Liberty Laws of the North, 1780-1861.* Baltimore, MD: Johns Hopkins University Press, 1974.

Murdock, Eugene C. *One Million Men: The Civil War Draft in the North.* Madison: State Historical Society of Wisconsin, 1971.

Murdock, Eugene C. *Patriotism Limited, 1862-1865: The Civil War Draft and the Bounty System.* Kent, OH: Kent State University Press, 1967.

Murphy, Jim. *The Boy's War: Confederate and Union Soldiers Talk about the Civil War.* New York: Clarion Books, 1990.

Murphy, Kevin P. *Political Manhood: Red Bloods, Mollycoddles, and the Politics of Progressive Era Reform.* New York: Columbia University Press, 2008.

Murray, Gail Schmunk. *American Children's Literature and the Construction of Childhood.* New York: Twayne, 1998.

Myers, Barton. *Rebels against the Confederacy: North Carolina's Unionists.* New York: Cambridge University Press, 2014.

Neely, Mark E., Jr. and Harold Holzer. *The Union Image: Popular Prints of the Civil War North.* Chapel Hill: University of North Carolina Press, 2000.

Neely, Mark E., Jr., Harold Holzer, and Gabor S. Boritt. *The Confederate Image: Prints of the Lost Cause.* Chapel Hill: University of North Carolina Press, 1987.

Neely, Mark E., Jr. *The Fate of Liberty: Abraham Lincoln and Civil Liberties.* New York: Oxford University Press, 1991.

Neely, Mark E., Jr. *Southern Rights: Political Prisoners and the Myth of Confederate Constitutionalism.* Charlottesville: University of Virginia Press, 1999.

Neff, Stephen C. *Justice in Blue and Gray: A Legal History of the Civil War.* Cambridge: Harvard University Press, 2010.

Nielson, Kim E. *Un-American Womanhood: Antiradicalism, Antifeminism, and the First Red Scare.* Columbus: Ohio State University Press. 2001.

Norris, John. *Marching to the Drums: A History of Military Drums and Drummers.* Stroud: Spellmount, 2012.

Olson, Kenneth E. *Music and Musket, Bands and Bandsmen of the American Civil War.* Westport, CT: Greenwood Press, 1981.

Orren, Karen. *Belated Feudalism: Labor, the Law, and Liberal Development in the United States.* New York: Cambridge University Press, 1991.

Pace, Robert F. *Halls of Honor: College Men in the Old South.* Baton Rouge: Louisiana University Press, 2004.

Palagruto, Ann. *Babes in Arms: Boy Soldiers in the Civil War.* Privately printed, 2010.

Parrott, David. *The Business of War: Military Enterprise and Military Revolution in Early Modern Europe.* Cambridge: Cambridge University Press, 2012.

Pateman, Carole. *The Sexual Contract.* Oxford: Polity Press, 1988.

Pearson, Susan J. *The Birth Certificate: An American History.* Chapel Hill: University of North Carolina Press, 2021.

Pearson, Susan J. *The Rights of the Defenseless: Protecting Animals and Children in Gilded Age America.* Chicago: University of Chicago Press, 2011.

Perry, Claire. *Young America: Childhood in 19th Century Art and Culture.* New Haven: Yale University Press, 2006.

Pinheiro, Holly A., Jr. *The Families' Civil War: Black Soldiers and the Fight for Racial Justice.* Athens, GA; University of Georgia Press, 2022.

Plant, Rebecca Jo. *Mom: The Transformation of Motherhood in Modern America.* Chicago: University of Chicago Press, 2011.

Poovey, Mary. *A History of the Modern Fact: Problems of Knowledge in the Sciences of Wealth and Society.* Chicago: University of Chicago Press, 1998.

Quigley, Paul. *Shifting Grounds: Nationalism and the American South, 1848-1865.* New York: Oxford University Press, 2012.

Rable, George C. *Civil Wars: Women and the Crisis of Southern Nationalism.* Urbana: University of Illinois Press, 1989.

Rael, Patrick. *Eighty-Eight Years: The Long Death of Slavery in the United States.* Athens: University of Georgia Press, 2015.

Reid, Richard M. *Freedom for Themselves: North Carolina's Black Soldiers in the Civil War Era.* Chapel Hill: University of North Carolina Press, 2008.

Reneau, Susan C. *The Adventures of Moccasin Joe: The True Life Story of Sgt. George S. Howard.* Missoula, MT: Blue Mountain Publishing, 1994.

Riney-Kehrberg, Pamela. *Childhood on the Farm: Work, Play, and Coming of Age in the Midwest.* Kansas: University Press of Kansas, 2005.

Ringel, Paul B. *Commercializing Childhood: Children's Magazines, Urban Gentility, and the Ideal of the Child Consumer in the United States, 1823-1918.* Amherst: University of Massachusetts Press, 2015.

Roberts, Warren. *Jacques-Louis David, Revolutionary Artist: Art, Politics and the French Revolution.* Chapel Hill: University of North Carolina Press, 1989.

Rorabaugh, W. J. *The Craft Apprentice: From Franklin to the Industrial Age.* New York: Oxford University Press, 1986.

Rosen, David M. *Child Soldiers: A Reference Handbook.* Santa Barbara, CA: ABC-Clio, 2012.

Rosen, David M. *Child Soldiers in the Western Imagination: From Patriots to Victims.* New Brunswick, NJ: Rutgers University Press, 2015.

Rosen, Robert N. *Confederate Charleston: An Illustrated History of the City and the People During the Civil War.* Columbus: University of South Carolina Press, 1994.

Rosenberg, Chaim M. *Child Labor in America: A History.* Jefferson, NC: McFarland & Co., 2013.

Ross, Dorothy. *G. Stanley Hall: The Psychologist as Prophet.* Chicago: University of Chicago Press, 1972.

Roth, Sarah N. *Gender and Race in Antebellum Popular Culture.* New York: Cambridge University Press, 2014.

Rotundo, Anthony E. *American Manhood: Transformations in Masculinity from the Revolution to the Modern Era.* New York: Basic Books, 1993.

Rowe, Mary Ellen. *Bulwark of the Republic: The American Militia in the Antebellum West.* Westport, CN: Praeger, 2003.

Ruddiman, John A. *Becoming Men of Some Consequence: Youth and Military Service in the Revolutionary War.* Charlottesville: University of Virginia Press, 2016.

Ryan, Edward. *Paper Soldiers: The Illustrated History of Printed Paper Armies of the 18th, 19th and 20th Centuries.* London: New Cavendish Books, 1995.

Ryan, Mary. *Cradle of the Middle Class: The Family in Oneida County, New York, 1790-1865.* Boston, MA: Cambridge University Press, 1981.

Sanchez-Eppler, Karen. *Dependent States: The Child's Part in Nineteenth-Century American Culture.* Chicago: University of Chicago Press, 2005.

Scaife, William R., and William Harris Bragg. *Joe Brown's Pets: The Georgia Militia.* Macon, GA: Mercer University Press, 2004.

Schantz, Mark S. *Awaiting the Heavenly Country: The Civil War and America's Culture of Death*. Ithaca: Cornell University Press, 2008.

Schmidt, James D. *Industrial Violence and the Legal Origins of Child Labor*. New York: Cambridge University Press, 2010.

Schwartz, Marie Jenkins. *Born in Bondage: Growing Up Enslaved in the Antebellum South*. Cambridge, MA: Harvard University Press, 2000.

Shammas, Carole. *A History of Household Government in America*. Charlottesville: University of Virginia Press, 2002.

Shannon, Fred A. *The Organization and Administration of the Union Army, 1861-1865*, 2 vols. Cleveland: Arthur H. Clark, 1928.

Shorter, Edward. *Women's Bodies: A Social History of Women's Encounters with Health, Ill-Health, and Medicine*. New Brunswick, NJ: Transaction, 1991.

Shuttleworth, Sally. *The Mind of the Child: Child Development in Literature, Science, and Medicine, 1840-1900*. New York: Oxford University Press, 2010.

Shy, John. *A People Numerous and Armed: Reflections on the Military Struggle for American Independence*. New York: Oxford University Press, 1976.

Sinha, Manisha. *The Slave's Cause: A History of Abolition*. New Haven: Yale University Press, 2016.

Sinha, Manisha. *The Counterrevolution of Slavery: Politics and Ideology in Antebellum South Carolina*. Chapel Hill: University of North Carolina Press, 2000.

Silber, Nina, and Mary Beth Sievens, eds. *Yankee Correspondence: Civil War Era Correspondence between New England Soldiers and the Home Front*. Charlottesville: University of Virginia Press, 1996.

Skeen, C. Edward. *Citizen Soldiers in the War of 1812*. Lexington: University Press of Kentucky, 1999.

Smith, Carl. *Urban Disorder and the Shape of Belief: The Great Chicago Fire, the Haymarket Bomb, and the Model Town of Pullman*. Chicago: University of Chicago Press, 1995.

Smuts, Alice Boardman. *Science in the Service of Children, 1893-1935*. New Haven, Yale University Press, 2006.

Snay, Mitchell. *Gospel of Disunion: Religion and Separatism in the Antebellum South*. New York: Cambridge University Press, 1993.

Souter, Gerry. *American Realism*. New York: Parkstone Press, 2015.

Stagg, J. C. A. *The War of 1812: Conflict for a Continent*. New York: Cambridge University Press, 2012.

Steinfeld, Robert J. *The Invention of Free Labor: The Employment Relation in English and American Law and Culture, 1350-1870*. Chapel Hill: University of North Carolina Press, 1991.

Steinfeld, Robert J. *Coercion, Contract, and Free Labor in the Nineteenth Century*. Cambridge: Cambridge University Press, 2001.

Stevenson, Brenda. *Life in Black and White: Family and Community in the Slave South*. New York: Oxford University Press, 1992.

Stott, Richard. *Jolly Fellows: Male Milieus in Nineteenth Century America*. Baltimore, MD: Johns Hopkins University Press, 2009.

Stearns, Peter N. *Childhood in World History*. New York: Routledge, 2006.

Stone, Lawrence. *The Family, Sex and Marriage in England, 1500-1800*. London: Weidenfeld and Nicholson, 1977.

Syrett, Nicholas L. *American Child Bride: A History of Minors and Marriage in the United States*. Chapel Hill: University of North Carolina Press, 2016.

Tatar, Maria. *Off with Their Heads! Fairy Tales and the Culture of Childhood*. New Jersey: Princeton University Press, 1992.

Taylor, Alan. *The Civil War of 1812: American Citizens, British Subjects, Irish Rebels, & Indian Allies*. New York: Alfred A. Knopf, 2010.

Taylor, Alan. *The Internal Enemy: Slavery and War in Virginia, 1772-1832*. New York: W.W. Norton, 2013.

Toll, Robert C. *Blacking Up: The Minstrel Show in Nineteenth Century America*. New York: Oxford University Press, 1974.

Tomlins, Christopher. *Law, Labor, and Ideology in the Early American Republic*. New York: Cambridge University Press, 1993.

Tomlins, Christopher. *Freedom Bound, Law, Labor, and Civic Identity in Colonizing English America, 1580-1865*. Cambridge: Cambridge University Press, 2010.

Tompkins, Jane P. *Sensational Designs: The Cultural Work of American Fiction, 1790-1860*. New York: Oxford University Press, 1985.

Turner, J. M. *A History of the Study of Human Growth*. Cambridge: Cambridge University Press, 1981.

Tuveson, Ernest Lee. *Redeemer Nation: The Idea of America's Millennial Role*. Chicago: University of Chicago Press, 1968.

van Wyck Buel, Richard, Jr. *America on the Brink: How the Political Struggle over the War of 1812 almost Destroyed the Young Republic*. New York: St. Martin's Press, 2005.

Vickers, Daniel. *Farmers and Fishermen: Two Centuries of Work in Essex County, Massachusetts, 1630-1850*. Chapel Hill: University of North Carolina Press, 1994.

Wasyliw, Patricia Healy. *Martyrdom, Murder, and Magic: Child Saints and Their Cults in Medieval Europe*, 2 vols. New York: Peter Lang, 2008.

Weigley, Russell F., Nicholas B. Wainwright, and Edwin Wolf. *Philadelphia: A 300 Year History*. New York: W.W. Norton & Co., 1982.

Weir III, Howard T. *A Paradise of Blood: The Creek War of 1813-14*. Yardley, PA: Westholme, 2016.

Welke, Barbara Young. *Law and the Borders of Belonging in the Long Nineteenth Century United States*. New York: Cambridge University Press, 2010.

Wert, Justin J. *Habeas Corpus in America: The Politics of Individual Rights*. Lawrence: Kansas University Press, 2011.

West, Elliot, and Paula Petrik, eds. *Small Worlds: Children and Adolescents in America, 1850-1950*. Lawrence: University of Kansas Press, 1992.

Werner, Emmy E. *In Pursuit of Liberty: Coming of Age in the American Revolution*. Westport, CN: Praeger, 2006.

White, Jonathan W. *Abraham Lincoln and Treason in the Civil War: The Trials of John Merryman*. Baton Rouge: Louisiana State University Press, 2011.

White, Richard. *The Republic for Which it Stands: The United States During Reconstruction and the Gilded Age, 1865-1896*. New York: Oxford University Press, 2017.

Wilcox, Vanda. *Italy in the Era of the Great War*. Leiden: Brill, 2012.

Wiley, Bell Irvin. *The Life of Billy Yank: The Common Soldier of the Union*. New York: Book of the Month Club, [1943] 1994.

Wiley, Bell Irvin. *The Life of Johnny Reb: The Common Soldier of the Confederacy*. Baton Rouge: Louisiana State University Press, 1943.

Wilson, Charles Reagan. *Baptized in Blood: The Religion of the Lost Cause, 1865-1920*. Athens: University of Georgia Press, 1980.

Wyatt-Brown, Betram. *Southern Honor: Ethics and Behavior in the Old South.* New York: Oxford University Press, 1982.

Yearns, Wilfred Buck. *The Confederate Congress.* Athens: University of Georgia, 1960.

Julia Grant, *The Boy Problem: Educating Books in Urban America.* Baltimore: Johns Hopkins University Press, 2014.

Zelizer, Viviana A. *Pricing the Priceless Child: The Changing Social Value of Children.* New York: Basic Books, 1985.

Zelner, Kyle F. *A Rabble in Arms: Massachusetts Towns and Militiamen in King Philip's War.* New York: New York University Press, 2009.

Ziegler, Valarie H. *The Advocates of Peace in Antebellum America.* Bloomington: Indiana University Press, 1992.

Zipf, Karin L. *Labor of Innocents: Forced Apprenticeship in North Carolina, 1715-1919.* Baton Rouge: Louisiana State University Press, 2005.

Zürcher, Erik-Jan. *Fighting for a Living: A Comparative History of Military Labour, 1500–2000.* Amsterdam: Amsterdam University Press, 2013.

Articles

Abbott, Richard H. "Massachusetts and the Recruitment of Southern Negroes, 1863-1865." *Civil War History* 14:3 (September 1968): 197–210.

Ablavsky, Gregory. "Empire States: The Coming of Dual Federalism." *Yale Law Journal* 128 (2018): 1792–1868.

Allardice, Bruce. "West Points of the Confederacy: Southern Military Schools and the Confederate Army." *Civil War History* 43:4 (1997): 310–331.

Ashwin, Clive. "Graphic Imagery 1837-1901: A Victorian Revolution." *Art History* 1:3 (1978): 360–370.

Ashton, Susanna. "'The Sense of That Crush I Feel at Certain Times Even Now': Jacob Stroyer and the Defense of Fort Sumter." *South Carolina Law Review* 46:2 (2014): 135–139.

Atkinson, Evelyn. "Out of the Household: Master-Servant Relations and Employer Liability Law." 25 *Yale Journal of Law & the Humanities* (2013): 205–270.

Atwater, Edward C. "'Squeezing Mother Nature': Experimental Physiology in the United States before 1870." *Bulletin of the History of Medicine* 52 (1978): 313–334.

Auman, William T. "Neighbor against Neighbor: The Inner Civil War in the Randolph County Area of Confederate North Carolina." *North Carolina Historical Review* 61:1 (1984): 59–92.

Bahde, Thomas. "'Our Cause is a Common One': Home Guards, Union Leagues, and Republican Citizenship in Illinois, 1861-1863." *Civil War History* 56:1 (March 2010): 66–98.

Bailey, Fred. "The Textbooks of the 'Lost Cause': Censorship and the Creation of Southern State Histories." *Georgia Historical Quarterly* 75:2 (Summer 1991): 507–533.

Barnes, Wayne. "Arrested Development: Rethinking the Contract Age of Majority for the Twenty-First Century Adolescent." *Maryland Law Review* 76 (2017): 405–448.

Bensel, Richard. "Southern Leviathan: The Development of Central State Authority in the Confederate States of America." *Studies in American Political Development* 2 (Spring 1987): 68–136.

Berry, Stephen W. "From Household to Personhood in America." In Lisa Tendrich Frank and LeeAnn Whites, eds., *Household War: How Americans Lived and Fought the Civil War.* Athens: University of Georgia Press, 2021, 287–292.

Berry, Stephen W. "When Mail Was Armor: Envelopes of the Great Rebellion, 1861-1865." *Southern Cultures* 4:3 (1998): 63–83.

Beutler, Keith. "Emma Willard's 'True Mnemonic History': America's First Textbooks, Proto-Feminism, and the Memory of the Revolution." In *Remembering Revolution: Memory, History, and Nation Making from Independence to the Civil War*, ed. Michael A. McDonnell, Clare Corbould, Frances M. Clarke, and W. Fitzhugh Brundage. Amherst: University of Massachusetts Press, 2013, 152–167.

Blanco, Richard L. "Henry Marshall (1775-1851) and the Health of the British Army." *Medical History* 14 (1970): 260–276.

Blassingame, John W. "The Recruitment of Colored Troops in Kentucky, Maryland and Missouri, 1863-1865." *Historian* 29:4 (August 1967): 533–545.

Bloch, Ruth H. "Changing Conceptions of Sexuality and Romance in Eighteenth-Century America." *William and Mary Quarterly* 60:1 (January 2003): 13–42.

Boime, Albert. "Thomas Couture's Drummer Boy Beating a Path to Glory." *Bulletin of the Detroit Institute of Arts* 56:2 (1978): 108–131.

Boucher, Ronald L. "The Colonial Militia as a Social Institution: Salem, Massachusetts 1764-1775." *Journal of Military History* 37:4 (1973): 125–130.

Boyd, Mark F. "The Battle of Marianna." *Florida Historical Quarterly* 29:4 (April 1951): 225–242.

Bradford, James C. "The Citizen Soldier in America: Militia, National Guard, and Reserves." In *A Companion to American Military History*, 2 vols. Malden, MA: Blackwell Publishing Ltd., 2019, 1:472–496.

Braun, Lundy. "Spirometry, Measurement and Race in the Nineteenth Century." *Journal of the History of Medicine* 60 (2005): 135–169.

Brown, R. Blake. "'Every boy ought to learn to shoot and to obey orders': Guns, Boys, and the Law in English Canada from the Late Nineteenth Century to the Great War." *Canadian Historical Review* 93:2 (June 2012), 196–225.

Capozzola, Christopher. "Minutemen for the World: Empire, Citizenship, and the National Guard, 1903-1924." In Alfred W. McCoy and Francisco A. Scarano, eds. *Colonial Crucible: Empire in the Making of the Modern American State*. Madison: University of Wisconsin Press, 2009, 421–430.

Carlson, David. "'The Distemper of the Time': Conscription, the Courts, and Planter Privilege in Civil War South Georgia." *Journal of Southwest Georgia History* 14 (Fall 1999): 1–24.

Chamberlain, Robert S. "The Northern State Militia." *Civil War History* 4:2 (June 1958): 105–118.

Clark, Elizabeth B. "'The Sacred Rights of the Weak': Pain, Sympathy, and the Culture of Individual Rights in Antebellum America." *Journal of American History* 82:2 (September 1995): 463–493.

Clark, Jack Allen. "Thomas Sidney Jesup: Military Observer at the Hartford Convention." *New England Quarterly* 29:3 (September 1956): 393–399.

Clarke, Frances M., and Rebecca Jo Plant. "No Minor Matter: Underage Soldiers, Parents, and the Nationalization of Habeas Corpus in Civil War America." *Law and History Review* 35:4 (November 2017): 881–927.

Clarke, Frances M. "So Lonesome I could Die: Nostalgia and Debates over Emotional Control in the Civil War North." *Journal of Social History* 41 (2007): 253–282.

Cooper, Jerry M. "The Army as Strike-Breaker: The Railroad Strikes of 1877 and 1894." *Labor History* 18:2 (1977): 179–196.

Costa, Dora L., and Matthew E. Kahn. "Surviving Andersonville: The Benefits of Social Networks in POW Camps." *American Economic Review* 97:4 (2007): 1467–1487.

Cox, Walter T. "The Army, the Courts, and the Constitution: The Evolution of Military Justice." *Military Law Review* 118 (1987): 1–30.

Cress, Lawrence Delbert. "An Armed Community: The Origins and Meaning of the Right to Bear Arms." *Journal of American History* 71:1 (1984): 22–42.

Day, John Kyle. "The Federalist Press in the Age of Jefferson." *Historian* 65:6 (Winter 2003): 1303–1329.

de Schweinitz, Rebecca. "'Waked Up to Feel': Defining Childhood, Debating Slavery in Antebellum America." In James Marten, ed. *Children and Youth During the Civil War Era*. New York: New York University Press, 2012, 13–28.

DiGirolamo, Vincent. "Newsboy Funerals: Tales of Sorrow and Solidarity in Urban America." *Journal of Social History* 36:1 (Autumn 2002): 5–30.

Douma, Michael, Anders Bo Rasmussen, and Robert Faith. "The Impressment of Foreign-Born Soldiers in the Union Army." *Journal of American Ethnic History* 38:3 (Spring 2019): 76–106.

Daw, S. F. "Age of Boys' Puberty in Leipzig, 1727-49, as Indicated by Voice Breaking in J.S. Bach's Choir Members." *Human Biology* 42:1 (February 1970): 87–89.

Doyle, Patrick J. "Replacement Rebels: Confederate Substitution and the Issue of Citizenship." *Journal of the Civil War Era* 8:1 (March 2018): 3–31.

Duemer, Lee. "The History of Antebellum Military Academies in the North: 1803-1865." *American Educational History Journal* 26:1 (1999): 128–133.

Edwards, Laura F. "Rights that Made the World Right." *Judicature* 102:2 (Summer 2018): 15–26.

Edwards, Laura F. "Sarah Allingham's Sheet and Other Lessons from Legal History." *Journal of the Early Republic* 38:1 (Spring 2018): 121–147.

Emberton, Carole. "'Only Murder Makes Men': Reconsidering the Black Military Experience," *Journal of the Civil War Era* 2:3 (2012), 369–393.

Fahs, Alice. "Remembering the Civil War in Children's Literature of the 1880s and 1890s." In Alice Fahs and Joan Waugh, eds. *The Memory of the Civil War in American Culture*. Chapel Hill: University of North Carolina Press, 2004, 79–93.

Faith, Robert O. "Public Necessity or Military Convenience? Reevaluating Lincoln's Suspensions of the Writ of Habeas Corpus." *Civil War History* 26 (2016): 284–320.

Field, Corinne T. "Are Women . . . All Minors? Woman's Rights and the Politics of Aging in the Antebellum United States." *Journal of Women's History* 12:4 (Winter 2001): 113–137.

Foster, John Michael, Jr. "'For the Good of the Cause and the Protection of the Border': The Service of the Indiana Legion in the Civil War, 181-1865." *Civil War History* 55:1 (March 2009): 31–55.

Franz, Manuel. "Preparedness Revisited: Civilian Societies and the Campaign for American Defense, 1914-1920." *Journal of the Gilded Age and Progressive Era* 17 (2018), 663–676.

Freeman, Joshua B., and Geoffrey Field, eds. "Special Feature: Labor and the Military." *International Labor and Working-Class History* 80 (Fall 2011): 3–147.

Frost, Jennifer. *"Let Us Vote!" Youth Voting and the Twenty-Sixth Amendment*. New York: New York University Press, 2021.

Furneaux, Holly. "Children of the Regiment: Soldiers, Adoption, and Military Tenderness in Victorian Culture." *Victorian Review* 39:2 (Fall 2013): 79–96.

Gallagher, Gary W. "Disaffection, Persistence, and Nation: Some Directions in Recent Scholarship on the Confederacy." *Civil War History* 55:3 (2009): 329–353.

Gilfoyle, Timothy J. "Street-Rats and Gutter-Snipes: Child Pickpockets and Street Culture in New York City, 1850-1900." *Journal of Social History* 37:4 (2004): 853–862.

Gilje, Paul A., and Howard B. Rock. "'Sweep O! Sweep O!': African-American Chimney Sweeps and Citizenship in the New Nation." *William and Mary Quarterly* 51:3 (July 1994): 507–538.

Glatthaar, Joseph T. "Everyman's War: A Rich and Poor Man's Fight in Lee's Army." *Civil War History* 54:3 (September 2008): 229–246.

Golden, Michael J. "The Dormant Second Amendment: Exploring the Rise, Fall, and Potential Resurrection of Independent State Militias." *William & Mary Bill of Rights Journal* 21:4 (2013): 1021–1079.

Goldin, Claudia, and Kenneth Sokoloff. "Women, Children, and Industrialization in the Early Republic: Evidence from the Manufacturing Censuses." *Journal of Economic History* 42:4 (December 1982): 741–774.

Grant, Julia. "A 'Real Boy' and Not a Sissy: Gender, Childhood, and Masculinity, 1890-1940." *Journal of Social History* 37:4 (Summer 2004), 829–851.

Greenstone, Daniel. "Frightened George: How the Pediatric Educational Complex Ruined the Curious George Series." *Journal of Social History* 39:1 (Fall 2005), 221–228.

Grinspan, Jon. "'Young Men for War': The Wide Awakes and Lincoln's 1860 Presidential Campaign." *Journal of American History* 96 (September 2009): 357–378.

Grossberg, Michael. "Who Gets the Child? Custody, Guardianship, and the Rise of a Judicial Patriarchy in Nineteenth-Century America." *Feminist Studies* 9:2 (Summer 1983): 235–260.

Guardino, Peter. "Gender, Soldiering, and Citizenship in the Mexican-American War of 1846-1848." *American Historical Review* 119:1 (2014): 23–46.

Haller, John S. "Civil War Anthropometry: The Making of a Racial Ideology." *Civil War History* 16 (1970): 309–324.

Hamer, Marguerite B. "Luring Canadian Soldiers into Union Lines During the War Between the States." *Canadian Historical Review* 27:2 (June 1946): 150–162.

Hamilton, J. G. de Roulhac. "The State Courts and the Confederate Constitution." *Journal of Southern History* 4:4 (November 1938): 425–448.

Hamilton, J. G. de Roulhac. "North Carolina Courts and the Confederacy." *North Carolina Historical Review* 4:4 (October 1927): 366–403.

Hatcher, James Brush. "The Patriotic Envelope in Civil War Days." *American Collector* 12 (May 1943): 12–13.

Heerman, M. Scott. "'Reducing Free Men to Slavery': Black Kidnapping, the 'Slave Power,' and the Politics of Abolition in Antebellum Illinois, 1830-1860." *Journal of the Early Republic* 38:2 (Summer 2018): 261–291.

Hess, Earl J. "The Early Indicators Project: Using Massive Data and Statistical Analysis to Understand the Life Cycle of Civil War Soldiers." *Civil War History* 63:4 (December 2017): 377–399.

Jung, Patrick J. "The Volunteer Military Companies of Antebellum Milwaukee." *Midwest Review* 14 (1992): 1–22.

Karcher, Carolyn L. "Rape, Murder and Revenge in 'Slavery's Pleasant Home': Lydia Maria Child's Antislavery Fiction and the Limits of Genre." *Women's Studies International Forum* 9:4 (1986): 323–324.

Kearney, Anthony. "Savage and Barbaric Themes in Victorian Children's Writing." *Children's Literature in Education* 17:4 (1986), 233–240.

Keetley, Dawn. "The Injuries of Reading: Jesse Pomeroy and the Dire Effects of Dime Novels." *Journal of American Studies* 47:3 (2013), 673–697.

Kerby, Robert L. "The Militia System and State Militias in War of 1812." *Indiana Magazine of History* 73:2 (June 1977): 102–124.

Kern, Stephen. "Freud and the Birth of Child Psychiatry." *Journal of the History of the Behavioral Sciences* 9:4 (1973), 360–368.

Kruman, Marc. "Dissent in the Confederacy: The North Carolina Experience." *Civil War History* 27:4 (1981): 293–312.

Kuebler-Wolf, Elizabeth. "'Train Up a Child in the Way He Should Go': The Image of Idealized Childhood in the Slavery Debate, 1850-1870." In James Marten, ed., *Children and Youth During the Civil War Era*. New York: New York University Press, 2012, 29–45.

Landrum, Shane. "From Family Bibles to Birth Certificates: Young People, Proof of Age, and American Political Cultures, 1820-1915." In Corinne T. Field and Nicholas L. Syrett, *Age in America: The Colonial Era to the Present*. New York: New York University Press, 2015, 124-147.

Laver, Harry S. "Rethinking the Social Role of the Militia: Community-Building in Antebellum Kentucky," *Journal of Southern History* 68:4 (November 2002): 777–816.

Leider, Robert. "Federalism and the Military Power of the United States." *Vanderbilt Law Review* 73:4 (2020): 989–1076.

Liaropoulos, Andrew N. "Revolutions in Warfare: Theoretical Paradigms and Historical Evidence." In Gary Sheffield, ed., *War Studies Reader: From the Seventeenth Century to the Present Day and Beyond*. New York: Continuum, 2010, 129–157.

Luskey, Brian P. "Special Marts: Intelligence Offices, Labor Commodification, and Emancipation in Nineteenth-Century America." *Journal of the Civil War Era* 3:3 (September 2013), 360–391.

McClintock, Megan J. "Civil War Pensions and the Reconstruction of Union Families." *Journal of American History* 8 (1996): 456–480.

MacDonald, Cheryl. "Canada's Secret Police." *Beaver* 71:3 (1991): 44–49.

McCunn, Ruthanne Lum. "Chinese in the Civil War: Ten Who Served." *Chinese America: History and Perspectives* 10 (1996): 149–181.

McDonnell, Michael A. "Class War? Class Struggles during the American Revolution in Virginia." *William and Mary Quarterly* 63:2 (2006): 305–344.

McGrath, A. Hope. "'A Slave in Uncle Sam's Service': Labor and Resistance in the U.S. Army, 1865-1890." *Labor: Studies in Working-Class History of the Americas* 13:3–4 (2016): 37–56.

McPherson, "James M. The Whole Family of Man:' Lincoln and the Last Best Hope Abroad." In Robert E. May, ed., *The Union, the Confederacy, and the Atlantic Rim*. West Lafayette, IN: Purdue University Press, 1995, 131–158.

McLaughlin, Joshua. "'Few Were the Hearts . . . that did not Swell with Devotion': Community and Confederate Service in Rowan County, North Carolina, 1861-1862." *North Carolina Historical Review* 73:2 (April 1996): 156–183.

Marshall, Nicholas. "The Great Exaggeration: Death and the Civil War." *Journal of the Civil War Era* 4:1 (March 2014): 3–27.

Marten, James. "Fatherhood in the Confederacy: Southern Soldiers and Their Children." *Journal of Southern History* 63:2 (May 1997): 269–292.

Massey, Mary Elizabeth. "The Civil War Comes to the Campus." In R.C. Simonini, ed. *Education in the South: Institute of Southern Culture Lectures* (Richmond, VA: Cavalier Press, 1959), 11–37.

Masur, Kate. "'A Rare Phenomenon of Philological Vegetation': The Word 'Contraband' and the Meanings of Emancipation in the United States." *Journal of American History* 93:4 (March 2007): 1050–1084.

Mayers, Adam. "Stolen Soldiers." *Civil War Times Illustrated* 34 (June 1995): 56–59.

Maza, Sarah. "The Kids Aren't All Right: Historians and the Problem of Childhood." *American Historical Review* 125: 4 (October 2020): 1261–1285.

Mechling, Jay. "Boy Scouts, the National Rifle Association, and the Domestication of Rifled Shooting." *American Studies* 53:1 (2014): 5–26.

Medford, Edna Greene. "'I was always a union man': The Dilemma of Free Blacks in Confederate Virginia." *Slavery and Abolition* 15:3 (1994): 1–16.

Murdock, Eugene C. "New York's Civil War Bounty Brokers." *Journal of American History* 53:2 (September 1966): 259–278.

Neely, Mark E., Jr. "Legalities in Wartime: The Myth of the Writ of Habeas Corpus." In Stephen D. Engle, ed., *The War Worth Fighting: Abraham Lincoln's Presidency and Civil War America*. Gainesville: University of Florida Press, 2015, 110–126.

Negus, Samuel. "'Conduct Unbecoming of an officer': Fraudulent Enlistment Practices at U.S. Navy Recruitment Rendezvous During the American Civil War." *The Northern Mariner/le Marin du Nord* 22:1 (January 2012): 27–52.

Nelson, Paul David. "Citizen Soldiers or Regulars: The Views of American General Officers on the Military Establishment, 1775-1781." *Military Affairs* 43:3 (1979): 126–132.

Newton, Steven H. "The Confederate Home Guard: Forgotten Soldiers of the Lost Cause." *North and South* 6:1 (December 2002): 40–50.

Nias, J.B. "Aitken, Sir William (1825-1892)," rev. Jeffrey S. Reznick. *Oxford Dictionary of National Biography*, Oxford University Press, 2004. http://www.oxforddnb.com/view/article/257, accessed March 20, 2017.

Norman, John P. "'Self-Preservation is the Supreme Law': States' Rights vs. Military Necessity in Alabama Civil War Conscription Cases." *Alabama Law Review* 60:3 (2009): 727–749.

Ofek, Adina. "Cantonists: Jewish Children as Soldiers in Tsar Nicholas's Army." *Modern Judaism* 13:3 (October 1993): 277–308.

Oveson, Catharine S. "Civil War Envelopes." *Antiques* 13 (June 1928): 490–492.

Park, Roberta J. "'Taking Their Measure' in Play, Games, and Physical Training: The American Scene, 1870s to World War 1." *Journal of Sport History* 33:2 (Summer 2006): 193–217.

Parker, Geoffrey. "Military Revolutions, Past and Present." *Historically Speaking* 4:4 (2003): 2–14.

Pasulka, Diana, "A Somber Pedagogy—A History of the Child Death Bed Scene in Early American Children's Religious Literature, 1674-1840." *Journal of the History of Childhood and Youth* 2:2 (Spring 2009): 117–197.

Pearson, Andrea G. "*Frank Leslie's Illustrated Newspaper* and *Harper's Weekly*: Innovation and Imitation in Nineteenth Century Pictorial Reporting." *Journal of Popular Culture* 23:4 (Spring 1990): 81–111.

Pearson, Susan J. "'Age Ought to Be a Fact': The Campaign against Child Labor and the Rise of the Birth Certificate." *Journal of American History* 101:4 (March 2015): 1144–1165.

Pettys, Todd E. "State Habeas Relief for Federal Extrajudicial Detainees." *Minnesota Law Review* 92 (2007): 265–322.

Pizarro, Judith, Roxane Cohen Silver, and JoAnn Prause. "Physical and Mental Health Costs of Traumatic War Experiences Among Civil War Veterans." *Archive of General Psychiatry* 63:2 (2006): 193–200.

Raney, William F. "Recruiting and Crimping in Canada for the Northern Forces." *Mississippi Valley Historical Review* 10:1 (June 1923): 21–33.

Reid, Richard. "Raising the African Brigade: Early Black Recruitment in Civil War North Carolina." *North Carolina Historical Review* 70:3 (July 1993): 266–301.

Robbins, John B. "The Confederacy and the Writ of Habeas Corpus." *Georgia Historical Quarterly* 55:1 (Spring 1971): 83–101.

Rorabaugh, W. J. "Who Fought for the North in the Civil War? Concord, Massachusetts, Enlistments," *Journal of American History* 73:3 (December 1986): 695–701.

Rye, W. Bruce. "Why a Physiologist?—The Case of Henry P. Bowditch." *Bulletin of the History of Medicine* 56 (1982): 19–29.

Sacher, John. "The Loyal Draft Dodger?: A Reexamination of Confederate Substitution." *Civil War History* 57:2 (June 2011): 153–178.

Schmidt, James D. "'Restless Movements Characteristic of Childhood': The Legal Construction of Child Labor in Nineteenth-Century Massachusetts." *Law & History Review* 23 (2005): 315–350.

Schwalm, Leslie A. "'A Body of Truly Scientific Work;' The U.S. Sanitary Commission and the Elaboration of Race in the Civil War Era, *Journal of the Civil War Era* 8:4 (2018), 647–676.

Scofield, Merry Ellen. "Yea or Nay to Removing the Seat of Government: Dolley Madison and the Realities of 1814 Politics." *The Historian* 74 (2012): 449–466.

Scott, Sean A. "'Good Children Die Happy': Confronting Death During the Civil War." In James Marten, ed., *Children and Youth During the Civil War Era*. New York: New York University Press, 2012, 92–109.

Shaw Kathleen. "'Johnny Has Gone for a Soldier': Youth Enlistment in a Northern County." *Pennsylvania Magazine of History* 135:4 (October 2001): 419–446.

Shammas, Carole. "Anglo-American Household Government in Comparative Perspective." *William and Mary Quarterly* 52:1 (January 1995): 104–144.

Shy, John W. "A New Look at Colonial Militia." *William and Mary Quarterly* 20 (1963): 175–185.

Shelden, Rachel A. "Measures for a 'Speedy Conclusion': A Re-examination of Conscription and Civil War Federalism." *Civil War History* 55:4 (2009): 469–498.

Siegel, Reva B. "'The Rule of Love,': Wife Beating as Prerogative and Privacy." *Yale Law Review* 105 (1995): 2117–2207.

Simon, John Y. "Grant, Lincoln, and Unconditional Surrender." In Gabor S. Borritt, ed., *Lincoln's Generals*. New York: Oxford University Press, 1994, 163–198.

Smith, Daniel Scott. "Parental Power and Marriage Patterns: An Analysis of Historical Trends in Hingham, Massachusetts." *Journal of Marriage and the Family* 35 (1973): 31–35.

Smith, Daniel Scott, and Michael S. Hindus. "Premarital Pregnancy in America, 1640-1971: An Overview and Interpretation." *Journal of Interdisciplinary History* 5 (Spring 1975): 537–570.

Smith, Joshua M. "The Yankee Soldier's Might: The District of Maine and the Reputation of the Massachusetts Militia, 1800-1812." *New England Quarterly* 84:2 (June 2011), 234–264.

Smith, Michael Thomas. "The Most Desperate Scoundrels Unhung: Bounty Jumpers and Recruitment Fraud in the Civil War North." *American Nineteenth Century History* 6:2 (June 2005): 149–172.

Spraggins, Tinsley Lee. "Mobilization of Negro Labor for the Department of Virginia and North Carolina, 1861-1865." *North Carolina Historical Review* 24:2 (April 1947): 160–197.

Stearns, Peter N., and Timothy Haggerty. "The Role of Fear: Transitions in American Emotional Standards for Children, 1850-1950." *American Historical Review* 96:1 (1991): 63–94.

Stearns, Peter N. "Girls, Boys, and Emotions: Redefinitions and Historical Change." *Journal of American History* 81:1 (June 1993): 36–74.

Suttles, Dennis E. "'For the Well-Being of the Child': The Law and Childhood." In Daniel W. Stowell, ed., *In Tender Consideration: Women, Families, and the Law in Abraham Lincoln's Illinois*. Urbana: University of Illinois Press, 2002, 46–70.

Sword, Wiley. "'Our Fireside in Ruins: Consequences of the 1863 Chattanooga Campaign." In Evan C. Jones and Wiley Sword, eds., *Gateway to the Confederacy: New Perspectives on the Chickamauga and Chattanooga Campaigns, 1862-1863*. Baton Rouge: Louisiana State University Press, 2014, 227–53.

Szabó, Eszter. "The Migration Factor in the American Civil War: The Impact of Voluntary Population Movements on the War Effort." *Americana: E-Journal of American Studies in Hungary* 12:1 (Spring 2016), available at: http://americanaejournal.hu/vol12no1/szabo.

Steckel, Richard H. "The Age at Leaving Home in the United States." *Social Science History* 20:4 (Winter 1996): 507–532.

Takentani, Etsuko. "The 'Omnipresent Aunt' and the Social Child: Lydia Maria Child's *Juvenile Miscellany*." *Children's Literature* 27 (1999): 22–39.

Tanenhaus, David. "Between Dependency and Liberty: The Conundrum of Children's Rights in the Gilded Age." *Law and History Review* 351 (2005): 351–385.

Testi, Arnaldo. "The Gender of Reform Politics: Theodore Roosevelt and the Culture of Masculinity." *Journal of American History* 81:4 (March 1995): 1509–1533.

Thavenet, Dennis. "The Michigan Reform School and the Civil War: Officers and Inmates Mobilized for the Union Cause." *Michigan Historical Review* 13:1 (1987): 21–46.

Thornbrough, Emma Lou. "Judge Perkins, the Indiana Supreme Court, and the Civil War." *Indiana Magazine of History* 60 (March 1964): 79–96.

Turley, Jonathan. "The Military Pocket Republic." *Northwestern University Law Review* 92:1 (2002–2003): 1–134.

Urdal, Hendrick. "A Clash of Generations? Youth Bulges and Political Violence." *International Studies Quarterly* 50 (2006): 607–629.

Vinovskis, Maris A. "Have Social Historians Lost the Civil War? Some Preliminary Demographic Speculations." *Journal of American History* 76:1 (June 1989): 34–58.

Walker, Mack. "The Mercenaries." *New England Quarterly* 39 (September 1966): 390–398.

Warner, John. "Physiology." In Ronald L. Numbers, ed. *The Education of American Physicians: Historical Essays*. Oakland, CA: University of California Press, 1980, 48–71.

West, Mark I. "Not to be Circulated: The Response of Children's Librarians to Dime Novels and Series Books." *Children's Literature Association Quarterly* 10:3 (Fall 1985): 137–139.

Weston, Helen. "Jacques-Louis David's 'La Mort de Joseph Bara': A Tale of Revolutionary Fantasies." *Paragraph* 19:3 (November 1996): 234–250.

Whisker, James Biser. "The Citizen Soldier Under Federal and State Law." *West Virginia Law Review* 94 (1992): 947–988.

White, Edward. "Recovering the Legal History of the Confederacy." *Washington and Lee Law Review* 467 (2011): 467–554.

Wiecek, William M. "The Great Writ and Reconstruction: The Habeas Corpus Act of 1867." *Journal of Southern History* 36:4 (1970): 530–548.

Wilkes, Donald E., Jr. "From Oglethorpe to the Overthrow of the Confederacy: Habeas Corpus in Georgia, 1733-1865." *Georgia Law Review* 45 (2010-2011): 1015–1072.

Wilson, Charles Reagan. "The Religion of the Lost Cause: Ritual and Organization of the Southern Civil Religion, 1865-1920." *Journal of Southern History* 46.2 (May 1980), 219–238.

Wilson, Mary L. "Profiles in Evasion: Civil War Substitutes and the Men who Hired Them in Walker's Texas Division." *East Texas Historical Journal* 43:1 (2005): 25–38.

Woolhandler, Ann and Michael G. Collins. "The Story of *Tarble's Case*: State Habeas and Federal Detention" (August 11, 2003). *Federal Court Stories,* Vicki C. Jackson and Judith Resnik, eds., Thomson/West. Available at SSRN: http://ssrn.com/abstract= 1447422.

Young, Robert E. "Young American Males and Filibustering in the Age of Manifest Destiny: The United States Army as a Cultural Mirror." *Journal of American History* 78:3 (December 1991): 857–886.

Zagarri, Rosemarie. "Morals, Manners, and the Republican Mother." *American Quarterly* 44:2 (June 1992): 192–215.

Zeiger, Susan. "The Schoolhouse vs. the Armory: U.S. Teachers and the Campaign Against Militarism in the Schools 1914-1918." *Journal of Women's History* 15:2 (Summer 2003): 150–179.

Zeiger, Susan. "She Didn't Raise Her Boy to Be a Slacker: Motherhood, Conscription, and the Culture of the First World War." *Feminist Studies* 22.1 (1996): 6–39.

Zipf, Karin L. "Reconstructing 'Free Woman': African-American Women, Apprenticeship, and Custody Rights during Reconstruction." *Journal of Women's History* 12:1 (Spring 2000): 3–31.

Thesis and dissertations

Bowes, Julia. "Invading the Home: Children, State Power, and the Gendered Origins of Modern Conservatism, 1865-1933." PhD diss., Rutgers University, 2018.

Bray, Christopher Alan. "Disobedience, Discipline, and the Contest for Order in the Early National New England Militia." PhD diss., University of California, Los Angeles, 2012.

Carlson, Robert D. "'Breach of Faith: Conscription in Confederate Georgia." PhD diss., Emory University, 2009.

Cooper, Abigail. "'Lord, Until I Reach My Home': Inside the Refugee Camps of the American Civil War." PhD diss., University of Pennsylvania, 2015.

Crocker, Jared Anthony. "An Average Regiment: A Re-Examination of the 19th Indiana Volunteer Infantry of the Iron Brigade." MA thesis, Indiana University, 2016.

de Vera, Samantha Q. "A Freedom No Greater than Bondage: Black Refugees and Unfree Labor at the Dawn of Mass Incarceration," PhD diss., University of California, San Diego, 2022.

Geserick, Marco Antonio Cabrera. "The Legacy of the Filibuster War: National Identity, Collective Memory, and Cultural Anti-Imperialism." PhD diss., Arizona State University, 2013.

Green, Jane Fiegen. "The Boundaries of Youth: Labor, Maturity, and Coming of Age in Early Nineteenth-Century New England, 1790-1850." PhD diss., Washington University in St. Louis, 2014.

Hochstettler, Paul S. "Suspension of the Writ of Habeas Corpus in the Confederacy during the Civil War." MA thesis, Ohio State University, 1932.

Hoptak, John David. "The Influence of Socio-Economic Background on Union Soldiers During the American Civil War." MA thesis, Lehigh University, 2003.

Kopp, Laura Elizabeth. "Teaching the Confederacy: Textbooks in the Civil War South." MA thesis, University of Maryland, College Park, 2009.

Krug, Donna Rebecca. "The Folks Back Home: The Confederate Home during the Civil War." PhD diss., University of California, Irvine, 1990.

Lager, Eric Andrew. "Radical Politics in Revolutionary Times: The South Carolina Secession Convention and Executive Council of 1862." PhD diss., Clemson University, 2008.

McGovern William., "Street Children: St. Louis and the Transformation of American Reform, 1832-1904." PhD diss., University of California, San Diego, 2016.

McGrath, Autumn Hope. "'An Army of Working Men': Military Labor and the Construction of American Empire, 1865-1915." PhD diss., University Pennsylvania, 2016.

Margis, Matthew. "America's Progressive Army: How the National Guard Grew out of Progressive Era Reforms," PhD diss., Iowa State University, 2016.

Mosvick, Nicholas Matthew. "Courtroom Wars: Constitutional Battles over Conscription in the Civil War North," PhD diss., University of Mississippi, 2019.

Pitcavage, Mark. "An Equitable Burden: The Decline of the State Militias, 1783-1858." PhD diss., Ohio State University, 1995.

Sanftleben, Kurt A. "A Different Drum: The Forgotten Tradition of the Military Academy in American Education." PhD diss., College of William & Mary, 1993.

White, Holly Nicole Stevens. "Negotiating American Youth: Legal and Social Perceptions of Age in the Early Republic." PhD diss., College of William and Mary, 2017.

Websites

Civil War Washington, http://civilwardc.org.

Richard Dobbins, Civil War Research Database, www.civilwardata.com.

Encyclopedia Virginia, https://encyclopediavirginia.org/.

Francis Davis Millet, "Civil War Diary," entry for July 15, 1864, Millet Family Papers, Smithsonian Archives of American Art, Washington DC. Available online at https://www.aaa.si.edu/collections/francis-davis-millet-and-millet-family-papers-9048.

Jim Sundman, "And Your Age Is?" guest post on Emerging Civil War website, https://emergingcivilwar.com/2011/12/01/and-your-age-is/.

Index

For the benefit of digital users, indexed terms that span two pages (e.g., 52–53) may, on occasion, appear on only one of those pages.

Note: Page numbers followed by *f* indicate a figure on the corresponding page.

abolitionism/abolitionists, 99–100, 142–44, 167
Adams, Samuel, 32–33
adolescence, defined, 13
Adolescence (Hall), 271
adolescent brain development, 22
African American. *See also* Black boys and youths, Black enlistment
    free African Americans, 238–41, 257
    recruitment of, 252–54
    United States Colored Troops, 113, 135, 257–58, 293–94
    as veterans, 266
age. *See also* enlistment age calculations
    of conscription, 3, 16, 44, 71, 78*f*, 81, 197–99, 220, 221–22, 283–84
    documentation of, 17, 307n.45
    of majority, 28, 144, 305n.39
    median age of home leaving, 12, 304n.31, 305n.37
    minimum age of enlistment, 3, 16, 21–22, 62–63, 70–71, 79–81, 176, 308n.51
    mortality associated with, 73–74, 75–76, 77–78, 86, 87
age consciousness, 12–13, 16–17, 70–71, 268–77, 304n.32, 304–5n.34, 355n.7
Aide Memoire de l'Officier de Sante, 78–79
Ainsworth, F. C., 280
Aitken, William, 76–79
Alabama Beacon, 241–42
Alexander, John, 257–58
Alexandre, Claude, 73
Allen, Stanton P., 151–52
Allison, John, 250–51

Allison, Joseph, 171–72
American Anti-Slavery Society, 99
American Defense Society, 282
American Revolution, 6, 28–29
analogies between slaveowners and parents, 36–37, 41, 43–44, 167–68, 179–80, 277–78
Andrews, Andrew Jackson, 157–58, 162–63
Anti-Slavery Alphabet, 99
anti-war Democrats, 259–60, 286
anti-war songs, 119
Appletons' Journal, 139
apprentice/apprenticeship, 14, 29–30, 36–37, 38–43, 60, 146–47, 163, 179–80, 315n.48
Army and Navy Chronicle, 55–56
Army Medical School, 76
asylum inmates, 252
Ayers, James, 252–53

Baker, Lafayette C., 245–46, 257–58
Banks, Nathaniel P., 185
Bara, Joseph, 126–29, 334n.42
Bardeen, C. W., 232–33
Barnard, George G., 183
Barnes, J. S., 208–9
Barney, C. Henry, 162–63
Barton, C. S., 22–24
Barton, Joseph, 22–24
Bates, Samuel P., 292
Battle of Antietam, 116–18
Battle of Bull Run, 106–7, 171–72, 174–75
Battle of Cedar Creek, 23–24
Battle of New Market, 206*f*
Battle of North Carolina, 208

Battle of Shiloh, 2
Battle of Vicksburg, 108–9
Battle of Yorktown, 157–58
Bedford Gazette, 259–60
Belknap, William W., 191–92
Bell, John, 154–55
Bernath, Michael, 103
Birkhimer, William, 56
Black, John C., 273–74
    Black boys and youths. *See also* African
        Americans, Black enlistment
    exploitation of, 18–19, 228–29, 252–58
    racist depictions of, 113, 134–
        35, 138–39
    hazardous labor by, 11–12, 231, 237
    impressment of (Confederacy), 11–12,
        229, 235–41,
    impressment of (United States), 11–12,
        249, 252–58
    as substitutes (United States), 257
Black enlistment. *See also* African
        Americans, Black boys and youths
    in Confederate Army 198, 224
    in US Army, 178, 252–54
Blake, William, 93–94
Blakeney, George W., 62–63
Blood, George P., 173–74
Boardman, George, 208–9
Boissoit, Alfred, 251
Bonaparte, Napoleon, 34–35, 129
Boone and Crockett Club, 272–73
bounty brokers, 245–47
bounty jumping, 243–45
boyhood. *See also* boy soldiers and
        drummer boys
    and political participation, 152–57
    and labor, 146–52
    and military education, 155–58
    and the allure of war, 144
    relationship to older men, 145, 146, 164
boy soldiers and drummer boys, of Civil
        War. *See also* boyhood.
    celebration of, 6, 9–10, 112–13, 152
    cultural representations of, 111, 114–19,
        139–41, 265, 332n.10
    and racial politics, 134–41, 266
    as U.S. icons, 112, 113, 124–34
    as white martyrs, 113, 119–21, 138–39

    as symbols in Europe and Latin
        America, 113–14, 126–30, 139,
        334n.42, 334n.45
    British representations of, 129–30,
        334n.46
    Confederate representations
        of, 131–34
    redemptive deaths of, 119–20
    introduction to, 9–11, 18–19, 21
    military importance of, 169, 187–88
    self–Conceptions, 68–69, 85–86
boy soldiers, after Civil War. *See also*
        memory of Civil War boy soldiers
    age consciousness and, 268–77
    celebration of, 261, 262, 263–68
    childhood vulnerability, 277–79
    infant army myth, 280–87
    introduction to, 262–63
    cultural transformation of, 268–77
    tracing lives of, 260–61
    World War I, 262–63, 277, 280–87
Boyers, Alden, 172–73
Boyers, Elijah, 172–73
Boyers, Mary, 172–73
Boykin Chesnut, Mary, 210, 225, 226
The Boy's War (Murphy), 290
Brandt, Dennis, 292
Brewer, Holly, 29
Brown, Albert Gallatin, 219, 253–54
Brown, Henry, 83–84
Bull, William, 49
Burdette, Robert J., 85
Bush, George W., 19
Byrnes, James, 283–84

Cameron, Simon, 174
Camp Jackson Affair, 154–55
Canada, 35–36, 251
Canebrake Cadets, 156
Cappahoosie Military Academy, 157–58
Chadwick, Edwin, 73–74
Chase, Salmon, 195–96
Chicago Daily Tribune, 130–31
Child, Lydia Maria, 96
child deaths, 120
child labor, 146–47, 230–31
child martyrs, 9–10, 113–14, 120, 131–32
child psychology, 94, 271–72, 279

child soldiers, 9.

childhood. *See also* child psychology,
    children's literature
  conceptions of 17
  human rights, 111, 278–79, 303n.23
  in Victorian art and literature, 111
  meanings attached to, 111–12
  and psychology, 94, 271–72, 279
  and race, 133–34

The Child's Instructor (Ely), 100–1
  children's literature, 93, 95–97, 101–3,
    105–7, 268

Chinese immigrants, 251

Citizen Soldier, 53

Clapp, Jeremiah, 212–13

Clausewitz, Carl von, 34–35

Clem, Johnny, 2–3, 4*f*, 127*f*

Cohen, Morris, 227–28

Cole, Orsamus, 184

Coleridge, Samuel, 93–94

Collamer, Jacob, 178–79

"The Colored Volunteer" (Nast), 135–38,
    136*f*, 137*f*

Committee on Military Affairs, 36

common law, 13–14, 15, 43, 49–51, 172–
    74, 183, 304n.32
  and concurrent jurisdiction, 50–
    51, 58–59

Commonwealth v. Cushing, 175–76

Commonwealth v. Downes, 59

Confederate Army. *See also* Confederate
    conscription policy; Confederate
    substitution policy
  and demographic anxieties, 199, 226
  conscription policy, 198, 211–
    13, 218–19
  support for underage
    enlistment, 200–1
  debates over enlistment age, 210–
    11, 218–20
  prohibition of underage substitutes,
    214, 241–42
  opposition to youth enlistment, 202–3,
    211, 214–15, 223–24

Confederate conscription policy, 198,
    211–13, 218–19

Confederate home guard and reserve
    units, 202–3, 223–24, 364n.102

Confederate substitution policy, 214,
    241–42

Conkling, Roscoe, 174

Conscription Act (1862), 200–10

conscription/draft. *See also* impressment;
    Confederate conscription policy
  exemption from, 81, 203–4, 210
  introduction to, 3, 7–8
  in Confederacy, 198, 211–13, 218–19
  minimum age, 3, 16, 44, 71, 78*f*,
    81, 283–84
  in Europe, 73, 77–78

Continental Army, 32

cooks, 11–12, 113, 231–32

Copp, Elbridge, 149–50

corrupt recruiters, 257–59

courage, 93, 94–95, 98, 99, 116–18

court martials, 8–9, 82–85, 235, 324n.44

Courture, Thomas, 139

Crane, Stephen, 268

Cravens, James A., 174–75

Crawford, James Henry, 248

Crimean War (1853-1856), 129

Crockett, John, 212–13

Crowder, Enoch, 285

Crowder, John H, 149–50

Cunliffe, Marcus, 31

Daily Dispatch, 200–2

Daily Evansville Journal, 130–31

Dana, Richard Henry, 167

Darley, Felix O. C., 116–18, 118*f*

Davis, Garrett, 254

Davis, Jefferson, 6, 65, 143, 202–3, 208,
    209, 210–11, 215–16, 219, 223–24

Day, Gerry, 240–41

De Greer, P., 121

De Marsan, Henry, 118–19

De Schweinitz, Rebecca, 99

DeBord, James K. P., 153–54

Democratic Republicans, 27–29, 35–
    36, 40–41

desertion/deserters, 49, 54–55, 168–69,
    183–84, 221–22, 227–28, 232, 234–
    35, 245–46

Dickens, Charles, 94, 111

dime novel scare, 276

Dinkins, James, 158–59, 160*f*, 207

discharge of underage soldiers. *See also* parental appeals for discharge of children
  age of majority and, 51–52, 56–57, 175–76, 212–15, 217, 320n.38
  court cases over, 61–62, 64–66
  debate over, 27, 35, 217–18
  in Confederacy, 199–200, 202–3, 204–5, 218–19
  lawsuits demanding, 168–70, 171–72, 174
  parental appeals for, 1–2, 5–6, 8, 22–23, 58, 59–60, 112–13, 182–96, 208–10, 213, 214–15, 221–23, 234, 343n.11, 357n.41
  physical incapacities of youth and, 71, 82–84, 86–87
  resistance to, 247, 249, 258–59
Dix, John Ross, 121, 122*f*
The Dixie Primer, 103–4
Douglass, Abraham, 254
Drago, Edmund, 293
The Drummer Boy: or the Battle-field of Shiloh (Muscroft), 266–67
"The Drummer Boy of Antietam" (Fleming), 116–18
"The Drummer Boy of Nashville" (Johnson), 121
"Drummer Boy of Shiloh" (Hays), 4*f*, 130–33, 132*f*, 138, 335n.53
"Drummer Boy of Vicksburg" (De Greer), 121
"The Drummer Boy's Farewell" (Dix), 121, 122*f*
dual military system. *See also* US Army (Regulars); militia system; National Guard
  introduction to, 20–21
  creation of, 31–35
  transformation of, 21–22, 52–56, 168, 177–81, 188–96, 284–86, 317n.4, 317n.5, 318n.8
Dubrulle, Hugh, 292
Duncan, Thomas, 205
Dunn, Allen, 195–96
dysentery, 69, 109

Early Indicators of Later Work Levels, Disease, and Death database, 87–88, 291, 295–99, 296*t*, 298*t*

Edes, Edward, 68–70, 71
Edmonds, John Worth, 62
Edwards, Laura, 306–7n.44
Eliot, George, 94
Ellis, William, 164
Ellsworth Phalanx, 161–62
Ely, John, 100–1
Emancipation Proclamation, 252, 254
Émile: or Treatise On Education (Rousseau), 93–94
enlistment age calculations. *See also* military medicine
  health concerns, 68–71
  introduction to, 68–71
  summary of, 86–88
enlistment contracts, 234
Enrollment Act (1863), 80–81, 243–44
Estienne, André, 129, 334n.44
evangelical Christianity, 130
Evans, Richard, 221–22
exemptions from militia duty, 317n.5
exploitation of youth, 18–19, 243–61

Fahs, Alice, 112, 267–68
family law, 277–78
Faulds, D. P., 130–31
Fayetteville Weekly Observer, 203
federalism, 168, 193–94, 195
Ferneyhough, Edgar, 209–10
Field, Stephen, 193–94
filial obedience, 8–9
First Book of History; for Children and Youth (Goodrich), 97
The First Reader, for Southern Schools, 104
Fleming, Albert, 116–18
Flynt, Nicholas, 27, 35
Foote, Corydon, 85
Foraker, Joseph B., 269*f*
Forbes, John Murray, 253
Frank Leslie's Illustrated Newspaper, 114–15
fraudulent enlistment. *See also* Black boys and youths, impressment of involving kidnapping charges, 247–48, 250–51, 253–54
  of asylum inmate, 252
  of minors, 239–41, 248–49
  of Native American youth, 249
  of immigrant youth, 250

of Canadian youth, 250–51
of Chinese youth, 251
investigations into, 251–52, 258–59
of Black boys and youths, 252–58
free labor ideology, 30, 277–78
French, S. G., 217
French Revolution, 113–14
fugitive slave cases, 15
Fugitive Slave Law (1850), 306n.43
Furneaux, Holly, 130

"The Game of the Soldier Boy" (Parker
    Brothers), 267
Gardner, Charles Howard, 162
Garnett, Henry Highland, 257
George, Samuel, 249
Georgia Supreme Court, 216–17
Ghent, William, 281–82
Gholson, Thomas, 64
Gilded Age, 277
Gilmore, Pascal, 156
Glatthaar, Joseph, 293
Goldthwaite, Robert, 170–71
Goodrich, Samuel Griswold, 96–97
Gould, Benjamin, 271, 289–90
Grand Army of the Republic (GAR), 266–
    67, 268, 273–74, 276–77
Grant, Fred, 108–10, 110f, 155
Grant, Nicholas B., 85–86
Grant, Ulysses S., 108–10, 110f,
    155, 220–21
Gregg, Oram, 180–81, 325n.47
Gregg, William, 82–83, 180–81
Grimes, James W., 191
Grinspan, Jon, 144–45
Grosvenor, Thomas P., 43
Gudgell, John, 1–2, 8–9
Gudgell, Julian M., 1–3, 8–9
Guild, Simon C., 162

habeas corpus
    in Confederacy, 210–18
    in United States, 5–6, 7–8, 19, 20, 50–51,
        56–57, 168, 171–72, 182–88, 192–
        94, 284
Hagerty, Timothy, 95
Hale, John, 176–77
Hall, G. Stanley, 271–72
Hamilton, Alexander, 32

Hammer, Nimrod Bramham, 162–63
Hammond, William, 79–80
Hampton Institute, 274
Hanks, Cypress, 232
Hardee, William J., 218–19
Harper's Weekly, 114–16, 134–35
Hartford Convention, 45
Hasty, Noah, 56–57
Hathaway, Annette, 84
Hathaway, William, 84
Hays, William S., 4f, 130–32, 132f, 138,
    335n.53
Hayward, Charles W. L., 244–45
heroic youths, 6, 129–30
Hill, Daniel H., 158–59
Hinman, Wilbur, 265–66
Hints to Young Medical Officers of the
    Army on the Examination of Recruits
    (Marshall), 75
History of Pennsylvania Volunteers
    (Bates), 292
Homer, Winslow, 115–16
Homestead Act (1862), 23–24, 250,
    353n.108
Hopkins, Luther W., 158, 280
Hopkins, William F., 264
Houghton, Edgar, 147
household governance. See also
    parental rights
    introduction to, 13–14
    sectional politics and, 30
    importance of young male labor to,
        169, 174
    in Confederacy, 204–10
Houston, Henry C., 289
Howard, George S., 5
Hubler, Thomas, 263–64
Hudson, Peter, 248
human rights, 9, 111
Humphreys, A. A., 232
Hunt, William Morris, 139, 140f
Hunter, David, 252
Hurd, Rollin, 317n.2

Illustrated London News, 114–15
Ilsley, E. Clarke, 131–32
Imboden, John D., 220
immigrants, 53–54, 241, 249, 250–52,
    321n.47

impressment. *See also* conscription/draft
    of African Americans, 11–12
    common law and, 64
    of enslaved persons, 253–54, 255*f*, 256*f*, 260
    of foreign minors, 250–52
    into Royal Navy, 31, 35–36, 51
    of Native Americans, 249
infant army myth, 280–87
*Infantry Tactics for Schools: Explained and
    Illustrated for the Use of Teachers and
    Scholars* (Root), 156, 159–61, 161*f*
Inter Ocean, 263–64
*Investigations in the Military and
    Anthropological Statistics of American
    Soldiers* (Gould), 271
Irwin, Robert, 232

Jackson, Andrew, 28–29, 46–47
Janeway, James, 120
Jefferson, Thomas, 32–33
Jesup, Thomas Sidney, 45–46
John Tommy, 251
Johnson, Eastman, 116–18, 117*f*, 139, 141,
    332n.14, 336n.74
Johnson, Robert, 121
Johnston, David E., 154
juvenile fiction. *See also* children's
    literature, 98, 267–68
Juvenile Miscellany, 96

Kent, James, 317n2
Kent, John B., 104–5
kidnapping of youths into military,
    22–23, 27–28, 51, 172–73, 248,
    370–71n.61
Kieffer, Harry, 162–63
King, Cyrus, 42–43
Knox, Henry, 44

Ladd, Luther C., 9–10, 10*f*
land bounties for service, 36
Lane, James Henry, 81
Latrobe, Benjamin Henry, 42
Lee, Robert E., 203–4
Lee, Robert E., Jr., 203–4
Lenroot, Irvine, 283–84
Lieber, Francis, 187–88
The Life of Billy Yank (Wiley), 289

Lincoln, Abraham
    discharge of Native Americans, 249
    habeas corpus suspension, 182–
        88, 189
    Militia Act and, 169–70
    parental appeals to, 82–83, 172, 180–81,
        351n.87
    plan for compensated
        emancipation, 179
    pro-Lincoln organizations, 142
    on war losses, 225–26
Lincoln, Edwin Hale, 91–92
Lincoln, Robert, 156
Lincoln, Thomas, 13–14
Lipscomb, George, 64
"Little Major" (Works), 118–19
Little Pet's Picture Alphabet, 102
"Little Sam" (Hays), 138
Locke, John, 94–95
Lord, John H., 59
Lost Cause myth, 15–16, 225, 274

Macarthy, Harry B., 131–32
MacLeod, George, 77–78
Madison, James, 27–28, 32
Magnolia Weekly, 133
manly competence, 146–52
*Manual of the Medical Officer of the Army
    of the United States* (Tripler), 78–79
Marshall, Henry, 74–76
Mason, Jeremiah, 43
Massachusetts Reform School, 197
Masur, Kate, 134–35
Mather, Cotton, 120
McCalley, Eli, 174–75
McCandless, Wilson, 183–84
McClellan, George, 123–24, 138,
    210, 223–24
McClung, Richard, 189–90
McCunn, John, 184, 185
McDougall, James A., 81
McKinley, William B., 153–54
McLoughlin Brothers, 101–2, 268–70
McMicken, Gilbert, 251
McPherson, James, 197
measles, 69
median age of home leaving, 12, 304n.31,
    305n.37

medical studies on physical limitations of young soldiers, 71–81
memoirists/memoirs, 145–46, 151–52, 231–32, 266, 268, 338n.20
memory of Civil War boy soldiers, 268, 280–81, 377n.25
Messmore, Isaac, 185–86
Mexican American War, 62–63, 78–79, 178, 320n.42
military academies, 158
military drill, 262–63, 273–77
military mobilization (Civil War), 168–71, 177–78, 194–95, 230
Military and Naval Magazine, 55–56
military colleges, 274–76
Military Enlightenment, 71–72
military labor
    compared to non-military labor, 231, 366–67n.11
    legal conditions of, 234–35, 258
    market in, 229, 230, 243–44, 246–47, 260–61
    nature of, 231–35, 258
military medicine. *See also* underage enlistment, medical criticism of
    and underage enlistment, 68–71, 74–80
    and age-based enlistment and conscription policies, 71–73, 78–81
    and examinations of underage recruits, 170–71
Militia Act (1792), 33–34, 44, 52, 346n.40
Militia Act (1795), 169–70
Militia Act (1862), 177–78, 252
Militia Act (1903), 285
militia system. *See also* dual military system
    difference from regulars, 14, 28, 318n.10
    classification debates, 44
    transformation of, 20–21, 52–56, 66–67, 175–76, 177–81, 194–95, 285
    legal discussion of, 49–51
Miller, Charles, 61–62
Miller, Delavan, 170–71
Miller, Francis Trevelyan, 281
Miller, Morris, 44–45
Millet, Frank, 164

Milnor, James, 38–39
Mims v. Wimberly, 216–17
minimum age of enlistment, 3, 16, 21–22, 62–63, 70–71, 79–81, 176, 308n.51
Mobile Advertiser, 200–1
Monck, Charles, 251
Monroe, James, 42, 45–46
Moore, A. B., 156
Moore, Josiah Staunton, 154
mortality, age-associated, 73–74, 75–76, 77–78, 86, 87
Moses, Robert, 252–53
mother-blaming, 282–83
mumps, 85–86
Murphy, Jim, 290
Muscroft, Samuel, 266–67
musicians in the military, 14, 70, 71–73, 231–33, 301n.9, 319n.25, 322n.14, 366–67n.11

Nagel, Charles, 241
Napoleonic Wars, 35–36
Nashville Daily Union, 220
Nast, Thomas, 115–16, 135–38, 136f, 137f, 332n.10
National Defense Act (1916), 285
National Detective Bureau, 245–46
National Guard Association, 284–85
National Guard, 285
National Intelligencer, 189
national preparedness movement, 282
National Rifle Association (NRA), 272–73, 276–77
National Security League, 282
nationalism, 61, 103–4, 113, 130, 133
Native Americans, 124–26, 249, 277
Nesmith, James, 80–81
New Orleans Crescent, 202
New York Daily Herald, 248
New York Daily Times, 65–66
New York House of Refuge, 248–49
New York Times, 171–72, 184
New York Tribune, 61–63
Nicholson, Hooper, 57–58
North Carolina Military Institute, 158–59, 160f
nostalgia, 68–69, 321n.2

Notes on the Surgery of the War in the Crimea (MacLeod), 77–78
Nott, Charles C., 105–6

On the Enlisting, Discharging and Pensioning of Soldiers (Marshall), 75–76
On the Growth of the Recruit and Young Soldier (Aitken), 76, 78f, 323n.25, 324n.29
Optic, Oliver, 267–68

pacifism, 53–54, 98–99, 282–83, 318n.9
parens patriae, 13–14, 278–79
parent–Child bond, 43
parental rights. *See also* household governance
    introduction to, 14, 167, 302n.17, 306n.42, 338n.22
    erosion of, 29–30, 168, 180, 195, 277–79
    parental appeals for discharge of children. 1–2, 5–6, 8, 22–23, 58, 59–60, 112–13, 182–96, 208–10, 213, 214–15, 221–23, 234, 343n.11, 357n.41
Parker Brothers, 267
Parley, Peter, 96–97
Parley's Common School History (Parley), 96–97
Pasulka, Diana, 120
patriotic stationery and envelopes, 111, 114–15, 121–23, 123f
peace activists, 276
peace societies, 53–54, 318n.9
Pearson, Susan, 278–79
Peirce, Edward Burgess, 232, 233f
Perkins, Samuel, 187
photography, 114–15
poems, 111, 118–19
Pomeroy, Samuel C., 81
posse comitatus, 56–57, 184–85
Post, Alfred, 79
Powell, Lazarus, 176–77
Pritchard, Henry Clay, 258–59
Progressive Era, 277
Providence School of Reform, 249

Quételet, Lambert Adolphe Jacques, 73–74, 76
Quincy, Josiah, 37, 39, 40, 41

Randolph, George, 212
Randolph, John, 41
Red Badge of Courage (Crane), 268
Redeemer governments, 284–85
Richmond Dispatch, 155–56, 264
Richmond Enquirer, 202–3
Richmond Examiner, 220–21
right to vote, 12–13
Roberts, Emmanuel, 57–58
Robespierre, Maximillian, 126–29
Robinson, Arthur J., 148–49
Roosevelt, Theodore, 272–73, 283
Root, N. W. Taylor, 159–61, 161f
Rotundo, Anthony, 272
Rousseau, Jean Jacques, 93–94
Royal Navy, 31, 35–36, 74
Rutherfurd, Winthrop, 215–16

Saulsbury, Willard, 179
Saxton, Rufus, 252
School Amusements; or, How to Make the School Interesting (Root), 159–61
school facilitation of enlistment, 157–64
Schouler, James, 277–78
Scott, Winfield, 156
secessionism, 1, 45–46
Second Confiscation Act, 179
Seddon, James, 214–15, 221–22
Selective Service Act (1917), 283
Seven Years' War, 28–29
Seward, William, 250
Shaw, Kathleen, 292, 293–94
Shaw, Lemuel, 59
Shay's Rebellion (1786), 33–34
Sherman, John, 179
Sherman, William Tecumseh, 9–10, 109
Shuttleworth, Sally, 94
Sigel, Franz, 220
The Slave's Friend, 99
sleeping on post, 83–84
small-scale enslavers, 30
smallpox, 69, 79
Smith, F. G., 79
Smith, Will B., 155
social Darwinists, 265–66
Southern Illustrated News, 133
Spangler, Edward, 171
Springfield Cadets, 156

"The St. Domingo Orphans" (Child), 96
Stanbery, Henry, 192–93
Stanton, Edwin, 82–83, 188, 189–91
Statutes Relating to the Army of the United States, 21–22
Staunton Spectator, 220
Stearns, Peter, 95
Steele, J. B., 189–90
Stephens, Alexander, 214–15
Stephenson, Philip, 154–55
Stevenson, John D., 61–62
Stillé, Alfred, 79
Stillwell, Leander, 17–18
Stockwell, Elisha, 146, 147–48
Story, Joseph, 31, 58
Stow, Silas, 36–38, 39
Stowe, Harriet Beecher, 99–100, 111, 120
Strong, Melzar B., 234–35
Strother, Edward, 209
Stroyer, Jacob, 237–39
Sullivan, James, 153
Sundman, Jim, 292
Sutherlin, William T., 224–25

Tanenhaus, David, 278
Tarble's Case, 193–94
Thayer, William, 106, 330–31n.49
The Life of Billy Yank (Wiley), 5
Thoughts Concerning Education (Locke), 94
A Token for Children (Janeway), 120
Townsend, E. D., 176
Treatise on Hygiene (Hammond), 79–80
A Treatise on Man and the Development of His Faculties (Quételet), 76
Treatise on the Law of Domestic Relations (Schouler), 277–78
Tripler, Charles S., 78–79
Troup, George, 40
Trumball, Lyman, 178–79, 190
typhoid, 69, 109

Ulmer, George, 150, 151–52, 232–33
Ulshoeffer, Michael, 61–62
Uncle Tom's Cabin (Stowe), 99–100, 120, 142, 266–67
underage enlistment. *See also* military medicine

1812 debates over, 35–41
1814 debates over, 42–48
1820s–1850s debate over, 56–67, 321n.47
contemporary understanding of, 21–22, 91–92, 163–64
legal conceptions of, 19–20, 321n.47
long-term health effects of, 87–88
medical criticism of, 68–70, 71, 86–87
military labor and, 231–43
nineteenth century understanding of, 22–24,
regulations relating to, 170, 191–92, 352n.95
The Union ABC, 102–3
United Daughters of the Confederacy (UDC), 274
United States Army (Regulars). *See also* dual military system, militia system
and unauthorized minority enlistment, 51–52, 56, 60–39
centralization of, 52
age regulations in, 170, 176
United States Colored Troops (USCT), 113, 135, 257–58, 293–94
United States Military Academy in West Point, 34–35
United States Navy, 302n.13, 322n.16
United States recruitment policies, 243–44
United States Sanitary Commission (USSC), 79, 289
United States substitution policy, 247
United States v. Bainbridge, 58, 59–60
United States v. Blakeney, 63
University of Illinois, 275
University of Virginia, 203–4
University of Wisconsin, 275
Upson, Thomas, 142–44, 153–54, 336–37n.1
US Census, 13
US Constitution, 50–51
US Supreme Court, 50–51, 58–60

Vail, Enos B., 150–51
Van Buren, William, 79
Van Winkle, Peter, 190–91
Vanderpoel, Aaron, 61–62
Vermont Supreme Court, 178

Viala, Joseph-Agricola, 126–29, 334n.42
Vietnam War, 21–22
Villermé, Louis-René, 73–74
violent imagery. *See also* children's
    literature
  in children literature, 93, 95–97, 101–3,
    105–7, 268
  imagined impact on children, 93–94
  pedagogical uses of, 92, 98–101, 107–8
  critiques of, 98–99
  in Confederate literature, 103–4,
    330n.42, 330n.44
  in letters to children, 104–6
Virginia Military Institute, 157–58,
    197, 205
Virginia's Secession Convention, 154
voting requirements, 53, 307–8n.48,
    308–9n.56
voting rights, 12–13

War Department, 52, 58–59, 65–66, 170,
    171–72, 174
War of 1812 enlistment
  age-related opposition to, 69–70
  controversy/debate over, 27–28, 30,
    35–41, 47
  introduction to, 11
  pay rise during, 55
*War Powers Under the Constitution of the
    United States* (Whiting), 179–80
Wasburne, Elihu, 220–21
Washington, George, 69n.8, 6, 28–29,
    32, 156
Watts, Thomas H., 212
Webster, Daniel, 43, 44–45
Webster, Thomas, 59–60
Wellington, Duke of, 34–35
West, James Orson, 175–76
West, James S., 175–76
Wharton, Henry, 91–92

Whiskey Rebellion (1794), 33–34
Whiting, William, 179–80, 217
Whitney, Addison, 10*f*
Wickersham, John, 207
Wickham, Williams C., 154
Wide Awakes, 142, 156
Wigfall, Louis, 219
Wiley, Bell Irvin, 5, 289, 290, 292–93
Willard, Emma, 96–97
Williams, David, 36, 44
Wilson, Henry, 80–81, 174, 191
Wilson, Woodrow, 282–83
Wise, Henry, 205
Wise, John, 155–57, 205, 206*f*
Wordsworth, William, 93–94
working–Class youths, 146–47
Works, Henry Clay, 118–19
World War I, 21–22, 262–63, 277, 280–87
World War II, 21–22
The Wounded Drummer Boy (Johnson),
    116, 117*f*, 139, 332n.14, 336n.74
Wyeth, John Allan, 148–49
Wyoming Democrat, 257

yellow fever, 84–85
Young, Jesse Bowman, 161–62
Young, Samuel, 283
Young Men's Christian Association
    (YMCA), 272–73
youngest Civil War soldier
    competitions, 263
youth. *See also* Black boys and youths,
    boyhood, boy soldiers and drummer
    boys, underage enlistment
  defined, 12–13
Youth's Companion, 164
Youth's History of the Rebellion (Thayer),
    106, 330–31n.49

Zeiger, Susan, 282–83